D.J. TAYLOR

The Prose Factory

Literary Life in England Since 1918

VINTAGE

1 3 5 7 9 10 8 6 4 2

Vintage
20 Vauxhall Bridge Road,
London SW1V 2SA

Vintage is part of the Penguin Random House
group of companies whose addresses can be found at
global.penguinrandomhouse.com

First published in hardback by Chatto & Windus in 2016

penguin.co.uk/vintage

A CIP catalogue record for this book
is available from the British Library

ISBN 9780099556077

Printed and bound in Great Britain by Clays Ltd, St Ives plc

Penguin Random House is committed to a sustainable future
for our business, our readers and our planet. This book is made
from Forest Stewardship Council® certified paper.

In memory of John Gross 1935–2011

I often remember him in terms of the warmth and surprising depth of his speaking voice . . . the amusement in his twinkling brown eyes, the despairing sighs that rang through the house when he was at his typewriter. The little daughter of a friend once remarked to her mother: 'Mr Mortimer is a very *cuddly* man.' She was quite right, but woe betide the would-be cuddler who let drop an incorrect date or a fault in pronunciation or grammar! A debatable point would send him in hot haste to the next room, where he would be found down on his knees, consulting one of the stout volumes of the *Oxford English Dictionary*. Long conversations on these themes led to Crichel being nicknamed 'The Prose Factory'.

Frances Partridge recalling the critic Raymond Mortimer and his home Long Crichel House in Dorset, *Everything to Lose: Diaries 1945–1960* (1985)

If we wish to understand writers in our time, we cannot forget that writing is a profession – or at least a lucrative activity – practised within the framework of economic systems which exert undeniable influences on creativity. We cannot forget, if we wish to understand literature, that a book is a manufactured product, commercially distributed, and thus subject to the laws of supply and demand.

Robert Escarpit, *Sociology of Literature* (1958)

'Well, I trust everyone,' says Miss Callendar, 'but no one especially over everyone else. I suppose I don't believe in group virtue. It seems to me such an individual achievement. Which, I imagine, is why you teach sociology and I teach literature.' 'Ah, yes,' says Howard, 'but how do you teach it?' 'Do you mean am I a structuralist or a Leavisite or a psycho-linguistician or a formalist or a Christian existentialist or a phenomenologist?' 'Yes,' says Howard. 'Ah,' says Miss Callendar, 'well, I'm none of them.' 'What do you do, then?' asks Howard. 'I read books and talk to people about them.' 'Without a method?' asks Howard. 'That's right,' says Miss Callendar. 'It doesn't sound very convincing,' says Howard. 'No,' says Miss Callendar, 'I have a taste for remaining a little elusive.' 'You can't,' says Howard. 'With every word you utter, you state your world view.' 'I know,' says Miss Callendar, 'I'm trying to find a way round that.' 'There isn't one,' says Howard, 'you have to know what you are.' 'I'm a nineteenth-century liberal,' says Miss Callendar. 'You can't be,' says Howard, 'this is the twentieth century, near the end of it. There are no resources.' 'I know,' says Miss Callendar, 'that's why I am one.'

Malcolm Bradbury, *The History Man* (1975)

There's more to life than books you know, but not much more.

The Smiths, 'Handsome Devil' (1983)

Contents

Part Three: The Modern Age

Monetary Values

Much of this book is concerned with what writers earned for the material they supplied to publishers and magazine editors. For purposes of comparison, £1 in the mid-1920s would be worth approximately £43 today; the equivalent amounts for the mid-1930s, the mid-1950s and the mid-1970s are, respectively, £48, £18 and £9. Thus, to offer a few benchmarks, Arnold Bennett's income in the years after the Great War was, by modern standards, around £1 million; George Orwell's a decade later as low as £10,000. Twenty years later Evelyn Waugh was earning between £180,000 and £200,000 per annum. The £250 advance paid to Martin Amis for his first novel in 1973 would now be worth around £2,300.

INTRODUCTION

Taste: Awareness: Possibility

When the distinguished literary agent Deborah Rogers died in the spring of 2014, more than one obituarist, reckoning up the extent of her achievements, declared that she had 'shaped the taste of a generation'. Even allowing for the licence traditionally extended to the memorial-writer, this seems a very substantial claim. Certainly, at least half a dozen of the novelists who came to dominate mainstream English literary culture in the 1980s – Ian McEwan, Salman Rushdie, William Boyd and Peter Carey amongst them – did so under her direct supervision. On the other hand, she could not be said to have 'discovered' these bright gems in the diadem of Thatcher-era fiction. McEwan and Boyd, for example, made their initial reputation with short stories published in little magazines whose circulation rarely exceeded a few thousand copies. As a highly circumspect professional adviser, Rogers was integral to her clients' success: she polished up their work for mass publication, pressed it upon sympathetic editors and brokered deals that would allow it to obtain the widest possible exposure. But her relationship with the distinctive cultural and commercial environment in which the writers whom her agency represented made their mark was largely indirect. A book-trade historian, seeking to explain the 'success' of a McEwan or a Rushdie in the 1980s would probably point to a number of factors quite beyond their talent as novelists: unprecedented media interest in what was then beginning to be known as the 'literary novel', stimulated by marketing initiatives and closely fought prize adjudications; a reconfiguration and refinancing of the British publishing industry in which commentators frequently assumed that what the writer was thought to be earning was quite as important as what he or she wrote; and a reorganisation and expansion of broadsheet newspapers which led to more space for arts coverage. Books, to put it starkly, and for all kinds of socio-economic reasons, were more fashionable in the late 1980s than they had been in the late 1970s – when publishers despaired of their diminishing returns and an early number of *Granta* appeared under the banner 'Beyond the publishing crisis' – and for a substantial number of writers, several of them represented by Deborah Rogers, the going was good. But while she undoubtedly played a significant part in the literary culture of her day, to claim that she 'shaped its tastes' is radically to overstate the case.

The question of what Deborah Rogers achieved, and the writers by whom she was able to achieve it, stirs two enquiries that lie at the heart of this book. What is 'literary culture'? And what is 'taste'? The first I take to be the environment in which books – any kind of book, and not just those written by Ian McEwan and Salman Rushdie – are conceived, written, brokered, published, distributed, reviewed, received, brought to the book-buying public and, in rare cases, taken beyond it into the much vaguer and less strictly demarcated world of film and television. Naturally, when compared to other industries, in which success and failure tend to be measured in straightforwardly economic terms, literary culture works in peculiar ways. A book, for example, can enjoy an influence wholly disproportionate to its sales. A literary magazine can dispose of 1,000 copies an issue direct to its subscribers, never be seen on a newsagent's stand and yet have an incalculable effect on the young and impressionable minds that fall under its spell. All these tendencies are exacerbated if the author of the book, or the editor of the magazine, is a distinctive personality, capable of sending out disciples to spread the word. To the library browser of the 1950s the names of T. S. Eliot, F. R. Leavis and Cyril Connolly may not have meant very much. At the same time their interventions and their status in the literary world created a framework for the evaluation of contemporary literature that thousands of library browsers regularly discovered they were responding to, even if the response was indirect or the influence accidental. And if literary culture works in mysterious ways, then what about the abstract which literary culture ends up cultivating, usually in a number of different varieties and never with any great confidence that the evaluative methods employed are anything less than partial – *taste*?

What, when it comes down to it, is taste? The *Shorter Oxford* offers a number of definitions, the best of which is probably 'the mental perception of quality', to which could be added the refinement that this perception will generally be shared by a body of readers who believe that their definition of 'quality' is superior to most of the other ones available. Taste in the world of books is a more or less solid bloc of opinion – passive when expressed by the hundreds of thousands of purchasers of a paperback novel, much more aggressive when espoused by members of smaller and more exclusive groups and when employed as evidence in any kind of cultural debate, almost certainly not the expression of a majority preference, and capable of achieving its aims by way of a kind of osmosis. Richard Bradford has written interestingly about the way in which during the period after the Great War 'the consensus' shifted in favour of the modernist poets who had been routinely disparaged before it, a shift that, crucially, involved praising a writer such as T. S. Eliot for characteristics (incoherence, ambiguity, allusion and so forth) that had previously been used to damn him. 'Taste', as imagined by an Eliot, a Leavis or a Connolly, is by definition elitist. It is Eliot's taste, born of long hours of agonised brooding on the part played by literature in human existence: hieratic, Olympian and calculated to make anyone less well read than Eliot – the vast majority of the population, that is – feel faintly uneasy, and yet at the same time inspiring a terrific sense of partisanship in his admirers, sometimes extending to outright sectarianism. Some of the most subversive moments in literature arrive when a particular brand of fashionable, minority taste declares itself in ways that may be incomprehensible to the reader who hasn't yet cracked its code. There is, for example, an entry in Anthony Powell's *Journals 1987–1989* in which Powell records his friend the former Chancellor of the Exchequer Roy Jenkins' account of a conversation with Léopold Senghor, the decidedly literary-minded president of Senegal. Senghor asks Jenkins which twentieth-century French novelists he thinks the best. Jenkins chooses Proust and Simenon, to which Senghor responds 'Why Simenon?' After which Powell adds 'As Roy remarked, the more chic answer would be "Why Proust?"' To the less cosmopolitan domestic reader, brought up to believe that Proust is one of the great masters of modern literature and Simenon a detective novelist, all this will be faintly baffling. Why should 'chic' opinion plump for Simenon? What sort of perverse, highbrow parlour game is being played here? Clearly, the reader suspects, there are one or two badges of cultural affiliation briefly on display, impenetrable to general readers, which a little more knowledge, a little more information – a little more *taste* – might allow them to decipher.

A century and a half before, that information would have been much more readily to hand. If 'taste' in the early Victorian era was that much more assimilable, it was because there were so comparatively few people actively at work to promulgate it. The serious reading public of the 1830s and 1840s was tiny, consisting of no more than a few thousand people; the sales of even 'best-selling' books were correspondingly small: only Dickens, for example, could be sure of selling more than a few thousand copies. Even then, though, the palisades of post-Romantic-era taste were ready to be forced open by mass literacy, and in the case of Dickens's novels, whose monthly instalments were frequently read aloud to audiences gathered in the upstairs rooms of public houses, newfangled channels of distribution. Literacy rates doubled between 1840 and 1900 to the point where 97 per cent of brides and grooms were able to sign their names on the marriage register. The threat posed to the taste-making pundits of the *Spectator* or the *Quarterly Review* by this new reading public, further expanded by the reforms of successive Education Acts, lay in the fact that so much of it existed beyond the reach of serious criticism, and one of the features of the Victorian age is the rise of the influential amateur critic, quite often with religious affiliations, whose followers demanded the same kind of guidance that they expected to receive, in spiritual matters, from the pulpit. Many of the cultural wars of the later nineteenth century, consequently, are those fought out between two kinds of taste: respectable opinion rebuking what it imagined to be upstart nonentities who are either producing or promoting what respectable opinion imagined to be rubbish. Early Victorian novels are full of these kind of antagonisms making their presence felt among the tea-tables – see, for example, the scene in Mrs Gaskell's *Cranford* (1853) in which Captain Brown regales an audience of genteel spinsters with extracts from the current number of *The Pickwick Papers*. His hostess, a clergyman's daughter brought up on a diet of Johnson, will only allow that 'perhaps the author is young. Let him persist', while declaring that she considers it 'vulgar, and below the dignity of literature, to publish in numbers'.

As this exchange perhaps demonstrates, many of the battles fought by 'taste' of the brand espoused by Miss Deborah Jenkyns and her circle in early Victorian Cheshire had their origins in social class. As late as the 1890s, in certain quarters, it was thought proper to prefer Thackeray to Dickens on the grounds that the author of *Vanity Fair* was a gentleman and Dickens an arriviste.* There had been an all-too symbolic encapsulation of this stand-off in the famous Garrick Club row of the later 1850s, in which Thackeray, supported by half a dozen baronets, had Dickens's protégé Edmund Yates driven out of the premises for using gossip picked up in the club as the basis for a magazine profile. The attitudes struck by the Bloomsbury Group half a century later had a similar grounding in the assumption of a cultural supremacy which is, simultaneously, a form of social superiority. A visitor to a Gordon Square party in the 1920s was amused by the spectacle of a pair of guardsmen in scarlet tunics, invited in off the street, setting hungrily about the buffet while the other guests gathered around them exclaiming 'How they eat!' But the same kind of incredulity, manifest incomprehension of how other people lived, was frequently brought to books of which Bloomsbury disapproved written by authors from social spheres which Bloomsbury had not cared to penetrate.

Naturally, as the twentieth century wore on and the talent pool from which literature recruited became more diverse, these prejudices were capable of quietly inverting themselves. The great literary casualties of the early 1960s, for example, an age in which the shadow of the 'working-class writer' began to loom over literary London, were middle-class writers who were thought either to have lost touch with some of the social realities they were attempting to describe, or to be addressing parts of the societal fabric that were scarcely worth writing about in the first place. The publication of Elizabeth Taylor's *In a Summer Season* (1961) stirred a curious unanimity among its reviewers. The *New Statesman*'s critic admitted to 'a brutish dislike for gracious upper-middle-class charm, at least in novels'. A radio panellist alleged that the author's merits were seriously undermined by the fact that, in terms of subject matter, 'we cannot be sure that she herself understands how marginal and decadent this part of English

* An echo of this survives as late as Somerset Maugham's *Of Human Bondage* (1916).

society has become'. Even *The Times*, while acknowledging the 'skilled craftsmanship', noted that 'Perhaps the setting is too conventional. Perhaps the book is too much of a type.' Miss Taylor, in other words, is being damned on what are essentially non-literary grounds, for having the temerity to write a novel set in that sink of moral iniquity the Home Counties, awash with well-heeled middle-class characters, when the smart money is being laid out on disaffected young proletarians from north of the Trent.

Not, by this stage in the proceedings, that there was such a thing as a single, dominant taste. In his study of the Movement, the loosely affiliated band of university critics and ironising poets who feature so largely in literary histories of the 1950s, Blake Morrison talks about the impending dissolution of the mid-twentieth-century's 'homogeneous literary culture', but it could be argued that this culture had been disintegrating since at least the 1880s. Such late Victorian novels as touch on the workings of the literary world reveal an environment with numberless coigns of vantage, in which old-fashioned gentlemen of letters continue to write novels in three volumes for a select contingent of library subscribers while sharp-eyed careerists concentrate on the rewards offered by mass-circulation weeklies such as *Chums* and *Tit Bits*, and the magazine editors' offices are full of flint-eyed opportunists such as Gissing's Jasper Milvain, who frankly allows that he writes 'for the market' and despises the readers he is labouring to entertain. By the 1920s, consequently, with the gods of the Victorian circulating library on their way to superannuation, there is no such thing as old-style homogeneous 'taste' – if, that is, this desirable entity had ever really existed in the first place.

The gravamen of Q. D. Leavis's researches into literary sociology, after all, was that there had existed in the late sixteenth century a more or less uniform literary public, and that the uneducated seeker after pleasure was compelled either to watch Shakespeare or pursue some other leisure pursuit altogether. The evidence, on the other hand, suggests that such people, if they could read, devoured low-level pamphlet literature by which Mrs Leavis would have been righteously appalled had she ever deigned to acknowledge its existence. It was not, perhaps, that the cultural divisions of the 1920s were anything new; rather, that the antagonisms they provoked were fought out with an unprecedented violence. It was an age of modernists and traditionalists, of highbrows and lowbrows, of middle-class reactionaries, as Orwell once put it, thanking God that they weren't brainy. It was also, and perhaps necessarily, an age in which sophisticated arbiters of 'taste', rather than operating as literary journalists, were increasingly migrating to university English departments, where small groups of influential pundits talked up the merits of books and poets which less stringent readers congratulated themselves on being unable – or unwilling – to comprehend.

One can exaggerate these distinctions. Small-scale, and involving only a few thousand participants, the literary world of the 1920s was, at one level, so closely knit as to make the gaps between its constituent parts seem more flagrant on paper than they were in practice. And, perhaps even more important, the poets, essayists, dramatists and novelists who plied their trade in the immediately post-war years, whatever their aesthetic or ideological differences, were united by a shared tradition. It was not that most of them had been to the same schools, but that they had been brought up to read many of the same books: even the conservative critics of *The Waste Land* prided themselves on their ability to decode the classical allusions. Nearly a century later, on the other hand, the diffusion of 'taste' begun in the age of Eliot and J. C. Squire, the hidebound editor of the *London Mercury*, has made an exponential leap. Frank Swinnerton's *The Georgian Literary Scene* (1935) described a world that, for all its individual compartments, was broadly coherent. Such a survey could presumably still be written now, but it would be dated from the moment it appeared. Neither would it possess any authority, for the idea of the taste-broker, able to convince large numbers of people of the rightness of his, or her, opinions, has all but disappeared. Mass rallyings around the flag of major literary prizes are all that remain. Like Eliot's 'objective correlative' – the suggestion that it could be possible, with the right training, for every serious reader to acquire the powers of judgement necessary for them to formulate the correct opinions about books – he, or she, is the victim of a mass- and consumer-oriented and technologically driven marketplace where power is exercised by those who shout the loudest through the greatest number of portals. There are still influential critics, whether disseminating their opinions in newspaper review pages or from university lecture-hall podiums, but the days in which Arnold Bennett could sell out an edition with a scratch of his pen or F. R. Leavis ruin a reputation on the strength of a few well-chosen insults are two or even three literary generations behind us.

The average reader – not, of course, that there is such a thing – may very probably suspect that this is a step in the right direction. The 'objective correlative' always seemed to me an immensely dreary way of instilling uniformity, for it assumed that literature, in the end, was broadly susceptible to the laws of cause and effect, when one of the principal joys of the art of reading is that it is unregulated, that you can think what you like about the work presented for your inspection. At the other end of the scale, to inspect a clutch of Amazon reviewers going about their work can be a deeply unsettling experience, merely because so many of them have no conception of where the books they are pronouncing on came from, the contexts they inhabit, or even, in exceptional circumstances, whether the artefact they are contemplating is a novel or a biography. If it is unlikely that these evaluative holes will ever be filled, then at the same time certain remnants of the old, collective taste – a series of shared assumptions that were as much moral as literary – are still capable of making their presence felt. Anyone born into the English middle classes during the period 1955–65 who chances upon Francis Spufford's *The Child That Books Built* (2002), for example, is likely to emerge from it with a painful twinge of recognition, for the great formative influence on Spufford's mental life turns out to be the Puffin paperbacks of the 1960s and 1970s: a sensible, sensitive and no doubt bourgeois world populated by the Ingalls family of *Little House on the Prairie*, the Moomins, *Charlie and the Chocolate Factory*, Henry Treece's Viking sagas and much else besides. There are comparable modern examples – let us say the Harry Potter books – but it is notable that they inhabit the much more intimate and immediate landscape of children's literature. The number of modern adults brought up on and morally conditioned by, say, the works of Ian McEwan and Martin Amis is probably rather small.

This is a study of the recent development of literary culture in England, an enquiry into the diffusion of taste that was a part of that development, an examination of the influences at work – many of them in university English departments and the mass media – to bring these changes about, and an investigation into the ways in which those involved in the world of books over the last century have attempted to fashion, consolidate or reimagine 'taste' and use it for their own ends. Why in the English twentieth century did certain kinds of writing prosper only for others to fall by the wayside? Why did certain critics succeed in forming or altering the opinions of the literary public and others fail? What assumptions did a reader who picked up a novel in the 1930s, the 1970s, or the 2000s, bring both to the book itself and the figure of the person who wrote it? Inevitably, there are no definite answers to any of these questions, but in posing them we not only learn something about the complex process by which a book is brought to its audience; we can also address the well-nigh alchemical transformation which lies at the heart of reading – the way in which literature, of whatever kind, works its effect.

PART ONE

Tradition and Dissent

CHAPTER I

Landscape with Figures

> Oh, you heavy-laden who at this hour sit down to the cursed travail of the pen . . . Year after year the number of you is multiplied; you crowd the doors of publishers and editors, hustling, grappling and exchanging maledictions. Oh, sorry spectacle grotesque and heart-breaking.
>
> George Gissing, *The Private Papers of Henry Ryecroft* (1903)

> John Pickford, BBC World Service, came to interview me about George Orwell . . . I tried to think of any literary figure, comparable with Orwell in international reputation, interviewed by oneself in the 1930s, perhaps a friend of Wilde's. These imaginings brought home to me the utter impossibility of reconstructing any 'literary period' of the past.
>
> Anthony Powell, journal entry, 27 October 1983

If there was one shared assumption that the thousands of people involved in English literary life brought back from the Great War, it was that nothing would ever be the same again. As with politics, finance, domestic arrangements, relations between the sexes – all parts of the national fabric pitched irrevocably out of kilter by the events of 1914–18 – so with the much more limited purlieu of books. Naturally, these developments were felt in myriad ways. Some were instantly apparent; others took decades to leach into the public consciousness. The psychological effects of the Flanders campaigns, and their impact on the literary men who fought in them, were still making their presence felt twenty or even thirty years after the weapons had been set down. At bedrock level, the consequences of a long-drawn-out and attritional land war swiftly reduced themselves to a case of missing personnel, empty seats at the table, a casualty list that cut a swathe through the ranks of poets, novelists and essayists alike. As the critic

Edgell Rickword put it, in reviewing J. C. Squire's *Selections from Modern Poets* (1921), 'Had there been no war with Germany, and none with Ireland, it would have been reasonable to expect all the poets in Mr Squire's anthology to be alive today.' As it was, Brooke, Owen, Rosenberg and dozens like them were dead. Philip Larkin, hard at work in the Bodleian Library on the *Oxford Book of Twentieth Century English Verse* (1973) half a century later, noted how often his researches into individual poets of the Great War era led him to a slim and solitary volume whose author had died shortly after – if not shortly before – the date of publication. The removal, almost at a stroke, of substantial numbers of the personnel who might have been expected to populate both the bookshelves and the pages of the literary reviews in the 1920s may have created a wealth of opportunity for those who remained, but it also – again, almost at a stroke – forged a myth of titanic forebears, by whom the poets of the interwar era would be judged and in whose absence the majority of them would be found badly wanting. One of the great, insuperable drawbacks faced by a J. C. Squire, an Edward Shanks, a John Freeman or half a dozen other tinkling 'Georgian' poets was the simple fact that they had survived while Rupert Brooke had gone to his grave on Skyros.

And if the poet of the 1920s was uneasily conscious of the fact that he stood, as it were, on the shoulders of giants, that other men who had accomplished what he was trying to do had done it better, bequeathing as they went a subject of such magnitude that many a Georgian versifier opted to ignore it altogether, then the difficulties faced by the average novelist were quite as far-reaching. Again, some of them were located not so much in procedurals as in psychology, that great wave of mental anguish that hangs over the English novel in the 1920s, even before the fiction specifically dealing with the Great War had begun to be written, and gives it characters with hugely symbolic names such as 'Mark Sabre' and 'Ransom Heritage'. At the same time, many of them are horribly mundane, a matter of small but highly significant protocols, road maps into the heart of character and motivation, which virtually no novel written in the period 1918–39 could altogether ignore. Most strikingly, no male character could be introduced into the plot of a conventionally framed interwar-era novel without a description of what he had or had not done in the war. Simultaneously, four years of military conflict had a long-lasting, if sometimes surreptitious, effect on the novelist's ability to devise a plot.

As Alec Waugh once pointed out, for at least a decade after the war's end the cradle-to-grave novel that had been so popular in the late Victorian and Edwardian eras could no longer be written, if only because the reader, watching its male lead wander down Piccadilly in the early summer of 1914, would be able instantly to predict the course of his life over the next half-decade.

The Great War's shadow hangs over English fiction until deep into the second half of the twentieth century, creating in the end a kind of behavioural code of whose implications the majority of novel-readers would have been all too aware. When in Anthony Powell's *At Lady Molly's* (1957), a novel set in the early 1930s, Ted Jeavons is identified by the narrator, Nick Jenkins, as 'something left over from the war', the effect would have been to set off a chain of assumptions in the original reader's mind, a suspicion that in however indirect a way he, or she, knows the kind of person Jeavons is meant to be. Powell (born 1905) was too young to have fought in the war, but the ironies that sometimes sharpen up his descriptions of those who had harbour the seeds of another of war's incidental effects on literature: the difference between combatant and non-combatant. Alec Waugh (born 1898) had fought in Flanders; his brother Evelyn (born 1903) was several years too young. Evelyn, consequently, was able to populate his first novel, *Decline and Fall* (1928), with characters such as the pederastic Captain Grimes, who reminisces: 'You're too young to have fought in the war, I suppose? Those were the days old boy . . . I don't suppose I was really sober for more than a few hours' and regrets that the cheque he sent to the War Memorial Fund never got through. Alec, who had commanded a machine-gun unit and spent time in a prisoner-of-war camp, would not have wanted to go so far.

Meanwhile, from the angle of those who earned their living from the pen, there was the question of the war's effect on the literary world as a professional environment, the way in which it was organised and the hierarchies through which its business was conducted. Here, too, profound changes had been at work. It was not that 'literary culture' had ceased to exist during the Great War – books had continued to be published, and poetry in particular had enjoyed a tremendous vogue – rather that the conflict had an inevitable impact on the principal medium through which that culture was expressed. Newspapers had not stopped reviewing books but in the majority of cases they ceased to employ freelance critics and parcelled the work out among members of staff whose livelihoods would otherwise have been thrown into jeopardy. The *Daily Telegraph*'s war-time novel-reviewing, for example, was mostly undertaken by its golf correspondent. Many a senior literary figure, too, had been claimed by what was essentially propaganda work. Hilaire Belloc wrote a weekly column on military strategy for *Land and Water*; G. K. Chesterton was engaged by the *Illustrated London News*; H. G. Wells's *Mr Britling Sees it Through* (1915) declares itself, from the title down, as a Home Front novel: provisional, hopeful, tenacious, quite unable to see the reality of what lies ahead. On the other hand, in terms of its status as a leisure activity, a pastime or even a branch of the entertainment industry, 'literature' was about to undergo a seismic disturbance, the implications of which had been apparent to interested insiders well before the Great War began. What had once been a mass interest was teetering on the brink of long, slow and irrevocable decline. Philip Waller's survey of the late Victorian and Edwardian eras makes this point with some force: 'The late Victorian period ushered in an unprecedented phenomenon, a mass reading public. We may now want to add that this was both the first and the *only* mass reading public.'

We may indeed. Powered by Victorian educational reforms, the move towards mass literacy and the emergence of a new range of mass-market newspapers and periodicals, reading – once one leaves aside its chief rival, organised sport – had by the early years of the twentieth century become the principal British leisure activity. At the same time, this cultural dominance was extraordinarily short-lived. The mass take-up of radio and cinema was already in prospect. Ominously enough, once Waller has staked his claim about the existence of a mass reading public he straightaway goes on to quote a *New Statesman* statistic from 1914 suggesting that for the first time the number of books borrowed from public libraries in Edinburgh has fallen. The significance of the story lies not in the fact that this turning aside from literature took place in Edinburgh, 'but that it is said to have happened as a result of the popularity of cinematograph'. In strict, taxonomic terms, consequently, the history of English literary culture in the period after 1918 is a chronicle of dissolution. Radio, cinema – and later television – did not destroy reading. All three took much of their material from literature, forged what were in some cases symbiotic relationships with it and provided valuable employment for writers who had previously been confined to the decent obscurity of the printed page. But the heights that the book and the magazine had scaled in the later nineteenth century would never be reached again. Henceforward the world of books, for all its centrality to the idea of 'culture' and for all the abstract glamour with which it was attended, would be a minority pursuit, whose decision-making processes, protocols and subject matter would be largely controlled by a cultivated elite.

At one level – the level of direct cultural influence – there is nothing very astounding about this retreat. The eighteenth-century bookseller-publisher, busy compiling his subscription lists and flattering his aristocratic patrons, was just as much of an opinion-broker as the *New Statesman*'s founding editorial board. In the same way, any literary historian who examines the working environment of 1918 cannot fail to be struck by a lurking sense of continuity. This tendency was most marked in the area of personnel. By and large it was the under-35s who had got themselves killed in Flanders; in their absence most of the giants of the late Victorian and Edwardian eras pressed indefatigably on into the post-war world. A. C. Benson, whose quasi-philosophical essays, filed under such titles as *The Upton Letters* (1905) and *From a College Window* (1906) won him an enormous popular audience, died in 1925. George Saintsbury, 'King Saintsbury', the undisputed doyen of the late Victorian quarterly review, whose early work had appeared so long ago as to be praised by Matthew Arnold, went on until 1933. Sir Edmund Gosse, the greatest of all the Edwardian literary panjandrums, sponsor of countless up-and-coming reputations and the dispenser of high-class critical judgements to readers of the *Sunday Times*, survived until 1928: a totem pole around which the aspiring critics of a later generation were, as they acknowledged, more than happy to dance. As Geoffrey Grigson recalled: 'Those of us who were born after 1905 grew up into the world in which Sir Edmund Gosse wrote week by week . . . six feet above contradiction like an archdeacon in the pulpit or an auctioneer on the rostrum.'

And just as the denizens of an older literary world had survived to ornament the newfangled landscapes of the 1920s, so many of the young literary modernists who were to cause such an outcry in the post-1918 era had spent the war years quietly establishing their reputations – reputations that might only have been sustained by a handful of magazine readers, but were to prove invaluable weapons in the cultural wars that lay ahead. Eliot, Pound, F. S. Flint and Harold Monro were hard at work in the pages of the *English Review*, *Poetry and Drama* and *Art and Letters*, and the contents of Eliot's influential *Poems 1909–1925* (1925) go all the way back to the reign of Edward VII. But quite as much a fixture of the new literary world of the 1920s were the 'sages' of the Edwardian era – Chesterton, Belloc, Shaw and Wells – several of whom had twenty or even thirty years of professional life before them, and all of whom possessed bands of fanatical supporters ready to follow them from book to book while filling the subscription lists of the magazines in which they periodically set up home. Several of the planning meetings that preceded the launch of the *New Statesman* in 1913 were, for example, spent calculating just how many readers – the tally hovered between 500 and 1,000 – Shaw might bring with him if his name were secured for the masthead.

No doubt the readers of Shaw, Wells or Chesterton or half a dozen other post-Victorian behemoths were worth having. On the other hand, the days when the name of a famous writer was enough to guarantee a periodical's success – Dickens with *Household Words* and *All the Year Round*, Thackeray with the *Cornhill*, Trollope with *St Paul's Magazine* – were fast disappearing. *G. K.'s Weekly*, which pursued an erratic course through the 1920s and 1930s, was never a paying proposition. While there were still magazines that came stamped with their editors' personalities – Eliot's *Criterion*, Squire's *London Mercury*, even, to a certain extent *Time and Tide*, owned by the feminist Lady Rhondda – these tended to be small-scale affairs, frequently sustained by private subsidy, too idiosyncratic ever to move out into the mass market. There were other ways, too, in which the literary milieux of pre-war days were becoming increasingly prone to fracture. Eliot once remarked that when Gosse died he created a vacancy that would never be filled: the post of titular head of English letters had ceased to exist. In making this point Eliot was, however stealthily, comparing the author of *Father and Son* to himself: the one addressing a mass audience against a backdrop of standards which it was assumed that critic and reader shared; the other anxious, in an age of increasing specialisation, to set down authoritative judgements for the benefit of an ever more exclusive band of subscribers.

Both Gosse and Eliot, in their very separate ways, were by-products of that mass reading public brought into existence by the Victorian board-school reforms, which simultaneously increased the number of people in zealous pursuit of 'literature' while fragmenting their margins into an almost infinite number of splinter groups. Judged by the standards that prevailed a century later, the early Victorian reading public had been microscopic: *Vanity Fair* (1847–8), for example, sold a modest 10,000 copies in its author's lifetime. More to the point, perhaps, the book was bought, and read, by an audience whose cultural frame of reference was largely Thackeray's own, who could decipher his classical references and his cultural allusions and appreciate his in-jokes. If by the 1890s, while one part of the literary world had grown bigger and brasher, then another, and by no means less influential part had turned more exclusive, more stylised, more self-consciously detached. As John Gross once put it, if it was the decade of Lord Northcliffe, the self-aggrandising proprietor of the *Daily Mail*, then it was also Aubrey Beardsley's, a time of coteries and collectors' items, ornate trifles and exotic reviews, not only the *Yellow Book* and the *Savoy*, but the *Dome*, the *Pageant*, the *Quarto*, the *Hobby Horse*, the *Chameleon*, the *Rose Leaf* and others so exquisitely obscure that there is no mention of them to be found even in the index of Holbrook Jackson's *The Eighteen Nineties*. The gap between the mass-market periodical that sold 500,000 copies and the recondite quarterly backed by private money that sold 500 is not always as wide as early modernists sometimes like to insist – after all, the one professional marker flag that unites Joyce, Virginia Woolf and Conrad is that each of them at some point in their careers submitted work to *Tit Bits* – but by and large fragmentation was the order of the day.

Come the 1920s this divergence had become an unsealable fissure, to the point where one sometimes breezes through the contents page of an obscure highbrow magazine wondering exactly who, other than the editorial staff, could be expected to take an interest in it. If all this made literary culture steadily less homogeneous at the professional level, then it also had serious implications for the leisure pursuit that ultimately sustained and financed it. To be 'fond of reading', as so many of the respondents to interwar social surveys clearly were, meant different things to different readers. Even in the infinitely narrower spectrum of book reviewing, the gap between a highbrow periodical such as the *Athenaeum* under John Middleton Murry's editorship and a magazine like *John O'London's Weekly*, aimed squarely at the Boots Library-subscribing traditionalist, could sometimes seem all but unbridgeable.

One effect of these oscillations back and forth along the intellectual scale was to limit – in some cases severely limit – the usefulness of certain hitherto valuable terms of cultural reference. 'Taste' in the 1920s, for example, has so many meanings that the word is probably best left out of literary criticism altogether. There is the 'taste' of T. S. Eliot and the 'taste' of the hundreds and thousands of predominantly female readers who enjoyed the work of Herbert Allingham, who contributed short stories at the rate of three or four a month to a variety of women's magazines for the best part of half a century. There is the 'taste' of the left-leaning public school poet scrabbling for a foothold in the columns of *Twentieth Century Verse*, and the 'taste' – a precise and well-nigh forensic taste – of the patron of the Hampstead bookshop library staffed by Gordon Comstock in Orwell's *Keep the Aspidistra Flying* (1936) who demands 'something – well *you* know – *modern*. Sex-problems and divorce and all that, *you* know', and is finally appeased with a copy of *Seven Scarlet Nights*. All this had a predictable effect on the opinion-formers who spent much of their time debating what 'taste' ought to consist of. When Eliot, to take an obvious example, talks about 'standards' he is using the word in an exclusive, if not cultist sense, for Eliot's benchmarks, it goes without saying, are not those of the overwhelming majority of people engaged in the act of reading books and there is no plausible way in which they ever could be.

But while the literary world was already fragmenting into a dozen different interest groups and coteries, and the modern free-for-all of the Amazon discussion forum was not yet in view, there were still a number of influences – some of them organisational, others bound up in the ways in which literature had traditionally been brought to the public – conspiring to stabilise the situation, to ensure that, in the end, at least some degree of centralisation and its concomitant, literary authority, prevailed. One of these had to do with the nature of the literary world itself: small-scale, mostly based in London, staffed by people – predominantly men – who shared the same kind of social background and whose aesthetic interests, however ultimately diverse, had been forged in the same cultural furnace. A world whose dimensions and propensity to multitasking were such that its individual members could come to occupy positions of enviable power. Thus W. L. Courtney, a former fellow of New College, Oxford inveigled into journalism in the 1880s, later doubled up as a director of the publisher Chapman & Hall and literary editor of the *Daily Telegraph*, a dual role that allowed him, on the one hand, to decide what kind of books ought to be published by his own company and, on the other, to comment, albeit indirectly, on the merits of a wide range of books published by his competitors.

But there were other powerful influences hard at work to ensure that much of the literary culture of the 1920s remained firmly wedded to its previous affiliations. The tendency of popular taste to lag dramatically behind more sophisticated espousals of the new and glamorous is a feature of every literary age. Beyond the Bloomsbury drawing rooms and the Garsington lawns, on which Lady Ottoline Morrell held her famous salons, the books that ordinary people read and enjoyed were frequently half a century out of date. Mrs Braddon; Marie Corelli; 'Ouida'; Mrs Humphrey Ward: many of the best-selling authors of the late Victorian era maintained their constituencies well into the interwar years. Historians of Everyman's Library, the decidedly upmarket reprint firm founded by Ernest Rhys in 1908, have remarked the regular appearance on its lists – together with Grote's *History of Greece* in twelve volumes and a translation of Livy in six – of extraordinary items long since vanished from fashionable bookshelves but still capable of pulling in huge subterranean audiences: one might instance the curious posthumous life enjoyed by the Rev. George Gilfillan's *Gallery of Literary Portraits*, much of the contents of which dates back to the 1840s, and which was still going strong as an Everyman Classic in the era of Pound and Eliot.

Inevitably, Gilfillan's survival is only one part of a general tendency to preserve and venerate the Victorian classics into an age whose superior intellects were bent on debunking them. Thackeray's centenary had been widely celebrated in 1911, as had Trollope's four years later. The early Everyman classics are stiff with the ornaments of the mid-nineteenth century, while the financial problems experienced by Chapman & Hall in the interwar years were largely caused by an over-reliance on the Dickens copyrights, which expired on the fiftieth anniversary of the author's death in 1920, leaving the firm embarked on a desperate quest for new revenue streams. And to an immense, residual Victorianism could be added another factor which lay at Victorianism's core: the enormous popularity of religious literature, whether produced by straightforwardly propagandist firms such as the Religious Tract Society or the Society for the Propagation of Christian Knowledge, which had long since cornered the market in

Sunday-school prizes, or mainstream concerns anxious to subsidise riskier commercial undertakings. Hodder & Stoughton's religious list included Hugh Redwood's Salvation Army chronicle *God in the Slums* (1930), which sold a quarter of a million copies in a year, and an equally successful two-volume translation of the Old Testament by James Moffatt.

The popularity of religious books gestures at another aspect of the post-Victorian reading public: its profoundly Nonconformist slant. It was not just that many of its members had come late to literacy, but that they had been brought up in a tradition that held most of secular literature in the deepest suspicion. Undoubtedly this helped to sustain another cherished late Victorian attitude that was still making its presence felt in the early twentieth century: the hostility towards fiction, routinely stigmatised on the grounds that it was trivial, undemanding, encouraged idle fancies and light-mindedness. When the aged Canon Jocelyn in F. M. Mayor's *The Rector's Daughter* (1924) enquires of his daughter's friend 'I wonder if Dora Redland ever reads. I am not speaking of the volumes of light fiction which young ladies devour at all hours, but does she ever *read*?', he is voicing a very common post-Victorian complaint that the vast majority of novels are simply aimed at shop girls. These prejudices endured deep into the interwar era: my 16-year-old father, applying for a clerical job in 1937, and asked what sort of books he liked, was careful to reply that he never picked up anything as vulgar as a novel.

All these factors – the lure of a bygone age, the persistence of bygone moral standards, the rise of a new mass-market audience in which the ability to discriminate was sometimes less important than the desire to consume – could, once combined, lead to startling confusions that would have appalled the tastemakers of the previous century. There is a rather revealing scene in Mayor's *The Rector's Daughter* in which Mary pays a visit chez Redland, a domicile containing Dora's elderly mother and her three spinster sisters, all of them engaged on pious good works, whose evenings are spent manufacturing articles for charity bazaars and reading aloud. As a treat for Mary they read *Bleak House*, and as a treat for one of the sisters they read Jessie Fothergill's *The First Violin*, a fine old display of *echt*-Victorian sentiment first published in 1877: 'they classed them together as the same sort of book'. But even the benighted Redlands, here in their Southsea backwater in the early years of the twentieth century, are seduced by the tang of novelty: 'it seemed there was thought to be an added intellectual aroma in what was new.' As for the type of books they borrow from the library, anything the assistant gives them suits as long as it is not 'indecent':

> but the American sentiment and the vulgarity! And they themselves were the reverse of vulgar. Their books seemed as unlike them as their drawing room. They were ready to take things as they found them; they liked what people round them liked; whereas Mary thought all her own opinions. She might have been happier if she had not. She would have had more in common with her generation.

The Redlands, it becomes painfully clear, are the products of a mass-market, *Daily Mail*-reading age, happy to follow majority opinion, to take what is offered, respecting tradition but hankering after 'newness' and, it is implied, no longer able to distinguish between a good book and a bad one. Mary, brought up in an environment of exacting literary standards and encouraged to think for herself, is consequently a woman, and a reader, out of her time.

And yet, as the evenings around the Redlands' fireside make plain, this is still, for all the blandishments of radio and cinema, a society that read – widely, copiously, even lavishly. A society, too, in which reading was a social activity, in which private diaries groan under the weight of their reading lists and no letter to a friend omits a description of the book that was set down last thing on the previous night. One of the remarkable aspects of the correspondence sent back from Flanders is how often it refers to reading. The future prime minister Harold Macmillan spent his spare time in the trenches ploughing his way through Dickens, Scott and Browning, in inexpensive editions sent out from London, handing the books on to comrades when he had finished them and eventually establishing an unofficial lending library. Badly injured by a German machine-gunner, he lay in a shell-hole awaiting rescue while reading a copy of Aeschylus which he happened to have in the pocket of his battledress. The recently published letters of Henry Deacon Ritchie, who died on the Western Front in September 1918, shortly before his twentieth birthday, tell a similar story.

Ritchie's taste ran to the popular novels of the day, works by Hugh

Walpole, Compton Mackenzie, E. Temple Thurston and Stephen McKenna. Writing from his training camp, prior to embarkation, he tells his sister Madge that he has just finished Alec Waugh's *succès de scandale*, *The Loom of Youth* ('I thought it very boring and I think you would find it coarse') and, a week or so later, offers his mother an impression of Arnold Bennett's *The Pretty Lady* ('unfortunately spoiled by intimate details about an innocent woman: but the other characters are very interesting – and a good picture of wartime London'). But his real discovery, it turns out, is Mackenzie's *Sinister Street*: 'It has to be taken as a whole: perhaps even then you will think it coarse. I'm afraid it is – but oh! So brilliant.' These may be conventional remarks about a series of highly conventional middlebrow novels, but at the very least they serve to demonstrate quite how firmly the spirit of literary appreciation had been inculcated into a well-educated teenaged boy in the period 1914–18. As to where 'Hal' had acquired his literary sensibility, it was hardly likely to have come from school – he was educated at Eton, which still devoted much of its curriculum to the classics. One can only assume that it derived from his family background, that he lived among people who took books seriously and regarded them both as an aspect of the social milieu in which they operated and as a suitable subject for discussion, even as one sat in a military training camp awaiting a summons to almost certain death.

Hal's other great enthusiasm, it scarcely needs saying, was the poetry of Rupert Brooke. For this was a literary culture in which poetry continued to play a dominant part. As Penelope Fitzgerald once remarked: 'Certainly at the beginning of the twentieth century, the English people still liked poetry.' The proof of this statement lies strewn all over the 1920s literary scene, but at a very basic level it can be detected in the large number of successful mid-century novelists who began their careers with the aim of being a poet. Graham Greene's first publication, at the tender age of 20, was a slim volume entitled *Babbling April*. Alec Waugh's *Resentment* (1918) falls into the same category – the early work of a young man who has not yet decided where his true vocation lies but is conscious of inhabiting a literary marketplace where much of the smart money is still being placed on verse. Orwell's Burma notebooks from the 1920s are full of amateur versifying, and he continued to publish occasional poems until as late as the Second World War. And if young men (and women) wanted to write poetry for aesthetic reasons, they were also aware of the considerable financial rewards it could attract. John Masefield's *Collected Poems* (1923) sold 80,000 copies, a figure which many a reputedly best-selling novel would struggle to match. Although Masefield had the advantage of being a household name, it was also possible for much less celebrated practitioners to record sales figures that would have been unthought of half a century later. A trawl through the advertisements of the successive volumes of *Georgian Poetry* confirms what relatively big business early 1920s poetry publishing could be: Flecker's *The Old Ships* is in its third 1,000; Harold Monro's *Children of Love* is in its fourth, along with his *Strange Meetings*. Even so unexceptionable a bloom in the Georgian garden as Ralph Hodgson's *Poems* (1917) went through eight printings by 1930.

The boom in poetry may have begun to diminish by the end of the 1920s – Edmund Blunden noted in 1928 that *Retreat* had been 'fairly well received' by the book trade with sixty copies of the fine edition disposed of and 260 copies of the standard – but to a certain degree the evidence of sales figures is beside the point, or at any rate secondary to the existence of a wide-ranging poetic culture which gathered up all generations and social classes in its net. It was an era of Popular Reciters, of children being encouraged to learn party pieces ('The Rime of the Ancient Mariner', 'How Horatius Held the Bridge', 'The Boy Stood on the Burning Deck'), of schoolmasters entertaining their charges with wistful stanzas from Andrew Lang, of writers asked to identify the formative influences that worked on them as children unhesitatingly setting down half a dozen volumes from the mid-Victorian poetry shelves; E. M. Delafield, for example, writing in 1935, listed her favourite books from childhood as *Idylls of the King*, *Enoch Arden*, *Marmion*, the *Poems of Jane and Ann Taylor*, *The Young Reciter* in two volumes and a bumper compendium entitled *1,001 Gems of Poetry*. All this worked its effect. As Rose Macaulay once put it, 'there was a kind of poetry intoxication going round', next to which the attractions of the average popular novel could sometimes seem painfully second rate.

Nothing symbolised the extraordinary intergenerational pull of certain kinds of verse, not to mention the intensely communal atmosphere in which so much poetry was conceived and appreciated, more than the success of the Poetry Bookshop, established by Harold Monro shortly before the war and still in business, albeit in diminished form, until the mid-1930s. Monro (1879 – 1932) was an odd character altogether, a twice-married homosexual of Scottish ancestry – the family owned a private lunatic asylum – who, arriving in London in 1911, rapidly became an habitué of the Bloomsbury salons: Virginia Woolf noted that 'his weakness, and paleness, did not impress us, but then, perhaps weakness and paleness are the necessary qualities'. The success of his newly founded journal, the *Poetry Review*, and his work for the Poetry Society led to an approach from the great contemporary talent spotter Edward Marsh and the first of the five volumes of *Georgian Poetry*. By 1913 Monro was established in premises at 35 Devonshire Street, where he began to publish his own illustrated rhyme sheets and preside over twice-weekly readings attended by everyone from Yeats, Lawrence and Wilfred Owen to Georgian staples such as Rupert Brooke, John Drinkwater and Walter de la Mare. If poetry in London during the Great War had a nerve centre it was here in Devonshire Street, where a coal fire burned in winter, seating was provided for browsers and the general atmosphere seems to have been halfway between a private subscription library and an exceptionally well-appointed gentlemen's club. Something of its enormous *réclame* may be divined from the newly conscripted Richard Aldington's account of the day in 1916 when, on informing the quartermaster sergeant that he was a poet, he was asked: 'Oh, are you? Have you ever heard of the Poetry Bookshop?'

A more astute businessman would have made better use of these advantages. But Monro, for all his private income, had no capital. And there were private demons forever on hand to drag him down. Eventually these went beyond his conflicted sexual life (his second wife was left 'terror-stricken' after he tried unsuccessfully to explain) to take in alcoholism, and thereafter the enterprise declined. By the time of the mid-1920s removal to Great Russell Street, opposite the British Museum, the shop's fortunes were on the wane. Walter Allen, paying a visit as a schoolboy in July 1928, found the premises empty and Monro lolling in a swivel chair, his feet on the desk in front of him: the proprietor neither looked up nor uttered a word. But seen in the round, Monro left an impressive trail. Whatever one may think of the Georgian anthologies a century later it is something to have been the impresario of Aldington's *Images* (1910–1915), and Robert Graves's *Over the Brazier*. And all this is to ignore the quarterly magazine *Poetry and Drama* and the shop's monthly *Chapbook* miscellanies. If, in the end, his greatest legacy was sheer goodwill then this is not to skate over the question of his influence. Eliot was a fan – despite having one of his poems rejected – and contributed editorial notes to the posthumous *Collected Poems*. Elizabeth Bowen remembered listening 'after dark, in a barn-like room, to Ezra Pound reading aloud what was hypnotically unintelligible to me by the light of one candle'. John Lehmann's memoirs talk of the 'magnet-pull of the Poetry Bookshop under Harold Monro'. One vital aspect of the shop's success was its appeal to children. A large proportion of the rhyme sheets were specifically designed for younger readers, while the premises themselves left an overwhelming impression of heat, comfort and solidarity. Penelope Fitzgerald left an affectionate account of her own early visits to the Devonshire Street site:

> The shop itself was on the ground floor of a dilapidated eighteenth-century house, with only one cold-water tap for the whole building. However, as you came through the swing door you felt the warmth of a coal fire burning at the other end of the room. There was a dog stretched out there and a cat, which sometimes sprang about the shelves, apparently deliberately, knocking down piles of books. The furniture had been made by the Fabian master-carpenter Romney Green, and was exceptionally solid, the curtains were of sacking, and there were cushions in 'jolly' colours. Across the walls rhyme sheets were displayed in rows, a penny plain, twopence coloured, and bought mostly for children. A whole generation learned to love poetry from these rhyme sheets.

In old age Fitzgerald wrote to a friend: 'I'm perhaps the last person who used to go to sleep as a child with a coal fire and the PB rhyme sheets on the wall.' Throughout her long life, Harold Monro's creation figures as a talisman, a kind of literary King Charles's head, forever driving her on towards commemoration. She schemes to write a full-length study of it, but is repulsed by a less than enthusiastic publisher. Undeterred, she conceives a biography of the poet Charlotte Mew, for which the shop will act as a backdrop. In her 70s, she produces a tremendous introduction to Howard J. Woolmer's exhaustive bibliography of Monro's teeming shelves. What is being commemorated, it seems fair to say, is not so much the Poetry Bookshop's physical reality – its welcoming fires, its assembly of 'all the poetry in print by every living English poet' – as its symbolic significance: an enduring example of the effect that a certain kind of literary culture could have on the sensibilities of those who came to worship at its flame.

Meanwhile, there is another question to be canvassed, which conventional studies of 'literary life' are sometimes prone to ignore: *who were the writers?* Investigations of this sort are, naturally, a statistician's nightmare. John Sutherland once wrote an essay entitled 'The Victorian Novelists: Who Were They?' in which he proposed that the number of individual novels published in the period 1837–1901 might be in the region of 50,000, and put the number of writers who laboured to produce them at 3,500. At the end of the century Walter Besant, in his capacity as founder of the Society of Authors, calculated that the number of novelists at work in Britain approached 1,200, of whom perhaps 200 were entirely self-supporting (Sutherland observes that 'this seems somewhat on the low side'). And these, it may be pointed out, were only the novelists: by and large the Victorian poets, essayists and all-purpose men of letters await their taxonomist. The most obvious point to be made of them as a professional bloc is that, encouraged by the increase in periodicals and publishing opportunities, their number was sharply on the rise. The 1881 census lists 3,400 'authors, editors and journalists'. By 1911 the figure had shot up to 14,000, and was set to rise higher still.

Inevitably the blanket description 'author' gives no idea of the very different gradations of status that applied, from Arnold Bennett to the penny-a-liners on obscure provincial weeklies, but even the penny-a-liner – *especially* the penny-a-liner – would have known that if anything distinguished his craft, here in the second decade of the twentieth century, it was a growing sense of respectability. The days when Thackeray's Major Pendennis could warn his nephew that literature was barely considered an occupation for a gentleman had long since disappeared – almost as remote as the moment when Thackeray himself, coming away from an evening party at Holland House and remarking to a fellow guest on the free and easy atmosphere that prevailed was informed that, yes, it was so free and easy that even Mr Thackeray had been invited. The effects of this transformation can be glimpsed in those late Victorian novels which touch on the question of the literary marketplace. In Gissing's *New Grub Street* (1891), for example, the veteran hack Alfred Yule sees his hopes of an editorship dashed by the appointment of a serious young man fresh out of university. Gissing returns to this theme in one of his last books, *The Private Papers of Henry Ryecroft* (1903), the melancholic narrator of which, himself a retired writer, devotes several pages to the relative prestige that his profession now enjoys. Ryecroft, who, like Gissing, served a long apprenticeship in the garrets of the Tottenham Court Road, surmises that the path of 'literature' is being made too easy:

> Doubtless it is a rare thing nowadays for a lad whose education ranks him with the upper middle class to find himself utterly without resources should he wish to devote himself to the profession of letters. And there is the root of the matter; writing has come to be recognised as a profession, almost as cut-and-dried as church or law; a lad may go into it with all parental approval, with ready avuncular support.

None of this would have appealed much to Gissing, who was once heard enquiring of some up-and-coming young talent 'But has he starved?' Twenty years after these words were written, what Ryecroft calls the 'carpet author' was becoming the rule rather than the exception, and 'authorship' emphatically a middle- to upper-middle-class pursuit. Of the seventeen contributors to a symposium edited by Graham Greene in which a group of well-known authors were invited to reminisce about their education, only one, Walter Greenwood, had attended a state school. For the vast majority of recruits to the profession, a private establishment was de rigueur. Here, as in so many areas of national life, Eton was in a class of its own. Of the literary men who made their debuts in the interwar era, well over a dozen – their number included Orwell, Powell, Cyril Connolly, Brian Howard, Harold Acton, John Heygate, Henry Green, John Lehmann, Robert Byron and Peter Fleming – were Old Etonians. This is unprecedented, but most public schools of the period were able to add a name or two to the roster: Harrow (L. P. Hartley), Winchester (John Sparrow, William Empson), St Paul's (Patrick Hamilton, Julian Maclaren-Ross), Marlborough (Beverley Nichols, John Betjeman), Wellington (Harold Nicolson), Gresham's (W. H. Auden), Sherborne (Alec Waugh, E. Arnott Robinson), Lancing (Evelyn Waugh, Dudley Carew), the Perse (F. R. Leavis) and Berkhamsted (Graham Greene).

All this may make the world of post-Great War literature seem desperately exclusive. But simultaneously the cadre of lower-middle-class grammar school boys who would cut such a swathe through the literary world of the 1950s was already beginning to swell the talent pool. By the early 1930s its number included Walter Allen (Aston Grammar School, Birmingham), Louis Golding (Manchester Grammar School), J. B. Priestley (Bradford) and H. E. Bates (Kettering). And this is to ignore both the steady rise of determinedly working-class writers such as B. L. Coombes, Harry Heslop, James Hanley and Jack Hilton, generally educated at council schools in the north of England, and the occasional maverick who came more or less from nowhere – the rather older A. E. Coppard (born 1878), say, who left school at the age of 9 to support his family and pursued a variety of day jobs ranging from Reuter's messenger to clerk and professional athlete before taking a job in an Oxford foundry that brought him into contact with literary-minded undergraduates. Female education, on the other hand, tended to be more exclusive. Some women writers, such as Nancy Mitford, were still being educated at home by governesses. Other nurseries of fledgling female talent included Downe House School (Elizabeth Bowen), Cheltenham Ladies College (Theodora Benson) and the mixed-sex 'progressive' establishment of Bedales (Julia Strachey).

Victorian literary society had bequeathed a dynastic tradition, in which successive generations of sons, and sometimes daughters, pursued what was virtually regarded as the family calling. Dickens's eldest son Charley worked on his father's magazines. Thackeray's daughter Anny became a successful novelist in her own right, and his posthumously acquired son-in-law Leslie Stephen was, by way of a second marriage, the father of Virginia Woolf. Both Mrs Frances Trollope's sons Anthony and Thomas followed her into the trade. By the interwar era, in a profession that had expanded three or fourfold, the question of parental occupation did not loom so large. Orwell's father worked in the Indian Civil Service; Anthony Powell's was an army officer; Graham Greene's the headmaster of his son's school. Of the two dozen names mentioned in the previous paragraph, only one – Patrick Hamilton – had a parent who had published novels. On the other hand, this did not mean that the Victorian tradition had altogether lapsed. Many of the new generation of writers of the 1920s and 1930s had grown up in an atmosphere in which books were a part of the family's professional compass. John Lehmann and his sister Rosamond were the children of Rudolph Lehmann, the celebrated

Punch journalist. Alec and Evelyn Waugh were the sons of the publisher Arthur Waugh, chairman of Chapman & Hall. Each, in later years, published books with the firm and at one time or another served on its board of directors. The force of these associations could be felt on much less exalted rungs of the publishing ladder. The magazine writer Herbert Allingham's father, for example, was the proprietor of a religious newspaper called the *Christian Globe*.

If the writers who populated the literary world of the interwar era tended to share similar backgrounds, to have attended the same kind of schools and universities (Oxford by far the most common destination) and to operate in the same kind of social landscapes, then the jobs they took while attempting to establish themselves were generally concentrated on a small range of activities more or less associated with their literary ambitions. Publishing was a frequent pre-career choice: Norman Collins worked for the firm of Victor Gollancz; John Lehmann served a bracing apprenticeship with Leonard and Virginia Woolf at the Hogarth Press. Numbers of aspiring writers trained as journalists: Graham Greene laboured on *The Times*; Dudley Carew on the *London Mercury*; Patrick Balfour as a gossip columnist on the *Daily Sketch*. Nancy Mitford reported for the *Lady*. A handful, such as S. P. B. Mais, a former Sherborne master, and Evelyn Waugh, who worked in a succession of down-at-heel prep schools, had graduated from teaching. Academe was not yet the draw it was to become, but several writers, including Louis MacNeice (Birmingham), Edward Shanks (Liverpool) and Edmund Blunden (Oxford) held down positions in universities. The author whose day job had no connection at all with the world of his creative imagination – the novelist G. U. Ellis, for instance, who worked in a bank – was becoming a rarity, although many a writer at the start of his career, notably in the Depression-hit early 1930s, was forced to take whatever he could get. Julian Maclaren-Ross was reduced to hawking vacuum cleaners door to door in Bognor Regis. Alternatively, there was the writer whose early career seems to have been chosen in the not quite conscious assumption it might at some future point offer useful material. The experience of serving as a policeman in Burma gave Orwell the subject matter for his first novel, *Burmese Days* (1934), while Patrick Hamilton's *Tuppence Coloured* (1927) derived from his own early experiences working for provincial repertory companies. In the same way, Henry Green's decision to work at the Birmingham office of his family's engineering firm in the late 1920s provided the background to his second novel, *Living* (1929).

At the same time, the job that sustained the fledgling writer while he, or she, incubated their early works was only as good as the professional circles in which they moved and the networks whose successful infiltration would guarantee them exposure. Occasionally these alliances could go as far back as school or university. An Etonian mafia was much in evidence in the late 1920s, whose members shamelessly reviewed each other's books and finessed introductions to sympathetic editors. The merits of a novel written by one of the characters in Nancy Mitford's *Christmas Pudding* (1932) are apparently such that, as Mitford puts it, even the reviewers who hadn't been to Eton and Oxford with him had praised it. Even Orwell, usually the epitome of professional scrupulousness, was not immune to this kind of wire-pulling, reviewing his old Eton contemporary Cyril Connolly's *The Rock Pool* (1936) for the *New Statesman*, while telling his friend 'You scratch my back and I'll scratch yours.' To the vigilant and mostly academic outsider – the Leavises, say, in their Cambridge fortress – literary London was perennially degraded by its obsession with the coterie spirit: Bloomsbury; the circle gathered around Eliot and the *Criterion*; Squire and his henchmen at the *London Mercury*; the rapt disciples of the Sitwell school; the Catholic tendency represented by Chesterton, Belloc and their acolytes – frail alliances, perhaps, sometimes capable of shifting imperceptibly into each other, but when heads needed to be counted, in some case of character assassination or controversy, able to flex their collective muscle to considerable effect. Even the highly disparate collection of intellects and enthusiasms assembled by the Bright Young People, the name that posterity has bestowed on the social circles frequented by Evelyn Waugh and his friends in the late 1920s, was a force to be reckoned with not merely in the literary weeklies but in the publishing world that lay behind them. Between 1927 and 1933, for example, Duckworth, where Anthony Powell worked as an editor, published books by at least half a dozen members of the group, including Waugh, Robert Byron, Cecil Beaton, Inez Holden and Powell himself.

Beyond the coteries lay a much less adversarial and contested world of clubs, institutions and semi-official meeting places through which the majority of novelists and journalists forged the alliances that would enable them to develop their careers: the lunch and tea parties hosted by such prominent figures of the interwar era literary circuit as Mrs Belloc-Lowndes (Hilaire Belloc's sister), the novelist W. L. George or J. D. Beresford, literary adviser to the firm of Collins, who entertained lavishly at his house in St John's Wood; gatherings at the PEN Club, founded in 1921 by Mrs Dawson-Scott, or the Tomorrow Club, whose members would assemble each week at premises on Long Acre to hear talks by the leading personalities of the day. If this was a much more fragmented landscape than its Victorian equivalent, then it was still small and centralised enough to be negotiated by anyone with the right kind of connections. Alec Waugh's accounts of his first forays into literary London, for example, are a testimony to just how heterogeneous a universe the specimen early 1920s bookman could inhabit: trips to the left-wing 1917 Club in Gerrard Street; invitations to Harold Monro's parties, where he met the Sitwells, Ford Madox Ford, Eliot and F. S. Flint; eventual graduation to the entertainments presided over by the three great hostesses of the era, the Ladies Morrell, Colefax and Cunard. If they were not, ultimately, Waugh's kind of people – they were certainly not the kind of people who would have read and admired his novels – then he was, at any rate, able to meet them socially on more or less neutral ground and burnish up the memory of them in later life.

Many-mansioned, and yet subtly – sometimes not so subtly – interconnected, capable of displaying a powerful sense of solidarity if its professional integrity seemed threatened, it was a community able to take full advantage of the media opportunities with which it was constantly presented. Led by middle-market newspapers such as the *Daily Mail* and the *Daily Express*, the popular press of the 1920s was busy developing a new kind of journalism, less respectful, less hidebound, keener on personality and controversy, drenching in artificial light the individual figures it thought suitable for its readers' edification. While it is overstating the case to say that in 'The Dragoman', the society column that Tom Driberg contributed to the *Express* in the late 1920s, one can detect the first glimmerings of modern celebrity culture, this was an environment which a substantial proportion of writers, particularly the younger and more publicity-conscious, were anxious to exploit. To a certain extent the fashionable writer had always been a celebrity – Dickens had been feted wherever he went; Stevenson could be purchased in bronze statuette; Thackeray's daughter Anny was so overcome by her first glimpse of the young

Swinburne reading his poems that she burst into tears on the spot. But the arc light that picked out the celebrated writers of the 1920s was that much more powerful. Press symposia found them debating the issues of the day. Newspapers reprinted their addresses to public bodies (Graham Greene left a notably jaundiced account of having to subedit transcripts of J. M. Barrie's speeches for *The Times*) and offered collected editions of their works as competition prizes: in old age Anthony Powell still possessed a leather-bound pocket set of the *Collected Works of John Galsworthy*, won as a schoolboy courtesy of the *Morning Post*.

Their opinions constantly solicited and invoked, their photograph regularly featured in both professional and non-professional milieux – it was as usual to see Evelyn Waugh's picture in the *Tatler* as in the *Bookman* – the writer was a conspicuous figure in the 1920s media scrum, and, as a result, able to benefit from a degree of exposure otherwise extended only to a successful politician or sports personality. And it was not simply the young and opportunistic who were able to prosper. Even A. C. Benson, by now a barnacled veteran from a bygone age, was gratified to discover that 1,500 people had turned out to hear him speak on a visit to the Birmingham Institute and that an enthusiastic fan had snipped his signature out of a training college visitors' book. It was the same with Hugh Walpole, whose readers could, on visiting the Lakeland village where he periodically retreated to write his books, purchase souvenir mugs on which his features were embossed. This kind of attention naturally gave the well-known writer a considerable status in the social circles of the period: rarely a household name, save in exceptional circumstances – Beverley Nichols, say, who was commissioned to advertise de Reszke cigarettes – but one who could expect to be recognised and use this recognition to his advantage. Evelyn Waugh's diary for May 1930, shortly after *Vile Bodies'* appearance on the best-seller lists, contains the entry: 'After dinner I went to the Savoy Theatre and said "I am Evelyn Waugh. Please give me a seat." So they did.'

But these accretions of glamour and, by implication, prestige, did not merely turn a proportion of the 1920s-era literary community into celebrities. They also worked on a more abstract, if not mythological level, to create what might be called 'the idea of the writer' – a series of elemental reference points, some of them patently absurd but nearly all of them having at least some vestigial tethering in reality, by which literary men and women could be conceptualised by the reading and non-reading public. Above all, there was an expectation of what a writer ought to look like. 'Author?' a customs official once demanded of Anthony Powell as he presented his passport. 'Where's your pipe?' These stereotypes, many of them gleefully exaggerated by newspapers and *Punch* cartoons, are a feature of 1920s popular culture. Seen variously in the column inches devoted to Bloomsbury affectation and to the 'Georgian' hankering for cricket, foaming tankards and Sussex-by-the-Sea, they are at their most pronounced in the field of poetry. Here the assumption of a down-at-heel romanticism unhesitatingly prevailed. When the hero of P. G. Wodehouse's *Leave it to Psmith* (1923) infiltrates Blandings Castle in the guise of the well-known Canadian poet 'Ralston McTodd' the attendant bright young things, though acknowledging his personal resonance, are disappointed by the shortness of his hair. Turgis, the pimply clerk in Priestley's *Angel Pavement* (1930), sprucing himself up in the hope of impressing his lady-love, instantly becomes the butt of the office wits: his former shabbiness is said to be reminiscent of a 'spring poet'. The young Penelope Fitzgerald could never believe that the respectable-seeming Walter de la Mare wrote verse: 'I knew how poets ought to look because at that time they walked about the streets of Hampstead.' It was the same with the veterans of the pre-war age. Powell's *What's Become of Waring* (1939) carries a description of an ageing man of letters named Minhinnick. A 'square-looking elderly man with a lot of white hair trimmed on Roundhead principles'; got up in a gentleman-farmer suit with a broad-brimmed black hat, gnarled walking stick bobbing at his side, he looks 'every inch an unsuccessful literary man'. After this, it is hardly necessary to add that Minhinnick is the author of the soon-to-be-pulped epic poem *Aristogeiton: A Harmony*.

Nowhere, it might be said, were these conceptions of how writers ought to look and behave more pronounced than in the field of female authorship. *Punch* had been having fun with the bluestocking – sometimes severe, sometimes shock-haired, at all times engaged in obscure pursuits that compromised her femininity – since at least the 1850s. Seventy years later, this interest had become focused on the figure of the successful woman novelist, sometimes found in her Mayfair dining room or, if younger, in her sophisticated metropolitan flat, but more often than not pictured abroad in comfortable Mediterranean exile. *Angel Pavement*'s ground-down Mrs Dersingham, daydreaming about an ideal life while waiting for her dinner guests to arrive, pictures herself as 'a terribly successful woman writer with a villa somewhere on the Riviera with orange trees and mimosa and things and lunch in the sunshine and marvellous distinguished people coming to call' (the male equivalent of this vision would be the 'shit in the shuttered chateau' of Larkin's poem, writing his 'six hundred words a day', or Compton Mackenzie, who eventually retreated to the Isle of Capri). Wodehouse, always a reliable guide to literary fads, catches something of these prescriptions in the short story 'Best Seller'. Its hero is Egbert Mulliner, a former employee of the *Weekly Booklover* currently recuperating from the strain of having to interview lady novelists with names like Mrs Goole-Plank and Laura la Motte Grindlay: 'For six months, week in and week out, Egbert Mulliner had been listening to female novelists talking about Art and their ideals. He had seen them in cosy corners in their boudoirs, had watched them being kind to their dogs and happiest when amongst their flowers.' When this casualty from the battlefront of light literature asks Evangeline Pembury if she will marry him, his first task is to ensure that she never has written, and never will write, a novel. Then, against all expectation, Evangeline betrays him. Her debut, *Parted Ways*, which recounts their courtship in intimate detail, is an instant sensation. On the strength of this she acquires a Byronesque literary agent, is interviewed in the press ('Her art, she told them, was rhythmical rather than architectural, and she inclined, if anything, to the school of the sur-realists') and is invited to talk to literary societies on 'Some Tendencies in Modern Fiction'. In the end the couple are reconciled, but it is a near-run thing: what remains is a burlesque of certain aspects of the early twentieth-century literary scene whose paraphernalia – and whose animating spirit – is sometimes uncomfortably close to reality.

Inevitably, some novelists contributed, knowingly or unknowingly, to this mythologising process. Much of the publicising done on authors' behalf in the 1920s and 1930s focused on the circumstances in which they had begun their careers, the struggles encountered along the way and the – occasionally – romantic situations in which they had produced their breakthrough books: the enormous success of A. J. Cronin's debut *Hatter's Castle* (1931) was greatly enhanced by press accounts of its composition in the study of a rented holiday home by Loch Fyne, where Cronin, a doctor diagnosed with a duodenal ulcer, had been sent on furlough, and its despatch to the firm of Victor Gollancz after the author's wife had stuck a pin at random into the *Writers' and Artists' Yearbook*. But to read eyewitness accounts of the successful interwar era writer in action – an Arnold Bennett, a Hugh Walpole, a Michael Arlen – is to become instantly aware both of the relatively exalted nature of the milieu (the Savoy supper party, the chauffeur-driven car, the Mayfair mews flat) and the high degree of stage management that was involved. When Paul Pennyfeather, back at Scone College, Oxford, in the final chapter of *Decline and Fall*, is hailed by his former associate Philbrick from the back of an open Rolls-Royce, it seems perfectly logical that, when asked who his opulent friend is he should reply 'Arnold Bennett', for this is precisely the image that Bennett had built up for himself. Even the Eliot seen dining by himself in a West End restaurant on the way to literary parties – aloof, mysterious, impregnable – was helping to sustain his own mystique.

But if it was an age in which the ambassadors of literary culture were becoming more self-conscious about their activities, then it was also one in which they became more self-conscious about the business of writing itself. The years during and after the Great War brought a shoal of what, for all their varying levels of theoretical intensity and intellectual engagement, would now be described as 'how-to' books, operators' manuals for the aspiring student of literature: Sir Arthur Quiller-Couch's *On the Art of Writing* (1916), Percy Lubbock's *The Craft of Fiction* (1921), Edwin Muir's *The Structure of the Novel* and E. M. Forster's *Aspects of the Novel* (both 1927). If the first principles they set down sometimes seem rather obvious – Lubbock's 'the beginning of criticism is to read aright, in other words to get in touch with the book as nearly as may be' – then, in an age which was still disposed to regard most fiction as a form of light entertainment, it is a relief to see them set down at all. Neither were such primers without their influence on later generations of novelists: Graham Greene, for one, paid tribute to *The Craft of Fiction*, with its emphasis on the Jamesian 'point of view'. There was a price to be paid for this absorption in the mechanics of writing, and it came in jargon – Miss Pembury, again, whose art is 'rhythmical rather than architectural'. On the other hand it had the welcome advantage of bringing questions of style, narrative structure and technique a great deal closer to the averagely intelligent reader than they ever had been before. And in this insistence on complexity – the prospect of alternative readings needing to be pinned down before they disappear, Lubbock's talk about the audience 'making' the novel – lies an awareness of the part played in literary culture by a constituency whose existence can sometimes be grievously overlooked: the reader.

CHAPTER 2

The Georgian Twilight

> Readers 200 years hence will be hunting up the Georgian books as we do the old songs and miscellanies.
>
> J. C. Squire

> For some reason you have been regarded as the head of a reactionary conspiracy, hostile to almost every modern tendency in literature.
>
> Robert Lynd paying tribute to Squire in *John O'London's Weekly*

Even now, three-quarters of a century after the last bona fide Georgian poet laid down his pen, there is still no real agreement as to what the adjective stands for. However technically accurate, Somerset Maugham's definition of a piece of poetry or prose written during the reign of George V comes nowhere near to conveying the myriad uses to which the word could be put, let alone the well-nigh mythological trappings with which it eventually came to be decorated. Neither does the formal record of 'Georgian' literature – the five volumes of *Georgian Poetry*, the collections of *Georgian Stories* which went on appearing until the late 1920s – offer any real impression of its impact on the book-world culture of the day. There were Georgian literary scenes, as anatomised by the critic-novelist Frank Swinnerton. There were Georgian nurseries, with their attendant 'bad boys', Georgian summers, Georgian prodigies, Georgian pastiches and, in the fullness of time, when one or two of those involved had got round to writing their autobiographies, a whole raft of Georgian adventures, Georgian boyhoods and Georgian summings-up. And this is to ignore the *Punch*-endorsed popular conception of Georgianism as a kind of compound of briar pipes, foaming tankards, cricket matches on village greens, rolling English drunkards and rolling English roads. Above all, there were Georgian readers, thousands of them, for whom a magazine editor like J. C. Squire or a poet like Walter de la Mare were potent allies in a fight to preserve the literary standards of the past against the devitalising influences of the post-war era.

Some of the writers responsible for this mythologising might sometimes complain about what they regarded as a bad case of conceptual straitjacketing: Squire once lamented that the members of 'the Georgian School' were merely 'a certain number of younger poets, selections from whom were gathered together in a series of volumes by Mr Edward Marsh, an anthologist of genius'. But not all these evocations, it should straightaway be said, were hostile. Neither was the chance to join this vast if rather diffuse movement necessarily disdained by representatives of an older generation anxious to show that they were still in the swing and of the moment. Desmond Coke, on reading a favourable mention of one of his early novels in *The Times*, wrote to inform its author, not altogether humorously, that he was thinking of altering his *carte de visite* from 'Last of the Edwardians' to 'First of the Georgians'. But none of this is to disguise the fact that by the mid-1920s – even earlier in sophisticated circles – 'Georgian' was a term of abuse. There were two explanations of this critical about-turn. The first was the sheer extremity of the depths plumbed by Georgian poetry in a world that was already becoming the province of Pound and Eliot. The second was the widespread resentment attracted by the impresarios and opinion-formers who cultivated 'Georgian' literature as a form and brought it to the public.

The first volume of *Georgian Poetry* (1912), edited by Edward Marsh, with contributions from James Elroy Flecker, Rupert Brooke, John Masefield and W. H. Davies, had cleared a great deal of dead wood from a late Victorian forest floor still stalked by Rondeliers, decadents and the polished exponents of *vers de société*. If there was no consensus over poetic first principles – how, a critic once wondered, can one meaningfully claim that the verse of Walter de la Mare *and* John Masefield is authentically Georgian in terms of its style and content? – then at least everyone could agree on a general predisposition towards simplicity, straight-talking, 'medium' and, of course – a prerequisite of practically all home-grown literature produced since the 1890s – anti-Victorianism. But by the appearance of the third volume, cracks had begun to appear in the varnish. *Georgian Poetry 1916–1917*, billed as 'the preselection of chosen examples from the work of contemporary poets belonging to the younger generation', is a pantomime horse of a book, half of it composed of reportage from the Flanders trenches, the other half apparently written by poets for whom the Great War and its attendant horrors might just as well not have existed. A century later, the juxtaposition of a poem like Sassoon's 'They', which contrasts a bishop's talk of 'just causes' with some of its practical consequences ('For George lost both his legs; and Bill's stone blind / Poor Jim's shot through the lungs and like to die') and the self-conscious escapism of Harold Monro's 'Weekend' can make uncomfortable reading:

> The train! The twelve o'clock for paradise.
> Hurry, or it will try to creep away.
> Out in the country everyone is wise:
> We can be only wise on Saturday.
> There you are waiting, little friendly house:
> Those are your chimney-stacks with you between,
> Surrounded by old trees and strolling cows,
> Staring through all your windows at the green.
> Your homely floor is creaking for our tread;
> The smiling tea-pot with contented spout
> Thinks of the boiling water, and the bread
> Longs for the butter. All their hands are out
> To greet us, and the gentle blankets seem
> Purring and crooning: 'Lie in us, and dream.'

And so on for a further nine stanzas. It is not just that the contrasts on which Monro so breezily insists – rural authenticity versus urban artifice, genuine pleasure only being obtainable at one remove from the rat race – would have struck a Caroline sonneteer as hackneyed; it is not that the pathetic fallacy begins to clang in the reader's ear (and Monro had form in this department – see his 'Every Thing' which imagines the 'little cries' of household objects); merely that the whimsicality seems, in the end, to be entirely self-conscious, the poem's point rather than its vehicle, a matter of shutting your eyes to what is really going on in the world and taking refuge in archness. Plenty of poetic movements, naturally, have ended their days in stylisation but the stylisation of the later Georgian poets was of a peculiarly rarefied cast: finding expression in a handful of symbols – moons, parrots, teeming jungle verdure – in lyrical evocations of landscapes (real and imagined) and their fauna that do not so much describe as simply enumerate. In his invaluable *The Georgian Revolt*, the critic Robert Ross is careful to separate 'Georgian' and 'neo-Georgian', to draw a line between – in effect – a first wave of poets who had something to say, and a second wave who were boiling down the original ingredients of Georgian poetry into a succession of stock formulae; a separation which doesn't ignore the fact that there are distinctions to be made. W. J. Turner ('When I was but thirteen or so / I went into a golden land / Chimborazo, Cotopaxi / Took me by the hand') was a genuine exotic, whose fantasy worlds, with their shimmering evocations of white feet paddling in tropical seas, seem properly strange. On the other hand, far too much later Georgian poetry tried to extract a mystical significance from what were effectively stage props. Take, for example, John Drinkwater's 'Moonlit Apples' from *Georgian Poetry IV 1918–1919*:

> At the top of the house, the apples are laid in rows,
> And the skylight lets the moonlight in, and those
> Apples are deep-sea apples of green. There goes
> A cloud on the moon in the autumn night.
> A mouse in the wainscot scratches, and scratches, and then
> There is no sound at the top of the house of men
> Or mice; and the cloud is blown, and the moon again
> Dapples the apples with deep-sea light.

At one level – that fundamental level at which a poet squares up to his, or her, subject matter – one can appreciate the Georgian dilemma, or rather the dilemma faced by those poets who, unlike Sassoon, were not directly involved in fighting a war. The temptation to ignore something so cataclysmic and terrifying that it did not seem assimilable by conventional poetic forms occurred to much better poets than John Drinkwater. But the consequence was that when a neo-Georgian sits down to address a definite 'war subject' – a tribute, say, to a friend killed in action – what results is usually accompanied by a terrific sense of strain.

We shan't see Willy any more, Mamie.
He won't be coming any more:
He came back once again and again,
But he won't get leave any more.
We looked from the window, and there was his cab,
And we ran downstairs like a streak,
And he said 'Hullo, you bad dog,' and you crouched to the
floor,
Paralysed to hear him speak.

No one is doubting Squire's sincerity, nor that of his editor (who assured his contributor that 'I want the Bulldog frightfully! I see you don't put it very high in your own list, but I think it's a wonderful thing'). And no doubt it would be perfectly possible, in the right hands, to construct a memorial to a dead friend seen through the eyes of a dog to whom the deceased can never return. It is not that 'To a Bulldog' is mawkish, or that its bluffness – the sense that there are deeper things lying behind it to which the poet doesn't care to admit – eventually grates, merely that the reader leaves it with a feeling that some vital part of the poetic jigsaw has been purposely excluded, and that in trying to confront the death of *W.H.S., Capt. [Acting Major] R.F.A; killed April 12, 1917*, Squire has in some strange way only evaded it.

By this time, in any case, a critical reaction had set in. Eliot had already sniffed at *Georgian Poetry 1916–1917*, but the first really serious assault on the Georgian circle came with Middleton Murry's *Athenaeum* review of Volume IV. Murry's main argument, remorselessly developed during the 1920s, was levelled at the Georgians' deep-dyed innocuousness. In an age that was reaching out to embrace upset and psychological unease there was a suspicion that Georgian verse had become spiritless and defensive, frightened by the prospect of a long climb to the summit of Parnassus and content to exist on a subsidiary crag. 'There is nothing disturbing about them. They are kind, generous and even noble' Murry deposed. 'They sympathise with animals and inanimate nature. They have shiny foreheads with big bumps of benevolence . . . and one inclines to believe that their eyes must be frequently filled with honest tears, if only because their vision is blurred.' Simultaneously, Murry was one of the first critics to voice the conviction that much Georgian poetry, by this stage, was a matter of keeping the ball rolling, going through the motions, settling for the easy goal of facility rather than genuine engagement. Having taken apart Squire's 'The Moon' from his 1920 collection of the same name, he decided that 'the suspicion hardens into a certainty that it is not really a poem, because it did not have its origin in any compulsive emotion, but was the outcome of a desire to write poetry rather than the urgent need to express a perception'.

This was incendiary stuff, for Murry meant to offend – he wrote privately to Katherine Mansfield that 'There's no doubt it's a fight to the finish between us and them . . . It's a queer feeling I begin to have now; that we're making literary history' – and even paid-up Georgians, Sassoon in particular, began to suspect that the real action was going on elsewhere. Marsh failed to help matters by continuing to reject submissions on grounds of obscurity: 'You c'd have pulled Blake to pieces in much the same way' the Poet Laureate Robert Bridges complained when his protégé Herbert Palmer failed to make the cut. Sales declined to 15,000 for Volume IV and 8,000 for Volume V, after which even Marsh was compelled to acknowledge that the project had stalled. At this point, too, what had begun as a protest against a particular poetic style, or rather that style's degeneration, had turned, imperceptibly, into a full-blown assault on the handful of literary personalities who were thought to be responsible for its failings.

Nearly sixty years after his death, J. C. Squire (1884–1958) – Sir John Squire as he somewhat improbably became in 1933 – remains one of the great bogey-figures of recent English literature, a byword for reputation-fixing, coterie politics and false standards from the pages of *Scrutiny* to the successive volumes of Eliot's *Collected Letters*. Lytton Strachey called him 'that little worm, Jack Squire'. To Virginia Woolf he was 'more repulsive than words can express, and malignant into the bargain'. Leavis thought him 'the epitome of all that men mean by the word philistine'. Inevitably, it takes a special kind of talent, or a special kind of exposure, to attract this kind of obloquy, and part of the almost fathomless hatred that Squire inspired in his enemies was a result of sheer ubiquitousness. He is simply everywhere in the literary 1920s, with a list of public engagements that includes starring appearances in any arts-world controversy worth the name to a commission to deliver the first live BBC commentary on the Oxford–Cambridge Boat Race. There was, needless to say, a permanent place reserved for him in the correspondence columns of *The Times*, and, as the decade wore on, a series of cameo roles in its literature. He appears, for example, as 'Jack Spire of the *London Hercules*' in *Decline and Fall* (1928) and as 'Hodge', the cricketer-poet in A. G. Macdonell's *England, Their England* (1933), which describes, with a kind of impressionistic faithfulness, the adventures of his famous cricket team 'The Invalids'. The potent hold he exerted over the young in his capacity as editorial sponsor and reputation-broker gives him a walk-on in many a literary autobiography of the period, several of which begin with hopeful forays to the *London Mercury*'s ramshackle premises at Poppins Court, east of Fleet Street. Geoffrey Grigson remembered calling on him at the age of 22 ('So I was going into Fleet Street. How? Was I interested in politics? No? Humph. Which, with some vague promises, was all'). And to ubiquity could be added a crusading spirit on behalf of traditional causes which mingled outright belligerence with an even less ingratiating tendency to patronise. A poet may just be able to tolerate being informed that his poems are bad, but very few people can stand being told, as were Pound ('Where he is incomprehensible he would not, I suspect, be found much less silly if one had the key to his cipher'), Edith Sitwell and countless others, that they were merely making themselves look foolish.

Squire's early career is an object lesson in defying your ancestral limitations. The son of a hard-drinking and family-deserting West Country veterinary surgeon ('What a swine my pater was'), he proceeded by way of Blundell's School in Tiverton to a history scholarship at St John's College, Cambridge. Ominously, his pronounced nostalgic side never really got over these early experiences: in old age he confessed to a friend that his two great regrets were a failure to win his First XV rugby colours and to occupy a college room that looked out over the Backs. At this point, however unlikely it may seem in the light of his later career – he stood as a Liberal in the general election of 1924 before switching his allegiance to Mussolini – he considered himself a socialist, and indeed his first publication, written in the intervals of working on the *Western Daily News*, was a pamphlet entitled *Socialism and Art*. There had already been some poems and translations from Baudelaire, but Squire's initial reputation, once he had moved to London and been taken up by A. R. Orage's *New Age*, was forged as a parodist: anyone brought up on the legend of Squire the arch conspirator briskly dispensing beads of poison from his Fleet

Street lair could spent a profitable half-hour with *Tricks of the Trade* (1917). Among other highlights, this contains a first-rate spoof of the *Tono-Bungay*-era H. G. Wells, featuring a philandering politician ('And then it was that the Hon. Astarte Cholmondeley came into my life . . . And then I met Cecilia Scroop') whose career is ruined when a phalanx of ex-mistresses confronts him outside the House of Commons, and a horribly acute burlesque of some of the paraphernalia of the Celtic Twilight ('There's a grey wind wails on the clover', etc.). The parodies display an aspect of Squire sometimes obscured by the anti-modernist diatribes – playful, imaginative, acidly acute. See, for example, his bitter pastiche of the first wave of stay-at-home Great War poets:

O to be in Flanders
Now that April's there
Where the water's drying up in the trench
To make more room for the summer stench
With General Joffre and Marshal Foch
In Flanders now

Curiously, Squire distrusted his facility in this medium – 'a not wholly admirable art' he advised his friend Robert Lynd – and with the exception of a full-frontal assault on Ezra Pound the parodies dry up by the early 1920s. By this point, in any case, Squire had bigger fish to fry. In 1913 he had managed to get himself appointed literary editor of the newly founded *New Statesman*, where, under the signature of 'Solomon Eagle' he wrote a highly influential column of book-world punditry entitled 'Books in General'. The editorship followed four years later, together with a productive friendship with Gosse, who amongst much other social adventuring introduced him to Winston Churchill ('I have met many politicians: this is the first who was *alive*') and by 1919, still only in his mid-30s, he had been given control of his own publication, the *London Mercury*.

The *Mercury*'s first number maintained that it was determined not to fall into the snare of partisanship, or attempt, as Squire rather grandly put it, 'to make universal the shibboleths of some coterie or school'. On the other hand, Squire's remarks on the condition of modern poetry would have left no potential reader in any doubt as to where he stood. Year after year, he complained, 'we have new fungoid growths of feeble pretentious impostors who, after a while, are superseded by their younger kindred; and year after year we see writers who actually have some intelligence and capacity for observation and exact statement led astray into the stony and barren fields of technical anarchism or the pitiful madhouse of moral antinomianism'. It is the usual conservative lament about aesthetic novelty – the idea that innovation necessarily implies a collapse in standards and an obsession with technique, together with warnings about the danger of modishness for modishness's sake. 'We have had "styles" which were mere protests and revulsions against other styles,' Squire lamented, '"styles" which were no more than flamboyant attempts at advertisement akin to the shifting lights of the electric night signs; authors who have forgotten their true selves in the desperate search for remarkable selves.' Praise for Hardy, Bridges and Conrad ('traditional yet experimental, personal yet sane') was balanced by criticism of the 'large number of writers who have strayed and lost themselves amongst experiments, many of them foredoomed to sterility', and – ironically in the light of what came later – a call for 'better and more enlightened criticism', capable of discriminating between the traditional and the free-for-all, sincerity and out-and-out pretension.

One might expect – magazine contributors generally taking their cue from their editor – that the *London Mercury* would be awash with Georgian time-servers and placemen. Remarkably the opening number contains work by Hardy, Brooke, de la Mare and W. H. Davies, as well as bibliographical notes by no less a modernist upstart than Aldous Huxley, while the next eighteen months brought poems by Belloc ('Tarantella'), Graves and Bridges and short stories by Virginia Woolf, Katherine Mansfield and Max Beerbohm. At the same time, anyone who comes across one of Squire's dogmatic assertions to the effect that 'people read poetry for the sake of beauty and for an appeal to the highest of appreciation and aspiration that is in them' will doubtless be struck by their odd sense of constraint, of hulking secret proscriptions of what can and can't be said, of stifling blankets of convention and respectability being flung over the participants when it looks as if the party may be getting out of hand. Squire would make an interesting case study of the psychology of conservatism: the man who is intelligent enough to see that many of the things he protests about have merit, that not all experimenters and free-formers are charlatans, that there are other kinds of poetry beyond the lyric, but is temperamentally unable to abandon the promontory he has carved out for himself even as the tides begin to roll in. His notorious review of *The Waste Land*, which appeared in the *Mercury* in October 1923, is a case in point. Squire puzzles over Eliot's verse. He frankly admits that he cannot make head or tail of it, yet he is conscious that the poem, when read in its entirety, 'must leave the impression on any open-minded person that Mr Eliot does mean something by it, has been at great pains to express himself, and believes himself to be pursuing a new avenue . . . of poetic treatment'. It is the same with Eliot's extensive footnotes, which, while they might explain where the poet gets his quotations and symbolism from, 'do not explain what these allusions are there for'. What, Squire wonders, having wrestled with 'Shantih, shantih, shantih', is language but communication, or art but selection and arrangement? 'It is a pity that a man who can write as well as Mr Eliot does in this poem should be so bored (not passionately disgusted) with existence that he doesn't mind what comes next, or who understands it.'

There was to be plenty more of this in the course of the next ten years, most of it distinctly of a piece with the war-era critic who thought the Vorticists 'a heterogeneous mob suffering from juvenile decay' and congratulated himself on turning up an alternative definition of Wyndham Lewis's *Blast* in *Webster's Dictionary*: 'a flatulent disease of sheep'. In fact, once allowances are made for wounded vanity and the peculiarly ad hominem aspects of early 1920s literary politicking, Squire had a point. He saw very well the likely consequences of the fragmentation of the poetic mainstream for the ordinary reader ('All this can lead to is a small public getting the dry, unmelodious husks it wants, the great public consoling itself with "Annie Laurie", and the hungry sheep in between, who are anxious to be up with the times and look for guidance where there is none, pretending to admire what it does not admire'), while his remarks on the difference between faddishness and genuine engagement can seem horribly prescient. It was not merely that the conservatively minded reader of the 1920s feared modernism as he feared 'Bolshevism' or 'cubism' – dangerous manifestations of instability – but that he suspected that its emergence was the result of spirited conspiring by pundits who should have known better. There is a rather revealing passage in *The Honeysuckle and the Bee* (1937), one of the several volumes of reminiscence with which he beguiled his later years, in which Squire is given a lift to Bath by a young couple whose female half interrogates him about the leading literary figures of the day. Admitting 'his various degrees of acquaintanceship with Mr T. S. Eliot, Mrs Woolf, Mr Aldous Huxley, several Sitwells, and various devastating and daring authors of both sexes', Squire at first finds the woman rather tiresome, only for her to ask, 'with a slight tremor in her voice', about Rupert Brooke. Squire realises that the degree of emotional connection has changed and that 'she was now speaking of a poet whom she had read and loved as a girl before she took up with the intellectual life', and that a certain kind of war poetry engages her attention in a way that 'Prufrock' never can.

In ordinary circumstances no one would have been much irked by Squire's conservatism, his pronouncements on the nature of poetry or even his complaints about fashionable young critics who deplored the pursuit of beauty. Rather, it was the conspiring that he did, or that was practised in his name, which united his enemies against him. A conspiracy, more to the point, of which the *London Mercury*, whose circulation never exceeded 10,000 copies even in its balmiest days, was only an incidental part. Even Squire's friends were prepared to concede that the influence he wielded in the London literary world of the early 1920s might be faintly injurious. In addition to his editorial duties he was engaged, towards the end of 1920, to write a weekly book review for the *Observer*. His friend Edward Shanks, the *Mercury*'s assistant editor, also wrote for the *New Statesman* and the *Saturday Westminster Gazette*. Another friend, W. J. Turner, reviewed poetry for *Land and Water*, while Squire's brother-in-law had a job on the *Outlook*. The friendship with Gosse gave him the ear of the *Sunday Times*, where Gosse was critic-in-chief. Another chum, Robert Lynd, was literary editor of the *Daily News*. Within three years of the war's end, consequently, Squire and his satellites had control, or at least substantial influence, over eight or more of the principal literary organs in Britain. Somebody came up with the nickname 'The Squirearchy' and the damage was done. Everywhere Squire's opponents looked they saw caballing, reputation-mongering and the boosting of inferior work by minor Georgians who happened to be part of the gang. As Alec Waugh once put it: 'A monopoly had been established for the placid pastoral poetry of John Freeman, Francis Brett Young, Martin Armstrong, Edmund Blunden; excellent of its kind, but there were others. A whole group of poets lacked a forum.'

Squire's influential anthology, *Selections from Modern Poets* (1921) with its no-nonsense assumptions about the poet's duty 'to exercise a clear and powerful influence on the thought of mankind with regard to the main problems of our existence' exacerbated this tendency by including, together with work by Hardy and Housman, two poems by his associate Iolo Williams, six by his childhood companion Francis Burrows and four by his Cambridge *convive* A. Y. Campbell. Squire had a particular genius for fixing literary prizes – a closing of the Georgian literary ranks which prompted Osbert Sitwell, writing as 'The Major', to offer a tipster's guide to the 'Hawthornden Stakes', a reference to the Hawthornden Prize, won in 1919 and 1920 by, respectively, Edward Shanks and John Freeman:

> Mr Freeman writes for the *London Mercury*
> Mr Shanks writes for the *London Mercury*
> Mr J. C. Squire is editor of the *London Mercury*
> Mr J. C. Squire is chief literary critic of the *Observer*
> Mr Iolo (or I.O.U.) Williams, a poet, writes for the *London Mercury*, of which Mr J. C. Squire is editor, and reviewed Mr J. C. Squire's book of poems for the *Observer*, of which Mr J. C. Squire is chief literary critic. Mr Squire has now written a preface to an anthology edited by Mr Iolo Williams. The Major, wiring from Newmarket, advises sportsmen to back Mr Iolo Williams as a future Hawthornden Prize Winner.

A sharper operator than Squire – one less caustic in his pronouncements, less quixotic in his enthusiasms – could have built this network of associates up into something really significant. But the enemy was too persistent, too contemptuous of everything Squire stood for and what he had to say. There was a suspicion, too, that he was storing up trouble for himself, had too many irons in the fire to make a success of the *London Mercury*, or indeed of anything at all. J. B. Priestley noted that 'He had a wide knowledge of literature, but from the '20s onward I suspect he cared more about architecture and cricket.' The *Mercury* had always been keen on crusades – the urgent need for a Ministry of Fine Arts, better government design standards, a National Theatre and so forth – but gradually these campaigns came to dominate its editorial notes to the exclusion of all else. The editorials of the mid-1920s are full of schemes to save public monuments as various as Stonehenge and Waterloo Bridge and support for an initiative sponsored by *The Times* to preserve wild flowers, not to mention 'a very useful little pamphlet issued by the Stationery Office entitled *A Brief Guide to Government Publications*'. There were still high-grade contributions – the number extolling *The Times*'s plan to secure the nation's flora also included 'A View from a Hill', one of the most macabre ghost stories that M. R. James ever wrote – but the magazine was becoming uneven. A short story might be published because its author needed encouragement, played cricket, or was a member of Squire's immediate family, his secretary or his boyhood friend.* None of these temperamental failings was helped by Squire's weakness for the bottle, the break-up of his marriage and, in 1931, the loss of his *Observer* job. Meanwhile, the range of literary projects on which he continued to embark – these included a stage version of *Pride and Prejudice* and a three-volume study of Shakespeare – did nothing to salve the growing awareness of his isolation both as a critic and as literary personality. Badly hit by the Depression, the *Mercury* struggled on into the early 1930s, by which time its editorials came more and more to consist of obituary notices of Squire's friends and news of the exciting political developments in Italy. His resignation was finally made public in 1934.

Squire's later years were a decline. For a time he kept precariously afloat by writing garrulous books of memoirs and acting as Macmillans' literary adviser, but the drink made him unreliable – he once excused his failure to deliver a commission on the grounds that the manuscript had blown out of the taxi window – and the BBC and the periodicals where he might still have commanded a hearing grew less inclined to take the risk of employing him. There was a regrettable incident when he was arrested for being found drunk in Regent Street. Come the Second World War, when the house in which he was living suffered bomb damage, he was effectively destitute. A fire at the cottage to which he later removed destroyed most of his possessions. Squire accepted these reversals with great fortitude. He grew a beard and, while residing in a hotel in the south-west London suburbs, quite liked

* T. C. Worsley remembered calling at the *London Mercury* as an aspiring teenage poet, to be greeted with the salutation 'Not *the* T. C. Worsley?' It turned out that Squire was recalling Worsley's cricket scores from *Wisden*. 'Of course I'll publish your poems,' Squire assured him. 'Leave them with me.' See *Flannelled Fool: A Slice of Life in the Thirties* (1937).

to be referred to as 'the Sage of Surbiton'. Friends rallied round and he spent his final decade living in the country, producing a weekly column for the *Illustrated London News* and angling for a collected volume of his poems: a gnarled survivor of the age of Brooke and de la Mare incongruously at large in the world of Kingsley Amis, John Wain and Philip Larkin.

Not all Georgians were like Squire: when closely inspected, Georgian solidarity is sometimes a good deal less impressive than it seems. To read the recently published correspondence of Siegfried Sassoon and Edmund Blunden is to appreciate not only quite how embattled was the literary landscape of the 1920s, but also the strain that its alliances placed on a writer of sensibility and spirit caught up in its periodic shifts and realignments. If the general effect is of a kind of non-stop guerrilla warfare, then the hostilities are made worse by the fact that they are being fought simultaneously on half a dozen fronts on a terrain in which the rules frequently seem to be being made up as you go along and where the loyalties of the people who wear your uniform are sometimes seriously in doubt. Squire, for example, though clearly a useful ally in standing up to the outrages of modernism, is made to seem faintly ridiculous in his caballings. Robert Graves, of whom most Georgians thoroughly approved, is regularly criticised for his Great War classic *Goodbye to All That* (1929), which reeks of 'grandiose delusions and arrogance' ('Haply I may remember / And haply disremember' runs an annotation in Blunden's copy), while Hugh Walpole and John Drinkwater are simply figures of fun. 'Sixteen pages of sawdust' was Sassoon's verdict on Drinkwater's *Persephone*.

And if not all Georgians were like Squire, then not all Georgian criticism approximates to the editorial notes of the *London Mercury*. While the Sassoon/Blunden exchanges leave an abiding impression of a milieu in which every book and its author have to be judged by the benchmarks of the old-fashioned, lyrical-satirical poetic orthodoxy to which both men punctiliously adhered, then they are always alert to the possibility that a book may have merit in spite of the public attitudes of its author, or that the private personality might harbour something very different at its core. Edith Sitwell was 'quite a simple and gentle person in "real life"', Sassoon thought, her public image marred only by an unnecessary combativeness ('Why *must* she always be "scoring off" people?'). The same hint of ambiguity distinguishes the work of one of the more substantial Georgian critics, Squire's *chef de cabinet*, the much-excoriated Edward Shanks. As a critic Shanks is the driest of old sticks: a failing which, to do him justice, he had the grace to acknowledge. Chided by the reviewers of his first volume of essays for making no attempt to encourage anyone actually to read the authors about which he happened to be writing, he retorted that there was a place for the critic who states quite coolly, 'and the more coolly the better', what a masterpiece seems to him to be.

In pursuing this highly desirable quarry across the conservative reviews of the 1920s, Shanks combined brazenly old-fashioned tastes with a rueful appreciation of the reasons why the books he disliked should have found an audience. On the one hand he is keen on every traditionalist master from Flecker to Galsworthy (the *Forsyte Saga* 'fulfils the conditions of great art: the persons in it are recognisable human beings, true to the requirements of time and place, but they are also symbols of forces which will continue in battle until human nature has evolved into some form which we should not be able to recognise at all'). On the other, he is perceptive about Lawrence, of whom he disapproves ('the solutions he offers of the great problem oppressing him are empty and false') while noting the existence of 'a flame of poetry, smoky, strange and disconcerting as it may be, which is at least genuine and which is hardly paralleled by any of the novelists of his generation'.

All this might seem to place him in a direct line of descent from an arch-conservative critic of the previous generation like Saintsbury – happy to delight in the form of a Rabelais or a Baudelaire while pointedly deploring the content. But Shanks, at least, had a sense of historical perspective, and his account of the late Victorian 'boom' in poetry, whose after-effects were still being felt in his own time, is eerily astute. One disabling legacy of the Victorian period, he suggests, is its self-consciousness, that eternal search for the 'great poet' which became even more frantic in the years after Tennyson's death when great poets seemed horribly thin on the ground. Brooke's life, not to mention his death, had 'rehabilitated' poetry. At the same time Shanks is shrewd enough to appreciate some of the differences between Brooke and the poets who followed him. Comparing 'If I should die think only this of me' with Sassoon, he notes that 'Brooke's subject is the impact made on his mind by the imagined possibility of death in certain circumstances. Mr Sassoon is moved by something a great deal more definite.' Brooke's poems, we infer, deal in abstract possibility; Sassoon's with blown-out trenches and bullets in the head.

All the same, there is no getting away from Shanks's prodigious conservatism, his quoting of Chesterton to the effect that *vers libre* is no more a revolution in poetry than sleeping in a ditch is a revolution in architecture, or his claim that 'H.D.' was the only great Imagist poet (Amy Lowell? Robert Frost? F. S. Flint?). Like many another conservative critic of the period, his Rubicon was Eliot. He is appropriately respectful: 'The critics who demand that modern poetry should render more fully and more richly the modern consciousness, and the world it lives in, stand on surer ground. The most able of the critics who have made this demand, Mr T. S. Eliot, is also the most formidable of the poets who have attempted to comply with it.' He concedes that Eliot is not just a 'mechanically excellent intellect' which has mistakenly strayed into poetry. He recognises a 'genuinely singing note' that might have realised beautiful work in the conventional manner. But in the end the pleasures of *The Waste Land* seem 'almost exclusively intellectual', a kind of highbrow crossword puzzle rendered synthetic by its magpie borrowings from other styles. And this before one even came to consider Eliot's fatal disillusionment ('Now disillusionment may be a source of poetic emotion like any other, but it is an infertile source'). It is the same with Edith Sitwell's poetry, of which Shanks tartly observes that one can only regret that what would seem to be so important a revolution in human consciousness should have resulted in poems of so little importance. There is something rather breathtaking about Shanks's claim – made in 1926 – that 'at this moment English poetry is in a depressed and languid, but by no means a hopeless, condition'. The equivalent would be a critic of 1848 looking up from his copies of *Dombey and Son*, *Vanity Fair* and *Alton Locke* to declare that English fiction has been treading water since the days of Sir Walter Scott.

The problem with Georgian poets – and with Georgian critics – is that, in the last resort, they demanded, or tolerated, only a very limited number of things from poetry: anyone who failed to supply them could be written off as, at best, merely obtuse, or, at worst, a dangerous trifler with the eternal verities. By this time, in any case, the intellectual battle was already lost. On the other hand, beneath the stratosphere of the literary reviews and the clever young men who populated them, the Georgian group still counted for a great deal.

For a substantial part of the middlebrow reading public, the poetry of such Georgian beau ideals as Drinkwater, Monro and Lascelles Abercrombie remained a potent draw well into the 1940s. As more than one of her biographers has related, it was the efficient recitation of Drinkwater's 'Moonlit Apples' and Walter de la Mare's 'The Travellers' that won the 9-year-old Margaret Roberts, later Thatcher, a silver medal at the Grantham eisteddfod. In much the same way, Drinkwater's *Collected Poems* turn up in Orwell's *Keep the Aspidistra Flying* (1936), as the Christmas gift bestowed on Gordon Comstock by his sister – exactly the kind of book that an unsophisticated reader of the 1930s would have given a relative known to be 'interested in poetry'. Squire, too, enjoyed a robust afterlife in the work of the mid-century literary autobiographers. In half a dozen memoirs of the Georgian literary scene there comes a moment when our hero first clambers up the rackety staircase to the room in Poppins Court, with its pulsing stove, its stuffed boa constrictor hanging on the wall, its maid of all work, Squire's secretary Grace Chapman, going efficiently about her duties and Squire himself, smelling faintly of brandy, huddled over a set of page proofs at his desk or writing one of his letters to *The Times*. Whatever one may feel about later manifestations of Georgian poetry – 'frail, frail, divorced from reality, frail and damnable' as Dudley Carew once ruefully put it – this, in its circumscribed and determinedly partial way, was clearly a Mecca of a sort.

CHAPTER 3

Dancing on the Hecatomb: Modern Movements

> I have said that Eliot spoke for his age. That is true if you think of the age as a comparatively small body of men and women generally described as persons of culture.
>
> Frank Swinnerton, *Figures in the Foreground* (1963)

> I have been reading a lot of back numbers of the *Criterion* – a paper I don't usually see as it costs seven and sixpence . . . I must say that for pure snootiness it beats anything I have ever seen.
>
> George Orwell, Letter to Brenda Salkeld, 7 March 1935

It is said that George V, invited to greet the first Labour Cabinet in 1924, arrayed himself in a scarlet tie and, on entering the room in which Ramsay MacDonald and his colleagues were assembled, remarked 'Gentlemen, we are all socialists now.' Given that literary history, like most other kinds of history, tends to be written by the victors, it is tempting to assume that the same blanket respectability was instantly conferred on the modernist writers of the 1920s – that here, in fact, was an unstoppable juggernaut which only the very old or the incorrigibly hidebound attempted to resist. But while there were any number of popular novelists keen to advertise their conversion to the modernist line, the hostility with which innovations in literary form were received by the great majority of middlebrow readers in the years after the Great War can sometimes seem rather startling in its violence. A hostility, more to the point, that takes in not merely stream-of-consciousness and *vers libre*, that rapt mythologising stare brought to the processes of ordinary life by Virginia Woolf's novels and Eliot's verse, but almost any critique, direct or indirect, of existing arrangements. The style and subject matter of

Ulysses (1922) were such that it had to be published by a private sponsor, well beyond the reach of the British censors, but even Alec Waugh's *The Loom of Youth* (1917), which ventures some very mild criticism of the public school system, was denounced from pulpits and banned from sixth-form common rooms by sensitive headmasters.

Neither was there anything generational about this resistance. Just as the aged Professor Saintsbury could decline to review Joyce's masterpiece on the picturesque grounds that 'when you're always expecting to have to run to the side of the ship as you turn the page, it ceases to be delightful', so the 17-year-old Patrick Hamilton turns out to have beguiled his leisure with an unpublished verse epic entitled 'Modernism', characterised by one of his biographers as 'an indictment of all those trends, chiefly in poetry but also in the whole field of contemporary creation, that seemed to him to be leading away from simplicity and sincerity'. To browse the memoirs of all those mid-century literary men who were at school and university in the age of Joyce, Pound and *Façade* is to appreciate quite how reluctant so many of them were to give up their attachment to Georgianism and lyric poetry and how regretful was their abandonment of older and less self-conscious forms of enjoyment. Dudley Carew, who became one of Squire's under-strappers in Poppins Court, left a wistful account of how the volumes of Georgian verse which 'greatly suited him' were 'put aside with a sigh' for *The Waste Land*. Geoffrey Grigson recalled that at the time he went up to Oxford in the mid-1920s, modernism meant virtually nothing to him: 'I had scarcely begun to suspect the *London Mercury*.' Enlightenment dawned after an encounter with Osbert Sitwell's anti-Squire pamphlet *Who Killed Cock Robin?*. Instantly Grigson transferred his allegiance to Eliot, whose poems, he discovered, were 'tense enough to pick up and use'. Grigson's Oxford contemporary Stephen Spender experienced a similar revolution in his literary tastes, starting his university career by inviting Walter de la Mare, Squire and J. B. Priestley to lecture at the English Club and ending it as a devotee of Eliot, Joyce and 'Hugh Selwyn Mauberley'.

But perhaps the most serious antagonism to experiment came from the clubman's armchair and the senior common room dining table. John Betjeman, an undergraduate at Magdalen College, Oxford, remembered that his tutor, C. S. Lewis, was far more hostile to Eliot in private conversation than he allowed himself to be in print. There were even the makings of an anti-Eliot conspiracy, in which Lewis and his collaborators – these included Henry Yorke, later the novelist Henry Green – devised a free-verse pastiche which would be sent to the *Criterion* under the pseudonyms 'Rollo and Brigid Considine'. The plot eventually fizzled out, but no one should doubt the conviction with which Lewis set about inaugurating it. To Lewis, as to the teenage subscriber to *Public School Verse* who preferred Flecker to 'The Love Song of J. Alfred Prufrock', the contempt in which the diehard held this fast-accelerating revolution in the arts had a number of causes. The most dramatic rested on modernism's implications both for the literature it was bent on superseding and the cultural assumptions that lay behind it, the sense of a well-nigh revolutionary irruption whose consequences extended beyond the library shelf. Anthony Powell once observed of the great biblical scholar M. R. James, provost of King's College, Cambridge and author of *Ghost Stories of an Antiquary*, that 'he represented the peak of one kind of civilisation, and to read about him is to see how inevitable was that intellectual revolution loosely known as the Modern Movement'. Henceforth, the old kind of high-mindedness that James had epitomised – a brand of studiousness which, it might be said, excluded as much as it embraced and could be actively hostile to new ideas ('Gentlemen, no thinking' James is once supposed to have admonished his students) – was in incremental retreat. And with it, inexorably, went much of the literature it had favoured. In terms of straightforward literary affiliation, modernism was sharply divisive. If it was a question of choosing between Arnold Bennett's *Anna of the Five Towns* and Firbank's *Concerning the Eccentricities of Cardinal Pirelli*, then Firbank invariably took the *pas*. The idea canvassed during the Great War that a fragmented and essentially unknowable modern world, no longer amenable to the cartography of the Victorian sages, demanded a new kind of supercharged consciousness to make sense of it was deeply unsettling, for it involved the discarding of huge amounts of superannuated lumber, and acknowledging, in C. K. Scott Moncrieff's words, that 'the arts were killed by war, and peace seems to express herself by dancing on the hecatomb'. As Frank Swinnerton (1884–1982) once put it, the war had drained significance from the life he had once known, which could no longer be seen as either symptomatic or historically interesting. 'Easy chronicles of pre-war life were finished; the life itself had been disrupted.' This did not mean that the easy chronicle would cease to be written, only that a certain kind of taste had moved on, leaving Swinnerton and his friends to reflect on the 'divorce between literature written as approved by persons of culture and an adulterate compound fit only for the amusement of nursery governesses'.

Swinnerton was never a paid-up member of the interwar avant-garde – his novels, he tells us in his fertile source-book *The Georgian Literary Scene*, sold 20,000 copies a year in the US and he was, additionally, a publisher's reader, which encouraged an interest in cash rather than cachet. At the same time, he saw very well some of the implications of this new air of exclusiveness with which a liking for such writers as Eliot, Joyce and Woolf would always be associated. It was taken for granted that such newfangled 'apostles of culture' – Swinnerton's phrase, again – would only appeal to a tiny minority, and the assumption was one that more combative modernists did nothing to dispel. Rather than envisaging art as a way of bringing readers together in pursuit of shared goals, they were sometimes only determined to use it as means of driving them apart. Of the 'Nine Propositions', an anti-philistine diatribe contributed by Frank Rutter to *Art and Letters*, Number VII claimed that 'Of any given subject the number of persons possessing knowledge is smaller than the number of uninformed', and Number VIII 'A minority is not always right, but right opinions can be held only by a minority.' The *Art and Letters* gang wanted to annoy (see, for example, Osbert Sitwell's middlebrow-baiting poem 'We will not buy *Art and Letters*') but even Edgell Rickword, a critic more interested in building bridges than identifying intellectual caste marks, conceded that 'modern work appeals necessarily to a restricted audience, of no particular class, but with a common sensibility, and there is no object in trying to expand this audience artificially'. That the 'modern work' might be appearing in a very limited format, in little magazines or in the catalogues of private printing presses, was of no comfort to intelligent mainstream writers who were sharp enough to appreciate that the real action was going on elsewhere, in low-budget periodicals where they themselves could not be found. All this produced a bewildering variety of 'popular' responses, ranging from the wistfully myopic and the timorously associative to the downright belligerent: C. S. Lewis, for example, simply solved the problem of modernism by ignoring it altogether, and could be found proclaiming – this in 1921 – that 'our best moderns' were Brooke, Flecker, de la Mare, Yeats and Masefield. There were popular writers who made strenuous claims to modernity while continuing to write novels about evening parties and country-house weekends in the approved Edwardian manner. None of them, however, neither the popular novelist nor the university don, the middlebrow columnist or the little magazine editor exulting in his 500 readers, was in any doubt of the elemental cultural separation that characterised both the production and reception of literature in the 1920s, and the attitudes of the reading publics who sustained this divide.

The war against the obfuscations of premodernist literature was fought on a number of fronts: in creative work, naturally, but also in the review sections of literary magazines. If this process had been set in train during the war, when Eliot, Pound and Harold Monro had begun to colonise the pages of the *English Review* and *Poetry and Drama*, then it was consolidated, shortly after the war's end, by such new arrivals to the scene as the *Monthly Chapbook*, the *Tyro*, the *Adelphi* and the *Criterion*. These were 'little magazines', some of them very diminutive indeed – for all its prestige, *Criterion* never got beyond a circulation of 1,100 copies – and their combative spirit was sometimes too much even for nominal allies. Eliot, for example, complained of the six numbers of *Wheels* (1916–22) that they were merely Georgianism's polar opposite: 'Instead of rainbows, cuckoos, daffodils and timid hares, they give us garden-gods, guitars and mandolins.' Born of a general suspicion that most establishment papers were run by conservatives, each of these radical counterweights brought a distinctive twist to arguments about the 'new writing'. The forty numbers of the *Chapbook*, which ran between 1919 and 1925, included barely a handful of Georgians, and the three critics whom its editor Harold Monro invited to consider the state of poetry in the early 1920s were Eliot, Huxley and F. S. Flint. *Art and Letters* (1917–20) trumpeted the exclusivity of the artist, while *Coterie* (1919–20), edited from Jesus College, Oxford and much favoured by more sophisticated undergraduates (one of Louis Golding's student-era squibs talks about a contemporary enticed by 'Canonisation in the *Coterie*') offered a more visual slant, with drawings by Nina Hamnett and William Rothenstein accompanying the poems by Eliot, Huxley and Edith Sitwell. Yet by far the most determined effort to see off the forces of reaction and introduce the 'new criticism' to a substantial body of informed readers came from a paper that, fifty years before, had been a byword for mid-Victorian staidness. This was the *Athenaeum*, rescued from a state of near-insolvency towards the end of the war by Arthur Rowntree and relaunched with John Middleton Murry (1889–1957) as its editor.

Murry's lustre has, understandably, dimmed in the century or so after his early 1920s heyday – he tends to be remembered for his famous friends and his relationship with Katherine Mansfield – but in his time he was a considerable figure. An unusual one, too, in the context of the Georgian literary scene, for his grandfather had been a publican; his parents kept lodgings in Peckham and he made his way to Oxford on the back of a scholarship to Christ's Hospital. This relatively humble upbringing was no barrier to the liberal and decidedly upper-class circles in which he aspired to move, and during the Great War, which he spent at the Ministry of Information, he and Mansfield were fixtures at the Garsington salons conducted by Lady Ottoline Morrell. There was an inevitable attachment to D. H. Lawrence and an equally inevitable falling-out. Murry's early vehicles were *Rhythm* and the *Blue Review* – small-circulation modernist prototypes – but the *Athenaeum* was an altogether more serious proposition: crusading, contentious, anti-Edwardian, resonant with intellectual éclat. Mansfield, Eliot, Woolf, Lytton Strachey, Clive Bell and Roger Fry all featured in its pages, and there was a concerted attempt to clear out the contents of the late Victorian lumber room by inviting Strachey to take on Matthew Arnold and encouraging Eliot to criticise William Archer, the translator of Ibsen, and the distinguished classicist Sir Gilbert Murray.

Not everyone approved – Hugh Walpole thought Murry 'simply ephemerally petulant' and his magazine 'a gloomy pretentious affair written entirely by cranks' – and even regular contributors could be taken aback by Murry's undisguised hostility towards 'them', his blanket term for the establishment forces he imagined to be permanently conspiring against him. On the other hand, the *Athenaeum*'s real difficulties stemmed from what Eliot called Murry's 'erratic and intuitive nature'. In literature, as in other parts of his life, he was a notably passionate man, and his quick-fire taking ups and laying downs of reputations could sometimes work to his disadvantage. Swinnerton noted that he 'represented the effects of successive enthusiasms for Lawrence, Dostoevsky, Hardy, Santayana and others who appealed to his emotions'. None of this was likely to appeal to a mass audience, and the *Athenaeum*, having failed to attract advertising, was forced to merge with the *Nation*. Murry reappeared at the head of the *Adelphi*, but enthusiasm for his brand of propagandising had declined, and many potential purchasers transferred their allegiance to the *Criterion*. If there was one rule that editors of little magazines learned to their cost, here in a landscape of minority cultures and carefully cultivated intellectual positions, it was that there were rarely enough subscribers to go round.

Murry was an inconspicuous figure, unknown beyond a relatively small circle of intellectuals and magazine readers. If literary modernism had a public face in the 1920s, it belonged – singly and collectively – to the Sitwells. It was said that had a variety-hall comic of the era gone on stage and imitated either Edith (1887–1964), Osbert (1892–1969) or Sacheverell (1897–1988), the subjects would instantly have been identified by hundreds of people who had never read a line of their works. Their genius for publicity – and it is not an exaggeration to call it that – kept up until the end, and Dame Edith, as she subsequently became, survived to ornament an early edition of *This is Your Life*. Detaching the Sitwells from the reams of press coverage that attended their frequently self-defeating stunts is not always easy; neither is getting to grips with the rather sinister clannishness of the early days. John Pearson, who wrote the best collective study of them, observed that they reminded him of a mafia family, sustained by a communal myth, each member pledged to assist the others until death. Certainly the Sitwells in one of the group rages that ensued whenever Edith or Osbert had been attacked in print or suffered some momentary slight could be an impressive spectacle: an instant closing of ranks and quest for vengeance with no quarter given or asked. At the same time, and despite these regular displays of solidarity, there were substantial differences in their respective positions: Osbert the front man, chief publicist, impresario, satirist and Liberal politician; Edith the poet and editor of *Wheels*; Sacheverell quieter, more scholarly, less enamoured of the volleys of self-advertisement that his siblings gleefully despatched towards the enemy lines.

The idea of there being an 'enemy' in the literal sense, whose every manoeuvre and reconfiguration had to be tracked with unrelenting vigour, was central to the Sitwell mythology, their sense of who they were and the kind of treatment they could expect from the world around them – and vice versa, of course. Again, it is not overstating the case to say that they imagined themselves to be engaged in a never-ending battle in which gangs of middle-class philistines, newspaper editors and literary traditionalists fired salvoes of abuse at an alliance of leftish-leaning politicians, dandy aesthetes, 'intellectuals' and experimental poets. One difficulty in conducting these engagements lay in the ramshackle nature of the alliances: an engrained touchiness meant that one or other of the family was always falling out with people on whose loyalty they theoretically depended (there was an early separation from Bloomsbury). Another lay in a deliberate courting of scandal and controversy which, inevitably, tended to detract from the seriousness of at least some of the things they had to say. The first public performance of Edith's *Façade,* a selection of her poems set to music by William Walton at the Aeolian Hall in 1922, is a case in point. According to Sitwell myth, actively promulgated in the months that followed, large parts of the audience had come to barrack. The reality was that an amateurish performance on a hot summer afternoon in an airless room was, understandably, received without great enthusiasm. Significantly, a later version, staged at the Chenil Galleries in 1926, was much more successful.

The problem with this relentless hunting of the philistines – Osbert's hobby, as stated in his *Who's Who* entry – was that it encouraged neutrals to overlook *Façade*'s considerable importance. With its curious and almost syncopated rhythms, its Jazz Age gloss, its queer half-rhymes and assonances and a backdrop pitched somewhere between the rustic arbour and the cocktail bar, it emerged into a modernist landscape where Huxley and Firbank had already set up camp while *Ulysses* and *The Waste Land* were hourly anticipated. If distance has diminished some of its original impact, then its symbolic importance is far harder to shunt aside. A not entirely far-fetched comparison would be with the Beatles' *Sgt Pepper's Lonely Hearts Club Band*, several of whose individual pieces no longer stand up to detailed scrutiny but whose cumulative cultural effect still seems dazzlingly impressive. All this naturally contributed to Sitwell legend, a mystique which Edith exacerbated by dressing herself in flowing, mock-medieval shifts and turbans and having herself photographed in a series of immensely studied poses by the young Cecil Beaton (Beaton, who knew he was on to a good thing, characterised her as a tall, graceful scarecrow, with the hands of a medieval saint). Inevitably, the reality of an invitation to tea at Edith's Bayswater flat sometimes undercut this illusion of poise and sanctity. The 16-year-old Brian Howard, summoned from

Eton on the strength of some manuscript poems – 'your promise is far too much for me to risk your future by publishing these poems of yours *in their present state*' Edith informed him – confessed himself 'very disappointed indeed . . . I got *one penny bun, and three-quarters of a cup of rancid tea in a dirty cottage mug*. Also, I don't like her apartment, or, rather, room. It is small, dark, and I suspect, dirty.' Another younger friend, Allanah Harper, remembered arriving at the flat to find Virginia Woolf, with whom some kind of truce had been established, among the guests, the two women sitting companionably on the sofa 'like two praying-mantises putting out delicate antennae towards each other'.

Once the fog of self-promotion and score-settling has lifted, there is a great deal to admire about the Sitwells as a creative unit. One might point, for example, to their insistence that the arts were there to be enjoyed, not doled out as sociopolitical palliatives; to their diligent and disinterested propagandising of a whole tribe of continental artists in whose merits they unhesitatingly believed; to their determination that young people with any kind of potential should be encouraged by their elders from the moment they began to exhibit it (other Sitwell protégés included the fledgling composers William Walton and Constant Lambert); to an unswerving commitment to pursuing their own aesthetic line in the face of public indifference and diminishing returns. Certainly, none of them found the commercial success with which, in an earlier epoch, this kind of studied avant-garderie might have been accompanied, at all easy to find. Osbert's American earnings from his first work of fiction *Triple Fugue* (1924) were a far from princely £18, while the print order for one of the cantos of Sacheverell's immensely recherché poem *Doctor Donne and Gargantua* was set at all of sixty-five copies. To set against this intent communal resolve is a feeling of collective insecurity and wounded vanity that amounted almost to paranoia. 'I have been having a *terrible* time' runs one of Edith's letters from early 1922, 'what with the boycott on the part of the Squire-controlled press and the insults on the part of the press which is so controlled. I know Squire is no good as a writer . . . Meanwhile, he is preventing any new work obtaining a hearing in England.' *Any* new work? *All* of England?

If Edith was merely plaintive, then Osbert sometimes seems simply neurotic. One or two of his more venomous sallies might even be taken as a form of displacement activity: a surface contempt for philistine editors and middlebrow novelists beneath which courses an altogether deeper enmity. Aldous Huxley captures this side of him in a short story called 'The Tillotson Banquet', where Osbert features as 'Lord Badgery', behind whose 'heavy waxen mask' of a face, Hanoverian nose, lustreless pig's eyes and pale thick lips, 'there lurked a small devil of happy malice that rocked with laughter'. This sort of thing, alas, was all too easy to guy, and early Sitwell history, consequently, is a matter of slights – real and imagined – being repaid at exorbitantly high rates of interest. C. K. Scott Moncrieff's *The Strange and Striking Adventures of Four Authors in Search of a Character* (1926) is a classic example of Sitwell mockery from the opening line onward ('Once upon a time there were four dear little children whose names were Frogbert, Sacharissa, Zerubbabel and Lincruston, inhabiting a stately home in the country entirely surrounded by every attention that natural affection could prompt or luxury afford'), and there was a corking row over the 23-year-old Noël Coward's revue *London Calling* (1923) which featured the actress Maisie Gay in a sketch entitled 'The Swiss Family Whittlebot' as 'Hernia Whittlebot' reciting her poems to an accompaniment provided by her brothers 'Gob' and 'Sago', and, later in the decade, an altogether fantastical episode in which Edith, news having reached her of *Lady Chatterley's Lover*, decided that Sir Clifford Chatterley was a caricature of Osbert.

The thought of a familial solidarity that might at any moment tip over the edge into outright hysteria, explode in the faces of unwary confidants, was apparent to many of the literary personalities who came across them in the 1920s. Frieda Lawrence, who had met Edith and Osbert in Tuscany, remarked that they seemed 'oversensitive, as if something had hurt them too much, as if they had to keep up a brave face to the world, to pretend that they didn't care and yet they only cared too much'. To balance this is the thought that it was a consciousness of Sitwell myth, that luminous collective childhood on the Derbyshire estate in the care of their eccentric parents, Sir George and Lady Ida, that gave much of their creative work its peculiar resonance. In particular, there is 'Colonel Fantock', Edith's luxuriant projection of bygone Sitwell life into a remote, hallucinatory fantasy world, which, while overhung with all the aesthetic foliage of the era – sleeping gardens, sad summer grass, musical boxes – manages to say something profoundly important about the kind of person she imagined herself to be:

But Dagobert and Peregrine and I
Were children then; we walked like shy gazelles
Among the music of the thin flower-bells.
And life still held some promise, – never ask
Of what, – but life seemed less a stranger, then,
Than ever after in this cold existence.
I always was a little outside life –
And so the things we touch would comfort me;
I loved the shy dreams we could hear and see –
For I was one dead, like a small ghost,
A little cold air, wandering and lost.

Ominously, this is the strain in Edith's work most disparaged by F. R. Leavis: 'sentimental reveries, reminiscences of childhood and so on', a judgement which presupposes that reminiscences of childhood aren't somehow a fit subject for poetry and that for people to be interested in their own past lives is a mark of emotional immaturity – presupposes, too, that a poem like 'Colonel Fantock' is 'sentimental', whereas what seems to lie at its core is a feeling of isolation, life never quite fulfilling its early promise, secret sorrowing in bright light.

Perpetually hard up, and at certain points reduced to the most mundane hack-work, Edith spent much of her time in the early 1930s writing book reviews and somewhat pot-boiling literary studies. As a critic she was a proselytiser, fond of picking winners, sensitive to subtlety (Empson's language was 'full, intense and charged with meaning') and even when overstating her case – she described Walter Greenwood as 'the Dickens of our time' – wanting desperately to engage with the alternative worlds set out before her. If she had a weakness it was her habit of fixing the evidence to make even the most unpromising subjects amenable to the straitjacketings of her literary taste. Orwell, to name only one detractor, professed himself baffled by her attempts to reclassify Pope as a Romantic. As he remarked, when you saw such phrases as 'smoking and appalling beauty' applied to a writer of Pope's urbanity, you began to wonder whether there wasn't something in the classical, non-musical view of poetry after all.

Unfortunately, the closer Edith veered to home the more suspect her judgements became: she was, for example, convinced that Sacheverell was 'one of the greatest poets our race has produced in the past 150 years'. In the quarter-century since his death a certain amount of critical ink has been expended in attempting to prove that 'Sachie', all things considered and with due regard for shifting tastes, was the most talented of the clan. Certainly, he took himself with an immense seriousness, telling the girl he was to marry that 'I am, though I say it myself, about the cleverest young man of my age in the country' and even at the age of 91, when asked to name his most treasured possession, unabashedly voted for himself. In the end, much of his interest lies in his ability to break free of the constricting embrace of brother and sister and 'the Gingers' (the junior Sitwells' name for their parents), on the one hand by marrying young, and on the other by disassociating himself from the perennial publicity hunts. In his wife, Georgia, he evidently found a boon companion, someone who not only understood him (rather too well, judging from the letter in which the bride-to-be complained that 'it is not my presence or affection that you love, but your isolated personal moments that give you pleasure') but shared his considerable capacity for enjoyment. There followed a life of high-class tourism interspersed with fallow periods on the Northamptonshire estate, much of it conducted on a shoestring. Chronically out-at-elbow until Sachie inherited the family money in the 1960s, the Sitwells led a heavily subsidised existence, their patrons including the Duke of Westminster, Siegfried Sassoon and a number of foreign governments persuaded of the publicity value of Sachie's travel books. Children – there were two sons – seem to have been regarded as an occupational hazard, and 3-year-old Francis nearly found himself abandoned in France with his nanny on the outbreak of war in 1939.

Meanwhile, there were the books. Sachie began as a poet, soon branching out into exercises in cultural rediscovery (*Southern Baroque Art* was a notable trailblazer in 1924) and, as the family star waned a little, travelogues. The poems are full of good lines while failing to disguise a suspicion that they are mostly about the poet himself and the highly stylised sensations he happens to have experienced: his biographer quotes a rather revealing passage in which he praises Edith's poetry for its 'degree of selection and separation from the dross of living'. But this, it might be said, is exactly the quality that makes his own work so distant and intangible. It is a wholly personal art whose reference points are narrowly aesthetic, whose preoccupations have a habit of spilling over into his inner life. In a letter which mourns his mother's death, for example, he notes that 'she had such a wonderful appearance. I long to see her hands, which were most beautiful', which, however heartfelt, has the odd effect of making Lady Ida seem like a china doll. In strict category terms, Sachie was an old-style aesthete self-consciously adrift in a world where art for art's sake had come to count for very little. It is an interesting exercise to compare the Sitwell view of Morocco, recorded on a visit in 1938, with Orwell's essay 'Marrakech', written at almost exactly the same time. Sachie sees the quack-doctors' pharmacopeia, 'a tray of disgusting objects, concoctions of bat or frog . . . the carcass of a raven looking like a body which had been dragged through town at the horse's tail', a row of prostitutes from whose white dresses and the thin lawn of their veils 'comes all the illusion of a thousand years ago'. Orwell sees poverty, marching men, half-starved Jewish tailors for whom the gift of a cigarette is an unimaginable luxury. None of this is to contest the accuracy of Sachie's observations or the liveliness of his reportage, merely to say that if you wanted a guide to some of the realities of life in a North African city on the eve of the Second World War you would choose Orwell over *Mauretania: Warrior, Man and Woman*.

By this time the Sitwells had long ceased to function as an effective fighting unit. Their collective golden age was the early 1920s: by the end of the decade they had begun to disintegrate – Sachie married and determined to detach himself from the injurious effects of the publicity machine; Edith luxuriating in the success of *Gold Coast Customs* (1929); Osbert buoyed by the reception of his novel *Before the Bombardment* (1926), more interested in his personal life and the advent of his long-term companion, David Horner. Such influence as they exerted on the post-1945 world took place in areas far removed from the cutting edge of avant-garde intellectual life. Osbert cultivated a friendship with the widowed Queen Mary and busied himself with a compendious autobiography, while Sachie was briefly employed to write the 'Atticus' column for the *Sunday Times*, a characteristically exotic affair in which he dilated on such topics as rare bulbs and European chocolate shops, while venturing ingenious comparisons between Field Marshal Montgomery and Louis XI. By the early 1960s they were museum pieces, and treated as such. On the other hand, the *Scrutiny* critics who wrote them off as triflers, dilettanti art-worshippers prostrating themselves on the altar of 'culture' were guilty of a fundamental misrepresentation. One can criticise the Sitwells for their clannishness and their belligerence, that trademarked refusal to understand that to attack somebody's poem is not necessarily to insult them personally, but their seriousness – a deeply felt belief that art should matter and does not matter enough – is rarely in doubt.

The Sitwells were early supporters of T. S. Eliot. In fact it is to Osbert and Sacheverell that we owe the existence of a 'side' to Eliot rarely recorded in formal accounts of his life: the off-duty bachelor manqué lurking in the rented flat in the Charing Cross Road where he went to write, known to his landlord as 'Captain Eliot' and anointing himself with green cosmetic powder. If the Sitwells were one kind of literary modernism's public face, then Eliot was its high priest, a figure of paralysing celebrity, the very sight of whom could inspire apprentice writers with a sense of hero worship. Fifty years after chancing upon him in a Charlotte Street restaurant in the late 1920s, Anthony Powell could still remember the feeling of excitement stimulated by the appearance of 'a figure whom the Sitwells, Bloomsbury, even Wyndham Lewis treated with respect'. The layers of prestige that Eliot collected around him here in the era of *Ulysses*, *Mrs Dalloway* and Hart Crane's *The Bridge* were all the more extraordinary in that the cultural war he embarked on in the mid-1920s was being conducted, simultaneously, on three or possibly even four separate fronts.

To begin with there was his status as a poet, or rather *the* poet, who, if not quite single-handedly, had brought modernism somewhere near to the literary mainstream. To the achievement of *Poems 1909–1925* could be added his decisive influence on the crowd of home-grown versifiers who followed in his wake. Brian Howard, compiling a never-to-be-published anthology of up-and-coming talent for the Hogarth Press in the early 1930s, noted the 'numberless variations, generally in the treble key, upon Mr Eliot's renowned poem, *The Waste Land*'. Edgell Rickword thought that 'if there were to be held a Congress of the Younger Poets and it was desired to make some kind of show of recognition to the poet who has most effectively upheld the reality of the art in an age of preposterous poeticising, it is not possible to think of any serious rival to the name of T. S. Eliot'. Then, in an age where literary criticism was ceasing to be a matter of scansion, metre and motive, there was his status as a critical hierophant, imparting a zealous, neoclassical acuity to a discipline which had previously got by on belles-lettrist laxness. Finally there was his position as a kind of aesthetic *idée fixe*, a potent symbol of the continuing post-war revolt against Georgianism, the lyric, Romanticism (up to a point), whimsicality, pastoralism – all that dead wood in which the jungles of the literary 1920s abounded. Small wonder that Powell, eyeing the austere, dinner-jacketed figure dining by himself in the Etoile, was impressed.

Latter-day students of the criticism are sometimes deterred by the occasional sonority of the tone. Eliot acknowledged this failing, and the preface to the 1928 edition of *The Sacred Wood* (1920) apologises for 'a stiffness and an assumption of pontifical solemnity which may be tiresome to many readers'. On the other hand, a pontifical solemnity seems to be what many of those readers wanted: in establishing some of the ground rules on which much interwar literary criticism came to be based, there was no room for anything that might be construed as light-mindedness. Almost from the very first page, Eliot is setting out marker flags for the highly exacting route by which he thought serious criticism ought to proceed. There is approving mention of Matthew Arnold's remark that the English poets of the Romantic age 'did not know enough'. Painful distinctions – painful, that is, to anyone who regarded the contents of the average Victorian library as a uniform entity – were made, as when he remarks how astonishing it would be if Arnold had shown his contemporaries exactly why George Eliot was more serious than Dickens and how Stendhal was more serious than both of them.

The undergraduate reader has barely stopped wondering when some first principles are going to be established – what, for example, is meant by 'serious'? – when Eliot switches his attention to the sages of the Edwardian era. The temptation to anyone who is interested in literature and ideas, he tells us, is to put literature in the corner until he has cleaned up the whole country first. 'Some persons, like Mr Wells and Mr Chesterton, have succeeded so well in this latter profession . . . that we must conclude it is indeed their proper role, and that they have done well for themselves in letting literature aside.' It is not just that the Wells–Chesterton kind of critic is being tempted outside his proper sphere of influence, rather that the whole apparatus by which he evaluates and judges literature is suspect: 'The criticism proper betrays such poverty of ideas and such atrophy of sensibility that men who ought to preserve their critical ability for the improvement of their own creative work are tempted into criticism.' This was not simply a call for critical authority – that was as old as the critic – it was also a demand for the exclusivity of the critical function. If the standards brought to the appreciation of contemporary literature were fundamentally flawed – Sir Edmund Gosse is hauled in here as an expert witness – then was it the younger generation's fault that it was aware of no authority it could respect?

Authority. Standards. Respect. These are pedagogic terms, and Eliot's schoolmasterly side is never very far away from his pronouncements on critical rules and manners. Interestingly, when Anthony Powell met him again, nearly twenty years after the Charlotte Street sighting, in the North Devon village where Powell was on post-demob furlough, he noted that the off-duty Eliot, taking tea with friends or drinking pints of cider in the local pub, 'had just a touch of the headmaster, laying aside his dignity for a talk with the more intelligent boys'. And yet standards, it might be said, are only as good as the mind that formulates them. What Eliot really wants, it soon becomes clear, is not so much a collection of hard-and-fast rules about how literature may or may not be supposed to work, but an awareness that intelligent judgements can only be reached at the end of a long and arduous reasoning process. The true generalisation, he insists, is not a shot in the dark, a flash of intuition, something breezily superimposed on a mass of contending materials. Rather, in a really appreciative mind, it is the final step in a series of patiently acquired insights which, collectively, 'form themselves as a structure'. Criticism, consequently, is 'the statement in language of this structure; it is a development of sensibility'. The same scrupulousness, naturally, was enjoined on the poet, who discovered in the essay 'Tradition and the Individual Talent' that not only were his pretensions to originality being called into question, but that the originality itself might be largely unwelcome, that he, or she, might only be called upon to consolidate the achievements of mighty ancestors. When we approach a poet 'we shall often find that not only the best but the most individual parts of his work may be those in which the dead poets, his ancestors, assert their immortality most vigorously'. Never mind the cultivation of an historical sense – 'nearly indispensable' to anyone who presumes to write poetry beyond their mid-20s – the true poet performs with a feeling that the whole of the literature of Europe from Homer onwards is stacked up at the end of his study desk.

Bracing as these prescriptions undoubtedly were – and are – they pose an insuperable difficulty for anyone involved in the day-to-day world of literary production, and the difficulty lies in the absolutely vertiginous crag from which they were dispensed to the smaller fry writing their criticisms and compiling their poems on the ground. The standards, it goes without saying, are too Olympian, the bar raised so high that only a handful of writers in a generation – perhaps only Eliot himself – can have any hope of clearing it. The average poet – the above-average poet if it comes to that – does not, by and large, sit down with the entirety of European literature since Homer burning in his mind; he, or she, is much more likely to be engaged on devising a rhyme for 'bare', which has exercised every poet since Chaucer. In the same way, a reviewer put to work on the novels of the moment may just about concede the proposition that change in the European mind 'is a development which abandons nothing en route', and that an appreciation of aesthetic continuity runs through most new work like the lettering through a stick of rock, but his, or her, first response will, likely as not, be an instinctive judgement as to whether it succeeds on its own terms. One suspects that Eliot knew this and that he did not, even in his rosier moments, imagine a world in which his kind of criticism was practised by more than a very small number of people.

At the same time the need to formulate these principles about tradition and the individual talents labouring in its shadow proceeded out of an insistence that critical practice – sometimes very workaday critical practice – should be encouraged to improve, even if the ideals with which this improvement was hedged about were impossibly lofty. Eliot being Eliot, there was no shortage of attempts to bring this theory triumphantly to the page, and from 1922 he had his own literary magazine to help him with the task. The *Criterion*, at first backed by Viscountess Rothermere, who thought that it might be a chic successor to *Art and Letters*, was originally a quarterly, then a monthly, and from June 1928, by which time it was being underwritten by the publishing firm of Faber & Gwyer, a quarterly again, with a prohibitive 7s6d cover price. On the other hand, if the *Criterion*'s circulation rarely exceeded a few hundred copies, then its readership was a great deal more substantial: cash-strapped undergraduate readers, for example, found that they could replenish their collection by obtaining sample numbers for the cost of postage.

The critic Julian Symons once suggested that the most interesting literary magazines are generally those which support an idea, or a group of ideas, very often embodied in an individual temperament.

If the *Criterion* – the *New Criterion*, as it became after its relaunch – was stamped with the dye of Eliot's personality, then the implications of that personality took a certain amount of time to emerge. The fourth issue (February 1924) talked about literary reviews maintaining principles 'which have their consequences also in politics and in private conduct', but it was not until 1926 that the editor proposed his 'Idea of a Literary Review', with its mention of 'tendencies' and the inadvisability of printing good material irrespective of the form that particular tendency took. The contributors, by this stage, included Proust, Virginia Woolf, Cavafy, Hugh Walpole, Eliot himself (with *The Waste Land*) and Pound, but what kind of tendency did they embody? There were predictable references to Classicism, Reason, the advantages of Authority over Liberalism (a decade later, at the height of the Spanish Civil War, Eliot could be found condemning the 'irresponsible anti-fascists, the patrons of mass-meetings and manifestos', whose minds were 'doctrinaire without being philosophic'). The increasingly hard-line nature of Eliot's conservatism is well known, but in some ways the most disconcerting aspect of the *Criterion* – certainly the aspect most conspicuously revealed by the succeeding volumes of Eliot's collected correspondence – is the distance between Olympian ideal and practical reality.

No doubt in its day-to-day routines the supervision of a highbrow literary review (a job Eliot combined with his duties at Faber & Gwyer) is no less humdrum an activity than any other branch of journalism, and yet the atmosphere of the *Criterion*'s editorial sanctum can sometimes seem horribly mundane. Eliot was uncomfortably aware of this tendency to pour his immortal spirit down the drain a pint at a time ('one sometimes feels that the work of editing a literary review is quite useless and makes no difference in the world' he told a well-wisher). All the same, his sedulousness, not to say obsequiousness, as a solicitor of contributions looks exaggerated even by the standards of the 1920s. Eliot's extreme deference to an older generation of literary gentlemen to whom he was professionally indebted has often been remarked, but the letters to such Grub Street veterans as Charles Whibley and the former Liberal MP J. M. Robertson practically lay on the flattery with a trowel. Amid a riot of invitations to tea and supper parties – these were grim-sounding entertainments involving select bands of *Criterion* faithful – and the sober commissioning of articles with titles such as 'Shakespeare's perception of the functional importance of the brain', the more playful, crony-haunted Eliot, capable of signing off his letters to Pound 'in haste, Possum', gleams rather fitfully out of the murk.

'It is not in any sense a popular review', Eliot assured one of his correspondents, 'and desires only to present the best thoughts of the best minds.' One of the most cheering aspects of the *Criterion*, consequently, was the way in which the best minds were not above haggling for better terms. Contributors' fees were a source of endless dissent: Virginia Woolf received a gracious apology in February 1926 after the editor had forgotten about the special rates, 'which, as a matter of fact, have never been applied to anyone but Joyce and yourself'. Ezra Pound got rather shorter shrift ('I thought I had made it quite clear that the payment would be at the rate of £10 per 5,000 words. The essay comes to 3,545 words'). Who was counting? Eliot himself? All this, together with the letters angling for copy ('I think you did not receive the proposal unfavourably') or exulting over the merits of what has been so kindly vouchsafed ('I anticipate very eagerly the effect it will have') suggest that it must have been a very rewarding experience to edit the *Criterion*, but not infinitely so.

But there is a wider cultural parable going on here, beyond the usual editorial obligation to expand the contacts book and keep the rates down to two guineas a thousand. This is the sheer difficulty of editing a highbrow literary magazine – or indeed any sort of literary magazine – at a time of cultural fracture. In an age where fragmentation was the order of the day and gangs of *vers libre* poets and outraged traditionalists fought running battles through the pages of the weeklies, Eliot's flexibility is one of his most engaging characteristics. Squire once described himself as 'a centipede with a foot in a hundred camps'. The same is true – up to a point – of Possum, here found encouraging the Auden-generation poets, there seen petitioning Housman to write about Wilkie Collins; an ally of the Sitwells but on friendly terms with Bloomsbury, and yet however prudently diplomatic and discreetly feline never quite aloof from the rough and tumble of literary in-fighting. 'We shall be able to deal with J.C.S . . . when Sir Edmund is safely interred in the abbey' he suggested to Edith Sitwell at one point in the mid-1920s, thereby yoking together two of the main obstructions to the rapt, colonising spirit coming up from the *Criterion*'s offices in Queen Square. As for the dignity – to go back to Powell's image of an off-duty headmaster hobnobbing with the senior boys

– one never knows quite how much of it was laid aside, what with the semi-, but only semi-jocular rebukes to F. Scott Fitzgerald for misspelling his name, or the gentle put-downs administered to the inadequately serious ('It does not seem to me that the subject matter is of sufficient importance to justify the *Criterion* in recognising the existence of Mr Michael Arden'). Eliot, on the evidence of his 1920s output, was, in the end, a tough cookie, a sharp operator, preparing a face to meet the faces that he met while acknowledging that his inner life, as represented by his increasingly volatile wife Vivien, was stalked by the grisliest private demons. All the same, you suspect that the lasting importance of the *Criterion*, even when Joyce, Proust and the matter of Shakespeare's cerebration have been given their due, is the fact that Eliot edited it.

If the literary 1920s were an age of intergenerational conflict, then in some ways Eliot – nearing middle age as the decade wore on, and a political conservative to boot – stood at the head of an older alliance that, even now, was finding the going more arduous than it had been in the immediately post-war years. There were newcomers knocking at the door, many of whom, while innately respectful of Eliot and what he symbolised, offered a more distinctive slant on the modern movement's engagement with the literature of its time. A letter from September 1927 in the third volume of Eliot's *Collected Letters* to his friend Thomas McGreevy, for example, makes passing reference to his 'not knowing' a Mr Rickword, 'who was the Editor of the late *Calendar*'. While Eliot, by this stage in his career, was modernism's high priest, Rickword (1898–1982) was its coming young man. A Great War veteran with an MC, invalided out of the army shortly after the Armistice, Edgell Rickword's early pronouncements about the need for critical standards would not have looked out of place in a *Criterion* editorial: he notes, for example, in what is clearly a dig at the Squirearchy, that 'taste' is being 'seriously misled and even increasingly undermined by many established literary pundits'. But if the public had never been so 'confused and debased' in its opinions during a half-century 'in which the discussion of literary questions has become general', Rickword's solution was not to retreat into a world of small-circulation highbrow magazines but to build bridges between the general reading public and the finest minds of the age.

Much of Rickword's early work, consequently, came in the form of short reviews for popular newspapers such as the *Daily Herald* and the *Sunday Referee* – object lessons, it might be said, in how to address a mass audience without compromising the principles you claim to be bringing to the mass audience in the first place, while also advertising some of the interests that would characterise his critical stance over the next decade and a half. As an accomplished lyric poet – see his *Behind the Eyes* (1921) – he had strong views about Romanticism, in particular a conviction that one of its most injurious effects had been to detach the poet from the minutiae of day-to-day existence. His remarks on the quintessential Georgian poet Lascelles Abercrombie are emphatic on this point: 'Since Crabbe there has been hardly a poet who could versify the details of ordinary life . . . poets have lost that innocence of eye which enabled them to accept every detail with impartiality and to dignify what was intrinsically uninteresting though necessary to their tale, not by periphrasis, but by its fusion with the current of their verse.' Like practically every major critic of the period, Rickword could not avoid saying what he thought about Eliot, and he contributed a particularly tough-minded review of *The Waste Land* to the *Times Literary Supplement*. Here, beginning with some suggestive remarks about the cultural layer 'of more or less density' which exists between a poem and its reader, he notes the way in which Eliot's emotions hardly ever reach his audience 'without traversing a zig-zag of allusion'. Eliot, in other words, is conducting a magic-lantern show, but being too reserved ever to expose in public the impressions stamped on him by his journey through the wasteland, he uses slides made by other people, 'indicating with a touch the difference between his reaction and theirs'.

By 1925, together with his friends Douglas Garman and Bertram Higgins – he described the editorial committee as 'a sort of discontented club' – Rickword was ready to start work on a collective enterprise. This was the *Calendar of Modern Letters*, at first a monthly, then reduced to quarterly appearances, whose subsequent influence was out of all proportion to its two-year existence and tiny circulation. That the editors meant business is evident in the opening editorial, 'Instead of a Manifesto', in which that highly desirable abstraction the 'liberal reader', that open-minded and ideologically unattached pursuer of truth and beauty, is marked down as 'not one with whom we share any particular admirations or set of beliefs'. From the outset the *Calendar* was keen on social and political issues, anthropology, psychology, nearly all of them pointing the way to the specifically

Marxist preoccupations that would occupy Rickword in the 1930s. The Victorian 'religion' of the great man had broken down. Now there was only race, the biological and economic environment and the individual. This, on the other hand, was by no means a paean to Romantic exceptionalism: 'perhaps there are not so many individuals as there are men and women with names and addresses'. The artist's job, consequently, was to help the ordinary person to work on his or her individuality – a task rendered that much more difficult by the collapse of shared critical values – and Rickword wrote an interesting review of Virginia Woolf's *The Common Reader*, insisting that the best essay in it was 'The Pastons and Chaucer', on the grounds that its theme was the influence on a writer of the society in which he lived. The Victorians, he argued, had produced 'the last examples of the literature which retains its expressive value along the whole scale of group perspective'. Since that time the prospective audience had split into a small body of 'educated, sharp-witted readers for whom a small spark of intelligence sometimes flickers' and the great reading public, forever at the mercy of 'the high-class literary-journalist-poet type' and capable of being grotesquely led astray.

How did the *Calendar* propose to redress this imbalance? A search through its opening numbers discloses a high degree of analytical sharpness. Douglas Garman contributes a devastating review – devastating, that is, in some of its implications – of a book of poems by Harold Acton, convicting Acton of an aestheticism whose detachment means, among other defects, that it never looks closely enough at any given subject that strays under its lens. Various Georgians are taken out and roundly chastised, with Lascelles Abercrombie's *The Idea of Great Poetry* coming in for particular hostility ('This attitude of sustained admiration is deadening') and there are approving notices of Eliot's *Homage to Dryden*, Joyce ('Mr Joyce has both enriched literature and potentially widened its scope') and I. A. Richards' *Principles of Literary Criticism*. But the *Calendar*'s most distinctive contribution to the intellectual debate of its time came in a series of 'Scrutinies', in which some of the great names from an age now presumed to be hurtling towards extinction were taken out and punctiliously exposed to a new brand of scrupulous and at times decidedly disrespectful judgement. Following the tone of the magazine's leading articles, the touchstone is 'relevance and the connection of the artist to the society from which he springs'.

And so Rickword, setting to work on J. M. Barrie, notes the 'fidelity' with which he describes what 'he felt in life' while stressing that its 'irrelevance to the world as we see it deprives us of a pleasure which our elders undoubtedly enjoyed'. Douglas Garman places de la Mare in the dock on a charge of 'simulated childishness', which 'results in the divorce of art from life, for the poetry which dictates it is incapable of creating a valid attitude to life and does not, therefore, fulfil its essential function'. Masefield (Bertram Higgins) goes much the same way, while Arnold Bennett (Edwin Muir) is let off with a caution on the grounds of his authentic sociological sweep. Bennett's novels may be dated, Muir argues, but the characteristics which make him an anomaly as an artist work to his advantage as a literary personality. 'He has brought into literature qualities which are seldom found there, which perhaps should not be found there, but qualities which, nevertheless, are interesting as well as admirable.'

Much of this, understandably, caused great offence: there were complaints from the *Times Literary Supplement* about 'the low standard of literary courtesy on display'. But the *Calendar*'s achievements, in the brief two-year span of its existence, were formidable. Richards' essay 'The Returning Hero' may be said to have set out some of the ground rules for the new wave of post-war poetry. 'A Note on Fiction' by C. H. Rickword, Edgell's brother, was singled out by Malcolm Bradbury for marking 'the transition of modernism into literary criticism of the novel'. The 'Scrutiny' tag was picked up by Leavis. And this is to ignore the magazine's focus on contemporary fiction, its sponsorship of A. E. Coppard and L. P. Hartley, the poems by Sassoon and Blunden, the bright idea of getting Bertrand Russell to review Huizinga's *The Waning of the Middle Ages*, the enthusiasm not only for Forster and Lawrence but Americans such as Hart Crane and John Crowe Ransom who at this stage were scarcely known in England. Rickword, Garman and Higgins may have lacked Eliot's intellectual gravitas and his sagacity – they certainly lacked his resources – but between them they created something which the *Criterion* was not – a genuinely *literary* magazine.

From the angle of the Boots Library subscriber, much of this – the *Criterion*, 'Scrutinies', the outer reaches of Sitwelldom – was so much intellectual sky-writing. Eliot did not become a national figure until two or even three decades later when a new and predominantly

Anglican audience began to discover *Four Quartets*. With rare exceptions, the Sitwells' books enjoyed such modest print runs that, as one of their editors recalled, once the complimentary copies had been disposed of, there were not a great many left to be sold. Rickword's own engagement with a genuinely popular audience had to wait until his editorial work on *Our Time* (1944–7), which has some claims to be regarded as Britain's only mass-circulation left-wing weekly magazine. None of this, though, is to ignore the way in which modernist principles, and modernist practice, began to colonise, or at the very least to infiltrate, the literary mainstream during the interwar era. Naturally, this process was very far from uniform, let alone directly measurable in its effects. Much popular awareness of newfangled developments in literature and the arts came through what was essentially comic disparagement: the satirical cartoons in *Punch*; the P. G. Wodehouse characters desperate to seem in touch with the latest manifestations of the avant-garde. But there were plenty of real-life popular novelists keen to establish at least some kind of accommodation with Bloomsbury and Garsington. Hugh Walpole, for example, pursued a courteous, admiring and rather puzzled friendship with Virginia Woolf, and was occasionally given to praising modernist novels not because he liked them but because they were the kind of books of which his intellectual friends might be expected to approve. In Anthony Powell's *The Acceptance World* (1955), set in the early 1930s, Nick Jenkins is startled to find the veteran literary man St John Clarke writing 'at least by implication favourably' about one of his novels in an American newspaper. Jenkins assumes that this is merely a case of St John Clarke discerning merit. It is left to his friend Barnby to diagnose an opportunistic conversion to modernism ('I fear it is all part of a larger design'). This episode mirrors the fortunes of Powell's own debut *Afternoon Men* (1931) and the 'scrap of implied praise' flicked towards it by Walpole, a writer not previously known for his encouragement of left-field talent but irrevocably mired in the world of the mainstream world of the *Times* Book Club and the *London Mercury*.

Inevitably, the rush to detect 'influence' can sometimes throw up more problems than it solves. Who, in the end, is able to quantify the precise impulse which causes one writer to leave discernible traces of another in his bloodstream? A. C. Benson once complained that if you asked a transatlantic critic who was the most influential writer currently at work in America, he would infallibly come up with a name of which neither you nor anyone else had ever heard. Nonetheless, to the clever young man or woman scrabbling for a foothold on the lower reaches of the interwar era's literary north face, certain names predominate. Joyce was an intoxicant, but also impossible to imitate (see, for example, the Trafalgar Square scenes in Orwell's *A Clergyman's Daughter* (1935), which mimic the 'Nighttown' sequence in *Ulysses*). Brian Howard, embarking on one of his many fruitless schemes to produce saleable literary work, decided that 'the descriptive parts must be poetry, rather in the manner of Virginia Woolf'. Anthony Powell, looking back from the vantage point of 1973, thought that it was 'difficult now to express the prestige attached to the name of Aldous Huxley in the 1920s'.

If the proto-modernist young man has a symbolic projection, it is Anthony Blanche (partly modelled on Howard) in *Brideshead Revisited*, who recites *The Waste Land* from his Christ Church balcony to the sweatered throng as they proceed to games field and river beneath him, is found reading Huxley's *Antic Hay* when the hearties arrive at his rooms, bent on throwing him in the college fountain, dines with Proust and Gide and is 'on closer terms with Cocteau and Diaghilev'. Few of these fan clubs, though, get us any nearer to the question of motivation. When Powell, for example, declares himself to have been 'prostrated' by the brilliance of Huxley's early novels, what lessons did he imagine he was learning from it and what would have been the effect of this immersion in the modernist high style on his own work? The answer, invariably, is a means of communicating that is so oblique that at times it scarcely seems to communicate at all, 'stories' whose plots proceed by way of stealthy insinuation, deft touches on barely visible threads, decisive twists and reversals of fortune. *Afternoon Men*, consequently, is a kind of elliptical tour in which a group of disillusioned bohemians idle their way through a round of futile love affairs and professional setbacks, only to end up where they began, and, as such, exist to file a statement of aesthetic intent calculated to make a critic less indulgent than Walpole seethe in his galoshes.

But one of the decisive modernist influences on the 1920s and 1930s, certainly on the Oxford aesthetes who clustered around Anthony Blanche's real-life equivalents, was a writer yet more recherché than Woolf, Huxley or Joyce. This was Ronald Firbank (1886–1926), a figure so unregarded in the annals of the early twentieth-century avant-garde that even now, ninety years after his premature death, he awaits a proper biography. Shy, dandyish, homosexual, reclusive and, apart from a brief mid-1920s vogue in the United States, where he was taken up by the influential critic Carl Van Vechten, compelled to publish his works at his own expense, Firbank's slender *oeuvre* includes, in such novels as *Caprice* (1917) and *Prancing Nigger* (1924), some of the high points of mid-period English modernism. Set in brightly hued never-never lands or in more recognisable environments twisted radically out of shape, they advertise a wit so delicate that it can scarcely be identified, borne forward by scraps of rococo dialogue, the whole stealthily undercut by intimations of deep unease, often extending to outright tragedy. As one, bright young men and women with literary aspirations rushed to acclaim Firbank as their mentor. Evelyn Waugh wrote an essay for *Life and Letters* (1929) in which he suggested that Firbank 'achieved a new art form' as a way of 'bringing coherence to his own elusive humour'. Brian Howard thought *Concerning the Eccentricities of Cardinal Pirelli* (1926), at whose climax the cardinal drops dead while in hot pursuit of an attractive choirboy, 'the wittiest book ever written. A triumph of indecent sophistication.' Anthony Powell, while working at Duckworth, and discovering that Firbank had left money in his will to finance the scheme, managed to contrive a posthumous collected edition. When Firbank's admirers began to publish books themselves, references to him tumble through the pages as statements of aesthetic intent. Bobby Bobbin, the dissolute Eton schoolboy in Nancy Mitford's *Christmas Pudding* (1932), keeps a set of Firbank's novels in his room. Anthony Blanche, alternatively, receives his copies direct from the author 'with fervent inscriptions'.

If the majority of modernist influence on the interwar novel is general – a matter of style and stance, a hankering after the Joycean set-piece or an awareness of the poeticism which Howard so admired in the novels of Virginia Woolf – then Firbank's is narrowly specific. As a novelist, it is fair to say that he bequeathed three main legacies to fiction. The first is his ability to recreate 'talking heads' – two- , three- or even four-way conversations in which no speaker is ever named after their introduction but where the author's ear for speech patterns immediately enables the reader to distinguish between them. His second technical advance is the way in which his style, by this time utterly stripped down and composed, manages to convey a tumult of impressions – movement, scene, talk – in a minimum of words. The removal of the Haitian Mouth family to Cuna-Cuna in *Prancing*

Nigger is announced in a single sentence: 'Little jingly trot trot trot, over the savannah hey – .' At the same time, Firbank perfected a trick of advancing the plots of his novels through allusive dialogue. In the *Life and Letters* essay, Waugh highlights the case of the Ritz hotel versus Lady Something in *The Flower Beneath the Foot* (1923) as 'typical of the Firbank method'. At a dinner party King William of Pisuerga observes of some piece of news that 'he could not be more astonished than if you told me there were fleas at the Ritz'. Lady Something mishears. 'Who could believe it?' she exclaims. 'It's almost too appalling . . . Fleas have been found at the Ritz.' The hotel goes unmentioned for the next forty pages, until a character called 'the Hon. Eddy' tells Lady Something that had he known he was going to be ill, he would have gone to stay at the Ritz. 'And you'd have been bitten all over' she assures him. There is another long silence, broken only by an aside in which 'an eloquent and moderately victorious young barrister' is represented as being 'engaged on the approaching suit with the Ritz'. A few pages later comes a casual remark that the Ritz is empty, save for a solitary guest.

V. S. Pritchett, who wrote a sagacious essay noting that Firbank had 'laid down the pattern for contemporary dialogue', characterised his novels as 'antics in a void left by life, elegies on burst bubbles'. One sees what he means and, by extension, the futility of subjecting him to the kind of sustained critical investigation which such talismans invariably attract. Here, simply through a handful of tangential remarks, tiny fragments of intent concealed in a vast mosaic, Firbank has manufactured a plot line that has the additional subtlety of taking place more or less offstage. As the chain of events set in motion at the Llanabba school sports day in *Decline and Fall* demonstrates, Waugh was not above borrowing this technique himself. The sequence begins when Mr Prendergast, drunk in charge of the starting pistol, inadvertently grazes little Lord Tangent's ankle with a stray bullet. Somewhat later in the proceedings a guest enquires of Tangent's mother, Lady Circumference, how her son has been performing, only to hear that he has been injured in the foot. 'Dear me! Not badly I hope. Did he twist his ankle in the jumping?' No, Lady Circumference explains, 'he was shot at by one of the assistant masters'. Twenty pages later someone casually remarks that Tangent's foot has swollen up and turned black. There follows another ten-page gap until an account of the bigamous union between Captain Grimes and the headmaster's daughter concludes with a reference to the regrettable absence of Lord Tangent, 'whose foot was being amputated at a local nursing home'. It is the authentic Firbankian note – sly, subversive and bleakly hilarious, brought out of the modernist shadows and put to work in one of the ornaments of twentieth-century British fiction.

Hugh Walpole: The Perils of Success

If not quite in the way he would have wanted, Hugh Walpole (1884–1941) is an exemplary figure: a genre-defining representation of the writer who, not content with worldly success, craves the intellectual recognition that will give it savour, and, as a result, spends much of his career making himself miserable over its absence. Despite his titanic sales, despite a much-coveted niche at the upper end of literary society that lasted a quarter of a century, despite a knighthood and the incidental satisfactions of any prestige assignment he cared to undertake – his report on the coronation of King George VI was syndicated around the world – he was a man born out of his time, a novelist condemned to operate in the endlessly contested territory of the 1920s and 1930s, when he would have been far better suited to a bygone age. How happy he would have been, he once reflected, if he had been working from 1890 to 1910, when Romanticism was all the rage. As it was he was forced to live out his days, half envious and half bewildered, in the world of imagism, Bloomsbury and *vers libre*. And to the awareness that he was, essentially, an anachronism could be added a suspicion, later hardening into certainty, that the tents of fashion had moved on, that the smart money was no longer being placed on the kind of books he wrote, but had migrated to an artistic high ground whose upper levels would always hang tantalisingly out of reach: one of the proudest moments of his life came when Eliot decided to serialise his novel *The Old Ladies* in the *Criterion*. The conviction that, deep down, he aspired to write a different kind of book nagged at him and made him unhappy. His only trouble, he once declared, was that he was definitely old-fashioned: 'Now I'd *like* to be modern. I'd rather be a male Hugh Walpole to a female Virginia Woolf than anything else on earth.' This insecurity was his undoing, and when it coincided with a practical joke played on him by another writer, the effect, for all his seeming indifference, was to ruin his life.

The depths to which Walpole's reputation had been reduced by the time of his death in 1941 – he was a long-term diabetic whose already weak health was fatally undermined by the strain of the Blitz – were all the more marked in the light of his early triumphs. A shy, sensitive parson's son, whose homosexuality expressed itself in passionate attachments to heavily married men, his early career was a kind of object lesson in how to get on. There was a valuable connection with Henry James, who devoted two-thirds of a column to his interesting young friend in a celebrated *Times Literary Supplement* article of 1915 on 'The Younger Generation'. Arnold Bennett maintained that 'the hand of the born and consecrated novelist' was apparent in *Mr Perrin and Mr Traill*. But many of the public relations campaigns he was capable of orchestrating went on behind the scenes. He was a great despatcher of deferential letters; a writer of humble but appreciative notes to reviewers who had yet to fall under his spell; a tyro who manifestly wanted to learn from his mistakes. Emerging from the Great War – latterly spent at a press bureau in Moscow – with an OBE and a contract from Macmillan, he seemed to have the world at his feet: ambitious and forceful, but simultaneously emollient and forgiving, never one to miss a short-term advantage, but there for the long haul. The critic who disparaged him usually received not a sharp note of rebuke but an invitation to lunch. This technique did not always work, and there were wounding brush-offs from Rebecca West and Katherine Mansfield, but the general effect was to burnish Walpole's status as the coming man of English letters.

In strict taxonomic terms Walpole tended to write two main kinds of novel: long, romantically conceived historical sagas, and shorter and somewhat macabre psychological thrillers. In a literary world where the cult of the best-seller was gaining ground, and alliances of publishers, booksellers and critics caballed to increase circulation, his sales were simply prodigious. *Harmer John* sold 40,000 copies in America in 1924 – an era in which many English novels sank without trace – as well as attracting a serialisation deal worth £4,000. As late as 1939 sales of the single-volume edition of the *Herries Chronicles* – his four-book Cumbrian epic – went into six figures. All this brought material success, and in particular an almost unparalleled collection of contemporary art, but already there were signs that the edifice of good fellowship, bland optimism – the 'apple-cheeked Hugh' persona created for him by admiring journalists – might not be indefinitely sustainable. He was a cultivator of the secret enmity, a champion of the quiet vendetta. The critic L.A.G. Strong remembered telling him that an editor he had attacked for printing a hostile review had tried to tone down the original script. 'Don't tell me that, you mustn't, you mustn't' Walpole is supposed to have lectured him. 'Don't take away my enemy.' This sensitivity extended to his social life. Alec Waugh once attended a supper party at which Walpole, having said his goodbyes but found his chauffeur missing, returned with the words 'Well, what were you saying about me behind my back?' One of the diners volunteered that they had all been agreeing what a happy man he was. It was said with affection, but Walpole was aghast. In the mazy intellectual landscapes of the modern novel, wasn't suffering, surely, the only proper condition to which the contemporary artist ought to be seen to aspire?

These anxieties, inevitably, took their toll – on Walpole's nervous system, on his personality and on his relationships with other writers. He was a generous man, happy to subsidise less fortunate colleagues who had fallen by the wayside. At the same time it was suggested that he had a habit of performing kindly acts that had the additional benefit of drawing attention to himself. Even his geniality, his well-intentioned speechifying, his willingness to propose toasts and to lead delegations came in for criticism. As Waugh, who held Walpole in genuine esteem, once put it: 'Need he always look as if he were the guest of honour at a party at which Life and Literature were the host and hostess?' But this was as nothing compared to the evening in 1932 when Walpole picked up a copy of Somerset Maugham's newly published *Cakes and Ale*. The character of 'Alroy Kear', a literary careerist whose passage through the world of English letters is a gargantuan exercise in nest-feathering, is not an exact portrait but it was near enough to Walpole to make anyone who knew him mark the resemblance, not least in its account of the young writer who sends his first novel 'with a pleasant letter to all the leading writers of the day', telling each one in turn 'how greatly he admired his work, how much he had learned from his study of them, and how ardently he aspired to follow, albeit at a humble distance, the trail his master had blazed'. To anyone who had watched the young Walpole at work, and the middle-aged Walpole capitalising on his success, this was unignorable. As Waugh drily observed, 'Everything was there: the appealing charm that Walpole could lavish on those who were successful and might be useful, and the bland indifference with which he could treat old friends who had betrayed him by being neither, and most unkind of all his complete lack of talent.'

Walpole's immediate reaction was one of heart-rent despair. According to one report, he began to read the novel while changing for dinner at the country house where he was staying, and was found half an hour later by his anxious host, trousers around his ankles, the book still gripped in a shaking hand. But in the longer term, *Cakes and Ale* presented him with an almost insuperable dilemma. He could not laugh it off: it was too big for that, too premeditated; too intimately connected to the front he offered to the world. A libel writ would only draw attention to the frailties Maugham had presumed to expose. In the end a pained letter was sent, to which Maugham disingenuously replied that 'Kear is made up of a dozen people, and the greater part of him is myself.' A prudent man would simply have kept quiet in the wake of this exchange. But Walpole overdid it. In fact, such was the curious psychological motor that drove his reactions that he not only pretended that nothing had happened but went out of his way to conciliate Maugham and defend him in situations where he was perfectly capable of looking after himself. Not long after the *Cakes and Ale* debacle, there was published, anonymously – the author was later revealed as the novelist Elinor Mordaunt – and in America, a lightly veiled attack on Maugham entitled *Gin and Bitters*. The question of English publication arose, whereupon Walpole weighed in with a letter to Maugham urging him to take legal action ('the book is *foul* and you ought to stop it') and offering to give evidence on his behalf. Walpole's biographer assumes that the letter meant exactly what it said, that a short-lived and misguided passion had burnt itself out. On the other hand, there hung for many years in the offices of Mordaunt's American publisher a cartoon captioned 'The noble art of self-defence', in which a small, frail woman is shown holding a book in front of her face to protect herself from a gigantic male attacker. The book is *Gin and Bitters*; the assailant unmistakeably Walpole, and the shout-line 'Now, no one can say that *Cakes and Ale* was meant for me.'

It is not overstating the case to say that this episode cast a shadow over the rest of Walpole's life, or, rather, that it destroyed his credibility among the people he most wished to impress. The letters he exchanged with his friend Frank Swinnerton in the 1920s are full of comforting but rather uneasy jibes about 'highbrows' (Walpole: 'Can it be that I am turning highbrow?'; Swinnerton, on putting down Walter Raleigh's *Letters*: 'Somehow I hate this bloody supercilious highbrow'). *Cakes and Ale* destroyed any aspirations that Walpole had towards this exalted state. What Maugham had written – and what Maugham had implied – made no difference to Walpole's receipts, his trips to Hollywood and his top-of-the-range commissions, but it finished him with the intelligentsia. Thereafter, nearly every scheme he embarked on seemed subtly tainted. He became a target for the highbrow joke (Constant Lambert, speaking at a Foyles Literary Luncheon in 1934, told the story of a fellow musician who, seeing a dust jacket in a bookshop window bearing the words *English Comic Characters. J. B. Priestley*, enquired if they had Walpole in the same series). Were he to attend a supper party given by Maugham at Claridge's, there would be whispered comments as he moved from table to table: dignity, it was felt, should have kept him away. If he accepted an invitation to contribute a books column to a daily newspaper, there were people on hand to wonder why he felt that he had to bother, to point out that he was no Arnold Bennett, and the *Graphic* – where Walpole's causeries appeared – was not the *Evening Standard*. The knighthood conferred by George VI did his prospects no good at all. As to what the specimen highbrow thought of him, Isaiah Berlin's account of a visit to his Cumbrian hideaway, given in a letter to Elizabeth Bowen, may be taken as representative:

> You know Mr Walpole? He says he admires your books immensely – a fat, rosy, happy largeish dimpled man came bouncing out to meet us, and then served tea coyly, like a shy provincial spinster, anxiously enquiring about milk and sugar . . . Mrs Woolf – who plainly persecutes him & plays him & turns him over & over – he said was a very humorous woman . . . he gave one to understand that he lived with her on easy, gay, unconcerned terms, each a head of a non-competitive profession . . . He is absolutely uncritical: he thinks 'The Waves' splendid & his own books also splendid: above all one should enjoy oneself, & not be gloomy.

Later, when Walpole came to tea with Berlin and his host, he developed the portrait further:

> Not a name was mentioned but soft streams of praise would begin to flow from his lips . . . His pleasure when anyone is run down is also full of innocent delight. How he has managed to survive embitterment, in spite of periodic dips into Bloomsbury where he must be spitted & roasted with regularity, is truly astonishing.

The fascination of Berlin's account lies in its hint that Walpole's personality existed on several levels, and that for all his delight in Mrs Woolf's friendship he knew exactly how Bloomsbury felt about him and how zealously they belittled his books. Certainly, the literary acquaintances who kept him company in his last years, and the unusually sharp memorial notices that followed his death, were convinced that he died an unhappy man: an unmourned casualty of the 1930s culture wars; a writer who, however successful on his own terms, strained every sinew in pursuit of a goal which respectable opinion had long ago decided was scarcely worth the having.

CHAPTER 4

Highbrows, Lowbrows and Those In Between

> The public has never been so confused and debased in its tastes as during the fifty years in which the discussion of literary questions has become general.
>
> Edgell Rickword, review of *The Common Reader, Calendar of Modern Letters,* 1925

> Middle-class culture has never been an adventure of the mind or soul.
>
> Douglas Jerrold, *Georgian Adventure* (1937)

The commercialisation of literature is as old as Caxton: a sharp-eyed exploitation of publishers' assets that began long before the late twentieth-century explosion of dump-bins and three-for-two promotions. Anyone who imagines the Victorian literary scene to have been a repository of high-mindedness and good taste, deferring to minority interests and at all times displaying a conscientious determination to protect and nurture left-field talent, is invited to inspect the 1880s diaries of George Gissing or the biography of a publisher like Richard Bentley or T. Fisher Unwin: in each case the atmosphere is cut-throat, the glamour tarnished, lofty ideals ripe to be sacrificed on the altar of profit. There are several explanations as to why, come the 1920s, this process should have quickened up. At the demographic level, the mass audience brought into being by the educational reforms of the later nineteenth century was, by this stage in its development, truly massive, capable of transforming a book that 'caught on' into a public obsession, with sales to match. J. B. Priestley's *The Good Companions* sold so many copies at Christmas 1929 that a fleet of vans had to be laid on to deliver fresh stock to booksellers. Simultaneously there lurked a suspicion that this new army of readers, whether clerks looking to be edified or housewives looking to be entertained, was potentially traitorous, all too ready to be lured away by the blandishments of radio, cinema and, as the interwar era wore on, television. Even here, in an age where a six-figure copy sale of a novel that captured the public's imagination was not unusual, it was feared that the book might soon revert to its former status as a minority interest, one among a dozen contending leisure activities, always likely to lose out in the race for novelty or be swept away by the latest fashionable gadget. If the conditions of the 1920s encouraged publishers to publicise their wares more aggressively, then they also inspired them to take advantage of the newfangled promotional techniques brought in on the back of the advertising boom of the Edwardian era. Understandably, the assumption that better sales were the result of better marketing had an echo beyond the publishing community. One of the features of the 1920s publishing scene is the considerable effort expended to construct a united front, consisting not only of those who produced books but those who wrote them, brokered their sale and distributed them, with the aim of maximising receipts all round. Hugh Walpole, for instance, could be found in 1920 urging a gathering of the Whitefriars Club – an ancient booksellers' trade organisation – to encourage co-operation between different parts of the industry. This led to the foundation, a year later, of the Society of Bookmen, and subsequently to the establishment of a National Book Council, later renamed the National Book League (among other achievements, the society came up with the idea of the Book Token and helped to finance its launch among booksellers). From here it was but a short step to a Book of the Month Club, based on the immensely successful American model, with support from Arnold Bennett and Walpole officiating as chairman of the selection committee.

With a greater degree of organisation came, inevitably, a greater concentration on commercial success. There had always been best-sellers – Robert Montgomery's epic poem *The Omnipresence of the Deity* went through twenty-eight editions in the 1830s – but the new environment of the interwar era saw them cultivated as never before, with publishers competing with each other to devise lists that benefited from their recognition factor: the public knowing in advance that the books they bought, frequently produced in uniform formats, would fulfil the kind of criteria they expected from fiction, and writers whose publishers had failed to adapt complaining about their out-dated sales techniques: 'he does so little to make way for his books amid the bustle of the publishers and journalists' Edmund Blunden lamented of his own sponsor, Richard Cobden-Sanderson. 'He becomes less and less interested in publishing, he sits on a sort of throne inscribed "A DISTINGUISHED PUBLISHER".'

It was all a far cry from Messrs Hodder & Stoughton's yearly output – brought out in identikit yellow jackets, carefully designed to fit into pockets and handbags, and dealing in titles that left no genre category in the nation's bookshelves unfilled. To begin with, they were sponsors of the 'big five' – A. S. M. Hutchinson, A. E. W. Mason, John Buchan, 'Sapper' (H. C. McNeil) and 'O. Douglas', the pseudonym of Buchan's sister Anna. Romance was represented by Ruby M. Ayres and Mabel Barnes-Grundy, westerns by Rex Beach, Max Brand and Zane Grey, thrillers by E. Phillips Oppenheim, Edgar Wallace and William le Queux. A tightly run distribution network, able to talk up a particular book's chances, prepublication, with the major circulating libraries – W. H. Smith, Boots and Harrods – allowed Hodder to pull off what were, by the standards of the 1920s, extraordinary feats of salesmanship. Hutchinson's *If Winter Comes* sold over 100,000 copies in its first year. All this gave the firm an unparalleled influence when it came to securing sought-after new titles – they were able to offer T. E. Lawrence an unheard-of advance of £30,000 – and it was not until the economic downturn of the 1930s that their power began to wane: even in 1935 their annual turnover stood at £400,000 Naturally, there were drawbacks to this approach. More idiosyncratic talents were sometimes unimpressed by the thought of being published to format, and tended to migrate to smaller firms. On the other hand, the loss of a Rose Macaulay or a Phyllis Bottome – reliable performers but by no means best-sellers – was something that Hodder were prepared to tolerate.

None of these achievements, whether it were 'Sapper's' best-selling debut *Bulldog Drummond* (1920) or the sensational success of *If Winter Comes* despite its pulverisation by the critics, could have been accomplished without the existence of a wider supporting network and a series of cultural affiliates capable of bringing literature to the market and commending it to the reader's attention. These developments had been in train for several decades – *New Grub Street* is full of complaints about a world in which gossip about a book sometimes seems more important than the artefact itself – but by the 1920s they had evolved into a large-scale and essentially mainstream literary culture: undemanding, conservative and conciliatory, whose various departments, singly and collectively, were at work to demarcate, regulate and sustain the public taste. It was the age of the middlebrow literary magazine, exemplified by the *Strand*, which published the short stories of Conan Doyle and W. W. Jacobs, and *John O'London's Weekly* with its causeries about the Browning courtship and Byron's love affairs. Bob, the literary-minded barman in Patrick Hamilton's *The Midnight Bell* (1929), is a *John O'London's* fan, and in consequence a victim to what Hamilton calls 'popularised' great literature ('He even began to read tabulated outlines of it and to acquire a Great-Short-Story-Of-The-World mentality. Like an idle playgoer with the drama, he became, with literature, even more interested in the names and picturesque personalities than in the actual achievements thereof'). It was also the era of the light essay, of the overexcitable dust jacket with its constant intimations of 'genius'; of the 'puff' or over-the-top review in which all pretence of objective standards went out of the window and the potential reader was assured that his soul would 'scream with delight'. The Book of the Month Club, which launched in 1929, was all too representative of these constituencies, with a board including a publisher (A. S. Frere of Heinemann) and a newspaper editor (Alan Bott of the *Graphic*), and a selection committee consisting of Walpole, Priestley, George Gordon, Clemence Dane and Sylvia Lynd – three best-selling novelists, the Oxford Merton Professor of English Literature and the wife of a popular essayist. To one kind of 1920s literary man all this meant choice, education and enlightenment, but to another it implied uniformity of taste and standardisation of output. As Douglas Jerrold tartly observed: 'Once you set out to sell books by national advertising the books you sell must be as popular, over the field of the potential demand, as any other goods offered for sale in the advertising columns of the national newspapers.'

Jerrold was a publisher himself – in the 1940s he would wind up on the board of Eyre & Spottiswoode with Graham Greene – and, as such, personally implicated in the new publicity techniques of the 1920s. He was, for example, at one point employed by the firm of Benn Brothers, who pioneered the stratagem of the double-column press ad, and it was his former colleague Victor Gollancz, who, when establishing his own imprint later on in the decade, extended the advertisements to include what Jerrold called 'the sabotaging of public taste by a barrage of uncritical opinion'. Under the watchful eye of their chairman, and sometimes at his instigation, Gollancz's publicity department extracted and arranged reviews 'to create the suggestion that no one could afford not to read this book'. Such was his determination to provoke a response that he once printed an advert upside down. On another occasion the sales pitch ran: 'Be careful. On Friday the most important book of the century is coming out. You will look a fool at dinner if you haven't got a copy and read at least the first few pages.' If Gollancz's knack of manufacturing eye-catching copy was not, in the end, quite as revolutionary as his critics insisted – his fellow publisher Grant Richards had played a similar trick before and during the war, sometimes printing unfavourable notices if he wanted to make a point – then he was orchestrating a decisive shift in the perceived value of the product he had for sale: the idea of the purchase of a book not as a milestone on the path to self-fulfilment, but as a kind of social obligation.

Peer pressure has always played a certain role in literary aspiration – Anthony Blanche in *Brideshead Revisited* struggling to get through Huxley's *Antic Hay* on the grounds that it will be discussed on his forthcoming trip to Lady Ottoline Morrell's salon at Garsington – but the idea that one would suffer social shame by a failure to have read the book of the moment was a novelty. Not content with tugging at basic psychological levers, Gollancz next had the bright idea of employing Gerald Gould, chief literary critic of the *Observer*, as his adviser. From the angle of the publisher anxious to bring his wares to market, this offered a dual advantage. It meant that Gollancz had Gould's supposedly expert opinion to guide him when it came to selecting manuscripts for publication, but it also meant that he had Gould's imprimatur, the praise of a man who appeared each week in the review pages of a reputable Sunday newspaper, to help him promote the finished work. Other publishers took the hint, while literary editors began to employ those quoted to write reviews, with the result that, as Jerrold puts it, 'on Sunday mornings you could hardly hear yourself speak for the noise of popular novelists and biographers calling to each other across the wide open spaces of the *Observer* and the *Sunday Times*'.

The idea of the 'star reviewer', the literary celebrity who signed his name at the foot of a column whose author had previously been clothed in decent anonymity, was not altogether new, but by the later

1920s it had become an essential part of the literary culture of the day. In strict hereditary terms the concept goes back to the Edwardian era, when Arnold Bennett began to contribute a column entitled 'Books and Persons' to the *New Age* under the signature 'Jacob Tonson'. When, nearly twenty years later, Lord Beaverbrook suggested to Bennett that he should start a new series in the *Evening Standard*, both parties to the transaction were conscious that the tone, formerly broad to the point of irreverence, had to change. There was also a need to capitalise on Bennett's celebrity. The result was a signed column, still brisk but also magnanimous and keener on talent-spotting than the ur-Bennett of twenty years before, which not only succeeded as journalism – the collected volume is worth reading even today as an example of how to convey the essence of a novel in a few hundred words – and sold books, but also created a shock wave that ran the length of Fleet Street. The *Evening News* signed up Priestley, later replaced by Frank Swinnerton, novelist and adviser to Chatto & Windus. Not to be outdone the *Daily Mail* engaged Compton Mackenzie as its chief reviewer, while Hugh Walpole was rapidly absorbed by the *Daily Sketch*.

Few of the celebrated pens taken up by daily newspapers at the end of the 1920s, often at fantastical salaries – Bennett was paid an annual retainer of £3,000 – imagined that they were making a contribution to criticism: it was accepted that the judgements on offer would be resolutely ad hoc. As Swinnerton once observed, 'a writer for the diurnal press has no time to formulate an elaborate critical theory; he relies upon experience based on everything he has read, and upon the resultant intuition of the hour'. Nonetheless, once one discounts the more obvious instances of friends doing each other favours, there was a great deal to be said for star reviewing. As was frequently pointed out in the celebrity critic's defence, the specimen library-browser of the late 1920s could have done worse than to go to J. B. Priestley for advice. Simultaneously, the star reviewer, though at all times expected to radiate stardom, was generally given a fair amount of leeway. Looking back on his three-year stint on the *Evening News*, Swinnerton remembered that, while being encouraged to review stock middlebrow best-sellers such as Dorothy L. Sayers and Francis Yeats-Brown, he was also allowed to write about George Moore, Bertrand Russell, Evelyn Waugh and Kafka. These were substantial advantages, as was the considerable professional prestige that the job attracted: 'I liked seeing my name in large type across a wide page . . . I liked being told by journalists that what I wrote was "damned good journalism", and seeing Squire buy a copy of the paper to see what I had written.'

The star reviewer prided himself on his relationship with his readers, a gradual process of identification, built up column by column, that encouraged them to value the opinions offered to them to the point where they were very often prepared to go out and buy the books on display. There is abundant evidence, at any rate from the very top of the pile, that this kind of arbitration had a direct impact on sales. Bennett, for example, could increase a book's circulation merely by mentioning it in a parenthesis. Anthony Powell, then working at Duckworth, remembered an otherwise obscure novel called *Sun and Moon* by Vincent Gowan selling '200 copies or more' on the strength of an *Evening Standard* puff, while the short-story writer Malachi Whitaker recalled that, on the basis of a half-column review of her first collection, *Frost in April*, 'for a week or two my name seemed to be in every paper I picked up. I was surprised to discover that I was a printed genius'. Swinnerton, similarly, writes of the fortunes of a Chatto first novel in which he had an interest being transformed by a favourable notice by W. L. Courtney, doyen of the *Daily Telegraph*'s reviewing panel. Gosse's *Sunday Times* sanction was equally worth having. On the other hand, all these compacts, real or imaginary, were altogether eclipsed by the relationships forged between the popular essayist and his audience. Newspaper historians generally agree that by this stage in its development the 'light essay' was no more than a debased survival from the world of Victorian periodical journalism, and yet the popularity of the essayist, whether unleashed on the pages of a daily newspaper or operating at the slightly more elevated level of an intellectual weekly, knew no bounds.

Perhaps 'light essay' is the wrong term for a form which the editors of the 1920s were beginning to refer to as 'middle articles' (Gordon Comstock in *Keep the Aspidistra Flying* can be found disparaging the 'dinky little books of reprinted middles' that clutter his employer's shop). Between 800 and 1,500 words in length, meditative, sometimes topical, nearly always humorous, so varied in its subject matter that no hard-and-fast theoretical rule applies, the essay, it was generally agreed, could be about practically anything – the advantages of travelling by underground, the prime minister's pipe, the difficulty of wearing a hat on a windy day – the whole consolidated, by way of literary quotation, allusion and the sense of learning lightly worn, into an immensely stylised piece of literary entertainment. Somebody once remarked of Priestley's adventures in the form that he was 'a snapper up of unconsidered trifles', which conveys very well the combination of disparate subject matter, mock solemnity and unabashed whimsy which the genre's upper-level exponents brought to their art.

If, indeed, it was an art to begin with. Seen in its historical context, the middle article, like the mass-circulation weekly and to a certain extent the star reviewer himself, was another by-product of the newspaper revolution of the 1890s and a newly literate readership who demanded material that was not overly demanding in its scope but at the same time not wholly devoid of uplift. Matthew Arnold – to name one of the light-essayist's remote ancestors – would doubtless have marked his survival into the 1920s down as a Regrettable Modern Tendency, but even Arnold's shade might have approved the efforts to construct a bridge between writer and reader on which he was embarked. At the same time he would certainly have nodded his agreement at Leonard Woolf's description of the specimen middle-article-filer as 'one of those impeccable journalists who every week for thirty or forty years turn out an impeccable essay . . . like an impeccable sausage, about anything, or everything or nothing'. Over and above the demands of weekly journalism, there was a deliberation about much of this – a sense, almost, of common purpose – that manifested itself in claims of universality, inclusiveness, like-minded sensibility speaking to like-minded sensibility across highly familiar terrain. The essayist's determination to be as much representative as narrowly individual often led him to adopt a pseudonym: A. G. Gardiner, long-term ornament of the *Daily News*, masqueraded as 'Alpha of the Plough'; Priestley, in his early days, was 'Peter of the Pomfret'. Equally, whether writing about anything, everything or nothing, the essayist was careful not to venture too far away from what were assumed to be the preoccupations of his audience. According to the *London Mercury*, 'Alpha's' subjects were 'those that the common man delights in – the common man of five-and-forty, suburban subjects set in a suburban world'. If this makes 'Alpha' seem like the last word in privet-hedged complacency, the elegist of the neatly manicured lawn and the Sunday joint, of Strube's City-bound 'little man' with his subfusc suit and bowler hat emerging from a terraced house in Beckenham or Petts Wood, then the voice in which he described these routines was a peculiarly resonant one.

Meanwhile, the number of similar voices sounding from their Fleet Street columns would have been sufficient to fill a decent-sized choir: Belloc, Chesterton, E. V. Lucas, 'Beachcomber' of the *Daily Express*, half a dozen more besides. The essay's omnipresence in certain quadrants of interwar literary life was reinforced by its attractiveness to publishers. It was not unusual for a specialist in the genre to produce two or even three collections a year of his weekly articles. Even more significant were the strenuous efforts to talk up the form's importance as literature, by way of selections and 'best ofs' and anthologies designed to impart a quasi-canonical status. All this gave the essay a distinctive social and educational presence: much favoured by schoolteachers with one eye on general-paper questions; its pedagogical sheen enhanced by newspapers who set competitions in which readers could send in their own compositions on given themes. And unlike certain other genres, the essay proved thoroughly adaptable to new media. By the 1930s, fine-tuned and even more expressly calibrated to the demands of a mass audience, it had migrated to radio. The hope among certain essayists was that it could travel even further: 'I want to write something that at a pinch I could read aloud in a bar-parlour' Priestley ambitiously declared.

Inclusivity. Universality. Tolerance. Diversity of subject matter. These were liberal values, and much of the light essay's allure, as practised by a Chesterton or an A. G. Gardiner, stemmed from its allegiance to an older and increasingly endangered political tradition: the *Daily News*, to which both Chesterton and Gardiner contributed, was a liberal paper in decline, whose merger with the *Westminster Gazette* in 1928 was all too symbolic of the waning fortunes of the Liberal Party in Parliament. No less attractive was the deliberate attempt to forge an alliance with its readers, founded on such desirable abstracts as good fellowship, shared interests and common humanity. It was Priestley, again, who remarked of his fellow practitioners that 'the reader who entertains them on his shelves will discover to his delight that he has forever at his elbow, at his command, a most notable company of talkers . . . whose very pages will soon begin to look like the faces of old friends'.

Some of these friends could be very ancient indeed. Consider, for example, the career of Robert Lynd (1879–1949) whose first contributions to the Fleet Street charivari went back to the Edwardian era and whose tenure on the *New Statesman* lasted for a third of a century. If there is something faintly remorseless about Lynd's pursuit of his craft, week in and week out for over forty years – he calculated his lifetime output at 1.6 million words, which sounds a serious underestimate, and his collected works run to thirty volumes – then the feeling of an endless conveyor belt running on into the distance is, to a certain extent, relieved by his lightness of touch, not to mention his undoubted sincerity. A Presbyterian minister's son from Belfast who, as one of his contemporaries put it, 'found life more amusing than self-display, and the enjoyment of it better than more conventional disgust', Lynd was in some ways a much odder character than the formal record of his progress among the weekly magazines of the Great War era suggests: the inner conflicts aroused by his Protestant nationalism produced a moving and pretty much unique essay, 'The Orange Idealist'. By 1913, having arrived in London by way of Manchester, he was literary editor of the *Daily News*, and as 'Y.Y.' already favouring the *New Statesman*'s readers with reflections on everything from the personalities of his native land ('G.B.S. as Idol', 'William Butler Yeats') to literary portraits ('Keats in His Letters') and the light essayist's customary stock-in-trade ('Aunts', 'Railway Stations I Have Loved', 'Arguing', etc.). Much of this, inevitably, had a comic side: his continual attempts – as a hundred-a-day man – to give up smoking encouraged loyal readers to send in gifts of acid drops and snuffboxes, and, like many compulsives, he seems to have enjoyed creating the pretence that he disliked the business of writing altogether and would be grateful if he were forced to stop.

If Lynd, both on paper and in much of his social life, is a pattern representative of the successful middlebrow journalist of his day – his professional acquaintances tended to be rather old-fashioned bookmen, and he was a friend of Squire – then there were always more exalted connections lurking in the background. Joyce and his wife Nora held their wedding lunch at Lynd's Hampstead house in 1931, and he produced an interesting critique of his friend's work ('James Joyce and a New Kind of Fiction') written from the angle of one who suspects that *Ulysses* has merit but can't altogether see it himself ('Q: Why does Joyce write in the way he does? A: He may be thought of as a predestined Protestant . . . a Protestant who, with the most dutiful zeal in the world, sets to defacing images and wrecking the lovely glass of tradition'.) On the other hand, once one gets beyond the faint air of bewilderment, the distinguishing mark of the Joyce essay is its subtlety. He insists on the importance of temperament. He compares *Portrait of the Artist* to *Stalky & Co.*, wondering (not wholly humorously) whether if Kipling had gone to Joyce's school, and Joyce to Kipling's, the end results would have been the same. And then there is his assault on the 'problem' of *Ulysses*, where he worries about the novel's defiant impenetrability ('The ordinary man, I imagine, will always feel, if he tries to read it, like a man exploring the depths of the Cheddar caves with the aid only of a box of matches'), notes Joyce's sense of humour, beauty and psychology, and then takes issue with his attempt to 'give the unspoken, unacted thoughts of people in the way they occur'. One can't help wondering, Lynd concludes, whether these unspoken, unacted thoughts occur in real life in quite the way in which novelists represent them as occurring, and he has his doubts about Molly Bloom.

In the end, though, Lynd is a critic of his time, or rather, it might be said, the generation slightly before his time, for whom self-conscious psychologising would always be faintly suspect. One might take as evidence of the comfort he took from the tradition into which he was born his essay on 'The Critic as Destroyer' – not a category he ever occupied himself – where he begins by examining the idea that all good criticism is praise. This leads him to the grand, and highly old-fashioned, conclusion that true criticism is a search for beauty and truth which culminates in the announcement of them: 'It does not matter twopence whether the beauty of their revelation is new or old, academic or futurist. It only asks that the revelation shall be genuine.' Lynd's real enemy, it turns out, is want of style ('It is to combat the stylelessness of many contemporary writers that the destructive kind of criticism is just now most necessary'). But the lasting value of 'The Critic as Destroyer' lies in its painfully honest attempt to forge a path between the *Criterion/Scrutiny* critic, to whom all popular art was anathema, and the middlebrow book-lover who required only a faithful representation of the entity he or she imagined to be 'ordinary life'. There is no point, Lynd insists, in sneering at the work of honest journeymen, and E. Phillips Oppenheim should be left to write his thrillers in peace: 'I do not think literature stands to gain anything even though all the critics in Europe were suddenly to assail this kind of writing.' What is needed is for authors 'to write well'. To which the modern sceptic will probably reply that it depends what you mean by 'well'. On the other hand, Lynd on the supposedly 'good' literature of his day is full of sharp discriminations – recognising, for example, Galsworthy's talent for naturalistic description but disliking 'the essential second-rateness and sentimentality of much of his presentation of ideas'. Not all of Lynd's contemporaries were capable of making this kind of distinction, and very few of them, having made it, would have felt entirely happy about conveying it into print.

Three decades before, Lynd and his compatriots would have been left to themselves, largely ignored by the powerful intellectual forces operating above their heads. As it was, the essayist of the interwar period was destined to spend a considerable part of his time defending himself and the medium in which he laboured from increasingly partisan attack. That the essay, like the star reviewer and indeed practically every expression of middlebrow taste, should become a kind of cultural battleground in which highbrows took potshots at what they considered to be the poverty of mainstream aspirations, and were assailed in their turn by belligerent populists, is a mark of the profound change that had come over the intellectual landscape since the Edwardian era. The great figures of the age of Balfour and Campbell-Bannerman – Chesterton, Wells and Shaw – might sometimes have worried about the depths to which an unfettered popular taste could sink: in the same way, they would certainly have been aware of the implications for the literary world which they inhabited of current developments in culture. But they had not the slightest doubt that they themselves were, in the end, popular writers, bent on reaching the widest possible audience and addressing its constituent parts in a language they could understand. By the 1920s this attitude was in sharp retreat. It was not only that modernism – by and large and notwithstanding the efforts of the Rickword school of bridge-builders – had detached itself from popular comprehension by way of its abstruseness; it was also that the new-style intellectualism of the interwar era was in many cases openly disdainful of popular taste.

In his celebrated polemic *The Intellectuals and the Masses* (1992), John Carey argues that this stance arose out of a contempt for 'ordinary' life that was both an aesthetic and a political prejudice. Illiberal and anti-democratic – Eliot's notorious remark about a society 'worm-eaten with liberalism' is pertinent here – the interwar modernist, if we believe Professor Carey, walked arm in arm with the autocrat and the eugenicist. No doubt Carey is right, and the volley of disgusting remarks uttered by nearly every modernist writer south of Eliot is quite indefensible. And yet the serial assaults on middlebrow literary culture, those accusations of lowered standards and a marketplace conducted along entirely commercial lines, whose cumulative effect was to encourage the trumpeting of the second-rate, were not confined to Bloomsbury and Mrs Leavis. It is worth pointing out, for example, that many of the criticisms of such interwar purveyors of middlebrow orthodoxy as the Book Society, the newspaper puff and the popular novelist, came not from Virginia Woolf and the *Criterion* but from book-trade insiders, distressed by what they saw as a blurring of the lines between critic and publisher, writer and reviewer, a tearing down of fences that had the effect of hoodwinking the impressionable reader into grotesque lapses of taste and annoying the serious writer who had little respect for the judgement of the critics who reviewed his books. Orwell's complaint about the reviewing climate of the 1930s, made in his essay 'In Defence of the English Novel', is that the 'disgusting tripe' produced by the blurb-writers means that few intelligent readers take novels seriously. Graham Greene, too, looking back on his early treatment by the reviewers, suggested that 'The reviewing of novels at the beginning of the thirties was at a far lower level than it has ever been since. Gerald Gould, a bad poet, and Ralph Straus, a bad novelist, divided the Sunday forum between them. One was not elated by their praise nor cast down by their criticism.'

Some industry veterans agreed. To Douglas Jerrold, who, as a publisher, might have been expected to approve of these alliances, the Book Society existed merely to appease booksellers. Newspapers, meanwhile, existed to appease their readers, which meant confirming their assumptions about art rather than calling them into question. 'And so the public gets what it likes, and is told by eminent men that they like the best.' As for the blandishments with which the average Book Society choice was brought to the Boots Library window, 'these novels have been chosen, consciously or unconsciously, because they are precisely the ones which critics will regard as works of genius. The critics, the authors, the publishers and the readers are, in fact, the same people, not merely spiritually, but in the flesh'. It is not that Jerrold wants the readers of *John O'London's Weekly* to try their hands at *The Waste Land*, merely that he knows that 'serious publishing' means 'good solid unspectacular books' will be fatally undermined by the low-level conspiring of which middlebrow literary life had increasingly come to consist.

While there were distinctions to be made here, they did not always work in the popular essayist's favour. For while the star reviewer tended to be regarded merely as a superior blurb-writer – even Bennett was attacked on these grounds – the essayist was generally accused of something much worse: nothing less than corrupting a once noble tradition, zealously calibrating whatever he had to say to the requirements of the market and being conditioned by it as he went along. Virginia Woolf's 'The Modern Essay', one of several elegant variations on this theme, convicts the modern essayist of having lost touch with the form's essential character by abandoning the 'personality' which lay at its core. In their defence, essayists of the Lynd-Priestley type expended a great deal of ink in proclaiming their authenticity. Motivation, impulse, moral compass, identification with audience – these, the argument went, were unaltered since the days of Charles Lamb. All that had changed was the paraphernalia of the world they wrote about, and if Belloc, Chesterton and their friends published their work in the periodical press, then so, two centuries before, had Addison and Steele.

This was a seductive argument, which appealed both to the bookish, antiquarian side of the interwar literary world – always keen to demonstrate its ancestral ties with Old Noll Goldsmith and Henry Fielding Esq., – while carrying the war into the enemy's camp by stressing an essential consanguinity. From her Olympian perch in Bloomsbury Mrs Woolf might sneer at the columnists of the *Daily News*, but surely there was more to bring them together than to drive them apart? Recent critical work on the essayist has tended to focus on his determination to carve out an authentic space in the literary marketplace of his day, halfway between the penny-a-liner and the academic critic and beholden to neither of them. Caroline Pollentier has even suggested that the middle article 'encoded an ethics of familiarity, which constituted a distinctive ideological response to the cultural antagonisms of the time'. This kind of terminology probably overstates the case – Lynd and co. were weekly journalists with deadlines to meet – yet there is in their work the definite sense of a united front, defensive positions needing to be taken up as the howitzers rain fire from behind the Bloomsbury trenches. Lynd, for example, once wrote a critique of superior attitudes entitled 'Highbrows'. Priestley, meanwhile, praised Lynd's eclecticism, his absorption in human idiosyncrasy, his attempts to combine the essayist's constant search for new material capable of stirring the jaded palates of his readers with an awareness of where he came from genealogically and some of the responsibilities involved in continuing, week in and week out, to give the public what it wanted. 'Mr Lynd is essentially a writer of today, that is, he writes of the things we know, of buses, race-meetings, cricket matches, seaside hotels, patent medicine, and anything that happens to interest him in life stirring around him . . . Yet he is incontestably in the tradition of the great English essayists.'

One can accept this claim while noting quite how stylised the essay had become in its early twentieth-century incarnation, how prone to feeding off itself, how determined to emphasise its lightness, how keen to exaggerate armature at the expense of brick. One of Belloc's collections was entitled *On Nothing*. A. A. Milne produced a miscellany under the heading *Not That It Matters* – ironic, of course, but not an entirely convincing way of talking up the merits of something one presumably wishes to defend. And if the essay seemed increasingly to be turning into an exercise in form, then its claims to universality and exclusiveness were equally suspect. Doubtless 'Alpha of the Plough's' middle-aged suburbanite was a significant part of the interwar demographic, but what about the other three-quarters of the adult population? And on strictly literary grounds, when set against some of the best periodical writing of the 1920s and 1930s, these reflections on the wisdom of cats, or the contents of men's pockets or the seaside holiday one took in 1913 can look horribly threadbare. Compare Lynd's literary portraits with V. S. Pritchett's weekly turns for the *New Statesman*. It is not just that Pritchett has an eye for an aphorism, that his sense of historical context immediately sets his subject in the sharpest of reliefs, that each generalisation or summarising remark has the effect of pulling the reader up short; it is simply that Pritchett's work always seems to stem – to borrow Leavis's phrase – from the pressure of something that needs to be conveyed.

It is the same with perhaps the greatest essayist of the whole interwar period, Virginia Woolf. On one level the gap between *The Common Reader* and one of Lynd's innumerable collections is not so very great. There is the same whimsicality, often enhanced by use of the first person plural. There is the same delight in oddity for oddity's sake, the same sense of embarking on an immensely sophisticated circular tour that eventually returns you to the point of entry. But there the resemblance ends. Woolf may, as Frank Swinnerton once complained, suffer from a sensibility that is entirely literary, but her best work is the product of a highly original mind fastening on the psychology of her subjects in a way that, for all the elevation of the view, emphasises the existence of universal principles. The famous essay on Jack Mytton, the nineteenth-century Shropshire squire, begins and ends with the prospect of 'Madame Rosalba' diving into the ocean at Brighton to bring up soup plates and prompting the watching holidaymaker on the pier – presumably Woolf herself – to feel a profound sense of gratification: 'It is because of this, she says, that I love my kind.'

Most of the highbrow assaults on mainstream literature concentrated on the particular forms that literature had been unwise enough to colonise: Mrs Woolf, after all, is discreet enough not to name any names. But if it was the era of the blanket condemnation, then it was also the era of the bitter personal attack, a search for representative figures at whose door the blame for some of this alleged cultural debasement might be laid. Curiously, as the 1930s wore on, these complaints took on a single point of focus in the bluff yet reliably combative figure of J. B. Priestley. It was Priestley's misfortune – a lasting, personal misfortune from which he never wholly recovered – to achieve vast commercial success at a time when the whole concept of commercial success was being called sharply into question. In an age when the matter of a writer's cultural affiliations loomed very large, Priestley (1894–1984), with his Georgian upbringing and his titanic sales, was always going to be a target for this sort of snootiness: what was really remarkable, as the decade wore on, was his emergence as a kind of all-purpose intellectual hate-figure, a symbol of degenerating public tastes and a byword for everything that was wrong with the contemporary novel and, by extension, the literary scene that authenticated it.

The contempt in which Priestley was held by some of his fellow writers can sometimes seem rather startling in its intensity. Virginia Woolf bracketed him with Arnold Bennett as 'the tradesman of letters'. The young Graham Greene caricatured him in *Stamboul Train* (1931) as the pipe-smoking popular novelist 'Mr Savory', and was promptly threatened with a libel writ. Orwell, alarmed by his influence on other writers, noted of Patrick Hamilton's Priestley-haunted *Twenty Thousand Streets Under the Sky* (1935) that 'he [Hamilton] has set out . . . to write a novel about "real life", but with the Priestleyan assumption that "real life" means lower-middle-class life in a large town and that if you have packed into your novel, say, fifty-three descriptions of tea in a Lyons Corner House, you have done the trick'. Anthony Powell not only put Priestley into his novels as a malign cultural signifier (as when half-witted Jasper Fosdick in *From a View to a Death* (1933) tries to impress a girl by offering to lend her the family copy of *The Good Companions*) but was still, half a century later, seeding his diaries with references to the 'stupefying banality' of Priestley's mind and his complete unsuitability for a Westminster Abbey memorial.

All this was, and is, horribly unfair – there were far more plausible candidates for highbrow disdain in the 1930s than the author of *English Journey* (1934) – and yet, as nearly always happens when the intelligentsia takes against a particular behemoth of the book clubs, a certain amount of the mud tends to stick. Thirty years and more after his death, although Priestley's plays are regularly revived and there remains a folk memory of his considerable impact as a wartime broadcaster, his novels are usually regarded as the quaintest of period curios: sprawling, sentimental, and the forerunner of every post-war metropolitan best-seller from Norman Collins's *London Belongs to Me* (1945) to R. F. Delderfield's *The Avenue Goes to War* (1964). Priestley's own verdict – see his 1962 essay collection *Margin Released* – was that he was a victim of straightforward snobbery, that fixed English idea, as he put it, 'that anything widely popular must necessarily be bad. Criticism . . . borrowed "best-seller" from the book trade, where it means what it says and nothing more, and made it pejorative'.

However heartfelt, this is also faintly disingenuous, for a close inspection of what was being written about him at the time suggests that he was being punished less for his success than for the sometimes wildly exaggerated claims made on his behalf. Orwell's review of *Angel Pavement*, another best-seller from the autumn of 1930, is particularly revealing in this respect. In ordinary circumstances one would not feel like attacking such a 'competent and agreeable novel', Orwell decides, 'if Mr Priestley had not been so extravagantly praised. He has been likened to Dickens, and when a novelist is likened to Dickens one must stop and ask the reason.' Once this 'absurd praise' has been discounted, it is possible to hail Priestley 'for the qualities which he really possesses, and take *Angel Pavement* for what it is: an excellent holiday novel, genuinely gay and pleasant, which supplies a good bulk of reading material for ten and sixpence'. What Priestley, who took himself and his art very seriously, thought about being described as a holiday novelist can only be imagined: at any rate it is one step up from being damned as a tradesman of letters by a woman who lived on dividend payments.

Angel Pavement's storyline can be given in a paragraph. Mr Golspie, an 'able rogue' (Orwell's phrase) arrives in London out of the blue on a Baltic cargo ship with a display case full of veneer samples in his trunk, and the sole UK agency for an innovative new manufacturing process ripe to make fortunes for the lucky men he selects as his business partners. Descending, apparently at random, on the moribund City firm of Twigg & Dersingham, he proceeds to shake up the business to devastating effect: swindling its vague and ineffectual owner, Mr Dersingham, wreaking havoc in the heart of Miss Matfield, its genteel secretary-typist and ruining the prospects of Turgis, its pimply clerk, who makes the mistake of falling for his vampish daughter. Written from the angle of each of Twigg & Dersingham's original employees – Golspie is simply a meteoric force of nature, coming and going as he pleases – the novel is a study in milieux: the Earls Court maisonette which Mr Dersingham shares with his not very enticing wife; the joyless routines of the 'Burpenfield Club' on whose melancholy premises Miss Matfield occupies a bedsitter alongside three or four dozen other neurotically ground-down spinsters; Turgis's gloomy lodgings in down-at-heel Camden; and the six-room terraced house in Stoke Newington inhabited by the desiccated accountant Mr Smeeth and his ingrate brood.

At the same time, *pace* Orwell, *Angel Pavement* is only incidentally a story of lower-middle- and middle-class London life. Its real subject is detachment, the absolute conviction expressed by most of its characters that their lives would be better lived out elsewhere, doing other things and in the company of other people. Priestley may not have been the first English novelist to appreciate the morale-sapping effect that living in a big city at the dawn of the machine age can have on an averagely sensitive human being, but it is extraordinary how often during the course of the novel's 600 pages, this tocsin begins to clang, and how many of the people caught up in it are sustained not by the material realities of their existence but by the careful cultivation of what might be called their personal myth. Miss Matfield's imaginative life, for example, is spent almost exclusively among romantic novels set in the South Seas ('jungles, coral reefs, plantations, hibiscus flowers, the scent of vanilla, schooners on the wide Pacific, tropical nights'). Turgis, alternatively, is a lovesick solitary, convinced, in spite of his unprepossessing exterior, that the relationship of a lifetime is just around the corner. Mr Smeeth, haunted by fear of the sack and its consequences for his family's well-being, takes refuge in classical-concert reveries with 'the strings in a rich deep unison sweeping on, and you were ten feet high and had a thousand glorious years to live'.

Gradually, as all these dreams are quietly brought out to be investigated, gently mocked or in one two cases ambiguously resolved in the dreamer's favour, *Angel Pavement*'s other key theme begins to declare itself. This is the thought of a generational divide, brought about by the tumultuous changes in post-war popular media. Mr Smeeth's children, hot for cheap sensation, tolerant of the old parental adages about hard work and duty but completely unmoved by them, are products of the cinema age ('They were the children of the Woolworth stores and the moving pictures'). His daughter's appearance, grimaces and gestures are, as Priestley notes, 'temporarily based on those of an Americanised Polish jewess' – one assumes this is Greta Garbo – 'who, from her nest in Hollywood, had stamped them on these young girls all over the world'. There is a rather significant moment, in terms of this intergenerational incomprehension, in which Mr Smeeth lectures Twigg & Dersingham's office boy on the subject of his own alternative life, in this case a leisure given over to detective magazines and the 'shadowing' of innocent members of the public.

'The best thing you can do, Stanley,' Mr Smeeth blandly advises, 'is to drop these silly tricks. They'll get you into trouble one of these days. Why don't you do something sensible in your spare time? Get a hobby. Do a bit of fretwork. Collect foreign stamps or butterflies or something.' Stanley, unimpressed, retorts that 'Nobody does them things now. Out of date.' Contemporaneity, up-to-dateness, the idea that one is obligated to do something merely because thousands of other people do it, rampages through the novel like a forest fire. Mr Smeeth and Stanley may be north-east London cockneys living within a mile or two of each other, who travel on the same buses, talk the same slang and listen to the same radio programmes, but the gap between their respective childhoods is widening into a chasm, and each of them knows it.

For all the chaos unleashed by the depredations of Mr Golspie – a character whom of course it is impossible to dislike on account of his sheer animal vigour – the novel ends on an up, with most of its cast galvanised into some kind of new relationship with a world that had previously held them in its thrall. Even Turgis, bruised, beaten and dismissed, his romantic dreams crushed into fragments and his person flung down the office stairs by his indifferent lady-love's outraged father, finds solace in the regard of Poppy Sellers, the junior typist. All the same, the thought of a world that is changing out of all recognition and bringing with it a set of daunting existential challenges is difficult to ignore, and the general effect is rather as if *The Waste Land* had been rewritten for the variety-hall stage. As for the novel's place in the literary canon of the 1930s, one can accept that everything Orwell, Greene and Virginia Woolf said and thought about Priestley is true, while registering the fact that *Angel Pavement* is a terrific example of the mainstream novel's occasional habit of defying its limitations, noticing some of the features of ordinary life that more highbrow productions routinely ignore and veering off into psychological territory where the much abused entity known as 'popular fiction' rarely strays.

None of this, alas, cut much ice in the cultural climate of the 1930s. Its consequence, among a certain type of mainstream writer, was a kind of inbred defensiveness in which individual opinions could be all too readily subsumed into the party line: anti-highbrow, concentrating its ire on a series of symbolic irritations, darkly conscious that its intellectual firepower was increasingly inadequate for the task in hand. In his memoirs, Geoffrey Grigson records a rather symbolic encounter with Priestley in the Café Royal in the summer of 1936. Here, after discussing his wide readership – the audience for his journalism was thought to run into seven figures – Priestley moved on to criticise such abominations of the modern movement as Henry Moore ('I don't know why all this modern stuff needs to be lumpy'), Eliot ('Bob Lynd wrote a review about *The Sacred Wood* which showed it really up') and surrealist art. It was mean to go on listening, Grigson concluded, and it was mean to report a private conversation. On the other hand, he had a feeling that it was not Priestley speaking, that the words issuing from his mouth had become entirely figurative: 'It was the public, honest, puzzled, not quite confident, successful, generous, but generous to mediocrity and bitter to the nonconformists of the small battalion.'

CHAPTER 5

The Pink Decade

> My own view is that support of the Soviet Union at the present juncture is (as the one hope of avoiding war) of such overwhelming importance that anything that can be quoted by the other side should not be said.
>
> Victor Gollancz, 1937

> On the whole the literary history of the thirties seems to justify the opinion that the writer does well to keep out of politics.
>
> George Orwell, 'Inside the Whale' (1940)

Most political historians would probably contend that the 1920s, and indeed a whole stretch of British history extending deep into the nineteenth century, reached a climacteric in the autumn of 1931. These were the months in which Ramsay MacDonald's National Government, which had come to power in order to protect the pound, went off the gold standard (19 September) and then called a general election (27 October) in which it triumphed over the remnant of the Labour opposition with a majority of more than 500. Keen to reflect the public mood – apparently one of grim determination and steely resolve – *Punch* produced a cartoon labelled 'The Splendid Sword' which sees John Bull, triumphant at his anvil, handing MacDonald a sword marked 'National Majority' while assuring him that this is 'the best job I've ever done. I feel sure that you can be trusted to use it well.'

How did the nation's literary men and women respond to a crisis whose immediate effect was to cut the value of certain investments in half, and whose symbolic importance was, if anything, even greater? Harold Nicolson's diaries show him wholly absorbed in electioneering work for Sir Oswald Mosley's New Party, which was to be even more decisively rejected at the polls than the Labour rump under Arthur Henderson. Virginia Woolf, determined to put art before economics, noted that 'We're off, & I write about Donne, Yes; and what could I do better, if we are ruined, & if everybody had spent their time writing about Donne we should not have gone off the gold standard – that's my version of the great crisis, &c &c &c.' George Orwell, so far as we can determine from his published writings, took no interest in the events of autumn 1931 despite his geographical proximity. Back from the hop-picking excursion to Kent that furnished a backdrop to *A Clergyman's Daughter* (1935), he and his friend Ginger fetched up in a cheap lodging house in Tooley Street, SE1. From this location they made pre-dawn trips to the fish market at Billingsgate – only a quarter of a mile from the Bank of England's headquarters in Threadneedle Street where the governor, Montagu Norman, sat in conclave – in search of casual work. The payment for helping a porter to push his barrow up the hill towards Eastcheap was twopence, but there was insufficient reward for the time spent hanging about. Orwell recalled that 'standing there from five to nearly midday I never made more than 1s 6d'.

One writer to whom the crisis in Threadneedle Street seemed an event of more than usual significance, and one requiring some kind of personal response, was Alec Waugh. Come the third week of September 1931 Waugh was staying at the Easton Court Hotel, Chagford, Devon, busily reworking a serial story he had written for the *Daily Mirror* into a novelette intended for a series of ninepenny paperbacks to be published by the firm of Ernest Benn (the venture was stillborn, but is of interest to publishing historians as the precursor of Penguin Books). For Waugh and, as he supposed, anyone born before 1910, the retreat from the gold standard was 'the biggest shock that we had known and were to know'. After a few days spent in London watching the situation develop at first hand, Waugh returned to Devon, but the file of magazine stories on which he was embarked did not go well, owing to 'the hourly excitement of public events'. Inspired by what he decided was 'the climax of post-war England', he began work on a miscellany of short stories and commentary designed to show 'the transition of English life from the excitement of the Armistice celebrations to the general election of 1931'. Although, necessarily, something of a hotchpotch, the result – the grandly titled *Thirteen Such Years* (1932) – is one of Waugh's better books. It concludes with an imaginary, and intensely symbolic, character sketch of an expatriate Englishman living in the south of France, a veteran of the Great War, gassed on the Western Front and compelled to seek a softer climate for medical reasons, who now thinks it his 'duty' to return. Inevitably, the London fogs are too much for his damaged lungs.

Cultural change is rarely a straightforwardly linear process. Literary periods blend into each other; a 'significant' writer seldom stops being significant overnight. Equally, best-selling novelists have a habit of maintaining their sales from one decade to the next; popular reading habits have their own rules, invariably divorced from the ukases of fashionable taste. In one of his pieces of mid-1930s reputation-brokering, Cyril Connolly demanded of Galsworthy, Bennett and Strachey 'Who reads them now?' The correct answer was hundreds of thousands of readers beyond the tightly knit and rather rarefied world inhabited by Connolly and his intellectual friends. On the other hand, the profound differences between the 1920s and 1930s as literary epochs were instantly apparent to the people caught up in them. At their most fundamental level, these changes were to do with the infiltration of left-wing politics into the literary mainstream. Douglas Jerrold noted in 1937 that 'to go Right is to go wrong in journalism today'. Orwell thought that as early as 1934 or 1935 it was considered 'eccentric' in literary circles not to be more or less on the left. To Anthony Powell it seemed that 'there was a moment at the beginning of the 1930s when anybody who didn't belong to the Left was totally swept off the book pages'.

However resonant Powell's memory, this transformation did not happen overnight; its roots go back deep into the previous decade, when as Orwell puts it in 'Inside the Whale', 'the wind was blowing from Europe, and long before 1930 it had blown the beer-and-cricket school naked, except for their knighthoods'. At the same time, its significance was not merely to do with the inevitable changes of personnel. It was not just that the pages of the literary weeklies came crammed with Auden, Spender, Isherwood and Cecil Day Lewis, but that seasoned observers were able to detect a change of temperament, an almost spiritual detachment from the world that had gone before. To many of the younger writers of the 1930s, 'modernism', though still basking in its contemporaneity, seemed determinedly backward-looking, often anti-progress, or at best non-committal, at times downright reactionary. The rising literary stars of the 1930s tended to be young – too young, for example, either to have fought in the Great War or to feel guilty about their absence – more optimistic, less stifled by tradition. The specimen *New Statesman* contributor ceases to be an all-purpose literary man with a fondness for Housman and becomes what Orwell, again, typifies as 'an eager-minded schoolboy with a leaning towards Communism'.

Like much of what Orwell has to say about the literary 1930s this is an exaggeration, filed for effect, and yet the scent of uplift that rises off the self-consciously leftist literature of the period, the feeling that one has inadvertently strayed into the pages of an exceptionally sophisticated Marxist school magazine, is impossible to ignore. A great deal of ink has been expended over the last three-quarters of a century in establishing the debt that 1930s literary Marxism – Marxism per se, if it comes to that – owes to the world of the schoolroom, and how the authority figures being rebelled against are often not much more than disguised versions of public school headmasters. If the Battle of Waterloo was won on the playing fields of Eton, then there is a case for arguing that some of the great literary engagements of the 1930s were won there too, or at any rate on the playing fields of Gresham's and Wellington College. But in making this unavoidable connection, one should also note the depth of the psychological thraldom in which certain English writers who swallowed the Marxist bait allowed themselves to be held. Bruce Hamilton, for example, returned from a fact-finding visit to the Soviet Union to discover that his younger brother Patrick had both 'gone left' and was in the process of assembling a library consisting of works by Marx, Engels, Lenin and Stalin. Left-inclined himself and tolerant of his sibling's vagaries, Bruce was forced to admit that Patrick's brand of Marxism was horribly intense, contemptuous of back-sliding and proceeded out of a need for belief so strong that at times it reduced itself to mere Stalin-worship. Sending Bruce a copy of a speech that the great man had delivered in 1939, he wrote:

> I don't imagine you will have seen this, and it is *magnificent*. Written in that lucid, dignified, semi-paternal style of his, it is the most refreshing and reassuring thing in the world. I am happy to say I have never had any doubts of this great man, and this should shame anyone who had during the Trotskyist business. As the years go on I get more and more respect for him as having original genius instead of being a mere Lenin-follower.

The conviction that Stalin was an honourable man who meant well persisted, unsullied by the Nazi–Soviet pact or the fact that of the 700 writers who had attended the first Congress of Soviet Writers in 1934 only fifty survived to ornament the second twenty years later, and as late as 1959 he was recording his good impression of Khrushchev ('I particularly like the way in which he is incessantly rebuking those who go too far in their denigration of Stalin'). It seems scarcely necessary to add that the stress laid on Stalin's paternal qualities is almost the exact antithesis of Hamilton's relationship with his own father, that the heroism he sought from politics was conspicuously absent from his own life, or that, as he grew older, his unreconstituted Marxism existed side by side with a determination to, as he put it, 'feel entirely justified in selfishly pursuing my own *material* and *cultural* interests'. To complain about all this is as futile as to rebuke Auden, say, for dressing for dinner, and if there is one criticism that can be levelled at practically every public school boy who joined the Communist Party in the 1930s – a step which Hamilton himself never managed – it is their habit of carrying huge amounts of psychological-cum-cultural baggage in this brave new world of whose inherent contradictions they were largely unaware.

The comparative exclusivity of a great deal of 1930s literary Marxism worked both for and against it. On the one hand, the fact that it was promulgated by ex-public school boys encouraged other, not necessarily sympathetic, ex-public school boys to take an interest, with the result that an awareness of left-wing viewpoints spread deep into the mainstream. It would be absurd to credit Alec Waugh with any kind of political vision – as a professional operator his gaze was fixed on America rather than Europe, and his views were nearly always those of a benign conservative – and yet he was sufficiently aware of the ideological crises of the day to spend several weeks in Russia in the mid-1930s, to read his Auden and to cultivate several left-wing literary friends, such as the novelist Arthur Calder-Marshall and his wife Ara in the hope that they could keep him in touch with what the younger generation was thinking. On the other hand, the fact that so much literary Marxism grew out of what was largely a social hierarchy tended to keep proletarian elements at bay. Such genuinely working-class writing that appeared in mainstream periodicals of the 1930s was largely there on sufferance, and most of the attention it received was careful to stress its representative qualities rather than its individual distinction. Orwell's review of *Caliban Shrieks* (1935), the autobiography of the former cotton operative Jack Hilton, does not go quite so far as this – he praises Hilton for seeing his subject 'from the inside' and for his 'considerable literary gifts' – but it is remarkable how quickly the reviewer proceeds from the particular to the general:

> Books like this, which come from genuine workers and present a genuinely working-class outlook, are exceedingly rare and correspondingly important. They are the voices of a normally silent multitude. All over England, in every industrial town, there are men by scores of thousands whose attitude to life, if only they could express it, would be very much what Mr Hilton's is.

Excellent as Mr Hilton's book is, you see, he is only doing what thousands of other men like him would do if they had the talent.*

The issues at stake in the literary in-fighting of the 1920s had largely been aesthetic, and the cement that held them in place frequently social: a few transcendent figureheads excepted, it was possible to judge a writer not merely by the kind of periodicals he, or she, wrote for, but also by their dinner companions. In contrast, the polarisation of attitudes that characterised the 1930s was firmly ideological. It was an age in which writers 'took sides', to borrow the title of Nancy Cunard's famous collection of responses to the Spanish Civil War, the fervour of whose rhetorical flourishes still has the capacity to startle (Brian Howard: 'With all my anger and love I am for the people of Republican Spain'); an age in which declarations of intent – a writer joining the Independent Labour Party or being received into the Catholic Church – were prized pieces of literary intelligence. Even more than the 1920s, with their furores over Squire and the Sitwells, it was an age of hate figures, emblematic repositories for the contempt of both left and right, who, as time went on, began to assume an almost mythological status. By far the funniest aspect of the letters exchanged between Siegfried Sassoon and Edmund Blunden, by this stage wholly Procrustean figures, is their almost

* As a member of the National Union of Unemployed Workers, Hilton offered Orwell advice on the writing of *The Road to Wigan Pier* (1937), but thought the book a 'travesty'. His own travelogue, *English Ways* (1938), is essentially the same journey made in reverse, from Rochdale to Epsom.

fathomless dislike of Stephen Spender, invariably referred to as 'S. Spender' and seen as the embodiment of everything that is politically, if not personally, objectionable. Thus a visiting E. M. Forster is reported by Sassoon to have received a letter from his younger friend, 'so we are *in actual touch with the crux of human affairs*'. A brisk review by Spender of one of Sassoon's books provokes the comment: 'I understand S. Spender has somehow been giving me "a piece of his mind"; glad he can spare any.' But it was not quite so political that the left could not occasionally turn on self-proclaimed allies. Edgell Rickword, too, left some withering remarks on Spender's involvement in the Spanish Civil War ('Of course, Spender was in Spain . . . Running around making a fearful fuss'). And all this is to ignore Orwell's famous tirade, scribbled on the back of the *Spain: Authors Take Sides* questionnaire, about 'fashionable pansies'.

But the question of motivation, 'commitment', the whole panoply of ideological engagement by which many a 1930s writer was eventually suborned, runs much deeper than Patrick Hamilton's search for a father figure, or the series of rebellions waged by former school prefects against a legion of phantom headmasters. What kind of environment, when it came down to it, produced a figure like Spender, son of the Liberal journalist J. A. Spender and the author of *Forward from Liberalism* (1937), a work which incorporates one of the great dilemmas of 1930s political life in its title? To a large extent the ideological fractures of the 1930s were provoked by an awareness of what was going on in continental Europe – Orwell's 'cold winds' blowing in from the Danube and the Rhine – but its stimulus was also much more narrowly domestic. In 1929, the year of the Wall Street Crash, unemployment in the UK had reached 1.2 million. By 1930 it had reached 2 million; by 1931 3 million. As the international market for manufactured goods dried up, entire communities, especially in the industrial north, existed on the brink of destitution. The human consequences of the Depression pervaded every stratum of 1930s literature. Just as the novels of the 1920s had turned on the question of what their male characters had, or had not, done in the war, so much of the fiction of the 1930s is dominated by the hunt for paid employment, or the fear of losing it. These anxieties extend to every social class. Even in the exalted landscapes of a 'society' novel such as Evelyn Waugh's *A Handful of Dust* (1934), Brenda Last's unappetising boyfriend Beaver is a redundant adman compelled to live off his mother. Anthony

Powell's early novels are crammed with more or less unemployable young men waiting for the chance to take up golf-club secretaryships, and anxious mothers enquiring about the prospect of jobs at the BBC.

At the middle-class level this alarm bell clangs yet more insistently. In one of *Keep the Aspidistra Flying*'s early chapters, Gordon Comstock composes an Eliot-style poem about clerks 'who hurry to the station / look, shuddering over the eastern rooves / thinking'. What do they think, Gordon wonders? 'Winter's coming. Is my job safe? The sack means the workhouse . . . Suck the blacking off the boss's boots.' The same terror stalks Edgar Hargraves, the ground-down haberdasher of Walter Greenwood's *His Worship the Mayor* (1934), uncomfortably aware that his account at the warehouse is overdue, the bank pressing and the only thing keeping him solvent is his wife's money. 'A million dreads clamoured in his heart, opening his eyes to the cold, imperturbable fact that business – his in particular – was definitely bad.' But it is also detectable down at the bedrock level of popular magazine stories which, though traditionally escapist in the solutions they brought to elemental human problems, acquire a much harder edge in the early 1930s. Herbert Allingham's serial stories, for example, contributed to such mass-circulation weeklies as the *Home Companion* and the *Family Journal*, are finely attuned to some of the deprivations of the interwar era, and exhibit a pronounced sympathy for the underdog and an insistence on the decency and solidarity of backstreet life. If their pictures of exquisitely shingled ingénues declaring that they 'won't let their children starve' owe something to Hollywood, then they are still an effective antidote to the capitalist plot view of working-class literature peddled by Orwell or the assumptions of consumer-materialist-model decline filed by the literary sociologist Richard Hoggart two decades later.

Just as the effects of the Great War took several decades to work their way out in fiction, so the legacy of the Depression ran deep into the 1950s. The post-1945 novels of Alan Sillitoe, Philip Callow and Sid Chaplin are full of anguished glances back to the world of jobless families living six to a room, the memory of old man Seaton's face in *Saturday Night and Sunday Morning* (1958) turning 'black from want of fags'. Ironically, one effect of the slump was to encourage reading in areas of high unemployment. A *Time and Tide* article from 1931 by a Welsh miner from the Pontypridd area noted how library borrowings had increased in a community harbouring 6,500 jobless men with time on their hands. Another effect was to create opportunities in the world of books for genuine proletarians – Leslie Halward, for example, who began writing after losing his job as a plasterer, or Greenwood himself, made redundant by a Manchester department store. By the mid-1930s most of the unemployment black spots in the north were home to a cluster of predominantly working-class writers: Harry Heslop, Chaplin and J. C. Grant in Durham; Walter Brierley, author of the classic *Means Test Man*, and F. C. Boden in Nottingham; Lewis Grassic Gibbon, George Blake and James Barke in industrial Scotland. There was even a rural strain, as represented by Jack Lindsay in *End of Cornwall* (1937), which charts the collapse of living standards in the agricultural south-west.

Not too many claims should be made for this very disparate group of writers as a movement. Their books were small-scale, framed, as the socialist literary historian Andy Croft once put it, 'in a small locality, a family, a place of work, a street, or a short space of time'. Frequently the achievement of their leading lights rests on a solitary book, such as Heslop's *Last Cage Down* (1935), with its evocation of a moribund Tyneside with 'Not a battleship being built. Not a crane moving. Not a man hitting a rivet with a hammer. A great, stultifying death.' At the same time, those who achieved any kind of long-term success tended to do so by extending their social range and making their work more acceptable to middle-class audiences. Greenwood's *Love on the Dole* (1933) is a genuine slum classic, in which a bourgeois face barely intrudes, but *His Worship the Mayor* is written from the point of view of the small tradesman who, while resenting the wealthy town councillors to whom he has to kowtow, despises his working-class customers and is grateful for the modicum of status allowed him in the hierarchies of the district.

As to why so many of the working-class writers of the period failed to achieve any kind of lasting success, the explanation very often lay neither in lack of talent, nor restricted range, but in the want of social and professional contacts. The widow of Sid Chaplin – one of the few pre-war proletarians to make a career in the post-1945 era – used to recount the symbolic tale of how her husband, invited to a party at Orwell's house in Kilburn in the early 1940s, stood for several moments on the doorstep regarding the shadowy figures glimpsed through the window and then, not feeling up to the task of confronting literary London on its home territory, turned on his heel and fled. The distance

– real and metaphorical – between middle-class and working-class response is even more marked in much of the reportage stirred by evidence of social and economic blight in the industrial north. The interwar era was a great age for voyages of exploration into a supposedly lost England, where industrialisation, ribbon development and numbers of widely reported conservation battles had fuelled an urge to celebrate the landscape beyond the ever-creeping suburbs. This had originally been one of the great Georgian themes, and as late as 1937 J. C. Squire proposed to write a book entitled *The Way to a Horse*, in which he would ride around England à la Cobbett, dilating on whichever scenes and incidents took his fancy.

The conditions of Depression-era Britain gave this tendency a particular focus. Priestley's *English Journey* (1934), Orwell's *The Road to Wigan Pier* (1937), the series of East End excursions that made up Hugh Massingham's *I Took Off My Tie* (1936) all belong to this increasingly crowded genre. Even Beverley Nichols, hitherto given to writing books about his garden and the smartest kind of society journalism, announced in 1933 that he was to spend several weeks studying the conditions of the unemployed in Glasgow and managed to endure ten days in a two-room tenement before booking into a hotel. However well intentioned these travelogues – and Nichols's biographer is careful to stress that his researches were abandoned because 'he found it impossible to articulate his anger and despair in any way that would result in action' – the sense of journalists in search of copy was sometimes rather too strong for comfort. When Orwell set out for the north of England in the early part of 1936 he did so not to have his opinions about politics confirmed but to amass the material for a book. His attitude to members of the Labour Party met in the course of his journeys around Wigan, Sheffield and Liverpool is more that of an anthropologist than an ideologue. As Robert Colls remarks in his excellent book about Orwell's idea of Englishness, at this stage in his political development he knew no Labour history, seemed to regard socialism as some sort of fad and took no interest in any of the institutions such as socialist Sunday schools and Leagues of Youth that were trying to make life better for the people he had come to observe.

If, as a humorist once remarked, you could scarcely throw a stone outside a Yorkshire pithead in the 1930s without hitting a journalist engaged on a study of working-class life, then the cumulative effect of these influences was unignorable, even to the right. But what were its practical consequences? One of them, inevitably, was a conscious absorption in working-class themes on the part of writers with middle-class backgrounds that genuine proletarians tended to treat with a certain amount of cynicism. As Rayner Heppenstall observed, from the vantage point of the early 1970s, 'I could have done the proletarian stunt as well as the next man and was somewhat tempted to do it in the pink decade before the war.' Broadly speaking, the bulk of left-wing novels of the 1930s fall into three categories: heavily slanted reportage; dramatised sociology (a novel like Alec Browne's *Daughters of Albion*); shading at its outermost fringe into bizarre forms of allegory. Patrick Hamilton's most avowedly 'political' novel, for example, is the immensely odd *Impromptu in Moribundia* (1939), in which an anonymous narrator travels by 'Asteradio' to the country of the title. Here he discovers the mythological underpinnings of twentieth-century English life to be literally true. He arrives to watch the cricket match in Newbolt's 'Vitaï Lampada' being played ('Ten to make and a match to win'), and spends time with a working-class family whose members embody every current middle-class assumption about the feckless, overindulged poor by idling and keeping coal in their bath. Meanwhile, the supposedly exemplary bowler-hatted 'little man' of Strube's newspaper cartoons metamorphoses into a gang of malignant dwarfs. Wells is ticked off for criticising the Soviet Union and the literary celebrities of the 1920s, Eliot, Joyce, Huxley and Lawrence, judged to be 'for the most part hopelessly and morbidly turned in upon themselves, and sterile in consequence'.

Much more successful, in that it avoids merely scoring points off the bourgeoisie and has more of an understanding of the social structures it is criticising, is *His Worship the Mayor*, in which a small shopkeeper in perpetual fear of insolvency hits the jackpot when his aunt dies and leaves him a fortune. Hitherto the target of contemptuous patronage from the local dignitaries, Edgar is instantly taken up and made much of by his peers, admitted to the town's most select circles, elected to the local council and finally lowered into the mayoral chair (with a knighthood in prospect after the impending royal visit) on the grounds that, as one of his fellow councillors puts it, 'You can't keep a good lad down.' Greenwood's point, naturally, is that Edgar is anything but a good lad. He is weak, ineffectual and dominated by his termagant wife, and it is only his newly acquired wealth that makes him powerful. If the novel has a weakness, it is the flaws that disfigure – to name a slightly similar book from a previous generation – Robert Tressell's *The Ragged-Trousered Philanthropists* (1913): all the bourgeois characters are vain, duplicitous and conniving, and all the working-class characters impossibly virtuous. To set against this is Greenwood's thoroughgoing grasp of the way in which wealthy people in the conurbations of the early twentieth century – the setting here is Salford – band together to defend the interests of their class and the moral sleight of hand that accompanies this process of self-aggrandisement. In his innermost heart Edgar is conscious of his inadequacies and his inexperience. On the other hand, he is aware, from his observation of it, that civic life is essentially a sham. And so, in visiting the local workhouse hospital, where one of the inmates is the husband of his former charlady, though puzzled as to what is expected of him, he is 'determined to act as though he wanted it to be understood that he Knew All About It'.

The real distinction of *His Worship the Mayor* lies not in its detail, or the painstaking observation of milieu, but in its intimate relation to its time. Naturally, Salford being Salford, and municipal corruption being the same from one era to the next, it would have been possible to write a novel along the same lines ten years before, but it would have lacked the political awareness Greenwood brings to it, the sense of a new set of analytical techniques brought to an age-old problem. And if the gap between the fiction of the 1920s and the fiction of the 1930s grew steadily wider, then the implications for poetry were even more emphatic. The typical young poet of the 1920s, the Eliot-sponsored aesthete haunted by the imagery of the *commedia dell'arte* or the backward-looking Georgian trying to shut his eyes to the paraphernalia of the machine age, had given way to Auden:

> On that tableland scored by rivers
> Our thoughts have bodies; the menacing shapes of our
>   fevers
> Are precious but alive . . .
> Madrid is the heart. Our moments of tenderness blossom
> As the ambulances and the sandbags;
> Our hours of friendship into a people's army.

To a certain kind of young, politically committed 1930s writer – usually one hailing from the same social background as his own – Auden's brand of demotic emotional reportage was irresistible. Isaiah Berlin recalled Stephen Spender's father complaining about his fatal influence: 'It's Mr Auden. Always, everywhere, this Auden. It's he, I am sure, who makes him write about decaying teeth and so on. I am sure Stephen doesn't really think of them at all.' This kind of translation was both widely resented – the short-lived weekly magazine *Night and Day*, which ran from July to December 1937 with a stellar cast of contributors including Graham Greene, Evelyn Waugh and Constant Lambert and backing from the publishing house of Chatto & Windus, was expressly designed as a response to 'the Auden circle' – and hugely susceptible to pastiche. Osbert Lancaster's *Draynflete Revealed* (1949) is a spoof historical guide to an imaginary south of England town. One of its architectural ornaments is a house known as 'Poet's Corner', the outpourings of whose successive occupants allow Lancaster to compose a burlesque of recent tendencies in English poetry. By the 1890s the building is in the possession of Casimir de Vere-Tipple, author of *Samphire and Sardonyx* and contributor to *The Yellow Book*, who, the author observes, in a nod to the Wilde scandal, 'did not long enjoy his property as he was forced, for private reasons, to live abroad after 1895 and thenceforth resided on Capri'. Casimir's heir, on his death in 1929, is his nephew Guillaume de Vere-Tipple, who, though still an Oxford undergraduate, has already made a name for himself with a collection entitled *Feux d'artifice* (1927), from one of whose poems, 'Aeneas on the Saxophone', Lancaster tantalisingly quotes:

> Delenda est Carthago
> (ses bains de mer, ses plages fleuries,
> And Dido on her lilo à sa proie attachée)
> And shall we stroll along the front,
> Chatting of this and that and listening to the band?

Come the 1930s, alternatively, de Vere-Tipple, who, we learn, 'was socially conscious to a remarkable degree and had long entertained doubts as to the security of capitalist society', has reinvented himself as Bill Tipple, author of *the liftshaft* (1937) and its *pièce de résistance*, 'crackup in barcelona':

Among the bleached skeletons of the olive-trees
Stirs a bitter wind
And maxi my friend from the mariahilfer strasse
Importunately questions a steely sky
His eyes are two holes made by a damp finger
In the damp blotting paper of his face.

The mark of Lancaster's sureness of touch is that both these effusions should bear such an uncomfortably strong resemblance to actual poems of the period. With its Jazz Age classicism, its quotations from foreign languages and its persistent interrogation, 'Aeneas on the Saxophone' would not look out of place in Harold Acton's *Aquarium*, published in 1924 when Acton, like his fictional alter ego, was still an undergraduate. 'crackup', too, Audenesque, low-key and hardbitten, looks as if it was robbed wholesale from a back number of *Twentieth Century Verse*. And Lancaster is not merely satirising a tendency: in the career of Brian Howard (1905–58) he has a real-life model in view. A precocious teenage poet of unimaginably avant-garde tastes ('Who is this Proust? Huxley was telling me about him. I ought to read him', etc.), co-editor, while still a schoolboy and with Acton, of the defiantly modernist *Eton Candle* (1922), he spent the 1920s attending parties of the kind used by Evelyn Waugh as the raw material for *Decline and Fall* (1928) and *Vile Bodies* (1930) and writing poems in the approved sub-Eliot manner. There was a solitary collection, *God Save the King* (1931), privately printed by his friend Nancy Cunard. But by this time the stream of personal destiny had been muddied by politics. According to his own account, the laughter which greeted an incautious remark about Hitler, made at a lunch party of Thomas Mann's in Munich in 1931, persuaded him to study the German situation. These were early days for the pansy pinks of Orwell's demonising (although Orwell seems never to have met Howard in the flesh, there are good grounds for suspecting that he knew all about him). Of all the 1920s aesthetes who 'went left' in the era of Jarrow, Spain and rearmament, he was, if not the first, then certainly one of the noisiest, bringing news of Hitler to the Labour Leader of the House of Lords, Arthur Ponsonby, interviewing the Nazi press chief Dr Hanfstaengl for the *New Statesman*, helping Nancy Cunard to assemble *Spain: Authors Take Sides*, and contributing one of his better poems, 'For Those With Investments in Spain 1937' to the series *Les poètes du monde défendent le peuple espagnol*.

This transition from Bright Young Person to Serious Left-Wing Figure required a degree of harmonisation that was sometimes rather beyond this fugitive from the era of 'stunt' parties and elaborately planned practical jokes. Some of the juxtapositions of his diary jottings from Sanary-Sur-Mer in the south of France, where he lingered in the summer of 1939 trying to extract his German boyfriend Toni from the displaced persons' camps, must have seemed incongruous even to their author ('24th August – War almost inevitable; 25th August – End of everything for us; 31st August – Home from party 3.30 a.m'). Howard, in fact, is an example of that characteristic 1930s figure, the aesthete who tries to convert himself into an ideologue using what were essentially the same materials. None of this escaped the notice of contemporary satirists, several of whom were negotiating the same challenges themselves, and if Howard has a lasting memorial it is his starring role in 'Where Engels Fears to Tread' (1937), Cyril Connolly's account of the career of 'Christian de Clavering', a pseudonym which combines two of Howard's forenames, author of *From Oscar to Stalin. A Progress*, an autobiography which Connolly purports to review.

'Why am I doing this, my dears?' deutero-Howard is reported as demanding. 'Because I happen to be the one person who can do it. My dears, I'm on your side! I've come to get you out of the wretched tangle of individualism that you've made for yourselves and show you just how you can be of use in the world.' There follows a tour of de Clavering's early life, a precocious apprenticeship at Eton ('What is that book, de Clavering?' '*Les chansons de Bilitis*, sir'), balmy days at Oxford with Waugh and Betjeman, partygoing with the Bright Young People ('Dear Evelyn, *of course* put me into it') and carousing with Picasso, Hemingway and Firbank. Only in the early 1930s, wandering into a left-wing bookshop near Red Lion Square, does he see the light. The shelves are full of slim volumes 'by unfamiliar names. Who were Stephen, Wystan, Cecil and Christopher?' Happily 'these blunt monosyllables spoke a new kind of language to me'. There is the additional advantage that 'some of these young poets, I realised, had even attended my university!' One quatrain, in particular, haunts him:

M is for Marx
And Movement of Masses
And Massing of Arses
And Clashing of Classes

('It was new. It was vigorous. It was real. It was chic!') Reinventing himself as 'Cris Clay' ('I realise I shall never understand eclectic materialism but I'm terribly terribly Left!') he joins a protest march that winds up in St James's in the heart of London club-land. Here in the bay window of White's are his old friends 'Peter' (Fleming), 'Robert'(Byron) and 'Evelyn' (Waugh). The sketch ends with 'Commissar' Clay warning his reviewers that they had best be careful. 'A line is being drawn . . . Yes, my dears, bullets – real bullets, the kind they keep for reviewers who step across the party line.'

The peacock tone of 'Engels' – an absolutely faultless reproduction of the manner in which Howard spoke and conducted himself – can sometimes obscure the seriousness of the charges which Connolly is levelling at one part of the literary left: the cultivation of left-wing views because they happen to be fashionable; the contempt for objective standards; careerism disguised as ideological purpose. Even more significant, perhaps, is the fact that, as Anthony Powell once pointed out, the pretensions which Connolly gleefully exposes are, in a certain sense, his own.

However reddish-tinged the 1930s, and however great the disquiet of certain right-wing or politically neutral writers who imagined that they were being forced off the books pages, the chances of the literary left ever offering a united front to its enemies were, in practical terms, extremely limited. One reason for this failure to coalesce was the impossibility of organising such wayward spirits as Howard and Connolly into anything resembling a literary movement. Another was the ideological straitjacket that hung around 1930s literary Marxism, and a series of prescriptions and prohibitions which many middle-class intellectuals associated with the left found it very difficult to swallow: an orthodoxy that took its cue not merely from the principles of Soviet Socialist Realism, with its emphasis on the representative and the communal, but the famous speech delivered by Maxim Gorky at the inaugural Congress of Soviet Writers held in 1934:

> Party members who work in literature must not only be teachers of the ideology that organises workers of all lands for the final battle of freedom. In all its behaviour party leadership must be a morally authoritative force; this force must above all inculcate in writers a consciousness of their collective responsibility for everything taking place in their midst.

Certainly very few of the writers associated with *Left Review* (1934–8) would have dissented from this view. If anything united the editorial team – originally Montagu Slater, Amabel Williams-Ellis and Tom Wintringham, with Edgell Rickword assuming control in 1936 – it was that they were middle-class enthusiasts for proletarian literature. This in itself would have been enough to compromise the critical standards on display – even Rickword later admitted that most of the material sent in via the Workers' Educational Association was 'very bad'. Far worse was the uncritical worship of the Soviet Union that expressed itself in windy propagandising, the inevitable volte-faces when former heroes of Soviet Socialist Realism were thrown over by the regime, and the more or less unspoken assumption that if a writer happened to be serving in Spain then his poems deserved respectful treatment in the review pages. Eight decades later there are still things that can be said in *Left Review*'s favour – Rickword and Slater kept up the critical level, and there was short fiction from Edward Upward and James Hanley – but Rickword's claim, made in the 1960s, that there was a line of descent to post-war social radicalism, that 'the Weskers and the Sillitoes' were reading their elder brothers' copies, is far-fetched.

How did it happen, Julian Symons once enquired, that the *Left Review* editorial committee, 'these sensitive and intelligent men', so often confused literature with tub-thumping and 'printed so much that now looks derivative, dishonest and dull?' In literary Marxism's defence, the view from the study window or indeed the room on the upper floor of the Fitzrovian pub in which *Left Review* was conceived, with its bleak vistas of Franco-inclining Spain, a reoccupied Rhineland and a National Government, encouraged the essentially romantic gesturing of which so much literary Marxism consisted. As for the official Marxist literary texts of the period – Alick West's *Crisis and Criticism*, Ralph Fox's *The Novel and the People* and Christopher Caudwell's *Illusion and Reality*, all published on the flood tide of 1937 – a certain amount of ink is sometimes expended on the task of trying to demonstrate English Marxism's separation from the Soviet model, the idea that, as Philip Bounds puts it, 'British communism created a distinctive form of Marxist criticism by combining Soviet theory with ideas from the English tradition of thought about literature and culture.' No doubt there were unorthodox thinkers at large on the leftist uplands – Jack Lindsay, for example, who at least appreciated some of the emotional consequences of the Marxist assault on religious faith – but to examine the careers of the principal home-grown theoreticians is to note the high degree of psychological damage: West with his almost neurotic sense of self-division, the four years spent interned in Germany (where he happened to be innocuously holidaying in the summer of 1914), the tuberculosis, the restless wanderings in continental Europe; Fox with his determination to combine painstaking scholarship with the career of a man of action, who seems more or less to have deliberately thrown his life away in Spain in 1937.

So much of what got written, too, seems a rather desperate attempt to shoehorn existing styles and tendencies into the newly sanctioned official forms. Thus we have West insisting that what he defines as the 'anti-individualism' of an Eliot or a Lawrence can have only one logical consequence – that is, conversion to communism – or Fox patiently analysing the qualities of 'bourgeois' fictional heroes in the hope that some of these attributes may help in the creation of the more socially responsible characters that 1930s orthodoxy now demands. Even 'Caudwell', the pseudonym of the former aviation specialist Christopher St John Sprigge, author of *Fly with Me: An Elementary Textbook on the Art of Piloting* (1932) – whose reputation has worn less badly than most of his contemporaries – stands or falls on his 'bourgeois illusion of freedom' as an explanation for the cultural decline brought about by capitalism. If none of this had much effect beyond a limited circle of ideologues, it was because – rather in the manner of literary theory half a century later – it bore so little relation to the average creative artist's experience of how that creativity worked. All the same, when raking through the ashes of so much that, in retrospect, seems bogus or simply misdirected, it is worth remembering some of the individual struggles involved and the intellectual uncertainties, sometimes amounting to trauma, suffered by people who were anxious to do the right thing and to put their talents at the disposal of a political creed which they believed to offer the prospect of genuine social reform. Asked, in his 80s, how he looked back on his involvement with *Left Review*, Rickword – generally thought to have committed intellectual suicide when he joined the Communist Party in the 1930s – would say only that he wanted to encourage new writers, that he accepted it was possible to display literary merit while not toeing the party line, but that he detected in the work of Strachey, Fox, West and Caudwell the beginnings of 'a native Communist literature'. As for his own failure to write any more poems, he denied that Marxism had constituted any kind of psychological brake: 'Lyric poets tend to finish early, you know.'

Nothing wrong with commitment, of course – and Rickword noted that he could understand the manner in which certain writers could only come to terms with their work in this way: 'It's a sense of revelation almost. That being committed makes you a poet, or even becomes a very worthy subject for poetry.' On the other hand, as the only real attempt to organise the British artistic left in the 1930s, *Left Review*, for whom Pasternak's work was inevitably 'far removed from Soviet actuality', cannot be counted a success. Much more tangible and wide-reaching were the achievements of the Left Book Club, originally envisioned by Victor Gollancz and his co-founders John Strachey and Stafford Cripps as a weekly magazine aimed at revitalising and educating the British left but swiftly reconfigured as a left-wing version of the Book Society intended to 'help in the struggle *for* world peace and a better social and economic order, and *against* fascism'. Take-up confounded even Gollancz's expectations: 6,000 subscribers joined in the first month; by the end of 1936 there were 40,000. The number of readers prepared to pay 2s 6d for a book – a third of the published price – each month for six months allowed phenomenally large print runs – 42,000 copies of *The Road to Wigan Pier*, for example, in 1937 – and substantial advances (Spender received £300 for *Forward from Liberalism*) while a nationwide chain of discussion groups was soon in place; one of them is attended by George Bowling, the hero of *Coming Up For Air*. Astute commercial operator that he was, Gollancz knew that a straightforward diet of uplift would not suit the mainstream audience he was bent on retaining, so the list oscillated between reportage (the ex-jailbird Wilfred Macartney's Parkhurst memoir, *Walls Have Mouths*), to politically slanted fiction (Murray Constantine's *Swastika Nights*) and the occasional theoretical work such as Rajani Palme Dutt's *World Politics 1918–36*.

Attempting to explain the club's success, Strachey noted that 'it could only have happened at the present time' – in a kind of political vacuum, that is, where the National Government's huge majority meant that effective criticism of the Tory-dominated administration tended to be extra-parliamentary. In terms of the organisation's precise political underpinning, most research seems to indicate that if at the executive level the Left Book Club was not a Communist Party front then it came very close to it: two of Gollancz's colleagues – Sheila Lynd and Betty Reid – were party members, and the ideological line rarely deviated from that put out by the Communist Party of Great Britain's King Street headquarters. Certainly Gollancz himself was in no doubt that the Soviet show trials of 1936 were a highly necessary expedient. On the other hand, communist influence among the subscribers was much less marked: estimates put the number of readers with party membership at around a fifth of the total. Yet if these allegiances offered the club its early dynamic, then they were also to prove its undoing. As the overthrow of the Republican government was followed by the Munich Agreement, many sympathisers – and Gollancz in particular – began to feel that they might have been wrong, and that Neville Chamberlain and his ministers were not quite the gang of fascist barbarians that party orthodoxy required them to be. The decisive blow was administered by the Nazi–Soviet pact of August 1939, which was too much even for the organisation's sponsoring publisher to stomach. Although the club kept up until the post-war years, the original impetus was gone. None of this, though, is to detract from its influence on left-leaning literary thought, or its role – together with Allen Lane's Penguin Specials – in helping to create what Richard Crossman was to call the 'psychological landslide to the left' whose consequences were finally to be glimpsed in the general election of 1945.

Naturally, the kind of mobilising tactics endorsed by Gollancz and his commissars were not confined to the left. There were Right Book Clubs, Centre Book Clubs, National and International Book Clubs, Religious Book Clubs, so many as to be described by one bookseller as 'the greatest innovation in the history of bookselling which this decade can show'. All the same, the efforts of the literary right to organise itself in the 1930s were always complicated by extra-political factors, which is to say that much of the noise was made by Catholic writers whose hostility to Soviet propagandising was very often couched in exclusively religious terms, and whose fear of godlessness was as least as strong as the fear of egalitarianism. In fact, even to list the substantial collection of Catholic literary men and women of the period – their number included Waugh, Greene, Maurice Baring, Alfred Noyes, Roy Campbell and Christopher Hollis – is to summon up endless questions of definition, ancestry, core belief and readership.

Both Chesterton and Belloc, the great Catholic sages of the era, had begun their careers as Liberals – in Belloc's case as Liberal MP for Salford – and while their views tended to grow more autocratic over time, the message of Belloc's *The Servile State* (1912), which he continued to preach until the end of his life, was that capitalism and socialism are two versions of the same thing. Belloc, to enlarge on this singularity, was not only anti-industrial and anti-capitalist, he was anti-modern; a position which orthodox and non-Catholic right-wingers of the decade would have found largely untenable. Chesterton's medievalism grew out of the same suspicion of oligarchies: capital and organised labour are expressions of the same subordinating impulse, and the only guarantor of freedom is the spread of private property. For all the sheen imparted to the movement by high-profile converts of the Evelyn Waugh type, this gave the militant, tract-writing Catholicism of the 1930s a determinedly fusty air. Like Wells and Shaw, whom they continued to engage in debate, Chesterton and Belloc were survivors from a bygone era who sometimes found the going, here in an age of totalitarian realpolitik, uncomfortably hard.

The sanctifying process that preserved so many early twentieth-century writers in the public imagination never really caught up with G. K. Chesterton (1874–1936). Wells is briskly reinvented every half-decade or so, Shaw's shade marches on through Michael Holroyd's three fat volumes, but until the appearance of Ian Ker's voluminous biography in 2011, the standard life of the author of *The Man Who Was Thursday* (1908) dated back to the year of the Normandy landings. There are several reasons for this neglect. One of them is that there is so much to sanctify: as a friendly critic once put it, even the most fervent Chestertonian might wish that he hadn't written so much, so rapidly and under such unrelenting pressure. The other is that Chesterton spent the greater part of his life as a Christian, specifically Catholic apologist – he abandoned Anglicanism in 1922 – with the result that most of the proselytising done on his behalf has been done by and for the converted.

None of this is to detract from the extraordinary resonance of Chesterton's writings to the 'believer' of the interwar era, his stance or the impact of his very considerable personality. The most obvious point to be made in his favour is that he was a genuine democrat. Unlike most of the writers with whom he had cut his journalistic teeth in the pre-1914 era, he believed not only in giving the ordinary men and women a vote but in listening seriously to their opinions. His disillusionment with the Liberal Party, which he might have regarded as his natural home, was mostly a consequence of his having grasped that its animating spirit was oligarchical and that working-class electors were there to supply ballast rather than direction. Undoubtedly the conviction that 'democracy' meant more than simply offering the newly enfranchised a ballot box led him into some cul de sacs – it informs the trademarked medievalism, against which even the diehard Chesterton-fancier sometimes wants to rebel – and like practically every other idea which he produced it was founded on a paradox (we approve of the 'common man' because no such person exists, etc.) but set against some of the high-minded Fabians at large on the early twentieth-century lecture hall circuit the sight of Chesterton in full flow can be a bracing experience.

The second point in his favour is his sense of humour. Again, this endlessly cultivated comic side is undercut by paradox. It takes a very serious man, he might have said, not to take himself with complete seriousness. Significantly, the humour extends to his apologetics – the truly religious person, he insisted, is more likely to laugh than to turn a disapproving face to the world – but it also lies at the heart of his egalitarianism. 'Whenever you have got hold of a vulgar joke, you may be certain that you have got hold of a subtle and spiritual idea' he once maintained, for to see a joke is to see 'something deep' which can only be expressed by something 'silly and emphatic'.

Clearly a writer with this kind of stylistic armoury at his disposal would have flourished in any age, but the early twentieth-century literary world was peculiarly suited to someone of Chesterton's industry and temperament. With the old Victorian certainties as moribund as the people who had proclaimed them, it was an epoch in search of sages, and Chesterton, a failed artist from middle-class west London with an intensely romantic view of the Fourth Estate, fitted the bill. An apprenticeship on the *Speaker* led to an influential weekly column on the *Daily News*, and by his early 30s he was hobnobbing with such titans of renascent Liberalism as Herbert Asquith and the former prime minister Lord Rosebery. Meanwhile, the books continued to pour forth, sometimes at the rate of two or three a year. The difficulty with Chesterton's enormous output, kept up almost to the moment of his death, is not so much to separate the wheat from the chaff – the pioneering work on Dickens, say, from the routine collections of newspaper articles – as to acknowledge that the millions of words which remain are all of a piece. Rather like Wells, everything he wrote, from the Father Brown detective stories to the leading articles in *G.K.'s Weekly*, good, bad or indifferent, is in the end an argument for himself.

As for his 'thought', here in an age of intellectual constraint and rigorous toeings of party lines, one is struck, eighty years after his death, by the sanity of most of his judgements, his idea that convention is actually a form of freedom as it offers a framework in which a subject can be developed, or his rebuke of Shaw's solemn refusal to celebrate his birthday: 'Mr Shaw is quite clearly aware that it is a very good thing for him and for everyone else that he is alive. But to be told so in the symbolic form of brown-paper parcels containing slippers or cigarettes makes him feel a fool; which is exactly what he ought to feel.' The ideal Chestertonian, you sometimes suspect, will be one less seduced by the totality of his output than by the half-dozen areas in which the really striking contributions he made to twentieth-century letters are in danger of being forgotten. It may be that these distinctions are simply impossible to make, and like the great Victorian panjandrums from whom he descends, the mounds of pitch are a price worth paying for the radium gleams within. But whatever view one ends up taking of Chesterton, it is always heartening, in an age of eugenicists and autocrats, to find a writer who believes that at least some of humankind's difficulties can be solved by the efforts of ordinary people.

Certainly Chesterton looks to have worn a great deal better than Hilaire Belloc (1870–1953), with whom he is inevitably compared and whose signal obduracy he altogether lacks. Much more so than with his younger colleague, whatever one feels about Belloc and the stream of apologetics that issued from his pen in the years before the Second World War is liable to be coloured by partisanship, and in particular his supporters' habit of overlooking quite how rebarbative he could be in the struggle to prove his point. Whether or not he was a nice man, he was definitely an indefatigable one, who seems to have spent most of his early career in a continuous ferment. A spell in the French army, a madcap dash to America to rescue his wife-to-be from a nunnery, the forced march to the Vatican that produced one of his best-known books, *The Path to Rome* (1902) – each seems to have been prompted by the same crusading spirit that drove him to pick up his pen: the most recent bibliography lists over a hundred volumes, and this is to ignore the vast amounts of uncollected journalism.

The restlessness that lay at the heart of Belloc's career may have boosted his phenomenal work rate – in 1928 and 1929 he produced two volumes of his *History of England*, biographies of James I and Joan of Arc, three or four novels, a travel book and several works of apologetics – but it was also his undoing, for it meant that practically every sustained endeavour was beyond him. Invited to run magazines, he invariably jumped ship after a few months in the editorial chair. A staunch party man when the occasion demanded it, Belloc was notoriously keen that the party should be his own. What he really liked doing, of course, was offering his opinions, whether to the armchair strategists of the Great War (in a celebrated column for *Land and Water*) or to the princes of the Catholic Church. His most recent biography quotes a wonderfully characteristic letter to Charlotte Balfour from 1922 on the subject of a forthcoming visit to Rome: 'We are to have our audience tomorrow, I believe. I want to tell the new Pope one or two things. I hope he believes them.'

No doubt most of Belloc's substantial constituency hoped so too. In the polemical shooting gallery of the interwar years, where materialism and religion took endless potshots at each other, he featured as a spiritual howitzer. The rows with Wells, in particular, offer a kind of caricature version of the debates between progress and reaction conducted with rather more subtlety elsewhere. Simultaneously, there is at least a social fascination in Belloc's ability to bring together the two distinct worlds in which he operated: on the one hand a Georgian quintessence made up of beer, briar pipes, long walks, drinking songs and Sussex-by-the-Sea – everything given a home in Squire's famous parody* – on the other, the salons of interwar literary Catholicism, descending from the aristocratic redoubts of Lady Lovat and Maurice Baring to H. V. Morton's 'Beachcomber' column and the apologists of the popular press. In the end, though, there is no getting away

* At Martinmas, when I was born,
Hey diddle, Ho diddle, Do,
There came a cow with a crumpled horn,
Hey diddle, Ho diddle, Do.
She stood agape, and said, "My dear,
You're a very fine child for this time of year,
And I think you'll have a taste in beer," etc. See *Tricks of the Trade* (1917)

from Belloc's autocratic, illiberal side, the almost indiscriminate enthusiasm for every right-wing cause or standard-bearer from Mussolini ('Meeting this man after talking to the parliamentarians in other countries was like meeting with some athletic friend of one's boyhood after an afternoon with racing touts') and Franco to Action française. Like many another young Catholic radical, the acolyte of Cardinal Manning and the economic reformer eventually became a quietist by default; his last years were spent lamenting the miseries of the world in which he was compelled to live while resting his hopes on the consolation of the afterlife. Doubtless there were things he wanted to tell his creator too. At any rate this blue-skies-deferred view of life left him happier than Wells, who ended his days in stark disillusionment. Somehow, though – to borrow the title of the book of nonsense verse for which he will probably be best remembered – what remains is only a cautionary tale.

If Chesterton and Belloc were by this time essentially figures from a vanished age, then, singly and jointly, they were still capable of whipping up a propagandist storm, both through *G.K.'s Weekly*, founded in 1925, to which Belloc contributed, and the Distributist League, formed as a vehicle for their anti-oligarchical theories of social reform and bringing together both radicals and traditional Tories to defend the liberties of the individual against spreading corporatism. 'Distributism' was a curious compound of libertarianism and social justice: it was, for example, violently in favour of private bus companies and fought a running battle against Lord Ashfield's London General Omnibus Transportation Company. At the same time it maintained that trades unions, instead of negotiating for pay increases, which made them wage slaves, should have joint ownership of industry. As Distributism's in-house journal, *G.K.'s Weekly* championed the small property-holder against socialism, communism and capitalist monopoly alike from a position that was Catholic, but not exclusively so, intended to be 'popular' while avoiding the stupidity that Chesterton detected in the tabloid press. Several thousand well-wishers contributed to the £10,000 needed as working capital, and friendly competitors such as Squire helped on the organisational side, but, rather like its founders, the enterprise seemed to belong to a bygone era. In particular, it assumed the existence of a loyal and more or less unquestioning readership largely attracted by the personality of its editor who would support the magazine to the death. Shaw warned that there was 'absolutely no public' for this kind of thing in the 1920s. Chesterton, who allowed himself £500 a year as editor – a frugality that horrified Squire – ended up injecting his own money to keep it going.

No doubt Chesterton was correct when he informed his subscribers – in one of the magazine's frequent appeals for support – that he was a victim of circumstances, as the 'movement towards a millionaire monopoly of the press' became unstoppable. But there is a suspicion that *G.K.*'s difficulties had at least as much to do with its editor. In the hotly competitive atmosphere of the interwar era, literary magazines needed a full-time staff. Chesterton, with his file of publishers' contracts and his ceaseless round of speaking engagements, was rarely seen at the paper's offices in the Strand and often left the work of selecting contributions to his secretary. He was chary, too, of being too closely associated with the magazine and had his portrait removed from the cover after the first few issues. On the other hand, lack of funds often forced him to supply large amounts of the content himself. None of this made the magazine attractive to the discerning reader ('What a dreadful production is *G.K.'s Weekly*' Sassoon complained to Blunden) or gave it any kind of consistent focus. Its contributors, consequently, tended to be hopeful apprentices – Orwell's first published piece appeared there in 1928 – or distinguished co-religionists offering their services gratis. An entry in Evelyn Waugh's diary from November 1936, shortly after Chesterton's death, when a short-lived attempt was made to keep the paper going by his friends, records an evening spent writing 'free stuff for Belloc: hope I get to heaven that way'.

There were, of course, secular Bellocs and Chestertons – younger critics, usually working on a relatively small scale, but able through sheer force of personality to establish a bridgehead for their own, sometimes highly idiosyncratic, view of the 1930s literary world. In an age where little magazines still counted for something – especially in the field of poetry – several of them were able to exert an influence out of all proportion to their meagre circulations, and in *New Verse* and *Twentieth Century Verse* they threw up two of the finest vehicles for poetry – and, equally important, for the criticism of poetry – of the interwar era. On the other hand, nothing could have been further apart than the origins and social backgrounds of their respective editors, Geoffrey Grigson and Julian Symons. Grigson (1905–85) was the son of an elderly Cornish clergyman – the seventh son, as he liked to remind people – who proceeded by way of Westminster to an Oxford English degree. Although the Lewis–Tolkien curriculum was not to his taste (his memoirs offer some choice remarks about the 'despicable school of English') he was able to see Virginia Woolf and Edith Sitwell in the flesh, talking to undergraduate literary societies, and enjoy the spectacle of Lord David Cecil mocking Gertrude Stein from the depths of the audience. Like many an aspiring literary man, he had difficulty in finding a suitable day job and there was a period spent marking time as a schoolmaster before he graduated to the *Yorkshire Post*'s Fleet Street desk, writing paragraphs for its 'London Letter'. From here it was but a short step to the literary editorship of the immensely right-wing *Morning Post*, which gave him a solid base from which to pursue after-hours work on *New Verse*.

To a modern reader, the fascination of *New Verse* lies in its caustic tone – an undercurrent of sometimes vicious asperity, which contemporary critics occasionally amused themselves by trying to explain, or at least to rationalise. Was it, someone once briskly suggested, because he was unhappily married? No, Grigson countered, it was because he was unhappily born. Although, in later life, he confessed that he disliked looking at old numbers – 'the fun and the slaughter now make me, if I recall them, rather sick' – then there is no point in pretending that what one critic called the magazine's 'picric flavour' wasn't a substantial part of its appeal. As Symons once observed, it is a great thing in any period to have a critic who will deal incisively with what seems to him to be meretricious, imitative or shabby writing. If the charge sheets sometimes filed by *New Verse*'s editorials can sometimes seem over-extensive – they included journalistic slickness, 'burrowing academicism', Grub Street, historians, biographers and nearly every kind of literary theorist – in other words, almost anyone working in the field of literature with the exception of Grigson himself and a few like-minded friends, then the list of his admirers was surprisingly eclectic: Connolly, for example, not to mention the milder type of Leavisite. As for the poets he was prepared to tolerate – Dryden, Crabbe, Auden – the temptation is to find in them a kind of literalism and distaste for phoniness that seems to underlie Grigson's sometimes rather complex personal life.

Set against Grigson's claims to outsider status (which are presumably reflected in the late-period attacks on contemporaries whom he imagined to have 'sold out') Julian Symons (1912–94) looks the genuine article: the son of a second-hand clothes shop proprietor who bequeathed his heirs an estate valued at £4. Brought up in working-class south London and afflicted with a stammer so paralysing that he was at one point sent to a school for backward children, Symons was eventually engaged as a shorthand typist at 27/6d a week. His strategy at this stage in his career was to take mundane clerical jobs while cultivating his literary interests by hanging around the Fitzrovia pubs, reading Eliot, Joyce, Pound's early *Cantos* and Wyndham Lewis, and sending poems to *New Verse*, with whose aims – and with Grigson personally – he felt an immediate affinity, and one of the attractions of the account he left of these early days is the series of distinctions it draws between the various strata of 1930s poets. Beneath the empyrean occupied by Eliot, Auden and co. there were, according to Symons, three main groups: the Grigson gang; bohemian romantics represented by Dylan Thomas, David Gascoyne and George Barker; and a lower order whose verse appeared in the 'Poets' Corner' of the *Sunday Referee*, then edited by Victor Neuberg, who printed three or four contributions a week, adjudged to be the best in heavy type. 'It may seem strange that anybody took him seriously' Symons recalled, remembering the editorial comments sometimes appended to these selections, 'but the prevailing poetic climate was such that young poets were pleased to find verse printed anywhere at all.'

It was in this decidedly low-rent atmosphere that Symons, with the help of Herbert Mallalieu, founded *Twentieth Century Verse*. Looking back on the early numbers from the vantage point of his 60s, Symons was struck by his own 'parochialism and ignorance'. All the same he is ready to admit that editorial blind spots over what was and was not fashionable gave the poems by Thomas and Barker their originality. Few magazines, as he pointed out, are as dull as those run in the service of an easily pleased aestheticism: judged by this yardstick, one of *Twentieth Century Verse*'s great merits is that not all of its contributors sound like Auden. If Symons made common cause with Grigson – although he always maintained that his own efforts never did more than 'palely reflect' *New Verse*'s virtues – it was in his stand against what the critic Hugh Gordon Porteus called 'the grosser and more manifest deceits of the day', their dislike of cliques and their enthusiasm for what Symons later termed 'commonsense standards in English Letters'. It would be an exaggeration to argue that the post-war movement towards exactitude and sceptical plain speaking starts here in the world of the 1930s little magazine. On the other hand, a letter written by Philip Larkin to his girlfriend Monica Jones over twenty years later – 'I've always had an admiration for Grigson . . . *And* he's a significant editor into the bargain' – suggests that at least one 1950s poet was conscious of the debt he owed.

Orwell in the 1930s

Between 1934 and 1939, long before the out-of-kilter dystopias with which he made his name, George Orwell published four downbeat and determinedly realistic novels. Each one, whatever the nature of the camouflage, is in some way autobiographical. *Burmese Days* (1934) draws on the five years spent as a servant of the Raj in the Burma Police; *A Clergyman's Daughter* (1935) combines an unsparing portrait of the Suffolk coastal town to which his parents had retired with reportage from his tramping days and adventures in the shabby-genteel world of private schoolteaching; *Keep the Aspidistra Flying* (1936) reprises his time as a bookseller's assistant in Hampstead; while *Coming Up For Air* (1939), though written from the vantage point of a middle-aged insurance salesman, returns us to the Thames Valley greensward where he wandered as a child. But in all four books there is something else going on, at once more oblique and, in the end, more overpowering. All, whether set in the colonial east, the flyblown provincial backwater of 'Knype Hill', Mr McKechnie's north London bookshop, or amid the turn-of-the-century Oxfordshire verdure, hint at some of the influences to which a somewhat conventionally minded young English novelist of the 1930s was subject, comment – either directly or indirectly – on the literary world in which that writer moves and, ultimately, offer a withering critique of the literary culture of the day.

In some ways Orwell's emphatic 'literariness' – the sense, common to all his books, of a vast private library lurking in the shadows of plot, scheme and character – is simply a matter of derivation. *Burmese Days*, for example, is drenched in essence of Maugham, and in the metaphorical charge of many of its scenic descriptions looks back to the poets of the Wilde-era avant-garde. *A Clergyman's Daughter* taps into the interwar era's fascination with the 'superfluous female' of the Victorian census return explored by Katherine Mansfield's story 'Daughters of the Late Colonel' and F. M. Mayor's *The Third Miss Symons*. Gordon Comstock, the embittered ground-down anti-hero of *Keep the Aspidistra Flying*, forever inveighing against the editors who won't print his work and the backstairs intrigues that supposedly stymie his chances of recognition, is essentially a refugee from *New Grub Street* pushed forward into the twentieth century. *Coming Up For Air*, meanwhile, is H. G. Wells's *The History of Mr Polly* (1910) brought up to date, one of whose key scenes Orwell deftly reanimates by having his hero walk into a down-at-heel tobacconist's shop and come face to face with his first girlfriend, now, inevitably, turned into a slack-jawed hag.

But if Orwell is wearing his influences on his sleeve – very old-fashioned influences they are too – then the view he takes of the literary world and the uses to which he puts it are by no means clear-cut. To Flory, the hero of *Burmese Days*, sequestered in a remote village with only the philistine inhabitants of the Kyauktada Club for company, 'literature' is a kind of hopeless dream, the symbol of a good and wholesome life that hangs tantalisingly over the far-off horizon. Part of the attraction of Elizabeth Lackersteen, the novel's love interest, is the fact that she 'adores' reading and has lived in Paris, which enables her besotted swain to conjure up enticing visions of a woman who has 'talked of Marcel Proust under the Paris plane trees'. Alas, Elizabeth's literary tastes are quite as conservative and traditional as the bores and sots of the club, and there is a revealing moment in which Orwell invites his higher-brow readers to judge her by way of the books she reads. Thus at one point she is found lying on the sofa reading Michael Arlen's *These Charming People*. 'In a general way Michael Arlen was her favourite author' Orwell chips in, 'but she was inclined to prefer William J. Locke when she wanted something serious.' Arlen was a fashionable 'society' novelist whose *The Green Hat* (1924), with its man-eating heroine Iris Storm, cut a swathe through the Mayfair drawing rooms of the 1920s, but it is that 'wanting something serious' which is really intended to damn Elizabeth in the knowing reader's eyes, William J. Locke being an archetypically best-selling middlebrow writer of the period and, at any rate to the Orwells of this world, of no serious interest whatsoever.

Burmese Days' other literary reference point is Flory's friend the Indian doctor Veraswami, with his fondness for Shaw and his habit of quoting Stevenson ('I see the British as torch-bearers upon the path of progress') – extinct volcanoes, we are encouraged to believe, and of no real relevance to the concerns of the early twentieth century. *A Clergyman's Daughter*, on the other hand, is less obviously weighted in its gestures to literature. At one stage there is mention of Dorothy reading Gene Stratton-Porter's *A Girl of the Limberlost* to the Mothers' Union sewing circle, while designing Mr Warburton gamely invents a writer named 'Ronald Bewley' – horribly plausible, it has to be said – author of the controversial novel *Fishpools and Concubines*, as a means of persuading her to pay an unchaperoned late-night visit to his house, but the book's real signifier is its reference to Dorothy spending a lonely Christmas Day at Burnham Beeches with a copy of *The Odd Women*, Gissing's late Victorian classic about a family of spinster sisters thrown on hard times. Dorothy is an odd woman herself, and her choice of festive reading material offers an instant context for her travails.

For all the precision of Dorothy's literary grounding, it is difficult not to think that this is a preliminary, a minor skirmish in the preparations for the really serious cultural engagement that is *Keep the Aspidistra Flying*, one of those books which, like Thackeray's *Pendennis*, *New Grub Street* and, a bit later, Powell's *Books Do Furnish a Room*, doubles up as novel and running commentary on the literary marketplace in which it is set. Gordon Comstock's date of birth is given as 1905, a couple of years after his creator; as a schoolboy he is said to have published his first poem in Orage's *New Age*. We first see this moth-eaten 29-year-old, author of the collection *Mice*, in his employer's front window, bringing to the loaded shelves not so much literary criticism as blanket opprobrium. The classics of the Victorian age (Scott, Carlyle and Meredith); religious books ('Father Hilaire Chestnut's latest book of R.C. propaganda'); contemporary works ('Priestley's latest. Dinky little books of reprinted "middles"') – all are brought out merely to be mocked. There is a special place reserved in this demonology for 'smart pseudo-Strachey pre-digested biographies. Snooty, refined books on safe painters and safe poets by those moneyed young beasts who glide so gracefully from Eton to Cambridge and from Cambridge to the literary reviews.'

If this sounds uncannily like Mrs Leavis riding one of her hobby horses, albeit in slightly less temperate language, then the author of *Fiction and the Reading Public* would probably have taken a keen interest in what happens next: the entry into the Booklovers' Corner library section of two middle-aged women, Mrs Weaver and Mrs Penn, who might be supposed to represent the tastes of 'ordinary' readers. Neither, alas, comes anywhere near to the standards that Gordon espouses. Mrs Penn bears her copy of *The Forsyte Saga* title outward so passers-by may 'spot her for a highbrow' – a double-edged sneer as Galsworthy's reputation by this stage was calamitously in decline. Mrs Weaver, meanwhile, is returning Ethel M. Dell's *Silver Wedding*. Subsequently Mrs Penn engages Gordon in a literary conversation, exposing herself as a hopeless middlebrow from one sentence to the next with her encomia on Priestley and Walpole ('There's something so *big* about him. And yet he's so human with it'). Having ushered them out of the shop, Gordon next turns his attention to the poetry shelves. Here, already on their way to heaven and oblivion, are the stars of his youth – Yeats, Housman, de la Mare and Hardy – superannuated but by no means inferior to 'the squibs of the passing minute', a category in which Eliot, Pound, Auden, Campbell, Day Lewis and Spender are all unhesitatingly lumped. 'Shall we ever again get a writer worth reading?' Gordon concludes, before deciding that 'Lawrence was all right, and Joyce even better before he went off his coconut' – that is, moved on from *Ulysses* to the experimental wordplay of the work-in-progress that eventually became *Finnegans Wake*.

Having negotiated this barrage of insults and litany of complaint, this dismantling of practically every literary reputation acquired in England since about 1820, the circumspect reader will be beginning to wonder about Gordon and the role that he imagines himself to play in this jungle of false standards and middlebrow enthusiasms. The answer is that he is the outsider to end all outsiders, the man on the margin who regards nearly every critic, editor and publisher in London as a band of conspiratorial halfwits. Just lately, with *Mice* behind him, desultorily at work on a vast, anachronistic-sounding poem ('two thousand lines in rhyme royal, describing a day in London'), Gordon has been taken up by Ravelston, the editor of a small-circulation magazine called *Antichrist*; the former modelled on Richard Rees, the latter on the *Adelphi*. His ambition is to ascend to the dizzying heights of the *Primrose Quarterly* ('one of those poisonous literary papers in which the fashionable Nancy Boy and the professional Roman Catholic walk *bras dessus, bras dessous*. It was also by a long way the most influential literary paper in England'). If this sounds suspiciously like the *New Criterion*, then the critic Paul Doring, who invites Gordon to his weekly get-togethers, sounds uncannily like the *Observer*'s major-domo Gerald Gould. Neither of them, alas, is much use to Gordon who, when he receives the manuscript of his rejected poem back from the *Quarterly*, is reduced to well-nigh apocalyptic rage: 'The sods! The bloody sods! Why be so mealy-mouthed about it? Why not say outright: "We don't want your bloody poems. We only take poems from chaps we went to Cambridge with. You proletarians keep your distance." The bloody, hypocritical sods!'

It is worth pointing out that Orwell, in the year of *Keep the Aspidistra Flying*'s composition, was getting his work printed by Rees (a fellow Old Etonian) and re-establishing contact with his old school chum Cyril Connolly, whose own novel *The Rock Pool* Orwell would gamely endorse in the pages of the *New English Weekly*. It takes a backstairs intriguer to know one. This extraneous knowledge makes *Aspidistra* a rather curious artefact: a novel about the corruption and venality of the literary world by someone who, far from being an outsider, is up to his neck in it. Yet the evidence of Orwell's letters and journals shows that he both believed in the existence of literary cliques – see the letter despatched to the compilers of the pamphlet *Spain: Writers take Sides* noting that 'I am not one of your fashionable pansies' – and imagined himself to be free of their taint. In the end the explanation can only be psychological, a matter of Orwell filling his books with projections of himself: ground-down, paranoiac, constantly being spied on, regulated and patronised by grotesque and vengeful adversaries. The Orwell who worked at Booklovers' Corner, Hampstead, between late 1934 and early 1936 had notably indulgent employers, a busy social life and an expanding professional range – amenities carefully denied to his resentful alter ego. The novel's most convincing pieces of reportage come at Doring's parties, in Gordon's fulminations on the doormat, in the scenes where Gordon, having lost his job for drunkenness, takes a starvation-level job in a 'mushroom library' in Lambeth, one of a kind that are springing up all over London 'deliberately aimed at the uneducated', displaying books churned out by half-starved hacks 'at the rate of four a year, as mechanically as sausages and with much less skill'. Installed in the library's single narrow room, Gordon charges his patrons 2d a time to borrow such items as *Secrets of Paris* and *The Man She Trusted*. What gives this episode its fascination is the sense of Orwell sowing some of the seeds of the 'Fiction Department' in *Nineteen Eighty-Four*, but there is an exactness about the detail which convinces the reader that the writer knows what he is talking about. In a curious way the Lambeth scenes are more convincing than Gordon's diatribes against the literary establishment:

the one is punctilious observation; the other a writer indulging in the dangerous game of twisting his own personality slightly out of shape.

Coming Up For Air, too, though couched in far more temperate terms, is also an argument with the literary culture of the interwar era. George Bowling, its decidedly non-literary hero, is not a resentful and marginalised poet but a self-confessed middlebrow who, at the same time, knows that there are better things available if you look in the right places. A Boots Library subscriber who 'always falls for the best-seller of the moment' – titles mentioned include Priestley's *The Good Companions* and Cronin's *Hatter's Castle* – he is also, rather unexpectedly, a member of the Left Book Club. At the start of the novel Bowling is reading a Boots selection entitled *Wasted Passion*, pilloried for its detachment from the way in which ordinary people think and behave. 'The chap in the story finds out that his girl has gone off with another chap. He's one of those chaps you read about in novels that have pale sensitive faces and dark hair and a private income.' This leads Bowling to pastiche a scene in which the hero flings himself down 'in a paroxysm of weeping' and reflects 'That's how people – some people – are expected to behave. But how about a chap like me?' If his own wife, the mirthless Hilda, were to abscond for a weekend with another man, 'it would rather please me to find she'd still got that much kick in her'. On the other hand, if he did care, would he fling himself down in a paroxysm of weeping? 'You couldn't, with a figure like mine.'

But how did Bowling, a grocer's son from the Thames Valley, forge a path into literature in the first place? It turns out that his imagination – like that of his creator, to judge from Orwell's account of his juvenile reading habits – was fired by boys' weeklies of the pre-Great War era such as *Chums* and the *Boy's Own Paper*, but also by the adventures of Sherlock Holmes and E. W. Hornung's Raffles. As a young shop assistant Bowling joins a reading circle – the early twentieth-century equivalent of a book group but with the emphasis on uplift. Yet the Damascene moment comes when, during the war, he is sent to north Cornwall to oversee a remote ration dump whose previous inhabitants have left a small collection of books behind them, including works by Wells and Compton Mackenzie and 'a back number of some magazine or other [this sounds like the *English Review*] which had a short story of D. H. Lawrence's in it'. This unexpected encounter has a galvanising effect. It is not, Bowling hastily explains, that he goes on to discover Proust, but that the knowledge acquired enables him in his subsequent trips to the library to discriminate between good books and less good ones. Starting out with piles of middlebrow bestsellers by Barry Pain, Pett Ridge, Oliver Onions and Elinor Glyn, he is eventually able to separate 'tripe and non-tripe'. In the latter category are *Sons and Lovers* ('I sort of half-enjoyed it'), and George Moore's *Esther Waters*, but in the end 'Wells was the author who made the biggest impression on me.'

Why should Orwell, an Old Etonian whose formative years were utterly unlike those of George Bowling, devote large parts of a novel about England in the run-up to the Second World War to a ventriloquial survey of the reading habits of the lower middle classes? The answer, perhaps, is that it is there to prove a point that is often ventilated in his literary journalism of the period – the long essay 'In Defence of the English Novel' contributed to the *New English Weekly* in 1936, say. The average literary sensibility, according to this argument, is constrained by the process which brings literature to the paying public, aspires to higher things but is everywhere rebuffed by cosy middlebrow bookmen of the Gerald Gould/Ralph Straus sort, wants to read good books with something to say about the world which reader and writer inhabit, but lacks the information and the technical nous that would enable it to make proper judgements. Bowling, you infer, is too susceptible to the blandishments flung at him by newspapers and book-club propagandists. He is not a highbrow, but neither is he a fan of the averagely good Priestley-and-water English novel. These tastes were not easily satisfied, either in the 1930s or in the decades ahead.

CHAPTER 6

Making a Living I 1918–1939

I could die with envy of Proust and Virginia, my dear. They never had to do *anything*.

Julia Strachey to her friend Frances Partridge, 1962

The decision to rely wholly upon his pen is the one really dramatic step in a novelist's career.

Alec Waugh, 1935

One of the fascinations of *New Grub Street*, George Gissing's immensely gloomy conspectus of the late Victorian literary scene, is the almost forensic quality of the detail. Gissing knew that if you are going to write a novel about what by this time in its development was essentially an industrial process then a paramount task is to establish what everybody earns. At the same time, this dutiful weighing up of profit-and-loss accounts – how many words written, how many guineas banked – is lent an even deeper resonance by the feeling that everything on display here is, in the end, personal, that the struggles of the book's ineffectual novelist hero Edwin Reardon are ultimately the author's own. Reardon's first novel, for example, is sold for £25 and published on the 'half-profits' system, with publisher and author sharing the proceeds. *On Neutral Ground*, the book that makes his name, fetches £100, after which his star declines: the mark of its successor's failure is that he should only be offered £75.

These meagre returns are remarkably similar to the prices that Gissing's early work attracted in the 1880s. His first novel, *Workers in the Dawn* (1880), underwritten by an authorial subsidy of £125, realised a cheque for exactly sixteen shillings. Even *New Grub Street*, the first of his books to achieve any sort of popularity in his lifetime, was sold outright for £150. And, interspersed with Reardon's travails – his permanent anxiety, his paralysing case of writer's block, the inevitable collapse of his marriage – comes a great deal of hard information as to the rewards available to the switched-on professional writer here in the age of Gladstone and Lord Salisbury. At one point Reardon's thrusting young friend Jasper Milvain, who writes only 'for the market', and will go on to marry the older man's widow, calculates that he has made ten guineas for a day's journalism. Meanwhile, the best-selling novelist who advises the young Reardon to take up fiction beams as he utters the word: 'It meant a thousand a year to him.'

The other fascination of *New Grub Street*, at any rate to those professionally enmired in the world of literature, is the extent of its demographic reach. Metaphorically, the world it describes is a kind of layer cake, whose strata extend from fashionable novelists in their West End town houses to indefatigable hacks in their suburban lodgings, and from broken-down old book reviewers to Flaubertian art-for-art's-sakers happy to shiver in their underheated garrets above the Tottenham Court Road – Gissing's own bolthole in his early days – if it allows them to preserve their integrity. But the questions Gissing poses about the literary market of the 1880s are no less interesting half a century later. Specifically: how did the average, and not so average, literary man or woman make a living in the 1920s and 1930s? How much could he, or she, expect to earn and from what kind of commissions in which kind of markets? A senior clerk working in a City office in the early 1930s – Mr Smeeth, say, the desiccated cashier of Priestley's *Angel Pavement* – could expect to earn £350 a year; a junior clerk half to two-thirds of this; a secretary-typist between £2 and £3 a week. Beyond London, the wage scales plunged even lower. Respectable middle-class incomes of the kind that allowed their beneficiaries to keep a servant and educate their children privately hovered in the £1,000 to £1,200 a year bracket. How, when set against these yardsticks, did the literary world of the interwar era compare?

At the top end sat a collection of writers – most, but not all, best-selling novelists – capable of earning what, to the average clerk, were wholly fantastic sums. Arnold Bennett's income, for example, rose from £15,783 in 1920 to a phenomenal £22,000 in 1929, a sum achieved not only by way of his best-selling novels but through journalism paid at a rate of two shillings a word (occasionally rising to 2s 6d) and short stories for which, as he informed his agent in 1928, 'I can always get £100 per 1,000 words . . . without counting the book rights.' Hugh Walpole was not quite in the Bennett category, and lacked his powers of self-promotion, but his annual income in the mid-1920s was put at between £3,500 and £4,500; it continued to rise for the next decade and a half. Shortly before his death in 1925, A. C. Benson, whose books of quasi-philosophical essays sold in their hundreds of thousands to meditative middle-class readers, estimated his personal fortune at £100,000. Half of this, admittedly, took the form of unsolicited gifts from a wealthy American admirer, but at least £50,000 had sprung directly from his pen. Benson, having started out in the late Victorian era – his first success was an edition of Queen Victoria's letters – had been able to benefit from lower rates of taxation: it was only in the later 1920s that the figure of the authorial tax exile – Maugham in his villa at Cap Ferrat, E. Phillips Oppenheim in his refuge by the seventeenth hole of the Nice golf course – became a gossip columnist's staple. Walpole, Maugham and Oppenheim were exceptions, but, at any rate in comparison to a senior clerk on his £7 a week, there were substantial incomes to be earned lower down the scale. Alec Waugh, a middlingly successful novelist, published on either side of the Atlantic and prepared to supplement the income received from his books with short stories and journalism, calculated that he earned £1,500 a year in the early 1930s. As for the purveyors of upmarket literary journalism, J. C. Squire's income in the year 1920–1 was put at £1,158, although the apparent security of his position was weakened by the *London Mercury*'s precarious financing. His editorial salary, which at one point rose to as much as £1,200, was eventually reduced to £600 and come the early 1930s disappeared altogether. There were decent pickings, too, to be made out of magazine journalism. Herbert Allingham, for example, who worked for half a century on a succession of popular women's and children's weeklies, regularly updating his plot lines to suit the requirements of succeeding generations of readers, amassed as much as £1,500 a year in the decade before his death in 1936.

Below the level of the acknowledged titan, the rewards were a great deal less impressive. A literary journalist, permanently in search of work and not over-fastidious about the kind of commissions he took on, might hope to earn between £400 and £500 per annum. John Hayward, later to find fame as the confidant of T. S. Eliot, set up as a jack of all trades in the late 1920s. In 1930 he estimated that he earned £89 for thirty-four articles. By 1932 his output had increased dramatically to 155 pieces, bringing in £388. A year later, 177 items realised £394. A fixture in the pages of *The Times*, the *Times Literary Supplement*

(200 contributions between 1929 and 1937), the *Daily Mirror*, the *Observer* and the *New Statesman*, Hayward calculated that at this period in his life he wrote a review at the rate of one every two days, balancing more highbrow editorial work on Donne and Rochester with notices of thrillers at five shillings apiece. Inevitably this level of industry recalls the disillusioned hack of Orwell's famous essay 'Confessions of a Book Reviewer', slouched at his desk beneath a fog of cigarette smoke while blearily appraising the half-dozen ill-assorted books his editor thinks 'ought to go well together' – these include *Palestine at the Crossroads* and a treatise on dairy farming. Yet if Orwell's portrait of a wraith in a moth-eaten dressing gown who is 30 but looks 50, glumly sequestered in a bedsitter littered with overflowing ashtrays and half-drunk cups of tea is a caricature, then the kind of work he is performing and the financial rewards available can be located in an age-old historical context. Book reviewing, as John Gross once pointed out, is one of the last surviving houses of Grub Street, and a trawl through the relevant volume of Peter Davison's *George Orwell: The Complete Works* soon discloses that Orwell's earnings in his post-Spanish Civil War period, when he was living in the Hertfordshire village of Wallington, were barely above subsistence level, between £2 and £3 a week, most of it obtained via book reviewing. The dressing-gowned drudge, vainly searching among the piles of unanswered letters for a cheque for two guineas 'which he is nearly certain he forgot to pay into the bank' is not quite Orwell, but he is near enough to him to provoke a twinge of recognition.

But there were factors at work in the interwar era capable, on the one hand, of making the professional writer's circumstances a great deal easier and, on the other, strewing the path with obstacles. On the plus side, the incidental expenses of the freelance life were a great deal cheaper than they would become. When Walpole arrived in London in 1908 at the beginning of his career, his Chelsea bedsitter cost him four shillings a week, whereas the fee for his weekly novel round-up in the *Daily Telegraph* came to three guineas. Similarly, when Leonard and Virginia Woolf founded the Hogarth Press in 1917 the combined annual wages of their cook and parlour-maid were £76 1s 8d – comfortably exceeded by the £95 9s 6d Virginia earned in that year from reviewing. Even in the 1930s accommodation could still be found in the poorer districts of London for under ten shillings a week.

While the freelance life was certainly precarious, founded on editorial whims and unflinching authorial reliability, then the number of outlets for literary work, if slightly reduced from its late Victorian high-water mark, was still highly diverse. There were six London evening newspapers prepared to pay both for signed articles and for anonymous paragraphs, six literary weeklies and fashion papers that commissioned feature articles and short fiction, and a large number of sixpenny magazines avid for copy. As Alec Waugh once put it, a short story had to be either very bad or very good (that is, exceptionally highbrow) not to find a purchaser. A writer's need for ready money was also more easily satisfied by a publishing industry built on high turnover and authorial zeal. Most mainstream novelists brought out a book a year; occasionally, if they dabbled in short stories or travel writing, two or three. Walpole's biographer puts his output between 1918 and 1930 at twenty-two books. Alec Waugh, no slouch at putting pen to paper, managed twenty between 1917 and 1932. Books were published quickly – the gap between receipt of a manuscript and the finished volume's appearance in a bookshop was often as little as eight weeks – meaning that writers rarely had to wait for their money. While advances were low, publishers were correspondingly keener on commissioning projects in advance. Sharp operators, knowing what might tickle an editorial palate, were skilled in negotiating down payments for work that in many cases remained unwritten. Malcolm Muggeridge remembered that merely to pass a publisher's office was enough for his friend the biographer Hugh Kingsmill to start reckoning up the likelihood of a contract. 'Do you think', Kingsmill once demanded, as the two of them passed the name plate of a particularly obscure publisher, 'if I went in now he'd give me an advance?' After Kingsmill's death in 1949, Methuen's accountants discovered numbers of agreements on the strength of which he had received money upfront but delivered nothing in return.

These conditions, and in particular the widespread availability of low-level journalism, offered considerable scope for freelances who knew what they were doing. A writer with talent and the right connections, prepared to exert him or herself in areas where fashionable pens disdained to linger, could soon establish the foundations of a reasonable income. Take, for example, the later career of the novelist and critic Ralph Straus (1882–1950). If Straus is remembered at all nearly seventy years after his death it is as a log-rolling book reviewer

– Orwell once declared that his name conjured up 'blurb' in much the same way as 'chicken' conjured up 'bread sauce' – but in his day he was an immensely powerful broker of reputations and all-purpose literary man. An accomplished wire-puller and friend of the famous – 'Straus seemed to know everyone' one of his memorialists recalled – he began in a small way, publishing biannual novels, contributing a weekly books page to the society magazine the *Bystander*, and supplementing the £800 a year that these activities brought in with a private income from the family business. Then, in the early 1920s, catastrophe struck, when his father had a fatal stroke and it was discovered that the capital had almost run dry. Straus, now in his 40s and accustomed to a fairly indolent lifestyle, was forced dramatically to reinvent himself. His first resort was the women's page of the *Daily Chronicle*, where, as 'Gertrude Belt', he dispensed sagacious advice to female readers. Meanwhile he increased his reviewing output by way of a column for the *Sunday Times*. Here, christened 'Uncle Ralph', on account of his cosy, avuncular style, he filed equally sagacious and infallibly upbeat summaries of the week's new novels. Younger friends were sometimes disposed to snigger – he once came down to breakfast in the course of a cricketing tour to discover half the team amusing themselves over a paragraph that began 'We women, and those of us with nephews and nieces' – but in general Straus's exploits, and his tenacity, were treated with respect.

However secure the average freelance existence in the interwar years – once, that is, the writer in question had obtained a foothold and provided he or she had the necessary staying power – conditions in the publishing industry were still far from encouraging. Book publishing, having boomed in the early post-war period, then went into sharp decline: the pronounced long-term effect of the 1930s slump can be seen in Hodder's diminishing turnover figures, which fell from £637,000 in the early 1930s to £380,000 in 1935 and as low as £289,000 in 1939. Yet the industry's problems went well beyond the general economic malaise. Douglas Jerrold's *Georgian Adventure* (1937) has some useful statistics from the 1930s balance sheet, whose effect is to demonstrate quite how difficult it was for a publisher, here in an era of high taxation and increased competition, to resist the pressure on his margins. Best-sellers excepted, it was the 'intermediate' author – sales between 2,000 to 3,000 copies but with occasional upward shifts – on whom the publisher traditionally made his money. But even here the process was fraught with danger. A novel by a relative unknown which achieved a sale of 5,000 copies might cost its backer £500 to publish and promote. The publisher's return would be just over £1,000. With a standard author's royalty of 15 per cent of published price, the writer would receive something over £850 and the gross profit to the publisher weighed in at £250. On the other hand, the publisher's net profit, Jerrold calculated, was no more than £20. As for the author, if he did other things as well as write fiction he could reckon on a profit of 75 per cent of his receipts. If he wrote full-time then, Jerrold argued, 'he has no business to be writing novels which sell 5,000 copies only occasionally – and only in England'. Only if he produced two a year, and sold his copyrights in the US, could he anticipate the £1,200 or so per annum which Jerrold regarded as an acceptable middle-class income.

In filing this jeremiad, Jerrold overlooks the fact that, historically, very few writers – certainly very few 'serious' writers – have ever been able to support themselves by fiction alone. The average advance for a first novel in the 1920s and 1930s ranged between £50 and £100. For certain specialised forms of non-fiction the figure was even lower. Empson, for example, pocketed £25 for the manuscript of *Seven Types of Ambiguity*. There were enterprising publishers prepared to take a risk on what they diagnosed as rising young talent, but sometimes these gestures could look merely quixotic. Graham Greene's first novel, *The Man Within*, published by Heinemann in 1929 for a £50 advance, on a royalty of 12½ per cent, sold a highly impressive 8,000 copies, after which Heinemann's Charles Evans offered his protégé £600 a year for three years (half to be supplied by his American publisher) for three more books. Greene promptly resigned from his subeditor's job on *The Times*, retired with his wife to a thatched cottage in Chipping Campden ('that pastoral Georgian dream of the industrial Twenties') and set to work. But *The Name of Action*, his second novel, sold barely a quarter of its predecessor's tally, and *Rumours of Nightfall*, his third, even fewer. It took the fluke of *Stamboul Train*'s selection by the Book Society in 1932, with a guaranteed sale of 10,000 copies, to rescue Greene's career.

What was much more common was for an apprentice writer to be offered tiny incremental advances. Patrick Hamilton, having sold his moderately successful first novel to Constable for £50 in 1925, was then offered a five-book contract worth £500. Orwell's 1930s novels generally brought him £100 each, but the advance for his collection *Inside the Whale and Other Essays* (1940) was only £40; shortly before its publication he had turned down an offer from the publishing house Nelson to write a book about poverty for £50. As for sales, it is instructive to discover quite how few copies some of the great works of twentieth-century English literature managed to ship in their early days. Orwell's *Down and Out in Paris and London* (1933) sold 3,000 copies in its UK edition and something under 1,500 in the US, while *Coming Up For Air* (1939), judged a 'modest popular success', made its author all of £140 less agent's commission. Anthony Powell's early novels, now regarded as high points of mid-period English modernism, stirred a similarly lukewarm response. Even Evelyn Waugh's *Vile Bodies* (1930), which reprinted eleven times in its year of publication, formed only a percentage of an income otherwise bulked out by journalism

The vast majority of interwar novelists found it hard to get by on books alone. How were they to make a living? A very few writers pursued lucrative side-lines, ripe to subsidise the production of more 'serious' work. Patrick Hamilton made his real income from two long-running stage plays, *Rope* (1929) and *Gaslight* (1938), whose proceeds enabled him to live comfortably for the rest of his life. Beverley Nichols, alternatively, was engaged, with varying degrees of success, by the impresario C. B. Cochran to work on his revues. When it came to part- or full-time employment, jobs on the fringes of the literary world predominated. Several writers spent time working in publishing itself: Swinnerton as an adviser to Chatto & Windus (on a salary of £550 a year); Anthony Powell as an editorial dogsbody at Duckworth (£300); Alec Waugh as a 'reader' for his father's firm, Chapman & Hall. But by far the most common resort of the literary freelance anxious to inflate his receipts was journalism. Here, as in book publishing, the rewards available varied enormously depending on the celebrity of the writer, the circulation of the newspaper or magazine in question and the nature of the material. At the very top of the ladder, prestige commissions for mass-circulation papers offered stratospheric rates of pay. The 3,000-word description of the coronation of King George VI contributed by Hugh Walpole to the *Daily Mail* in 1937 realised £150. Evelyn Waugh was reputed to receive thirty guineas per 1,000 words from the *Daily Express*: his freelance earnings from journalism in the

1930s were estimated at £2,500 a year. Far beneath these exalted redoubts, run-of-the-mill features generally fetched five guineas per 1,000 words A short story printed in an evening newspaper might make £4, rising to £8 in a specialist periodical solely devoted to short fiction such as the *Royal*.

Inevitably, straightforward 'literary' journalism such as book reviews and critical articles paid a great deal less than mass-market commissions, yet even here the rates varied prodigiously. The £3,000 a year Arnold Bennett received for his weekly page in the *Evening Standard* was unprecedented; Squire's £750 per annum for his column in the *Observer* was much nearer to the sum a well-known literary figure could expect for giving his opinion of a book in a weekly newspaper, although Squire once claimed that he was offered the same salary as Bennett to decamp to one of the *Observer*'s rivals. As a general rule, the more highbrow the paper the less it was able to dispense in contributors' fees. The *Criterion*'s standard rate – much haggled over – was £10 per 5,000 words, although the *Listener*, on its foundation in 1929, ran to as much as twelve guineas for 2,000. Even in its balmy days the *London Mercury* never offered more than £25 for a single piece, and there were embarrassing incidents, later on the in the 1920s, in which Squire was sued for underpayment. As for routine 600- to 700-word notices of novels and biographies, which made up the bulk of the average newspaper's books pages, these brought the reviewer between £2 and £3, rising to £5 if one were working for a well-established weekly such as the *Spectator*, falling to a fraction of this if the critic had been hired by a poorly funded political paper where the thought that contributors were writing 'for the cause' was used as an excuse to keep the rates low. The novelist Peter Vansittart was paid £1 for his first contribution to the left-wing weekly *Tribune*.

At the same time a whole new range of literary activities and markets had sprung into existence which Reardon and his friends had never had the opportunity to exploit. One of these was the intensely competitive world of the newspaper 'serial': a full-length story, in fifteen to twenty instalments, commissioned by a popular newspaper, usually at a fee of £300 to £400 and extensively advertised, which could then be worked up into a book. Another was the newly established BBC, which from the outset was keen to employ writers to deliver 'talks' and take part in topical discussions. A third was the burgeoning American market, usually envisaged by the aspiring novelist of the

1920s as a kind of greenback-strewn land of plenty with the potential, should all go well, to transform their life.

Generally speaking, the financial opportunities offered by the US to British writers took three forms. In exceptional circumstances the man or woman who stepped westward could be offered a full-time job: working in a university English department, for example, or editing a magazine. Beverley Nichols spent a miserable few months in the late 1920s running the American *Sketch*. Much more common was the transatlantic tour – now much more developed from the days when Dickens and Thackeray had tramped their way around the big-city lecture theatres – in which a well-known British novelist would spend two or three months working his way up and down the eastern seaboard with occasional excursions to the South and Midwest, speaking to literary societies and women's clubs, and taking the opportunity to negotiate lucrative deals with American publishers and magazine editors along the way. Walpole's visit of 1920 turned into a kind of triumphal progress, in which he delivered thirty-five lectures for fees ranging between $200 and $400. All in all, he reported to his mother, adding to his lecture fees the various commissions secured en route, he expected to make £8,000 from the trip.

A third source of income came not so much from forging alliances with American publishers – although these could be immensely rewarding if the resulting book became a best-seller – as in breaking into the vast transatlantic magazine market. If a short story sold to a British literary magazine fetched between £10 and £15, then one unloaded on an American periodical such as *College Humor* might attract a fee of $150 (£30). Further up the scale, *Redbook* paid $750 (£150) and was prepared to offer several thousand dollars for its 15,000-word novelettes. In the course of his 1920 tour, Walpole managed to negotiate the sale of ten stories to the *Pictorial Review* for the then stupendous fee of $1,350 per item. While there were sometimes technical difficulties involved – upmarket American magazines tended to favour a particular kind of plot line, often about US tourists searching for Old World sophistication amongst the European tourist sites – a British writer who cracked the procedural code could expect to earn substantial sums of money.

And all this is to ignore perhaps the greatest transatlantic El Dorado of all: Hollywood. Not only were film companies, through their London representatives, prepared to pay huge amounts for the rights to best-selling books, they were also anxious to employ celebrated authors to adapt literature for the screen. But while film money could sometimes be acquired with almost absurd ease – Ralph Straus once received £700 for a film for a novel entitled *Married Alive*, merely so that the studio could capitalise on its arresting title – the experience of working in Hollywood itself was much more problematic. The practice of importing British literary celebrities to work on film scripts, pioneered by Paramount in the years after the Great War, was rarely successful: the new medium was too much of a departure, and even successful dramatists found themselves unable to refine their techniques. Somerset Maugham, bidden to Burbank in 1920 on the assumption that he would be commissioned to produce a series of storylines, ended up being paid $50,000 for a script that was never used. Although the money was gratefully received, Maugham disliked having to work with 'the obscene Cecil' (his name for Cecil B. DeMille) and later declared that he 'looked back on my connection with the cinema with horror'.

Walpole, who arrived in California in 1935, experienced similar frustrations. The original idea had been that he would work on *Kim* and *Oliver Twist*, but by the time he reached Hollywood the studio had switched its attention to Mark Twain's *The Prince and the Pauper*. Two months later, after several false starts on a variety of miscellaneous projects, he calculated that he had been paid £2,000 for doing nothing. But at least Walpole was a celebrated figure who could command high fees whether he worked or idled. At the lower end of the scale the prospects could be much less enticing. Anthony Powell, who arrived in California two years later hoping to break into screenwriting on the strength of an apprenticeship spent devising 'quota quickies' at the Teddington studios, found each offer of his services flatly refused.

Statistic-mongering never quite conveys the reality of the literary life, or the vagrant impulses – sometimes decidedly vagrant – that lie at its heart: it is recorded that as an 80-year-old, with half a century in the trade behind him, Professor Saintsbury's fingers still twitched in anticipation as he bent over the latest parcel of books sent in for review. To get an indication of what the specimen literary existence was like *as lived* it is necessary to examine the careers of individual writers. Outwardly, nothing could be more distinct than the early careers of Walter Allen (1911–83) or Alec Waugh (1898–1981). The former was a self-made provincial; the latter a middle-class publisher's son for whom the picking up of a pen was simply to join the family trade. And yet taken together there are odd points of contact, in terms of both aspiration and professional horizons, above all the hint that some kind of harmonising process was at work: a set of influences and assumptions to which practically all writers of the interwar period were susceptible.

Allen, in particular, is a thoroughly representative example of the new breed of literary men thrown up by the 1930s – of relatively humble origins (his father was a silversmith's engraver from Birmingham) but keen to take advantage of the educational opportunities now available to the upwardly mobile working class. Not that Allen's motivation was any less romantic than that of the Victorian journalist lured into the profession by repeated readings of Thackeray's *Pendennis*: his imagination was gripped by the classics in his early teens, and he was soon contributing causeries to *John O' London's* and *T. P.'s Weekly* under such headings as 'Autumn in the Poets'. A grammar-school boy, sensitive to the mockery that went with his free place, his first literary hero was Shaw, but the decisive influence on his development came from Arnold Bennett. D. H. Lawrence, his first 'unaided' discovery, produced exactly the same sense of fellow feeling, a view of the world expressly calculated to appeal to 'a working-class boy with no advantage but his talents'. Fifty years before, the talent might have gone unrecognised or been led down uncongenial paths, but as Allen's memoirs make clear, if certain doors were closed to provincial newcomers, then others were newly ajar. Poems written in the approved Eliot manner and sent to the *Criterion* were returned without comment, but there was a certain amount of mild encouragement from Middleton Murry at the *Adelphi*, and in 1932, fresh from an English degree at Birmingham University, he set up as a freelance, writing sketches and essays for the *Birmingham Post* and broadcasting his short stories on the BBC Midlands Region. Allen estimated his weekly income at this time at around £4 – by no means a fortune, but well above the average income of the West Midlands labouring class.

The real interest of Allen's early career, on the other hand, lies less in his social origins than in the discovery that he was involved in a bona fide provincial literary culture, with its own distinctive networks and conventions. His friends at this time included Auden (whose wedding he attended) and John Hampson, author of *Saturday Night at the Greyhound*. It was E. J. O'Brien, editor of *English Story*, who had the bright idea of christening Allen and Hampson, together with Peter Chamberlain and Leslie Halward, the 'Birmingham Group' – a loosely knit gathering, perhaps, but a genuine confraternity in a way that one or two self-proclaimed literary alliances of the later 1930s were demonstrably not. While provincialism in these days was uncomfortably associated in the public mind with the parochialism of Scottish kailyards and folk poetry, Allen at least was always looking to expand his horizons: in the mid-1930s, when work was scarce, he contrived to secure a post as a visiting lecturer at the University of Iowa. A first novel, accepted at the tenth time of asking by Michael Joseph, brought him to London where he secured lodgings at fifteen shillings a week, largely funded by a *Daily Telegraph* column entitled 'A Hundred Little Homes'. The novel sold a mere 420 copies and he was reduced to reading manuscripts for the UK arm of MGM, 'about the lowest form of life in literary London'. His weekly earnings from all sources at this point amounted to £3 10s – less than he could have got from working in an office – but enough of an incentive to keep his mind fixed on a career that would last for the next four and a half decades.

If anything distinguished the 'born man of letters', Alec Waugh suggested in one of his garrulous volumes of autobiography, it was his 'immense resilience'. The description would fit Walter Allen, but it is even more applicable to Waugh himself: a consummate literary freelance whose six decades of adult life were supported entirely by his pen. Unlike Allen, Waugh began with the built-in advantage of a family connection. At the same time, he was honest enough to admit that his was a modest talent ('I have no illusions about the quality of my work. I know myself to be a very minor writer') which would need constant recalibration to suit the commercial demands of the age. His early career, consequently, is a kind of masterclass in writerly opportunism, built on a determination to find out what the public wanted, colonise new markets and find niches which only he, or a very few people like him, could fill. It was also one burdened with a substantial handicap, in the shape of a much more successful younger brother, whose resentment of his sibling dated back to nursery days, and who was not above seeding his author biographies with references to his kinship with 'the popular novelist Alec Waugh', in feline disparagement of Alec's potboiling trifles.

But forward planning and an eye for the market could only take one so far. Much of Waugh's early success was founded on the lucky break, in his having produced something which, however transitorily, caught the public's mood and enabled him to advance to the next rung of the literary ladder. *The Loom of Youth*, written at the age of 17 and published shortly before he left for Flanders as a junior officer in the Machine Gun Corps, appeared in the summer of 1917, at a time when the Great War was bogged down in stalemate. A lightly disguised account of Waugh's formative years at Sherborne, its criticisms of the educational methods used to train up the nation's officer class guaranteed an appreciative audience. Wells and Bennett approved, the latter writing to Waugh's father, Arthur, to assure him that it was a 'staggering performance'. *The Loom of Youth* did not make its teenage author a great deal of money – Waugh calculated his lifetime earnings from it at something over £1,100 – but it set him up as a writer in a world where, as he remembered, 'it was not difficult to pick up four or five pounds a week with journalism, and five pounds went a long way in 1920'. In his early 20s, already married to his childhood sweetheart and holding down a part-time job in Arthur's office, his literary earnings amounted to £400 a year. On the other hand, this kind of momentum was difficult to keep up. Books descended on to his publisher Grant Richards' desk at the rate of one or two or a year – two more novels, a book of short stories, an account of his experiences as a prisoner of war – but none of them sold more than 2,500 copies, and he worried that his friends would write him off as that fatal literary casualty, the 'one-book man'.

Then, in 1925, his fourth novel, *Kept*, became a modest best-seller. An account of a disillusioned set of youngish men and women bent on squandering the moral and financial capital they had accumulated in the pre-1914 era, this, too, chimed with the reading public. Its relative success – 6,000 copies sold – enabled Waugh to strike out in unexpected directions. He spent the next four years travelling the world, going wherever the fancy took him but always keeping one eye firmly fixed on the United States. Part of Waugh's fascination with America was straightforwardly romantic – he had fallen in love with an American woman – but as least as much of it was to do with an awareness of commercial possibilities. He admitted, he 'thought of America as a country that would rain showers of gold on me, through its book clubs, its magazines, its lecture tours, through Hollywood . . . I saw it as a market.'

In fact the showers of gold would have to wait another quarter of a century. In the interim Waugh had to make do with the royalties for *Hot Countries* (1930), a West Indian travelogue, which was taken by the US Literary Guild. Back in England in 1931, living in a four-room flat in Chelsea (annual rent £225) he put his income at £1,600, consisting of £600 advances for his novels ($1,000 in the US), short stories at £30 or £40 a piece for *Nash's Magazine* and *Harper's Bazaar*, and journalism at £10 to £15 per article. A US lecture tour under the auspices of the well-known agent Colston Leigh for an advance of $1,000 narrowly broke even. Meanwhile, as the 1930s wore on, Waugh had begun to differentiate himself from the circle of English and predominantly Georgian writers in which he had grown up, becoming more cosmopolitan, less constrained by the conditions that had formed him. While he continued to write long, cradle-to-grave 'English' novels, and made a half-hearted attempt to embrace domestic routines in a house on the Hampshire/Berkshire borders purchased by his wealthy second wife, his career was galvanised by the American agent Carol Hill, who encouraged him to break into the US 'glossy' market. Benefiting from Hill's expert tutelage, and assured that he was 'bilingual as regards America', he was taken up by magazines such as *Redbook* and *This Week*, which paid $750 a story. A *Redbook* novelette brought in $1,500. His instructions from his commissioning editors were to 'give us something our own writers can't'. Waugh obliged with such topical items as 'It Happened in 1936', in which a disaffected American couple on holiday in London are reconciled by means of a new mode of transport: the wife makes a solitary transatlantic crossing by boat, only to be beaten to the dockside by her reconciliation-bent husband, who has reserved a berth on the *Hindenberg* airship.

Was this an effective way of conducting a literary career? In the intervals of congratulating himself on his newfound transatlantic success, Waugh had already begun to worry about the precariousness of his income. One disadvantage of concentrating on the US magazine market was its volatility – what suited one editor might not suit the next – and another lay in Waugh's engrained habit of inserting material from his short stories into his full-length novels. Waugh himself was unhappy with *Going Their Own Ways* (1938), a study of 'the marriage question', which exemplified some of the pitfalls of this technique. Reaching his fortieth birthday in 1938, he was conscious that professionally he was at a low ebb. Sitting in a public library in the West Indies, he came upon an almanac which contained a discussion of the year's literature: the references to himself were unflattering. His younger brother Evelyn, on the other hand, had just published the highly successful *Scoop*. By his own account, Waugh wondered whether this might not be a good time to give up the life of literature altogether, go back to England and his – or rather his wife's – fine Queen Anne house and become 'a full-time village squire'.

PART TWO

Citadels of Power

CHAPTER 7

University English I

We never quarrelled with anyone.

Q. D. Leavis, interviewed late in life, by the *Cambridge Evening News*

That is what Henry James says about the novels of Arnold Bennett, and I think you will agree, Greenham, that it is final.

F. R. Leavis to the artist painting his portrait, 1962

Although neither man would perhaps have thought the accolade worth having, the two most influential academics involved in the teaching of English literature in British universities in 1918 were Sir Walter Raleigh (1861–1922) and Sir Arthur Quiller-Couch (1863–1944), respectively Merton Professor at the University of Oxford and King Edward VII Professor at Cambridge. By the standards of the early twenty-first century – the standards of the early twentieth century, if it comes to that – neither was at all a conventional literary don. Raleigh, who took up his post in 1907, had come to Oxford via a circuitous route that included stints at Liverpool, Glasgow and the Mohammedan Anglo-Oriental College, Aligarh, and published very little once he arrived there. 'Q', as Quiller-Couch was invariably known, was a political appointment, urged on Asquith by his henchman Lloyd George, whose knighthood was a reward for services to the Liberal Party rather than for the popular novels and journalism by which he was known to the general public. The suspicion that he was, in some sense, an impostor hung over his early days in the job, and the introduction to the published version of the Clark Lectures delivered in the year after his appointment talks modestly about their contents 'bewraying a man called unexpectedly to a post where in the act of adapting himself, of learning that he might teach, he had often to adjourn his main purpose and skirmish with difficulties'. Not the least of Q's achievements, it might be said, was the air of self-deprecation he brought to a professional calling in which half a dozen titanic egos were already beginning to contend.

Raleigh and Quiller-Couch were, in their separate ways, provisional critics at work in a discipline whose ground rules were largely being made up as they went along – posterity might think the title of one of Q's early collections, *Adventures in Criticism*, all too apt – and the institutional foundations on which they were building were positively inchoate. Oxford had boasted a professor of Anglo-Saxon since the late eighteenth century, but the Merton Professorship had been established as recently as 1885, and the whole tenor of 'Oxford English' was determinedly philological. Cambridge English, too, was a recent creation, dominated by linguists, strongly opposed to the study of modern texts, offering a one-part English tripos in two sections and an official teaching complement of exactly three staff: Q, the professor of Anglo-Saxon and a solitary lecturer, the medieval historian G. C. Coulton. Doctorates had been available since 1883, in consideration of previously published work, but the PhD was not introduced until 1919 and learning resources were pitifully sparse: many of the books in the original faculty library were donations from the master of Magdalene, A. C. Benson. The impression that English literature was there on sufferance, clinging parasitically to the skirts of more sober disciplines, was reinforced by the lack of specialisation. Until 1923 no lecturer destined to achieve a permanent appointment had so much as studied English as a first degree. These conditions persisted deep into the interwar era. I. A. Richards, for example, began his academic life as a social scientist and William Empson completed Part II of the mathematics tripos before jumping ship.

The resistance offered up by Oxford and Cambridge to the idea of teaching 'modern' literature – a category that sometimes extended to anything written since the late Renaissance – is entertainingly outlined in Stephen Potter's *The Muse in Chains*. The principal objection was not only that the books studied, and the way in which they were approached, were likely to be trivial ('chatter about Shelley' as one late nineteenth-century eminence put it) but that the ground set out had already been covered. English literature, according to the orthodoxies of the Cambridge combination rooms, was something that an educated gentleman picked up in his spare time: the undergraduate simply acquired a working knowledge of Milton and Dryden in the same way that he acquired an evening suit. As to what the electors to Oxbridge chairs required of their professors, their published works clung firmly to the tradition of the late Victorian belles-lettrist. Q's *On the Art of Writing* (1916), those Clark lectures duly repackaged by the Cambridge University Press, addresses such topics as 'Jargon', 'The Difference between Verse and Prose' and 'Style', the advice given always benefiting from the lecturer's long apprenticeship in Grub Street. There are worse things, after all, than to be told by a professor of English literature that one should almost always prefer the concrete word to the abstract, almost always prefer the direct word to the circumlocution, and generally use transitive verbs that strike their object and use them in the active voice: Orwell, one feels, would have approved. There is a whiff of contemporaneity, too, in that the incidental references take in not merely Alcuin, Belisarius and *Beowulf*, but Mr Robert Bridges, Mr Gilbert Chesterton and Mr Frank Harris. By contrast Raleigh's *Some Authors* (1923), published posthumously in the year after his death, but assembled in accordance with his wishes, goes no further than Matthew Arnold, and you sense that Raleigh's sympathies are more actively engaged by a rereading of *Don Quixote* or his eighty-page reassessment of Sir Thomas Hoby, the Renaissance translator.

While Q and Raleigh were essentially gentleman critics, modestly at large in a world where the gentleman critic – at any rate one employed by a university – would shortly become extinct, their impact on the world around them was not altogether to be disregarded. If nothing else, Q's three versions of the *Oxford Book of English Verse* left an indelible stamp on the taste of the mainstream poetry-reading public, as profound in its way as that of Palgrave a generation or two before. Each, from his separate vantage point, was conscious that change was in the air, that new kinds of critical approaches were starting to make their presence felt, of a kind that university English departments could not very well neglect. Q, in particular, was responsible for introducing the two-part tripos, so that the undergraduate of the 1920s could at least study English for the whole of his, or her, degree. His aim, as he candidly admitted, was to encourage his pupils to put the information they had acquired to practical use, to send a generation of graduates out into the literary weeklies, and nothing gave him greater pleasure than to be able to declare, once the faculty reforms had got going in the 1920s, that 'already the work of several of our few first-class men – creative criticism especially – is being eagerly taken by London editors'. The stance taken by those Cantabrians who regarded 'London editors' as the great corrupting influence on the maintenance of literary standards would have puzzled him: literature, as far as he was concerned, was an endless frieze rather than a series of tightly demarcated compartments, and Hardy was just as capable of proving a technical point as Heine. He was, additionally, a talent-spotter, who encouraged Mansfield Forbes and Richards to turn his dreams for the development of the English faculty into reality, and even gave his backing to Leavis, of whom he later remarked: 'I would take a lot of trouble to get Leavis better placed, thankless as that trouble . . . would be, since no good fortune would easily equal his sense of his deserts.' Raleigh, too, bequeathed an impressive legacy both to the pupils who attended his lectures and to the undergraduates of a later generation who picked up on the provocative remarks with which his books are sprinkled. John Carey remembered being inspired to read Milton by an essay in which Raleigh declared that had the author of *Paradise Lost* been present in the Garden of Eden he would have eaten the apple and then written a pamphlet justifying his actions.

If Raleigh's unexpected death – of a fever contracted on a visit to Baghdad in his capacity as the official historian of the RAF – is especially to be regretted, it is because of its timing: precisely at the moment when Oxford was standing by to repel the modernisers. Raleigh, you suspect, would have been less keen on conciliating the language specialists than his successor George Gordon, author of *Medium Aevum and the Middle Age* (1925). As it was, C. S. Lewis, appointed a fellow of Magdalen in 1925, and J. R. R. Tolkien, installed as professor of Anglo-Saxon in the same year, though not unopposed, had the upper hand in a long-running faculty quarrel about the curriculum that ended in 1931 when – largely thanks to Lewis's part in the campaign – the study of Victorian literature was more or less abandoned. In strict historical terms this was not a new disagreement – its origins went back to the very beginnings of Oxford English in the 1880s – but in Tolkien, who as Lewis noted on their first meeting 'thinks the language is the real thing in the school', the advocates of post-Chaucerian literature encountered an immensely sophisticated opponent.

To categorise the author of *The Lord of the Rings* as an out-and-out reactionary in these debates, bent on promoting the dead at the expense of the living, is, strictly speaking, inaccurate. On the one hand, very few linguistic conservatives would have gone quite so far as to think *The Faerie Queen* unreadable and Shakespeare overrated. On the other, there was an undeniable logic to his stance. As scholars of language, much exercised by the problems of variant readings, the Early English specialists' principal complaint about Dickens was that no definitive texts of his work were available. Once the experts had collated the existing manuscripts, and weighed up the evidence of authorial interventions and editorial interference, then it might just be possible to study *Bleak House* in the same way as the *Finnsburg Fragment*, but until that time . . . Working from this template, and with Lewis squarely behind him, Tolkien decided to press for a remodelled syllabus in which undergraduates would be expected to read widely in Early English, while early and medieval specialists could pursue their chosen areas of enquiry without having to touch the 'modern' side. In practice this meant compressing the list of set books rather than extending them. Something, clearly, would have to go. In an article written for the *Oxford Magazine*, Tolkien recommended 'jettisoning certainly the nineteenth century' (unless parts could appear as an 'additional subject') and proposing the course that was in the end more or less adopted: that compulsory papers should stop at 1830.

It was not that studies of nineteenth-century literature wholly disappeared from Oxford English: Humphry House's *The Dickens World* (1941) is a pioneering study of Dickens's relation to some of the social currents of his time, and House was in at the foundation of the great Pilgrim edition of the novelist's works, completed long after his own death. But the consequences of the Tolkien–Lewis putsch were still being felt in Oxford English three decades later. Almost to a man – and woman – the generations of undergraduates who studied the subject in the 1940s and 1950s rose up to complain about a series of proscriptions and limitations that seemed to obscure the attractions of English as a degree course to all but the most committed specialist. John Carey, who was to acquire the Merton Professorship himself in the 1970s, recalled that the syllabus was 'a scandal or a joke, depending on your sense of humour'. Kingsley Amis, who arrived at St John's College, Oxford in 1941, left a bitter account of his forays into 'the almost-universally disliked area that included philology, the structure and history of the language, and the literature of the period roughly up to the death of Chaucer in 1400'. Just writing those phrases, Amis decided – they can be found in the Oxford chapter of his *Memoirs* (1991) – the bare thought of when Chaucer died, or that he lived at all, brought him 'a strong whiff of the depression the thing itself regularly brought me'. In much the same way the opening stretch of John Fowles's novel *Daniel Martin* (1977), an authentic portrait of undergraduate life in the Oxford of the late 1940s, finds its hero contemplating a bookcase full of texts, including 'the abominable *Beowulf* and a number of other ancient printed instruments of torture', together with a cartoon of Tolkien being trampled underfoot by a Stakhanovite bear carrying a lettered banner with the runic proclamation 'Down with Anglo-Saxon'.

The worst thing about these attitudes, perhaps, is that they were exportable, and that provincial university English departments, built on the Oxford model and frequently staffed by Oxford refugees, rushed to adopt them as their own. Walter Allen, enrolling at the University of Birmingham in 1929, discovered that he had fetched up in a teaching environment where Tolkien and Lewis would have felt very much at home – Old and Middle English 'turned into a philological grind', the novel barely respectable and seeming to stop with Fielding and Austen, the nineteenth-century paper dominated by Carlyle and Ruskin. Birmingham English did go on until 1890, and there was space for such dangerous moderns as Robert Bridges, but the faculty head, the redoubtable Professor Ernest de Selincourt (1870– 1943), then doubling up as Oxford Professor of Poetry, was famous for his disapproval of all contemporary writers. Allen left a devastating sketch of his lecture-hall manner: 'Mr (*sniff*) Aldous (*sniff*) Huxley says . . . Mr (*sniff*) T. (*sniff*) S. (*sniff*) Eliot (*sniff*) whom some of you young gentlemen profess to understand and admire'. If all this makes de Selincourt sound like J. C. Squire in an MA gown, then it should be pointed out that his scholarly credentials were impeccable – among other distinctions, he had discovered and edited the 1805 edition of *The Prelude* – but to a 20-year-old who had read Auden and could feel the new critical winds sweeping in across the fens from Cambridge, he seemed the worst kind of academic obfuscator. There is an apocryphal story of William Empson, invited to meet de Selincourt in the early 1930s to discuss a possible job opportunity, blowing his chances by remarking that he had just read the most wonderful book, Malinowski's *The Sexual Life of Savages*. Significantly, such encouragement as Allen received as an undergraduate came from E. R. Dodds, the professor of Greek – an Auden fan, who was responsible for getting 'Paid on Both Sides' printed in the *Criterion* – and Louis MacNeice, who joined the Classics department in 1930.

While the 1930s-era Tolkien was a profoundly influential figure, his impact was almost entirely confined to university teaching: from the angle of the literary public he was merely an obscure philologist, whose solitary children's book *The Hobbit* (1937) looked like an almost quintessential don's vagary. In Lewis, on the other hand, Oxford English possessed its most redoubtable ornament: a man who by dint of his taste for controversy and his introduction to the medium of radio talks had by the early 1940s turned into one of the most conspicuous public intellectuals of the age. At the same time, none of Lewis's personae – Lewis the doughty controversialist, Lewis the spiritual guide, Lewis the scourge of the modern movement – came *sui generis*, and Tolkien's impact on the positions he was eventually to occupy should never be discounted. One might note, in particular, the famous three-way conversation of September 1931 between Tolkien, Lewis and their mutual friend Hugo Dyson on the nature of myth. To Lewis a myth was self-evidently a lie, and therefore worthless, 'even though breathed through silver'. Tolkien disagreed. To ancient, pre-rational man the world was alive with mythological beings and the stars were living silver. Man is not ultimately a liar. He may pervert his thoughts into lies, but he comes from God, and it is from this source that he draws his ideals: his imaginative inventions, consequently, must originate from God and must, logically, reflect something of eternal truth. The storyteller, according to this interpretation, is not an autonomous inventor but a 'sub-creator'. This revelation was not only a giant step in Lewis's route march towards Christianity, but it also laid the foundation of his aesthetic theories, the idea – treated more elaborately in Tolkien's British Academy lecture on fairy stories – that the creative artist, whatever the results of his imaginative output, is merely reflecting the image of God.

The secular critic who stumbles across this view of literature very often tries to distinguish Lewis's undoubted critical acumen from his apologetics, to argue that Lewis's scholarly observations can, in certain circumstances, be detached from the ideological purpose that lies behind them. But this is to miss the point. Like one or two critic-theologians of the previous century – R. H. Hutton is an obvious comparison – Lewis's view of life itself, let alone the literature that reflects it, is determinedly theocentric. *The Pilgrim's Regress* (1933), after all, is an attack on modernism written to prove a spiritual truth. Lewis's hero fetches up in the realm of the 'Clevers', allegorical figures intended to represent the worst excesses of the 1920s (a later edition added running headlines identifying the various members as 'The Poetry of the Silly Twenties', 'The swamp-literature of the Dirty Twenties' and 'the gibberish-literature of the Lunatic Twenties'). Later, he finds sheltering in a hut three pale, ascetic men: 'Humanist', 'Neoclassicist' and 'Neo-Angular'. Here the connection between intellectual faddishness and what, to Lewis at any rate, seemed suspiciously emotion-free forms of modern religious belief becomes explicit. As he put it, when asked to explain some of his symbolism, 'What I am attacking in Neo-Angular is a set of people who seem to me to be trying to make of Christianity itself one more highbrow, Chelsea, bourgeois-baiting fad. T. S. Eliot is the single man who sums up the things I am fighting against.'

Unlike Tolkien, who greatly resented allegorical interpretations of *The Lord of the Rings*, Lewis was always a keen student of the figurative: his great 1930s success, *The Allegory of Love* (1936), was a scholarly study of the allegorical love poetry of the Middle Ages. And yet the really curious aspect of his critical writings from the 1930s is not so much their deeply reactionary tone – there were plenty of reactionaries doing the rounds of the literary weeklies – as the way in which the attempts to find an explanation in God nearly always contain a hint that much more tangible evidence may lie in Lewis himself. Take, for example, his resistance to the idea that a writer's personality may be deduced from his, or her, work. To Lewis this was at best pseudo-biography and at worst psychological muckraking, and the Cambridge scholar E. M. W. Tillyard's claim that *Paradise Lost* is 'really about the true state of Milton's mind when he wrote it' produced a devastating polemic in which Lewis declares that 'A poet does what no one else can do: what, perhaps, no other poet can do; but he does not express his personality.' There is respectable critical precedent for this idea, not least in the highly ironic connection to the Eliot of 'Tradition and the Individual Talent', but the student of Lewis the man, as opposed to Lewis the critic, might be entitled to wonder whether it doesn't have its origins in his own subterranean life. Lewis's biographers tend to emphasise his emotional shyness, his buttoned-up character, his deliberate lack of interest in the things that made him tick, diagnosing a reluctance on the subject's part to probe too deeply into his psyche for fear of disturbing what lay beneath. Undoubtedly some of this reserve leached into his manner as a writer and led him, in words that seem to rely for their effect on transparency and directness, into what is sometimes only concealment and artifice. His friend Owen Barfield noted that his rejoinder to Tillyard's reply in the Milton row ('An Open Letter to Dr Tillyard') was, when viewed by certain lights, really only a kind of pastiche. There is a rather revealing moment, for example, in which Lewis attacks the tendency of modern criticism to exalt poets just as it disparages what he calls 'common things and common men'. Modern verse, he continues, communicates a boredom and a nausea that has little place in 'the life of the corrected and full-grown man'. This, too, sounds uncomfortably like Lewis borrowing from elsewhere – from Squire, say, unleashing one of his thunderbolts at the excesses of *vers libre*, while his subsequent debunking of the notion of the poet's bravery ('What meditation on human fate demands so much "courage" as the act of stepping into a cold bath?') looks, as Humphrey Carpenter remarks in his book about Lewis's circle, uncannily like something out of Chesterton.

By the 1939 essay 'Christianity and Literature', Lewis had developed a full-blown Christian aesthetic. To assume that a poet's personality mattered in any consideration of his poems is the view held by a 'half-hearted materialist'. The modern critic fails to realise that if the materialist view of the universe is true, then 'personality' is as meaningless as anything else. The buzzwords of modern criticism – *creative*, *spontaneity* and *freedom* – are contrasted with their opposites – *derivative*, *convention* and *rules*. Leavis, as the heir to a tradition of 'educated infidelity', is damned for basing his position on subjective judgements. 'Unless we return to the crude and nursery-like belief in objective values we perish' Lewis trumpeted, a slogan whose effectiveness as a rallying cry is rather undermined by an awareness of just how very far from crude and un-nursery-like some of Lewis's own critical judgements could be. Not all of Lewis's polemics were hatched entirely on his own. Many of them were cooked up, or at any rate first ventilated, in the congenial company of the discussion group whose members, including Tolkien and Dyson (who succeeded to Gordon's Merton

Professorship) met in Lewis's rooms in Magdalen. Although the posthumous celebrity acquired by the 'Inklings', as this loose association of dons and their acolytes came to be known, is largely a consequence of the late twentieth-century Tolkien cult, this isn't to disparage their influence. On the other hand, the idea that they were a fully fledged literary movement rather than a small group of friends bent on prosecuting each other's interests is overstating the case. Even to file them under the convenient label of 'Oxford Christians' ignores profound differences in religious affiliation: Tolkien was a cradle Catholic; Lewis an Ulster Protestant. As academics, too, their interests wildly diverged, and the only shared professional viewpoint they could really muster was an abhorrence of modernism. While there was a certain amount of mild conspiring when it came to the promotion of published work – Lewis's enthusiasm for *The Fellowship of the Ring* (1954) was such that he managed both to supply a jacket endorsement and to review it for *Time and Tide* – the only serious piece of fixing the group was able to bring off was the election of the manifestly unsuitable Canon Adam Fox, author of a narrative poem in light verse entitled *Old King Coel*, to the Oxford Professorship of Poetry. Tolkien called the escapade 'our first public victory over established privilege', but this suggests a degree of organisational zeal that the Inklings never possessed. And if it came to that, Tolkien, Lewis and newer members such as Lord David Cecil were the beneficiaries of a fair amount of established privilege themselves.

In any case, by the mid-1940s the Inklings were beginning to fall apart. Lewis's role as a public apologist for Christianity was never one for which Tolkien felt much sympathy (he once rather cattily referred to his friend as 'Everyman's theologian'). But what really undermined the group was the introduction of Charles Williams to its meetings at the start of the Second World War. An all-purpose literary man who worked at the Oxford University Press's London office, a religious thinker whose vaguely supernatural novels were admired by Eliot, the author of a sub-Arthurian epic, *Taliessin through Logres*, Williams lacked only one quality demanded of an Inkling, and that was the regard of the association's joint senior partner. As it was, Tolkien remained wholly unsympathetic to Williams's mind. Over and above this impediment, there was a suspicion that the Tolkien–Lewis alliance was coming to the end of its natural life, that each had begun to pursue separate paths and interests: Lewis meditating his highly successful Narnia series (which Tolkien disliked); Tolkien embarked on *The Lord of the Rings*. Meanwhile, in terms of the university where he had now spent thirty years of his life, Lewis was a disappointed man. His failure to attain the Merton chair and his defeat in the 1951 Professorship of Poetry election at the hands of Cecil Day Lewis rankled: in 1954 he accepted the newly established Cambridge Professorship of Medieval and Renaissance Literature. Anyone expecting pyrotechnics from this translation to the enemy camp was to be gravely disappointed. By this stage the fire had burned out, and many of the antagonisms of the interwar era no longer seemed worth pursuing. Even the Sage of Downing, of whom Lewis had once remarked 'Leavis demands moral earnestness. I prefer morality', turned out to be 'quiet, charming and kindly'.

The irony of his transfer to Cambridge – not that much of a remove, as he still lived in Oxford and lost no opportunity of making the fifty-mile journey back – would not, one feels, have been lost on Lewis. After nearly three decades spent sniping from afar at this source of moral contamination he would now be able to observe it at first hand. But Lewis, during his long years at Magdalen, would have been darkly conscious that the real action was going on elsewhere, that compared to the hubbub emanating from Downing College – and other places – Oxford lay sunk in well-nigh medieval torpor. The distinguishing mark of Cambridge English was how rapidly it began to emerge as an institution: a process accelerated not merely by the increase in undergraduates and tutorial posts and an almost unheard-of interdisciplinary focus, but by its deliberate engagement with the wider literary world. The university-sponsored Clark Lectures of the 1920s, delivered by such fixtures of the London literary scene as Murry, Eliot, Forster and Desmond MacCarthy, became a recognised highlight of the intellectual calendar. A Literary Club made way for an English Club, and there was a surge in the number of student periodicals. And together with these structural developments came the first glimpse of what it would be overstating the case to call a collective sensibility, but was at the very least an indication that several first-class Cambridge minds were beginning to focus on the same kind of subject. Forster's Clark Lectures, whose material was later worked up into *Aspects of the Novel* (1927), went down particularly badly with an up-and-coming Cambridge literati bent on a more rigorous approach to literature. Leavis declared himself 'astonished' at their intellectual nullity and thought it a 'nuisance' that all the girls' schoolmistresses in England would now seize on Forster's distinction between 'flat' and 'round' characters. Empson, reviewing the book for *Granta*, lamented the 'commonplace limitations' of Forster's analysis, while offering a substantial foreshadowing of his own subsequent development as a critic: 'An attempt, successful or not, to include all possible attitudes, to turn upon a given situation every tool, however irrelevant or disconnected, of the contemporary mind, would be far too strenuous and metaphysical an exertion.'

Leavis's and Empson's strictures serve to emphasise the rather ambiguous relation in which 'Cambridge English' stood to smart metropolitan literary circles. On the one hand, the visit of a genuine literary celebrity whose principles one could respect would have members of the faculty out in force. When Eliot gave the 1926 Clark Lectures, Empson remarked that he felt 'like most other verse writers of my generation, that I do not know how much of my own mind I invented'. At the same time admiration for Eliot tended to be confined to younger dons and undergraduates. From the other side of the generation gap F. L. Lucas, an ex-classicist turned English don, reviewing *Essays for Lancelot Andrewes* anonymously in the *New Statesman*, could be found patronising 'a pleasant little volume by a man who is evidently fond of reading, generally reads with intelligence and always expresses his opinions with fire and lucidity'. And while certain members of the faculty had connections with the world of literary London, the Oxford belles-lettrist tradition – which could allow George Gordon to double up as chairman of the selection committee of the Book Society or Lord David Cecil rapidly to establish himself as a weekly reviewer – had only a limited take-up in Cambridge. Empson's brief foray into smart literary circles came after he was sacked from his college job, while Leavis's distrust of coteries, of judgements about literature founded on essentially social grounds made by young men who had known each other at Eton, was an animating force behind practically everything that he wrote.

The real progenitor of the Cambridge approach to literature, here in the mid-1920s, was I. A. Richards, whose *Principles of Literary Criticism* (1924) and *Science and Poetry* (1926) brought an almost fathomless degree of intellectual rigour to a medium – the criticism of poetry – that had previously got by on instinct and form. Richards, by his own admission, had two ends in view: 'first to supplant the easy-going and vaguely laudatory criticism that was still largely the vogue by something more rigorous, and secondly to apply the science of psychology to the processes of making and enjoying literature'. Achieving the second meant devising a formula that owed more to science than to metrical analysis: the Richards 'theory of value' rested on what he called 'the effort to obtain maximum satisfaction through coherent systematisation of the impulses'. Positive impulses were christened 'appetencies', and anything that worked to satisfy them must be regarded as good or valuable. All this – essentially the idea that literary criticism is ultimately a subsidiary branch of psychology – involved some very large claims, even more so when rival critics came to appreciate some of its implications for such casualties of the theory of value as organised religion. But even literary conservatives tended to approve of Richards' distinction between the language employed to define scientific absolutes and the 'pseudo-statement' of poetry, which although it cannot be proved is 'not necessarily false'. Eliot accepted that the theory was probably true, but only partly so. This was merely a psychological theory of value, whereas what we needed to complement it was a moral theory of value. The two were incompatible, but both needed to be held. 'If I believe, as I do believe, that the chief distinction of man is to glorify God and enjoy him for ever, Mr Richards' theory of value is inadequate: my advantage is that I can believe my own and his too, whereas he is limited to his own.'

Debates of this kind were perhaps of less interest to the Cambridge audiences than the sight of Richards in uninhibited lecture-hall flow. Christopher Isherwood, then an undergraduate at Corpus Christi College, remembered 'this pale, mild, muscular, curly-headed young man' with his 'plaintive, baa-lamb voice' announcing that it was quite possible that in fifty years' time people would have stopped writing poetry altogether. To Isherwood this apparition was 'infinitely more than a brilliant new literary critic: he was our guide, our evangelist, who revealed to us, in a succession of astounding lightning flashes, the entire expanse of the Modern World'. Another of these acolytes was William Empson (1906–84), of whom Richards thought sufficiently highly ('the best man I've ever had at Cambridge') to recommend to Eliot at the *Criterion*. Like Richards, Empson had come to 'English Studies' from across the disciplinary divide, and, also like Richards, he brought to it a quasi-scientific air that when applied to semantics – his particular area of interest by the early 1950s – had an almost revolutionary effect. The first fruits of this approach were revealed in *Experiment*, a student magazine begun while he was still an undergraduate, together with Jacob Bronowski, Humphrey Jennings and Hugh Sykes Davies. The official editorial policy was 'to gather all and none but the not yet too ripe fruits of art, science and philosophy' and the seven issues – Empson was in charge for only the first three – included essays, fiction, translation, paintings by Braque and photographs by Cartier-Bresson. Editorial standards were high – so high that Bronowski felt able to reject a submission from Ezra Pound: there were congratulatory letters from Eliot and Joyce.

While Empson was already incubating some of the ideas that would underpin his early critical work – see the remarks on Forster – he was also developing a line in spiky modernist poetry – Eliot-derived, but distinguished by some highly individual grapplings with syntax. The notoriously hard-to-please Leavis commended his contributions to *Cambridge Poetry 1929* ('he is an original poet who has studied the right poets (the right ones for him) in the right way . . . Mr Empson commands respect'), noting the influence of Donne and suggesting that he was 'as intensely interested in his technique as in his ideas.' A great Cambridge future beckoned, only for Empson, seven weeks into a junior fellowship at Magdalene, to be sent down from the university for what must count as one of the more bizarre curtailments of a fledgling academic career, when a college servant found a packet of contraceptives in his rooms. However petty-minded the decision, and however pusillanimous the response of some of his friends among the Magdalene dons, it is difficult not to suspect that, to a certain degree, this banishment worked to Empson's advantage, that he was, when it came to it, too *orageux* for a Cambridge in which even Leavis was regarded with deep unease for most of his career, and was better off elsewhere. As it was he departed for London, secured introductions to a great many people who mattered ('Mr Empson to see us' Virginia Woolf reported to Clive Bell in a letter of February 1930. 'A raucous youth, but rather impressive and as red as a turkey, which I like') and set to work, at lightning speed, on the 'grammatico-critical essay' that was to become *Seven Types of Ambiguity* (1930).

The danger in assessing the book's considerable influence on later

T. S. Eliot at his desk at the offices of Faber & Gwyer, 1926

'Bloomsbury says…' Virginia Woolf, who both denied Bloomsbury's existence and acted as its spokeswoman

J. B. Priestley, who claimed that his newspaper essays attracted a seven-figure audience, enjoys a cup of tea

A Georgian football XI, late 1920s, featuring J. C. Squire (seated, with ball) and J. B. Priestley (to his right). The celebrated literary agent A. D. Peters stands third left

George Orwell on Walberswick beach, Suffolk, 1932

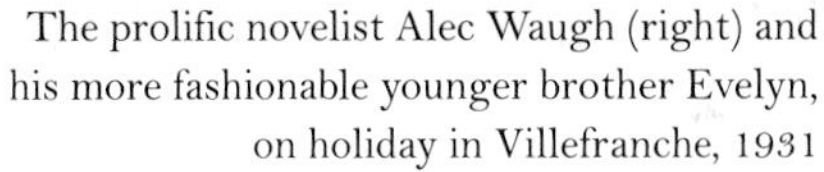

The prolific novelist Alec Waugh (right) and his more fashionable younger brother Evelyn, on holiday in Villefranche, 1931

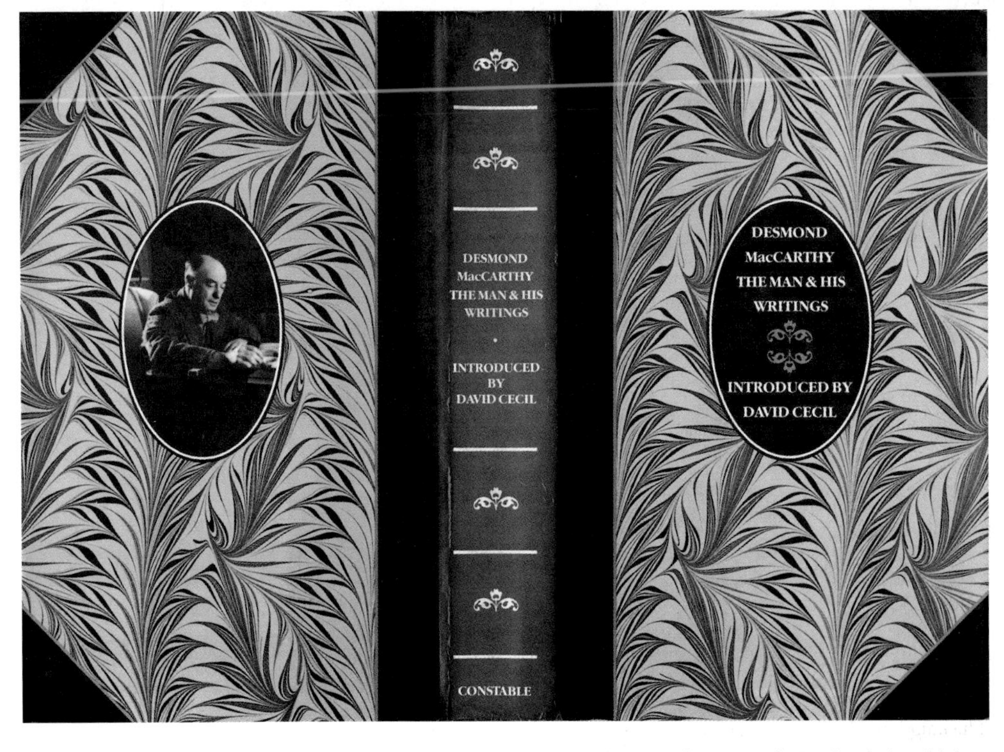

A posthumous selection of Desmond MacCarthy's criticism, introduced by his son-in-law, Lord David Cecil

Late 1940s literary society. Sachevevell Sitwell, Peter Quennell and Cyril Connolly stand on the extreme right

Broadcasting on the BBC's Eastern Service, early 1940s: left-to-right, seated, Venu Chitale, Tambimuttu, T. S. Eliot, Una Marson, Mulk Raj Anand, Christopher Pemberton, Narayana Menon, standing, George Orwell, Nancy Parratt and William Empson

Allen Lane, architect of the paperback revolution, with Penguins

Novelist E. M. Forster and critic Raymond Mortimer relax at the Bloomsbury haunt of Long Crichel

THE PENGUIN
NEW WRITING

8

Gordon Jeffery	*The Way We Live Now—VII*
Laurie Lee	*The Armoured Valley*
Fanfarlo	*Shaving Through the Blitz—VI*
John Sommerfield	*Nobody Got Roasted*
Robert Pagan	*The Maggot in the Apple*
Eric Wilfrid White	*Speak With His Mind*
Stephen Spender	*Books and the War—VII*

* * *

Dylan Thomas	*The Peaches*
C. Day Lewis	*Address to Death*
Beatrix Lehmann	*The £2,000 Raspberry*
Louis MacNeice	*Poem*
Louis Guilloux	*A Man and a Woman*
Frank Sargeson	*An Affair of the Heart*
Fred Urquhart	*To-Morrow Will Be Beautiful*
Ahmed Ali	*Morning in Delhi*
Georg Anders	*Song of the Austrians*

EDITED BY
JOHN LEHMANN

John Lehmann's *Penguin New Writing*, which at the height of its success, sold over 75,000 copies a month

generations of students lies in overemphasising its original impact. As Empson's biographer John Haffenden points out, it took well over a decade to sell out a decidedly meagre first edition of 1,500 copies, and its colonisation of unofficial student reading-lists had to wait until the 1940s. Kingsley Amis recalled of his time at Oxford that it was one of the two books people seemed to be reading (the other was its opposite, Lewis's *Allegory of Love*). On the other hand, it was extensively reviewed, as much, one suspects, for its self-evident modernity as for the technical advances it canvassed – Leavis judged it 'the work of a mind that is fully alive in this age, and such a book has a very unusual importance' – while Empson's habit of plucking individual lines from the texts that strayed beneath his lens and subjecting them to the most minute scrutiny provoked intense debates not merely over his approach to poetry but of what, when it came down to it, poetry might actually be supposed to consist. Middleton Murry, for example, complained that Empson's technique was simply machinery, and ignored the fact that a poem was not just a repository of meaning for the critic to tease out but an 'incantation', whose impact on the reader could only be weakened by over-reading. An over-reading, more to the point, that seemed to elevate the critic to a more important level than the thing being criticised. The assumption that he was a kind of advance guard for the American New Criticism – and by implication the continental structuralists – for whom the figure of the author had largely ceased to matter was one that haunted Empson for the rest of his career. So, too, did the assumption that he was a tiresomely self-conscious highbrow, determined on making literature more difficult for the averagely intelligent reader. In fact, this stance was more likely to be adopted by Empson's admirers – Leavis noted of *Seven Types* that 'those who are not capable of learning from it were not intended by Nature for an advanced education in letters' – than by the critic himself. His casual journalism from the early 1930s shows a rather melancholy awareness of the gulf welling up between the serious writer and the general public, and the implications for literary culture as a whole. One might note, in this context, an obituary of Harold Monro, written for a Japanese newspaper in 1932, in which he remembered Monro recalling how he was once given an hour by a newspaper to write a poem about a royal wedding: 'One may think the result was bad, but it shows there was some contact between a respectable writer and the large reading public: most poets now who can be taken as seriously as Harold Monro cannot imagine themselves doing such a thing. I feel that with his death the poet in England will become even more isolated than before.'

If Richards and Empson never managed to establish anything resembling a school of criticism, or at any rate a Cambridge school of criticism, then one reason lay in the fact that they spent so little of their professional lives in Cambridge. Richards ended up at Harvard. Empson pursued a long, peripatetic career in the Far East before coming to rest at the University of Sheffield. In Empson's case, too, there were personal factors at work to inhibit the alliances and meetings of true minds on which schools of criticism are usually founded. The reader of Haffenden's exhaustive biography of him is likely to emerge with the impression of a deeply eccentric character, afflicted by all manner of private demons, whose capacity for plain speaking could sometimes turn into downright rudeness. Eliot remarked his 'peculiarly twisted and tormented, but very painfully suffering soul'. Part of the trouble may well have sprung from his difficulties with women – there were struggles with his sexual orientation, and it is a fact that of the dozens of academics appointed to the Sheffield English faculty during his time there, only one was female. In his and Richards' absence the task of establishing a genuine critical movement devolved upon the third member of the 1920s Cambridge triumvirate, F. R. Leavis, of whom it can be safely said that no academic teacher of English during the period 1930–60 was quite so influential or quite so widely resented.

The resentment, of course, was a carefully cultivated aspect of Leavis's persona. From a very early stage in his career he was an example of that well-known paradox, the man who perpetually complains of being overlooked and excluded by the establishment but whose reputation depends, by and large, on that very exclusion, kept afloat, all the time, by his sense of inner worth. Q. D. Leavis, his equally redoubtable wife, is supposed once to have remarked that had he lived in the mid-seventeenth century he would have been one of Cromwell's generals. As the story goes, Leavis replied with absolute seriousness 'No my dear, I would have been Cromwell.' It would be wrong to pretend that the early years of Cambridge English 'explain' Leavis and the positions he came to assume. One of the clues to his psychological make-up must surely lie in the radical Nonconformist tradition in which he was brought up (his family was of Huguenot ancestry). There were personal traumas, too – Great War service in a Quaker ambulance unit, the death of his father in a road accident on the opening day of university finals. At the same time, the formative influence of Richards is impossible to discount. In 1925, for example, a PhD on the relationship between journalism and literature in the eighteenth century under his belt, we find him attending Richards' undergraduate lecture course on practical criticism, notable for its reliance on mass-survey methods in an attempt to discover what ordinary people, rather than authors or men of letters, thought about the books they read. Richards' view of *The Waste Land*, and his talk about 'the emotional logic of poetry' and the ideal 'right reader' left their mark, while Leavis's 1930 essay 'English Poetry and the Modern World: The Current Situation' clearly derives from *Principles of Literary Criticism*'s assertion that the poet 'is at the point at which the growth of the mind shows itself', or as Leavis put it – sounding rather like the nineteenth-century historian Hippolyte Taine – 'the most conscious point of the race in his time'.

The outlines of Leavis's long and combative career are an odd mix of formal accomplishment and private torment: the forty-year sojourn at Downing College; the stream of publications, beginning with *New Bearings in English Poetry* (1932); the perpetual establishment snubs that delayed a university readership until he was in his 60s; the cantankerous old age. If there are two aspects of his early days in academe that jump instantly to notice they are, first, what an exceptionally good teacher he was in conventional, exam-passing terms – Emmanuel College, with which he was associated in the late 1920s, achieved five first-class degrees in 1927 – and, second, how hard he had to fight to consolidate his position in a community whose staider members were still disposed to regard Richards, Empson and co. as dangerous lunatics. His stint in the pool of probationary lecturers, from which most inductees soon moved on to full-time posts, lasted six years, after which he was told he would not be reappointed, and Downing, where he was eventually appointed director of studies, was one of the poorest colleges in Cambridge. Already there were signs of the almost messianic dogmatism that would be associated with him in later life ('You're like Jesus Christ' an early pupil is supposed to have told him) and also of the fanatic enthusiasm he was capable of generating in the substantial part of the student population who were on his side. By this time, he had met and married Queenie: not merely a meeting of true minds in the accepted sense, but the coming together of two powerful intellects whose researches had led them independently to identical conclusions about the debilitating effect on literature of its exposure to commercialism. *Fiction and the Reading Public* (1932), her PhD thesis worked up into a book, is a volume-length elaboration of her husband's view, expressed in the essay on poetry and the modern world, that 'urban conditions, a sophisticated civilisation, rapid change in the mingling of cultures, has destroyed the old rhythms and habits, and nothing adequate has taken their place'.

Leaving aside some of the more eye-catching pronouncements – see, for example, the famous remark about Eliot's 'shocking essential ignorance of the possibilities of life' – there are two main aspects to Leavis the critic: the self-conscious assumption of Matthew Arnold's role as a scourge of the 'technologico-Benthamite civilisation' of modern consumer materialism and his status as the re-valuer and re-interpreter of modern English poetry and the novel in terms of what one admiring biographer calls his 'commitment to the value and significance of life itself'. It has to be said that Leavis the heir of Arnold is by far the less amiable of these guises. Never mind the remarks about only the fortunate few being able to appreciate Shakespeare or Donne or an airy judgement such as 'the potentialities of human experience in any age are realised only by a tiny minority' (and what exactly are 'the potentialities of human experience'? Leavis never says); there is something deeply dispiriting about the complaint, made towards the end of his life, that formerly quiet areas of Cambridge were being made hideous by working people listening to transistor radios. One might say in reply that the ability of university teachers to sit in comfortable houses and write books largely depends on disagreeable tasks performed by working people, who can presumably spend their leisure time as they like. This is a cheap shot, perhaps, but Leavis's determined anti-populism can sometimes be insufferable, and his detachment from, and incomprehension of, the greater part of human life is what – with certain exceptions – makes him such an unreliable critic of mass culture and its extravagances.

It is worth drawing attention to this awesome level of detachment, if only because Leavis's strictures on mass entertainment, even of conventional responses to art and music, so often seem to proceed from a sort of affrontedness. In his *F. R. Leavis: A Literary Biography,*

G. Singh reprises an argument conducted in the 1930s with the *Scrutiny* contributor D. W. Harding, who had suggested that there might be some value to the ordinary person in cheap music or the cinema. No, Leavis retorted, 'If too tired to engage the mind in fresh effort, why not reread a classic (something worth reading) with which one is already familiar, play good music one already knows, instead of taking trash?' And yet the exchange seems somehow fundamental to the view of the world and the exclusive position that literature assumed within it: it is possible, as somebody once remarked, to have a fully developed sense of moral responsibility without having read *Middlemarch*; there are ethical touchstones, surely, beyond George Eliot. It is there in the sentence in the first number of *Scrutiny* which refers to 'a necessary relationship between the quality of an individual's response and his general fitness for a human existence'. And then there is *Mass Civilisation and Minority Culture* and its insistence that it is upon the minority that depends

> our power of profiting from the finest human experience of the past; they finally keep alive the subtlest and most perishable parts of tradition. Upon them depend the implicit standards that order the finer living of an age, the sense that this is worth more than that, this rather than that is the direction in which to go, that the centre is here rather than there.

Inevitably, one would be a great deal more sympathetic to the spectacle of Leavis in pursuit of his ideals if he would only define what those ideals were. As it is, when he canvasses the desirability of

> a mind that will approach the problems of modern civilisation with an understanding of their origins, a maturity of outlook, and not a nostalgic addiction to the past, but a sense of human possibilities, difficult of achievement, that traditional cultures bear witness to and that it would be disastrous, in a breach of continuity, to lose sight of for good

one simply wants to ask Leavis to stop being high-minded and answer some fundamental questions. What is a sense of human possibilities? Is this writer any good? If not, why not? Should I read Meredith/Thackeray/Gissing or the various other writers disparaged in Leavis's work on the novel, several of whom he has conspicuously not bothered to read? These are questions that a critic with less exalted ambitions – a V. S. Pritchett, say, or a Middleton Murry – usually manages to answer in a way that Leavis does not. It is the critic René Wellek's point about *Revaluation* (1936) all over again: that here was a highly evaluative work which had no theory of evaluation and never troubled to explain the criteria on which its judgements were based. Certainly Leavis's defence – that spelling out requirements was fatal to the compact forged between reader and text, that words in poetry invite us not to 'think about' and judge but to 'feel into' and become – makes some valuable points about the effect of poetry on the individual consciousness, but from the angle of the man who talks constantly about the possibilities of human experience and implicit standards, it can look faintly evasive. In these circumstances it was all too easy to write Leavis off as a 'personal reactions' man (Stephen Spender's deadly phrase) whose impact was always likely to be softened by the manifest dullness of his prose style.

In all these arguments it is important to distinguish Leavis the practical critic from Leavis the critical hierophant. To read some of the early criticism of the kind that appeared in *New Bearings* and *Revaluation* can be a bracing experience. Here is Leavis on Auden's technique: 'not one that solves problems; it conceals a failure to grapple with them, or, rather, makes a virtue out of the failure'. Or, on the then fashionable comparison of Joyce's linguistic experiments with those of Shakespeare: 'Shakespeare's were not a product of a desire to "develop his medium to the fullest", but of a pressure of something to be conveyed'. This is excellent, as far as it goes: arresting, near-aphoristic, hinting at more solid things behind the glittering surface. It is when Leavis goes for the wider perspective that the canvas blurs. *The Great Tradition* (1948), with its bogus affiliations and paranoiac restrictions, was untenable then and it is even less tenable now. The same point might be made of some of the implications that could, by this stage in the proceedings, be detected in Leavisian critical enquiry in general, in particular the suspicion that the pursuit of 'standards' would ultimately lead to a comparatively small group of people laying down the law, with especial consideration being given to the views of their spiritual director – that is, Leavis himself.

There is no getting away from the sect-like qualities that Leavis and his circle had begun to assume by the 1930s, the thought that here was not so much an advertisement for the Cambridge English school as a second and much smaller school existing on its semi-detached flank. For a start there was *Scrutiny*, or, to give it its full title, *Scrutiny: A Quarterly Review*, launched in 1932 with L. C. Knights's and Donald Culver's names on the masthead but Leavis lurking in the background. Then there were Leavis's forays beyond Cambridge, notably in the monthly *Bookman*, where he could be found in the Christmas number of 1932 appraising the year's work in criticism and commending his wife for 'shattering' the argument that there was no difference between universality and popularity. Finally, and most important of all, there was his concerted effort both inside Cambridge and beyond it to assemble a group of disciples. Early pupils, sent out into the world of schoolteaching, were already supplying recruits, whose arrival at Cambridge would be met by a note slipped under the door ('We understand you are intelligent. A group of us meets . . .'). The somewhat rackety equipage of Downing College, meanwhile, was being whipped into gear, with a proportion of the endowment directed towards English scholarships and a circular ready for despatch to enquiring schoolmasters which advised aspiring Downing-ites to read Richards, Empson, Eliot and the Leavis-edited collection of *Scrutiny* essays, *Determinations*.

Bright undergraduates – Boris Ford, for example, and D. J. Enright – were already beginning to appear in *Scrutiny*. If the real impact of Leavis and his methods had to wait until the 1950s, when this generation of pupils were firmly established in academic posts, then what Leavis's biographers have a tendency to call 'the gifted Leavisian X' was already at work spreading the Sage of Downing's message. Already, though, there were ominous signs of trouble ahead, not the least of them Leavis's habit of falling out both with erstwhile supporters and the guiding lights who had helped him secure his first professional footholds. Even Richards was cast into the outer darkness after Leavis took against *Coleridge and the Imagination*. On the other hand, Leavis's early rise is truly astonishing. Within not much more than a decade and a half an institution that had barely existed in the 1920s was exerting a decisive hold on the idea of 'English Studies': an institution, more to the point, that had held the old belles-lettrist tradition of English letters in the deepest contempt and regarded most professional book reviewers as the members of a nest-feathering clique. All this would have profoundly important consequences for the shape of criticism in the second half of the twentieth century, pitting the don against the man, or woman, of letters, the professional against the amateur, close readings against impressionist generalisation, the textbook against the literary essay. Leavis may have helped to professionalise the world of English literature in the 1930s, but he also brought to it another version of the 'club spirit' he otherwise affected to deplore. In this lay his, and some of that literature's, undoing.

CHAPTER 8

Late Bloomsbury

> If a literary tradition does not keep itself alive, here in the present, not merely in new creation, but as a pervasive influence on feeling, thought and standards of living . . . then it must be pronounced to be dead.
>
> F. R. Leavis, 'What's Wrong with Criticism?' (1932)

> The next generation is likely to react vigorously against the intellectualism of Bloomsbury.
>
> Raymond Mortimer, 'London Letter' to the *Dial* (1928)

If one kind of 1920s reader – the kind represented by Hugh Walpole – imagined the Bloomsbury Group to be the epitome of style, sophistication and substance, then another kind, younger and less impressionable, was already keen to regard it as the oldest of old hat: the curious embalmed residue of previous ages, as Anthony Powell once put it, not altogether to be despised but self-evidently out of date and from certain angles scarcely less stick-in-the-mud than the philistines it had made its reputation by attacking. Part of this disapproval on the part of the cutting-edge young was simply a reaction to Bloomsbury's increasing commercial success, its ascent, as the 1920s wore on, from the highbrow *conversazioni* to the bookshelves of the middle-class drawing room: Lytton Strachey's *Elizabeth and Essex* (1930) sold 40,000 copies in the UK alone, and went on to become one of the biggest selling non-fiction books in interwar American publishing history. But another part rested on a genuine distaste for Bloomsbury attitudes, Bloomsbury manipulations and, down at the sharp end of literary practice, Bloomsbury methodology. The preface to Evelyn Waugh's *Rossetti* (1928), for example, offers some pointed remarks on developments in modern biography: the 'old-fashioned' life and times has gone, Waugh suggests, and in its place 'we have discovered a jollier way of honouring our dead. The Corpse has become a marionette. With bells on its fingers and wires on its toes it is jiggled about to a "period dance" of its own piping; and who is not amused?' Strachey is not mentioned, but the author of *Eminent Victorians* (1918) and *Queen Victoria* (1921) would have known exactly to which contemporary biographical eminence Waugh was referring. Perhaps, in the end, it was merely a question of guilt by association, that in its mass debunkings of Victorianism, Victorian beliefs and Victorian personalities, Bloomsbury could never really free itself from the taint of the institutions it was trying to discredit. For all her modernity, and her insistence that human consciousness was not the same in 1920 as it had been in 1890, it is impossible to travel more than a few pages into the world of Virginia Woolf without remembering that this is the granddaughter of Sir James Stephen KC, and that there are certain assumptions and traditions on display which are tampered with at one's peril.

Judgements of this kind necessarily presume an understanding of what Bloomsbury was, the personnel who staffed it and the principles by which it operated. None of this information was easy to come by in the 1920s, and with certain obvious exceptions it is not a great deal easier to supply it now. Bloomsbury's *locus classicus* might have been the Cambridge of the late 1890s, where Thoby Stephen, Leonard Woolf, Clive Bell, Lytton Strachey and Saxon Sydney-Turner encountered each other for the first time, but the assumption of a collective identity only began to make its presence felt in newspaper articles in the early 1920s, and the core membership was not described in public – by Raymond Mortimer, in an essay in the *Dial* – until as late as 1928. For all its air of revelation, its determination to name names and isolate standpoints, the piece turns out to be a characteristic exercise in Bloomsbury sleight of hand. Mortimer begins by talking about 'the Bloomsbury spirit'. This is never properly defined, 'but I would place first a belief in Reason, and a conviction that the pursuit of truth and the contemplation of beauty are the most important of human activities'. As for what this pursuit might entail, no subject, he assures us, is taboo, no tradition accepted without examination, and no conclusion evaded. In a hypocritical society, Bloomsbury has been indecent; in a conservative society, curious; in a gentlemanly society, ruthless; and in a fighting society, pacifist. Meanwhile, the complaint that Bloomsbury is narrow in its tastes, loose in its morals, 'irreverent, unpatriotic, remote and superior', is of course correct.

'For will not relentless reasoning and delicate discrimination make a man all these things?'

But then, fearing that he may have said too much, Mortimer instantly backtracks: 'such vivid personalities as the leaders of the group could never of course commit themselves to any composite direction of taste'. The retreat to straightforward personal attraction turns out to be typical of nearly every Bloomsbury effort at self-definition. To Leonard Woolf, who did more than most to create and sustain the Bloomsbury legacy, its members were simply 'a group of friends'. Frances Partridge, while acknowledging, on the one hand, that she and her husband Ralph regarded it as the only society they could imagine to be comparable to the eighteenth-century salon, wondered, on the other, 'why people could not just accept that Bloomsbury was never a superior closed circle, but just a loose collection of people who happened to be friends, some more talented than others, who pursued their occupations as much for pleasure and experiment as to make their mark'.

One senses that Partridge is genuinely bewildered by the late twentieth-century obsession with Lytton, Leonard and Virginia – and it should be noted that these remarks were filed many years later in response to the wave of anti-Bloomsbury criticism provoked by a millennium exhibition on 'The Art of Bloomsbury'. On the other hand, the reason why so many readers equated the societies of Gordon Square, or Charleston, or Ham Spray House in Wiltshire, with the idea of cultural superiority, or at the very least a determined closing of the cultural ranks, was that so many of Bloomsbury's private and public pronouncements encouraged them to do so. Virginia Woolf's diaries, for example, are crammed with references to 'what Bloomsbury says' and 'what Bloomsbury thinks'. As for the exclusiveness, one need only read a paragraph or so of Strachey's opinions on his fellow workers in the field to realise quite how paralysing it could be. Reporting back to Carrington on his attendance at Arnold Bennett's Anglo-French poetry society, founded with the aim of giving an interest to Bennett's young French wife, he pronounces the affair to be 'an incredibly fearful function', with a running order consisting of Edith Sitwell ('her nose longer than an ant-eater'), Eliot ('very sad and seedy – it made one weep') and finally Mrs Bennett herself, who recited 'with waving arms and chanting voice, Baudelaire and Verlaine till everyone was ready to vomit'.

Not, of course, that Strachey is the standard by which Bloomsbury demands to be judged. His snootiness could be off-putting even to paid-up members of the group. Vita Sackville-West suspected that 'the drooping Lytton' must have done its cause a great deal of harm, and even Frances Partridge wondered if the bitchiness of his letters wasn't sometimes taken to excess. All the same, his strictures on Edith Sitwell's delivery of 'her absurd stuff' chez Bennett serve to illustrate the belief to which Bloomsbury clung most tenaciously of all, which, it is fair to say, was its own exceptionalism. The most commonplace letter sent from one Cambridge combination room to another long before sender or recipient had achieved any kind of celebrity carries this subtext, the thought that there never had been anything like Bloomsbury before and never would be anything like it again. 'I sometimes feel as if it were not only we ourselves who were concerned,' Lytton briskly informs Leonard Woolf towards the end of the Edwardian era, 'but that the destinies of the whole world are somehow involved in ours . . . We are like the Athenians of the Periclean age.' The same high valuation of joint and collective worth emerges from a letter from Strachey to John Maynard Keynes about an emotional entanglement in which one them was caught up: 'Great God, it's more weird and more bad than anything that ever happened in the world before.' Later Bloomsbury apologists have tended to magnify this sense of detachment from ordinary life by their strenuous efforts to justify it. 'It would be wrong to talk about him as if he were an ordinary man,' Noel Annan once remarked of Keynes. 'He was not.' One sees what Annan means – that it pains him to imagine his hero domesticated, that he trembles lest the great man's unquestionable distinction should be reduced to the level of mere idiosyncrasy – but all this rather ignores the fact that Keynes presumably ate, slept, breathed and defecated like anyone else.

Yet exceptionalism could only be taken so far. Frances Partridge's invocation of the Augustan salon as a benchmark for Bloomsbury separateness and Bloomsbury solidarity works both ways: on the one hand conveying a succinct impression of the closed circles and shared tastes in which Bloomsbury dealt; on the other sharply exposing some of its limitations here in a world of mass-market aesthetics, where taste was ever more diffuse and the ideological context of cultural preferences grew ever more open to debate. A world, more to the point, where what the general public wanted from art and what the intellectual was prepared to allow it could take wildly differing forms. Frank Swinnerton's complaint about Virginia Woolf was that her terms of reference were entirely literary, that her particular brand of intellectualism could only deal with its own kind, and pulled up short in the presence of anything it could not understand: 'she knew what went on in her own mind; but she would not have crossed the street to shake hands with Dickens'. And behind this cordon sanitaire lurked the undeniable fact that Bloomsbury's brand of cultural superiority reflected what was essentially a social division. The fact that so many of its day-to-day activities relied on the existence of dividend payments and servants to bring in the tea is a critical commonplace, and yet one would be far more sympathetic to the exemplary liberal sentiments expressed by Frances and Ralph Partridge if they weren't so regularly accompanied by jokes about the domestic staff. Still, there is something to be said for a left-leaning bourgeois who, in an age in which bourgeois civilisation is supposed to be coming to an end, is both aware of his impending extinction and at the same time determined to stick to his ground. As Stephen Spender (1909–95) once put it: 'To them there was something barbarous about our generation. It seemed that with us the thin wall which surrounded their little situation of independence and which enabled them to retain their air of being the last of the Romans had broken down.' The wall might have collapsed, but some of the fragments were surprisingly sturdy.

This may make Bloomsbury sound impossibly hieratic, a handful of stratospherically well-read opinion-brokers lounging on the summit of Mount Olympus and occasionally tossing a newly minted critical judgement over the edge, but in practical terms it could be thoroughly down to earth, alert to, if disparaging of, shifts in the literary marketplace, eager to talk up the prospects of its champions, anxious to encourage the men (and women) in its ranks who seemed the most likely to succeed. Of these aspirants, none seemed likelier than Desmond MacCarthy (1875–1952) who, if only by dint of his long tenure on the *Sunday Times*, has claims to be regarded as the Bloomsbury critic with the greatest influence on the reading public at large. If Bloomsbury agreed on anything, it was the immense promise, almost amounting to genius, that MacCarthy displayed as a young man. Leonard Woolf recalled that 'when I first saw Desmond he looked like a superb young eagle who with one sweep of his great wings could soar to any height he chose'. It was confidently predicted that he could do anything, that some monumental work – ideally a novel – would issue from his pen the moment he could find the time to write it, and yet, as year succeeded year, despite the liberal encouragement of his peers – the celebrated Bloomsbury Memoir Club was founded with the deliberate aim of forcing him to write – all that emerged was several decades' worth of gentlemanly procrastination.

As time went on, this inability to produce the thing that really mattered became one of the great Bloomsbury puzzles. What was holding him back? What psychological impediment stayed his hand? Did he, as one admirer gallantly conceptualised his inanition, love life too much and literature too little? The truth would seem to be that, as Ian Hamilton once put it, he was simply a stylish and honourable Edwardian man of letters with a somewhat chaotic personal life, at large in an environment where the certainties of Edwardian-man-of-letterdom were being increasingly called into question. He was a social animal, too – his wife once accused him of neglecting everything around him except society – who combined an immense affability with a habitual improvidence ('I shall have to go on scribbling three articles a week to the end of my days' he told Lytton Strachey sometime in the 1920s – a forecast that proved to be all too exact). None of this made his domestic life easy, or fostered the working conditions that might have helped with the writing of that great lost masterpiece, and in some ways MacCarthy's greatest strength, given the various distractions that beset him, was merely his ability to keep his head above water.

Neither, from Bloomsbury's point of view, was he much of a purist, in either his affiliations or his critical opinions. For one thing he was a friend of Squire, whose *New Statesman* column he took over early in 1920, only parting company with his old colleague much later on when the Georgian paraphernalia became too much to bear (there was an uncomfortably frank review of one of Squire's volumes of autobiography, written in 1937, in which he confesses that 'I sometimes felt that I had really lost sight of my friend behind cricket-pads, pewter pint pots, pheasants, shotguns, runabout cars, footballs, committee agenda'). More important, when it came down to it, was the undeniable fact that the new critical atmosphere of the 1920s was deeply inimical to him. He read the *Criterion* with interest, and was polite about the *Adelphi*, but *Ulysses* struck him as a confused failure and he disliked Virginia Woolf's stream-of-consciousness techniques. He used to say that she could evoke very well the sensation of a train passing and the wind buffeting the watcher standing near the track, but could not describe the train itself. It was not, one hastens to add, that he failed to see the significance of Joyce, or Eliot, or even Gertrude Stein – he conceded that *Ulysses* contained 'more artistic dynamite than any book published in years' – merely that he did not enjoy them, and, as he once remarked, the first step to culture was to learn to enjoy, not to know what was best.

Perhaps there is something to be said for the critic who believes the interwar period to be a 'rather silly' literary epoch. On the other hand, judgements of this kind need more explication than MacCarthy was sometimes inclined to bring to them. No doubt had he been born half a century earlier, and furnished with the inestimable advantage of a private income, he would have settled down as a magazine essayist in the great mid-Victorian tradition. But this was the 1920s, and there were sides to be taken and livings to be earned. The *New Statesman* column, signed 'Affable Hawk' in succession to Squire's 'Solomon Eagle', brought plenty of prestige, but little in the way of regular salary. There were visits from the bailiffs, and the slapdash habits to which his biographers habitually draw attention seem to have stemmed from the constant effort to keep pace with the demands of his extensive social life. Certainly, by the mid-1920s he was combining his *New Statesman* post with the literary editorship of the *Empire Review*, reading manuscripts for Heinemann and contributing to a stack of publications as various as the *Daily Herald*, *World's Work* and the *Nation*. There were also regular engagements at the BBC. A Chesterton or a Priestley would have taken all this in his stride, kept the balls aloft with improvisatory fervour, but MacCarthy lacked the stamina for this kind of literary heroics: he could never raise his level of production and there was rarely enough money to go round. At one point friends subscribed £300 for him to take a three-month foreign holiday, but the temperamental failings soon reasserted themselves. 'Oh Desmond's hopeless,' his long-suffering wife Molly once complained; 'he's like a dog who runs out if the door is open.'

MacCarthy's prospects began to improve in the late 1920s when he severed his connection with the *New Statesman* and became chief literary critic of the *Sunday Times* at double the salary. Even more advantageous was an offer from his wealthy friend Oliver Brett, Lord Esher, to install him as editor of the newly founded monthly magazine

Life and Letters at £800 a year. As it was, MacCarthy's three-year tenure was symptomatic not only of his own professional shortcomings but of the wider literary climate in which he operated. Designed to rival the *London Mercury*, whose cover price it undercut, with 2,600 subscribers on board and a commitment by Esher to underwrite production costs to the tune of £4,000 a year, *Life and Letters* was pitched at a level to which most literary magazines of the period could only tentatively aspire. There was to be a series of foreign reports, space for longer pieces, celebrity contributors, monthly bibliographies aimed at bringing in subscriptions from libraries, book dealers and universities. MacCarthy did his best. He assembled a stellar line-up – Virginia Woolf, Bertrand Russell and Robert Graves were all pressed into service, and early numbers featured Cyril Connolly on Joyce and Evelyn Waugh on Firbank; he made a point of covering topics dear to his heart such as the dangers of censorship; but he could never get the best out of his distinguished contributors and Esher, having lost half his investment, turned it into a quarterly before closing it down altogether.

What had gone wrong? More even than the *London Mercury*, *Life and Letters* seemed to belong to a bygone era of English literary life, one of shared tastes and universal standards, that was fast being overthrown. Max Beerbohm, on receiving a copy, remarked that it made him 'ache to be living in those days of serious refinement and happiness! How it cheapens this thin, sad, hectic little era.' Connolly, who had a great deal to thank MacCarthy for in terms of personal kindness and encouragement, and was in addition paying court to his niece, once referred to it as 'the literary event of the late Twenties', but his diary of the time is sharply critical. Here the complaint is that MacCarthy, with his inbred fear of experiment, merely pandered to mainstream opinion and allowed the concern to degenerate into a type of literary *Punch*, 'as august and readable as any late Victorian arse wiper, and as daring and original as a new kind of barley water'.

MacCarthy was happier at the *Sunday Times*, where he enjoyed the advantage of a regular platform, a mass audience – the paper's circulation grew rapidly throughout the 1930s and reached half a million by the end of the Second World War – and what, for a weekly reviewer, was a generous quota of space: at one point his 'World of Books' column extended to 1,800 words. Even here, though, there lurked a suspicion that he was a makeweight, hanging on to the coat-tails of more distinguished forebears. One of his first jobs was to produce a tribute to his recently deceased predecessor, Sir Edmund Gosse. He was able to praise the texture of Gosse's prose style ('smooth as silk and shot with wit and iridescent with fancy') while hinting at his lack of creativity and his spiteful streak. Gosse's shadow hung over his early years on the paper: he complained that his editor, Leonard Rees, treated him as a man might treat a second wife ('Rees looks at Gosse's picture on the wall, looks at me, and says "How different from my dear Jemima"'). There were difficulties, too, with academic critics to whom a policy of enjoyment at all costs was deeply suspect. The second number of *Scrutiny* contains Leavis's celebrated article 'What's Wrong with Criticism?' – a question to which MacCarthy's *Criticisms*, a selection of various literary columns turned in over the past twenty years, alas, provides some of the answers. If there was consolation it lay in a social life which, to judge from the accounts of it left by other Bloomsberries, must have been quite as exhausting as his weekly deadlines. Virginia Woolf recalled stealing a look over his shoulder as he stood examining his engagement book. 'Monday Lady Bessborough 8.30. Tuesday Lady Ancaster 8.30. Wednesday Dora Sanger seven sharp. Thursday Lady Salisbury ten o'clock. Friday lunch Wolves and dine Lord Revelstoke. White waistcoat.' The last two words were twice underlined. The reason for the white waistcoat, Woolf later discovered, was that Lord Revelstoke proposed to introduce him to the king.

In the end, longevity saw him through. He might, by the final years of his career, have been a wholly antique presence on the margins of the London literary world – 'Oh what an amazing small parakeet birdie he does look these days,' Julia Strachey remarked, on meeting him in 1945, 'his crest flying out behind him . . . and seeming to hop along and shift up and down his perch as he chatters' – but he carried with him a vivid sense of the people he had known and a lack of pomposity that endeared him to younger colleagues. One of Leonard Rees's successors on the *Sunday Times* remembered him sitting in the composing room and discussing Ibsen 'as if he and I were old cronies'. Leavis might have described him as 'the journalistic middleman of cultivated talk' – although Leavis acknowledged that he reposed in a higher category than Squire or Lynd – but the talk had a very un-Bloomsbury-like warmth. The modern reader who takes the trouble to look at some of his best essays – the memoir of Henry James, say – published in the posthumous selection edited by his son-in-law, Lord David Cecil, may conclude that his work has survived rather better than contemporary estimates of it were apt to prophesy.

At the same time, it is worth pointing out that the troubles which afflicted him amounted to far more than improvidence or an inability to calibrate his work schedule to the demands of his engagement diary. As a young man he had given up orthodox Christianity for the 'natural' philosophy peddled by George Meredith – what mattered was to be true to oneself and trust to the fundamental goodness of 'the earth' – without realising that what attracted him to Meredith's vision was that it offered a kind of religion by default. The twentieth century, consequently, hit him hard. He had little of the agnosticism, or the polite scepticism, of the Woolfs and the Stracheys. 'The longer I live,' he told his friend J. L. Hammond, 'the more convinced I am that men must have a religion that, if it were true, would prevent them feeling insignificant.' Like some of his views on literature, or indeed his whole-hearted embrace of 'society', this is a very un-Bloomsbury-like attitude. All the same, it is one of the things that makes him interesting: a disinclination to follow the party line that, in the context of 'Bloomsbury thinks' and 'Bloomsbury says', does at least give him a life of his own.

MacCarthy died in 1952, knighted at the last for services to criticism. By this time much of the shine had come off Bloomsbury and some of the reputations forged in the 1920s were in lowish water: not helped by a sustained process of debunking exemplified by the series of articles contributed by F. A. Simpson to the *Cambridge Review* and the *Spectator*, which demonstrated quite how seriously Strachey's *Eminent Victorians* had misrepresented Cardinal Manning and the circumstances of his acceptance into the Catholic Church. But there was still a place for Bloomsbury critics, and what might be called the MacCarthy-ite line, with its emphasis on enjoyment, delight and the sensibilities of the educated gentleman, continued to be pursued through the pages of the *Sunday Times* by MacCarthy's trusted lieutenant Raymond Mortimer for the next quarter of a century. If Mortimer (1895–1980) survives at all these days it is as the long-time ornament of Frances Partridge's diaries, a depressive and somewhat pedantic figure forever jumping up from his armchair to dispute a mangled quotation with the aid of *Larousse* or the *Oxford Classical Dictionary*, but in his time he was an influential critic, much commended for the air of lightly worn learning he brought to his reviews – the cultivated man adrift in a world of philistines, perhaps, but always aware of the dangers of allowing this cultivation to get out of hand. And while he lost no opportunity to sing the praises of his distinguished forebear – he declared that most of the good literary journalism of the 1920s and 1930s owed something to MacCarthy's example – he was not above laying down a few laws of his own, or at least defining some of the critical principles on which his work was based. The selection from his journalism which he reluctantly allowed into print shortly before his death contains an amusing and self-deprecating 'autobiographical preface', in which the autobiographer describes himself as a 'shameless elitist', convinced that the well-being of the nation depends on the talents of a small minority, and that liberty is more important than equality, with which it is in any case incompatible. Metaphysics are beyond his grasp; his imagination is as limited as his intellect; he makes no claims to originality. Nevertheless, he is serious about what he does. 'His interest in the craft of writing has been acute' and he has strained, throughout his long career, 'to be lucid, concise and entertaining'.

Mortimer, one sometimes feels, is the ultimate belles-lettrist: prepared to write about almost everything that came his way – the collection from which these remarks are taken is called *Try Anything Once* – as at home with a book about the Zulu Wars as a study of Degas. Naturally he was an implacable opponent of academe, as alarmed by proposed increases in the number of undergraduates ('Whereas in a business generally expansion may be beneficial, it is harmful in our business, which is to produce civilised people') as by academic treatises on the classics compiled with one eye on the examining boards. A piece called 'Literature made Difficult' despairs of the volumes in the Macmillan *Casebook* series and their lists of 'dismal questions' along the lines of 'What would *Hamlet* lose if it were not a poetic play?' and hopes that no student will ever read through them. However, though he disliked academics and feared the consequences of specialisation, he was prepared to do them justice. His review of *The Common Pursuit*, for example, begins by dismissing the idea that criticism is a science rather than an art ('a delusion') only to pull up short with a tribute to Leavis's intelligence ('his mind, if narrow, is extremely acute; and he can be enlightening about the select authors he admires'). After this Leavis's inconsistencies – notably the complaints about Eliot failing to rein in his personal prejudices – become intolerable, but some of his most telling criticisms are based on his own private knowledge. Thus he can disprove Leavis's claim to have been Eliot's sole defender in the early 1920s – 'the bold solitary champion of a neglected untouchable' – with a remembrance of Virginia Woolf speaking about him in Cambridge in 1924, when it was taken for granted that everyone present was aware of Eliot's importance.

In the end, Leavis is convicted on a charge of being biased against enjoyment, with extra bad marks for his knotty syntax. 'Could such a sentence be published by a good critic, or indeed by anyone with a feeling for the English language?' Mortimer wonders at the end of one particularly abstruse piece of analysis. If there is something rather plaintive about this enquiry, it is because Mortimer was uneasily aware that the whole view he took of literature was ripe for superannuation, that there would be other and even less respectful Leavises whose influence would be much less easy to resist. The ship was sinking, and he knew it. But it would be a mistake to write him off as a literary dodo warily parading on the Mauritian strand. His particular merits (and also some of his limitations) are markedly apparent in his essay 'The Victorian Philistines', which while it works itself up into a terrific rage about *echt*-Victorian attitudes to art has some useful points to make about the importance of individual talent. Studies of the wider scene are all very well, he suggests, but Marx and Taine have exaggerated the extent to which genius is a product of circumstance. Writers and artists 'are interesting chiefly in so far as they are different from, and superior to, their contemporaries'. As for the topic under discussion, he is good on the background to Victorian middle-class puritanism ('this money-minded and arriviste asceticism') and determinedly witty at the expense of its religious beliefs ('To understand the Victorians, I believe, one must study Nonconformity. This is not a pleasing task').

Certainly Mortimer is displaying his own prejudices, and his complaints about Victorian 'complacency' can be met with the response that his own stance is itself highly complacent. When he rebukes the Victorian politician John Bright for an insufficiently respectful attitude to sculpture and for preferring the draped form to the nude ('This eminent man, because he had not trained himself to appreciate the Fine Arts, presumed that those who had done so were affecting emotions they did not possess') the result may look like simple patronage. Nevertheless, one leaves a piece like 'The Victorian Philistines' with a feeling that the critic has not only thought very hard about the subject that has strayed under his lens, but is himself personally affected – that the question of Victorian philistinism is supremely important to him because he grew up in its shadow. This may be part of the Victorian taint that younger critics detected in Bloomsbury in the 1920s, but then even Leavis and Eliot, in their different ways – Leavis especially – were products of the social and religious codes that formed them, and the critic who fails to respond to these stimuli will quite often end up feeling that, in their absence, it is not worth writing criticism at all.

Raymond Mortimer lived long enough to witness the Bloomsbury revival in full swing: a process in which, with certain reservations, he was happy to participate. By the time of his death, in 1980, the recovery of interest in Bloomsbury studies, in Bloomsbury personalities, in every aspect of the relationship between Leonard and Virginia and the workings of the Hogarth Press, had been gathering pace for nearly a decade and a half: an upward curve which, to those who had monitored the virtual collapse of the movement's share price in the post-war era, seemed almost inexplicable. By the early 1950s, Bloomsbury's fortunes had sunk very low. It was not merely that the major figures were dead, or that the intellectual climate of the immediately post-war era seemed much less hospitable to Bloomsbury preoccupations and Bloomsbury values. Rather, the shades of Lytton and Virginia were casualties in a generational conflict, prosecuted by a new wave of writers, many of them from much less exalted social backgrounds, whose instinctive dislike of Bloomsbury's intellectual methods was sharpened by an awareness of the social basis of their art. In Kingsley Amis's *Lucky Jim* (1954), for example, Jim Dixon's adversary Bertrand Welch is thought to resemble 'Lytton Strachey represented in waxwork form by a prentice hand'. Angus Wilson's *Hemlock and After* (1952) criticises Virginia Woolf for 'a withdrawn kind of sensibility which had little to impart to the modern novelist and the modern reader of novels'. Worse, the academic high-ground was shifting, as the pioneers of 'English Studies' at Cambridge and elsewhere began to occupy positions of genuine power. It was estimated that a third of the contributors to the highly influential *Pelican Guide to English Literature* (1955–61) had *Scrutiny* connections: sure enough, Woolf was written off as a minor talent with 'a fragmentary and inconclusive technique'.

The more objectively minded of Bloomsbury survivors were

uncomfortably aware that a certain amount of this criticism was neither spiteful, nor malicious, but accurate. A paper delivered to a 1952 meeting of the Memoir Club went so far as to suggest that at the root of Bloomsbury's downfall lay 'its intolerance of everyone and everything which was not all the time amusing'. In this deeply contested atmosphere new publications, whether by those still living or others lately dead, tended to be met with an indifference sometimes extending to outright hostility. The Strachey/Woolf letters, jointly edited by Leonard and Lytton's brother James, did nothing for either correspondent. The magic had all gone, Malcolm Muggeridge proposed, recalling that he had recently picked up a copy of *Eminent Victorians*: 'It seemed meretricious, shrill and unconvincing.' Virginia Woolf's *A Writer's Diary* (1953) also attracted adverse reviews, and a bracing letter to Leonard from his brother Edgar ('It is not for me to question the decency of a man selling his wife's tragedy for gold').

All this placed Leonard Woolf, as the principal guardian of the Bloomsbury heritage, in an awkward position. He had begun on his 'management of the past' – to use his biographer's phrase – as early as 1945, getting his wife's papers typed up and liaising with sympathetic friends in the conviction that the Bloomsbury ghosts needed careful handling, only to discover that nobody cared either way. Wounded by the hostile response to his long-meditated *Principia Politica: A Study of Communal Pyschology* (1953), of which the *New Statesman* remarked that its author 'strayed through the domains of child psychology, animal psychology, anthropology and classical scholarship with the lightest possible equipment and little reference to any detailed research', he began to suspect that future publications would not be worth the irritation they provoked. David Garnett, writing to him in 1959 to suggest a Bloomsbury photograph book, was firmly rebuffed: 'it would be met by the usual chorus of anti-Bloomsburiensis, which is more virulent among reviewers than elsewhere'.

Meanwhile, the ornaments of Old Bloomsbury continued to die off: Ralph Partridge in 1960; Vanessa Bell in 1961; Saxon Sydney-Turner, one of the original founding fathers, the following year; Clive Bell in 1964. Yet as the movement's key personnel dwindled into extinction, so there came hints that its animating spirit was very much alive. One mark of this resurgence of interest could be found in the enthusiasm of American book dealers. The Chicago firm of Hamill & Barker, for example, paid Leonard Woolf £12,500 – a very respectable sum for the late 1950s – for an assortment of Woolf items that included the diaries, then sold on to the Berg Collection. Some early drafts of *The Voyage Out* went for a further £600. Even more marked was the rise in scholarly interest. The standard bibliography, *Writings about the Bloomsbury Group* (1989), notes six entries from 1960, increasing to sixteen in both 1962 and 1963 and an unprecedented thirty-five in 1964. Sales of Woolf's novels, diligently kept in print by Leonard in his capacity of director of the Hogarth Press, now affiliated to Chatto & Windus, were similarly robust. The combined British and North American sales of *To the Lighthouse* amounted to 23,000 copies in 1963. Unexpectedly, Leonard's management of the past, now bolstered by the regular appearance of instalments of his multi-volume autobiography, looked as if it might be about to pay dividends. It was in this atmosphere of modest consolidation, if without great hope of financial reward – the advance was a mere £50 – that Michael Holroyd set to work on his compendious life of Strachey.

In the event, *Lytton Strachey* (1967–8), against all expectations and in the face of concerted lobbying from survivors alarmed by its intimate tone, raised public fascination with Bloomsbury on to an entirely new plane. As the Bloomsbury historian Regina Marler once put it, 'Before 1963, it would have required psychic attributes to foresee that the breakthrough in the Bloomsbury revival would be a two-volume biography of Lytton Strachey.' In the 1950s the author of *Queen Victoria* had been routinely criticised for failings as varied as his condescension, his patronising style, his pacifism, his sentimentality, his classicism, his elitism and – rather paradoxically – his popularity. Now, curiously enough, he seemed as relevant as an anti-Vietnam protest march on Grosvenor Square. What had happened? A reread of Holroyd's original – there was a single-volume recension in 1994 – soon establishes it as an odd book altogether: admiring of Strachey's accomplishment, but for all the vigour of the treatment failing to convince the reader that the works are anything more than period pieces, histrionic and top-heavy with laborious word play, much more comfortable in exploring the complexities of the life: the *echt*-Victorian childhood under the gaze of his father, the General; the fallow years at Cambridge; the early career as a reviewer flowering unexpectedly in the success of *Eminent Victorians*.

None of this is to disparage Holroyd's achievement, or even to note the irony that the methods used should be exactly the reverse of those favoured by Strachey himself – the coy ironist memorialised by the well-meaning fanatic. Rather, it is to wonder why such a magisterial account of so faintly insubstantial a figure should strike such a resonant chord with a reading public not exactly short of Bloomsbury heroes in whom to take an interest. And yet there were several excellent reasons for *Lytton Strachey*'s enormous success. Most obviously, it was, as Raymond Mortimer correctly diagnosed, 'the first post-Wolfenden biography', a book that not only went beyond the bedroom door but did so in the full knowledge that its subject was homosexual. More important even than this was its appearance in 1967, the 'Summer of Love', in which the prospect of sexual liberation was in the air and there were exciting parallels to be drawn between the kaftan-wearing hordes of the King's Road and the denizens of bygone Charleston lawns. Frances Partridge professed herself shocked by the vulgarity of the *Sunday Times* serialisation, a riot of outsize pictures and flaring headlines advertising 'Trouble at the Mill House' and 'The Abode of Love', but the effect of emphasising the sexual irregularities was to make Bloomsbury seem thoroughly up to date while fostering a belief that, as Clive James once jokily put it, 'the Bloomsbury people were the ur-hippies'.

In fact this was a travesty of Bloomsbury's relationship with the generations that followed it. It takes only a glance at Frances Partridge's 1960s diaries to establish quite how equivocal were her dealings with the beautiful people of Swinging London, and despite the repeated urgings of her sophisticated young friends she has no time at all for *Sgt Pepper's Lonely Hearts Club Band*. But in some ways this separation is beside the point. Mysteriously, Bloomsbury had contrived to satisfy the cultural expectations of a new constituency of readers. Much the same tendency characterises later and predominantly American approaches to Virginia Woolf, in which critics galvanised by the new feminist, historical and psychoanalytic treatments of famous women writers detected in her qualities of which she herself was very probably unaware. All this led to the odd spectacle of a praiseworthy attempt to determine new vantage points on Woolf gradually mutating into an ideological crusade. It is one thing to commend *Night and Day*, *Three Guineas* and *The Years* for their supposed radicalism, or even to claim that the earlier drafts of Woolf's novels are 'much more radical, more left-wing, more egalitarian, more lesbian and more feminist than the published texts themselves' – the words are Louise DeSalvo's – but the critic who argues that Woolf is not only a pacifist socialist but 'deeply committed to the revolution' is simply not being faithful either to the works or to the highly complex and ambiguous personality that created them.

Leonard Woolf died in 1969, two years after *Beginning Again*, the third volume of his autobiography, confirmed the strength of the Bloomsbury renaissance by winning the W. H. Smith Prize. If Bloomsbury had a chatelaine, here in the last third of the twentieth century, it was Frances Partridge (1900–2004). From the angle of Bloomsbury's early history and what might be supposed to constitute its presiding spirits, Mrs Partridge's credentials were irreproachable. As Frances Marshall she had been a member of the Ham Spray *ménage à quatre*, along with Lytton, Ralph and Ralph's former wife, Dora Carrington. She was a tenacious defender of Bloomsbury *amour propre*, who managed to see off a proposed Ken Russell version of *Lytton Strachey* and fought a long delaying action against Peter Luke's play *Bloomsbury*, which duly expired after a five-week run at the Phoenix Theatre in 1978. Finally, and conclusively, she had preserved a haul of letters and diaries which, in indefatigable old age, she was eager to use in defence of Bloomsbury heritage. To read any of her ten volumes in this line, beginning with *A Pacifist's War* (1978) and ending with *Ups and Downs*, which appeared shortly before her death, is an odd experience. It is not that she isn't horribly shrewd, or that her opinions on almost any subject that strays beneath her lens aren't worth having, merely that her sensibilities have been paralysed by the glamour of these past associations. No modern literary personality or contemporary cultural fad or change of generational standards is so singular that it can't in the end be judged by way of the old Bloomsbury standards.

And so, meeting Cyril Connolly for the first time in 1948, she reflects – disapprovingly – on how 'the modern smart intellectual falls so far below Old Bloomsbury, who knew that personal relations came before money, good food and luxury'. At Charleston, in the company of her daughter-in-law Henrietta and the latter's friend Georgia Tennant – the brightest of the 1960s bright young things – she can 'feel in them both how the influence of that extraordinary and ever-fresh civilisation had pulled against the superficial glamour of the dashing young people who live for their own beauty, sex-appeal and clothes and keep themselves in a state of hectic stimulation with drinks and drugs'. Charleston increasingly became her talisman, a place where 'real values have been aimed at and achieved, something lovingly created and kept alive. Even now when nearly all of them are dead, it is the same.'

No one, perhaps, among second-generation Bloomsberries, had seen so much of the movement from the inside or was better qualified to write about it: even as a very young woman, caught up in an exclusive world of intellectual debate and sophisticated repartee, she seems thoroughly at home, always up to her opponents' fighting weight. Yet the materials assembled in Anne Chisholm's sympathetic biography, though intended as a case for the defence, could equally well be used by a prosecuting counsel. Frances believed – and this is by no means an exhaustive list – in the pursuit of pleasure, however austerely defined, in 'reason', in the paramount importance of personal relations, in not interfering when those relations took an unusual or potentially threatening form, and, notoriously during the Second World War, in an exacting brand of pacifism whose full implications she sometimes shied away from pursuing. The knots that she and her husband Ralph tied themselves into in the early 1940s, snug in their Wiltshire house and taking little interest in the war effort, are, in effect, *A Pacifist's War*'s subterranean theme. What ought they to think of America's arrival in the conflict (Ralph is excited; Frances fears it will make things worse)? What about the soldiers manoeuvring nearby (Ralph, who had fought gallantly in the Great War, sympathises; Frances initially resents their 'bestial muffled shouts')? Press agitation over the Mosleys' release from prison prompts the comment: 'As neither Ralph nor I accept the principle that people should be shut up for their principles, the question doesn't arise for us.' It is the same with Lord Haw-Haw and his inflammatory broadcasts on Berlin radio: Frances dislikes him, naturally, but at the same time cannot doubt his sincerity.

All this raises fascinating questions about the limits of freedom, democratic values and collective will, from which Frances habitually steps aside when the going gets tough. The idea that in tolerating the activities of people who, if left to their own devices, will cease to tolerate you and, if given political power, will set about fashioning an environment in which the concept of tolerance is very soon extinguished scarcely occurs to her. Neither does the thought that the ability of well-bred intellectual types to debate the circumstances in which they will or won't support military conflict largely depends on the possession of a private income: one might even say that it was only the degree of isolation from the world that the Partridges managed to contrive that enabled them to be so high-minded about it. This is not to deny Frances's courage – the Partridges' pacifism did not enhance their popularity among their Wiltshire neighbours – merely to note that her conviction that what was needed, as the panzers swept across France in the summer of 1940, was a rational discussion of motive ignores any idea of how the world actually works.

The same kind of evasiveness applies to some of the mysteries of her private life. The most obvious puzzle is what led her to suppress so many of her natural instincts. Whenever anyone close to her died – Ralph in 1960, her beloved son Burgo of an unsuspected aneurysm in 1963 – their bodies were simply taken away for instant, unmemorialised despatch. Ralph's infidelities with a succession of London-based mistresses were sedulously unpicked in tea-table conversation. Admirable as all this self-possession may be on paper, there is a terrible chilliness at its heart. A wife who hurled dinner plates at her husband's fancy woman or sneered at her choice of lipstick might have had less dignity, but one would have liked her more. In the end, however resistant to some of the attitudes on display, one puts down an account of her life with a genuine admiration for the subject's integrity and indomitable spirit while wondering if the gap between right-thinking, no-nonsense rationalism and faint complacency isn't sometimes a little too occluded for comfort.

The diaries are full of sharp little judgements of the people who strayed into the Partridges' orbit. In the circumstances it was hardly to be expected that Frances and Ralph should avoid being judged themselves: Ham Spray, consequently, makes several appearances in late twentieth-century fiction – a source of amusement but also, to those who had difficulty in swallowing the Bloomsbury myth, sheer bewilderment. Cynthia Kee's novel *A Responsible Man* (1993) reproduces the living conditions of the late 1950s, when Cynthia had first been taken to the house by her husband, the journalist Robert Kee, their toings and froings conducted in an atmosphere of social and intellectual superiority. Frances and Ralph appear as 'Vivian' and 'Guy', joking about their servants, disdaining television and maliciously reading out their letters over the breakfast table. There is embarrassed naked swimming in the outdoor pool. 'Speaking seemed to be a sort of game to be played with initiates; an odd word here or there, a cue for general amusement.'

Much more devastating in some of its implications, in that it was written by a long-time Bloomsbury observer capable of cracking some of these ciphers, is V. S. Pritchett's story 'Cocky Olly', not published until as late as 1989 but describing the Ham Spray routines of the immediately post-war period. Intriguingly, Pritchett's narrator is not a version of himself but a girl named Sarah, whose conventionally minded parents disapprove of the queer company to be found in the house next door. Ralph is 'Glanville Short', Frances 'Emma' and Burgo 'Benedict', while the guests at their weekend parties are disparaged by Sarah's father as a 'Gang of traitors. Pacifists, long-haired pansies, atheists, bathing stark naked in that swimming pool. Friends of Hitler and Stalin.' Like Ralph, Glanville retains his military rank ('calls himself a major'), and has survived the experience of being blown up and buried alive during the Great War.

Warned off the precincts of 'Lower Marsh House' by her father and mother, Sarah is understandably fascinated by its inhabitants. Caught in a sudden rain shower and soaked to the skin she ends up sheltering from the storm chez Short, is introduced to Emma ('a short woman with small, brown, brilliant eyes'), invited to complete a jigsaw ('How beastly they are to put so much water in the thing. It's cheating. What a bore') and, by now intoxicated by the lives they lead, instructed to stay to tea. The visit culminates in the wild halloo of 'Cocky Olly', a chasing game played through the house, during which Benedict's weirdness ('There's a dead body in there', etc.) reveals itself. Glanville, meanwhile, is on the telephone to his bookmaker. The second half of the piece concentrates on Benedict, the boarding school in Dorset from which he periodically absents himself – as did Burgo – his eventual transfer to Newbury Grammar School (ditto) and a bizarre and rather frightening episode in which he entices Sarah on to the wrong train ('I'm running away. I hate that school. I hate Glanville. I'm not going back') from which they have to be rescued with maximal inconvenience to everyone involved.

It is not known whether Frances ever read 'Cocky Olly' – when questioned in later life she would say only that she preferred Pritchett's conversation to his books – but as an introductory guide to the late Bloomsbury hearth and home it stands in a class of its own. And in the end you suspect that what will survive of Bloomsbury in the popular imagination – selected works aside – is its social dimension, that endless pageant of picnics on summer greensward, Olympian conversations and informal chatter about who has run off with whom, in which so much of what is on offer reduces itself to gesture, inference, tantalising fragments whose ultimate design hangs slightly beyond the grasp of those who don't possess the ulterior knowledge required to decipher its code. Useless, of course, to reproach Bloomsbury for its exclusivity. It was their club: why should they be expected to let non-members through the door?

On the other hand, as with many a closed society, its protocols could be baffling to the non-affiliate. At exactly the same time that Frances Partridge was embarking on her Bloomsbury preservation campaign – writing her cross letters to literary editors who had chosen what she judged to be the wrong reviewers for Bloomsbury memoirs, fighting her battles against vulgarising theatre producers – the young Franco-Canadian novelist David Plante was making his debut in literary London. As might be expected from a young man on the make with a bulging address book, Plante's 1960s diaries are full of Bloomsbury shadings, but they also exhibit a keen interest in what Bloomsbury might be thought to consist of, what, in the last resort, made it tick. And so, coming back from a meeting with the elderly Duncan Grant, he decides that 'there is enough Bloomsbury left for someone to feel a part of it in its residue'. At the same time the Bloomsbury code of practice is sometimes all but inexplicable. Thus on one occasion he receives a visit from the mercurial Henrietta Garnett, Burgo Partridge's widow and Frances's daughter-in-law. Henrietta is wearing an antique ring which Ottoline Morrell had given to her grandmother. She had handed it on to her daughter who, according to Henrietta, 'found it in a drawer among dirty socks, put it in an envelope which she didn't seal, misspelled my married name and got my address all wrong, and sent it off to me, and it arrived. And that is Bloomsbury.' Finally, there is the occasion on which he reads Virginia Woolf's diaries. At first the young man is fascinated by the people who appear, only to discover that 'as I read my fascination diminished, and I see, not a world, but a room with blank, windowless walls and a low ceiling, Virginia's own room where she is locked in, locked in with people whom she gives no space to move about, to talk to one another, to be themselves'.

CHAPTER 9

Editors at War

An editor frays away his true personality in the banalities of good mixing, he washes his mind in other people's bathwater, he sacrifices his inner voice to his engagement book.

Cyril Connolly

It is very proper that you should have proud memories of *Horizon*. It was the outstanding publication of its decade.

Evelyn Waugh, letter to Cyril Connolly, 23 October 1961

Surveys of the literary scene of the early 1940s have a habit of reducing themselves to questions of ownership, aggrandising tendencies that left inferior forms trailing in their wake. Was this – a classification frequently offered at the time – a highbrow's war? A poet's war? An essayist's war? A short-story-writer's war, even? All these attributions have something to be said for them, quite as much as the representative figures – a J. Maclaren-Ross, a Dylan Thomas – whose lives are regularly brought forth as a means of illustrating the effects of six years of military conflict on the individual and collective temperaments caught up in it. On the other hand, one thing the period 1939–45 certainly was not is a novelist's war. By and large, most of the great fictions inspired by the experience of military service hung fire for ten or twenty years, and sometimes even longer. *The Military Philosophers*, the final volume of the wartime trilogy included in Anthony Powell's *A Dance to the Music of Time*, did not appear until 1968. Part of this dereliction was to do with straightforward separation from the literary world, a self-enforced absence from the desk brought about by military service or various kinds of war-work. Evelyn Waugh served in a commando unit; Powell in Military Intelligence; Graham Greene in the secret service. Waugh was an exception, managing to amass sufficient leisure time to allow the writing of two full-length novels, but most of his serving contemporaries found their duties so onerous that they neither had time to put pen to paper nor to keep up with the literary controversies of the day. Asked by an interviewer late in life whether he thought 'intellectuals' had deplored Auden's and Isherwood's flight to America in 1939, Powell would only point out that he 'was almost immediately in the army when war broke out' and remained in khaki for six years. There were more pressing concerns than Auden's navel-gazing in New York.

Even more important than the absence of many writers on active service were the conditions that prevailed on the Home Front and their effect on the colleagues left behind. War-work, whether in government offices or in a 'reserved occupation' thought to be keeping up the nation's morale, generally involved long hours and left little time for writing. Orwell's two years as a talks producer on the BBC's Eastern Service severely restricted his availability for freelance work. Patrick Hamilton, who found himself contributing continuity dialogue for popular-music shows, got off comparatively lightly, but even he produced only a single novel between 1939 and 1945. The novelist who spent his days labouring in Bomber Command's press office or, like Beverley Nichols, touring armaments factories in the service of propaganda journalism, might possibly devote his evenings to book reviewing, but it took an unusually high degree of stamina to embark on any sustained creative work. More demoralising even than this was the general atmosphere in which the war – the early years of the war, especially – was fought. Orwell's diaries constantly refer to the impossibility of producing anything of lasting value against a backdrop of falling bombs and gloom-ridden newspaper headlines. More than one novel-reviewer filing his weekend round-up in the days after France fell in the early summer of 1940 reflected on the utter incongruity of his task. The detachment of a Hugh Walpole, who, arriving in Cornwall a month later for a working holiday, professed himself 'tranquillised . . . I feel that I could stay here for months, and the war far, far away', was altogether exceptional.

This uncertainty gave such novels as were written during the war an oddly provisional quality, the feeling that, however purposeful the unravelling of the various individual and collective lives on display, what follows can only aspire to the status of an interim report, ripe to be modified or overthrown altogether by information that is not yet to hand. Waugh's *Put Out More Flags* (1942) ends in limbo and the hope that, as one of the characters puts it, there is 'a new spirit abroad'. Even when the war's outcome could be confidently predicted, the novelist could be found looking two ways at once: forward to the likely arrangements of a post-war world; backwards to a milieu whose incidental pleasures loomed all the larger in a landscape of rationing and blackout curtains. Little of this allowed for a realistic treatment of what was immediately to hand. Looking back at *Brideshead Revisited* (1945) from the vantage point of the late 1950s, Waugh noted that it was conceived in a period of 'threatening disaster'. In consequence, the book is 'infused with a kind of gluttony, for food and wine, for the splendours of the recent past, and for rhetorical and ornate language, which now with a full stomach I find distasteful'.

Had Waugh not been writing his novel at breakneck pace in a few months' leave cadged from a sympathetic commanding officer, it would presumably have been written in a very different way, or rather – at least this is Waugh's implication – it was only the peculiar circumstances of the war and the shadow of what might happen after it that caused it to appear at all. *Brideshead* is a prophetic novel, which envisages the post-war world as a kind of socialist holiday camp, and, as a panegyric preached over the coffin of the stately home, is thoroughly inaccurate: the role of the National Trust in preserving the nation's historic buildings was, as Waugh conceded, something he was unable to foresee. Much more common in the fiction of the war is a preoccupation with particular domestic talking points which the war had thrown up: evacuees, say, or the prevalence of fifth columnists, the whole quickly subsumed into the spectacle of groups of sometimes very different people quietly and dutifully getting on with their lives, with the conflict itself only a distant rumour in the background. A representative specimen might be Monica Dickens's *The Fancy* (1942), set mostly in a west London munitions factory, where the constraints of rationing and the fractured personal lives lived out against a constant threat of displacement are presented with absolute matter-of-factness.

If it was not a novelist's war, then whose was it? Certainly, to return to the idea of the 'highbrows' war', it was an era in which the circulation of 'serious' books increased, fuelled by the availability of cheap paperbacks and their popularity among the armed services. British Army battledress incorporated a pocket above the left knee known as the 'Penguin pocket'; *Penguin New Writing*'s fifth number carried a footnote asking readers to leave the book at post offices for forwarding 'so that men and women in the services enjoy it too'. The intelligent, articulate soldier, deeply concerned about the state of the world to which he will return after the cessation of hostilities, is a feature of much of the fiction written in the war's aftermath (see, for example, Kingsley Amis's 'I Spy Strangers', set in the run-up to the 1945 general election, in which a mock-Parliament debates the shape of post-war social arrangements). Certainly, it was an era in which a vast amount of poetry was written and read, although its abundance could not disguise the fact that the old poetic mainstreams were breaking up into dozens of tiny tributaries. To read a chapter or two of one of the great period sourcebooks – Derek Stanford's somewhat score-settling *Inside the Forties*, say – is to be plunged head first into a terrific sub-world of subgroups and alliances, full of New Romantics and Neo-Apocalyptics zealously conspiring against each other, 'challenges to Possum' and pitched battles at the Poetry Society, and a feeling that the best seats are being reserved for the people with the loudest voices or the most efficient publicity machines. As Nicholas Moore put it, some time afterwards, 'The Forties were not a good time for poets. They were a good time for hangers-on, for literary gossips, for mediocrities, for people who wished to gawp at the great or the would-be great or the play actors.'

In an atmosphere of constantly shifting personnel, of promising careers put on hold by the arrival of conscription papers or cut short by death, the best of what remains in the wartime anthologies has the air of reportage: Henry Green's impressionist renderings of his time in the Auxiliary Fire Service; Maclaren-Ross's gamey short stories of army life, which have a habit of reducing themselves merely to descriptions of milieu: Kafkaesque encounters with army bureaucracy; two soldiers trying to remember details of an anonymous comrade who has killed himself for the benefit of his grieving father. For all his idiosyncrasies (the mirrored sunglasses, the death's-head sword-stick, the brothel-creeper shoes) Maclaren-Ross is a characteristic early 1940s figure, commanding and in some sense created by the environment he inhabited – in this case wartime Soho, with its restless congeries of resilient bohemians, its servicemen home on leave, its long-term population of drunks and prostitutes. It was not just that the war offered Maclaren-Ross a focus for his admittedly rather wayward talent, and a backdrop in which he felt at home, but that its working conditions, its profusion of little magazines and more or less enthusiastic sponsors, were suited to the kind of material he aspired to write. According to his biographer, in the nine-month period between summer 1944 and spring 1945 Maclaren-Ross's stories appeared at the rate of almost one a month, in periodicals ranging from well-known weeklies and monthlies such as *John Bull*, the *Strand Magazine* and *Lilliput* to *Summer Pie* and *Christmas Pie* – charity fund-raisers published by Messrs Hutchinson – and wholly obscure publications such as the *World Digest of Fact and Comment*.

Maclaren-Ross's range seems exceptional, even for the print-hungry 1940s. On the other hand, Angus Wilson, only half a decade later, was able to submit his early work to a vast array of outlets, including the *Cornhill*, *Occident*, the *Windmill*, *Argosy*, *Life and Letters* and the *Wind and the Rain*. Clearly, in terms of medium and influence, the war belonged not so much to the poet or the short-story writer but to the man or woman who sponsored them: the editor. Yet the considerable impact made by the leading literary magazines of the day – *Horizon*, *Penguin New Writing* and *Poetry London* – is also a mark of the way in which the wider cultural environment surrounding them had begun to change. The three great modernist magazines of the 1930s – *New Verse*, *Twentieth Century Verse* and the *New Criterion* – had all ceased publication in 1939. Their successors were conscious that they occupied different territory, that their editorial policies were founded more on general expertise than sharply delineated principle. What might look like a willed eclecticism was often no more than a practical necessity. 'However much we should like to have a paper that was revolutionary in opinions or original in technique', Connolly wrote in *Horizon*'s opening number, 'it is impossible to do so when there is a certain suspension of judgement and creative activity . . . Our standards are aesthetic, and our politics in abeyance.' While it would be a mistake to take this statement at face value – and no analysis of Connolly's editorial pronouncements can ignore his habit of overstating his case – the *Criterion* subscriber turned *Horizon* reader who came across his musings on 'ivory shelters' or the artist's responsibilities during wartime would have been instantly aware that he, or she, had arrived on an entirely different planet.

Connolly returned to this theme nearly a quarter of a century later in an essay entitled 'Fifty Years of Little Magazines'. Here he distinguishes between the 'dynamic' and the 'eclectic' (the modern equivalents would doubtless be 'proactive' and 'reactive') – editors with exclusive ideological purposes, and editors compelled by force of circumstance to settle for a catch-all pluralism ('Some flourish on what they put in, others by what they keep out'). The dynamic editor, Connolly concluded, 'runs his magazine like a commando course where men are trained to assault the enemy position; the eclectic editor is like a hotel proprietor whose rooms fill up every month with a different clique'. Again, you suspect Connnolly of overstating his case, ignoring the fact that the most ideologically driven editor is motivated, first and foremost, by the need for good material: even Orwell, submitting 'Shooting an Elephant' to John Lehmann's *New Writing* in 1936, and aware of the magazine's political stance, wondered quite how 'anti-fascist' his subject matter might be. All the same, this is not mere posturing: Connolly, for all his world-weariness, would have liked nothing better than to be a 'dynamic' editor had circumstances allowed it. Meanwhile, there were definite advantages in eclecticism, not least relative commercial success. *Horizon* sold an average of 8,000 copies a month; the October 1942 number of *Poetry London* with a cover by Henry Moore boasted a print order of 10,000 – both respectable figures, but altogether eclipsed by *Penguin New Writing*, whose circulation, at its peak, hovered at 75,000 and whose *readership* must have extended to three or four times this. And yet, like some of the dilemmas of Connolly's plaintive editorialising, this, too, was in some sense artificial, a product of its time. To a very large degree the war had created the intellectual and environmental conditions in which *Horizon*, *Penguin New Writing*, *Poetry London* and magazines like them could flourish. Without war's stimulus they fell away into extinction, and if one factor unites their editors – Connolly, Lehmann and Tambimuttu – it is the difficulty they found in adjusting to the post-war world.

The Second World War may have given Cyril Connolly (1903–74) his first taste of unadulterated success, but the spadework had been done ten or fifteen years before. As an Old Etonian protégé of Desmond MacCarthy, he made his debut in the *New Statesman* as far back as 1927 with a long and claim-staking review of the seven-volume *Works of Laurence Sterne*. The piece is uncannily prophetic of the mature Connolly: the praise for 'irresponsibility' and 'exhilaration'; the enthusiasm for Sterne's 'serene utopias'; the fervent embrace of style ('his beauties are lost on those who contract intellectual hay-fever from fine writing'); the nods to *Lycidas* and Gray's 'Elegy', each a key element in the unfolding Connolly canon. And if Connolly had the talent, then he was also able to make use of an extraordinary range of highly placed wire-pullers at work on his behalf. To inspect the early part of his career is straightaway to wonder whether in the course of English literary history quite so many fairy godfathers had ever hung over a single cradle. His Balliol tutor, the legendary F. F. Urquhart, forgetting the embarrassment of Connolly's third-class degree, commended 'a man of unusual ability', encouraged him to find a publisher for his undergraduate journals and volunteered to show them to Eliot. John Buchan and Henry Newbolt, two of the grandest literary eminences of the day, consented to meet him and pronounced the sample of his correspondence he brought along to the interview 'very vivid and interesting'; it was agreed that, were he to write any travel pieces, Buchan, in his capacity as a director of Nelson's, would try to get them published. The wealthy American man of letters Logan Pearsall Smith engaged him as confidential secretary, allowed him £8 a week whether he turned up or not, lent him money and went so far as to pay off his duns. Connolly seems to have regarded all this as the most natural thing in the world. There were complaints about his pushiness – even the mild-mannered MacCarthy delivered a lecture or two on these lines – but by the late 1920s he was safely installed as one of the *New Statesman*'s regular novel-reviewers and lost no opportunity in making his fortnightly appearances as arresting as possible.

Auberon Waugh once suggested that a book reviewer stands or falls on the liveliness of his, or her, response. Judged on this scale, Connolly scores very high. Amid a riot of obscure enthusiasms and mandarin pronouncements, he never forgot that his first duty was to entertain, and that a book aimed squarely at conventional mainstream taste may still have merit. One of his great advantages as a reviewer is his awareness that there are novels and novels, that the critic who ventures into the bear pit of the fortnightly fiction round-up has to leave a certain part of his soul at the door, that to judge everything set before you by the benchmarks of a Joyce or a Woolf is to court disaster, not to mention alienating the vast majority of your readers. Orwell's remark about the reviewer needing a spring balance capable of weighing both an elephant and a flea clearly struck a chord with the man who could write: 'The great difficulty in reviewing novels is to maintain a double standard – one to judge novels as fiction, and the other as literature. Luckily very few novels pretend to be literature, but when they do it is necessary sometimes to slate them by one rule and praise them by another.' What might be called Connolly's fascination with mediocrity, his concern to distinguish good popular novels from bad ones, is an essential part of the astuteness he brought to his surveys of the 1930s literary scene. As his biographer Jeremy Lewis notes, much of the interest of his pre-war work lies in the insights it offers into the dreams of the period as reflected in middlebrow fiction. The tendency is most marked in a series of sketches he contributed to *Night and Day*, which follows the adventures of the solidly middlebrow Arquebus family, as anatomised by their daughter Felicity. Arquebus *père* works as blurb-writer for the publisher Mr Goulash; his wife's favourite authors, housed in a glass-fronted bookcase, include Phyllis Bentley, Beverley Nichols, Theodora Benson 'and some of the new young authors who left one rather breathless and whose books had lovely cold names like *Open the Sky* and *Armed October*'.

Not, of course, that this habit of lounging in the courtyards of the enemy ever encouraged Connolly to forget which side of the cultural barricade he was on. His bugbear, through nearly half a century of reviewing, was what he called 'the worthy second-rate'. Taxed with the rigour of his onslaughts against popular writing of the day, he declared that the real problem was one of surplus personnel: the train of fiction was already hopelessly overcrowded and all the comfortable seats were occupied by people with third-class tickets. It might seem surprising, in these circumstances, that he approved of Arnold Bennett, but then Bennett exhibited that crucial requirement, catholicity of taste: 'he has resisted the sclerosis of the imagination which drives elderly novelists into the last Tory refuges of English society, so that while Mr Galsworthy and Mr Walpole are borne down the stream of time, humped anxiously in slabs of property like Eskimo dogs marooned by the thaw on crumbling pack-ice, Mr Bennett is appreciating Proust and Joyce, and even inducing other people to read them'. What he emphatically did not approve of was sentimental Englishness, nature-worship, pastoralism, all that part of post-war writing which seemed to be putting itself at the disposal of the heritage industry. No one took greater delight in reinforcing the stereotype of the Georgian than Connolly. A diary entry from 1929 finds him striding along the downs at Lulworth Cove and castigating the 'awfulness' of the people who wrote about them: 'Kipling's thyme and dewponds, Belloc's beer and Chesterton's chalk, all the people writing poems at this moment for the *London Mercury*.' In a flash all the things he most disliked about English literary life and the social arrangements that abetted them ran riot through his imagination:

> I thought of all the ardent bicyclists, the heroic coupleteers, the pipe-smoking, beer-swilling young men on reading parties. The brass-rubbers, the accomplished morris dancers, the Innisfreeites, the Buchan-Baldwin-Masefield and Drinkwatermen, the Squires and Shanks and grim Dartmoor realists, the advanced tramp lovers.

Tirades of this sort undoubtedly added to Connolly's professional stock, but they did not make him popular: the nickname 'Boots', bestowed on him by his friends, was a truncation of Virginia Woolf's complaint about 'that smartiboots Connolly'. Already, in his mid-20s, the first signs of the Connolly legend were triumphantly on display. The Connolly myth, burnished up by its protagonist for the next thirty or forty years, resists exact definition, but it has its roots in Connolly's immensely complex attitude – at once realistic, fanciful and self-pitying – to the business of writing: the natural need, were anything to be accomplished, to try hard, balanced by the earnest desire not to be seen to be trying too hard, the awareness that many of the works of art he admired had been created by the ascetically single-minded always compromised by his need for idleness and sensual pleasure. At one level the thing Connolly most wanted to write was a masterpiece. At another, he seems to have realised that a fundamental part of his psychological make-up was satisfied by not writing it, by procrastination, the filing of thousands of words about the difficulty of writing thousands of words, the creation of artificial dilemmas – solitude versus conviviality, cash versus cachet, self-reliance versus sponging – which could be picked away at to the point where the endless, self-incriminating discussion of how one ought to live one's life sometimes seems to become an alternative to the life itself. A journal entry from 1927 sets these anxieties in sharp relief:

> Damn life, damn love, damn literature! In other words, damn journalism! Live out of London, drop journalism – yet to quit

> one made impossible by loneliness, the other by finance. Make £1,000 a year, make pots of money out of a novel! Too soft for journalism, too rough for literature. I should be wretched abroad, bored in the country – what can one do?

Unable to find the creative environment in which he could prosper, and already conscious that a certain part of him positively luxuriated in its absence, Connolly trod water for much of the 1930s, esteemed as a critic – the *New Statesman* berth was supplemented by work for the *Daily Telegraph* and the *Sunday Times* – but left far behind in the race for celebrity by Oxford *convives* such as Evelyn Waugh. Then, too, there was the question of his emotional life, in which early homosexual leanings were replaced by marriage to an American heiress named Jean Bakewell, destined to inherit £6,000 a year, but at this point sustained by a monthly $200 allowance. The Connollys departed for the south of France to try 'living for pleasure' and 'living for beauty', but Connolly was restless in the Gallic heat. *The Rock Pool* (1936), the novel inspired by this sequestration, featuring a gang of listless expatriate bohemians uncomfortably like himself, full of private jokes and considered obscene by English publishers, was eventually issued by Jack Kahane's Obelisk Press in Paris. A visit to Barcelona in November 1936 produced a brisk analysis of British support for Republican Spain: 'The typically English band of psychological revolutionaries, people who adopt left-wing political formulas because they hate their fathers or were unhappy at their public schools or insulted at the customs or lectured about sex.'

By this time there was another paradox intermittently on display, which might be defined as the difference between what Connolly thought of himself and the view taken by those who regarded him, on a scale somewhere between irritation and envy, from afar. From the vantage point of Cambridge English, or even that of the grammar school boy making his slow ascent up the rungs of Fleet Street, he was the embodiment of the coterie spirit, kept afloat by indulgent patrons, hedged about by well-placed friends keen to do him favours. Q. D. Leavis, in her review of *Enemies of Promise* (1938), the book in which Connolly finally managed to make a paying proposition out of one or two of his neuroses, offers some withering remarks about the personal element in his work. It was all very well for Connolly to praise Spender's study of Henry James. To Mrs Leavis, who lacked the advantage of knowing Spender personally but had, as she pointed out, been reading Henry James's novels for fifteen years, 'the only way in which his study affected me was as a botched-up piece of journalism by somebody who not only had no capacity for examining James's novels artistically but who had not even read them with ordinary care or intelligence'.

Horizon, whose debut number appeared in December 1939, attracted similar complaints. Its sponsor was Connolly's fast friend Peter Watson, an immensely wealthy Old Etonian whose grandfather had paid Maundy Gregory £30,000 for a peerage that was never delivered. The regularity of its paper supply, here in a world of requisition and shortage, owed everything to Connolly's contacts at the Ministry of Information, and the keen-eyed observer could not have failed to spot the presence in its columns of half a dozen writers with whom the editor had sat in classrooms at Eton or attended parties at Oxford. Faced with accusations of cronyism, Connolly would probably have replied that an editor gets nowhere by being over-fastidious, that it is better for a literary magazine to exist rather than not to exist, even if the money came from the Watson family's margarine fortune, and that the editorial clique included Waugh and Orwell as well as Brian Howard. Nonetheless, imputations of gentlemanly blandness occasionally stuck: even when the magazine espoused the cause of proletarian solidarity by publishing a piece about working in a coal mine its author, Gully Mason, was eventually revealed as an Old Etonian whose parents owned the mine.

To do Connolly justice, *Horizon*'s advance publicity signalled a determination to escape from some of these constraints. There was talk of encouraging unknown writers, of disregarding both the feuds of the past and the inertia of the present, of an effort to 'synthesise the aestheticism of the Twenties and the puritanism of the Thirties into something better'. And to a certain extent, Connolly lived up to his promise: the publication of 'A Bit of a Smash in Madras' made Maclaren-Ross's name. On the other hand, neither Forster, Woolf or Eliot could come up with anything for the opening number – Woolf contented herself with noting in her diary that the magazine was 'small, trivial, dull: So I think from not reading it' – and the well-known writers piped aboard in their place were Maugham, Walpole and Priestley: stalwarts of the Georgian old guard, whom Connolly himself could have been found mocking five years before. Meanwhile, attentive readers of the magazine's editorials could watch a different aspect of the Connolly myth slowly uncoiling itself: the spectacle of Connolly luxuriating in his guilt (at not having joined up), agonising over his attitude to the war effort and delighting in the complaints about indecision and inconsistency which were such a feature of the letters page.

At the heart of these anxieties lay a suspicion that armed conflict was not conducive to good writing. A *New Statesman* piece from the early months of the war declared that 'the best modern war literature is pacifist and escapist, and either ignores the war or condemns it'. As ever Connolly proposed to make a principle out of his vacillation: 'Our doubt is our passion and our passion is our doubt.' There was also a certain amount of jeering at those in uniform – 'dashing', 'stern', 'intrepid' and so, incriminatingly, on. The difficulty was that Connolly would have liked to be all these things himself, and the efforts made on his behalf by others reduced him to genuine, if still highly self-conscious, misery. As he put it in an 'Open Letter' to a serving soldier: 'Of course, all the time you had to fight. Don't think I am unaware of all this fighting, it is just that which churns the guilt round and round until it thickens into a kind of rancorous despair . . . Oh, why can't I fight for myself?'

There was something playful, to the point of teasing, in much of Connolly's relationship with his readers. Spender, who worked with him on the magazine, described these transactions as a kind of 'flirtation', in which frequent bouts of provocation were invariably followed by a return to probity and decorum. Complaints about his insistence that writers should turn their backs on the war – see Goronwy Rees's 'Letter from a Soldier', printed at the front of the July 1940 issue – brought concessions: 'We cannot afford the airy detachment of earlier numbers' Connolly conceded. 'We have walked through the tiger-house, speculating on the power and ferocity of the beasts and looked up to find the cage doors open.' On the other hand, his 'commitment', if that is what it was, was essentially backward-looking, anxious to preserve old values and masterpieces until such time as they were needed again: the bright, hard future held little interest for a man who, as *Enemies of Promise* revealed in rather painful detail, was still getting over his childhood. None of this, though, was enough to undermine Connolly's conviction that, for all his occasional disillusionment, he was engaged on a heroic task, for which posterity could be expected both to judge and reward him. Spender recalled his asking:

'Are you certain that anyone will want to read it in twenty years' time?' whenever a poem came up for discussion.

And the eclecticism, which he later lamented, had its advantages. Whatever one may think of Connolly's attitudes, his manifest absurdities, his striking of poses that he later came to regret, there is a great deal to be said for a publication whose index runs from Aragon to Waugh by way of Orwell, Henry Miller, Osbert and Sacheverell Sitwell and Octavio Paz. All of this, too, is to ignore the distinctive personal resonance which Connolly brought to his editorial duties. Maclaren-Ross's portrait in *Memoirs of the Forties* gives an idea of the powerful magic he brought to his dealings with aspiring contributors: the 'housemaster's outfit' of tweed jacket and baggy flannel trousers; the lunches at the Café Royal, the rolls of galley proofs brought out and corrected on his knee. It was something to have him on your side. Typical of his admiring supplicants was the fighter pilot Rollo Woolley, who scratched the words MY STORY ACCEPTED IN HORIZON ('The Pupil', 1942) across an empty page in his diary shortly before his death in the skies above North Africa.

The objections to *Horizon*'s stance, its editorial ruminations, its European reference points, and the talent pool from which Connolly acquired his contributors, were twofold. The first band of detractors, taking their cue from Mrs Leavis, complained of an elitism that was as much social as aesthetic: the same faces engaged on what were, more or less, the same routines; resistance to whom amounted to a symbolic skirmish in a much wider struggle then beginning to be fought out in British cultural life. Julian Symons once remarked that a study of the magazine's attitudes and its general preference for 'the bland over the abrasive' was essential to anyone who wished to understand the literary 1940s in England. To Symons and the other survivors of the previous decade's *galère* of little magazines, *Horizon* seemed, among other defects, to be insufficiently avant-garde. To another kind of reader, alternatively, the difficulty lay in its proudly worn sophistication. Waugh's *The Loved One*, printed in its entirety in the February 1948 number, and with Connolly as one of its dedicatees,* begins with

* 'I anticipated ructions & one reason, apart from the predominant one of my affection for yourself, for my seeking publication in *Horizon* was the confidence that its readers were tough stuff.' Evelyn Waugh to Cyril Connolly, 2 January 1948. See Mark Amory, ed.,*The Letters of Evelyn Waugh* (1980), 265.

two expatriate Englishmen washed up on the desolate shores of Hollywood puzzling over a specimen table of contents: 'Kierkegaard, Kafka, Connolly, Compton-Burnett, Sartre, "Scottie" Wilson,' Sir Francis Hinsley complains. 'Who are they? What do they want?' Dennis, his young friend, can only explain that he has 'heard of some of them. They were being talked about in London at the time I left.' Sir Francis is an Edwardian belles-lettrist ('"Arnold Bennett's debt to Zola"; "Flecker's debt to Henley". That was the nearest I went to the moderns'), but there were younger critics prepared to find Connolly's eternal Francophilia, his habit of interrupting a newspaper review to declare that he yearned to be loitering in some formal garden with great Corneille, sombre Racine and honest Molière, not only escapist but fundamentally bogus. And yet even the harshest younger critic would find it hard to overlook his one really singular achievement, here in the highly unpromising circumstances of early 1940. This, it might be said, was to find a vessel for his tastes and contrive to keep it afloat for the best part of a decade.

It was not to be expected – Connolly being Connolly – that this level of commitment could be indefinitely maintained, and one of the most remarkable things about *Horizon*, given the personality of the man who edited it, is that it lasted so long. Come the later 1940s Connolly was losing interest, accepting and then declining tempting offers from the *Observer*, pursuing vagrant literary enthusiasms that seemed to depend on which part of the world he happened to be staying in. By this stage the editorial spadework was being left to underlings. It was Sonia Brownell, shortly to become the second Mrs Orwell, who could claim the credit for discovering Angus Wilson, whose short story 'Mother's Sense of Fun' appeared in December 1947.* But by December 1949 it was all over, with a tenth-anniversary issue on the news-stands, and the (unfulfilled) hope of a reopening in the following year if conditions improved. Connolly's account of the last rites, filed some time after the event, is determinedly elegiac: 'We closed the long windows over Bedford Square, the telephone was taken, the furniture stored, the back numbers went to their cellar, the

* Miss Brownell's judgement was not infallible. She returned a poem by Theodore Roethke with the comment 'It seemed to us that your poetry was in a way very American in that it lacked that inspiration, inevitability or quintessence of writing that distinguishes good poetry from verse.'

files rotted in the dust. Only contributions continued to be delivered, like a suicide's milk.'

Like many a survivor from the gilded 1920s and the more puritanically minded 1930s, Connolly found the dispensations of the post-war era much less to his taste. Comfortable berths were secured – he inherited his old mentor Desmond MacCartney's column in the *Sunday Times* on the latter's death in 1952 – and bridgeheads established, but the tenor of the age was against him. The new academic criticism, especially of the kind peddled on American university campuses, greatly distressed him. 'Mr Blackmur teaches at Princeton,' he lamented of R. P. Blackmur's *Language and Gesture* (1955); 'he is a don; he writes to startle and impress; it would not do if he were too simple, or if what he wrote about was too simple.' There were similar complaints about the critic Hugh Kenner, who, Connolly declared, failed to grasp that Eliot's greatness lay not in the sum of his influences ('imitating Laforgue or digesting Bradley or restoring neoclassicism to the moribund Georgians') but from the deep awareness of unhappiness that breaks through the formal conventions of his verse. None of these strictures is disinterested, for running through them is the realisation that in this brave new world of jargon and tenure the kind of role that Connolly himself had occupied was tending to extinction:

> at the opposite end to the university teacher of 'creative writing' is the literary journalist. He cannot afford to be obscure; he is not subsidised; he has to compress his views into a few hundred words; he must grade, explain and entertain all at once, and his work is immediately forgotten, totally ignored except for those who write in to correct a name or a date.

In his 60s, now embarked on his third marriage, perpetually hard up and never less inclined to apply himself to the serious business of his craft, Connolly found himself ever more caught up in academic crossfire. The campus specialists would have liked him more had he not pronounced his judgements from behind a mask of self-deprecation. Meanwhile the books he continued fitfully to produce – mostly collections of rehashed journalism – lost him the respect of a new generation of writers who had grown up in his very considerable shadow. Kingsley Amis, reviewing *Previous Convictions* (1963) in the *New*

Statesman, thought that few judges born after 1920 would award him 'anything but a stiff sentence'. A paid-up member of the cultural establishment, a London literary racketeer, a propagandist on behalf of abroad and its inhabitants, a dilettante . . . 'one can write out the charge sheet with one's eyes shut'. It was the same with *The Modern Movement 1890–1950* (1965), the choice of a hundred key books which had inspired or consolidated modernism, criticised not only for its superficiality and want of rigour but for the large number of mistakes which Connolly had inadvertently admitted into the text. By the time of *The Evening Colonnade*, published shortly before his death, he had become almost wholly an elegist, memorialising and re-memorialising the landscapes of his 1920s youth ('Besides, the world was small. There were few Americans. All London was contained in one telephone book. The literary worlds met: Gide was Bloomsbury, the genial Stulik at the Eiffel Tower had his private rooms decorated by Wyndham Lewis. There was no thumbs-down jury of unfrocked Leavisites to stifle our modest exhibitionism. No rumble of a distant drum').

Assembling a final judgement on Connolly is far from easy. From one angle he is the worst sort of critic: vague, impressionistic, always letting a personal association or a pleasant memory get in the way of his disinterestedness, all too ready to make a performance of his attitude to the books on which he was asked to pronounce. From another this reliance on the personal touch is what gives much of his work its impetus. Even the most sentimental of his essays on the 1920s, and the constant chiming of their familiar names – Firbank, Eliot, Stulik in his glory – rarely fail to convey the sheer excitement of being a literary man on the make in the era of *Ulysses* and *The Flower Beneath the Foot*. And if *The Unquiet Grave* (1945), the selection of aphorisms and classically inspired fine writing by which he would probably prefer to be remembered, now seems simply redolent of its time, as much a product of the age of Spam and Nissen huts as *Brideshead Revisited*, then there is the question of influence. 'Sir,' Philip Larkin is supposed to have said to him when they met at Auden's memorial service, '*you formed me*.'

The full weight of the Connolly legend took some time to accrue. But the clouds of mythological glory that hung around the figure of Tambimuttu (1915–83) – Meary James Thurairajah Tambimuttu, to allow him his full name – seem to have been there from the start.

There were several explanations for the swathe which 'Tambi' cut through the literary world of the early 1940s. One of them was the sheer exoticism that he brought to the Soho backstreets and Bloomsbury squares in which most of his working life was spent, a whiff of the tantalising unknown that extended both to his antecedents and his whole approach to the art form in which he pined to distinguish himself. A Sinhalese émigré, of supposedly royal descent – he claimed to be able to trace his familial line back to the last king of Jaffna – he arrived on the boat from Colombo early in 1938 bearing a letter of introduction to Eliot and a determination to follow every known prescription of how a poet ought to look and behave. With his blue-black hair, long and apparently boneless fingers, shivering beneath a habitual Melton overcoat buttoned up to the chin, he became a fixture of the Fitzroy pubs and coffee shops, a kind of high-priest of poetry preaching what was not so much souped-up romanticism – although there was plenty of that – but universalism. 'Every man has poetry in him' he once declared, in a characteristic piece of windy editorialising. 'Poetry is the awareness of the mind to the universe. It embraces everything in the world . . . It is a universal force and like God it can never be discovered, although it will always be present, directing thought.'

Even at this stage, not everyone was convinced by what Maclaren-Ross called his 'Holy Fakir of Poetry side'. But the introductions bore fruit ('T. S. Eliot says I'm going to be a great poet,' he reported to sympathisers. 'I could have cried when he said that') and by the end of 1938, with the help of his friend Anthony Dickins, he had scraped together sufficient funds for the first number of *Poetry London*. Featuring the work of Dylan Thomas, George Barker and Stephen Spender, neatly produced on quarto pages and with imaginative use of illustrations, this drew warm compliments from cognoscenti: Lawrence Durrell congratulated the editors for 'creating a format capable of accommodating every kind of poet writing today'. There was more trouble about money – intended as a monthly, the magazine had managed only six numbers by June 1941 – but by this time Tambi's star was firmly in the ascendant. On the strength of *Poetry London*, in which his epic poem 'Out of this War' had begun to appear, Eliot invited him to compile a yearly anthology for Faber (only a single volume, *Poetry in Wartime*, appeared). Then, in 1942, came an association with the newly founded firm of Nicholson & Watson, who declared themselves willing both to underwrite the magazine and finance a publishing imprint. This was eventually given the grandiose and Gallic-sounding title of Editions Poetry London. Things were quiet at first – only two books appeared in 1944 – but the following year brought the bumper 264-page *Poetry London X* and a publishing programme that included Henry Moore's *Shelter Sketch Book* and works by Henry Miller, Anaïs Nin and Vladimir Nabokov. Not the least of Tambi's achievements was that he came within an ace of publishing the first UK edition of *Lolita*.

On the one hand, Editions Poetry London came drenched in the scent of a new-fangled bohemian cosmopolitanism. On the other, it harked back to a much older poetic tradition. Like Harold Monro a quarter of a century before, Tambi was keen to foster links between artists and poets. Nicholas Moore's *The Glass Tower* (1945) contained drawings by Lucian Freud. Graham Sutherland was commissioned to illustrate David Gascoyne's *Poems 1937–1942*. The critics, meanwhile, were divided. Eliot might have remarked that it was only in *Poetry London* that he consistently expected to find new poets who mattered, but there were frequent onslaughts by those unimpressed by the 'every man is a poet' line, who detected in Tambi's eclecticism only a barely disguised free-for-all. As Geoffrey Grigson put it: 'The axis which runs through *Poetry London* is that all poems are poems, and equally worth printing. The only axis is to have no axis, beyond the faith in muddle and contradiction.'

Already, though, the achievement had begun to take second place to the legend. Maclaren-Ross recorded the eyewitness account of a girl who, engaged as the magazine's secretary, was taken to a basement room containing a half-collapsed camp bed, a kitchen chair and a work table on which lay a bottle of blue-black ink, a chewed Post Office pen-holder and stacks of embossed crested paper. She was told that she would be paid fortnightly on Friday, whereupon Tambi borrowed a five-pound note she happened to have with her to go out to lunch with Eliot. An employee of Editions Poetry London left a similarly fraught description of working conditions at the firm's Manchester Square office, with Edith Sitwell lurking on the staircase and Elizabeth Smart, whose *By Grand Central Station I Sat Down and Wept* appeared in 1945, arriving together with a baby and a note from the child's father, George Barker, reading '& this is my angel . . . Take care of her for me.'

Even more so than Connolly, Tambi was a creature of the war and the unprecedented professional environment that came with it. Come the post-war atmosphere of falling book sales, risk avoidance and fiscal prudence, he cut a much less confident figure. In 1946 Nicholson & Watson decided to review their investment. A new backer, Richard Marsh, put in £5,000 and acquired 51 per cent of the business; by 1949 Editions Poetry London's presiding genius had been forced out. Thereafter, although there were still publishing projects and talk – seldom more than talk – of eye-catching arts world schemes, Tambi's fortunes underwent a long, slow decline. There was a relocation to America, but *Poetry London/New York* never really moved beyond first base, despite the confident note struck by its editorials: 'Poetic compression of the highest order is only possible within a culture which expresses the total man, and is universally understood.'

On the face of it the 1960s and Tambi were made for each other, but while there were visits to Timothy Leary's LSD centre at Milbrook and two issues of *Poetry London/Apple Magazine*, forged out of a meeting with the Beatles, much more representative of the decade was a despairing letter from 1968 to the poet Michael Hamburger asking him to get his memoirs serialised in the *Sunday Times*, on the grounds that 'telephone and gas will be cut off next week unless I pay, and the rent is due on the first'. Still, though, he persisted, loyally kept afloat by friends who admired his ideals and cherished his absolute indifference to the practicalities of business. His last, unrealised, scheme was to produce a book in celebration of the royal wedding between Prince Charles and Lady Diana Spencer.

Hindsight, abetted by the large number of volumes of 1940s memoirs through which he vagrantly wanders, has tended to write Tambimuttu off as a kind of high-grade confidence trickster, but in his defence that is not – or not quite – how he appeared at the time. A 1971 reprint of some of the *Poetry London* material provoked the *Times Literary Supplement*'s reviewer to bemoan the 'vatic posturing of charlatans and mediocrities' and suggest that whatever good verse could be found 'here and there in the quagmire' was a result of the law of averages holding up in exceptional conditions. To set against this is a certain amount of flair and a great deal of disinterested propagandising on poetry's behalf. As Derek Stanford once remarked: 'Tambi was not an original thinker, but the manner in which he took over our English bohemian ideas and approaches and strained them through his Tamil make-up resulted in something which appeared both novel and very exotic.' All the same, it is rather significant that Stanford follows this encomium with an anecdote about a mislaid poem by Dylan Thomas being finally discovered in a brimming chamber pot. We ought not to grudge him his Festschrift, Ian Hamilton pronounced, on the appearance of a memorial volume six years after his death: if nothing else, the book gave us an idea of how he got away with it.

And perhaps the lasting symbol of Tambi's undoubted influence on the teeming literary world of the early 1940s is the famous photograph taken during the recording of a wartime broadcast on the BBC's Eastern Service and featuring the editor of *Poetry London* alongside Eliot, Orwell, Empson and the Indian novelist Mulk Raj Anand. Eliot, grave-faced and austere, might be a don who has strayed into the proceedings by mistake. Empson, bespectacled and engrossed, has the appearance of a benign civil servant. But Tambi, long fingers poised over his script, lock of hair falling over his forehead, looks every inch a poet.

Like Connolly, his bitter rival in the early *Horizon* days, John Lehmann (1907–87) could look back on a career extended deep into the pre-war era. His first proper job was as manager of the Hogarth Press, and the Woolfs had published a collection of his poems, *A Garden Revisited*, as long ago as 1931. Much less defatigable than Connolly, much more habituated to the writing of books, the whole business of putting words on paper that the author of *The Unquiet Grave* found so demoralising, Lehmann made a virtue out of his staying power, and yet there lurks a suspicion that his great days belong to that overpopulated corner of the 1930s in which homosexuality and a belief in the unstoppable rise of proletarian socialism sat side by side. A champion satyromaniac with a string of working-class boyfriends, Lehmann was, additionally, keen to harness his sexual tendencies to the forward march of radical politics. 'Through sexual activity,' as his biographer puts it, 'he might at last reach the inner sanctum of the proletariat.' If one of the indirect consequences of any biographical sketch of Lehmann is to demonstrate quite how personally – let alone creatively – disastrous the results of this intermingling could be, then, in the end, it is Lehmann's representativeness that makes him interesting. Seen in the round, his fifty-year career as a man of letters – poet, editor, critic, autobiographical novelist – conveys a terrific sense of a determined, if not particularly likeable man relentlessly pursuing the kind of twentieth-century literary life that might have been expected of someone of his talents, connections and background.

Much more than Orwell, Powell or Henry Green – to name only three of Lehmann's Old Etonian near-contemporaries – the question of upbringing looms dramatically over his early years. The idyllic childhood, the family money, the establishment connections (his father was a *Punch* staffer and Liberal MP), the range of sibling talent (Rosamond became a well-known novelist, Beatrix a respected actress), emotional tutelage at Cambridge courtesy of the ubiquitous G. H. Rylands: in some ways Lehmann looks exactly like the kind of doomed apprentice whom Connolly anatomised in *Enemies of Promise*, compromised by sheer weight of expectation. Lehmann may well have been secretly aware of this constraint, for he turned miserable towards the end of his time at Eton and the cultivated aloofness that characterised his emotional life can seem infinitely chilly. At the same time, all this provided a free admission ticket to the enticing world of literature. The Woolfs thoroughly approved of him; he was their sort of person from their sort of milieu ('Lehmann may do,' Virginia noted, 'a tight, aquiline boy, pink, with the adorable curls of youth; yes, but persistent, sharp'). The offer of a partnership had to be turned down for want of capital, but as manager of the firm's operations at their Tavistock Square HQ, he was responsible for the *New Signatures* anthology edited by Michael Roberts. Already, though, the central dilemma of his professional life was moving inexorably towards him: was he to be the impresario of other people's creative work or a creative writer himself? On the other hand, even being an impresario had its risky side, as he discovered when attempting to steer his friend Stephen Spender's novel *The Temple* into print. The Woolfs were unimpressed. Judging them too 'emotional' in their attitude to their publishing activities, Lehmann quit in August 1932, took himself off to the continent and began to formulate some of the principles that would characterise the editorial thrust of *New Writing*.

The 1930s were the great age of the manifesto, literary and otherwise. Poking fun at 'Johnny Hoop', a burlesqued version of Brian Howard who meanders through the *Vile Bodies* charivari, Evelyn Waugh notes that one of his principal reasons for not joining the Communist Party was that its manifesto had been written, once and for all, by somebody else. The fascination of Lehmann's various blueprints lies in their eagerness both to bite the hand that fed him and pour scorn on fashionable panaceas from beyond the Atlantic:

> Wanted: a new kind of journalism in London to drive the elderly softnesses and condescensions of the *New Statesman* and *Spectator* off the stage, and to usurp the pretence-new of the pseudo-American.
>
> Wanted: a new kind of art to blow the spunkless complacencies of Bloomsbury sky-high.
>
> Wanted: a new kind of writing that has really caught a spark from the true machine of modern life.

As to how this might work in practice, the distinguishing mark of *New Writing*'s early numbers – the first two were published in 1936 – was the volume of working-class writers (Charles Harte, George Garrett, Leslie Halward) and the pronounced ideological slant, including a contingent of Soviet writers recommended by Ralph Fox. These tendencies were yet more emphatically displayed in the following spring, when the magazine began to be underwritten by the communist publishers Lawrence & Wishart: the third number had a much more political tone, contained a tribute to Fox – by this time dead in Spain – and, under the heading 'Workers and Fighters', a collection of pieces on the Spanish war, Polish oppression and the great Hunger March of 1922. Subsequently Lehmann renewed his ties with the Hogarth Press and produced three numbers of *New Writing New Series* 'with the assistance', as he put it, of Isherwood and Spender and featuring further working-class talent in the shape of B. L. Coombes and James Hanley.

The war began badly, with Spender's defection to *Horizon* (it was impossible to have a direct and natural relationship with him as a friend or even close collaborator, Lehmann sniffed, 'pathologically eaten up as he is with jealousy, vanity, egotism and utterly corrupted by years of extravagant self-deception'). On the other hand, there were worse drawbacks than treacherous aides-de-camp, in particular a hint that Lehmann's radicalism could go only so far, was liable, in the end, to be compromised by external factors that went beyond both literature and politics. Just as Lehmann's homosexual slumming nearly always ended in emotional turmoil, so its literary equivalent – the championing of working-class writers – was always liable to be undermined by sheer good manners. The autumn 1940 number, now retitled *Folios of New Writing*, and including Orwell's 'My Country Right or Left?' and V. S. Pritchett's story 'Aunt Gertrude', also contained 'The Leaning Tower', the text of a lecture given by Virginia Woolf to the Brighton branch of the Workers' Educational Association. If not exactly patrician in its tone, this analysis of some of the cultural assumptions on which English literary life was based spoke loftily of writers occupying a raised chair, of benefiting from gold and silver: 'To breed the kind of butterfly a writer is you must let him sun himself for three or four years at Oxford or Cambridge.' Yeats and Eliot were charged with abandoning the heritage bequeathed by their predecessors; new writers learned that they were trapped in a tower from which they could not descend. Three responses were received, from Louis MacNeice, Edward Upward and the former miner Coombes, the latter respectful but unenthused by what he regarded as Woolf's blatant snobbery. Lehmann's own response to Coombes, published after Woolf's death, is unconvincing; the snobbishness reimagined as whimsicality, the class assumptions never interrogated, Woolf defended on grounds that were as much social as literary.

None of this, happily, could dent the assurance which Lehmann brought to the triumphs of his professional life. Perhaps, on the other hand, it was merely the unquestioning acceptance of his social advantages that secured them in the first place ('When the all-clear came, Lehmann went to the Athenaeum, had a bath and ordered breakfast' runs his biographer's account of a typical morning during the Blitz). By this time, in any case, he had fallen in with Allen Lane, who, having commissioned *New Writing in Europe* (1941) and sponsored an anthology of *New Writing* highlights, informed his protégé that he wanted Penguin to have its own monthly literary magazine. At 6d a copy, and benefiting both from Penguin's generous paper allocation and the efficiency of its sales force, *Penguin New Writing* was an instant success. It was reported from Blackpool that Polish forces billeted there rushed to Boots to buy it. The first number sold 80,000 copies, after which sales levelled out at 75,000. To examine some of the early contents pages is to note the sureness of the editorial touch, the merits of regular features such as 'Shaving through the Blitz', reportage filed under the general heading of 'The Way We Live Now', Spender – with whom some sort of rapprochement had been established – and others on 'Books and the War'. Lehmann alleged that the best contributions about the war were the result of his intervention: 'when I could make a direct suggestion to a writer whose capabilities I already knew; rare indeed has been the unknown author who showed that his imagination has been at work on his material with any intensity. And yet I find it very difficult to believe that people are not thinking and feeling about the war in a far more interesting way than gets into the words that arrive on my table by every post.'

Certainly by the end of 1942, *PNW* had attracted an immense prestige, the high quality of the material – the June 1941 number offered poems by Laurie Lee, MacNeice, Cecil Day Lewis and Dylan Thomas – balanced by a growing awareness of the difficulty, here in wartime, of producing such a thing as a literary magazine at all ('Fanfarlo's typewriter may have been put out of action by Mrs Greenbaum's landmine, and Robert Pagan's beautiful handwritten manuscript may have met with Nazi fires on its way through the post, and arrive charred and soggy a week late'). Like Tambi, a part of Lehmann's success lay in his being at the right place at the right time. On the other hand, his declared aim of 'bringing forward the right writer at the right moment' took careful management. One of the most impressive aspects of *PNW*, consequently, is Lehmann's ability to juggle up-and-coming but essentially mainstream talent with more esoteric contributions still capable of appealing to a mass audience. The December 1942 number, for example, featured stories by Robert Westerby and Pritchett, Maclaren-Ross's 'Y List', the Tyneside pitman Sid Chaplin's 'The Pigeon Cree', together with Harold Acton parading his knowledge of Chinese literature ('Lu Hsun's resemblance to Chekhov is more apparent than real') and the art critic Michael Ayrton on John Minton's designs for Gielgud's *Macbeth*.

As with Connolly, though, there is a sense that the war represented Lehmann's high-water mark, and the highly artificial conditions he had been able to take advantage of were unlikely to be replicated in the post-war era. Certainly, the Lehmann of the later 1940s was full of ambitious schemes. These included *Orpheus*, billed as 'A Symposium of the Arts' – elegant, super-refined, with contributions from Acton on 'Modern Painting in Mexico', Peter Brook on 'Style in Shakespeare production' and a well-nigh Tambi-esque forward claiming that 'The deep need today is to assert the lyrical and imaginative spirit against materialism and the pseudo-sciences . . . the poet is the creator, and the work of the poet is the mainspring of history.' Most ambitious of all was the launch, in 1946, with money borrowed from members of his family, of a fully fledged imprint backed by the printing firm of Purnell & Co., whose financial resources and paper supply, here in a world of shortages and post-war privation, allowed for an ambitious publishing programme. Both these ventures were built on the assumption of continuity, a conviction the mass audience brought into being by the exceptional circumstances of 1939–45 would endure, and that it would be interested both in Mexican painting and in the roster of decidedly highbrow writers assembled by John Lehmann Ltd, whose inaugural lists included Saul Bellow, Paul Bowles and a young Gore Vidal. Neither, when it came to it, proved to be the case. There was a silent abandonment of pre-war principle, too, in the move into trade publishing and elegant arts magazines, which tended to feature the work of Lehmann's friends and had little space for upwardly mobile proletarians.

Still, Lehmann persisted. By 1947 he was no longer a free agent but a salaried employee of Purnell, who had advanced funds to pay off the family investment, and was busy expanding the firm's output to include a series of upmarket reprints called 'the Holiday Library' and 'the Library of Art and Travel'. But the boom years for literature were over, and by 1950 John Lehmann Ltd was losing money. Its difficulties coincided with the decline of *Penguin New Writing*, cut to three issues a year in the spring of 1948 and then extinguished altogether. Purnell waited until 1952 to cast Lehmann off, rejecting his offer – with the financial support of Robert Maxwell – to buy back the firm, and sitting out the resultant media storm, which included a multi-signature letter to *The Times* and a lunch given in his honour at the Trocadero at which Eliot proposed the toast. He managed one final magazine-world fling in 1954, with the launch of the *London Magazine*, backed by Cecil King, owner of the *Daily Mirror*, in a gesture that owed at least something to Lady Rothermere's support of the *Criterion* three decades before.

Expected to be chic, highbrow and low-circulation, the magazine surprised everyone, not least its proprietor, by selling 23,000 copies of its first issue. Subsequent numbers were almost as successful, but by this stage there was a feeling that Lehmann had lost his edge, seeming to believe that, as one of his assistants put it, literature was simply 'a huge, immoveable, incontrovertible part of culture, there was nothing progressive about it'. The eventual decline in circulation confirmed all Lehmann's worst suspicions about cultural drift in the post-war era. 'There is not nearly so much creative ferment as twenty years ago' he complained. Neither, he believed, was there a receptive middle-class readership 'who really care for literature as literature and part of life, for the creative imagination first wherever it comes from'. The complicated series of financial manoeuvrings that followed King's withdrawal of support ended with Lehmann relinquishing control in 1961. The removal of his name from the masthead was 'a sort of death' and he was naturally appalled by the first manifestations of post-war consumer materialism, of which the *London Magazine*'s fate seemed all too symbolic: 'in spite of all that is so much better and healthier . . . the promise of 1945 has been horribly lost in complacency, vulgarity and the exploitation of all that's lowest'.

And here Lehmann strikes a note common to nearly every decade of recent English literary history: the lament of the cultivated literary gentleman who finds himself marooned on an inhospitable strand by the changing tides of public taste. Thereafter Lehmann's star began irrevocably to wane. His various volumes of autobiography received a certain amount of attention, but by the time of *The Ample Proposition* (1966), he was indisputably a figure from the past, an ageing Homintern ghost grimly stalking the corridors of the 1960s. A late novel, *In the Purely Pagan Sense* (1976), confirmed his interest in working-class boys, who, one critic thought, 'in (and often out) of their lederhosen, become as indistinguishable and characterless as girls in a high-kicking chorus'.

As to what remains of Lehmann, anyone who follows his trail for very long is liable to stumble up against his prodigious self-absorption and the belief that the importance of his literary gifts transcended all other obligations. Writing up his farewell to his Austrian lover Sikyr, for example, as the clouds gathered over pre-war Vienna, he could only pat himself on the back: 'And he went on to speak of my books, and said no, not propaganda, that wasn't my business, but to reveal just this real face of life, the human side, that was the great service I could do.' There is something faintly impenetrable about this, the sense of a mind fenced in by the expectations it has of itself, soured, in the last resort, by an awareness that these expectations may not, in the end, amount to very much, in which that old Eton schoolmaster's warning about punching above your weight clangs like a leper bell. In fact Lehmann's real service to literature was his work on the various incarnations of *New Writing*. He may not have had Connolly's all-consuming introspection, that constant urge to expose, defy and conciliate his deepest feelings which could turn his editorials into dazzling high-wire acts, but in some ways his detachment worked to his advantage. Compared to *Horizon*, *Penguin New Writing* is much less of a performance, much more the product of a sophisticated intelligence printing the best of what he has before him on the understanding that it may, to some degree, reflect and amplify the circumstances in which it was written. And if Lehmann was unable, or perhaps only unwilling, to follow Connolly's trick of turning his creative frailties into an essential part of his personal myth, then there is still something impressive about his doggedness, his persistent refusal to settle for the lower rung and the second-rate. Whatever one thinks of some of his evasions and inconsistencies, the literature of the Second World War would have been a vastly different place without him, and of how many editors – let alone novelists and poets – can that truthfully be said?

CHAPTER 10

Waiting for the Barbarians

It is the end of a civilisation . . . There is no point in resisting any longer. It is the decay of civilisation that I study – like Leland and Aubrey before me . . . Yes, it is a vanishing culture that I pursue, the debris that I lovingly cherish.

A. L. Rowse quoted in Martin Green, *A Mirror for Anglo-Saxons* (1961)

Thank God the People aren't interested in letters.

Evelyn Waugh, letter to Nancy Mitford, October 1948

Whatever the precise nature of the relationship between military conflict and art, the end of the Great War had a profoundly liberating effect on literature. To name only its most conspicuous ornaments, the early 1920s brought the publication of *Ulysses*, *Façade*, *The Waste Land*, *Mrs Dalloway* and *The Flower Beneath the Foot*. Simultaneously, there came a rapid expansion of the media in which works of this kind could be discussed, however unfavourable the resulting treatment. The *London Mercury* might have been expressly designed for the propagation of undemanding, middlebrow taste, but no one could doubt the vigour with which it fought its corner. In much the same way, posterity might regard Squire and his circle as the authentic voice of cantankerous poetic reaction, but it seemed to them that they operated at the heart of a newly reanimated tradition, that the cultural objectives on which they were bent during the 1920s were worth fighting for, and that literature itself would be the loser if they failed.

By contrast, the literary world of the later 1940s looked a stagnant affair. The market for 'serious' books and magazines went into irreversible decline. The Penguin Specials that had fitted so neatly into so many a serviceman's battledress pockets ended with the cessation of hostilities. The final publication of the Left Book Club,

G. D. H. Cole's *The Meaning of Marxism* (1948), sold a feeble 6,250 copies: a far cry from the abundant circulations of *The Town that Died* and *Forward from Liberalism*. It was a world of paper shortages, austerity design and crippling production delays, in which authors returning from military service with the aim of resuming long-interrupted careers did not like what they found. Alec Waugh, who had spent the latter stages of the war working in Military Intelligence in the Middle East, arrived at his agent's office in July 1945 assuming that he could straightaway step back into his old routine to receive the stark warning: 'A number of new writers have come up. You'll have to be regraded.' There were new categories, into which a 47-year-old veteran of the trade might not easily fit. His first post-war novel, *Unclouded Summer* (1948), was a victim of book-trade economising, not published until nearly two years after it was written, released to a stony silence and declared out of print very soon afterwards. And to the practical difficulties of shepherding one's work into the booksellers' windows could be added a newfound technical impediment that to Waugh seemed quite as daunting as the proscriptions of 1918. How could one set a novel in 1938 when its public outcome, at least, was implicit from the opening page? Ultimately Waugh made the fortunate discovery that the six years spent in khaki had given him a breathing space, as well as providing valuable material for future books, but the short-term prospect was a great deal less promising.

Waugh's literary agent, the redoubtable A. D. Peters, had made a point of warning him of the threat of 'new writers'. In fact, upstart newcomers were thin on the ground. Observers of the post-war literary scene tended to be struck by how closely its arrangements conformed to those of the pre-war world. Some of the great best-sellers of 1946 – a million copies sold – were the ten Shaw plays repackaged by Penguin. Anthony Powell's novel *Books Do Furnish a Room* (1971), with its chilly evocations of snowbound literary London in the winter of 1946–7, describes a landscape of left-wing publishing firms picking up where they left off, still fighting the battles of the 1930s, however sharp the additional resonance given to them by the events of the past six years, still hastening to publish foreign propaganda novels with titles like *The Pistons of Our Locomotives Sing the Songs of Our Workers* and having their losses underwritten by the apparatchiks in King Street. So backward-looking is the collective gaze that Howard Craggs, the major-domo of Boggis & Stone, is said scarcely to recognise that the books he publishes are propagandist. 'It all gives him a nostalgic feeling that he's young again, running the Vox Populi Press, having the girls from the 1917 Club.' The hero of the hour, one of the few new writers indisputably thrown up by the war, is the novelist X. Trapnel, Powell's projection of the real-life Maclaren-Ross. But Trapnel, like his alter ego, has no staying power. Maclaren-Ross, after the success of his novel *Of Love and Hunger* (1947), described the 1950s as 'a decade I could have done without'.

When a promising newcomer did appear, on the other hand, it was noticeable how often his, or her, characters seemed to be stuck in limbo, uncomfortably poised between the old world and the new. The people in Angus Wilson's second collection of short stories, *Such Darling Dodos* (1950), tend to be battered survivors from bygone eras, living precariously off diminished capital, their lifestyles threatened by punitive taxation, trying to cast off shackles that are as much symbolic as actual: rootless, vagrant and – like a good many writers in the post-war period – searching for a milieu that is prepared to accept them for who they are. The heroine of 'Hearts of Elm', for example, knows that the impending death of her aged servant will mean the break-up of her family, and for her a chance to depart for London where she can 'do things for themselves, not for their associations or memories'. Most symbolic of all is Wilson's title story, which turns into a long and by no means unsympathetic argument with the exacting brand of pre-war liberalism espoused by Robin and Priscilla, two ancient progressives sequestered in a north Oxford suburb. By the close, their unquestioning support for the good brave causes of a bygone age has been sharply exposed. The future, we infer, lies with their courteous but matter-of-fact younger relatives, for whom Robin's and Priscilla's high moral line on the great issues of the 1930s veers dangerously close to sentimentality.

The staleness of this post-war environment occurred even to those who existed somewhere fairly near to its heart. Cyril Connolly's fictitious American novelist 'Harold Bisbee', paying a first post-war visit to London, is surprised to find that the cocktail party to which he is invited contains no guest under the age of 30 and that the names dropped into the conversational pool are those of John Lehmann, Peter Quennell, Raymond Mortimer and Elizabeth Bowen – antediluvian figures, as far as Bisbee is concerned, reoccupying positions they had first taken up ten years before. Connolly himself, according to

Evelyn Waugh, had been offered $1,500 by an American magazine for an article on the topic of 'Young Writers Swing Right', but, having failed to find anyone under the age of 35 of either right or left, was forced to decline the commission.

Naturally, none of these failings went unnoticed by anti-metropolitan critics beyond the Home Counties margin. F. R. Leavis devoted several pages of the December 1948 issue of *Scrutiny* to a piece entitled 'The Progress of Poesy', attacking the *Times Literary Supplement* and *Horizon* for their praise of Auden, C. M. Bowra and Edith Sitwell – the usual inward-looking coteries, Leavis declared, feeding off each other – and, for good measure, disparaging John Hayward's newly published British Council pamphlet *Prose Literature since 1939* on the grounds that it perpetuated the dominance of a clique sustained by alliances formed at school and university ('nothing could be worse for the prestige and influence of British letters abroad than Mr Hayward's presentment of the currency values of Metropolitan literary society and associated University milieux as the distinctions and achievements of contemporary England').

It is the easiest thing in the world, of course, to denounce the influence of metropolitan literary cliques if you don't happen to be a member of one of them yourself, and in many ways 'The Progress of Poesy' is a typical piece of Leavis bombast – trumpeting 'currency values' at the expense of genuine differences of alignment which would have occurred to anyone who had studied the writers involved at close hand, and conveniently ignoring the various alliances and wire-pullings that Leavis was capable of orchestrating on his own behalf. Yet Leavis's point – that many of the ornaments of the post-war literary scene not only knew each other but had been to school together and reposed, with various minor gradations, in the same social drawer – was incontestable. First-hand accounts of the evening in 1950 when the *Times Literary Supplement* gave a party to celebrate the first half-century of its existence, and crowds of hitherto anonymous reviewers flocked to the magazine's offices at Printing House Square, suggest that the air was full of delighted cries of recognition. The importance that Leavis attached to this assault on Metroland back-scratching may be gathered from his decision to make it the final essay in *The Common Pursuit*: 'What particularly characterises our time in England is the almost complete triumph of the "social" (or the "associational") values over those which are the business of the critic.'

What was one to do, he enquired of a correspondent, in the aftermath of a debate along these lines at the ICA in July 1952, 'in a world in which what was once the Sitwell Circus has become a constellation of genii and Spender has been a major writer for twenty years and Desmond MacCarthy writing up his friends . . . is a great critic and Cyril Connolly is credited with both critical and creative gifts'?

It was a good question, that would have taken someone with a better knowledge of how the London literary world worked than Leavis to answer. John Hayward, to whom these remarks were addressed, had a chance to observe the bracing spectacle of Leavis in action when he became involved in some of the literary aspects of the 1951 Festival of Britain. A certain amount of this – providing the text for Bill Brandt's black-and-white photographs of buildings and landscape – was routine, but Hayward was also required to judge a poetry competition, to which the newly created Arts Council, together with the festival organisers, had allotted prizes to the value of £1,000. The panel, which included Sir Kenneth Clark, Bowra, Lord David Cecil, G. H. Rylands and Professor Basil Willey – Oxbridge establishment figures to a man – was disparaged by Leavis on the grounds that none of them knew anything about poetry. Again, this is Leavis overstating his case – Bowra and Rylands, at least, were highly suitable candidates to judge a poetry competition – but these objections might have been more strongly overcome had the competition thrown up evidence of genuine accomplishment. Unhappily the standard of entries was low, although a degree of amusement was provided by a poem from 'a Lady of Title', which began 'The pansy lying by thy side / Is happier far than I'. Pundits in search of youthful exuberance gloomily calculated that the average age of the winners was over 40 and the average age of the committee charged with selecting them over 50. Introducing the commemorative volume *Poems 1951*, Hayward decided that 'the future of English poetry is darker than it has ever been', that old-style patronage was long gone, leaving a gap that only the state could fill. 'In the end poetry cannot survive unless the public can be induced to read it.'

There were plenty of threnodies of this kind, silver-age laments for passing glories, doing the rounds of the later 1940s – see, for example, Connolly's valedictory editorial in the final number of *Horizon*, a year before, with its remarks about 'closing time in the gardens of the west'. In this context, the Festival of Britain's piecemeal efforts on behalf of the printed word have a symbolic ring: damned for the exclusiveness of those called in to assist; criticised by vigilant academe; incorporating (in the shape of the Arts Council) state-funded bodies who would play an increasingly important role in the direction taken by 'literature' in the post-war years. And Leavis's considerable shadow can be glimpsed elsewhere in the proceedings, notably in Priestley's novel *Festival at Farbridge* (1951), whose visiting academic, Mr Mortory, who comes to lecture on 'The Novel: A Revaluation' may be taken as an exact portrait.

But there were other shadows hanging over the literary cocktail parties of the immediately post-war era. Several of them were cast by the representatives of a generation that the fashionable world might have assumed no longer to exist. Take, for example, Dudley Carew, whose memoir of his early life, *The House is Gone*, was published in 1949 by the far from modish firm of Robert Hale. A former school friend of Evelyn Waugh, with whom he later fell out over a slighting reference in the latter's autobiography,* and an editorial assistant on the *London Mercury*, Carew eventually graduated to the post of cricket correspondent of *The Times*. The fascination of his autobiography lies not simply in the sharpness of its reports from the late 1940s freelance coalface – the lack of column inches, the frustrations of having to combine weekly journalism with the writing of 'serious' books – but in the unabashed conservatism of most of the aesthetic judgements on display. For Squire's apprentice, it scarcely needs saying, the past twenty years are not much more than a depressing interregnum. A self-styled 'romantic conservative', brought up on the giants of the Edwardian age, Carew is unimpressed by practically all literature written since 1930. His complaint about modernism is that it forces both its practitioners and the subjects about which they write into a private room shut off from the greater part of human experience. 'The case against modern writing in general is not so much that it is bad writing, but that it is limited writing' he briskly decides. But bad writing it is, 'and other men than Chesterton have felt the instinct to defend the purple passage'. From the Carew angle, Wells, Bennett and co. offer a richness and a solidity, 'and the discards are from strength, not weakness'.

* *A Fragment of Friendship* (1974) repays the slight with interest.

Significantly enough, the only writer Carew exempts from this blanket condemnation is Orwell, but his respect derives less from the political subtexts of *Animal Farm* and *Nineteen Eighty-Four* and more from the Orwell of 'Why I Write' and its insistence that books are written for aesthetic as well as political reasons.

It would be easy enough, on the strength of his paean to Compton Mackenzie's *Sinister Street* (1914) – about which he remarks that 'a novel written today to the same pattern would be a very different thing, spare, taut and angry where *Sinister Street* is full, ripe and tolerant' – to mark him down as a middlebrow pure and simple. But if he is, it is of a curiously discriminating sort, for *The House is Gone* fairly bristles with its author's dislike of the modern best-seller and its rigid stylisations ('In Book I old grandfather Tom wears a cloth cap and the mill is a little one-man business and there is a lot of broad Yorkshire and a page or two about the Crimean War'). All this presumes a homogeneity among books of the moment that close inspection generally reveals not to exist. It was Frank Swinnerton who, having read Q. D. Leavis's *Fiction and the Reading Public*, noted that 'from outside, like cats at night, all best-sellers look the same'. In fact, if properly deconstructed and seen in its commercial and literary contexts, a best-selling novel can sometimes shed more light both on its audience and on the literary tradition in which it reposes than many a more abstruse work. Consider, for example, the case of Norman Collins's prodigiously successful *London Belongs to Me* (1945), a novel which not only discloses a great deal about its audience's expectations of fiction but also gestures at some of the cultural assumptions that hovered above the author's desk when he wrote it.

Collins (1907–82) has altogether fallen off the literary map in the three and a half decades since his death, but he bestrode the landscapes of his time in a way that might seem rather startling to some of his more narrowly focused descendants. A best-selling novelist since his 20s – his debut, *Penang Appointment*, was published as early as 1934 – he served, successively, as aide-de-camp to Victor Gollancz, a BBC radio talks producer, director of the Light Programme, an immensely successful controller of BBC television, a lobbyist for commercial broadcasting and, finally, deputy chairman of ATV. Only Melvyn Bragg, perhaps, among his twenty-first-century epigoni, could boast the same degree of switched-on and thoroughly transmedial expertise. And if the parallels with Lord Bragg can seem faintly eerie, then Collins's persistent shadowing of George Orwell through the 1930s and 1940s looks eerier still. As the Gollancz employee charged with seeing *Keep the Aspidistra Flying* (1936) through the press, for example, Collins was one of the few people who can be said to have taken on Orwell in a quarrel and emerged his moral superior. The bad feeling left over from the Gollancz days burned on, and Orwell's *Complete Works* contains several notably terse memoranda that buzzed back and forth along the Broadcasting House corridors in the period 1941–3.

Seven hundred pages long, dense, compendious, and well-nigh heroically diffuse, *London Belongs to Me* represents the high-water mark of what might be called the middlebrow panorama of capital life: one of those almost interminable novels in which the incidental detail is heaped on with a trowel and even a visit to the funfair realises a page of technical information about the electric cranes and What the Butler Saw machines on display. Its most obvious debts are to J. B. Priestley's no less compendious *Angel Pavement* (1930) and, to a slightly lesser extent, Patrick Hamilton's trilogy *Twenty Thousand Streets Under The Sky* (1929–35), but some of the echoes go back even further to the kind of lodging-house reportage pioneered by George R. Sims's *Memoirs of a Landlady* (1916). At the same time Collins's work prefigures late-period variations such as Monica Dickens's *The Heart of London* (1961) and in particular R. F. Delderfield's *The Avenue Goes to War* (1964) whose 'people's war' theme it shares. There is even a German spy, Dr Otto Hapfel, who, while masquerading as a research student, files punctilious reports to his superiors in Berlin about the Englishman's love of cricket and his reluctance to stand up in cinemas when the national anthem is played.

Like many another London panorama, the action in *London Belongs to Me* takes place, by and large, at a single address – 10 Dulcimer Street in Kennington. Here, first assembled on the arbitrary date of 23 December 1938, can be found Mrs Vizzard, the establishment's vigilant and exacting landlady, the retired clerk Mr Josser and his wife (with and without their daughter Doris), the widowed Mrs Boon and her car-mechanic son Percy, the esurient tinned food hoarder and tea-brewer Mr Puddy, and an elderly woman named Connie, nightly ornament of a cloakroom in a West End speakeasy. Soon inflated to nine by the arrival of Mr Squales, a nest-feathering medium who occupies the back basement, Dulcimer Street's human cargo is thereafter prey to dispersal and decline. It is about everything – which is to say that its cast are busy marrying, dying, making speeches at the 'South London Parliament', whose debates mirror the progress of the war, creating life and on one occasion snuffing it out – and nothing. It is about London, of course – and the geographical coverage extends as far as Mayfair and the City – and yet the organism that stretches out on all sides beyond Dulcimer Street is curiously undifferentiated. So, too, are the people, who for all their generational divisions – Doris and Percy are interesting specimens of restless, machine-age youth – talk in the same way, think many of the same thoughts and, in social situations, operate as a kind of catch-phrasing Greek chorus. They are sure they look a perfect fright. They have met his (or her) type before. They insist that visitors must take them as they find them. Diffidently, but with a certain *affairé* pride, they banter the signature remarks of the day back and forth. 'Where was Moses?' Mr Josser wonders at one point when the lights fail. It is one of the novel's most authentic moments, a perfect example of how people really talked to each other in 1939. The answer, which nobody gives, but which I can remember my father (b.1921) reciting a dozen times, is 'In the dark.'

All this makes *London Belongs to Me*, with its cinema fantasies, its minutely itemised car fleets, its farewell parties in EC2, very true to life, without perhaps being true to any of the individual existences fugitively at large in it. Gas-ring haunting, baked-bean swilling Mr Puddy, who remembers even his late wife only for her culinary skills, is a case in point. Mr Puddy's distinguishing marks are his colossal appetite and his adenoidal vocal tones ('If the drains are still rudding – if it isn't dodal war by then', etc.). The reader knows that this cannot go on for ever, that these hopeful stake-outs in the grocery queue can't be indefinitely sustained, that there will come a moment when Mr Puddy must quit his gas ring, his tin opener and his comfy night-watchman's basement and perform some heroic act. And yet when he pulls an injured fireman from the flames during an air raid (while returning to rescue the packet of ham booked for his supper) the result is oddly unsatisfactory, as if by jumping out of his stereotype for a moment he has somehow jumped back into it merely by confirming our expectations of him.

What are the materials from which Collins's complex social tapestries are woven? On the one hand, these are straightforwardly literary

– a sub-Dickensian insistence on the human spirit's ability to prosper beneath a topsoil of washed-out mornings, minor privations and the rent being due. Mrs Vizzard, for example, has her eye on hard-up, prosy Mr Squales, an idyll only punctured by his flight into the arms of a rival admirer and a breach-of-promise suit. The Jossers pine for a country cottage. Mrs Boon's dreams are vicarious, bound up in her slinking son. Mr Puddy, alternatively, merely schemes to accumulate enough provisions to see out the war. On the other hand, they are more contemporary, more obviously tethered to newer media that had grown up in the past half-century of London life. A scene in which Percy tries to chat up the blonde at the funfair change booth ('"Ever have any time off?" "No, I go straight on. All day and all night." "What's your name?" "Oh, call me Mrs Simpson"') sounds exactly like a couple of cross-talk comedians plying their trade on a variety-hall stage. Collins's audience are Boots Library subscribers and weekly magazine readers; they may well have handed-down copies of *Little Dorrit* and *Martin Chuzzlewit* on their shelves; they will certainly have read Priestley; but they are also, as many of the novel's incidental references make clear, cinemagoers, radio-listeners and catchphrase-hoarders, and here in the 1940s the cultural signposting necessary to attract them to a work of literature has no single source.

And in its roundabout way, *London Belongs to Me* answers a question that has always hung over urban English novels of the 1930s and 1940s: their (comparative) lack of susceptibility to American influence. This, after all, was the age of classic American naturalism, of Theodore Dreiser, James T. Farrell and John Steinbeck, of grim, biological imperatives, suicides in Bowery flophouses and remorseless journeys towards the electric chair. We know that the Priestley–Hamilton–Collins school of metropolitan panorama was aware of these transatlantic determinists to the extent of occasionally namechecking them (Bob, the literary-minded barman in Hamilton's *The Midnight Bell*, has ambitions to write a novel that 'would put you in a class with Hugo, Tolstoy and Dreiser'). If nothing else, Collins demonstrates the absolute impossibility of producing the English equivalent of, say, Farrell's *Studs Lonigan* trilogy here in a world of Lyons cafés, social security and the ceremonious routines of the South London Parliament. As it happens, *London Belongs to Me* has one violent death (the funfair blonde, whom Percy pushes out of a stolen car) and one unexplained drowning, a son missing in action, a trial scene and a death sentence later commuted to life imprisonment. None of Percy's mental anguish, though, quite dispels the faint air of cosiness that hangs over the proceedings. Collins is not a sentimentalist, but neither is he a realist, and the stagecraft that novels of this type require quite often descends into stage management.

The particular social milieu occupied by Mrs Vizzard, Mr Puddy and the others turns even more distinctive when viewed from the vantage point of the twenty-first century. To anyone brought up on the London cosmopolitanism of a Zadie Smith or a Hanif Kureishi, *London Belongs to Me* may seem less a novel than a piece of dramatised sociology or even an anthropological study. Like an old-fashioned situation comedy, it is predicated on a shared vernacular, a geographical precision, a social uniformity that is only reinforced by the faint variations up and down, and a series of assumptions about human behaviour that the intervening seventy years have called sharply into question. Its most attractive feature is its communality, its nervous protocols, its endless politenesses, its inches given and received, its sense of a group of people brought together by unexpected contingency, and driven to solidarity, their surface frostiness nearly always dissolving into an inner warmth. In this context, it isn't in the least surprising to discover that Collins's chief legacy to the Light Programme was the commissioning of *Woman's Hour*. Both as a writer, and in his role as one of broadcasting's first grey eminences, he clearly envisaged popular art as a kind of societal glue, designed to bring people together rather than to drive them apart. But of all the assumptions about human behaviour put under the microscope in the seven decades since *London Belongs to Me*, the idea that popular culture is a unifying rather than a divisive force is perhaps the most questionable of all.

Orwell reviewed *London Belongs to Me* for the *Manchester Evening News* in November 1945, tracing its line of descent through Priestley and Walpole to Dickens, noting the existence of dead wood and signs of hasty composition, but concluding that it 'could be numbered among the few novels published this year that are worth reading'. There was nothing unusual about Orwell's enthusiasm for a book of this kind. He had a taste for middlebrow literature, and when the Boots Library-subscribing George Bowling in *Coming Up For Air* talks about 'falling for' the successive best-sellers of the 1920s the reader is invited to suspect that Orwell had fallen for them himself. On one level this fascination was simply a by-product of livelihood. The greater part of his income until the middle 1940s was acquired by reviewing run-of-the-mill books in sometimes equally run-of-the-mill publications: it can come as rather a shock to discover that in February 1941, one of the darkest months of the Second World War, he was sitting down to appraise John Llewellyn Rhys's *England Is My Village*, Nina Fedorova's *The Family*, Dan Wickenden's *Walk Like a Mortal* and Bruce Marshall's *Delilah Upside Down* for the *New Statesman*, and deciding that 'the novels coming out at present are at a terribly low level, the lowest, probably, in living memory'. At the same time, left to its own devices, without the resonant allegorical and dystopian twists imparted to *Animal Farm* and *Nineteen Eighty-Four*, Orwell's fictional compass invariably returned to the kind of territory hitherto populated by the writers he had enjoyed in his youth: Bennett, Wells and Maugham. From the fragments he left behind, it seems clear that the novel he had started work on shortly before his death in 1950 was intended as a rather old-fashioned piece about a young man coming back from the East in the 1920s: a trajectory that exactly parallels Orwell's own return from Burma in 1927. This absorption in the way that 'ordinary' people live their lives, and the assumptions that underlie them, informs much of his routine critical work – he is nearly always more interesting on Priestley than Sartre – as well as providing the spur for his pioneering investigations in the field of cultural studies, a discipline he may be said to have helped create. As with Bowling and his popular-novel orgies, this resonance is all the more emphatic for being personal: asked to consider the elemental attraction of the blood-and-thunder boy's adventure story and the type of response it stirs among its juvenile audience, the reader is instantly aware that at least half of Orwell's judgement is to do with the excitement he himself felt as a child in the presence of Dick Dauntless and the heroes of the *Boy's Own Paper*. Like Andrew Lang, to name a critic of an earlier generation, he realised that the appeal of a Stevenson or a Henty goes very deep, and that it is not always explained by conventional methods of literary criticism.

In trying to account for Orwell's unprecedented influence on the English literary world from the late 1940s onward, one ought to begin by pointing out that for the majority of Orwell-fanciers this voyage of discovery was at best incremental. Much of his early work appeared in highly obscure publications. The four-volume edition of essays, journalism and letters edited by Ian Angus and Orwell's widow Sonia did not appear until 1968, and Peter Davison's magisterial *Complete Works* hung fire for another thirty years. Undoubtedly, the presumption of Orwell's importance had much to do with his premature death. Reading the obituaries by, among others, Koestler, Pritchett and Julian Symons, Malcolm Muggeridge felt that he saw in them 'how the legend of a human being is created'. If much of the legend, here in the early days of the Cold War, attached itself to *Nineteen Eighty-Four* – a staple of politicians' reading lists in the 1950s, and adapted for the small screen in 1954 – then there were already plenty of people ready to draw attention to Orwell's wider significance. A special number of *World Review*, featuring selections from the unpublished notebooks and commemorative essays by Bertrand Russell, Huxley and Spender, appeared as early as June 1950. Naturally, not all this coverage was favourable. Six and a half decades after Orwell's death, with most of the political questions on which he campaigned decisively won in his favour, it is easy to forget the suspicion with which he was regarded by certain parts of the left in the era of Churchill, Eden and Suez. As Kingsley Amis once put it, long after his own conversion to the free market and proto-Thatcherism:

> I think that in the late '50s, when I still retained considerable vestiges of my early leftism, I was made uncomfortable by Orwell's writings about Communism. I could not dismiss him as dishonest and callow, so found an 'out' by calling him hysterical. I think now (understandably) that Orwell had made a better prediction in 1949 than I was capable of in 1957, and my reading of *Nineteen Eighty-Four* as political writing is much higher now than it was then.

Some on the left never forgave him, or, more accurately, were concerned to play down the importance of the political crucible in which some of his best work was forged. As has been several times remarked of Raymond Williams's account of him in *Culture and Society* (1958), it would be impossible to gather from it that there was ever a man called Stalin or that Orwell wasn't reacting against very specific lies and atrocities. And in some ways Williams's 'Modern Masters' volume, published in 1971, is even more evasive. Take, for example, this passage describing the situation in Spain in 1937, where the beginnings of a social revolution, supported by the POUM, for whom Orwell fought, were brutally suppressed by the Spanish republicans:

> To move in that area at all is like moving into a minefield. Certain historians have taken the view that the revolution – mainly anarcho-syndicalist but with the POUM taking part – was an irrelevant distraction from a desperate war. Some, at the time and after, have gone so far as to describe it as deliberate sabotage of the war effort. Only a few have argued on the other side that the suppression of the revolution by the main body of Republican forces was an act of power politics related to Soviet policy, which amounted to a betrayal of the cause for which the Spanish people were fighting.

Again, it would be impossible to gather from Williams's innocuous phrasing that warrants had been issued for Orwell and his wife's arrest, that a report to the Tribunal for Espionage and High Treason denounced them as 'confirmed Trotyskites', that the private papers stolen from Orwell's hotel room ended up in the NKVD archive in Moscow, and that had he and Eileen stayed in Barcelona rather than escaping over the border they would almost certainly have been shot. If this isn't power politics, involving the specific intervention of the Soviet Union to enforce its own ideological protocols, then what exactly is it?

In Williams's defence, it could be said that Orwell was misrepresented quite as much by right-wing enthusiasts as by warier, if not positively hostile, voices on the left: not the least of the shadows that hung over his deathbed was the realisation that he had given post-war conservatives a valuable propaganda weapon in the battles of the Cold War. If his general outlook was so acceptable to large numbers of readers who would have counted as his political opponents, the explanation lies in its grounding in a tradition of native radicalism that passes back through Chesterton to the great exponents of Victorian social reform: significantly, his celebrated essay on Dickens owes far more to Chesterton's pioneering study of 1906 than he would perhaps have cared to admit. Orwell's quarrel with England is not that its controlling forces are corrupt – his complaints about the upper classes are notably even-handed in their nods to the hanging judge who declines to take a bribe or the ducal heirs killed on the beaches at Dunkirk – merely that the wrong people are in charge. Similarly, his strictures on the sensibilities and the institutions 'steeped in the worst illusions of 1910', as he put it, gain an extra resonance from the reader's suspicion that he was steeped in many of them himself. Certainly the raw material that inspired most of his best essays – 'Boys' Weeklies', 'Raffles and Miss Blandish', 'The Art of Donald McGill', 'The Decline of the English Murder' – nearly always returns us to the Edwardian world of his boyhood. Here, as in the atmospheric middle section of *Coming Up For Air*, Orwell is the small boy curled up on the hearthrug with his copy of Jules Verne or H. G. Wells, or rather the adult who regards the atmosphere of sensationalising American sub-literature as morally inferior to the Billy Bunter stories and believes that a left-wing children's comic is inconceivable for the simple reason that no child could ever be persuaded to read it.

Orwell's effect on the writers and readers of the 1950s and 1960s is all the more significant for the number of different levels on which it operated. To take only one area in which his influence can still be felt, quite apart from the impact of *Nineteen Eighty-Four* or the forays into cultural studies, there is the series of explorations he conducted into non-canonical areas of English literature. John Carey has noted how when he came to take an interest in Thackeray's early journalism – an aspect of his work that most critics now rate as highly as *Vanity Fair* – the only piece of criticism that seemed in the least to anticipate his own views was Orwell's essay 'Oysters and Brown Stout'. The same point could be made of Gissing, or Smollett, and if a novel like Leonard Merrick's *The Position of Peggy Harper* (1909) survives anywhere in the public imagination it is because Orwell took the trouble to write about it sometime in the mid-1940s. From the angle of the 1950s, the sheer profusion of Orwell's output was a point in his favour. It spoke of necessity, the urgency of something to be conveyed rather than self-conscious and subsidised artistry. This, too, was an era of plain speaking and common sense, when a writer who assured his posthumous audience that good prose was like a windowpane would always have the edge over Bloomsbury obfuscations. The windowpane analogy is not one of Orwell's better *obiter dicta* – one can think of half a dozen novelists, from Firbank to Joyce, many of them admired by Orwell himself, whose prose is anything but. On the other hand it is the seductiveness of the tone, that sharp, decisive, uninhibited statement of what one believes, coupled with an absolute defiance of anyone who happens to think differently, that is Orwell's chief legacy to the generation that followed him. As Amis, again, put it, on this occasion from the vantage point of 1957: 'Of the writers who appealed to the post-war intelligentsia, he is far and away the most potent . . . No modern writer has his air of passionately believing what he has to say and of being passionately determined to say it as forcefully and simply as possible.' Anthony Hartley, in *A State of England* (1963), goes even further than this, arguing that 'the "no-nonsense" air of an entire generation came from Orwell'.

The modern reader, determined to see the post-war era in the round, as the age of Angus Wilson and Iris Murdoch as much as Amis and Larkin, may suspect that this is an overstatement, an attempt to pursue solidarity where none exists. On the other hand, elements of Orwell's prose style wind through some of the literary criticism of the 1950s like loosestrife through a hedge. Here is John Wain discussing the audience for poetry in a magazine article written in 1953:

> In the seventeenth century it was not even necessary for your work to be printed before you became famous as a poet: manuscript copies would reach all the people you wanted to reach . . . And the important feature of this small audience was that it was clearly visualised . . . Whether or not the poet liked his readers (and Augustan poetry, which enjoyed the tidiest set-up of all, was largely satiric), he knew who they were. He was not shouting at a hole in the wall.

What gives this paragraph, written for the relatively highbrow audience of *Twentieth Century*, its intensely Orwellian tang? First, there is the air of authority that burns off the page – an authority, more to the point, constructed out of huge generalisations (was the Augustan audience quite as restricted as Wain supposes? What about the broadsheet balladeers?). Then there is the degree of contact that Wain manages to establish with his reader, not merely by addressing him, or her, as 'you', but by the choice of imagery that has some kind of kick in it. In this context, that 'shouting at a hole in the wall' is a masterstroke: not quite in the same league as Orwell's description of book reviewing as 'kissing the bums of verminous little lions', but strikingly visual. Essentially Wain is using the same technique as the

Orwell of *The Road to Wigan Pier*, who, to emphasise the squalor of his lodgings, condemns the landlord for peeling potatoes into a bucket of dirty water – as if any water in which potatoes are peeled can be expected to remain clean – playing a rhetorical confidence trick whose powers of persuasion are such that it would take an exceptionally courageous reader not to acquiesce.

And Orwell's tone was quite as seductive as his subject matter. Malcolm Bradbury, who made his own debut in the 1950s, has noted the 'ordinariness' of the post-1945 fictional landscape, its intimate relation to the worlds of *Keep the Aspidistra Flying* and *Coming Up For Air*, a coign of vantage that can sometimes seem purely anthropological. In Wain's first novel *Hurry on Down* (1953), the picaresque hero Charles Lumley is invited home by the working-class girl he is courting. Charles is drawn to Rosa's father, but dislikes her brother on the grounds that Stan, determined to better himself by rising out of the world of manual labour, is 'learning the technique of cheap smartness', talks a different language from his father ('demotic English of the mid-twentieth century: rapid, slurred, essentially a city dialect and, in origin, essentially American') and lacks the 'genuine dignity' of a man whose speech and habits were formed before 1914. Again, this use of fiction as a vehicle for brisk little sociological lectures strikes the authentic Orwell note. But there is another ideological edifice being erected here that, like tone and subject matter, was crucially important to a literary generation which, by and large, was hostile to the era that had preceded it. This was the idea of the interrupted tradition. With Orwell's *Critical Essays* (1946) in one hand, back numbers of *Scrutiny* in the other and the collected works of D. H. Lawrence reposing on the shelf behind you, it was just about possible to forget that the confusions of the past half-century – modernism, dissociation, detachment, man alone rather than man-in-society – had happened, to return to a world of genuine moral seriousness by way of what Martin Green has called 'the true transmitters of the Victorian heritage'. Naturally, this concertina-ing of literary history ignores the fact that a great deal of Orwell's work is consciously reacting against Victorianism. On the other hand, one can combine this inherent scepticism with the knowledge that, as with several of the Victorian sages, the opinions to which he clung most fiercely had been obtained at great personal cost. When the former servant of the Raj and convinced anti-imperialist informed his readers that an India governed along the lines suggested by E. M. Forster would last a fortnight, you are instantly aware that this is a man who has seen how the empire works at first hand rather than as private secretary to a maharajah. Orwell's twenty-first-century status as a secular saint would probably have puzzled him, but the personal authority on which it rests is rarely in doubt. And in the end his insistence that one effects changes in the way that societies organise themselves by making ordinary people re-evaluate some of their most cherished beliefs takes us back to the essay on Dickens. Here his conclusion is that Dickens's 'message', so often hijacked by ideologues anxious to claim him for their own, can be boiled down to the two words 'behave better'. This, depending on your point of view, is either a gigantic cliché, or a profoundly important exhortation which we – politician, literary critic and reader alike – neglect at our peril.

CHAPTER II

Making a Living II 1939–1970

Try to earn £1,000 a year from publishing today and see what happens.

Stephen Spender, writing in 1946

I earn £10,000 a year, which used to be thought quite a lot. I live like a mouse in shabby-genteel circumstances.

Evelyn Waugh, writing in 1956

Literary editors have always relished the idea of the symposium. The state of fiction. The state of poetry. The writer and Leviathan. The writer and society. Such topics, and others like them, were as common to the little magazines of the post-war era as Audenesque poems or refutations of F. R. Leavis. But the readers who opened their copies of *Horizon* in September 1946 would have stumbled on something much more elemental – a survey that went to the heart of the practical business of being a writer. Gathered beneath the heading 'The Cost of Letters', the novelists, poets and critics sprung from Connolly's address book had been given six individual questions to answer. How much did they think a writer needed to live on? Could a serious writer earn this sum by his writing, and if so, how? If not, what was the second most suitable occupation for him? Does literature suffer from the diversion of a writer's energy into other employments or is it enriched by it? Should the state or any other institution do more for literature? Were they satisfied with their own solutions to the problems previously set out and did they have any specific guidance to offer to young people who wanted to make a living by writing?

Twenty-one of Connolly's contributors replied, ranging in status from the reasonably celebrated (Graves, Orwell, Pritchett) to the gamely up-and-coming (Maclaren-Ross, Robert Kee) and the relatively obscure (Alex Comfort, Robin Ironside). There were two women,

Elizabeth Bowen and Rose Macaulay. Naturally enough, the most extensive, and detailed, replies were attracted by questions one and two. None, perhaps, were as heartfelt as those supplied by Maclaren-Ross: 'Your questionnaire arrived at an opportune moment when I was at my wit's end to know which way to turn for money.' How much, when it came down to it, did the writer need? Leaving aside the egalitarian caution of John Betjeman ('as much as anyone else'), the free-handed whimsicality of Dylan Thomas ('as much as he wants to spend') and the singular extravagance of Elizabeth Bowen, who plumped for £3,500 a year, no one could be accused of wanting an especially luxurious life. Connolly's £5 a day is a reflection of his taxi-hailing, cigar-smoking metropolitan tastes. Cecil Day Lewis stresses the inestimable advantage to the writer of a small private income, but generally speaking a modest frugality is the order of the day. Maclaren-Ross, another compulsive taxi-hailer, thinks he could get by on £20 a week. Robin Ironside can make do on £15. William Sansom and Robert Kee are prepared to go as low as £400–500 a year. Orwell reckons £10 a week for a married man (after tax) and £6 for a bachelor. There is a faint suggestion that writers perform better in reasonable comfort with a certain amount of travel thrown in – even Orwell maintains that 'most of them probably benefit by travelling, by living in what they consider sympathetic surroundings, and by eating and drinking the things they like best and by being able to take their friends out to meals or to have them to stay' – but, equally clearly, most of them seem to be content with a standard of living that will enable them to practise their trade without anxiety or interruption. Modest middle-class comfort is better than a mansion, and peace and quiet preferable to noisy opulence.

But how is this money to be earned? The replies to question two – could a serious writer earn this sum by his writing and, if so, how – suggests that, with rare exceptions, it could only be amassed by means of some additional job beyond the world of books. Betjeman stresses the need to be 'established'. Connolly mutters darkly about the life rafts thrown out by Hollywood and the book societies. Spender, supposing that the standard rate for literary journalism is three guineas per 1,000 words, calculates that a novelist or poet who wanted to raise his, or her, income to £1,000 per annum would have to write three or four articles a week. If freelance journalism or what Cecil Day Lewis, never afraid to call a spade a spade, terms 'literary hack-work', is the answer then it carries a debilitating sting in its tail, or rather the makings of a catch-22, in which the conditions required to complete the great masterpiece can only be obtained by an outpouring of creative energy on inferior work that will leave very little time for the great masterpiece. 'It's very difficult' Maclaren-Ross, then at work on *Of Love and Hunger* (1947), his fictionalised account of selling vacuum cleaners on the south coast in pre-war days, complained. 'Suppose, like myself at the moment, you have written short stories but now want to write novels?' How was one to raise the sum of money needed to sit down and concentrate? 'You can't do it, except by more short stories, radio plays or what have you. The writing of which takes up most of your time . . . So the novel doesn't get written, that's all.' The solution in Maclaren-Ross's own case would have been to pursue a more frugal life, to live modestly in the country, away from the fleshpots of Soho and the residential hotels on which he squandered his substance. At the same time, the disadvantages of the Maclaren-Ross lifestyle shouldn't blind us to the difficulties with which many a writer far less extravagant in his habits was faced in the post-war era.

The *Horizon* symposium was one of Connolly's brighter ideas, for it reflected, with varying degrees of engagement, the sense of anxiety that hung over the great majority of literary existences in the years after 1945, the feeling – liable to be expressed by a best-selling novelist as much as by an underpaid apprentice – that this was not, by and large, a good time to be a writer. The newspaper columns of the late 1940s are full of anguished little variations on this theme. Orwell himself had already filed a piece for the *Manchester Evening News* in July 1945 ('Authors Deserve a New Deal') which explicitly connects what he imagined to be the poor quality of contemporary writing with the economic problems experienced by those charged with producing it ('it ought to be realised that the bad state of present-day English literature is in part due to the difficulty of keeping alive simply by writing books'). Interestingly, his solution to the problem of accumulating 'enough money to secure the spare time and peace of mind that writing books demands' is a very early version of Public Lending Right, state subsidy for the author by way of a fee for library borrowings ('The reading public, in fact, must expect to pay for its books, just as the drinking public expects to pay for its beer'), but these were early days for the concept of state subsidy for literature. Item five of the *Horizon* survey (Should the state or any other institution do more for literature?) brought in some violently mixed responses, ranging from Alex's Comfort's 'I don't think the writer should touch the state or its money with a barge pole' to the somewhat bizarre suggestion advanced by Robert Kee that the state should make £400 a year available to anyone who wanted to be a writer, renewable at the writer's request.

The ideological battles that accompanied state involvement in the practice of literature would come later. For the moment the problems were strictly economic. Essentially the novelists, poets and critics aiming to make a living out of their work in the first two decades of the post-war era would find this task made much more difficult, first, by the changing nature of publishing, and, second, by the fact that the value of literary earnings had failed to keep pace with the cost of living. This discrepancy would become more marked as the post-war period went on, but it was already evident in the late 1940s, when punitive tax rates and rising prices contributed to a sense of middle-class insecurity that went well beyond Grub Street. The figure of £1,000 to £1,400 suggested by V. S. Pritchett as an optimal literary income in the *Horizon* survey is prefaced by an acknowledgement that in the interwar era it would have been half that. But the fiscal winds of the post-war publishing scene blew both ways. The paperback revolution inaugurated by Penguin in the previous decade had ushered in an era of 'cheap books', but cheap books, unless they sold in exceptional quantities, meant less money for authors. If it was the age of the best-seller and volume sales unheard of in the 1930s – Paul Brickhill's *The Dam Busters* became the first million-selling paperback in 1956 – then it was also a time in which the old-style literary livelihood made up of a modest-selling annual book, supplemented by reviews for weekly magazines and the books pages of national newspapers seemed even more under threat. In his manual for the aspiring late Victorian writer, *The Pen and the Book* (1899), Sir William Besant, founder of the Society of Authors, had painted a roseate picture of the kind of openings available to what he called the 'good steady man of letters', in a burgeoning marketplace founded on the needs of a newly literate and educated reading public:

> This man, of whom there are many – or this woman, for many women now belong to the profession – goes into his study every morning as regularly as a barrister goes to chambers. He finds

> on his desk two or three books waiting for review: a MS sent him for opinion: a book of his own to go on with – possibly a life of some dead-and-gone worthy for a series: an article which he has promised for a magazine: a paper for the *Dictionary of National Biography*: perhaps an unfinished novel to which he must give three hours of absorbed attention. There is never any danger of the work failing as soon as the writer has made himself known as a trustworthy and attentive workman.

Half a century later there was an uncomfortable feeling that work of this kind was insufficient to go round, that the 'book of his own to go on with' might be a casualty of the decline in fiction publishing which had seen the volume of new titles fall to as low as 1,200 in 1945. One marked feature of the mid-twentieth-century marketplace was the collapse of the middlebrow literary magazine – the *London Mercury*, the *Strand*, *John O'London's*, the *Cornhill* – which had previously offered a refuge for a certain kind of literary man and his wares. But the world of belles-lettres was growing more restricted, more likely to be colonised by moonlighting academics on institutional salaries, more likely to be concentrated on the back end of the *New Statesman* or the review pages of the *Spectator*. G. K. Chesterton had been an anachronism in the 1930s. It was inconceivable that such a figure could exist in the age of Kingsley Amis and of Nicholas Monsarrat's *The Cruel Sea* (1951), which in the first six years of its lifespan sold 1 million copies at the original hardback price of 12s 6d with no cheap editions and no paperback sales.

Monsarrat's sales figures were exceptional, even for the hot-house conditions of the 1950s, and yet there is plenty of evidence to confirm the emergence of a new breed of super-selling international authors whose receipts were of only a slightly lesser order. As early as 1946, for example, the crime writer Peter Cheyney had revealed that his audited net English language sales for the previous eighteen months amounted to 1,563,441 copies, well over half of which had been racked up in the UK. Meanwhile, less well-known writers were facing what the *Bookseller*, in its Christmas issue of 1948, warned was 'a rapidly shrinking market'. All this had a significant impact on literary incomes, whose statistics, come the 1950s, show an ever-widening gap between the haves and the have-nots. In a survey carried out by the Society of Authors in 1955 – a much more forensic exercise than Connolly's canvassing of his friends – 15 per cent of respondents estimated that they earned between £500 and £1,000 (comparable to the rewards of a senior clerical job), 18 per cent earned between £250 and £500, and 40 per cent under £250 – that is, less than £5 per week. A more detailed survey, undertaken in 1957 and analysing over 600 replies, showed even greater disparities. Four per cent of the sample declared that they earned in excess of £2,500. Eight per cent computed their income at between £1,500 and £2,000, 10 per cent between £1,000 and £1,500, 15 per cent between £500 and £1,000, 18 per cent between £250 and £500 and 40 per cent beneath £250. No doubt a certain proportion of the survey base were enthusiastic amateurs happy to supplement their day jobs with work written in the evenings and at weekends. All the same, if one takes the ideal literary income as defined by Connolly's sample in 1946 as between £750 and £1,000, it is sobering to discover that, eleven years later, two thirds of the people describing themselves as authors are earning less.

A book-trade sociologist would probably retort that a certain kind of literary life has always been like this, that Gissing's *New Grub Street*, like Thackeray's *Pendennis* before it, positively teems with writers who are scratching a subsistence living from the soil of Victorian literature. This, though, is to ignore the sheer proliferation of outlets, a demand for printed material so extensive that it took an altogether conspicuous lack of talent to fail utterly. Even Gissing's Whelpdale, a whimsical opportunist than whom no character in the novel seems less likely to succeed, finds a niche as a 'literary adviser', on the strength of which he is able to establish his wife in a pretty house in Earls Court. But houses in Earls Court were not so easy to find sixty years later; and neither were jobs as literary advisers. Orwell maintains that he can 'just imagine . . . a bank clerk or an insurance agent going home and doing serious work in his evenings; whereas the effort is too much to make if one has already squandered one's energies on semi-creative work such as teaching, broadcasting or composing propaganda for bodies such as the British Council'. Naturally, there was precedent for the respectable day job – one thinks of Eliot in the Foreign and Colonial Department of Lloyds Bank, or Sir Edmund Gosse, who officiated as librarian of the House of Lords – and yet one of the truly striking characteristics of the 'serious' writers of the 1950s is how reluctant the majority of them were to commit themselves fully to literature. While the roster of secondary occupations included jobs in academe

(Kingsley Amis, D. J. Enright, Malcolm Bradbury) and broadcasting (Anthony Thwaite, Rayner Heppenstall and P. H. Newby, who ended his highly distinguished BBC career as controller of the Third Programme) it also extended to advertising (Roger Longrigg and later Fay Weldon and William Trevor) and the Civil Service (C. P. Snow and his protégé William Cooper). The poet Roy Fuller became a director of the Woolwich Building Society. Angus Wilson was superintendent of the British Museum Reading Room. Francis King spent nearly two decades abroad for the British Council. Anthony Powell, then at work on the early volumes of *A Dance to the Music of Time*, held down part-time appointments at the *Times Literary Supplement* and *Punch*.

If anything united this vast collection of bureaucrats, teachers and cultural eminences it was – at any rate as far as their literary careers were concerned – a high degree of caution. Rather than encouraging an instant throwing over of the reins, success tended to prompt an agonising period of reflection, a reckoning up of the disadvantages and pitfalls of full-time writing that could sometimes take several years to resolve. Paul Scott, then a successful literary agent with several well-received novels to his name, spent much of the later 1950s debating whether to give up his position at the firm of Pearn, Pollinger & Higham. When he finally resolved to set up as a full-time novelist on the day after his fortieth birthday, the omens could scarcely have been more promising. William Morrow, his American publisher, had offered him £1,800 a year for three years, while his agent had volunteered to manage a kitty, into which all his earnings from whatever source would be paid, allowing him a quarterly salary of £450. The manuscript of his new novel, *The Chinese Love Pavilion*, had been received with 'wild excitement' by his UK publisher Eyre & Spottiswood. And yet the events of the next decade offered an object lesson in the difficulty of making this kind of arrangement work. Despite a change of UK publisher – Secker & Warburg, who were prepared to pay him £2,000 a book – Scott, in writing the successive instalments of his great masterpiece *The Raj Quartet* (1966–75) found himself perpetually short of money, forced to take on hack-work and at one point reduced to applying for an Arts Council bursary.

At 40 Scott might have been thought a late starter. But there were other writers, many of them more successful, who delayed even longer. Kingsley Amis, for example, extricated himself from academic life at

Peterhouse, Cambridge as late as 1963. For Angus Wilson (1913–91), regarded in the mid-1950s as one of the most promising younger writers in England, to give up his institutional salary required a decisive effort of will. Francis King waited until his early 40s to take the plunge and then hedged his bets by asking the British Council for a year's sabbatical with the option of re-employment should his career fail to prosper. For some writers, even those with established reputations, the thought of leaving comfortable berths, the possible deterioration of their incomes or family arrangements, was too much to bear. William Cooper, forcibly retired from the Civil Service at the age of 67, seems to have spent most of his working life poised on a knife-edge between two worlds, ever conscious of the attractions of doing nothing but write fiction, at the same time desperately afraid of the consequences if it all went wrong. All the evidence of Cooper's later novels is that he came to regard the dual career as a mistake, undertaken for reasons that were as much to do with a sense of personal belonging as the need for success. As Cooper's alter ego Joe Lunn puts it in *Scenes from Later Life* (1983) during an emotionally charged conversation with his wife, Elspeth:

> In the Government Service I was always saying sharp, bright things that either maddened people or frightened them. Also, because I had a career as a writer, they never felt I was one of them . . . And it's been exactly the same on the other side of the fence. If I'd staked everything on my literary career, I should have had to buckle to and show myself, if nobody else, I really believed in my novels enough to live by them.

There is no community, Joe decides, of which he has ever been a part. Simultaneously Cooper was honest enough to admit, in the midst of these agonisings, that the Civil Service had given him most of his material: to deal convincingly about the corridors of power – always Cooper's special subject – it is perhaps necessary to have trodden a few of them yourself. It was the same with the campus novel-writing dons of the 1950s and 1960s, who occasionally chafed at the restrictions imposed on their creativity by the academic nine-to-five but were darkly conscious of the fact that without it they would have had very little to write about. If one emerges from a novel like Bradbury's *Eating People is Wrong* (1959) with a suspicion that some of Professor

Treece's students are scarcely worth the teaching, then it also has to be acknowledged that their presence on the post-war university campus is what makes it a subject for comedy in the first place. All this meant that the decisive step which propelled the specimen 1950s novelist from a lecture hall, or an office, or a school classroom into full-time writing was not easily taken. Sometimes it was not taken at all. And for those prepared to plunge headlong into the freelance life, danger lurked on every side.

After publishing his first novel, *A Day in Summer* (1963), J. L. Carr gave up his job as a Northamptonshire head teacher and set up on his own account as a publisher-cum-writer. At this point he and his wife Sally possessed a house and capital of £1,600, and supposed that they could survive for two years on these resources while they established the business. Within eighteen months the capital was down to £400, and though Carr's fiction was later successful – he was twice shortlisted for the Booker Prize – there was a period in the mid-1970s when remaindered copies of *The Harpole Report* (1972) went to pay the butcher's bill. Carr, who specialised in computations of this sort, once calculated that he earned seventeen pence an hour in the 1970s for writing novels. If this sounds a precarious existence, then it should be pointed out that many a household-name writer of the 1950s was beset by financial anxiety. V. S. Pritchett, rebuked by the fiction editor of the *New Yorker* for seeming to prefer writing travelogues for the mass-market *Holiday* ('Please, *please* write some stories for us. We need you in the magazine not just as a critic . . . but as a fiction writer'), could very well have replied that the travel pieces brought in far more money than even the notoriously free-spending *New Yorker* could afford to pay its contributors.

Like many another writer before him, Pritchett, come the early 1960s, was beginning to worry about the direction his work seemed to be taking, fearful that he was pouring his immortal spirit down the drain a gallon at a time while the great masterpieces his imagination yearned to produce lay unwritten. Yet the pressures to which even the most celebrated writers of the period were subject shouldn't disguise the fact that, to the 'serious' writer who struck lucky, the financial rewards available were greater than they had ever been. Somerset Maugham's biographers are invariably coy about the exact amounts of money he earned during his long and prolific career, but it is a fact that the sale of his picture collection at Sotheby's in the early 1960s fetched £592,000. And if Maugham, the bulk of his resources accumulated in a previous era, living in unharrassed tax exile on the French Riviera, is in some sense a bad example, then there were other, younger writers doing almost as well. Evelyn Waugh put his mid-1950s income at £10,000 a year – an impressive sum for the time, given that it was made from putting words on paper rather than from lucrative film deals. In fact Waugh's career in the last fifteen years of his life is a kind of triumphal progress around the publishing and newspaper offices of central London in which editors line up to throw money at him. In 1957, following the death of his old friend the Catholic theologian Ronald Knox, he decides to write a biography and, after a bidding war among the religious publishers of the day, is offered £3,000 by his usual sponsors, Chapman & Hall. Suggesting to his agent, in the early 1960s, that he might compose an autobiography in three volumes, he is presented with an extraordinary package, made up of UK and foreign rights and a newspaper serialisation deal, guaranteed to bring in nearly £30,000. Meanwhile, newspaper editors continue to court him. In 1960 the *Daily Mail* offers him £2,000 for five travel articles, based on a two-month, expenses-paid jaunt around Venice, Monte Carlo and Greece, following this up, a year or so later, with another £2,000 for a trip to Guiana. Waugh professed himself 'appalled' by the way in which the pieces were edited, but noted that 'It is no use quarrelling with one's bread and butter at my age.'

Waugh was not alone in his earning capacities. The popular historian A. L. Rowse, sitting down to calculate his yearly income in March 1964, estimated that he was receiving £1,200 from his All Souls fellowship, £1,000 from his British publishers, Macmillan, and £500 to £600 for editing the *Teach Yourself History* series. But the really big money came from America – $6,000 from the Huntington Library, $7,000 to $8,000 from lecturing, $5,000 a year from one US publisher and the same sum from another on account of a $20,000 advance for a book about the Battle of Bosworth. In all, Rowse calculated that he had accumulated and invested between $60,000 and $70,000 in the past few years. The difficulty with earnings of this magnitude, in an era of high taxation, was that liabilities could only be kept to a minimum by increasingly devious financial arrangements whose legality could not always be guaranteed. As early as 1947, for example, Evelyn Waugh had entered into an agreement with the editor of the American *Good Housekeeping* whereby he would be paid $4,000 for a short story (delivery date unspecified) half of which took material form in the shape of a new car delivered to him in Ireland as a way of avoiding tax.

Later, on the advice of his accountant, he began to pay royalties and advances into a trust, jocularly known as the 'Save the Children Fund', intended to pay school fees and household expenses, but regularly raided – with the apparent connivance of the trustees – to buy himself antique silver and pictures. But the accountant's death revealed that Waugh had been badly advised. With the Inland Revenue pressing him for several years' back tax, the package deal for his memoirs was essentially a stop-gap measure to shore up his straitened finances. Rowse, too, once he began to make money from his books, was keen to minimise his exposure to tax, but his efforts amounted to little more than avoidance. An arrangement with Macmillan, whereby they contracted to pay him £10,000 in forty quarterly instalments, collapsed when it became apparent that the publishers had retained capital they were not entitled to invest. There were other run-ins over the next decade, involving payments – by Rowse – of anything between £60,000 and £100,000. A diary entry from September 1967 records 'an appalling morning with the Income Tax authorities, louring like a cloud over the scene for months'.

Waugh and Rowse were established writers, with substantial backlists ripe for exploitation (the Save the Children Fund's first deposit was a £1,000 payment from Penguin) adept at transforming high-end journalistic commissions and book projects into working holidays: the trip that produced Waugh's final travel book, *A Tourist in Africa* (1961), was subsidised by a shipping line and involved an expenses payment of £1,500 – three times the nominal advance from Chapman & Hall. On the other hand, there were up-and-coming writers equally capable of flexing their financial muscle. For all his anxieties about giving up his day job, and some very humble beginnings – £50 for his debut collection, *The Wrong Set*, in 1949, £75 for *Such Darling Dodos* a year later – Angus Wilson was soon able to convert himself into a considerable financial proposition. A gross income of £1,441 in 1955 had more than doubled to £3,541 by 1956, and by 1958, two years into full-time writing, and with the help of a small legacy, his annual receipts amounted to £5,500. This was a very reasonable upper-middle-class income for the era of Anthony Eden and Harold Macmillan, yet there are several crucial caveats. A relatively small percentage of these sums came from books – *Anglo-Saxon Attitudes* (1956), the novel that may be said to have properly launched Wilson's career, attracted a £300 advance. The vast majority was picked up in journalism and radio and TV work. Similarly, as a homosexual bachelor, living in ad hoc accommodation – the rent on his Dolphin Square flat in the early 1950s was a mere £142 a year – Wilson's outgoings were modest. Fearful that this early promise might not be maintained, he continued to fret about the future. His first reaction when offered a part-time teaching post at the newly founded University of East Anglia in 1963 was to ask whether the job came with a pension.

Beneath these exalted redoubts, the pickings for the aspiring literary man or woman of the post-war era could be modest to the point of non-existence. Kingsley Amis received £100 for *Lucky Jim*, payable on publication, although a begging letter managed to produce £25 in advance from the legendarily stingy Victor Gollancz. For all his growing reputation, Anthony Burgess thought himself lucky to have prised £200 out of Heinemann for his eighth novel, *The Worm and the Ring*, in 1961. In an atmosphere of caution and frugality, the terms suggested by the newly established firm of Anthony Blond in 1959 for Simon Raven's debut novel *The Feathers of Death* – £25 down, £10 per week for the ten weeks during which the book was to be written, £50 on acceptance and a final £50 on publication – seemed almost absurdly generous to its author ('It was, by any standards, a magnificent offer for an unknown publisher to make to an obscure hack'). Not all of Blond's authors were so fortunate. *The Blackmailer* (1958), a novel by Isabel Colegate, a partner in the firm, attracted an advance of £50 against a royalty of 10 per cent on the first 2,500 copies sold. If Colegate had imagined that the path to literary glory ran rapidly upwards, she was mistaken. Her third novel, *The Great Occasion* (1962), was widely reviewed but made her only £18 above a meagre advance and a small fee for the paperback rights. 'I was enormously disappointed' she later recalled. 'I suppose I had still not got through that bit they tell you as a child about going on trying and gradually getting better and then everyone being very pleased with you.'

A 'name' writer, not above playing one publisher off against another and using his, or her, reputation as a bargaining tool, could sometimes raise substantial sums of money when the need arose. Gollancz, for example, anxious not to lose Kingsley Amis to predatory rivals, was persuaded to hand over what his agent, Graham Watson, called the 'huge loan' of £5,000 in anticipation of *My Enemy's Enemy* (1962) and *One Fat Englishman* (1963), but this kind of munificence was rare. Most writers who wanted to make a living out of literature in the 1950s and 1960s without taking a part-time job had to turn to that infallible resource of the interwar era, literary journalism. Here, though, the opportunities were proportionately fewer and the rewards substantially less. Worse, as with fiction-writing, the gap that had opened up between the star performers employed to write lead reviews and critical articles and the hack commissioned to file novel round-ups and run-of-the-mill belles-lettres continued to widen. Cyril Connolly, the doyen of post-war newspaper critics, was paid £800 a year during his brief stint as literary editor of the *Observer*, succeeded to Desmond MacCarthy's *Sunday Times* spot at a fee of £40 per weekly article and by 1971, when he had filled the post for nearly twenty years, enjoyed an annual contract worth £4,250. V. S. Pritchett received a yearly retainer of £1,500 from the *New Statesman* during the 1950s. But Connolly and Pritchett were titans of the trade. On the outer margins of the reviewing circuit, the rewards were much less generous. The *Listener* by this time was paying seventeen guineas for its fortnightly novel-review, but on an impoverished weekly such as *Time and Tide*, the fee could be as low as £2 or £3, a sum that even the perennially hard-up Raven was forced to reject as uneconomic. Moreover, work of this sort was always likely to be irregular: to earn £1,000 a year from the *Spectator* in the 1960s would have required the reviewer to write a piece every week of the year. Inevitably, there were writers prepared to work at this pace, but the regular columnist often found himself swamped under a tide of new books. Burgess, again, though grateful for his weekly slot on the *Yorkshire Post*, calculated that he had read 350 new novels in the space of two years.

Happily there were newer media to hand, whose formats encouraged the writer not to put pen to paper but merely to open his mouth. While the radio 'talk' had been part of the freelance author's repertoire since the late 1920s, its attractions soon came to be dwarfed, as the 1950s wore on, by the power of television. Here the work available tended to be of two kinds. 'Name' writers could expect to be invited on to early versions of the chat show, then springing up on the commercial channels ('The commercial television people approached me today, asking me to sign up for another series of personal appearances' runs an entry in Beverley Nichols's diary from January 1956;

'This time in the afternoon, and 65 guineas instead of 50 guineas. I turned them down, rather brusquely') or, in exceptional circumstances, to be subject to full-length interviews in the more august surroundings of the BBC. As with radio, the Corporation was not known for its free-handedness, but a combination of sticking to one's guns and a resourceful agent could produce substantial rewards. Evelyn Waugh was originally offered seventy-five guineas for his famous *Face to Face* grilling by John Freeman in 1960, but eventually walked away with £250.

Waugh, and to a lesser extent Nichols, were operating at the top of the scale, but lower down, especially when the BBC began to invest in a series of relatively highbrow arts programmes, opportunities for less well-known, and sometimes altogether obscure, writers began to increase. Simon Raven, at this point in his career no more than a journeyman book reviewer, found himself invited on to the new flagship programme *Monitor* in 1958 to interview Kingsley Amis. In the context of the late 1950s literary marketplace, Raven's account of this experience is rather revealing. He regards the medium with distrust, thinks his interviewing technique 'inept' and is not asked back for another three years. And yet, in a roundabout way, the appearance is judged to have done him good. 'I was known to have appeared, to have been paid to appear, on a prestige TV programme, never mind what I did or said on it. I had received, so to say, a licence to make public statements: I had become, in however ill-defined and dingy a fashion, an *authority*, which, in an age of authorities, is an important step.'

For a select handful of writers, and mostly irregularly, television offered a valuable new way of earning money without great effort, but other income streams were beginning to dry up. The market for short stories, so buoyant in the 1920s that it had been possible for a writer of the calibre of Stacy Aumonier to make his reputation without ever having to write a full-length novel, continued to decline: only a few specialist vehicles such as *Argosy* survived. The ancient tradition of the novelist who doubled up as playwright, which had brought small fortunes to Maugham, Priestley and Patrick Hamilton, had also begun to diminish. This was becoming a specialised art: most of the dramatists who established themselves in the 1950s were playwrights pure and simple. Priestley, on the other hand, continued to write plays well into the 1960s, and his collaboration with Iris Murdoch on *A Severed Head* brought Murdoch £18,000 in the course of its three-year run. As ever, America continued to hold out the prospect of enormous wealth, as attractive to the freelance journalist as to the writer of film scripts. Kingsley Amis, having contracted to write a film column for *Esquire* in the late 1950s, found that he was being paid at 2s 6d a word – three times the money offered by a mass-circulation British newspaper. Alec Waugh, selling a short story to Hollywood in 1953, was able to live off the proceeds for the next eighteen months. Only a handful of home-grown writers in the 1950s and 1960s were able to play the Hollywood game with any success – Nigel Balchin, for example, or Frederic Raphael – but the money available dwarfed anything that the domestic market was able to provide. By the end of the 1960s Anthony Burgess's agent had negotiated a rate of $50,000 per script; the film rights of *A Clockwork Orange* (1961) were bought by Warner Brothers for $200,000, although in time-honoured Burbank fashion little of this came to the author himself.

Burgess, in fact, is a textbook example of the resourceful post-war freelance's ability to mix traditional ways of earning a living with newer income streams, writing at an ever more hectic pace – one of his collections of occasional pieces was called *Urgent Copy* – and never afraid to get his hands dirty, alternating highly paid work for film and television with more mundane engagements with the *Listener* and, in the early part of his career, straying into the more exotic realms of corporate copywriting. One little-known addition to his bibliography is *London and the CLRP: A Centennial Tribute to the City of London Retail Property Co. Ltd 1864–1964*. Yet Burgess's versatility is exceptional.* There were other writers much less able to adapt to the changing conditions of the post-war literary scene. Take, for example, these few days in the late-period professional life of Julian Maclaren-Ross. It is March 1960 and our hero, now in his late 40s, great days manifestly behind him, burdened by a wife, child and numberless debts, his working capital further reduced by a burglary at his Bloomsbury hotel, is clearly

* See Martin Amis's *Observer* interview from 1980: 'I would go on to endure an authentically frightening hangover which lasted for half a week. At eight in the evening on the day after the day after, I was still sitting in an armchair with a hand on my brow saying, "Dear oh dear. Dear oh dear oh dear . . ." Whereas Burgess (I am sure) went home, did the kitchen, spring-cleaned the flat, wrote two book reviews, a flute concerto and a film treatment, knocked off his gardening column for *Pravda*, phoned in his surfing page to the *Sydney Morning Herald*, and then test-drove a kidney-machine for *El Pais* – before getting down to some serious work.'

on his uppers. Desperate for ready cash, he sets hastily to work on a radio dramatisation of an ancient short story, 'The Swag, the Spy and the Soldier'. On Wednesday 2 March a friendly BBC producer gives him a day's broadcasting work. This brings in £15, but the duns are massing. 'Driven by the abiding fear of eviction', in his biographer's courteous phrase, he works through the night with the aim of delivering the manuscript before the weekend. This Herculean feat is narrowly accomplished. With the £47 thus raised he chips away at his most pressing debts, hands over £10 to the hotel management – the family are now secure until Tuesday morning – and remits £4 to a former landlord and his wife, one of a tribe of creditors now packed into the cluttered margins of his life, to deter them from chasing him for unpaid rent. The weekend passes without incident. Come Monday 7 March, 'The Swag, the Spy and the Soldier' gets the BBC's stamp of approval, enabling Maclaren-Ross to pocket another £47. Three-quarters of this goes on the hotel bill, thereby guaranteeing the family's residence for another six days. Just as Maclaren-Ross is congratulating himself on this respite, in rockets a summons from the outraged landlord. Flustered by this further distraction and still anxious to keep the hotel management sweet, he unloads a cache of manuscripts on an obliging dealer for £40 and, encouraged by sales of a recent pot-boiling novel, meditates a TV adaptation, only to have to abandon the scheme a few days later for an attempt to persuade the BBC to commission a ninety-minute radio play.

The extraordinary thing about this deadline-haunted stretch of time, with its trackless hours spent working against the clock, its amphetamine-fuelled assaults on the stacked pile of exercise books, is how typical it was of Maclaren-Ross's late-period routine. But the author of the all too ominously titled *Of Love and Hunger*'s difficulty lay in his failure to adapt to changing circumstances, to comprehend that neither the working practices or the lifestyle that had seen him through the 1940s would pass muster a decade and a half later. Younger writers who had begun to colonise the literary marketplace could find the going equally hard. At more or less the same time that Maclaren-Ross's career began its final, precipitous descent – he died of a heart attack in 1964 with the manuscript of his best-known work, *Memoirs of the Forties* (1965) half finished – the aspiring novelist J. G. Farrell, then employed part-time by a language school, established himself in an Earls Court basement with the aim of completing his first book. The rent was £3 10s a week. Allowing himself 10s a day for food and personal expenses and taking his meals in a workman's café, Farrell reflected that he had 'never tried to live on so little'. After several rejections *A Man from Elsewhere* was accepted by Hutchinson for an advance of £50, with a further £100 payable on publication. On the strength of this Farrell took ship for Paris where he worked on a second novel and supported himself on the proceeds of a second part-time teaching job.

Both *A Man from Elsewhere* (1963) and its successor *The Lung* (1965) were well received, and Farrell, who on his return to the UK had been living in a conservatory annex in Kensington, was awarded a two-year Harkness fellowship. From New Haven, Connecticut in November 1966 he could report 'no shortage of money'. But the reviews of his third novel, *A Girl in the Head* (1967), were unsatisfactory, and by the following year he was once again in London, living in a cheap hotel, combining work on what was to become *Troubles* (1970) with reading manuscripts for publishers, and watching his capital diminish from one week to the next ('my meagre savings are vanishing at an alarming rate'). The book was finished by June 1969, but negotiations with Jonathan Cape, to whom Farrell had migrated with *A Girl in the Head*, took months to conclude, and he was infuriated to discover that the £200 he had expected from his paperback publishers had been reduced to a fraction of this amount by the time Cape had compensated themselves for unearned advances. Desperate for money, he accepted a 'hacking job' – writing careers leaflets for £50 – and began to write book reviews for the *Spectator* at £20 a time. Finally, in June 1970, there was a brief upturn in his fortunes when the Arts Council awarded him a grant of £750 'with which to go on writing'. In seven years, Farrell's income from all sources – four novels, one of them not yet published, casual journalism and part-time teaching jobs – cannot have amounted to more than £3,000.

Was this kind of life sustainable in the third quarter of the twentieth century? Farrell was a bachelor, careless of his own comfort, prepared to endure considerable hardships in pursuit of his dream of becoming a successful novelist. Men (and women) with families and mortgages were more willing to compromise. Many an aspiring female novelist – A. S. Byatt, for example, who remembered writing her first novel in a cramped Bloomsbury flat in the rare intervals when her two small children had fallen simultaneously asleep – would have welcomed the chance to do even that. Nonetheless, all the evidence of the late 1950s and early 1960s suggests that the living of the old-style Grub Street life – entirely from one's pen, without resorting to academe or a part-time job – was becoming steadily more problematic. Reviewing his prospects for the year ahead in 1962, Simon Raven strikes a faintly exasperated note:

> There is not to be penury, but no more is there to be a year of leisure. There is, as usual, to be work. *Close of Play* [his fourth published novel] must be finished. This present book must be collected together to settle last year's income tax (or is it the year before's?). I must think about an 'important' novel to impress a disillusioned American publisher. I must write plays for the BBC in order to educate my son. I must write reviews and essays to pay for the expensive lubricants which will provide peace of mind and at the same time help to jolt a tired imagination. I complain at none of this. I merely wonder, from time to time, how long it will go on.

In fact, Raven is being faintly disingenuous. He is, by his own admission, an extravagant man with a taste for foreign travel, fine wines and fashionable restaurants, with a gambling habit to boot. A little prudent management of his resources, the reader suspects, would enable him to live in modest comfort. A more reliable guide to the working condition of the 1960s freelance life is Jonathan Raban, whose memoir of his early days in London begins with its 27-year-old author giving up his teaching job at the University of East Anglia (£1,750 per annum) and coming to rest in Highgate, where a bedsitter cost £7 a week to rent, and a reasonable living could be put together by writing book reviews for *Encounter* and the *London Magazine* for between £15 and £30 a piece. 'In 1969 it was still – just – possible for a newcomer to scrape by on literary journalism' Raban decided, there in a room littered with newly arrived Jiffy bags and the scripts of half-written television plays. By coincidence, 1969 was the year in which Anthony Burgess, alarmed by a 95 per cent rate of super-tax which threatened to engulf his lucrative film earnings, disappeared to exile on the continent. In a world where disparities of income grew more marked from one publishing season to the next, the Corporation of the Goosequill, to borrow Thackeray's phrase, was losing its solidarity.

Alec Waugh: The First Best-seller

There have always been best-selling books, just as there have always been pundits to disparage them. As long ago as the 1570s Thomas Nashe could be found lamenting that 'treatises of *Tom Thumme*' were being 'bought up thick and three-fold, when better things lie dead'. The struggling hacks of the nineteenth-century book-world novels are, with certain exceptions, aghast at the rampant commercialism of the Victorian marketplace, and to be a titan of the circulating library pulling in your £1,000 a year is, to a disdainful classical gentleman like Edwin Reardon, merely to pander to the mob. By the late 1950s, as modern business methods and more sophisticated forms of advertising began to arrive from America, this process became steadily more concentrated and hard-headed, to the point where publishers vied with each other in trumpeting their sales figures. In January 1956, for example, the paperback firm Corgi Books proudly announced further reprints of their best-selling war novels John Brophy's *Immortal Sergeant*, Guthrie Wilson's *Brave Company* and Eric Lambert's *The 20,000 Thieves*, each of which had already sold more than 250,000 copies. Not to be outdone, Messrs Collins declared, four months later, that the forthcoming hardback printing of Hammond Innes's *The Mary Deare* was to be a staggering 75,000 copies, only for Victor Gollancz to trump this achievement with the revelation that they expected to unleash between 100,000 and 200,000 copies of Daphne du Maurier's *The Scapegoat* on to the market.

By the standards of the 1930s, these were impressive figures, made all the more significant by the fact that they were not confined to 'popular fiction': in the same year Heinemann advertised a sale in excess of 100,000 hardback copies for Graham Greene's *The Quiet American*. But as well as selling more copies of their books, promoting them more aggressively and acting with greater vigour to detach up-and-coming writers from the clutches of their rivals, publishers were also beginning to change the way in which commercially successful books were brought to the market. Many of the best-sellers of the 1920s had been released to a largely indifferent public, only mysteriously to 'catch on' in the months after their publication, to strike some chord with the reading public which their sponsors could not originally have foreseen. Famously, A. S. M. Hutchinson's *If Winter Comes* was made mincemeat of by the critics before achieving its six-figure sales in 1922. Thirty years later, by way of judicious manipulation of the media and the canny, prepublication sale of subsidiary rights, a book's success was, increasingly, guaranteed before a single copy was sold. One of the first beneficiaries of this revolution, somewhat to his own surprise, was Alec Waugh.

The early post-war years had not been kind to the author of *The Loom of Youth*. His marriage to an Australian heiress named Joan Chirnside had fallen apart, not least because of his serial infidelities. As a novel-a-year man back in the 1930s, he found the proscriptions of the later 1940s, with their paper shortages and their modest print runs, a serious brake on his earning power. Worse, he seemed to have lost the knack of writing short stories for the lucrative American market which had sustained him in the years before the war. All these factors worked their effect, and the early 1950s marked a descent into less elevated marketplaces: a life of Thomas Lipton, commissioned by the firm of tea-importers and grocers that bore his name, and a history of Gilbey's, the British wine merchants, were only two of his forays into the debatable territory of company history. Now deep in his mid-50s, Waugh was faced with the uncomfortable realisation that most of his bridges were burnt. Divorcing his wife, and transferring himself to America as an 'emigrant alien', he found his income sharply reduced. There was even the thought of suicide, by way of a hoarded cache of barbiturates on an obscure tropical island to minimise the embarrassment to family and friends. And then, not for the first time in his writing life, Waugh had an extraordinary stroke of luck.

It began with the news that Twentieth Century Fox had bought the rights to a short story – 'Circles of Deception' – the last piece of short fiction, it turned out, that Waugh would ever write. Having pocketed a substantial cheque – enough, he calculated, to keep him for nearly two years – Waugh resolved to live modestly and focus his energies on a single book that might, if adroitly managed, transform his prospects. The resultant manuscript, at this point headed *The Sugar Barons*, 900 pages long, set in the West Indies, and markedly more ambitious than anything to which he had previously set his hand, was ready by the early part of 1955. Although unenthusiastically received by his British agent, A. D. Peters, it was seized upon by his American publishers, Farrar & Straus. 'This, clearly, is the book we have been waiting for' the editorial director informed his US agent. Encouraged, but by no means exalted – Farrar & Straus proposed a first printing of 10,000 copies – Waugh departed to Nice with his current lady-love, Virginia Sorensen, and holed up in the Hotel Escurial.

To this address, some days later, came a message announcing that the *Ladies' Home Journal* had bought the serial rights for $22,500. By his own account Waugh was so overwhelmed by emotion that he sat on the hotel stairs in a daze. But better was to come. Three days later a cable arrived bearing the legend 'Literary Guild Selection January'. Twenty-four hours later the telegraph boy produced a third sheet of paper marked 'Readers' Digest Condensed Book Club'. At this point Waugh and Sorensen were about to leave for Geneva. Awaiting their taxi early one morning on the hotel steps, they were informed that New York had tried to telephone the previous evening. On their first afternoon in Switzerland a telephone call announced: 'Twentieth Century Fox. A hundred and forty thousand dollars.' The proud author, who had now amassed a quarter of a million dollars in the space of a few weeks, guilelessly remarked that 'he didn't know there was so much money in the world'.

By January 1956, the month of publication, *Island in the Sun*, as *The Sugar Barons* had been prudently recast, had racked up prepublication earnings of nearly $500,000 – enough, as Waugh gratefully acknowledged, to set him up for life. There was to be no more propaganda work for grocers. But what was it about the book that so awakened the interest of publishers, movie-makers (the film was eventually made by Darryl F. Zanuck), magazine editors and, once copies appeared in the shops, the paying public? In fact, *Island in the Sun* assembles several of Waugh's favourite preoccupations: murder, adultery, closely observed social interaction and racial tension. Essentially, the novel consists of five interrelated narratives. In the first a woman kills a man by mistake – he hits his head on a table-edge when struck by her in the course of an argument – but decides not to inform the police. The second strand involves a young American from the South who falls in love with the daughter of a West Indian planter only to discover that he has 'coloured' blood. A third takes in a man's suspicion of his wife's infidelity. To these domestic melodramas, Waugh adds two more general plot lines: a controversial new governor trying to impose his authority, and a reactionary planter who tries to discredit a young black agitator by inciting a riot in which he himself is killed.

Modest, as ever, about the novel's literary merits, which even his brother Evelyn grudgingly acknowledged, Waugh attributed its resounding commercial success to sheer topicality, suggesting that the interracial theme appealed to a post-war society that had begun to consider these issues, while the locations were becoming more familiar to an affluent new American audience for whom the Caribbean was now a viable tourist destination. The success of *The Loom of Youth* had offered Waugh a calling card to the literary world, but *Island in the Sun* changed his life. Evelyn's opinion that, in its aftermath, his brother 'never drew a sober breath' was an exaggeration. Alec Waugh had always lived frugally. He continued to publish books for the remaining quarter-century of his life, mostly spy novels and garrulous autobiographies, none of which sold remotely as well, and to pursue a vagrant and inconspicuous lifestyle. 'I was a scattered person. I liked my life the way it was. I had no wish to have it any different. *Island in the Sun* made it possible for me to lead the same life a little longer, a bit more amply.' On the other hand, his friends could not help noting that henceforth when he stayed in New York the studio apartment was abandoned in favour of a hotel suite.

CHAPTER 12

New Men

> I write an article for the *Spectator* on the subject of Urbanity. In a Beaverbrook periodical called *Books and Art*, a young man writing under the name of Humphrey Clinker has accused me in two successive articles of being cultured, snobbish and urbane. I rather like having the chance to answer him, although I do not really understand what his real grievance is. He says that 'virtuosi' such as Cyril Connolly and myself live in ivory towers and do not possess the common touch or understand the dust and roar of life. We should treat literature as a smart columnist treats life and should not discuss general ideas but concentrate on personalities and be more newsy. I say in my article that I am writing for an educated public and not for an uneducated public and that it would be absurd for me to put on a proletarian tone.
>
> Harold Nicolson, diary, 19 March 1958

> Who do you take with you on the long weekends in Sussex cottages? Kafka and Kierkegaard, Proust and Henry James? Dylan Thomas, *The Confidential Clerk*, *The Age of Anxiety* and *The Golden Horizon*? You belong to an age that is passing.
>
> J. D. Scott, *Spectator*, 27 October 1954

Orthodoxy tends to mark down the literary 1950s as an age in transition, if not tumult, in which many of the established reputations of the era went down like ninepins before an aggressively newfangled demographic assault. Bloomsbury was in sharp retreat; 'taste' was moving in unexpected directions as one band of cultural opinion-formers gave way to another – a transformation which, most onlookers agreed, was as much to do with the social provenance of the author as aesthetic preference. The 'Amis man', Simon Raven's shorthand for the new kind of fictional hero who came to populate the novels of the later 1950s ('honest, kind, loyal, intelligent and, in matters of politics or social welfare, the most ineffable prig . . . boozy, priapic and inept'), is as much a sociological construct as a figure out of literature, as Raven, to whom nearly all post-1945 arrangements were thoroughly anathema, no doubt intended him to be. Inevitably, this suggestion of changing guards or reshuffled packs, even – in staider quarters – of barbarians at the gates, tended to be confined to the world of weekly magazines and radio arts programmes. The general reading public, in so far as we can determine its tastes from Mass Observation surveys and the evidence of library borrowings, was still happily absorbed in the popular literature of a previous age. No self-respecting member of the intelligentsia, on the other hand, approached the age of Kingsley Amis, John Wain and Richard Hoggart with anything other than a profound suspicion that change was in the air. This feeling was especially marked among the young men and women who observed the era from school sixth forms and junior common rooms. Here, for example, is John Carey (b.1934), a product of a suburban grammar school and as class-conscious a critic as the whole post-war era ever threw up, on Martin Green's *Children of the Sun* (1976), a study of English 'decadence' in the first half of the twentieth century: 'This book is richly stocked with people whom any person of decent instincts will find loathsome. That is partly what makes it fascinating, but also what makes it shaming, because the characters Martin Green describes dominated English cultural life from the end of the First World War until the fifties.'

Carey is not, it should immediately be pointed out, a Leavisite – he once described the voice of Q. D. Leavis as that of a cultural dictator – but this is essentially the Leavis line, observable in the pages of *Scrutiny* and elsewhere at any time during the 1930s, insisting that literary society is populated and manipulated by a tiny coterie of writers perpetuating in print the alliances previously forged at school and university. If, on the one hand, the people Carey is complaining about – Brian Howard and Harold Acton among them – are what became known as the 'Brideshead Generation', then his sights are also fixed on Bloomsbury and indeed any well-connected impresarios of the modernist project – another endeavour which the literary 1950s seemed anxious to overthrow. The 1950s, on this reading – and Carey is writing with twenty years of hindsight – were an attack on standards that had their roots in social caste rather than literary value, that whole Connolly-sanctioned idea of superior 'mandarin' consciousness, a world in which new men, unhindered by superfluous social baggage, could safely luxuriate. Much of this is true, no doubt, and yet one notes just how tenaciously most of the old guard held on: Connolly and Raymond Mortimer continuing to occupy their niches on the *Sunday Times* (despite Mortimer's occasional fear, as expressed to Frances Partridge, that 'I can't give them what they want'); the *New Statesman* still offering a home to far-from ageing Bloomsberries; Harold Nicolson continuing to file his weekly 'Marginal Comment', a column much commended for its correctness of style, to the *Spectator*. Simultaneously, many of the newcomers were rapidly assimilated into literary-cum-social circles which – on paper at any rate – they were supposed to detest. A bona fide literary rebel would not perhaps have written with quite such unction as Kingsley Amis did to Edith Sitwell in the early part of 1954 ('It is very kind of you to want to arrange a luncheon party for me. I too am greatly looking forward to it . . . I do hope the indisposition you mention is now completely at an end') but much of Amis's insubordination was wished upon him by the journalists who wrote up his exploits for public consumption, and while he was capable of mocking the entertainment that followed in one of his regular letters to Philip Larkin ('rather like lunching with a kindly maiden aunt who wants to show that she's interested in all that writing you're doing'), another part of Amis is clearly exulting in the fact that, in more than one sense, he has arrived.

While some of the alliances of the immediately post-war era can seem unexpectedly heterodox – as, to go back thirty years, were many of the configurations of the Georgian twilight – demarcations of taste were similarly blurred. Somerset Maugham, induced to read *Lucky Jim* when its author won the award garnished with his name, might have been horrified by the apparent philistinism of some of its pronouncements, but card-carrying modernists such as Miss Sitwell and Anthony Powell warmly approved: Powell, in fact, went out of his way to cultivate Amis's friendship. All this could be highly confusing to media onlookers bent on breaking down the mass of material before them into recognisable shapes. Amis left an instructive account of an evening in 1955 in which he was invited to interview Powell on the Third Programme in the confident expectation that he would attack the author of the newly published *The Acceptance World* on social grounds ('It was not hard to guess that the interview had been intended to consist of a lower-class malcontent . . . having a good go at somebody whom he would see as an upper-class git'). Arriving at the studio Amis and Powell greeted each other by their Christian names: 'at once the BBC faces fell in disappointment, almost disgust'. This is not to disguise the fact that Amis and Powell came from very different social backgrounds – the one a middle-class boy from Norbury, the other an Eton-educated colonel's son – or that they wrote about very different people, merely that each applauded something in the other's work, and in the other's personality, that would not have been apparent to a radio producer who, as early as 1955, had swallowed some of the prevailing myths about the 1950s as a literary decade.

Whatever his precise social background, and whatever his attitude to the literary generation he aimed to supplant, the 'new man' is a feature of fiction of the 1950s and, as such, given a starring role in such genre-defining novels as C. P. Snow's *The New Men* (1954) and William Cooper's retrospective *Memoirs of a New Man* (1966). Snow's and Cooper's exemplars are bright, scientifically educated boys from petit-bourgeois backgrounds, purposefully at large in the engine room of the mid-twentieth-century establishment. Cooper's *The Struggles of Albert Woods* (1952) is a pattern example of the 'new man' novel, even if its resourceful, lady-killing lead is, in one sense, a rather old man, in fact not much more than an H. G. Wells hero from the early 1900s brought up to date and given greater room for manoeuvre: a sharp operator risen dramatically out of 'the lower middle class, that great repository of English energy, ability and talent'. A hard-working experimental chemist, whose exhortatory journal entries are straight out of *Love and Mr Lewisham* ('Today read 100 pages of *War and Peace*. Not enough, Woods. You must read and read and read'), Albert succeeds in battling his way to Oxford and securing a college fellowship. As the admission ceremony proceeds, kneeling at the warden's feet in the college chapel, he is overcome by emotion: 'If there is such a thing as the force of destiny, Albert felt it at that moment almost hurting as it carried him aloft, like a strong sustained kick up the seat.'

Like Wells's upwardly mobile young men, Albert's ambitions are at once social and romantic. Humble, schoolteaching Thelma – an archetypal Cooper girl, described as 'gay, lively, talkative, kind and friendly, completely democratic though extremely shy' – is eventually thrown over in favour of his academic mentor's palely aristocratic daughter. There is a significant scene in which Thelma, visiting her boyfriend's sumptuously refurbished college suite, doesn't know where to sit: the room is 'too grand' for her. Once wooed, on the other hand, frail, consumptive Margaret fades into the margins, leaving husband and father to continue their twenty-year game of follow-my-leader through a maze of professional appointments, Royal Society elections, government committees and epic set-tos over research endowments. Finally, having spent the war years successfully synthesising a new kind of nerve gas, Albert blows the chance of a knighthood by incautiously rebuking the wife of the Cabinet minister in whose gift it lies. The character and his social origins – his worldly ambition, his sensitivity, his go-getting – are essentially Wellsian, but the milieu in which he operates is something altogether different.

To begin with there is the technocratic background, in which the research lab and the Oxbridge common room shade effortlessly into the gentlemen's club and the Whitehall committee room. There are the human relationships proceeding by way of minute adjustments to the emotional thermostat. There are the dense bureaucratic tangles deviously unpicked by way of quiet words and zealous colluding. And yet the abundant charm of this parable of the new man's resolute tramp through the Whitehall corridors, its sense of how a certain kind of bureaucratic life can be understood by the people at large in it here in the machine age, is everywhere undermined by its lack of depth: an absorption in backstairs intrigue and power-broking that goes no further than a delight in power's incidental rewards. To put it another way, here is a group of highly intelligent men – academics, industrialists, senior civil servants – busily conspiring to influence the world of 'affairs' in the not quite conscious assumption that the whole business is an end in itself. The idea that anyone who works in a government office might have a destiny in view beyond a knighthood or the solace of the chairman's smile would be as stoutly resisted as a belief in God or a vote for Winston Churchill.

The great danger faced by the 'new man', consequently, whether in fiction or in the world inhabited by the person who had created him, was his habit of turning into a slightly different version of the obstructive forces he was bent on supplanting. Albert's complaint about the mid-century establishment, after all, is not that it exists, or that it is fundamentally undemocratic, but that it does not yet include himself. One need only consider the trajectories of one or two real-life new men – Kingsley Amis is an obvious example – to remark the relative ease with which a surly young 1950s iconoclast could transform himself into the entity he had begun his career by disparaging. At the same time, post-war novels about upwardly mobile young men heading off in pursuit of the glittering prizes had – or, more important, were assumed to have – a second and in some ways yet more luminous agenda. *The Struggles of Albert Woods*, like *Lucky Jim* or John Wain's *Hurry on Down* (1953), cried out to be interpreted not merely as a piece of literary art but as a social document – a guide to the evolving welfare state, say, or an expression of disillusionment with that state's development, to adapt Anthony Hartley's famous line about the 'limited revolt of the intellectuals'. Even if such books were not primarily conceived as pieces of reportage from a changing post-war world, then that is how they tended to be analysed by critics alert to sociological inferences and thinly disguised political comment.

These pressures affected each of the very different versions of new men (and women) on display in the literary 1950s, from the 'Movement' (formally identified in 1954, but arguably at work some years earlier), the 'Angry Young Men', a group so artificial that its members ranged from fashionable playwrights to a deeply obscure lecturer in the University of Hull's Department of Extramural Studies, to the new wave of predominantly working-class writers who began to make their presence felt towards the end of the decade, and even such minor and desultory political-cum-literary groupings as the Spartacists, whose manifesto called for 'a clean break and a fresh start under new men'. Their end result, inevitably, was a great deal of false taxonomy – Iris Murdoch, for example, marked down as an honorary Angry Young Man – and an interest in literature that, in contrast to the aesthetically conscious 1920s, stemmed from motives that had more to do with sociology, constructions of post-war social arrangements that were there to prove political or demographic points. The 1950s, you sometimes feel, have been subjected to rather more interpretation than they can bear, and the varied attentions of sociologists and media historians have sometimes tended to obscure a literary climate that can seem a good deal more open-ended than critical orthodoxy likes to insist.

On the other hand, for all this taxonomic shoehorning, the characteristic 1950s attitudes – its familiar names, its talismanic figures, its keenness, to particularise, on Leavis, Orwell, Lawrence and Amis rather than Eliot, Forster and Woolf, its admiration for what Martin Green calls 'the decent man – as opposed to the gentleman or the Anglo-Saxon moralist' – seem genuine enough. To Green, whose dislike of what he regarded as the sterility and artificiality of English life had prompted a 'voluntary exile' in the United States, Forster is an example of 'an upper-middle-class mind failing to meet the challenge of modern times'. Amis, alternatively, has created 'the lower-middle-class non-gentlemanly conscience'. His achievement has been to fashion

> a voice, a way of talking about everything, and about oneself as one does so, which contains every tone, every modulation of tone, of that mode of being; the naively puritan morality, the subtly scrupulous, almost nagging habit of mind, the suspicion of all pretentiousness and falsity, the cardinal importance given to genuineness, the strenuously unheroic posture, the strongly moral sense of humour, above all the sense of being at home in lower-middle-class England as nowhere else.

But what were the practical consequences of 'being at home in lower-middle-class England' – provided, of course, one could decide where lower-middle-class England actually was? One of them, once we except a few cosmopolitan figures such as Murdoch and D. J. Enright, was a profound insularity, or rather a dislike of the European influences to which English literary life had been subject in the interwar era, and in particular the Gallophilia cultivated by Eliot (an enthusiast for Laforge, Corbière and Baudelaire) and Strachey, the author of *Landmarks in French Literature*. Interestingly, it is possible to catch the scent of this disparagement much further down the cultural scale than Amis's novels, with their slighting references to Gide and their villains named 'Bertrand'. Anti-highbrow *Punch* jokes in the 1950s frequently turn on the pretensions of those who claim acquaintance with European literature, while Stephen Potter's satirical *Some Notes on Lifemanship* (1950) contains a section on 'New Statesmanship', suggesting that 'it is utterly un-New Statesmanlike to suggest that there is any branch of French literature with which you are unfamiliar'. There follows the cautionary tale of one 'K. Digby', banned from respectable journalism for stating in a middle article that he had 'never read a word of Rimbaud'. Digby, as Potter notes, had made a fool of himself, and yet 'everyone must respect the way in which he fought back' – publishing essays in obscure provincial newspapers, or prefaces to catalogues of exhibitions in Scottish museums, and contriving to refer to France every 250th word. To ram the point home, Potter then offers some hints on 'OK people to mention', in which Rilke and Kafka head the list ('it is doubtful whether there have been any more OK names in recent years'). Potter's inference, shared by Amis and Larkin in their 1950s correspondence and detectable in much of the literary journalism of the period, is clear: highbrow literary life is largely a matter of posturing, embracing what is modish rather than upholding the standards in which one genuinely believes and preferring suspect European names to home-grown talent.

If there was a self-conscious exaggeration about much of this Little Englanderism, then it proceeded from a sincere conviction that much of the modernist canon that the average 1950s novelist had been invited to admire when a schoolboy or an undergraduate was not only over-promoted, its merits deliberately talked up by cultural pundits who should have known better, but that it was, additionally, false to the life it purported to describe. This is Amis's complaint about Virginia Woolf, who, he crisply informs Larkin, 'seems to be *quite lacking* in the means for provoking my approval. I should like to *go through* [*Jacob's*] *Room* with you, pointing out all the *lies* she tells.' To many of the era's newcomers, modernism seemed little more than a conspiracy bent on excluding ordinary readers, founded on the individual ego rather than communal responsibility. Frequently their literary heroes were the kind of writers whom the modernist arbiters had tended to mock – Bennett, for example, on whom Wain wrote a series of laudatory articles – their rallying cries designed to emphasise their allegiance to an older and, as they saw it, more authoritative tradition. 'The Experimental Novel was about Man-Alone; we wanted to write novels about Man-In-Society as well' as William Cooper once put it, which rather ignores the fact that his own novels, highly autobiographical and self-mythologising to a fault, are largely about William Cooper.

In pursuing these lines of attack, they were keen to identify figures from previous generations whose influence on the formation of taste they judged to be malign. Just as Stephen Spender had, in the 1930s, found himself regarded by older, Georgian writers as a symbol of everything that was wrong with contemporary literature, so in the 1950s he was singled out as what Blake Morrison, in his excellent study of the Movement, calls 'the kind of poet who it was necessary to oppose' and, as such, excoriated by Thom Gunn in his poem 'Lines for a Book':

> I think of all the toughs through history
> And thank heavens they lived continually.
> I praise the overdogs from Alexander
> To those who would not play with Stephen Spender.

Which may, as Morrison notes, look like an undergraduate squib – it was originally published in the Cambridge student magazine *Granta* – until you recall that it follows a direct line of descent from Leavis's complaints about Spender's false metropolitan reputation.

But however socially detached, anti-European or anti-modernist their individual members may have been, if one characteristic united the 'new men' of the 1950s, it was the relationships they enjoyed with newspapers and the periodical press. These engagements were not uniformly successful – if the career of Colin Wilson, author of the 1950s cause célèbre, *The Outsider* (1956), was made by the newspapers, then it was ruined by them as well – but their very existence offers evidence of the way in which literary society had changed since the interwar era. Freed from the constraints of wartime paper rationing, competitive, aggressive, ever more susceptible to American influence, middle-market newspapers increasingly saw 'the author', not to mention the literary groupings in which the author might be caught up, as an important part of the fledgling celebrity culture in which they had begun to specialise.

To make this distinction is not to ignore the interest which pre-war Fleet Street had taken in literary men and women. Many a well-known writer had become a gossip-columnist's staple in the years between 1918 and 1939 – Evelyn Waugh is an obvious example – using this celebrity to build up a network of contacts capable of turning certain newspapers into message boards conveying information about their lives, opinions and work in progress. On the other hand, most popular newspapers of the 1930s stopped short of offering their readers exposés of Bloomsbury or insider guides to the Auden–Spender axis. If writers became 'news' in the 1950s it was largely because of the distinctive cultural conditions that prevailed in post-Attlee England, in which an increasing sense of economic well-being, combined with the arrival of American-style consumer materialism, led to an obsession with novelty, 'youth' and the overthrow of supposedly outmoded cultural models: an overthrow with which newspapers and periodicals felt themselves to be intimately connected. All this meant that the existence of literary groupings and alliances tended to be announced to the world at large by newspaper columnists. The discovery of the 'Angry Young Men', for example, a category that came to include everyone from John Osborne to Richard Hoggart, was first advertised in a series of articles in the *Daily Mail* and the *Daily Express*. Trails of this kind, even when they were followed by respectable weekly magazines, generally produced an intense scepticism in those closer to the realities of literary life as to whether these alliances actually existed, or whether they might have simply been dreamed up by journalists desperate for copy. There is no such thing as the Movement, the novelist Carey Willoughby (supposedly based on John Wain) tells his host, Professor Treece, in Malcolm Bradbury's *Eating People is Wrong* (1959), 'All made up by the literary editor of the *Spectator*.'

Inevitably, the overall effects of this exposure were mixed. On the one hand, it provided welcome coverage for writers who might otherwise have been confined to the review pages: it is conceivable, for instance, that at least a few of the readers of the Swansea paper who, in October 1954, were invited to inspect photographs of Kingsley Amis judging the local heats of a beauty competition sponsored by an electricity company would have gone on to borrow one of his books from their branch library. On the other, it meant that practically all the innovative work of the period was doomed to become a victim of – another of Thom Gunn's memorable phrases – the 'revolt into a style', the process by which anything genuinely insurrectionary becomes imitated, propagated and synthesised into wider cultural classifications from the moment it begins to exist. If there had been a revolution in British art and letters since 1945, Julian Symons once suggested, then it had been imposed from above with the connivance of the Arts Council and municipal leisure departments 'and with the enthusiastic co-operation of up-to-date magazines and newspaper editors'. A welcome development, it goes without saying, a pleasant change from stagnation and cultural drift, but not to be confused with the much more radical transformations in taste that spring up from the roots of a society in the wake of war or revolution and which had characterised the era of Pound and Eliot.

* * *

At first sight the identification of the group of poets, novelists and critics known as the Movement looks every inch an artificial construct. Not only was news of its discovery first brought to the world by a weekly magazine – the *Spectator* of 1 October 1954 – and not only did many neutral observers doubt that it even existed, or assume that it was merely a stunt aimed at promoting the careers of the writers involved; but even those sympathetic to some of the individual talents on display thought that they should be allowed to get on with their work in isolation, that collective tags were not only unhelpful but might end up as a positive obstruction. As Evelyn Waugh put it, in one of the many letters that followed the group's debut, 'Please let the young people of today get on with their work and be treated to the courtesy of individual attention. They are the less, not the more, interesting if they are treated as a "Movement".' As with many of the literary unveilings of the later 1950s, the immediate prompt to the *Spectator* piece – by the literary editor, J. D. Scott – came in a command from the editor, Walter Taplin, to produce something sensational that would reverse a declining circulation. This, as Scott later reflected, was not an easy task for a literary editor, whose main job is to commission reviews: as he rather plaintively noted: 'you can review sensational books, in a sensational way, but what can you do if people are not producing sensational books?'

Scott's solution was to take an existing judgement, pronounced in his own pages some weeks before, and develop it along more incendiary lines. Anthony Hartley's article 'Poets of the Fifties' had featured in the edition of 27 August 1954. Here Hartley, himself a poet, discussed the work of half a dozen poets whose verse had been appearing in the *Spectator*, and elsewhere, since the beginning of the decade. Names mentioned included Amis, Wain, Larkin, Gunn, George Macbeth and Donald Davie. What had struck Hartley in his explorations was 'a similarity of tone' that might be described as 'dissenting and nonconformist, cool, scientific and analytical'. Also diagnosing 'complication of thought, austerity of tone, colloquialism and avoidance of rhetoric' (and, it should be pointed out, stressing the existence of common dangers as well as common goals), Hartley had concluded that 'What is certain is that, for better for worse, we are now in the presence of the only considerable movement in English poetry since the thirties.' Scott's refinement, as he later conceded, was to take the movement in poetry, see how far it extended into fiction and consider the extent to which it represented 'some historic change in society'; a change which, if it existed, was thought to be reflected in such novels as *Lucky Jim* and Wain's *Hurry on Down*.

Looking back on what he had written from the vantage point of the mid-1970s, Scott could never quite decide whether the new literary species he had identified was wholly factitious, or if he had merely exaggerated the impact of something which, while genuine, was so small-scale and provisional as to call for Hartley's 'tentative delineations' rather than his own Madison Avenue approach. Six decades later it is possible to agree wholeheartedly with Blake Morrison's description of 'a literary group of considerable importance – probably the most influential in England since the Imagists', note the procedural similarities that bind together such individual talents as Amis, Larkin, Enright and Donald Davie and accept all the designated trademarks of toughness, sparseness, the underplayed effect and the ironic sign-off, while wondering whether, on one level, group solidarity consisted of not much more than Wain's remark to Thom Gunn, when they first met in 1953, that 'there are some other chaps in London who are writing like you, we must all get together' – a low-key organisation, whose shared points of view came about by chance rather than design. In fact, one of the Movement's most distinctive characteristics is the way in which almost any statement made about it needs to be qualified almost out of existence to have any value at all. It is true, for example, that the reviewers were debating the existence of 'a new poetry' by the end of 1952, the year in which Davie published his influential *Purity and Diction in English Verse*, with its talk of renewing old usages and 'conservation', but the fighting talk of new generations and clearing of decks indulged in by Wain when he took over the series of *New Soundings* broadcast on the BBC's Third Programme not only overstates his case but overlooks one or two salient continuities with previous arrangements. The editor of the first half-dozen *New Soundings* was John Lehmann. While his replacement by Wain in April 1953 was an all too symbolic changing of the guard, with Wain insisting that he presided over a unique event in English Literature, Lehmann could plausibly claim that the original impetus was his.

This deep-seated ambiguity turns out to be typical of nearly every aspect of the Movement's make-up, from its ideological underpinning – if such a thing existed – to the social background of its members. Much, for example, was made – at the time and subsequently – of

Movement connections to Leavisite Cambridge, where both Gunn, Davie and Enright had been educated. Davie was quoted to the effect that in the immediately post-war years '*Scrutiny* was my Bible, and F. R. Leavis my prophet', while Enright, published in *Scrutiny* while he was still an undergraduate, was one of the Sage of Downing's particular protégés. This, though, is to ignore the much less admiring view that Leavis's affiliates took of him as they moved through the 1950s and the years beyond: Davie's remark that Leavis's criticism was 'useless, because it takes its bearings from a state of culture such as, in the English-speaking world, no reader or writer will experience henceforward'; or Enright's intensely moving poem 'Standards', which remembers a barmaid who reads 'the shoddiest of she-girl magazines' (an obvious reference to Mrs Leavis's strictures on mass culture) but supports her invalid mother. Recollecting Leavis ('He was much concerned with standards') while watching the girl dealing with a drunk, Enright decides that he is 'appalled to recall / his cold and silent and derivative sneer'.

The same ambivalence cuts through the question of the Movement's social identity. Critics of an older generation, noting such characteristics as nonconformist religious upbringings, grammar school educations, the brisk exchange about redistribution of income between Jim Dixon and Bertrand Welch in *Lucky Jim*, diagnosed the stirrings of a lower-middle-class radicalism. A radicalism, more to the point, that seemed emphatically anti-metropolitan in tone, given that several of its exponents taught or worked in provincial universities (Amis, Wain, Larkin) and that a key Movement text was Cooper's *Scenes from Provincial Life* (1950) – a novel whose influence on *Lucky Jim* struck Cooper's wife so forcibly that, hearing an extract broadcast on the radio, she summoned her husband with a cry of 'Here's a man who's been reading your book.' But these surface affinities were deceptive. Jim Dixon's complaint about the social arrangements of the day is not that they exclude large percentages of the population, but that they exclude him; his saviour, at the novel's close, is Gore-Urquhart, a wealthy upper-middle-class patron of the old school, who offers him a soft private secretary's job at £500 a year.

The lack of any real insurrectionary spirit meant that Movement writers tended to absent themselves from efforts to stoke up the ideological furnace of the 1950s literary scene. Amis rather pointedly declined to contribute to *Declaration* (1957), a symposium edited by

Tom Maschler, a young publisher at MacGibbon & Kee, designed to bring together members of the new group of 'young and widely opposed writers' who were 'striving to change many of the values which have held good in recent years'. Maschler had to get by with Wain, Colin Wilson, Doris Lessing and Kenneth Tynan. It was the same with the much-vaunted provincialism. *Lucky Jim*, like many another 1950s novel, ends on the station platform with its hero awaiting the arrival of the London train. *Scenes from Provincial Life* may look back to its author's early career in pre-war Leicester, but by the time Cooper wrote it he was a civil servant living in Putney. Significantly, his next novel, its publication delayed for many years by the libel lawyers, was entitled *Scenes from Metropolitan Life*.

And if background, identity and location rarely follow any clear-cut pattern, then the same qualifications apply to even so specialised an area as the techniques and ambitions of Movement poetry. Much of the habitual distrust of modernism proceeded from a suspicion that it was founded on ego, that the universal principles hinted at by its self-conscious mythologisation of the processes of ordinary life was a sham, that Joyce, Woolf and co. meant, in the last resort, to stratify and demarcate the audience for literature, to talk to each other rather than the great mass of the reading public. Yet the original Movement audience – Third Programme listeners, the readers of those early 1950s poems published in the *Spectator* – was both woefully small and unlikely to be inflated by exposure to the delicately hewn ironies in which the specimen Movement poet habitually dealt. Here as much as plain man talking to plain man was don talking to don. Enright's 1953 essay 'The Poet, the Professor and the Public' might claim that 'We need not deceive ourselves into believing that real poetry can ever be grown in academic hot-houses', but the Movement's distinctly pedagogic tone is apparent in the polish of its verse, its more than occasional brusqueness, its buried references (see the line from Empson which weaves through *Hurry on Down*), its trick of laying down behavioural law. Equally contested, especially in the early days, is what later came to be regarded as the Movement's defining mark: its anti-romanticism. Certainly, there are the disobliging references to Dylan Thomas; the frequent complaints about the 'public, political' romanticism of the 1930s; the promotion of what Malcolm Bradbury was later to call 'a common and shareable reality'. But it was Anthony Thwaite, an Oxford undergraduate at the time J. D. Scott first put pen to paper, who declared, more than half a century later, that the post-1945 period did not easily give itself to generalisations, and that 'even now, in my late seventies, George Barker and Philip Larkin can, and do, coexist'.

Scott's final verdict on the modest literary juggernaut that he had sent creaking into gear was that 'I cannot feel that it was seriously wrong to promote the work of young poets, even factitiously.' As for those being promoted, leading members of the Movement, whether they acknowledged their status or not, were, by and large, adept at dealing with the media, keen on putting editors and interviewers to work as accessories in their campaigns for self-promotion. Amis and Wain, to take only the most obvious examples, quickly developed into all-purpose literary men with regular berths in weekly magazines and Sunday newspapers, and an opinion for every controversy that reared its head. Although press coverage had a beneficial effect in bringing a handful of very loosely connected *Spectator* poets to a wider audience, its consequences for some of the other manifestations of the 1950s literary scene were positively injurious. Media response to the northern and Midlands-based novelists who began to make their presence felt in the period 1957–9, for example, was little more than a catalogue of misrepresentation. As Harry Ritchie points out in his invaluable *Success Stories: Literature and the Media in England 1950–1959*, most of the reviewers of this new wave of fiction surging in from beyond the Trent assumed that the social origins of their authors – Stan Barstow, Philip Callow, John Braine, Keith Waterhouse, Alan Sillitoe – were broadly homogeneous. Similarly, the books they produced were acclaimed – when they were acclaimed – for what was presumed to be their documentary value, a social realism that was the literary equivalent of *cinéma-vérité*.

Neither of these assumptions was correct. In fact close inspection reveals at least half a dozen variations on the 1950s working-class demographic, ranging from the aspirational 'lace-curtain working class' (Barstow's phrase) rising from foundry or production line to solicitor's office or draughtsman's shop, the provincial bohemians of Callow's Lawrence-inflected *Common People* (1958) to the thrusting meritocrats of a novel like Braine's *Room at the Top* (1957) and the moody antinomianism of Sillitoe's Arthur Seaton in *Saturday Night and Sunday Morning* (1958). Seaton, in particular, is entirely detached from Barstow's or Braine's upwardly mobile heroes, concerned not so much with getting on and (by extension) getting out, but getting by and staying put, kicking against stagnancy, bringing sometimes anarchic resources to bear on conformity and routine. But these distinctions meant little to the self-appointed and occasionally nest-feathering taxonomists of working-class fiction at large in literary journalism. A disparaging early 1960s *Punch* series of journalistic 'types' includes a figure christened 'The One Subject Man', whose 'critical essay on "The Working Class Novel" gained widespread acclaim when he wrote it eight years ago' and who has written nothing else since, contriving to 'earn more from the works of Barstow, Sillitoe, and Braine than they do themselves'.

In Sillitoe's case the generalisations initially brought to the enticing figure of the 'working-class writer', whether he happened to be a sharp-eyed grammar school boy or a denizen of the East Midlands underclass who had left school at 14 to work in a bicycle factory, had a particularly unfortunate effect. English readers of his short story collection *The Loneliness of the Long Distance Runner* (1959) were invited to admire 'The Match', in which an embittered middle-aged man stamps home from a football game to pick the quarrel that will end his marriage, as a chilly exercise in social determinism, while assuming that it was another utensil afloat in the late 1950s kitchen sink. Sillitoe's French translator, on the other hand, marked him down as the heir to Camus. Similar pre-digestion attended the novels of Sillitoe's maturity, whose determination to go beyond dramatised sociology tended to baffle his reviewers, who either undervalued his achievement or merely failed to comprehend what he was trying to do. And so *A Start in Life* (1970) retains the old Nottinghamshire background while soon developing into a picaresque (Sillitoe maintained that his models were the Spanish novelists Diego Hurtado de Mendoza, Mateo Alemán and Francisco de Quevedo) which transports its hero to a hustler's life in Soho and concludes, amid a hail of bullets, as a skit on the idea of the existential hero.

Whatever he may have thought about this dereliction of critical duty, Sillitoe, at least, had staying power: he was there for the long haul. But there were smaller fry, keener on the idea of publicity as a means of advancing their careers, whose dealings with the press offer only a cautionary tale. One can see this tendency at work in the trajectory pursued by the small band of acolytes collected around the decade's most celebrated *enfant terrible*, Colin Wilson. By the later

1950s Wilson's star was already in perilous descent: the initial wave of enthusiasm for *The Outsider* had been replaced – at any rate among the critics – by a much more sceptical attitude to his markedly introspective brand of existentialism, and, at the lower end of the market, a determination to focus on the easily caricatured aspects of Wilson's erratic personal life. At this stage Wilson's principal disciples ('It's lonely work and I could do with some allies') were the novelist Bill Hopkins, author of *The Divine and the Decay* (1957) and Stuart Holroyd, whose *Outsider*-like manifesto *Emergence from Chaos* had appeared in the same year. Both inhabited a terraced house in Notting Hill, with a spare room which Wilson, alternating with John Braine, used as a pied-à-terre. Neither, even at this early juncture, could have failed to be aware that their association with Wilson and their supporting role in the press coverage that his exploits attracted, was a decidedly mixed blessing. 'Of course', Wilson cheerfully informed Stuart Holroyd at one point, 'you and Bill have suffered from the backwash of my publicity.'

To read accounts of the trio's adventures in the late 1950s is a peculiar experience, not merely for the earnestness of the exhortations ('We've got to put English existentialism on the map') but for the feeling that every utterance, and every scheme of work – single or collective – has been manufactured with one eye on the *Daily Mail*. This is not to question the sincerity of their beliefs – and when Holroyd went on television to declare that 'What we're all three agreed on is that the values, the attitudes and the traditions of liberal humanism are not relevant to the world we're living in today' he undoubtedly meant it – merely to note the underlying conviction that, for maximum impact, they had to be handed out in public. There are plays to be written for the English Stage Company at the Royal Court. There is Bill's new political party, the suspiciously right-wing-sounding Spartacists, which inclines to Wilson's view that power ought to be in the hands of the 5 per cent of the population equipped to exercise it. There is a plan to enlarge the group's reputation by means of a collection of essays for Gollancz, so that, as Wilson puts it, 'in the next two years we should really consolidate ourselves as a literary bloc in England'.

Stuart Holroyd, meanwhile, is trying – and failing – to get on with *The Dialectics of Despair*, superseded by the provocatively titled *Method in his Madness: An Essay on 'Contemporary Man'* ('a study of the manifold and ingenious ways in which men deceive themselves that they live purposefully') and finally a play to be premiered at the Royal Court. By this stage, unfortunately, such press coverage as the group continued to attract was taking an unwelcome turn. There was a rumour that the Spartacists were to join forces with Sir Oswald Mosley and intended to support his candidature at North Kensington in the forthcoming general election of 1959. In the end, his play *The Tenth Chance*, was given a solitary, Sunday night staging. Mosley was in the audience; several hostile critics made noisy exits, and there was a scuffle in a nearby pub. In faint mitigation the story made the front pages of both the *Daily Express* and the *News Chronicle*. To Holroyd the experience was profoundly disillusioning. 'To the newspapers we were just good copy, and for the television people we were cut-price performers. If there were going to be any battles of ideas and principles fought they wouldn't be fought through the media.' By the end of the decade, still only in his mid-20s, he had left literary London for good.

Evelyn Waugh once complained that the Auden–Spender–MacNeice axis of the 1930s had 'ganged up' and captured the decade. The same point could be made of certain Movement writers of the 1950s. One of the marks of the apparent centrality of Amis and Larkin to the immediately post-war period is the frequency with which they are invoked by social historians. The index to Dominic Sandbrook's *Never Had It So Good*, a study of the period 1956–63, contains thirty individual references to Amis and sixteen to Larkin: not bad going for a novel-writing lecturer at a Welsh university and a provincial academic librarian, neither of whose copious diaries and letters reveal any startling signs of social or political awareness. Doubtless this fascination with Amis and Larkin is coloured by the memory of their steady rightward drift during the 1960s and 1970s and their reimagining, come the 1990s, as totem poles of political reaction: Amis, in particular, is an almost genre-defining example of the Attlee-supporting Labour gradualist whose radicalism is wholly extinguished by the events of the following decade. From the angle of the literary historian, all this tends to invest the era with an irremediable taint of greyness, timidity and aesthetic conservatism, the thought of 'a decade so awful that the very thought of it makes me want to tear wallpaper off with my teeth' as Elizabeth Young once put it. In fact, judgements of this kind were being made at the time, often by observers of an older generation who, returning from foreign exile to what they imagined was the centre of the literary world, found it staid and purposeless. Christopher Isherwood, enjoying a six-month furlough in London with old friends such as Connolly, Lehmann and Forster, noted of an evening spent chez Spender that 'the chief impression I got from him was weariness . . . hates England because it is so dark; wants to get a job in Athens; is sick of the eternal need to make money'. Travelling to Manchester to take part in a televised literary quiz, Isherwood was interested to find that none of the three younger writers featured on the programme – A. Alvarez, John Mander and Hugh Thomas – claimed to read a book for enjoyment.

It was not only veterans of the 1930s who thought the 1950s literary scene enervated and self-regarding. To Martin Green, whose *A Mirror for Anglo-Saxons* (1961) sheds an intriguing light on transatlantic literary relations in the post-war period, the problem lay in the weight of accumulated tradition, that 'essential Britishness' which, to Green – a working-class grammar school boy who ended up at Cambridge under Dr Leavis – took no account of the realignments of the post-1945 world. England, he decided, 'had explained the different forms of life to me, but in a way that emptied them of colour, weight, magnetism'. Was there anything in English literature, he wondered, to compare with *The Catcher in the Rye*? To another kind of critic, alternatively, the difficulty involved not so much a stifling anti-Americanism as a 'hollow core', generally defined as a reluctance to address the complexities of contemporary life and stemming from an indifference to, or outright dislike of, the modernist techniques developed two or three decades before. This is essentially the argument of Gabriel Josipovici's *What Ever Happened to Modernism?* (2010), which develops a remark once dropped by the novelist Eva Figes to the effect that 'the horrors of her lifetime' could not be accommodated by the English social realist tradition to which, by and large, the novelists of the 1950s belonged. To put it bluntly – far more bluntly than Professor Josipovici would like, no doubt – Belsen, Auschwitz and Katyn need something more than the traditional English patternings of character, irony and sentiment to be done justice by art.

Far more common to the home-grown writers of the 1950s was the idea of Bradbury's 'common and shareable reality', which we can all possess. It is this that Raphael Faber, the émigré don of A. S. Byatt's

Still Life (1985), is complaining about when he rails against 'stories with character' and deplores 'whining . . . insularity . . . verbal sluggishness'. Most of Faber's family have been killed by the Nazis, and his response is a 'difficult' poem entitled 'Lubeck Bells' which contains no direct reference to the Holocaust. And yet, faced by a Raphael Faber, or Bradbury's Katya Princip, who informs the British Council's timorous envoy Petworth in *Rates of Exchange* (1983) that he is 'really not a character in the world historical sense. You come from a little island with water all round', or even Professor Josipovici with his distaste for realism and his sulks about overlooked talent, the specimen English novelist is entitled to protest that it isn't his fault he wasn't born with their disadvantages and that, in however general a way, a cultural tradition is only as good as the sum of its constituent parts, that studies in comparative literature can only go so far. The reason why, for example, in the interwar era the Americans had Dreiser and Dos Passos, with their sprawling accounts of big-city, machine-age diaspora, and we made do with Bennett, Priestley, Greene, Waugh and Auden, lies not in anything so grand as a defective aesthetic but in the fact that Priestley lived in London rather than Chicago. The point works both ways, and the modern-day library browser from Billings, Montana is likely to detect the same type of bizarre exoticism in Anita Brookner as British readers find in the novels of Annie Proulx.

In any case, shorn of its labels, much of the post-war literary tradition that took root in the 1950s turns out to be a great deal more variegated than it seems at first glance, much more inquisitive and forward-looking, much less susceptible, when it comes down it, to distinctions between conservative and progressive points of view. It can hardly have escaped Professor Josipovici's notice, for example, that his two great heroes, praised for carrying on the modernist baton into an inhospitable age, are Muriel Spark and William Golding, whose champions are, respectively, two of his great anti-modernist bogey figures, Evelyn Waugh and John Carey. Perhaps this is merely a way of suggesting that in the 1950s, far more so than in previous decades, the gap between official and unofficial views of literary culture, between what opinion-brokers assumed that people were reading and the subterranean literary life that went on beyond the reach of the literary weeklies grew steadily more pronounced. To read the academic John Lucas's recent memoir of his student days is to encounter a very different world from the somewhat restrictive cultural palisade inhabited by certain Movement poets, with a range of influence extending from Charlie Parker to Allen Ginsberg. And yes, Lucas has read *The Catcher in the Rye*, of which he states categorically that 'No novel, before or since, has had such a strong or lasting impact on a whole generation of readers as Salinger's did on the generation of the 1950s.' Clearly there were different kinds of new men out beyond the shadows cast by the Snovian technocrats, the provincial university English departments and the Notting Hill rooming houses, in whom a sensationalising press had yet to take an interest.

CHAPTER 13

Common Readers: The Mid-century Audience

> One great feeling though – I can read a book, taking interest and losing myself.
>
> Nella Last, diary, 13 September 1945

> After the war there will be a burst of intellectual curiosity of all kinds. Thousands of soldiers will feel that they have missed a lot and will turn eagerly to reading books.
>
> David Garnett, letter to Rupert Hart-Davis, 10 February 1941

Back to that eternally vexed enquiry: who were the readers? Or rather, to retreat a little from the view from Mount Olympus, as occupied by Eliot, Virginia Woolf and the Sitwells, what did ordinary people read, from the vantage point of its subsidiary crags? Even in the 1950s, when hitherto unexplored areas of popular culture were being opened up to academic debate, this was never an easy question to answer. Richard Hoggart's famous remark about the necessity of remembering that there never was any such person as the common man can equally well be applied to the idea of the common reader – an increasingly mythical being, you sometimes feel, to whom no generalisations apply, elusive, contradictory, alternately capable of astounding you with the narrowness or the catholicity of his, or her, taste. On the other hand, taste only reveals itself by way of solidarity, by a sufficiently large number of people liking something to make that communal judgement a factor in the commercial or aesthetic processes going on above their heads. How best to pin it down? Best-seller lists – at any rate the best-seller lists of the mid-twentieth century – are notoriously unreliable, assembled piecemeal and offering little in the way of verifiable data. Anthony Powell remembered the case of a volume of poetry published by Duckworth in the 1930s which appeared in a London newspaper's 'Books in demand' column in the wake of a total sale of exactly three copies.

And yet a best-seller list ought to tell us *something*. To examine some of the *News Chronicle* charts from 1937 (Margaret Mitchell's *Gone With the Wind*, Compton Mackenzie's *The East Wind of Love*, Rudyard Kipling's *Something of Myself*) is to suspect that they do indeed reflect purchasing trends among the book-buying public – *Gone With the Wind* was a publishing sensation, interest in Kipling's autobiography had doubtless been stimulated by his death earlier in the year – while appreciating just how fallible they are as a guide to collective preference, even more so in that one of the great givens of English literary life has always been the extreme reluctance of its patrons to spend money on books. By and large, the readers of the immediately post-war era obtained the novels they read from libraries – whether municipally run, or belonging to a private sector that began with the Boots Subscription Library and descended to the kind of mushroom establishments Orwell writes about in *Keep the Aspidistra Flying*, where the charge is twopence and the stock consists of 200 or 300 flyblown titles parcelled out into such categories as 'Crime', 'Wild West' and 'Sex'. And all this, naturally, is complicated by the regularity with which literature was pressed into service as an adjunct to social position. Until deep into the 1950s, a Boots subscription was as much a status symbol as membership of a book club thirty years later or the copy of *Captain Corelli's Mandolin* or *Birdsong* left out on the patio for the guests to admire thirty years after that. When the pretentious Mrs Plumleigh-Bruce in Patrick Hamilton's *Mr Stimpson and Mr Gorse* (1953) is described, by herself, as a 'voracious' reader, and by Hamilton as devouring 'every popular, illustrated and hysterically laudatory book about Marie Antoinette upon which she could lay hands', the contemporary reader instantly deduces that her literary interests are somehow secondary to the badge of gentility which ownership of them supposedly confers.

Much more directly revealing than best-seller charts are the Mass Observation surveys of the 1940s and 1950s, which reflect the likes and dislikes of a middlebrow, but by no means undiscriminating, audience still happily absorbed in the popular literature of a previous generation, and in many cases the generation before that. The post-war diaries of the Cumbrian housewife Nella Last, for example, show their *Sunday Express*- and *Woman's Weekly*-reading compiler beguiling her leisure with Galsworthy's *The Forsyte Saga*, Priestley, *Vanity Fair*, Dickens (a particular favourite since her father presented her with a Boots edition at the age of 9) and in 1951, greatly daring, risking a dip in Lawrence's *The White Peacock*. But her touchstone was the work of Hugh Walpole ('The Herries books to me are always a delight, beyond their style, bringing alive the places I love in the Lakes'). Paternal association, geography (the backdrops to Walpole's novels were only a bus ride away), the authenticating presence of non-literary media (Galsworthy's novels were serialised on BBC radio in the late 1940s, along with other favourites such as *The Count of Monte Cristo*) – all these are helping to shape Nella's taste in books. Like many a mid-century reader she worries that the 'classics' are losing their sheen – a rather plaintive entry from July 1947 wonders whether 'children now ever discover the rows of Dickens, Thackeray, Dumas, Harrison Ainsworth, Scott or Brontë on the higher shelves of the bookcase' – and yet her relish for the literature of the past is always capable of springing sharp distinctions. She dislikes Trollope, for example, on the grounds that he 'portrays a period from which sprang "socialism" in its more rampant form'.

In fact, Nella's anxieties over the decay of the English literary tradition were misplaced: all the evidence suggests that nearly a century after their first publication many of the Victorian classics were still going strong, and that there existed a general feeling that the principles of 'taste' could only be inculcated via recourse to the standards of the 1860s and 1870s. One of the very earliest Pelican reissues sponsored by Allen Lane, for example, was a revised edition of Arnold Bennett's *Literary Taste* (1909), whose recommendations include some extraordinary mid-nineteenth-century curios. There were several explanations for – to use only one piece of available data – the regularity with which characters in wartime fiction are discovered to be occupying their free time with Victoriana: General Liddament in *The Soldier's Art*, say, being discovered while out on manoeuvres with a copy of *The Small House at Allington*, or fire-watchers gamely recapitulating the plot of *Adam Bede*. The anti-Victorian fires stoked in the 1920s, and exemplified by the success of Strachey's *Eminent Victorians* (1918), had long since died down. To a renewed respect for the achievements of Victorian art and culture could be added a variety of commercial and social factors calculated to make Victorian and indeed pre-Victorian literature much more widely available to the middlebrow reader than it had been thirty or even fifty years before. One of them was the widespread recourse by newspaper proprietors to sets of the classics as ammunition in the circulation wars of the 1930s – the complete Dickens, for example, offered to readers of the *Daily Mail* for a few shillings and six coupons.

Another was the extent to which, during the early part of the twentieth century, the great Victorians had fallen out of copyright. Thackeray lapsed in 1913, Dickens in 1920, George Eliot in 1930, Trollope in 1932. In each case cheap editions came rapidly and lucratively on to the market: the Oxford World's Classics versions of Trollope – which included little-known items such as *Sir Harry Hotspur of Humblethwaite* as well as the Palliser sequence – was a staple of the book-hungry 1940s, which with its absence of paper for new titles, offered yet another reason to return to the solid landscapes of Barsetshire or Middlemarch. A third was the BBC's habit of adapting 'great works' for radio and broadcasting them to an audience extending far beyond such aficionados as Nella Last. Alan Sillitoe, for example, remembered the enthusiasm with which his impoverished Nottingham family sat listening to a version of Charles Reade's *The Cloister and the Hearth*, terrified all the while lest the set should be repossessed by the hire-purchase company whose payments they had failed to maintain. Subsequently this impetus would be kept up by television, which not only turned to standard works for inspiration (Simon Raven's BBC adaptation of the Palliser novels in the early 1970s, a BBC *Barchester Chronicles* in 1982) but had an abiding weakness for very minor aspects of the Victorian canon. If comparative obscurities such as Captain Marryat's *Children of the New Forest* or Mrs Dinah Craik's *John Halifax, Gentleman* have any kind of residual hold on the collective literary consciousness of the twenty-first century it is because, forty years ago, some enterprising BBC producer decided to adapt them for the Sunday teatime slot.

Among the gods of the Victorian circulating library who continued to appeal to the great-grandchildren of their original audience, one writer reigned supreme. Whereas Thackeray's reputation now rested on a single book – *Vanity Fair* – Dickens continued to dominate popular perceptions of literature in a manner only rivalled by Shakespeare, a kind of continuous tunnelling into the national subsoil in which the frame of reference was sometimes merely associative. The great Dickens scholar Humphry House, writing in 1941, talks about the

'Dickens atmosphere' and the very common early twentieth-century habit of applying the adjective 'Dickensian' to everything from a neighbourhood to a room – a process in which vagueness is nearly always trumped by the delight of the enthusiast convinced that material of this kind can be traced back to its source. Even more important, perhaps, for Dickens's enormous *réclame* were the multiple interpretations made possible by such a vast and sprawling body of work. In the early part of the century G. K. Chesterton could claim him as 'almost' a Catholic. Thirty years later T. A. Jackson was hailing him as practically a Marxist. House, writing the year before the Beveridge Report at a time when great interest was being taken in the probable shape of post-war social arrangements, is careful to stress his reformism, the connection between 'the attitude to life shown in his books and the society in which he lived' – an important part of Dickens's appeal to the serious-minded reader of the 1930s, no doubt, but at the same time giving no hint of his enormous standing further down the cultural ladder in what might be called the sub-literary world of cigarette-card portraits and comic sketches. Orwell notes in his essay of 1940 that a music-hall comedian who went on stage and imitated one of Dickens's major characters could be fairly sure that the audience would understand what he was doing. This tendency persisted, and as late as the 1987 general election campaign Neil Kinnock's assault on the Conservative government included a lavish Dickensian checklist in which the chancellor, Nigel Lawson, featured as Scrooge and Mrs Thatcher as a modern Miss Havisham.

Cinema, naturally, was important in maintaining this spell – see, for example, the enormously successful 1951 film version of *A Christmas Carol* with Alastair Sim as Scrooge – but so too was literature itself. The Dickensian strain runs through the mainstream best-seller of the era from Warwick Deeping to Priestley and Norman Collins to create an environment in which much of the popular writing of the age seemed to have been expressly fashioned in Dickens's image. The characterisation of, say, Priestley's *Angel Pavement*, with its flaring surfaces, its attention to paraphernalia, its hats, teeth, signature remarks and vocal tone, could only have been done by someone who had steeped himself in the atmosphere of *Martin Chuzzlewit* and *Dombey and Son*. As we have seen, much of the highbrow disdain for Priestley in the 1930s stemmed from the efforts made by popular journalists to build him up as a bearer of the Dickensian torch. In a literary culture still to a certain extent living in the nineteenth century, there would always be a place for the very large number of writers bred up in Dickens's shadow. Other Victorian shadows, too, for the great selling point of Angela Thirkell's 1940s and 1950s output, set in a reanimated Barsetshire and distinguished by an absolute contempt for the Attlee government, was its link to the world of Trollope.

At one level the regressive tendencies of the mainstream literary taste may seem difficult to square with the wider social climate, that whole noisy post-war insistence on the advantages of novelty and consumerism, the lure of the bright, shiny, mechanised future. They are certainly difficult to square with the one great transmogrifying force at work in the literary 1940s and 1950s – the paperback revolution inaugurated by Allen Lane's establishment of his Penguin imprint in 1935, which not only guaranteed the widespread availability of cheap books, but also broadened distribution channels to include newspaper kiosks and branches of Woolworths. Yet it would be a mistake to assume that cut-price paperbacks, however much they expanded the audience for literature or created almost overnight an enthusiasm for printed contributions to 'current affairs', would automatically foster a taste for contemporary fiction. Many hardback publishers were unenthusiastic; several refused altogether to participate in the scheme; in the early days, at least, Lane was reduced to taking what he could get, sometimes in job lots (half a dozen titles from the first Penguin batch came from the firm of Jonathan Cape). The early Penguin lists, consequently, are weighed down by ballast from previous eras: Beverley Nichols's juvenile autobiography *Twenty-Five*, first published in the year of the General Strike; Norman Douglas's *South Wind* (1917); even so gnarled a Victorian dystopia as Samuel Butler's *Erewhon* (1872), first ushered on to the circulating library shelves at the time of Gladstone's first administration. As late as the 1950s, when a majority of publishers had been brought round to the idea of mass-market formats, a determination to squeeze every last drop out of hardback sales could mean a gap of several years between hardback and paperback publication. *Lucky Jim* and John Wain's *Hurry on Down* took seven years to transfer into soft covers, and C. P. Snow's *The Masters* (1951) eight, while the book-buyer of limited means avid to get his hands on Angus Wilson's *Such Darling Dodos* (1950) found himself expected to wait an entire decade. It was only in the 1960s that the period between original publication and reissue was reduced to two years or, in exceptional cases, a mere twelve months.

None of this should blind us to the absolute contemporaneity of the Penguin project, the galvanic effect that it had on the mid-century book trade or its altogether prodigious sales (3 million copies disposed of in the first year). There had, of course, been paperbacks before – Messrs Hutchinson's vilely printed thrillers, Ernest Benn's sixpenny library and various experiments conducted by Gollancz – but none of these precursors had anything like the impact of the original Penguin catalogues or, as the brand developed, their effect on the wider literary consciousness, what *The Times* approvingly termed 'a new social habit'. The war, in which Lane's conscription-diminished staff managed to print nearly 600 titles, only consolidated their position. The Penguin colophon appeared on everything from archaeological primers to collections of crossword puzzles, from manuals of 'Planning, Design and Art' to books narrowly focused on the war effort, such as G. H. Goodchild's *Keeping Poultry and Rabbits on Scraps*. All this, and particularly the early move into non-fiction – Lane began his Pelican imprint with the aim of creating something 'similar to Penguin only a little more serious in tone' – raises the question of the Penguin readership, to whom, in the last resort, the books were intended to appeal, and the nature of the Penguin influence. From one angle the paperback – cheap, classless, mass-produced – was the last word in disposability: there were stories of passengers on cruise ships tearing out successive pages and throwing them over the side as they read. At the same time Lane's admirers tended to congratulate him for manifestly not conciliating the popular taste, for trying to educate it rather than, in the manner of contemporary American firms, merely appeasing its grosser appetites. As Bill Williams, the founding secretary-general of the Arts Council, put it in the early 1950s: 'Your entire success – and, indeed, your reputation, your knighthood too – has been built on a steadfast refusal to bid for the masses.'

Lane saw himself as an educator, a taste-broker keen to point his readers in the direction of books they might find intellectually or practically useful: his message was enthusiastically taken up by a later generation of critics who first came across his output as schoolboys or undergraduates. Although conceived more than a decade in advance of the BBC's Third Programme, the Penguin could sometimes seem very close to being its print equivalent. John Gross has noted how 'in the early days the imprint seemed rather like the BBC'. The books' appeal to that vital part of the pre-and post-war demographic, the scholarship boy from the poor home, avid for cut-price intellectual stimulus, was profound. Such people, according to the portrait offered in Richard Hoggart's *The Uses of Literacy*, 'own the Penguin selection from Eliot, as well as some other Penguins and Pelicans; they used to take *Penguin New Writing* . . . they probably own the Pelican edition of Freud's *The Psychopathology of Everyday Life*'. Hoggart himself possessed a collection of Pelicans, bought pre-war at the University of Leeds bookshop, which had then been lugged around North Africa and Italy during the war. Thousands of other servicemen could have told the same story. This audience had not, of course, been coaxed into being overnight. Its roots go back to the world of the Workers' Educational Association extension lecture, the Peace Pledge Union and the Left Book Club. All this suggests that despite their vast sales to all parts of the mid-century readership, Penguins appealed most directly to middlebrow and highbrow readers. Come the 1950s their hold on the best-seller market was much less secure in the face of competition from such determinedly commercial operators as Pan (founded in 1944) and Corgi, whose jacket designs brought a lurid gloss to even relatively highbrow work. And while Penguins remained an essential part of the cultural landscape of the 1950s, it is difficult not to conclude that their animating spirit belongs to an earlier epoch, the world of Priestley's wartime broadcasts, Beveridge and the Attlee government.

A profound attachment to the past; a delight in reading coupled with a practised disinclination to spend money on it; an ongoing paperback revolution; the onrush of new media; an educational system more and more reliant on 'set books': the influences to which the specimen mainstream book-fancier of the early post-war period was subject are so various as to be barely quantifiable. What he, or she, manifestly took no interest at all in were expensively produced hardback novels of a 'literary' cast of the kind reviewed in newspapers and weekly magazines. On the very rare occasions when a publisher from the early post-war era dishes the dirt on the sales figures, advances and expectations for modish literary fiction, the statistics are grim beyond measure. By the late 1960s, according to the independent publisher Anthony Blond, the sponsor of a hardback novel in a 3,000-copy edition who failed to sell paperback rights could expect to lose several hundred pounds in the process. Hardly any of these books made their way on to the shelves of the average middle-class post-war home, for the simple reason that they came from an environment with which the mainstream reader would not have been in the least familiar and at a price from which he, or she, would have instinctively recoiled.

So which factors governed that notional 'common reader's' approach to the world of books? First, one must note the effect of material picked up in childhood – anything from nursery rhymes to A. A. Milne and *The Wind in the Willows* in presentation sets – and at school. Then there were the items bequeathed by former generations, usually arranged in glass-fronted bookcases on display in lounges and sitting rooms, which could contain anything from nineteenth-century textbooks to 'improving' works sponsored by the Religious Tract Society and won as Sunday-school prizes. To this could be added whatever was available in local libraries and second-hand shops (the latter always a regular resort of non-bookish parents anxious to find something to occupy literary-minded children) and – much less frequent but important in terms of novelty – the kind of books which, however briefly, became the focus of sensationalising news coverage. Not only was the post-war era a period in which literature, however misinterpreted or trivialised by catchpenny social commentators, was thought to play a significant role in the cultural transformations to which Eden-era Britain was subject – a time in which writers as various, and as variously successful, as Kingsley Amis, Colin Wilson and Richard Hoggart became household names – it was also a time in which books were 'news' in a way that they had not been two decades before and a succession of causes célèbres were advertised to, and purchased by, the middlebrow public for essentially non-literary reasons. One of the funniest scenes in Penelope Fitzgerald's *The Bookshop* (1978), set in a Suffolk coastal town in the late 1950s, involves the unexpected sale of 250 copies of Nabokov's *Lolita*. Similar enthusiasm attended the Penguin publication of *Lady Chatterley's Lover*, which, after a highly publicised court case, sold 200,000 copies on its day of publication in 1960.

But how did all this work in practice? How, surrounded by all these contending stimuli, did flesh-and-blood readers get on? Judged by the criteria set out above, John Gross's account of his early reading habits in a middle-class East End home of the 1940s and 1950s looks thoroughly representative: a fascination with nursery rhymes leading to *The Golden Treasury*, a love of boys' school stories such as Talbot Baines Read's *The Fifth Form at Dominic's* and eventually the 'indispensable' Penguins. One potent source of inspiration was his mother, a fan of the stock best-seller of the 1920s and given to remarking 'I don't suppose people read Sheila Kaye-Smith anymore?', but also fond of *Vanity Fair* and sufficiently anxious to nurture her son's interest in books as to bring home job lots from second-hand shops, one of which turned out to harbour most of a collected edition of Kipling. And then there were his father's volumes from the old 'Thinker's Library', including a selection from the poetry of James Thomson, author of *The City of Dreadful Night*, which left him 'with an unforgettable impression of dark terraces, murky causeways, huge squares, grandiose monuments'. Random impressions, in other words, ranging from the thoroughly conventional to the tantalisingly exotic, sponsored by parents with little formal knowledge of literature – Gross senior was an émigré Jewish doctor – but sufficient, when taken together, to point their son in the direction of a Cambridge English scholarship. Much the same materials lie to hand in David Lodge's account of his lower-middle-class childhood in the south-east London suburbs: a Dickens-loving father with a collected edition courtesy of the *Daily Express* who, in addition, 'had excellent though selective taste in literary fiction'; Richmal Crompton's William books borrowed from Deptford public library; *Ivanhoe* alternating with cheap boys' magazines.

Even if the aspiring reader had little in the way of formal education, or came from a determinedly lower-class background, the same influences – or diluted versions of them – can be seen hesitatingly at work. The novelist and screenwriter Keith Waterhouse, born in 1929 and raised, like Richard Hoggart, in a grimy suburb of Leeds, remembered that his literary tastes relied on 'serendipity'. A friendly schoolmaster put him on to Conan Doyle, Jack London, Kipling and Bennett. His mother, rather 'scared' by his determination to become a writer but nonetheless determined to encourage it, came back from the local market with ancient copies of *Punch* and a battered volume of Barrie's plays. Pot luck at the library turned up W. W. Jacobs and Evelyn Waugh, and a second-hand stall old Penguins for a few pence each. Moving house in his teens, he chanced upon a new and more upmarket library that contained the *New Statesman* and the *Times Literary Supplement*. And at one time there was the guidance of *John*

O'London's Weekly, abstracted from the pannier of his delivery bike during the course of his morning newspaper round and handed over to its unsuspecting subscriber a day late. 'That a literary weekly crammed with articles on the likes of Hardy, Victor Hugo, Shaw, Wells, Arnold Bennett, could be successfully targeted at a night-school audience of aspiring clerks and office boys now seems incredible' the mature Waterhouse believed.

If there is a common thread to all these mid-century testimonies, it is a sense of the widespread availability of literature to those who cared to look for it and the large number of different sources from which guidance about it might be obtained, even if the readers in search of it came from the very bottom of the social heap. Though born into absolute poverty in pre-gentrified North Kensington, for example, the former Labour Cabinet minister Alan Johnson's early experiences have several points of contact with Lodge and Gross. His mother enrolled him as a member of the Ladbroke Grove branch library before he could read. There was a glass-fronted bookcase at the house of a friend, containing copies of Dickens's novels, *Treasure Island* and *Pride and Prejudice*, from which he was eventually allowed to borrow *David Copperfield*. Presents brought home from a local workingmen's club Christmas party introduced him to *Tom Sawyer*, *Little Women* and *Robinson Crusoe*, and again there was the encouraging schoolmaster, Mr Carlen, who recommended Wells, Bennett and C. S. Forester and gave him the money to buy four copies of any paperback he cared to choose for the school library. Johnson invested in *Keep the Aspidistra Flying*.

The odd, or not so odd, aspect of all these early reading experiences, Gross's and Lodge's especially, is how closely – *mutatis mutandis*, naturally, and at a quarter-century's remove – they mirror my own. As a child growing up in a middle-class East Anglian home, I was aware of the sensibilities of four adult readers: father, mother and maternal grandparents. All of them, though not remotely bookish, read novels of varying kinds and with varying degrees of enthusiasm and all of them, I believe, would have made a distinction between the books they had on display and those whose pages they actually wanted to open. The lock on the glass-fronted bookcase in my grandparents' front room was rarely turned but when it was (surreptitiously, by their grandson) turned out to contain moralising religious tracts from the late Victorian era – there was a particularly dreadful one called *Mother's*

Warm Shawl, about a servant girl being dragged back from the brink of perdition after squandering money earmarked for the garment of the title on finery for her own back – Macaulay's essays in red buckram awarded to my grandfather as a Bungay Grammar School prize; the occasional 1950s best-seller (these included *Island in the Sun*); books of reprinted 'middles' from the interwar era; and, so tightly pressed between two larger volumes as to give the impression it had been hidden there, a copy of the original Penguin *Lady Chatterley*, which suggested that my grandfather was a darker horse than he sometimes let on. As for the books which my grandparents allowed themselves to be seen reading in public, my grandfather was a fan of yellow-jacketed Gollancz crime novels – the merest skim through the opening pages confirming whether or not he had 'read it before'. My grandmother, on the other hand, liked doorstep-sized historicals of the kind tirelessly produced by Jean Plaidy, Victoria Holt and Philippa Carr, all of whom, I later discovered, were pseudonyms for the same person: the indefatigable Eleanor Hibbert, whose books my wife, at one stage in her publishing career, found herself editing.

It was the same with my mother and father. Neither of them had any formal training; neither of them had studied English beyond their mid-teens; but both of them, when time allowed, were keen, if miscellaneous, readers. The four novels that my father brought home each week from the local branch library, for example, were extraordinarily varied in tone: from P. G. Wodehouse to John Updike, from hard-boiled American thrillers to aggressively 'modern' novels with multi-clause titles and arresting psychedelia-style jackets picked up on a whim. My mother's idea of a 'good' book, on the other hand, repeatedly pressed on me in teen-dom, was Arthur Grimble's 1920s Pacific travelogue, *A Pattern of Islands* (who was Grimble? Enquiry reveals him to have been, amongst other things, a protégé of A.C. Benson at Magdalene College, Cambridge) or Agnes Yates's *Putting the Clock Back*, a curiously enticing memoir of life in a tough-sounding Quaker household of the 1870s. Again, the books they owned seemed to have been assembled according to wholly mysterious principles, betraying impulses that to anyone chancing upon these fairly meagre hoards seemed more or less random. My father's collection included the odd Dickens novel, presumably carried away from school, the occasional smutty paperback with the price on the back marked in dollars (where did they come from, I wonder?) and a shelf or two of children's anthologies from the 1930s with titles like *The Bumper Book for Boys*. My mother's cache, alternatively, was a treasure trove of post-war middlebrow standards – Priestley's *Festival at Farbridge*; Somerset Maugham's collected stories in four volumes – but it also contained two items for which I shall always be grateful, Penguin paperbacks of Orwell's *A Clergyman's Daughter* and Waugh's *Decline and Fall*.

When it came to children's books of the kind read to us at bedtime in the late 1960s, my parents were on much firmer ground. They knew about Barrie, Milne, *The Wind in the Willows* and Beatrix Potter and they were aware of Puffins, Penguin Books' juvenile imprint, with their entry ticket into the worlds as variously down-to-earth as Laura Ingalls Wilder's *Little House* series and Eve Garnett's *The Family from One End Street* or whimsically fantastic as Tove Janson's Moomin saga. So what was the extent of my literary knowledge at the age of fifteen? I had read every line of Tolkien's work then available, C. S. Lewis's *Narnia* series, a couple of hundred superior children's books, not all of them chosen for their silent reinforcement of middle-class values (the family from One End Street were a dustman's effervescing brood) and countless boys' school stories pillaged from my father's hoard, with titles like *The Liveliest Term at Templeton* and *Strickland of the Sixth*, in which steely-eyed soccer captains handed out socks on the jaw to shirking ingrates and fresh-faced teenagers enjoyed ripping teas in the shadow of the elms – books whose spell was such that when despatched to prep school at the age of nine I couldn't understand why it wasn't like Havenhall, North Yorkshire, where Strickland exercised such a healthy moral influence, and why the bullies didn't shrink away at my approach. Less edifyingly, I had taken a mild but lubricious interest in the dog-eared paperbacks handed round surreptitiously in the school playground in which Hell's Angels tore chunks out of each other with bicycle chains or flash-fisted Jim Hawkins, the hero of Richard Allen's *Skinhead*, polished up his Doc Martens.

As for the sort of books it was possible to respect, I admired Orwell, while at this point having read only two of his novels and *Down and Out in Paris and London*, knew about Dickens by virtue of his being part of the cultural furniture – routinely televised on the BBC, turned into musicals or updated by the Muppets; why, there were even a couple of pubs within walking distance called the 'Pickwick' and 'the 'Micawber'. I had even, thanks to a highbrow children's weekly called

Look and Learn, to which my parents subscribed, heard of Proust and Balzac. Beyond that, though, literature – however enticing – was difficult to access, a few swirling figures glimpsed through an otherwise impenetrable palisade. It was not taught at school until the sixth form, the English literature O level being reserved for the notional dimwits who were no good at German. Meanwhile, contemporary fiction might just as well have not existed. Who were the outstanding British novelists of the 1970s? As a teenager, I couldn't have told you, for I had no information. My only resource was the Earlham branch library, Norwich, where among the collected works of R. F. Delderfield, A. J. Cronin, Mazo de la Roche and Dennis Wheatley, I browsed impressionably on, sometimes making a discovery (John Fowles, Piers Paul Read) at other times (when chancing upon some piece of avant-gardery whose code could not be cracked) sadly conceding defeat. Modern literature only began at the age of 16 when, paying a visit to the University of East Anglia's campus bookshop, I chanced upon a paperback of Ian McEwan's *First Love, Last Rites*, read the first story – about the teenage boy who plots incest with his sister – and discovered that, mysteriously, here was a book unlike anything I had previously encountered. Sometime after that, driven by who knows what impulse, I started buying the *Spectator* and reading the book reviews in the back. Tantalisingly and incrementally, like some lost, sub-tropical island emerging out of a weed-strewn lagoon, a whole new world had begun to take shape.

Not all the influences at work on the middlebrow reader of the 1950s and 1960s were wholly backward-looking. Recent history, for example, was everywhere to hand in the shape of 'war books', a publishing trade staple for the next quarter-century and beyond, reinforced by the popularity of 'shot and shell' serials in mass-market newspapers. Science fiction, largely absent from the domestic scene since the days of H. G. Wells, had begun its long march out of the specialist magazines to the essentially mainstream and increasingly eco-conscious novels of John Wyndham and John Christopher and the respectability of the first semi-academic study, Kingsley Amis's *New Maps of Hell* (1960). Meanwhile, the devastating impact of American imports on nascent British consumer culture was reflected in post-war literary traffic. Dashiell Hammett's *The Thin Man* had been one of the first Penguins; swiftly followed across the Atlantic by Raymond Chandler.

Home-grown critics such as Orwell and Hoggart were sometimes inclined to deplore the likely effects of this new American brutalism – see Orwell's essay 'Raffles and Miss Blandish', which contrasts the moral codes of E. W. Hornung's 'amateur cracksman' and the sadistic villains of James Hadley Chase. On the other hand, hard-boiled native crime novels, of the kind written by James Curtis or Robert Westerby, date back to at least the 1930s. What all commentators could agree on was the increasing multilateralism of the popular best-seller. Evelyn Waugh, having analysed a copy of his brother's *Island in the Sun*, remarked to his friend Ann Fleming that 'it's rather good if you think of it as being by an American which he is really' – a back-handed compliment which neatly locates Alec's spiritual home somewhere in the mid-Atlantic.

Naturally, there was far more to mainstream taste than these vague outlines suggest. It was a body of opinion subject to myriad and sometimes contradictory influences: a world no doubt circumscribed by the Boots Library and the highly conservative books pages of the *Sunday Express*, but now and again capable of tugging free from its moorings to espouse a genuinely adventurous choice; a world in which the best-seller, much more cunningly marketed and publicised, would sell an increasing number of copies to an increasingly large number of readers, with the selling process ever more susceptible to the influence of other media; a world of the *Reader's Digest* condensed book anthology; of the short fiction-peddling *Argosy* magazine; of espionage novels whose villains, here at the onset of the Cold War, were increasingly likely to be thickset hoodlums with East European accents; of genteel travel books whose authors roamed around a planet which perhaps seemed less far-flung and more accessible than had previously been the case; of Nevil Shute, Nicholas Monsarrat, Agatha Christie, Lloyd C. Douglas and Daphne du Maurier; of Thor Heyerdahl and his *Kon-Tiki* expedition across the South Seas; of enduring library favourites such as Richard Llewellyn's fictionalised lament for the lost world of his South Wales childhood, *How Green Was My Valley* (1939), still in print in its thirty-seventh impression thirty-five years later; of Joy Adamson, Elsa the lioness and *Born Free*; of volumes of reprinted magazine sketches with illustrations by Ardizzone and Searle; of *Punch* annuals and field marshals' memoirs; of bird books and spotter's guides and railway manuals; of agreeable and sometimes undemanding novels that were read in their hundreds of thousands, and sometimes millions, by people whose motives can never be precisely quantified.

If one wanted a representative figure from this age, and to a certain extent the ages that both preceded and followed it, it might be A. J. Cronin, whose career runs back deep into the 1930s and extends almost to his death in 1981. And yet even the briefest inspection of Cronin's thronged and multitudinous *oeuvre* reveals how little he conforms to the stereotype of middlebrow blandness. Certainly he showed an uncanny ability to devise work that was acceptable to Hollywood and television and, perhaps more important, to continue to be acceptable thirty or forty years after its publication: *The Stars Look Down* (1935) was adapted for the small screen as late as 1975. Certainly, some of his best-known work – the short stories which went to make up the BBC's *Dr Finlay's Casebook*, say – verges on cosiness. Much of his early output, on the other hand, is reformist in tone. *The Citadel* (1937), which draws on his early medical experiences, is thought to have influenced Aneurin Bevan as he set about organising the National Health Service. *The Northern Light* (1958), alternatively, set in the offices of a high-minded newspaper with a declining circulation, is a bitter attack on yellow-press journalism. Cronin, in other words, is much more than a conventional stock best-seller than we might like to assume – more radical, more prone to risk-taking, more finely attuned to some of the sociopolitical preoccupations of his age. And whatever may be said about his dogged style and his repetitions, not many popular novelists have their passing marked by a leading article in the *News of the World*. The same point could be made of that other staple of the post-war library lists, R. F. Delderfield (1912–72), whose evocations of an unfallen England – one of his novels is actually titled *God is an Englishman* – are never quite what they seem, and who in *The Avenue Goes to War* produced a genuine 'people's war' chronicle, full of characters picked for their ability to transcend the divisions of class and status. Not the least of the middlebrow novel's achievements, it turns out, is, however stealthily and intermittently, and with due regard for the sensibilities of its readers, to exhibit one or two of the symptoms of what, again, is a Dickensian quality – the radical conscience.

PART THREE

The Modern Age

CHAPTER 14

Metropolitan Critics

> The literary editor of a great newspaper must be a man of wide learning, of great experience in the commerce of letters, a critic of intellectual force and a great administrator. His position is more responsible by far than that of the Head of an Oxford college or even of a great public school. His task should be to create an educated democracy, not to pander to the taste of the half-educated and thus stereotype and standardise it.
>
> Douglas Jerrold, *Georgian Adventure* (1937)

> The literary criticism that arose in this country after the Second World War was as judicial, as fault-findingly ambitious and as youthfully and generationally vengeful as any that has ever been.
>
> Karl Miller, *Dark Horses: An Experience of Literary Journalism* (1998)

Most literary journalism is, in the end, metropolitan in character. It may not be written in London; it may be composed by someone who prides himself or herself on not being part of the 'racket' so deprecated by Mrs Leavis (and others); but ultimately nearly everything about it – preoccupations, range of reference, tone – will tend to conform to an age-old pattern: a kind of coffee-house buzz of assumption, inference, reputation-brokering and fashionable yard-sticking, a small but vigorously maintained network capable of drawing in even those detached from it by geography or professional circumstance. Malcolm Bradbury, for example, spent the last quarter-century of his academic life at the University of East Anglia, but no one would have thought of referring to him as a 'provincial critic'. Unlike Dr Leavis – to take a rather obvious comparison – who turned his sequestration into a positive virtue, Bradbury was a book reviewer as much as an academic, his ear finely tuned to the latest Grub Street gossip, convinced – again, unlike Leavis – that, far from squandering their talent, dons who wrote reviews for national newspapers were contributing to an essential part of modern critical practice.

There was sound historical precedent for this migration of most of the available resources to a few square miles of central London and a dozen or so newspaper and magazine offices. One or two mid-Victorian critics had made a point of distancing themselves from the London charivari – one thinks of the Rev. George Gilfillan zealously prosecuting his career from the wilds of Dundee – but by Gissing's day the English literary world was thoroughly centralised. There was, and is, nothing particularly sinister about this concentration of talent. Most newspapers and periodicals are based in London; literary editors like to have face-to-face dealings with the people from whom they commission reviews. In the pre-internet days, and to a certain extent beyond them, the young man or woman who schemed to pursue a career in literary journalism was conscious of the fact that success in Grub Street to a certain extent depended on proximity to it. Many of Kingsley Amis's 1950s visits to London, on leave from the University of Swansea's English department, were pleasure trips, undertaken with the object of catching up with old friends or renewing his extra-marital sex life, but Amis also found time to cultivate contacts and look up potential sponsors who might offer him freelance work. A typical excursion from November 1954 sees him paying court to the assistant editor of the *Evening Standard*, and calling on J. D. Scott, literary editor of the *Spectator*. The young don shouldering his way into the review pages of the *Observer* and the *Sunday Times* would have taken the idea of the metropolitan critic for granted: it was only in later decades that it became a point of conflict, something to be argued over in Arts Council committee rooms and the source of anguished editorials in small-circulation poetry magazines.

One consequence of this understanding that English literary culture of the 1960s and 1970s was, by and large, London literary culture was a high degree of self-consciousness. Much of the literary journalism of the period is, on the one hand, aggressive – in that there were points to be made, positions to be taken both on the old kind of literature that was slipping away and on the new kind that was taking its place – and, on the other, narrowly defensive, aware that existing arrangements were not to everyone's taste, that certain arts world *hauts fonctionnaires* (Roy Shaw, for example, who succeeded to the secretary generalship of the Arts Council in 1975) might be keener on devolution than on the constant furbishing up of a central strand. Clive James wrote a cross letter to *Private Eye* at around this time, defending the *New Review* from the charge that it was run for the benefit of a small group of metropolitan wire-pullers living in each other's pockets and alleging that an Arts Council cabal wanted the magazine brought down 'so that they can redirect the money to those talentless regional poets who run in and out of Peak District pubs with carrots stuck up their noses in order to raise the consciousness of the indigenous fauna'. There is a suspicion here that James is not only overstating his case, in response to what he imagined to be the threat of a devitalising, devolutionary tide, but is simultaneously filing an argument that will call his stance as an independent cultural arbiter seriously into question. The hint, after all, is not only that those being invited to decide whether or not a regional poet is talentless are Mr James and his cronies, but that the regional poet who enquired if he could take part in the judging process would probably be denied a hearing.

In their defence, such remarks were uttered in the consciousness of rectitude. For whether aggressive or defensive, threatened by the idea of the regional poet or scarcely aware that such cultural tribunes even existed, the literary journalist of the 1960s and 1970s was generally convinced that he, or she, inhabited a professional golden age. The realisation was especially pronounced among industry veterans with bitter experience of the bad old days of the pre-war era. Julian Symons, whose career extended back to the little-magazine world of the early 1930s, declared that 'the standards of contemporary book reviewing are increasingly higher than they were in the days of Straus and Gould'. Younger reviewers with a knowledge of the wider historical context hastened to agree. According to Jonathan Raban, it was in reviews rather than in seminar rooms or foundation-funded colloquies 'that the main dialogue about modern literature is sustained, that new writers are discovered, old ones revalued, that standards of comparison are established and the essential small-talk of a literary culture goes on, often at a much more sophisticated level than was the case 50 years ago'. These are impressive claims, and they tend to be borne out by the literary autobiographies of the period. No reader of the memoirs of Claire Tomalin (literary editor of the *New Statesman* in the early 1970s) or Miriam Gross, who assisted Terence Kilmartin on the books pages of the *Observer* and later became literary editor of the *Sunday Telegraph*, could be left in any doubt of the seriousness of the task on which they imagined themselves to be embarked. Tomalin, in particular, believed her job 'was to engage as seriously with literature as the front of the paper did with politics'. Wit was encouraged, and licence allowed, 'but it was not a frivolous activity, being a reviewer' and the (unnamed) man who turned in a piece suggesting that he had not read the book in question from cover to cover was never asked again.

If the Wilson–Heath era was a good time to be a book reviewer, then what had brought these conditions into existence? The most obvious explanation was a practical one, specifically the end of paper rationing and the daily newspapers' return to the more spacious dimensions of a previous age. Keith Waterhouse's account of his struggles to acquire a foothold in the newspaper world of the 1950s carries some rueful recollections of the long, straitened aftermath of the war 'when the broadsheet papers were down to six pages and the tabloids to twelve'. By the late 1950s these restrictions were at an end, and the reviewer charged with anatomising the new Kingsley Amis or the latest Iris Murdoch could expect to be allowed a certain amount of elbow room. But a much more compelling reason lies in the range of personnel available. Star reviewers excepted, the pool of regular reviewers in the 1920s and 1930s had been limited in its scope. With the income literary men and women could anticipate from their books in the post-war era conspicuously failing to keep pace with inflation, a much larger group of comparatively well-known writers was anxious to take on reviewing work. Their ranks were at all times likely to be swelled by moonlighting academics, conscious of the meagre rewards on offer to junior dons – £1,800 a year or so in the late 1960s – and by more senior figures who might disdain the money but relished the cachet.

All this brought an undeniable expertise and glamour to what had previously, at any rate at some of its lower levels, been seen as a rather mundane activity. The *Observer*'s regulars in the early 1970s included Paul Bailey, Anthony Burgess, D. J. Enright, Angus Wilson, Philip Larkin and Lorna Sage; Anthony Powell contributed fortnightly to the *Daily Telegraph*; Francis King reviewed for its Sunday edition. Even weekly magazines, where rates of pay were lower and younger talent encouraged, were able to amass formidable reviewing teams. The *New Statesman*'s roster of fiction reviewers in the mid-1970s, for example, included Valentine Cunningham, Julian Barnes and Jeremy Treglown – respectively a future Oxford professor of English, Booker Prize winner and editor of the *Times Literary Supplement*. While several of the ancient houses of Grub Street – the round-up review, the transcribed blurb masquerading as objective criticism – survived unscathed into the 1970s and beyond, even by the standards of the great Victorian intellectual monthlies this is an impressive collection.

On the other hand, newspaper and magazine books pages are only as good as the editors who compile them. With certain prominent exceptions, the literary editors of the interwar era had not been conspicuous figures; neither were the duties they undertook regarded as being particularly glamorous. Peter Fleming, appointed assistant literary editor of the *Spectator* in the early 1930s, signed his letters 'literary subeditor', in tacit acknowledgement that his job was largely to correct typographical mistakes and defective grammar. With more space available for book reviews and a general feeling that high-profile reviewers played an important part in extending newspaper arts coverage, the literary editor's role became correspondingly more important. Incumbents tended to stay longer in the job, to possess, in some cases, quite as much intellectual kudos as their contributors (Terence Kilmartin devoted his spare time to a new translation of Proust), above all to dedicate themselves to their craft in a way that would have seemed superfluous to a Frank Swinnerton or an Arnold Bennett. One of Kilmartin's assistants once itemised the qualities that he brought to his task. They included an imperviousness to flattery, immunity to the corruptions of friendship, the habit of selecting books for review entirely on the basis of their intrinsic merits, a delight in confounding the expectations of anyone who attempted to lobby him, and a dislike of excessive praise, which often led to favourable reviews being reined back into apparent neutrality. Kilmartin's deputy once made the mistake of showing Clive James the unedited typescript of a glowing review of his first book, only for it to appear on the following Sunday with every favourable adjective removed. Taxed with this austerity, Kilmartin explained that James was a contributor; the *Observer*'s books pages did not, in his view, exist merely to gild the reputations of the people who wrote for them.

In other hands, this dedication expressed itself in a conviction that review sections, far more so than other parts of the newspaper, had a duty to serve minority interests. The *Daily Telegraph*'s David Holloway once declared that 'one is concerned about printing a good quality of review. One cannot consider the saleability of a book when one is considering its reviewability. If a book is desperately specialist, it won't be done, but even if one in a thousand of our readers is going to enjoy that book, we should review it.' To examine some of the deeply recherché items Anthony Powell noticed for the *Telegraph* at this time – fragments of 1890s memorabilia, selections from the letters of Ernest Dowson, portraits of Sir Arthur Quiller-Couch, Oxford table-talk – is to be grateful for Holloway's powers of discrimination while wondering, as John Sutherland once put it, if there was a single other part of the newspaper that tried to cater for such a tiny fraction of its readership.

If the cult of the literary editor had a presiding genius – not that he would ever have conceived of himself in this way – it was probably J. R. Ackerley (1894–1967), who became the founding literary editor of the *Listener* in 1935 and occupied the post for very nearly a quarter of a century. A nervous, acerbic and at times well-nigh misanthropic homosexual, fixated on his Alsatian bitch Queenie, the subject of *My Dog Tulip* (1956), Ackerley had the good fortune to discover that much of the spade work had been done before he arrived. Founded in 1929 on the premise that its contents should merely reflect and recycle the BBC's broadcast output, the *Listener* had rapidly sheared off from its original moorings to become a cheaper but surprisingly successful version (27,000 copies per week) of the *Spectator* and the *New Statesman*. Books coverage featured strongly in the prospectus and under the eye of the deputy editor, Janet Adam Smith, the magazine already had a reputation for highbrow poems of the Day Lewis/Spender/MacNeice school – the kind of material, in fact, to be found in Adam Smith's influential *Poems of Tomorrow* anthology, published a few months after she left to marry the poet Michael Roberts. On the other hand, the *Listener*'s considerable reputation as a sponsor of avant-garde poetry had been won at a cost. BBC executives were wary; Adam Smith took care to show experimental poems to the conservatively minded editor, R. S. Lambert, only after he had returned from lunch. But however much Lambert may have disapproved of experiment, or indeed controversy of any kind, Ackerley's appointment was a testimony to the seriousness with which the paper took literature, even more so in that his job, strictly speaking, was that of general reviews editor, with eight pages to fill, including art criticism, three pages of short, unsigned notices, a full-page critique of new fiction and poetry and short stories when conditions allowed.

The advantages of a relatively large amount of space, and a Corporation-funded budget – the contributors to his opening salvo, a series on the Grand Tour, were offered twelve guineas for 2,000 words – made Ackerley a power to be reckoned with in the world of literary journalism, but it was a power that he considered himself deeply unfitted to exercise: he maintained that he was entirely unsuited to the job and seems not to have understood that his innate curiosity ('I read everything in sight – histories of the Ottoman Empire, instructions on patent medicines, bus tickets, everything') was the key to his success. Geoffrey Grigson once described him as a cultivated man doing a journalist's job, which may not sound very flattering either to cultivated men or journalists, but conveys at least something of the combination of breadth of interest and practical nous that characterised his tenure. While it would be overstating the case to say that the assumptions he brought to the post in any way constituted a 'policy', there was, at the same time, a recognisable Ackerley way of doing things, a modus operandi in which high-mindedness and a certain amount of low cunning each had their place.

If he exhibited fairly conservative tastes and was sometimes reluctant to back his judgement, then he was always keen on new, or newish, writers, as happy to publish Auden, Spender and Isherwood as his predecessor had been and, additionally, a champion of the Audenesque 'short poem' on the grounds that such trifles could always be used to fill up odd corners when commissioned copy had run out. An enthusiast for provocative opinions – a review of a symposium by twelve public school headmasters by the progressive educationalist A. S. Neill was spiked by the BBC's controller of public relations – he was never an out-and-out troublemaker, even if his advice to reviewers that 'personal relationships cannot be allowed to enter into these matters' sometimes led to difficulties with grand literary eminences who assumed that he was on their side. In this spirit Roy Fuller was allowed to criticise Edith Sitwell's tribute to the Greek poet Demetrios Capetanakis in *New Writing and Daylight*, thereby offending both Sitwell and her editor, John Lehmann, each a personal friend of Ackerley, and compounded the offence by disparaging Sitwell's current collection of verse. A draft of her letter of complaint has survived: 'I expect to be treated with the respect that is due to my poetry, & to which (after many years of the insults to which all important artists are subjected at the beginning of their career) I am now accustomed.'

Inspecting the formal – and not so formal – accounts of Ackerley's career, and also his private comments about friends and fellow writers whom he imagined to have sold him short, one is struck, above all, by his tact. He wanted his critics to be honest, and not to feel that they had to notice a mediocre work 'unless some public interest is served', but he was opposed to cruelty for cruelty's sake. The reviewer was trusted to make whatever changes might be required ('I like the *exact* word always, and the exact meaning, but whether my changes are on or off the mark only you know what was in your mind') and suggestions were always offered tentatively. Ackerley is once supposed to have telephoned a contributor at midnight from the printer's to ask if he could drop a comma. All the same, tact could sometimes be jettisoned altogether if Ackerley thought that circumstances demanded it. The long-term encouragement bestowed on Fred Urquhart, whose fiction Ackerley admired and whom he would have liked to publish, was balanced by a growing suspicion that Urquhart was a bad judge of his own work, happy to abandon the qualities that made him distinctive in the effort to persuade the *Listener* to print him. The letters Ackerley exchanged with Urquhart would make a little volume in themselves: 'I don't know how necessary it is for you to publish your writings . . . but I do think you'll damage a reputation which I do agree with [Edwin] Muir is promising if you don't exercise a more careful judgement' he advised at one point. Comments on individual stories grew increasingly caustic: 'No, no, a thousand times no. This is a magazine story, sentimental, with bright chatter and a "surprise ending": its epitaph is, "Makes you think, don't it?" – or would be if one had not foreseen from somewhere about the middle the end you are so busily preparing behind your screen of chatter.' In the event, Urquhart's *Listener* debut hung fire for a dozen years.

If there was one thing that could be guaranteed of Ackerley's pages it was an absence of 'magazine stories'. Given the constraints of the medium, which prohibited a length of more than 3,500 words, the quality of the *Listener*'s short fiction was consistently high: A. E. Coppard, Francis King, Walter de la Mare, V. S. Pritchett, Elizabeth Bowen, James Hanley, Angus Wilson and Sean O'Faolain all published work there. All this may make the paper seem like the model of a liberal arts magazine and Ackerley the unfettered dispenser of critical

Anthony Powell (on left of raised platform) en route to Holland with the rest of the *Punch* staff for a cricket match arranged by its new editor, Bernard Hollowood (bottom right), 1958. Being forced to attend this trip was apparently 'the last straw' in Powell's relations with the magazine

Powell in old age, with a fan

D. J. Enright, poet, critic and epitome of the post-war man of letters

Alan Sillitoe, shortly after the publication of his best-selling *Saturday Night and Sunday Morning*

A Child's Guide to Modern Culture

Christopher Booker, William Rushton and Richard Ingrams

A is for

Kingsley AIMLESS. He is a typical modern in-tele-ctual. In the olden days intellectuals were poor men with beards, who lived in the British Museum and wrote nothing but enormous books on history which sold three copies and changed the face of civilisation. No one ever heard of them until after they were dead. But Mr. Aimless is very rich and good-looking. He lives mainly in TV studios, where he interviews Popular Singers. He also writes popular novels about sex which sell millions of copies. Sometimes they are made into even more popular films with P. Sellers and he becomes even richer. In between, he writes many articles about jazz, science fiction, etc. Mr. Aimless is a typical modern in-tele-ctual. And like most modern in-tele-ctuals, he has gone POP. (See POP-CULTURE PSEUDS.)

The One Subject Man

His critical essay on "The Working Class Novel" gained wide acclaim when he wrote it eight years ago, and he has been writing it ever since. Whenever anything remotely connected with "literature and the working class" arises, they turn to him for his essay. Occasionally his conscience prompts him to shuffle the sentences into a new permutation. Assured of a place on any panel met to discuss social problems, and with a steady stream of lectures to deliver as well as books to review, he feels he can mine this particular seam for a good many years yet. Because of his upper middle-class background he is considered by Hoggart to be not quite genuine; nevertheless he contrives to earn more from the works of Barstow, Sillitoe, and Braine than they do themselves.

An expert on the Sillitoe-era 'working-class novel' entertains his audience, as imagined by 'Hewison' of *Punch*

Younger and older literary generations of the early 1960s, as satirised by the *Spectator*. Above, members of 'the Senile Club' include Evelyn Waugh (standing, second left), C. P. Snow (seated, centre) Bottom left, Kingsley Amis.

Ian Hamilton, whose editorship of *The New Review* became the focus of a long-running controversy over state funding for the arts

Anthony Thwaite punts Philip Larkin along the river Tas, Norfolk, early 1970s

Alan Ross at the offices of the *London Magazine*, 1990s

J. L. Carr, author of the Booker-shortlisted *A Month in the Country* and *The Battle of Pollock's Crossing*, who calculated that in the 1970s novel-writing paid him an average of seventeen pence an hour

J. R. Ackerley, long-term literary editor of the *Listener*, working al fresco

A leather-jacketed Malcolm Bradbury and his friend David Lodge participate in a seminar on Bradbury's *The History Man*, University of Birmingham, 1978

Angela Carter (left) and Lorna Sage, University of East Anglia, 1980s

A. S. Byatt, publicity photograph taken at around the time of publication of her first novel *The Shadow of the Sun* (1964)

Iris Murdoch, early 1960s, doyenne of the new breed of post-war female novelists

The Arts Council-sponsored Writers' Tour of North Wales, March 1969. Left to right, Nell Dunn, Angus Wilson, J. O. Jones, Margaret Drabble, Charles Osborne and Christopher Logue

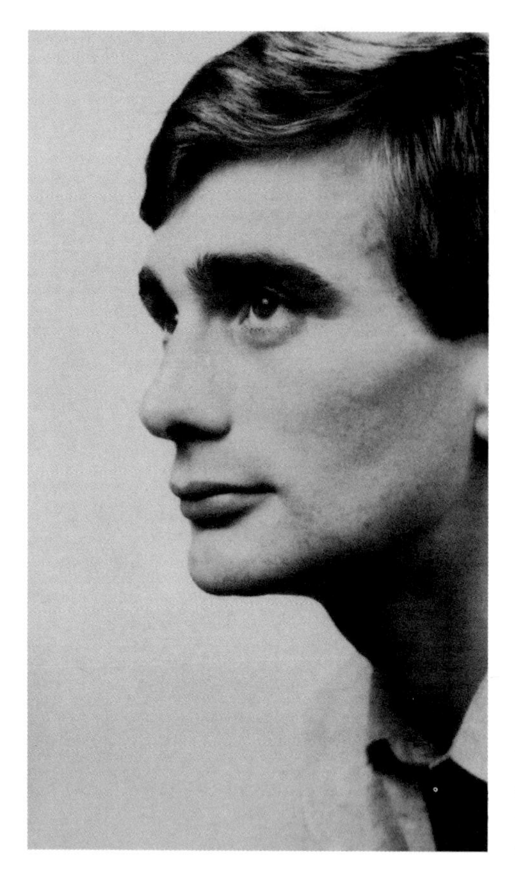

Richard Burns, author of *Fond and Foolish Lovers*, who killed himself at the age of 33

Critic John Carey encourages the younger generation, 1980

values to a large and discriminating audience: in fact its status as a state-sanctioned organ of the BBC meant that he laboured in constant fear of offending official policy. There were early difficulties with Sir Stephen Tallents, the controller of public relations, who kept an eye on the moral tone and complained of Henry Reed's use of the word 'brothel'. Further trouble was in store with the appointment of H. A. L. Fisher, warden of New College, Oxford, and a former minister of education, to the BBC's board of governors, who thought the poetry selections mediocre and, while finding the reviews 'intelligently done and generally competent', wondered why it was necessary for Edwin Muir to speak so highly of Aldous Huxley's 'inconceivably disgusting' *Eyeless in Gaza*. Far too much of Ackerley's time was spent in stand-offs of this sort, in conciliating the whims of the director general Lord Reith, who once suggested that 'literary reviews run as a comprehensive guide to reading, e.g. for country rectories, would be a good circulation point', or dealing with the fallout from a remark of Leonard Woolf to the effect that J. B. S. Haldane was too serious 'to win him the popularity which many politicians struggle for in comparison with film stars and little princesses'. The reference to the daughters of George VI had to be removed.

Ackerley was eventually persuaded to relinquish his post in 1959, three years beyond the standard BBC retirement age. He had hankered after a 'nice fat long-service cheque' in acknowledgement of his 'thirty years' hard labour', but was awarded a year's salary and a pension of £468 per annum, an arrangement he considered 'stingy'. His old friend E. M. Forster wrote a consolatory letter dwelling on the low value placed on literary ability in an age more disposed to worship mammon. If Ackerley had an heir – literally so, in that at one point he became the *Listener*'s editor – it was Karl Miller (1931–2014), who began his career on the *Spectator*, then moved on to the *New Statesman* and could be found thirty years later, still in harness, combining the editorship of the *London Review of Books* with the Lord Northcliffe Professorship of English Literature at University College London. It would be wrong to exaggerate the scent of kinship – Ackerley was a scion of the comfortably-off upper-middle classes (his father was the Fyffes banana king) while Miller was, as he put it, 'a working-class youth from Cambridge University who saw himself as some kind of bohemian professional'.

Much more so than the pragmatic Ackerley, Miller was convinced that the kind of journalism he wished to sponsor sprang from an authentic tradition that extended all the way back to the *Edinburgh Review*. To him, as to his great hero, the *Edinburgh*'s original editor Francis Jeffrey, 'literature' signified a universal field of knowledge which ran from politics to poetry, and was, ideally, to be approached by critics who knew that their responsibility went beyond the particular discipline under review to the wider cultural fabric that supported it. Significantly, one of his favourites among the *New Statesman* veterans was V. S. Pritchett, a critic whose rapport with the general reader he considered to be 'beyond compare'. Pritchett, Miller deposed, had the great merit of *liking* books, at a time when newcomers to literary journalism – this was the 1960s, with many of the pre-war old guard in danger of replacement – 'were blamed for disliking them and being philistine'.

There was another difference between the Ackerley-era *Listener* and the Miller-era *New Statesman*, and this was a suspicion, steadily increasing as the 1960s wore on, that the old cultural certainties about reading publics and shared values could no longer be taken for granted. One of Miller's early tasks at the *New Statesman*, for example, was to deal with some of the fallout from the celebrated 'Two Cultures' row between Leavis and C. P. Snow, in which the whole idea of a unified field of knowledge and the centralising mechanisms that might sustain it was called sharply into question. Naturally these interrogations were also taking place down at the bedrock level of literary journalism, where the blend of social and professional backgrounds on display could produce wildly differing editorial viewpoints. Trying to define the spirit that animated his colleagues here in a world where Sir Alec Douglas-Home, the former 14th earl, was about to give way to middle-class Mr Wilson, with his pipe, raincoat and weather eye for a photo opportunity, Miller judged that 'We were with the people in a number of literary ways, and yet professionally academic too, in temper, as well as bohemian and metropolitan and journalistic.' These are far from being mutually exclusive categories. Neither are they devoid of all historical precedent – the *Fraser's Magazine* of the 1840s had peddled a rather similar brand of Grub Street intellectualism. But brought together in the pages of the *Spectator* and the *New Statesman*, they could sometimes realise an odd kind of dualism, in which establishment and anti-establishment attitudes – two words then coming much into vogue – trailed each other from one page to the next. The *Spectator*, for instance, though traditionally Conservative, and owned in the 1950s by Sir Ian Gilmour, a former Guards officer who later became a Tory MP, counselled its readers to vote Labour at the 1959 general election. The *New Statesman*, too, was capable of bewildering shifts in standpoint, balancing general enthusiasm for new mass-cultural trends with regular salvoes of Bloomsbury-era elitism, as in Paul Johnson's celebrated attack on the Beatles and their working-class fans.

Inevitably, much of this confusion was the product of a wider awareness of some of the implications of the mass-cultural tendencies of the post-war age for the narrower, and at this point strictly hierarchical, world of books: a highly symbolic battleground in which some of the most telling interventions came from people with direct experience of the phenomena under review. It was Donald Davie, in a 1961 letter to the *New Statesman* complaining about a reference to a 'real if often raw culture of working-class life', who noted that 'the boy or girl who knows what working-class life is makes no such claims for it'. To Miller, with his shrewd historical sense, this was not so much a sociological rebuke but part of an age-old conflict between literature and the best-seller, a conflict in which it seemed important that excellence should not be confused with exclusiveness: 'We were people who liked the popular arts and who thought in terms of a general culture sustained by mutually enlivening subcultures, in terms of a "spectrum of taste".'

As Miller might have acknowledged, this was a difficult trick to pull off in an era founded on the principle of readers, listeners and viewers doing things for themselves, whose intellectual arbiters, whether highbrow journalists or academic theorists, were increasingly happy to assume that cultural values were relative and that the most fail-safe judgements could eventually be overthrown by sheer persistence: 'Judgement isn't what it was, but it is still in session' was Miller's icy comment several decades later. Many of the judgements Miller himself was promulgating had, necessarily, to do with the literary classics of the past half-century: with Eliot ('one part of what some of us came to be interested in expressing was an opposition to certain features of Eliot's journalism – to the politics, prejudice, and mugwump pretence of impersonality, that we were to find there'); Bloomsbury (a terrific assault from Brigid Brophy on Virginia Woolf); and Stephen Spender – a generational clash of such unrepentant hostility that there was talk of a 'Cold War' between Bloomsbury and its enemies with Miller in the role of intermediary and diplomatist.

The Miller who presided over these engagements, who carried olive branches back and forth and allotted space to injured parties, was not to everyone's taste – let alone the taste of those members of a senior literary generation who imagined, rightly or wrongly, that he had taken against them. Frances Partridge left a caustic account of the *New Statesman*-era editorial eminence: 'an intelligent, auto-intoxicated Scot; doesn't want to hear anything from anyone else, but just to do his own turn ad lib, which happens to be skilful and funny. But few people want to spend the whole evening laughing heartily at someone else's capers; it was like a night out with stockbrokers.' On the other hand, even Mrs Partridge would probably have admitted that the literary pages Miller edited throughout the 1960s and 1970s maintained an exceptionally high standard, both in straightforward criticism and creative literary work. Though his early days at the *Listener*, whose editorship he assumed in 1967, were dogged by controversy – in particular Thom Gunn's article 'Love, Love, Love' on 'The New Music' – the regular reviewers included Frank Kermode, Christopher Ricks and D. J. Enright, and the original poetry took in Larkin's 'The Old Fools', Derek Mahon's 'A Disused Shed in County Wexford' and Seamus Heaney's 'The Grauballe Man'. Understandably, Miller thought the magazine's enforced closure by the BBC in 1991 a disgrace, arguing that it had been 'a place where broadcasting and literature in the widest sense of the word could live together'.

Trying to define the brand of literary journalism which Miller and other kindred spirits were keen to sponsor in the 1960s and 1970s, one notes its intensely communal air. Miller's memoirs, for example, are a riot of first-person plurals, recurring names and nods to old friends. Although several of the weekly magazine and Sunday newspaper books pages of the era seem to be permanently staffed by members of the same bustling, interdependent collective, the tone of the criticism they produced was broadly homogeneous: urbane, tough-minded, debunking, serious, adversarial, eager to bolster its own standards and principles by framing them against the literature of the recent past. The string of reviews contributed by the young Martin Amis to the *New Statesman* in the early 1970s of novels by the generation of English writers who had, with one or two exceptions, begun their careers in the 1950s are a pattern demonstration of the up-and-coming tyro acknowledging certain debts to the literary ghosts who haunt his upbringing while, at the same time, emphasising his detachment from their influence. Iris Murdoch is advised to slow down, on the grounds that were she to pause to reflect awhile on her prodigious talent, 'she would, in short, begin to find out how good she is, that strange and fearful discovery'. Angus Wilson is briskly informed that the 'twinkly, walkabout exuberance' of *As If By Magic* isn't suited to his 'savagely direct talents'. Fay Weldon is chided for allowing cliché to spread 'inwards from the language of the book to its heart'.

While a certain amount of exception – sometimes violent exception – was taken to these judgements (Angus Wilson's biographer, Margaret Drabble, notes that the *As If By Magic* review caused 'deep and lasting offence' to her subject) they were nothing if not representative of the broader tone of the age: born of a critical environment that was both exacting and unimpressed, Olympian and street-sharp, capable of descending, in its less imaginative lower depths, to a stridency that had the advantage of being tolerated, if not positively encouraged, by some of its editorial sponsors. Miller notes that he 'went into it all' – 'it' being the experience of literary journalism – believing 'as Francis Jeffrey did, in the correction of taste and the wholesome discipline of derision', while suggesting that much of this newfound asperity had its roots in social class, the self-confidence of the new breed of upwardly mobile critics (a category in which he places both Kingsley Amis and himself) masking a deeply rooted insecurity. 'Fear and hurt, whatever their source, may go with an appearance of strength and a tendency to condemn.'

While there was plenty to condemn, there was also – as the example of Angus Wilson reminds us – plenty of fear and hurt. With it came a confident estimate of the value of literary journalism and an assumption that it was better able to achieve its aims than outwardly more elevated forms of literary criticism. It was a time when academics were beginning to colonise the review pages in even greater numbers than before, but this did not disturb a belief in certain quarters that the academy was part of the problem. Peter Ackroyd, the youthful literary editor of the *Spectator* in the mid-1970s, went so far as to talk about 'the death of the mind':

> Literary criticism . . . is now all but paralysed; this has nothing to do with book reviewers, who perform a useful public function, and who, in any case, would never aspire to the dizzy ranks of 'the critics', I am referring to those critics in the universities,

> who publish long articles in specialised journals, who write books about Henry James or Samuel Johnson, who, in short, are a cut above Grub Street and its environs. There has been nothing original from them in ten years. I have yet to read a contemporary academic critic who could write more intelligently, or read more carefully, than a good book reviewer.

It scarcely needs saying that Ackroyd was the former holder of a Yale research fellowship, and was the author of a formidably clever post-modernist treatise (*Notes for a New Culture*, 1976) that would put the ornaments of many a university English department to shame. Less combative observers, usually those who had been longer in the trade, saw the professionalisation of their craft as evidence of a widening gap between the production of literature and the analysis of it. D. J. Enright, opening a review of George Watson's *The Literary Critics* (1962), with a suggestion that there was too much criticism and not enough writing, was not being simply mischievous. Criticism, he argued, was getting 'better and better'. If this 'radical discrepancy' between criticism and creation was a fact, 'then it at once accounts for the precedence in prestige, and probably in quality, which criticism now takes over creation'. Enright, you feel, is having it both ways here – enjoying one of the rueful little jokes with which his work is periodically enlivened, while noting a development that many of his colleagues on the pages of the *Observer* or the *Sunday Times* would have greeted with deep unease: the rise of a new and increasingly sophisticated critical class with claims to a theoretical expertise calculated to make the all-purpose literary journalist look like an amateur. It was no wonder, in these circumstances, that reviewers and editors were keen to talk up the cultural value of what they did.

No doubt there is a way in which at least some of these distinctions are artificial. As John Sutherland once pointed out, if the 1970s-era Ackroyd was a cut above Grub Street, then the modern Grub Street was itself a cut above Grub Street as originally depicted by the Augustan satirists. If, as Richard Hoggart once suggested, there was no such thing as the 'common man', then, equally, for all the occasional homogeneity of tone, there is no such thing as the typical literary journalist, merely a mass of men and women with a variety of qualifications and stances who make a proportion of their income from reviewing books and to whom the standard professional categorisations simply fail to apply. Even marking down Enright (1920–2002) as a 'metropolitan critic' has its dangers, if only because he spent the period 1950–70 thousands of miles away from the metropolis teaching in the Far East, and for all the rigour of his literary journalism he was at least as well known as a poet. A postman's son from Leamington Spa, the privations of whose early life are faithfully recorded in the verse sequence *The Terrible Shears* (1973), a scholarship boy and student of Leavis, Enright was always conscious both of where he came from and of the implications of this question of upbringing for the view he took of the world. Whatever he might ultimately have thought of Leavis, he was quick to acknowledge that the Sage of Downing was one of the few teachers he had met who deeply *wanted* his pupils to follow what he was saying and treated them as something approaching equals – a lack of condescension that was all the more welcome given the wider context of 1930s-era upward mobility. 'Life was hard then' Enright recalled. 'It was hard for "scholarship boys" to get scholarships to enable them to go up to the university. It was hard to get published. It was difficult to start a magazine and difficult to keep it going. It was hard to find a post.' (Enright's first academic job was in Egypt, which provided the setting for his 1955 novel, *Academic Year*. In the rush to criticise the Leavises it was easy to forget the conditions in which they operated, an environment in which 'You had to be devoted and tough to survive.'

Enright's own toughness, his ruefulness, his lightly worn learning, his sedulously cultivated irony – all, as he would have conceded, exemplary 'Movement' characteristics – are some of his most attractive qualities. But if long-term immersion in academic life had furnished him with the greater part of his critical armoury, this did not make him any more indulgent of academic foibles. Much of his work in the 1960s and 1970s may be read as a critique of the modern critical process, and he wrote a pointed review of a collection of essays about Dylan Thomas complaining that such was the reliance on symbolism that by the end whatever was being interpreted had lost most of its charm and most of its interest. How odd, he mused, 'that in this age of precision instruments in literary criticism, it is still supposed that to call something a symbol is to make a meaningful statement'. The same reluctance to board the academic gravy train can be found in his review of Gunter Grass's *Dog Years*. Is Harras the German shepherd poisoned because he 'symbolises' Nazism? 'Nonsense. Harras is just a dog.' Whether dealing with *Scrutiny*, Dylan Thomas or the German avant-garde, Enright is a pragmatist, keener on determining what truly exists in a book than what the critic wants to find there, exercised above all by particularity. He produced an intensely revealing essay on Sir Herbert Read's autobiographies, which, according to Enright's interpretation, preach the homily that 'in a thousand ways the principle of anarchism will determine our practical policies, leading the human race gradually away from the state and its instruments of oppression towards an epoch of wisdom and joy'. To Enright, this kind of assertion is meaningless: the inquisitive reader, he argues, will want to hear about the thousand ways, and Sir Herbert's detailed accounts of his childhood are much more to the reviewer's taste.

A less sophisticated critic, you suspect, would not have been able to file this judgement with quite the same conviction, let alone the same panache. As it is, Enright's essays, for all their intellectual plumage, occasionally put one in a mind of a drummer who, having worked his way along the margins of bebop and free jazz, returns with a certain amount of relief to the staider satisfactions of standard time signatures. As a reviewer he is keen on humour, on seriousness that has the advantage of not taking itself too seriously, on writing that seems actually to be about something rather than conforming to the approved contemporary patterns – one of his regular complaints about the fiction of the 1960s, for example, is that for all its technical aplomb it has no subject. Thus he can write of John Updike that he is undoubtedly a highly skilled writer 'but to me seems hardly an author at all . . . It is all very neat and contrived, as if some sophisticate is amusedly performing for a psychiatrist of low intelligence.' What is to be applauded is the straightforward enjoyment of existence: reviewing Larkin, for instance, he confesses to a degree of impatience 'at the sight of so marvellous a skill at conveying the feeling of living joined with such a valetudinarian attitude towards life'. Significantly, the pragmatist in him was always brought back to the surface by anything that could be construed as an over-reliance on form. C. P. Snow, in his *Strangers and Brothers* sequence, might have 'the courage of his clichés', but Enright is distressed by the spectacle of naturalism taken to its logical extreme 'in what seems little more than a waxwork show'. Hansard ('presumably a naturalistic document') was distinctly more animated.

While Enright, with the memory of Downing College ever before him, took his seriousness for granted, for Brigid Brophy (1929–95) a self-proclaimed professional gravitas was always an essential part of her intellectual attack. 'People . . . often ask me whether my journalism interferes with my serious writing' she once wrote. 'As a matter of fact, my journalism *is* serious writing.' This, it turns out, is a highly typical Brophy-ism. Tart, brisk, astringent, much in demand by broadsheet newspapers throughout the 1960s for her contributions to the burgeoning genre of women's issue journalism ('The Immorality of Marriage', 'Monogamy', etc.), a pioneer of the animal rights movement and a zealous vegetarian, she can sometimes seem uncannily like the prototype for A. S. Byatt's Frederica Potter in *The Virgin in the Garden* and *Still Life*: ferociously intelligent, using both intelligence and ferocity as part of her selling point, but at the same time faintly defensive, getting her retaliation in first for slights that have yet to materialise. *Prancing Novelist* (1973), for example, her compendious study of Ronald Firbank, is full of oddly proleptic footnotes, anticipating objections that have not yet been made. To read more than half a dozen pages of her journalism is to be struck by the recurring enthusiasms – Firbank, Mozart, vegetarianism – her love of precision, economy, detail, her willingness to arrive at sharp moral judgements and, as a practising novelist herself, the immensely jaundiced view that she took of the state of post-war British fiction.

Enright might have complained that most modern novels had no proper subject. To Brophy, co-author (with Charles Osborne and her husband Michael Levey) of the no-nonsense *Fifty Works of English and American Literature We Could Do Without* (1967), the problem was that the subjects they did pursue were the wrong ones, or, rather, that they strove for an ulterior, sociological importance that gave their work topical relevance but weakened it as fiction. As she once put it, reviewing a novel by Gillian Freeman, 'too often the post-war novelist spreads his risk. Just in case his novel should turn out no good as a novel, he puts forward an extraneous claim as well – that his novel either documents or, by its very existence, exemplifies some social trend we can't afford to miss.' Naturally, no account of trends in contemporary fiction could ignore some of the stanchions on which contemporary fiction was founded, and she filed a devastating reassessment of Virginia Woolf for the *New Statesman*, criticising the vagueness of her detail – she was particularly cross to discover that in *Between the Acts* Woolf seems to think you need a corkscrew to open a bottle of champagne – and comparing her unfavourably to Simenon ('who has the literary good sense to approach the intangible through the concrete'), talking of her 'outstandingly defective' ear, and suggesting that her expressive form concealed a giant hole at its core: 'the absence of characters and incidents, those sheer gifts which are as indispensable to true novelists as tunes to true composers and which can only come, not be summoned'. She concedes that Woolf is 'a clever and thoughtful literary person', but confronted with *Orlando* her preference is for the Marmalade Cat – 'he makes so much less the impression of being neutered'.

Although barely into her 30s when the 1960s began, Brophy is in many ways a figure from an earlier age: her first novel, *Hackenfeller's Ape*, appeared as far back as 1953 and she kept a keen eye on popular attitudes to the 1950s phenomena whose emergence she had witnessed at first hand: see, for example, her tenth-anniversary dismissal of *Lucky Jim*, in which Amis is arraigned on a charge of appealing to 'the philistinism of a middle class which suffered from cultural claustrophobia, believing itself to be literate not through love of culture but as a badge of class'. Of genuine newcomers to the 1960s scene, by far the most influential – not least because he combined the dual roles of critic and editor – was Ian Hamilton (1938–2001). Like Miller, Hamilton was very much a 'new man': a grammar school boy from Darlington who made his way to Keble College, Oxford (where even the attentions of his admiring tutor, John Carey, could not prevent him from getting a third-class degree) and co-founded the *Review*, billed as 'a magazine of poetry and criticism', as early as 1962.

A decade and a half after his premature death, much of Hamilton's achievement is in danger of being obscured by the legends that accumulated around him: the saturnine bar-propper grimly informing a potential contributor who declined a large Scotch on the grounds that he didn't like drinking in the morning 'Good God man! None of us *likes* it'; the silent, authoritative presence at literary gatherings ('dark, heavy-faced, almost speechless' Rayner Heppenstall noted, on meeting him at the BBC in 1970). Once the mythological fog has drifted away from the Pillars of Hercules, the Soho pub in which, beneath a cloud of cigarette smoke, Hamilton held editorial court for the best part of a decade, something of his true nature looms into focus: a detached and almost painfully austere figure, much exercised by 'standards' and the question of poetic authenticity. Considering the stance adopted by the *Review* in the memoir that introduces Hamilton's anorexic *Collected Poems*, Alan Jenkins offers such adjectives as 'stringent', 'serious' and 'absolutist' – a hard-line and tact-free editorial policy designed to steer a course between 1940s neo-romanticism and Movement-era irony, both of which Hamilton greatly disliked. Issue nine, for example, featured the last poems of Sylvia Plath, and there were special numbers on Eliot and Empson and interviews with 1930s survivors such as Edgell Rickword and Edward Upward.

As for the literary qualities which Hamilton might be thought to admire, these are most obviously on display in his essay 'The Forties', with its praise of 'self-detachment', his anthology *The Poetry of War 1939–1945* (1965), which identifies Keith Douglas, Alun Lewis and Roy Fuller as the pre-eminent poets of the conflict, and the 1968 essay on Fuller written shortly after the latter had been elected to the Oxford poetry chair. The characteristic that he admires in Fuller turns out to be 'the self-deprecating habits of his verse and of his social conduct', and there is approving mention of his remark that 'if one is a reserved character who sees what a BF [bloody fool] he is, one can't be a personality poet'. Fuller, you suspect, appeals to Hamilton because he detects in him many aspects of his own poetic self: not only a belief in the advantages of self-effacement and letting the words speak for themselves, but a conviction that the belief should be taken out into the public arena. When Hamilton notes that 'Fuller the self-effacing poet and companion has surprised many with the astringency of his critical pronouncements. Hard on his own pretensions, he is free to be at least ungenerous to those of his contemporaries', he could equally well be talking about himself. The suspicion that Hamilton is using Fuller to fight some of his own battles in the 1960s poetry world hardens into certainty when he commends him for the sense he conveys of holding out against chaos, and goes on to note that Fuller was one of a handful of young poets whose criteria of objectivity, intelligence and social concern were formed in the 1930s, but whose reputation had to be made in the 1940s, 'a period of deplorable critical standards and slapdash poetical practice'.

After this it is no great surprise to find Hamilton insisting that Fuller would dislike the 'Black Mountain gang' and the Liverpool poets, if only because he was implacably hostile to them himself. 'Popsters and barbarians' was his description of the 1960s counter-cultural scene, and he was genuinely shocked when *The Mersey Sound*

(1967), a Penguin anthology showcasing work by Adrian Henri, Roger McGough and Brian Patten, notched up sales of half a million copies. If there was a distinction to be drawn, it was between poetry and entertainment. As he remarked in a later interview: 'Most of what is out there today isn't really poetry . . . It might be a form of writing that is engaging and sharp and entertaining, but it is not poetry.' Unsurprisingly, exposés of the ever-widening chasm between 'seriousness' and populism were a feature of the *New Review*, the *Review*'s much more substantial successor, which ran for fifty issues between 1974 and 1978. Older hands, who remembered not only the *Review* but the little magazines of the 1930s, were sometimes underwhelmed: 'nothing like as good' Julian Symons declared, diagnosing an inability on Hamilton's part to impose his personality on the larger format. Always mired in controversy, from its mockery of the anti-traditionalist putsch that briefly delivered the Poetry Society into the hands of a gang of sinewy experimentalists and sound poets, to the long-running debate about its public subsidy,* the *New Review* never quite absolved itself from a charge of cliqueishness, or of an unwillingness to cultivate the sensibility of anyone who was not on its fairly exclusive wavelength to begin with. Asked by an interviewer if he would like his meagre band of 2,000 subscribers to double, Hamilton offered the laconic reply: 'Maybe. But I'd like to know who the other 2,000 were.' This kind of thing went down very badly in the 1970s – officially an era of inclusiveness and openness in the arts world – and Hamilton's apparent eagerness to bite the hand that fed him – in this case the Arts Council – can sometimes seem a little too studied for comfort. On the other hand, it takes only a glance at the magazine's contributors during the five years of its existence to establish the range of talent that he was able to marshal on what was self-evidently a minority culture's behalf.

If there was a distinctive literary scene at this time, it could be found in the group of younger writers associated with the mid-1970s *New Statesman*, with satellite agencies in the *New Review*, the *Times Literary Supplement* and the *Spectator*, where the 23-year-old Peter Ackroyd had begun to shake up the somewhat antiquated equipage of the magazine's books pages on his appointment as literary editor in 1973. Certainly, an inspection of Hamilton's list of contributors, who included Clive James, Craig Raine, James Fenton and Martin

* This is discussed at greater length in Chapter 15.

Amis, established a link with each of these rivals, notably the *New Statesman*, where Amis was appointed deputy literary editor in 1973, eventually succeeding Claire Tomalin three years later. Subsidiary roles were occupied by such writers and critics as Christopher Hitchens, Julian Barnes, Ian McEwan and Lorna Sage. Clan gatherings, mainly at a kebab house in Theobald's Road, were distinguished by their self-consciousness. One junior *New Statesman* staffer remembered that 'the place and those associated with it took on a kind of clubbishness: exclusive in that you had to be clever and funny to become a member'. At any rate the sense of a collaborative spirit, defiantly opposed to other collaborations, was strong. Whereas most of the group were Oxford graduates, Clive James at least, who had read English at Cambridge, was still smarting from the wounds left in his sensibility by F. R. Leavis: 'his advocates still held that the London literary circuit was lightweight, modish . . . So we decided that we'd create an alternative to academia, based in London, something made up of people who were writers *and* critics.' As to what this amounted to in practice, the atmosphere tended to highbrow bohemianism, manifesting itself in private jokes and ribald *New Statesman* competitions, often won by staff members and their friends entering under pseudonyms. One notes, too, the magazine's enthusiasm for the newly modish brand of crisply observed, image-heavy 'Martian' poetry, symbolised by the triumph of Craig Raine's genre-defining 'A Martian Sends a Postcard Home' in the annual poetry competition for 1978.

Literary scenes invariably carry the seeds of their own obsolescence. Magazines change shape, or reassess their editorial priorities. Personnel move on. By the late 1970s the sense of London literary journalism as a coherent unit, with shared principles and affiliations to match, had begun to dissolve. The arrival of Bruce Page, much more exigent and left wing than his predecessor Anthony Howard, in the *New Statesman*'s editorial chair led to Amis's resignation, along with his deputy, Julian Barnes. The *New Review* closed in 1978. Ackroyd by this time had stepped down as the *Spectator*'s literary editor and reinvented himself as a cinema critic. Although perennially engaged as book reviewers, all three were increasingly occupied with their own literary projects. What survived, after the participants had moved on, were a great many collections of literary journalism and, above all, a tone: informal, ironic, unimpressed to the point of belittlement. 'Boisterously smartyboots in style and fake-Augustan in its grammar' Jonathan

Raban once remarked of one of Clive James's more exalted flights, awarding extra bad marks for sarcastic inversion, circumlocution, use of the ironic negative and leaving a general impression that the reviewer is 'a sight more clever than the man he's reviewing'. Certainly the reader who chances upon James's opinion of Richard Crossman's Cabinet diaries will wish that that the critic himself had been Secretary of State for Housing in the first Wilson government as he clearly knows exactly what needed to be done.

On the other hand, the weekly fiction masterclasses which Ackroyd conducted in the mid-1970s *Spectator*, though frequently disdainful in their judgements, are nearly always examples of a critic – however given to mockery – saying things that need to be said: accusing Erica Jong of stuffing herself with clichés in the same way that a scarecrow 'might have to wad himself with straw and pieces of old newspaper', convicting her, in the end, of 'inauthentic' prose and 'pervasive self-adulation'. Like Ian Hamilton, Ackroyd was wary of the insubstantiality of much of the literature of the 1960s and 1970s, whether it came courtesy of Liverpool poets or American auto-confessionalists, an insubstantiality, he believed, that had its roots in the eternal quest for the new. If, as the poet Alan Brownjohn once put it, this was a period of literary history 'soft on crap', then some of its most effective adversaries were the books page editor and his henchmen and women. And while the Wilson-era debate about 'standards' went far beyond the arts and entertainment into politics itself, one of the sturdiest defenders of orthodoxy turns out to be that unutterably prosaic figure, the freelance book reviewer.

Lady Writers

> Lady writer on the TV
> Talk about the Virgin Mary . . .
> She had all the brains and the beauty
> Dire Straits, 'Lady Writer' (1979)

On the very last day of 1965, Simon Raven published an article in the *Spectator* under the heading 'Scheherazade: The Menace of the Sixties'. Addressed to his fellow (male) novelists, its subject was the contemporary woman writer – symbolised by the heroine of *The Thousand and One Nights* invoked in the title – and its tone mock-humorous. 'I am well aware that lady novelists are not a new phenomenon' Raven sternly informs his readers, 'and as long as they kept their activities within decent bounds I was one of their warmest admirers.' Now, it turns out, and for all the excellence of Rosamond Lehmann and Margaret Mitchell, on whose Rhett Butler Raven modelled his undergraduate persona, matters have gone too far: 'for every prominent male novelist at present writing in the English tongue there are at least three females on the list. Gentlemen, we are being swamped.' And why is the woman writer so popular here in the age of Harold Wilson and Edward Heath? Raven has a number of ingenious, not to say sexist and patronising, explanations. The first is that the novelist is by definition a professional liar, and women are better liars than men, both inventive and plausible, while the 'self-righteousness with which they deceive themselves' lends a terrific air of conviction to their attempts to hoodwink other people.

Simultaneously, he alleges, a woman can bring off a feat which no man is ever able to achieve – write without scruple of a life which is exclusively given over to personal emotion. 'Such is a woman's biological conditioning that she can both think and write as if nothing existed . . . outside the home or the current love affair.' Third, there is the misplaced chivalry of reviewers, who will apparently allow the women writer a degree of procedural licence rarely extended to male competition: 'For all the critics care, a lady novelist can change the colour of her hero's hair as often as she dyes her own. She can debauch the rules of baccarat or chess, drive 1,000 miles or more without stopping for petrol, and enter Albania itself without a visa.' Finally there is the fact that sex, about which women novelists are prone to write, seems sexier if people have a mental picture of a woman sitting there writing it. In other words the success of the lady novelist is due, in almost equal proportions to 'chicanery, flirtatiousness, and freedom from intellectual principles and inhibitions'. And so the toast for 1966 is 'Death to Scheherazade – it is high time her head were off.'

What makes this condescension just about tolerable half a century later is both its air of grudging respect – Raven suspects that Iris Murdoch, the only woman novelist whose name he specifically mentions, is a major talent and, being an honest man, can't bring himself to belittle her – and the accuracy of its opening deduction. Far more so than the 1940s and the 1950s, and with due allowance made for the wretched working conditions in which she frequently had to operate, the 1960s and 1970s were an era in which the upmarket woman writer carried if not everything then certainly a great deal before her, an era in which such novelists as Murdoch, Doris Lessing, Brigid Brophy, A. S. Byatt, Margaret Drabble, Edna O'Brien, Gillian Freeman and dozens of others like them were taken very seriously by the critics and had their books treated with a far greater punctiliousness than had sometimes been allowed to their mid-century equivalents. If the pages of the literary weeklies were not exactly thrown open to them – of the fifty-two contributors to a mid-1960s *Spectator* anthology, eight are women, while Kingsley Amis's *Spectator–New Statesman* hybrid from 1977 manages exactly five – then she was an increasingly influential presence in the world of 1960s literature. But who was the woman writer? Where did she come from? What did she want? And what obstacles stood in the way of her achievement?

While one or two intellectual women tended to sneer at what they regarded as the easy consolations of the literary life – Zoë Heller remembered the disparaging tone which her mother, canvassing likely career choices for her daughter, brought to the words 'literary editor' – then, quite apart from the demands of hearth and home, the greatest impediment was men: male publishers such as Duckworth's Colin Haycraft, who referred to his firm's highly successful and predominantly female fiction list as 'the distaff side of the business' or 'a branch of gynaecology', male critics, always keen to shift women off into their own private zenana, and male novelists, never so happy as when caricaturing the female competition. What Raven, for example, really thought about the woman writer, or certain of her early 1970s incarnations, may perhaps be inferred from a bravura passage in *The Survivors* (1976), the final instalment of his ten-volume *Alms for Oblivion* sequence, in which the guests at a PEN Club party in Venice include two novelists, 'one middle-class and the other proletarian' called, respectively, Acarnania Mayling and Jessica Fubs. Subsequently Acarnania lectures the Marquis of Canteloupe, a partner in the publishing firm which sponsors her, on the iniquity of hereditary titles while Jessica recounts the plot of her next novel, 'which was to contain several blow-by-blow descriptions of intercourse between an agricultural labourer and his nine year-old daughter'. These cameos are brought to an end by the arrival of teenage Baby Llewellyn, the daughter of a Cambridge academic, who, when introduced, remarks '"I know about them. Poppa says your books are soft, sticky crap" – to Mayling – "and yours are hot, runny crap" – to Fubs.'

More dignified versions of this kind of burlesque could be found a great deal higher up the literary ladder, in a world where male (and female) ideas of how a woman writer ought to look and behave were frequently confounded by the physical reality. The 63-year-old Penelope Fitzgerald, having won the 1979 Booker Prize for her novel *Offshore*, found herself treated to a belittling interview by Robert Robinson on the BBC *Book Programme*, in which, referring to his guest as 'Mrs Fitzgerald', and conscious of a shortlist containing works by Thomas Keneally and V. S. Naipaul, he announced that 'the best book didn't win'. Admirers tried to categorise her in terms of prevailing styles of women's fiction. She noted that people told her she was in Barbara Pym's group, and that you either had to be in hers or Beryl Bainbridge's. But even the upper reaches of non-academic criticism were susceptible to this type of pigeonholing. One might take as evidence Gilbert Phelps's chapter on 'The Novel Today' in 1970s reissues of the final volume of *The Pelican Guide to English Literature*. Various female titans – Ivy Compton Burnett, Muriel Spark, Doris Lessing – are given their due, after which, tacked on to the section on Lessing, comes reference to 'another preoccupation which has become increasingly, and understandably, prominent among women writers during the last decade – the exploration of the ways in which modern society appears to offer freedom and equality to women, without any really worthwhile context in which these can operate – and which still, in point of fact, involve both injustice and violence to women's natures and talents'. Specialists in this genre are said to be Penelope Mortimer, Brophy, O'Brien, Drabble and Byatt, who have 'dealt with various aspects of the modern woman's dilemma with insight, honesty and unsentimental realism'.

You sense that Phelps (1915–93), a highly respectable mid-century man of letters and BBC mainstay, is doing his best in the face of well-nigh insuperable odds – in this case the need to say something coherent about a wildly diverse group of writers – but even so there is a limit to the value that can be got out of the claim that Penelope Mortimer and Edna O'Brien deal with various aspects of the modern woman's dilemma with insight, honesty and unsentimental realism. But if, by and large, the women writers of the 1960s and 1970s were constantly being judged in terms of their image and the presumption of their collective solidarity, then what did they think of that image and, by extension, that solidarity themselves? At one level – the basic, professional level at which contracts to write books are offered and accepted – they would have been conscious that the evaluative prism through which their work was brought to the world had undergone a profound change, and that a certain kind of women's writing – wry, reflective, unassuming and on occasion humorous – was much less hospitably received than it had been fifteen or twenty years before. It was not merely Elizabeth Taylor at whose work critics began to look askance for being middle class, localised and old-fashioned. Barbara Pym's career ground to a halt in the early 1960s when her publisher Jonathan Cape declined to sponsor her seventh novel, *An Unsuitable Attachment*. Friends pulled such strings as they could – it was a great shame if 'stories about sane ordinary people doing sane ordinary things' couldn't find a publisher, Philip Larkin complained when his own firm turned it down – but her renaissance had to wait until the late 1970s, fuelled by a *Times Literary Supplement* symposium in which Larkin and Lord David Cecil acclaimed her as a neglected talent.

Clearly a woman writer needed an 'image', a projection of herself capable of meeting the demands of television appearances and magazine interviews. But how was it to be constructed? There were, of course, 'anti-images' – refusals to participate in the media feeding frenzy that threatened to engulf many of the successful female novelists of the period, which become a kind of participation by default. Take, for example, the early career of Iris Murdoch, acclaimed by male critics as an honorary Angry Young Man on the strength of her debut *Under the Net* (1954) – Raven, a dozen years later, refers to 'that intelligent lady, Miss Iris Murdoch' and suggests that she qualifies as 'an honorary male' – and appearing to take no interest in how she looked or dressed. A guest at her marriage ceremony reported that he had 'just been to a wedding where the bride wore a mac', while some of her mid-1950s correspondence hints that she was simply bewildered by the necessity to talk to interviewers:

Press: Well, Miss M, do you intend to do so-and-so, such-and-such, and so-and-so?
Oneself: I don't really know – maybe, but I haven't made any plans at all . . .
Press report: Miss M told us that she intends to do so-and-so, such-and-such, and so-and-so.

On the other hand, Murdoch seems to have selected the photographs of herself that were released to newspapers with a certain amount of care – see, for example, the farouche, cigarette-smoking intellectual bent over her writing paper in Snowdon's famous portrait.

Here, perhaps, lay another snare for women novelists of the 1960s. Like Murdoch – a formidably clever woman who lectured in philosophy at St Anne's College, Oxford – many of the 1960s Scheherazades were essentially bluestockings who owed their advancement to a talent for exam-passing. Byatt and Drabble, for example, had Cambridge firsts and could have held their own in any university English department that cared to employ them. But however undimmed their intellectual lustre, they were painfully aware that the hothouse conditions of the 1960s, regulated as they were by a media fixated on novelty, beautiful people and the questioning of accepted roles, demanded something more. Contemporary young women's magazines of the *Cosmopolitan* and *Nova* type were keener on the *enfant terrible* (Brophy, with her attacks on marriage), the well-brought up girl who went slumming (Nell Dunn, author of *Up the Junction*) and the sexy transgressive (Edna O'Brien, whose novel *August Is a Wicked Month* offered an omnipurpose title for summer feature articles). Did Byatt and Drabble feel entirely at home here? The jacket photograph of Byatt's critical study of

Murdoch, *Degrees of Freedom* (1965), shows her wearing what looks like a superannuated gymslip, every inch the ornament of a women's college senior common room. Drabble, despatched by the BBC to investigate nightclub culture, looks faintly bemused by these new forms of entertainment, an anthropologist dutifully at large in a newly discovered society that certain intrepid travellers have just brought to her attention, anxious to attend to its rituals and observances but in no sense deeply engaged. And yet what is remarkable about both women's 'look', as the 1960s wore on – fashionable hairstyle, intent expression – is how closely it came to conform to the accepted view of the intellectual 1960s woman, as represented by, say, Vanessa Redgrave in Antonioni's *Blow-Up*.

But however strenuous the attempt to reach some kind of accommodation with period norms, to write columns for *Cosmopolitan* or debate divorce in the op-ed pages of the *Sunday Times*, there regularly arises from the 'women's novel' of the 1960s and 1970s a feeling of profound disillusionment, the suspicion that all this image-brokering is not, in the end, good for the writing which it is designed to sustain or for the writer empowered to create it. Byatt's chilling take on the 1960s media circus *The Game* (1967) hinges on the relationship between Julia, a fashionable novelist lured into TV presenting, and her sister Cassandra, an Oxford don. The title refers to a lavish Brontë-esque entertainment involving miniature armies and complex strategic adjustments devised by the sisters when they were children, and there is an anguished moment in which Julia suggests that 'nothing we can do now can possibly measure up to the – the sheer urgency, and beauty and importance of all – all we imagined', adding for good measure that she 'never meant to write the sort of stuff I write'. Julia, we deduce, is a lightweight, swimming into harbour on the tides of the time, yearning to write what she calls 'a real book – a complicated book – not about myself' but perpetually side-tracked by the 1960s charivari of which she is such a conspicuous ornament. In the end, fascinated by what she regards as Cassandra's academically self-absorbed detachment from the world, she determines to write a novel in which a thinly disguised version of her sister is the central character. On receipt of *A Sense of Glory*, Cassandra bolts the door of her college room, seals up the cracks and crevices, switches on the gas and kills herself.

CHAPTER 15

Reaching Out

> The ignorance I have so far encountered – and not simply of cultural matters but of the world lying beyond the borders of daily experience – has an almost medieval quality.
>
> Shiva Naipaul while on an Arts Council-sponsored writers' tour of Humberside, 1978

One of the highlights of Messrs Heinemann's catalogue for spring 1951 was the arrival onto the shelves of J. B. Priestley's novel *Festival at Farbridge*. It is not, strictly speaking, one of Priestley's better books: the jokes are a little too forced; the endless high spirits a little too willed; the cast a little too populous; and their characteristics a little – no, a great deal – too stylised. There is, moreover, as one passes from twinkling Commodore Tribe, with his plans to incorporate this somnolent South Midlands town into the Festival of Britain, to Laura Casey, the perennially resourceful girl who helps him to accomplish them, a sense that Priestley is beginning to feel the strain – not merely the understandable pressure applied to an author who has been working at full pelt for thirty years, but the anxiety of a man who suspects that he is about to be put out to grass, that the professionalisation of English literature which he sees going on all around is leaving him with very little room for manoeuvre. The novel's preface, cast in the form of an extensive dedication addressed to Priestley's long-term commercial sponsor, A. S. Frere of Heinemann, makes this point with some force, what with its remarks about a return to 'the old comic tradition of storytelling, which is not yet dead' and its baleful sign-off ('I don't suppose this book is a contribution to literature, which is rapidly becoming something that hardly anybody is allowed to contribute to'). As well as offering one of his panoramic treatments of the state of England, Priestley is also in hot pursuit of the state of English literature, and what he discovers, here inside the Farbridge lecture halls, is emphatically not to his taste.

Nowhere is this disillusionment with contemporary literary practice more marked than in the lecturers who are eventually chosen to add gravitas to a programme otherwise given over to drama and the popular arts. One of them is the poet Rufus Grope, who recites a set of verses entitled 'Menippus On Half-day Closing' – a fine old modernist hotchpotch in which 'Utter mendacities / Are almost suppressed / Except in the case of the girl with too many shoes'. But Grope, it turns out, is merely an incidental diversion. Priestley's real scorn is reserved for 'the very distinguished critic' and Cambridge don Leonard Mortory. Although Farbridge is represented as a cultural desert, one or two of the better-informed locals have heard of Mr Mortory. Laura, for instance, has been introduced to his work by her impeccably high-minded, *New Statesman*-reading, Third Programme-listening landlady. A 'dusty-looking man, who stared hard through heavy tortoise-shell spectacles and kept tightening his lips as if some dreadful crisis were on hand', Mr Mortory is the author of such critical works as *Disavowals*, *Rejections*, *Exclusions* and a new book, *Refusals*. His critical credo, somewhat haltingly expressed, is that the 'so-called great novelists' – names mentioned include Fielding, Sterne, Dickens and Thackeray – 'don't offer us the organised co-relation of critical experience and fantasy we demand. They lack the absolute integrity we insist upon'. Invited to Farbridge to lecture on 'The Novel: A Revaluation', Mr Mortory can be heard proclaiming the need for 'a small, distinct, self-conscious elite, entirely separated from the new mass culture . . . a few small groups here and there capable of appreciating', by which time the masquerade is complete. There is no doubt about it. Mr Mortory is a portrait of F. R. Leavis.

And here, for all its longueurs and its elegiac glances back to a more communal world which Priestley supposes to be fading away, *Festival at Farbridge* strikes a prophetic note, for it is one of the first English novels to hint that the future of English literature rests on its institutionalisation: that a genuinely popular taste is ripe to be replaced by something supervised by more exacting arbiters, that the future, or at any rate a substantial part of the future, lies in the spectacle of Leavis, with his proscriptions and his austerity, his jargon and his insistence that literary appreciation is something that can only be enjoyed by a very small percentage of the population. At the heart of Priestley's complaint is a conviction that ordinary people are being driven away from books by an excess of interpretation, that the fastidiousness of a Mr Mortory (or an F. R. Leavis) is, in the end, designed to limit entry to an arena that should be open to all. As Laura puts it when attending to one of Mr Mortory's harangues, 'I don't want to be one of a small, self-conscious elite. It sounds awful. Just an arty-smarty little gang, dreadfully pleased with themselves, out of touch with most of life.' (Mr Mortory's original would no doubt have countered that most of life was not worth keeping in touch with.) But whether the culprit was Leavis, or, as seems much more likely, the revolution in mass entertainment to which Leavis was reacting, an awareness that the world of books was rapidly being returned to the status of a minority culture hangs over the cultural landscape of the immediately post-war era.

The absence of the book – or at any rate the serious book – from most kinds of cultural activity practised beyond London is, for example, a feature of much of the fiction that touches, however incidentally, on post-war provincial life. In Penelope Fitzgerald's *The Bookshop* (1978), based on first-hand experience in late 1950s Suffolk, the shop's clientele is content with the memoirs of retired generals and SAS men; the titles supplied to the lending library come in three categories – sought-after, acceptable and 'frankly old and unwanted' – and the most desirable item among the new library stock is Harold Nicolson's biography of Queen Mary. In J. L. Carr's *How Steeple Sinderby Wanderers Won the FA Cup* (1975), set in a remote fenland hamlet, the pull of literature is even less distinct, sufficiently remote to obtain Joe Gidner, employed in devising verses for greeting cards, the job of producing a history of the local football team on the grounds that 'writing's your living'. Sinderby's only connection with the world of books is a woman who writes romantic novels and a long-dead folk poet whose anniversary is celebrated by the local schoolchildren. Even with the educated middle classes there is a sense that 'serious' literature exists in a remote, inaccessible vacuum – expensive, difficult to procure, fenced off by its producers. There is a rather significant moment in David Lodge's *How Far Can You Go?* (1980), set in the early 1960s, in which a couple named Michael and Miriam visit their old school friend Polly, now a successful journalist, and her television producer husband Jeremy in their newly converted Kentish oast house. Among the heap of desirable modern consumer artefacts that litter the shelves is 'a new hardback novel in its pale yellow jacket that had been widely reviewed in the past few days'. Like the Japanese hi-fi equipment and a kitchen 'straight out of the colour supplements', a hardback novel is, we infer, a luxury item, well beyond Michael and Miriam's modest middle-class resources.

And it was still in the hardback novel that the future of 'serious fiction' was thought to reside, however reluctant novel readers, seduced by the lure of cheap paperbacks, were to buy them. Anthony Blond's *The Publishing Game* (1971) offers an amusing account of the many reasons why the potential purchaser of a newly published hardback won't find it anywhere in their local W. H. Smith ('It is not the fault of that much-satirised, near-monopoly . . . that they haven't got *It Happened on Sunday*, published by Rosencrantz & Guildenstern at £1.95 and widely reviewed. It is rather the fault of the British public'). Blond, an enterprising independent publisher who devoted much of a family trust fund to underwriting a stream of first novels, once circularised his authors with a photocopied sheet explaining why their books were not available at the Didcot railway station bookstall. It might be wondered, amid all this evidence of exclusivity, this fundamental failure to connect, exactly how those people interested in 'serious' literature went about feeding their sensibilities, here in a world where hardback novels increasingly assumed the status of luxury goods, and the answer is that, generally, information was acquired piecemeal.

In the absence of any formal method of communication, how was serious literature to reach out to the vast subterranean audience whose members might possibly glance at the review pages of a daily newspaper or listen to a literary discussion on the Third Programme, but for whom the price of a hardback novel – 10s 6d in the 1950s, rising to 21s in the following decade – was prohibitively expensive? One solution was to send the writer out into places where potential readers might be found, thereby tapping into a tradition that went back to the middle of the nineteenth century. Many a high-minded Victorian celebrity had deplored what seemed to be the defilement of literature by commerce: Carlyle provoked a famous row with Thackeray by comparing the writing of *Cornhill to Cairo* – a travel book subsidised by free passage around the Mediterranean courtesy of the P&O – to a blind fiddler playing the Highland ferries. At the same time, especially in the aftermath of Dickens's immensely successful public readings, even the high-minded Victorian celebrity was uneasily aware that a great deal of money and personal goodwill could be generated by author appearances. Thackeray's own lecture tours of the late 1850s were a kind of triumphal pageant around the county towns, punctuated by public banquets and the presence of admiring crowds. Despite these early stirrings, nothing that we would recognise as bearing the least resemblance to the contemporary literary festival was in existence until the interwar years. Even then, the emphasis was on placing the author in front of his, or her, fans rather than selling books. On the other hand, the programme of the *Sunday Times*-sponsored 'Book Exhibition', staged at the Dorland Hall, Lower Regent Street, over a fortnight in the autumn of 1936, sounds remarkably similar to modern arrangements. Aldous Huxley reads from his work; Alec Waugh sizes up 'A Storyteller's Workshop', with Ralph Straus in the chair; Graham Greene, already marked down as a Catholic writer, investigates 'A Novelist's Belief', while at the popular end of the spectrum the England cricket captain Douglas Jardine examines 'Cricketing Fact and Fiction' and X. M. Boulestin – the 1930s equivalent of Jamie Oliver – appraises 'Cookery Books'.

Like most formal manifestations of the mainstream literary culture of the interwar era, the regular *Sunday Times* events took place in London. If the Festival of Britain – much derided at the time and bitterly complained of by Conservative newspapers – had one long-term effect, it was as the symbol of official determination to bring the arts to the public by way of regional and local networks. But while the Cheltenham Literary Festival (founded in 1949) actually pre-dates the celebrations at Farbridge, and elsewhere, it was not until the early 1960s that the paraphernalia associated with the modern festival – international visitors; minor controversy; commercial sponsorship – began to make its mark. The 'International Writers' Conference' convened by Orwell's widow Sonia at the 1962 Edinburgh Festival, with panel appearances from Malcolm Muggeridge, Rebecca West and Mary McCarthy, was a notable trailblazer. Not to be outdone, and conscious of the recent arrival of the Penguin paperback of *Lady Chatterley's Lover* in the bookshops, the Cheltenham Festival of the same year advertised an eye-catching seminar on 'Sex in Literature'. Of the four-strong panel, Kingsley Amis accused Jane Austen of writing 'pecuniary pornography', Joseph Heller suggested that the makers of mink coats had corrupted more young women than any book, and Carson McCullers, labouring under the disadvantage of being drunk, proposed that 'so long as a book is true and beautiful' it could not be obscene. The impact of this discussion was magnified in the public eye by one of its emotional by-blows. This was Amis's decision in 1963 to leave his wife of fifteen years for the festival organiser, Elizabeth Jane Howard.

If there was a drawback to these literary conventions, with their promise of personality clashes and intrigue, it was that they were largely preaching to the converted: the middle-class book-lovers who flocked to Cheltenham in the 1960s did not constitute a new audience. They were part of an existing audience whose curiosity had been piqued. Moreover, their rationale was determinedly commercial: the point of inviting Joseph Heller to address the Gloucestershire intelligentsia was to make money for the festival by selling copies of Heller's books. Behind the manoeuvring that led to the Festival of Britain in 1951, on the other hand, was a presumption that bringing 'culture' – fairly narrowly defined at this point – to the people was the duty of the state, especially when that culture seemed to be threatened by everything from imported American paperbacks to the Light Programme. But how was Leviathan to fulfil its obligations? If a single principle can be said to underlie public expenditure on literature in the three decades after the Second World War, it was that such things are better done at arm's length. While this modus operandi can be traced back to an understandable post-war distaste for the cultural commissars of totalitarian states, it meant that those charged with distributing whatever funds were available seldom appeared to their advantage when statements of intent were called for. It also meant that the Arts Council sometimes looked to be keener on shoring up existing arrangements, preserving what seemed to be fading away rather than searching for new audiences and different forms of engagement with the wider public. Pre-1966, for example, the tiny sums handed out to literature went entirely to individual poets or to organisations connected with poetry: a Poetry Panel (1949–50); the foundation of a Poetry Library at the National Book League HQ in Albemarle Street; the creation of a Poetry Book Society (both 1953). By the mid-1960s the total sum of something under £5,000 a year consisted of grants to the Apollo Society, an organisation which arranged verse readings, the Poetry Society, a handful of poetry festivals and the holder of the council's solitary bursary.

At this point two hitherto independent streams – one representing the publishing industry, the other the resources of the state – began tentatively to converge. In 1964 the Publishers' Association pressed the

Poetry Panel to recommend to the Arts Council that it should transform itself into a fully fledged Literature Panel with an expanded membership. This proposal was accepted, and the resultant body was charged with advising the council on ways of helping literature, particularly imaginative literature, including poetry. Meanwhile, a reforming arts minister, Aneurin Bevan's widow Jennie Lee, had published a government White Paper entitled *A Policy for the Arts*. This took the unusual step – unusual, that is, for a western democracy – of regarding the artist as a wage-earner like any other worker, and observed, additionally, that painters, poets, writers and sculptors were often lost to the arts for want of comparatively small sums of money which would subsidise their apprenticeships. In the following year, the government grant to the Arts Council was raised from just under £4 million to £5.7 million. Literature, under the supervision of the eminent musicologist Eric Walter White, was allotted £63,000. Trivial as this sum was – although it was to increase fourfold over the next decade – its administration clearly posed several problems for White's minuscule staff. The greatest problem of all, perhaps, was the need to establish some first principles. How should literature be subsidised? Should it support individuals or organisations? Which would be better for the condition of literature in Britain? And if one were to have a Literature Panel, who ought to sit on it? How were some of the considerable practical difficulties in underwriting literature to be overcome, and how was the Arts Council's return on its investment to be measured? Should the Literature Department be subsidising individual publications and, if so, which sections of the community should they be targeting? Should it be sending writers out into the community and, if so, to which communities and for what purpose?

Actions were eventually taken in all these areas: grants were distributed; writers were sent on tour; magazines were underwritten. Yet the lack of a guiding principle nearly always impeded any serious investment on literature's behalf. The Literature Panel – to take the department's most conspicuous public face – began its deliberations in January 1966. Long on personnel – twenty-one people sat down at the table – but short on administrative expertise, it began its existence not by concentrating its efforts on how literature might best be subsidised, or trying to discover where subsidy might be needed, but by deciding to extend the help previously given to poets and the number of grants and bursaries available to writers of fiction and non-fiction.

Here, in slight mitigation, it was merely following the stipulations of the annual report for 1965–6, which stated that the panel must go out and find the writers most deserving of help: a recommendation endorsed by the chairman, Cecil Day Lewis. Noting that there were 'good writers' who after ten or twenty years in the profession didn't earn more than £1,000 per annum, Day Lewis declared that 'If we are prepared to pay more than lip service to the art in which our nation has always excelled, we have to do something.'

To this end nearly £18,000-worth of bursaries was distributed in 1966–7; a series of disbursements which prompted critics to enquire: how exactly was this doing anything useful for literature? Significantly, much of this criticism came from within the Arts Council itself, courtesy of its assistant literature director, Charles Osborne, who, unlike the group of poets assembled on the Literature Panel, thought that state subsidy – following the policy of the Arts Council's other departments – should be aimed at organisations, not individuals. 'Spending hundreds of thousands of pounds on encouraging mediocrities to think of themselves as "full-time" writers was both pointless and cruel' Osborne argued. What was needed was a structural solution: a state publishing house, say, underwritten to the tune of £500,000 per annum. As it was, most of the panel's largesse in that year – £50,123 – went on a handful of bursaries, some awards and prizes, small grants to poetry groups and £5,000 in handouts to literary magazines.

The difficulty with Osborne's scheme was its radicalism. Even for the 1960s – a great age for cultural experiment and innovation – this was a step too far for a country that associated state publishing with the satrapies of the Eastern Bloc, and most of whose citizens believed that a writer who struggled to support himself had failed in his profession, like a plumber with an insufficient number of call-outs. Expert guidance from above might have helped, but Jennie Lee, quoted in the *Sunday Times* to the effect that her function was 'merely a permissive one . . . I want simply to make living room for artists to work', gave little indication of her priorities. And so the department soldiered on, often giving the impression that it was having trouble finding projects to spend money on – the secretary of the Poetry Society, which had managed to survive without state aid since 1912, was persuaded that he needed £1,500 a year – and playing into the hands of its free-market detractors with the introduction of four £1,000 Arts Council Prizes for Literature, widely supposed to be favouring anti-establishment material at the expense of anything comparable from the right. Meanwhile, there were problems with the panel itself. Some of its members, while complaining about their advisory role, showed little grasp of the practical realities of publishing.

The view of Osborne, who wrote an agreeably waspish memoir of his time at the Arts Council, was that generally, if asked to discuss an applicant organisation – a cash-strapped little magazine, say, with a precarious circulation – the panel would agree that it was worthless, only to be overcome by a wave of sentiment and urge a grant. That the old-fashioned standards of 'taste' to which Book Society selection panels had clung in the 1930s were becoming increasingly difficult to promulgate became even more evident in the case of individual writers, consideration of whose merits was often stymied by a reluctance to recognise the idea of 'merit' in the first place. 'Untalented' was not a word to be used lightly, Osborne remembered, and he was once rebuked by Maureen Duffy for arguing that one writer whose case had come before the panel was 'better' than another. 'Better', Ms Duffy is supposed to have growled, 'is an elitist word.' By this time, too, the idea of a state publishing house seemed less and less convincing. Not only did the prospect of state-subsidised competition terrify the domestic publishing industry, but the suggestion that such a body was urgently required to publish high-quality manuscripts that could not find a sponsor proved to be ill-founded. Writing to publishers for details, the department failed to find a single example.

Naturally, allowances have to be made. This was uncharted territory both for the state and for arts-world functionaries commissioned, with greater or lesser degrees of enthusiasm, to do the state's bidding. Worse, all of those involved knew that they were likely to attract a torrent of public criticism whatever line they decided to take and whichever contemporary writers and publications they opted to support. But, this caveat having been filed, it is difficult not to regard the early deliberations of the Literature Panel as, in some small sense, the 1960s in miniature: a combination of good intentions, lack of practical expertise and fashionable egalitarianism fatally undermined by a reluctance to take decisions or to establish a theoretical basis on which those decisions might be made. Osborne, who succeeded Eric Walter White in 1971, took a much less emollient line, suggesting in his letter of application that state intervention was required at three points: those at which literature was written, published and bought.

His specific proposals included wider outlets for literary work (including the creation of a first-class magazine exclusively devoted to literature), changes in publishing techniques, discussions with booksellers over the setting up of a proper training scheme, and a plan to sell books in libraries.

These were ambitious proposals – revolutionary, even – which reflected a genuine desire to move the take-up of 'literature' beyond its core audience, yet the prospects for putting them into practice grew hazier from one year to the next. Part of the problem, inevitably, had to do with inadequate funding. Looking at the sums of money laid out on literature, in comparison with the amounts available for other art forms, it is difficult not to conclude that the Arts Council barely advanced beyond tokenism. In 1973–4, for example, out of a total grant of £17 million, exactly £146,000 went to literature. In 1975–6 the figures were, respectively, £24 million and £255,000, the latter broken down into £103,000 to institutions, £26,000 to small presses, £45,500 to literary magazines, £8,190 in grants to publishers, £7,560 on two university creative writing fellowships, £35,000 in awards to thirty-five listed writers, and £9,705 on writers' tours and writers in schools.

All this, necessarily, had only a tiny impact on the Literature Department's aim of supporting writers, increasing the number of outlets available to them, expanding their audience and subsidising the publication of work that might otherwise have foundered on the rocks of commercial viability. The grants awarded were minimal – an average of £1,000 in 1975–6. Small publishers looking for help to underwrite their lists found that they were caught up in a spiral of increased outlay and diminishing returns. As Peter Owen put it in a mid-1970s jeremiad on the state of fiction publishing: 'The problem of ever-increasing costs – firmly linked with higher prices and reduced sales in a vicious circle – can only be solved, in part at least, by making available to publishers substantially more money in the form of grants through the Arts Council.' Significantly, such bona fide successes that the department did manage to chalk up came in the form of modest schemes, conceived with the aim of encouraging ordinary people to try their hand at writing. *New Poetry I* (1975), the first of ten such anthologies published in the course of the next decade, attracted 42,000 submissions from 10,000 poets, 170 of whom saw their work in print and were paid fees on a scale far higher than that of the average poetry magazine. There was also a series of international poetry festivals – high-profile and not without controversy, as when Joseph Brodsky, newly expelled from the Soviet Union, was invited to speak in 1972.

To lack of money could be added a difficulty endemic to any kind of arts funding in so comparatively small a country as the UK: the fact that as only a tiny percentage of the population is engaged in the creative arts, whenever its representatives are gathered together – whether to dispense largesse or judge literary prizes – many of them will know both each other and the people who stand to benefit from their decisions. If the supposed cliquishness of the panel provoked criticism in the matter of grants for individual writers, then the problem was far worse when it came to one of Osborne's most cherished projects: the funding of literary magazines. The long-running controversy over the *New Review*, fifty issues of which benefited from Arts Council subsidy in the period 1973–8, with the sum involved rising to £22,000 in 1975–6, hinged not so much on the merits of the magazine as the thought that it was merely providing employment for writers who were happily engaged elsewhere. Auberon Waugh, a thorn in Osborne's flesh throughout the decade, judged it no better and no worse than similar literary journals of the past. The drawback was that, apart from being more expensively produced, 'it is *exactly the same*. The same writers write just as boringly about the same people as they always have done.' Even panel members lobbied for a diversification in editorial policy that would allay the fear that the 'same old people' were colluding.

The case for the *New Review* naturally rested on the calibre of its contributors, but it could have been a great deal stronger had distribution arrangements come anywhere close to the lustre of the names on the masthead. As it was, sales hovered at around 4,000 copies at a cover price of 90p (later reduced to 75p) with circulation bumped up artificially by the Arts Council policy of supplying copies gratis to public libraries. W. H. Smith was reluctant to stock it, and advertising revenue rarely rose above a trickle – only three of the 128 pages of the summer 1978 number were devoted to adverts, and one of those was taken up by the Arts Council itself. Looking back, Osborne considered the five-year sponsorship one of his finest moments ('Those fifty issues . . . stand as a remarkable achievement, and one of which the Arts Council's Literature Department can be proud') and attributed its demise not only to poor business management but to envy, yet even he might have conceded the detrimental effect of its thoroughly unbusinesslike approach.

Exactly the same degree of controversy attended a highly ambitious scheme aimed at increasing the number of people reading 'serious' books and widening the demographic of the people who wrote them. This was the New Fiction Society – essentially a state-sanctioned book club offering newly published novels at discount prices. Such was the pitch of official enthusiasm that over £34,000 was spent on establishing the project in 1974–5, with a further £26,000 – over a tenth of the entire literature grant – a year later. A substantial fraction of this was laid out on a national advertising campaign, featuring an eight-question quiz beneath a portrait gallery ('Is this a working-class novelist?', etc.). Early signs were promising: 2,000 readers signed up; another 5,000 were confidently anticipated. Much hung on the attractions of the selected books, but these, for all the talk of rooting out promising unknowns, tended to reflect the contents of newspaper review pages. Critics complained that Doris Lessing, Malcolm Bradbury and Simon Raven already had their constituencies: why should they be buttressed by public subsidy? The suspicion that the society was just another upper-middlebrow book club neither added greatly to the sales of individual titles, nor, with 2,000 members (a figure that proved impossible to increase) choosing four books a year at 25 per cent discount on the published price, did it come anywhere near to covering its costs.

As for the overall statistics, a statement from January 1977, by which time the scheme was in its death throes, confirmed that since October 1974 the society had sold 13,000 books to the public at a cost to the taxpayer of £60,500. It would have been cheaper, one detractor alleged, for the Arts Council to have bought the books at full price and given them away to passers-by in the street outside their Piccadilly headquarters. Amid this volley of recriminations and counter-recriminations there is a certain amount to be said in the New Fiction Society's defence. Its selections were not entirely middlebrow – Dinah Brooke and Ian McEwan featured on early lists – although its encouragement of new and unpublicised authors was, at best, half-hearted. Informed critics declared that, given long-term support, it had the potential to transform the character of the patronage of fiction, creating a book club that could have taken over the role of public libraries at a time when these institutions were thought to be failing in their support of books with minority readerships. Where the scheme foundered was on the time-honoured reluctance of the educated public to spend money on books.

Like The *New Review*, the New Fiction Society was a promising idea that failed spectacularly, and the conspicuousness of the failure had serious implications for literature funding in the decade that followed. Meanwhile, there was another way in which the department could fulfil its remit of taking literature beyond its metropolitan base and out into the world at large. The concept of the 'writers' tour' was originally suggested by the novelist and playwright Julian Mitchell to the Literature Panel's incoming chairman, Angus Wilson, in the late 1960s. The idea was enthusiastically taken up, both by Wilson and the then Arts Council chairman, Lord Goodman, not least because it deflected attention from the continuing rows about bursaries and prizes, alternately stigmatised in the press as an old boys' network and a lottery. An initial excursion, led by Wilson, was arranged to North Wales; Mitchell, as the originator of the scheme, would direct a second trip to Lancashire. Assembling around him a praetorian guard of Nell Dunn, Christopher Logue and Margaret Drabble, Wilson arrived at the Bulkeley Arms Hotel, Beaumaris, Anglesey, early in March 1969 – not the ideal month, Drabble recalled, for a jaunt around the rain-sodden terrain. Undeterred, the team ventured boldly into draughty libraries where, as Drabble recalled, 'many a solitary librarian sat patiently amidst her quiet stock', delivered lectures in English to audiences in Welsh-speaking schools and, on entering branches of W. H. Smith to sign books, were invariably asked by customers where the greetings cards were kept.

Though Drabble, at least, found the experience 'hectic, non-glamorous and very stimulating', it was acknowledged that points of contact between these cultural tribunes and members of the public were sometimes hard to locate; when they existed, it tended to be a consequence of indirect exposure to the mass media. Some of the schoolchildren were familiar with Nell Dunn's work through having watched the film of her novel *Up the Junction*; others recognised Drabble for her appearances on a television programme called *Junior Points of View*. On several occasions, though, the tour members began their engagements with the vagrant humanity spread out before them in the stark awareness that no one present knew who they were or had read a line of anything they had written. Perhaps this was to be expected. Equally unpredictable was the audience reaction. When, at one gathering, Wilson announced that the theme would be 'Death' and, to that end, read from a suitable scene in *The Middle Age of Mrs Eliot*, several people came up afterwards to say that they found it 'helpful'.

Efforts to establish the precise impact of this attempt to take literature to the people were complicated by the absence of any benchmarks. A full classroom did not necessarily imply interest: many of the audience had simply been press-ganged into attending. More valuable were stray comments from listeners, such as the teenage boy who assured Wilson that 'I had got something across to them.' Nonetheless, the tour was judged to have fulfilled its objectives, after which Mitchell, Adrian Henri, John McGrath and Iris Murdoch were despatched to Bolton. Murdoch's biographer records that she undertook twenty-one school visits in a week. But for an account of the depths which the writers' tour could plumb when the going was bad, one need look no further than Shiva Naipaul's record of his trip to Humberside in early 1978 in the company of the poets Patricia Beer and Edwin Brock and his fellow novelist Gabriel Josipovici. Fuelled by a belief that art ought to be universal, and guiltily recalling his status as a past beneficiary of Arts Council largesse, Naipaul arrived in Hull to discover that cultural life had 'ground to a kind of standstill', that the staff of the local Arts Council office resembled 'a beleaguered garrison' and that the university – at this point harbouring Philip Larkin, Andrew Motion and Douglas Dunn on its staff – had no impact on the town.

The tour began on a Monday morning at a school in Snaith, where fifty 15- and 16-year-olds had been assembled. Even as he begins to read, Naipaul decides, 'I realise I have chosen the wrong passage. That it is all going over their heads.' There were no hands raised. In the end someone enquires: 'Do you live in a mud hut?' On the following day the caravan presses on to Hornsea School to entertain the A level English students. Here Naipaul is distressed to find that the teacher in charge knows nothing about him and that only one pupil can be persuaded to ask a question. Next stop is Kingston High School, where, after a long, post-presentation silence, a teacher wonders why poetry doesn't rhyme anymore. In the evening the team repairs to a local hotel to address an audience of twelve people. By Wednesday the party is negotiating the challenge of Newland High School, allegedly more academic in tone and rife with rumour 'of a girl who might actually go to university'. Alas, this paragon is 'too shy' to reveal herself. Later, at the university's adult education department, where forty people have braved the chill of the Humberside night, there seems the brief prospect of genuine cultural engagement, but it turns out that the students have been 'ruined by their academic training' and ask about technique and symbolism. Subsequently the path winds down and ever down. On Thursday morning at Market Weighton School Naipaul asks the English teacher 'What can I assume they know?' But all intellectual bets are off: 'You can assume nothing at all.'

Against considerable odds, the children respond well to a short story, prompting Naipaul to reflect that 'If it were all like this, my week in Humberside just might be considered worthwhile.' But this proves to be a false hope. That evening, at a public library, accompanied by Edwin Brock, Naipaul encounters an audience of five people. In the ensuing quarrel with Sandy, the Arts Council's representative, he is informed that 'We've got to go on *trying*.' But why go on trying, Naipaul wonders. 'We were achieving nothing. We were really no more than a circus, a collection of curious individuals. Humberside has no need of us.' Shortly afterwards, he and his fellow emissaries from the world of literary culture return to London. Later Naipaul receives a letter from Sandy assuring him that twelve of his books have been sold during the week and suggesting that 'there is interest in what you have to say, despite your fears to the contrary'.

Was there? Naipaul's is clearly a loaded account, the reaction of a man who is determined to find fault irrespective of the conditions in which he finds himself and makes no concessions to the difficulties experienced by the people he comes up against. The kindlier Angus Wilson, to whom Nell Dunn complained that a headteacher wasn't interested in her visit, suggested that she failed to take account of the pressure the man was under, a workload that allowed 'no possibility of an interest in anything else'. Generally speaking the apparent success – or failure – of the writers' tour rested on the temperament of the participants. Those who congratulated themselves that they were communicating something to their audience came away satisfied with the results. The Naipauls of this world, who arrived with a suspicion that they had fetched up in a cultural desert, were bound to have their worst suspicions confirmed. If there was a wider difficulty, it lay in the piecemeal nature of the enterprise. The writers' tours were one-offs, departing periodically to what appeared to be arbitrarily chosen parts of the country, travelling at lightning pace from one venue to another, often with only a sketchy plan of what they intended to do, or what response was required from the audience encouraged, or bidden, to attend. There was little in the way of follow-up. It was no wonder, in these circumstances, that the staff at some of the schools involved regarded them as an unwelcome distraction or that some of the children were either bored or cowed into silence.

Naipaul's trip to Humberside coincided with a determined effort to detach the Literature Panel from its anchorage in a world of genteel amateurism. Under the supervision of Melvyn Bragg, appointed chairman in 1977, there was at least an attempt to construct a proper literature policy, accompanied by moves to reduce the size of the panel. Still, most of the evidence suggests that what money the panel did dispense was largely being wasted. A report on the grant-awarding scheme concluded that no book written with the aid of a grant would not have been written without it. Osborne's bleak summary of the situation was that 'A number of mediocrities have received grants from us in the past few years, and we ought not to have been handing out money to these writers.' Who, it might reasonably have been enquired, was benefiting from literature funding? This was certainly a question that occurred to the compilers of the 1984 pamphlet *The Glory of the Garden*, which set out the Arts Council's plans for the coming decade. Here, in a climate of fiscal austerity, the Literature Department's budget was cut by almost half, from just under £1 million to £500,000 on the grounds that whereas drama and the opera would decline almost to extinction without public subsidy, literature, which would always be underwritten by a large and profitable commercial industry, would not. Other than its support for poetry, the impact of state subsidy for books, and any attempt to enlarge the audience for the literary culture they represented, was 'highly marginal'. Osborne, made redundant in the wake of this retrenchment, produced a telling valediction: 'If those who, over the years, have been crying out simply for more public money for literature had been able to produce sound reasons for spending more, then literature would no doubt have flourished in the Arts Council's development plans and we would now be contemplating perhaps a doubling rather than a halving of its spending on literature.'

What could be said about this decades-long battle to establish some first principles about the distribution of public money to writers, publishers and their audiences – a battle which, when it came to it, had ended in the downgrading (financial and symbolic) of literature's status? What, in the end, were the White-and-Osborne Literature Department's achievements? If we are to believe the ever-sceptical Osborne, it had subsidised the publication of a number of books which would probably have been published with or without the Arts Council's support. It had kept afloat, in some cases temporarily, a number of high-class, small-circulation literary magazines (unlike the *New Review*, the *London Magazine* appeared to live a charmed life and continued to receive subsidy during and beyond this period) which would probably otherwise have perished, and indirectly augmented the careers of several of the British novelists who made their debuts in the 1970s and 1980s, among them Ian McEwan, William Boyd and Graham Swift. It had taken writers out into the provincial margins and exhibited them, with varying degrees of success, to audiences of schoolchildren and the paying public. Perhaps most usefully of all, it had sponsored several anthologies of poetry and short fiction which offered a platform for talented amateurs who would otherwise have gone unpublished. Meanwhile, the controversies in which it had become embroiled had, however unfairly, reinforced the literary world's reputation for cliquishness and backstairs intrigue. At the same time, and however unwittingly, it exposed a dilemma with which nearly every intervention in the field of state subsidy for the creative arts eventually has to contend: the difficulty of striking a balance between the art itself and the interests of the people administering it. Put an entity charged with expanding public take-up of literature and the capacity of writers to produce it in the hands of a bureaucrat, and the literature itself is all too easily lost sight of. Put it in the hands of other writers, and the first casualty is likely to be a grasp of practical reality. No one came close to solving this dilemma in the period 1950–84, and it would be a very sanguine observer of the contemporary scene who suggested that anyone was close to solving it now.

A. S. Byatt and the 1960s

'Novels won't go away.'
'That remains to be seen.'

Conversation between Frederica Potter and Edmund Wilkie in *A Whistling Woman* (2002)

A. S. Byatt's four-volume novel sequence about life in post-1950 Britain, or rather certain specialised aspects of that life, begins with *The Virgin in the Garden* (1978), set mostly in the Coronation year of 1953. At this point the two main characters are the Potter sisters, Stephanie and Frederica, the one a charming and intelligent bluestocking lately down from Newnham, the other a gauche and irascible schoolgirl. By the time of *Still Life* (1985), the action is more or less divided between Suez-era Cambridge, where Frederica is getting into her intellectual and sexual stride, and the family home in North Yorkshire, where Stephanie has mysteriously (but not, we infer, mistakenly) married the brooding local curate. Here, with half the sequence still to run, Byatt takes the altogether dramatic step – fatal or foolhardy, depending on your point of view – of killing off nice, dependable Stephanie via the agency of an unearthed fridge. The remainder of the proceedings – *Babel Tower* (1996) and *A Whistling Woman* (2002) – is her younger sister's to command. While each contains a central situation that is somehow extraneous to her – a court case involving a supposedly obscene book, the founding of a 'new' university up on the North York Moors – it is she, self-consciously alert to the shifting tides of the Age of Aquarius, who operates at their core.

Both *Babel Tower* and *A Whistling Woman* are, in their various ways and with varying degrees of engagement, responses to the literary climate of the 1960s, its artistic 'happenings', its determined search for freedom of expression, its keenness on experiment, the lure, and the threat, of new media that may very soon replace the old. Not that the gaze which Byatt (b.1936) turns on the world of her young womanhood is in any way straightforward. *Babel Tower*, in particular, is built on a confidence trick, in which the illusion that this is Frederica reacting spontaneously to some of the cultural phenomena of her time is invariably trumped by the awareness that Byatt's is a long-term perspective, reflective yet in its way still provisional, but always arrived at by way of information acquired with hindsight. And so Byatt, who studied English at Cambridge in the 1950s and claimed to have begun her first novel as a respite from Leavis's lectures, is implicated in Frederica's passage through a particular quadrant of the literary world, in her view of fiction generally and the particular book she eventually writes, or compiles herself, while at the same time effortlessly transcending them. She knows more than her creation, is not above correcting some of the assumptions she brings to the world around her, and frequently concocts lines of dialogue which, while perfectly suited to Frederica's voice, are there to make retrospective cultural points. There is, for example, a dreadful moment – dreadful, that is, in its implications for anyone engaged in the teaching of English Literature – when a friend tells Frederica that she ought to write a novel. 'I don't have any ideas' Frederica crisply replies. 'I've been educated out of it. Have you noticed people who write novels never studied English Literature?'

There are two very substantial ghosts looming over the desk at which Frederica compiles her first readers' reports for the publishing firm of Bowers & Elder and writes her first, far from tentative, reviews for a magazine called *Spyglass*, represented as 'a cultural weekly founded by a minor member of Bloomsbury, surviving with a precarious circulation and a disproportionate reputation for wit and influence'. One of them, clearly, is Leavis, whose effect on her is made to seem far more ominous by being linked to a much more tangible authority figure: 'She felt about her father as most of her generation felt about Dr Leavis, that anything she could conceivably produce must fall short of his high requirements. Her writing was clandestine notes, out of his gaze.' Which, one might add, is a fair description of the early drafts of *The Shadow of the Sun* (1964), scratched out in the Cambridge lecture rooms. The other is Kingsley Amis. The undergraduate Frederica has already had her run-ins with Amis, attending his lecture to the university Literary Society, disliking *Lucky Jim* for its readiness to judge the female characters for 'bad make-up and arty skirts', dismissing with a flourish contemporary approval of Dixon's engagement with the snobbish pretensions of Bloomsbury or *Brideshead* cliquishness on the grounds that 'if you were going to set up childish irresponsibility as a model of innocence she supposed she would rather have Charles Ryder and Sebastian Flyte in the garden from which they would inevitably be expelled'. But he turns up again when Frederica, teaching the extramural class that is a refuge from a third authority figure – her soon to be ex-husband – chances upon a taxi driver who confesses that 'he laughed like a drain' over Jim's famous burning of the bedclothes, without being able to articulate why.

Frederica's real complaint, you presume, is not with Amis-style slapstick, or supposedly moral judgements which turn out to be entirely arbitrary – although she dislikes them both – but with stylisation, the subjugation of complex fictive material into preordained patterns: 1960s fiction, she implies, is a matter of identifying a small, individual constituency and appealing to it. Her novel-reviewing for *Spyglass* relies not so much on aesthetic judgements as the straightforward identification of milieux – Amis territory, Murdochian moral intricacy, Snow corridors. The need to classify is even more pronounced in the manuscripts Frederica appraises for Bowers & Elder, which seem to have had all the individuality squeezed out of them in the struggle to strike some kind of representative chord. The first batch includes *The Voyage of the Silver Ship*, a Tolkien-style allegory, *Mad Dogs and Englishmen*, a priapic picaresque and *A Thing Apart*, another of those sensitive young-woman-at-Cambridge novels which Frederica, as a former sensitive young woman at Cambridge herself, so roundly despises. A fourth typescript, *Daily Bread*, a transparently autobiographical novel about a clergyman who loses his faith, written by his despairing wife, turns out to be rather good and is accepted for publication. Later, when Frederica graduates to the helm of a highbrow television programme called *Through the Looking Glass*, one of her guests will be Julia Corbett, an older woman 'somewhere between a lady novelist and a woman novelist', the titles of whose books – *The Bright Prison* and *The Toy Box* – are 'witty variations on confinement'. Here Byatt is being scrupulously accurate about her source material – the mid-1960s harboured several real-life Julia Corbetts – but also acknowledging a tradition in which at least a small part of her own work resides. *The Virgin in the Garden* and *Still Life* contain several trapped women and Byatt, on the evidence of autobiographical fragments strewn around her early work, looks as if she may have been one herself.

Frederica's own first work, *Laminations*, is another scrupulous reflection of prevailing tastes: an example of the fashionable 1960s preoccupation with cut-and-paste and collage; an attempt not to pursue the old Forsterian ideal of connectedness but to insist on the advantages of separation and detachment. Its significance is both personal to Frederica, who has decided she can only create things by cannibalising other people's creations, and central to the era in its quest for a novelty that was inextricably bound up in 'experiment' and 'freedom'. *Babel Tower*, in particular, is full of despatches from the cultural front line, excited talk about the 1965 Poetry extravaganza at the Albert Hall ('They were all high, they were all spaced out. Adrian Mitchell read a poem about Vietnam. It was full of enthusiasm and incredibly tedious'), and emblematic figures determined to narrow the gap between literature and popular culture. Pride of place in this assemblage is 'Mickey Impey', a 'Liverpool poet and performer', author of *Naughty Poems for Bad Boys and Girls*, who makes a terrific nuisance of himself on the schools visit undertaken by the government committee investigating the teaching of English, prattles about Blake and is, we are given to understand, simply a disruptive influence.

More sinister than Impey's narcissism are the deliberations that accompany the launch of the new university in *A Whistling Woman*. Here the students demand to be allowed to study 'important new things. Theories. Literary theory. Political theory.' The vice chancellor, who argues that literary theory is meaningless without knowledge of more than one grammar and more than one syntax (the students aren't keen on languages, finding them 'hard') is told that the undergraduate body regards grammar as 'a control system'. Unlike many an anatomist of the 1960s – Kingsley Amis, say, in *I Want it Now* (1968) or Simon Raven in *Places Where They Sing* (1970) – Byatt never passes an explicit judgement on these assertions, on Mickey Impey, who appears to believe that school curricula are designed to brainwash children into serfdom, or on universities in which intellectual rigour is sacrificed for faddishness. On the other hand, *Babbletower*, the novel prosecuted for obscenity, which concerns an imaginary community bent on 'an experiment in freedom', ends with the imposition of a brutal tyranny, while the new university descends into anarchic chaos. Perhaps, in the end, Leavis had the last laugh.

CHAPTER 16

University English II

> The great fault of the Leavis position has been the belief that literature and its study can do more for us than is really possible.
>
> David Holbrook

> The only critical wisdom I know is that there is no method except yourself. Everything else is imposture – there is only oneself.
>
> Harold Bloom

A Movement-era journalist commissioned to write a feature article assessing the impact of the Oxford English school on contemporary literature would have been struck by a curious paradox. On the one hand, there were plenty of Oxford dons – half a dozen of them at least – busily at large in the review pages of the intellectual weeklies and contributing to the cultural debates of the day. On the other, scarcely any of them specialised in what was beginning to be known as 'English Studies'. John Sparrow was a distinguished Latinist; Hugh Trevor-Roper and A. L. Rowse historians; Maurice Bowra a classicist-cum-university administrator. The solitary exception was Lord David Cecil, an old-school belles-lettrist, the titles of whose critical works – *The Fine Art of Reading* or *The Stricken Deer*, his study of Cowper – perfectly convey the kind of gentlemanly and rather old-fashioned scholarship in which he dealt. This is not to disparage Lord David's accomplishments, either as critic or biographer – his life of Max Beerbohm (1964) is still the standard account – merely to note that the view of literature, and of developments in the study of literature, taken by Oxford in the 1950s and 1960s was at best backward-looking and at worst deeply reactionary. Sparrow was commonly known to the reading public for a series of BBC talks on such topics as 'Revolting Students', 'Equal Rights' and 'Beards' – none of which he approved of in the least. Trevor-Roper spent much of the late

1950s engaged in a controversy with Evelyn Waugh on obscure aspects of recusant history. Bowra had already begun to play a commanding role in the reminiscences of *Brideshead*-generation memoirists. Each of them exercised a significant influence over the minds, and by extension the behaviour, of several generations of devoted acolytes. The memorial volume put together after Bowra's death in 1971 is a kind of cataract of respectful goodwill. And Betjeman ('Shall any of us who knew him enjoy life so much as we did in his company?'), Osbert Lancaster and the other distinguished contributors are not simply being polite: Bowra clearly meant everything to them that they said he did.

Yet the form that this influence took, and the way in which it was transmitted, was a great deal more nebulous. Academically, Bowra was a popularising Hellenist, but the books lack the conversational sparkle that he brought to social life and have not survived. His real forte, you suspect, was repartee and through it the propagation of the values he held dear: the liberal humanism borrowed from his delvings in antiquity, rampant individualism, a view of human nature quite untrammelled by convention, and a view of Oxford that consisted of taking sides, burnishing grudges and getting your retaliation in first. To a 19-year-old fresh from the school sixth form the spectacle of Bowra on the warpath could be a bracing experience: one of the challenges facing any Bowra anatomist, consequently, is to establish what made him so different from the average ornament of an Oxbridge common room, and why, in an environment dominated by zealous personal cultists, he loomed larger than any. Part of it was his cosmopolitanism: the early years spent in China, where his father was a colonial official; the adolescent journeyings through pre-revolutionary Russia; horrific war service – about which he could seldom be got to speak – on the Western Front. Equally intriguing, to those caught in the blasts of Bowra's booming self-possession, was the existence of a much more diffident inner side. A cautious homosexual, a gregarious solitary, a frustrated poet, fearful of the slights of literary and social groups from which he felt excluded (Bloomsbury, 'smart' London), nervous of the patronage of 'serious' scholars, the Bowra who emerges blinking into the light of the post-war era can seem a much less confident proposition.

As to what Bowra thought about the literary causes he so vigorously championed, a faint and somewhat fusty air of benefit of clergy hangs over the proceedings, the suspicion that however much one believes in such desirable abstractions as equality of opportunity and harrying the establishment, the good things in life are best suited to oneself and one's friends. This is particularly evident in his serial musings on the duties and entitlements of 'the poet'. The noise of politics and politicians, he once wrote, 'impinges on the serene silence of his contemplation and their vulgar emotion spoils the delicate concentration of his vision'. In 1943, sounding like a proto-Ted Hughes, he could be found defining the poet as a 'shaman', who is 'no longer a man among other men' but instead 'in touch with some superior order of things'. This is not to charge Bowra with quietism – no one hated Hitler more – or even the kind of starry-eyed exceptionalism that burns through so many of the poetry magazines of the 1940s, merely to wonder whether one of the greatest impediments to an understanding of poetry isn't this disinclination to believe that poets pay their taxes and stir sugar into their tea like anyone else. But Bowra's undoing was not simply his romantic view of poetry, his unfulfilled emotional life or the professorships that never came his way. It was also that as he grew older, Oxford life was becoming more professionalised, less interested in the humanist pursuit of the good life, the scabrous anecdote and the witty dining companion – less interested, in fact, in Bowra himself. John Lowe's biography of his great friend Sparrow, whose wardenship of All Souls coincided with Bowra's long reign at Wadham, offers a symbolic episode in which the pair, returning from a university dinner sometime in the 1960s, walk past a group of 'obviously gilded undergraduates' who take no notice of them. 'How sad' Sparrow observes. 'Twenty years ago we should probably have known all of them.' No, Bowra corrects him. 'What is sad is that twenty years ago they would have recognised us.' The late-period nickname bestowed on Bowra by the Wadham students, it turns out, was 'Old Tragedy'.

If what did for Bowra and his kind was the post-war professionalisation of university life, in which the specialist succeeded the generalist and undergraduates became increasingly focused on paid employment rather than the gentlemanly pursuit of knowledge for its own sake, then little of this had yet to attach itself to the teaching of English. Many colleges still had no full-time tutorial staff. Faculty lecturers were frequently denied college fellowships and the perquisites that went with them: J. B. Leishmann, the translator of Rilke, for example, who taught English at St John's in the 1950s, was allowed to dine with his senior colleagues only on Saturday nights. Meanwhile, the administration of advanced degrees was often chaotic. Kingsley Amis left a caustic account of his attempts to get Lord David Cecil to take an interest in the supervision of his BLitt. But while efforts were being made to drag Oxford English into the twentieth century – F. W. Bateson had begun editing *Essays in Criticism*, W. W. Robson was at work on Leavis, Empson and Eliot, and there were younger dons working to promote syllabus reform – most neutral observers were aware that the faculty possessed only a fraction of the lustre of its Cambridge equivalent, an entity with which Leavis's name was still synonymous. But here, too, a paradox applies. On the one hand, Leavis's influence on the way in which English was being taught, whether as a university subject or in school sixth forms, had never been greater. On the other, Leavis himself seemed a much less confident figure, more turned in on himself, more sensitive to slights (real and imagined), more liable to be involved in eye-catching but spirit-sapping and professionally unproductive rows.

However much Leavis might complain about the 'club spirit' in English letters, his own private club, in which he officiated as president, membership secretary and occasionally chucker-out, was developing into an immensely powerful group of proselytisers and devotees. *Scrutiny* might have ceased publication in 1953, but *Scrutiny* principles were alive and well both in university senior common rooms and in the wider world of critical practice. The seven-volume *Pelican Guide to English Literature* came choc-full of Leavisites, with an editorial role for Leavis's former pupil, Boris Ford. Even more significant in its way was the annual migration of Cambridge graduates sympathetic to Leavis to jobs in the teaching profession, from which redoubts they hastened to supply candidates for the Cambridge entrance exams. An undergraduate who arrived at Downing in the early 1960s recalled that almost all his fellow pupils had been taught by English teachers who were either former pupils of Leavis or fashioned in his intellectual image. Meanwhile, the presence of Leavisites in university English faculties offered another conduit. After graduating, the same student discovered that he was able to acquire a teaching job at a new Australian university simply because of his connection with Downing. Arriving in Melbourne, he found himself welcomed by a band of Leavis enthusiasts.

But there was another side to this unstoppable forward march, and it lay in Leavis's increasing estrangement from the Cambridge English faculty. Understandably resentful of his halting progress through the university hierarchy – he was appointed to a readership as late as 1959 – his attitude to undergraduate teaching increasingly resembled that of the leader of an exclusive and barely penetrable sect. Incoming students were given to understand that university lectures were scarcely worth attending. David Ellis, whose *Memoirs of a Leavisite* offers a revealing portrait of the late-period Leavis in action, thought that he 'made reading English at Downing feel like an autonomous activity which was on occasion rudely interrupted by inappropriate teaching from outside'. This sense of cultishness was reinforced by Leavis's tendency to disparage all extraneous cultural forces, his conviction that to open a copy of the *Times Literary Supplement* – then being stylishly overseen by Alan Pryce-Jones – was to be instantly submitted to a process of intellectual debasement, a world of lapsed standards and self-perpetuating coteries, where literature was judged not on its merits but by a series of protocols never quite discernible to anyone who existed on the wrong side of the fence. It was also kept alive by Leavis's habit of falling out with former colleagues and contributors who had lost enough of their awe to start asking awkward questions. David Holbrook, who had been taught by Leavis in the 1940s and was later to occupy the post of director of English Studies at Downing, was careful to preserve two letters sent to him by Leavis separated by a remove of a quarter of a century. The first, a testimonial from 1952, noted that 'the high opinion I formed of his ability has been steadily confirmed. He is a man of distinguished intelligence, wide reading and very good cultivation.' The second, from 1977, ran: 'You'll not be surprised to learn that I've always had a low opinion of you, both of your intellect and your character . . . *it's time to let you have it*.' Holbrook also suffered the indignity of the 'cut direct', when Leavis, encountering him in a Cambridge backstreet, plunged defiantly on with his eyes fixed on a point some feet above his former colleague's head.

Holbrook's crime, he suspected, was merely to have disagreed with Leavis over his attitude to Lawrence, and to have protested about Leavis referring to him publicly as 'a well-known indefatigable publicist on the theme of pornography' – a curious complaint given his editorship of a symposium entitled *The Case Against Pornography* (1973).

Holbrook also seems to have made the fatal mistake, in conjunction with the philosopher Roger Poole, of asking Leavis to define what he meant by 'life' (as in 'the essential possibilities') and other esoteric terms such as 'Nisus' and 'Abnung' which had recently crept into the Leavis lexicon. Holbrook's conclusion, not published until a decade and a half after his mentor's death, was that the Leavises were 'extremely disturbed people', 'absolutist' in the view they took both of literature and of personal relations, and, in Leavis's case, filing judgements that could sometimes only be construed as 'deliberate wickedness'. In Holbrook's defence, he had observed Leavis in action – and been observed in his turn – over a period of several decades, and seems to have known, psychologically, what he was talking about. On the other hand, a glance at the collection of egotists, reality-deniers and score-settlers who have set up as professional critics in the past couple of centuries would seem to suggest that psychological trauma has never been a bar to producing first-class criticism. What seems to have rankled with Leavis, whenever a former colleague nerved himself to dispute his view of Eliot or *Lady Chatterley*, was the charge of subjectivity – the claim first made by Stephen Spender in the 1930s that he was merely a 'personal reactions man', dressing up his instinctive likes and dislikes in academic persiflage.

It was this that led Leavis to develop his notion of the 'third realm' – a kind of prejudice-free critical space or form of morphic resonance which, as he conceptualised it, is 'neither merely personal nor public in the sense that it can be brought into the laboratory and pointed to', an enticing intellectual palisade beyond individual subjectivity and objective thinking which is still capable of convincing the neutral reader who manages to obtain an entry. The 'third realm' is an attractive idea, while never quite negotiating the considerable impediments that lie in its path. The disinterested mental category Leavis describes can hardly be innate, unless we are back in the Lewis–Tolkien territory, where all forms of creative and critical expression derive ultimately from God. Therefore the ability to arrive, independently, at an individual judgement which, without obvious external pressures, is also a collective judgement must surely involve some kind of collaboration in which, critical practice being what it is, one opinion crowds out another through sheer force of will. And even if a hundred readers were induced to read *War and Peace* in a series of hermetically sealed rooms, and all arrived at more or less the same conclusion, this does not necessarily mean that their opinions are valid or that Tolstoy is a 'good' writer and J. B. Priestley a bad one. The same point, despite the activism of the post-war Leavisites and the chapter in his biography with the stark heading 'Helpers 1955–1960', can be made of Leavis himself.

Besides, the disinterested quest for universally accepted standards was not something with which the general reader of the 1950s and 1960s would necessarily have associated the author of *The Common Pursuit* (1952) and *D. H. Lawrence: Novelist* (1955). Leavis's public reputation in the post-war era was that of a controversialist, pursuing war to the knife with his enemies, trampling on those who failed to share his opinions at a moment's provocation and infuriating middlebrow book lovers who deprecated both his antagonisms and the asperity with which they were expressed. *The Lyttelton Hart-Davis Letters*, for example, six volumes of (mostly) literary chit-chat exchanged between the independent publisher Rupert Hart-Davis and the retired Eton master the Hon. G. H. Lyttelton in the period 1955–62, fairly seethes with execrations of 'the man Leavis'. Lyttelton writes in February 1962 to say that, having read a remark about Max Beerbohm in the *Spectator*, he is minded to respond by quoting Lamb's question to Coleridge 'whether the higher order of Seraphim *illuminati* ever sneer' on the grounds that 'a great deal of Leavis's line about poets or novelists that he doesn't like and their admirers is not that they are mistaken but that they are contemptible'. Hart-Davis picks up the torch six weeks later, quoting from Housman's preface to his edition of Manilius and lamenting 'If only Leavis could write like that! But he has no ear, no taste, no judgement. How *can* a man who writes as he does teach anyone *English*?' The last letter written by Lyttelton before his death from cancer of the liver in March 1962 contains a final objurgation: 'I say, Leavis! Have you ever known opinion so unanimous about a man's spite, bad manners, injustice, bad English and conceit?'

The particular disagreement to which Lyttelton refers is the 'Two Cultures' debate with C. P. Snow, born of Snow's contention, expressed in his Cambridge Rede Lecture of 1959, that the scientific mind was socially progressive and the literary mind reactionary, which continued for the next three years. Before it ran a series of bitter disputes – with the Oxford critic F. W. Bateson over the question of what it was necessary to know about the poems of past eras in order to understand them; with the young academic Frank Kermode over a somewhat dismissive Third Programme survey of Leavis's work (of which his biographer notes that Kermode's manner 'was that of one walking round a grand Victorian edifice in wonder, with piety just on the edge of sarcasm'); with Sir Allen Lane, even, over a copy of the Penguin *Lady Chatterley* which the publishing magnate wanted signed for a memorial collection, but was returned by Leavis unmarked, with the comment 'I do not think Sir Allen Lane did a service to literature, civilisation or Lawrence in the business of *Lady Chatterley's Lover*.' The 'Two Cultures' row is thoroughly representative of the late-period Leavis in action: a convincing argument that soon degenerated into personal abuse. No one could dispute the seriousness of Leavis's response, his warning that 'the advance of science and technology means a human future of change so rapid and of such hints of tests and challenges so unprecedented, of decisions and possible non-decisions so momentous and insidious in their consequences, that mankind . . . will need to be in full possession of its humanity'. Yet it took only half a minute of the lecture at which this riposte was delivered for Snow to find himself described as 'portentously ignorant'.

To Holbrook, who, as he concedes, had learned a great deal from Leavis but had also discovered some of his limitations along the way, the problem was simply that of an intellectual black hole, a failure to find anything to believe in except vague generalisations, a position kept up by way of a pretence – in this case the idea that a minority caucus with common standards existed or had ever done so – a belief that, in the end, the world of the classroom not only explained the life that went on beyond it but was of greater importance. To critical sophisticates, on the other hand, the Leavis cult sometimes seemed nothing more than an exercise in displaced religion. A religion, moreover, that had its origins in social class. Bowra, having heard Leavis speak in the early 1960s, reported to his Cambridge friend G. H. Rylands 'He had nothing to say, but the whole mystery was revealed. He is what our mothers would have called CHAPEL. The low, mousey voice, trailing into inaudibility at the end of each sentence, so suitable for the ministrations of the Lord's supper; the quotations from scripture in the form of Lawrence and James . . . above all the sense that if you sign with him on the dotted line, you are saved.' This is patronising, perhaps, although no more patronising than – say – Mrs Leavis lambasting the Virginia Woolf of *Three Guineas* for having too little experience of life to pronounce authoritatively on her topic, but its diagnosis of the spell which Leavis cast on some of his hearers, and the peculiar fervour that he managed to arouse and cultivate, can hardly be gainsaid.

By this time, in any case, he was losing his grip. There was a final, calamitous falling-out with Cambridge, after the appointment of Brian Vickers to a Downing fellowship, which Leavis interpreted as a snub to his henchman, the then Downing director of English Studies, Morris Shapira, and ultimately to himself: he resigned his fellowship in a huff and accepted a visiting professorship at York. Critical responses to his later work trod an uncomfortable line between recognition of past achievement and an awareness of what Julian Symons, in reviewing *Anna Karenina and Other Essays* (1968) called 'his narrow dogmatism, his lack of charity and his failure of imagination and sympathy'. And if 'Cambridge English' was changing, then so too was the academic world beyond it, and in ways that Leavis – and many pre-war educationalists – found deeply inimical. The decade and a half between 1950 and 1965 brought a significant expansion in university English departments. Before the Second World War the higher-education establishment south of the Tweed and east of the Wye had consisted of Oxbridge, London, successive groups of English civic and 'redbrick' universities (such as Bristol, Manchester, Hull, Durham, Sheffield and Birmingham) supported by various outlying 'university colleges'. Sussex was granted its charter in 1961, by which time the University Grants Committee, under whose aegis this expansion proceeded, was considering submissions from a further twenty-eight potential universities. Six of them were approved in yearly tranches – York and East Anglia (1963), Essex and Lancaster (1964), Kent and Warwick (1965). Meanwhile, the Robbins Report of 1963 had begun to clear the decks for an environment of vastly extended student numbers and a fundamental redefinition of the purpose of a university in the modern world; a milieu in which the old academic single-mindedness, the idea of communities of scholars with their (predominantly) non-utilitarian goals was replaced by a new educational corporatism.

Interestingly, as far back as the early 1940s, Leavis had produced what he called a 'Sketch of an English School' – his ideal conception of the way in which English literature might be taught and studied in the post-war world. It is a revealing document, not only for the assumptions it makes about the intellectual calibre of the participating undergraduates – concentrating, for example, on Part II of the Cambridge English tripos on the grounds that the students will be fully fledged literary critics by the time they emerge from Part I – but in its suggestion that the course should begin with 'the background to religious history'. As for the interpretative tools which Leavis insists that undergraduates should bring to Calvinism's transformation into Nonconformity, these should include 'tact and delicacy of interpretation, an awareness of complexities, and a sense of the subtle ways in which, in a concrete cultural situation, the spiritual and the material are related'. In essence this is a blueprint for much of the 'cultural studies' movement that sprang up in the mid-1960s – Richard Hoggart, E. P. Thompson, Raymond Williams et al. – but none of it would have cut much ice in the new university English departments of the 1960s where experiment was in the air and a newly appointed junior lecturer was more likely to be interested in the latest developments in the American novel than in Dickens's relationship with the puritan middle class. Margaret Drabble's biography of Angus Wilson contains a breathless account of the 'unconventional, creative' UEA in its bright, mid-1960s dawn: 'Out on its own East Anglian limb, it hoped to avoid the worst of the North–South, Redbrick–Oxbridge divide: yoghurt-eaters in Jaeger scarves mingled with Mancunian addicts of chips, peas and tomato ketchup.'

It also hoped, if not perhaps stating the fact in so many words, to widen the catchment area from which academic teachers of English had traditionally been drawn, a process that led not merely to Wilson's arrival in the role of visiting senior lecturer, but to the cultivation of a talent pool that was both non-Oxbridge and, even more important, non-male. Female literature dons had, of course, been making their presence felt in university English departments for nearly half a century – a representative specimen might be Oxford's Dame Helen Gardner, the anatomist of Donne and Eliot – but the young women borne on the tide of post-war social mobility who began to be appointed to junior lectureships in the 1960s were, by and large, cut from a very different cloth, and none more so than Lorna Sage (1943–2001) who spent her entire academic career out on Drabble's East Anglian limb.

Sage's fame came late, so late as to be largely posthumous. In fact, *Bad Blood* (2000), the best-selling account of her notably tough Flintshire childhood, won the Whitbread Biography Prize only a week before her premature death. If Sage as a memoirist is mostly concerned with getting by and keeping afloat, trying to forge some kind of career for herself against a backdrop of bygone familial trauma and her own teenage pregnancy – she was married at 16 and gave birth a few weeks before sitting her A levels – then the career academic, sitting down to consider her childhood, is keenly alert to the first glimmerings of a literary sensibility, the seeds sown by the volumes to hand in her wicked old clerical grandfather's library, the late-night book jags, the abiding love of Latin. Although her academic preoccupations ran as far as Milton and Thomas Love Peacock – see her *Peacock: The Satirical Novels* (1976) – it would be fair to say that, as a woman making her way through the world against considerable odds, her principal subject was the woman writer engaged on what was effectively the same task, and much of her best criticism returns with a kind of homing instinct to the figure of the post-war woman novelist.

Naturally, given her berth in a New University and the observation point it offered for the Women's Movement taking shape beyond, she is fascinated by the era's bright particular stars (Kate Millett, Erica Jong, Marilyn French) but her attitudes to them – to any other woman writer if it comes to that – are rarely clear-cut. *Women in the House of Fiction* (1992) opens with a teasing preface in which Sage declares that she admires Simone de Beauvoir, the great heroine of her youth in the Flintshire council bungalow, for her contradictions: a reluctance to see herself 'just as a woman' combined with an acute awareness of who she was and what might be expected of her; a writer of realist novels who invariably puts reality in figurative quotation marks. There follows a brisk engagement with textual theory – the principal quarry here is Roland Barthes – in which she notes, of the writers she intends to discuss, that 'their experience and their displacements are not to be accounted for in terms of some universal state of textuality'. Whereas to Barthes writing may be anybody's and everybody's and the text that results from this inclusivity a 'heterocosm', the books she has been reading 'aren't like that'. Whatever the theorists may say, fiction isn't placeless and what can sometimes look like a mass of narratival convention can sometimes turn out to be more subversive than it seems; the great talisman here being Iris Murdoch, praised for calling into question the power of the overview and for stuffing her books with the local, the particular, the unclassifiable – 'everything that makes the quotidian world of passion, habit, conflict and muddle seem real'.

While there is no way of 'placing' the woman writer and, by extension, no way of displacing her either, then when it comes to the individual novelists who stray beneath her lens, a curious contradistinction seems to apply, which is to say that Sage is sometimes less interesting on the talents you expect her unequivocally to admire and more convincing on the ones you expect her to have doubts about. Angela Carter, for example, is applauded for writing fantasy which is deliberately unglamorous rather than 'in opposition', but the paragraphs which she singles out for approving comment always seem thoroughly mundane. On the other hand, her account of Margaret Drabble's novels is an object lesson in demonstrating how a writer may defy some of the limitations imposed on her by the critical orthodoxies of the day. Drabble's bright, ambitious heroines, as Sage sees them, are reacting against the idea of the abstract individual: the 'stuff of human life' matters more than sexual or social encoding; individual destiny is always going to be caught up in and complicated by the extended communities into which her characters tumble. If this highly astute analysis of the way in which Drabble conducts her cast through these tangles of contingency has a drawback, it is the assumption of 'cosiness'. Is the background to a novel like *Jerusalem the Golden* (1967) quite so genteelly sequestered as Sage seems to think, what with the separations and tarnished dreams that lie at its core? But the point she makes about the complexity and ambiguity of Drabble's world recurs in her discussion of Murdoch's novels, whose social and sexual forces confine people, for better or worse, to the middle ground they share with each other, and which – at least, this is the implication – make them interesting. And Murdoch's methods are, when it comes down to it, polemical – a way of keeping abstract speculation and radical deconstruction at bay. *Under the Net* (1954), influenced by Sartre and dedicated to Raymond Queneau, might have a chronically self-absorbed male monologuist for a hero, but he ends up with both a character and a context. A quarter of a century later, in the Booker-winning *The Sea, The Sea* (1978), the untidiness of the landscape, the packed and sometimes contradictory detail, is its philosophical heart.

It is the same with Christina Stead, a writer with whom, you suspect, Sage profoundly sympathises, here acclaimed for not conforming, for not fitting herself into the niches her admirers have fashioned for her, inhabiting no particular group or tradition, disdaining feminism, literary experiment, the Old Left with equal tenacity. 'Placing' Stead's work is, you deduce, a matter of absorbing interest to Sage ('Is she the last great modernist? The last great realist? A female Joyce/Lawrence? An unwomanly Woolf?') even as she shakes her head over the futility of the task. It is uncanonical art, she decides, which perhaps ignores the fact that even uncanonical art ends up defining itself, if only in its absence from and opposition to the things from which it is detached, and that a writer who declines to define herself will eventually turn this reluctance into a kind of definition by default. At the same time there is a sense of something oddly personal burrowing away in the essay on Stead, and it is difficult not to think that when she praises her subject for, as she puts it, not worshipping art, for not setting the artist apart, for not distinguishing 'the struggle to invent literature from everyone's struggle', her own struggles aren't at least somewhere in the back of her mind.

The immense concentration of resources on the university teaching of English in the 1960s had two main consequences for literary culture. Most obviously, it began to professionalise and institutionalise literary criticism with the aim of converting certain aspects of it into the exclusive preserve of universities, magnifying its importance, in terms of academic hierarchies, but at the same time minimising its relevance to the greater part of the reading public. As David Lodge once put it, many years after the process had been set in train, 'Since serious literary criticism was virtually monopolised by the universities, it has become of all-absorbing interest to its practitioners, and a matter of indifference or incomprehension to society at large.' As Lodge helpfully points out, this has uncomfortable implications for academic critics who believe that universities have a civilising mission in society. Leavis, after all, expected to see his books reviewed in the *Spectator* and the *New Statesman*; the same exposure would be unlikely to greet Professor X of the University of Loamshire, author of *Lawrence's Hegemonic Structures.* But while institutionalisation created a body of specialists, whose interests increasingly lay beyond the traditional remit of English dons – in the New Criticism of the American campuses or the theoretical winds blowing in from the continent – it also produced a cadre of youngish academics who were happy to intervene in the upper reaches of the literary mainstream.

There had been teachers of English at large in newspapers and magazines well before the Second World War, but the 'media don' who begins to make his first appearances in the mid-1960s was a new phenomenon altogether, distinguished, above all, by the catholicity of his – or her – interests, as likely to write a best-selling novel as to appear at an academic symposium, to write the script for a late-night television series as to contribute a review to *Essays in Criticism*. Picking up a random copy of the *New Review*, for example, from the later 1970s one finds no fewer than five moonlighting academics, including the Oxford Yeats specialist John Kelly and the UEA's Helen McNeil. Neither was it the case that the media don flourished exclusively in the breeze-block-and-concrete campuses that were beginning to spring up in provincial cities around the UK. By the end of the 1970s both Oxford (Craig Raine, John Fuller, Valentine Cunningham, John Bayley) and Cambridge (Eric Griffiths, Colin MacCabe) had a complement of college tutors keen to balance workaday routines with the advantages of regular spots in the review pages of the national press. Naturally, several qualifications apply. Raine, Cunningham and co. were young dons with stances to take and points to prove. It would be absurd, on the other hand, to call John Bayley (1925–2015) a media don in the accepted sense: he was merely a veteran academic whose reviews appeared in periodicals as diverse in tone and circulation as the *London Review of Books* and the *Spectator*. Nonetheless, while not in the least constituting anything that could be described as a literary movement, each of them in their separate ways was an example of Oxbridge putting itself on public display, serving up opinions about literature – sometimes comparatively trivial forms of literature – in what could sometimes seem an overpopulated forum.

Seen in the round, and with the benefit of hindsight, the media don was a mixed blessing. Undoubtedly, he – and increasingly she – played a significant role in disseminating and popularising, on radio, television and in print, higher-brow material that would otherwise have struggled to find an audience, while his, or her, presence in more mainstream branches of literature frequently drew attention to more abstruse academic interests. Thus David Lodge, the comic novelist with his audience of hundreds of thousands of readers, is also David Lodge, MA, PhD, professor of modern English literature at the University of Birmingham and author of *The Modes of Modern Writing: Metaphor, Metonymy and the Typology of Modern Literature*. The bridge connecting these twin professional callings was a narrow one, but it did exist. At the same time the moonlighting academic frequently brought his jargon with him, sat in late-night television studios talking about 'sequential narratives' when he meant stories, and to the non-academic writer fetched up in close proximity could be a thoroughly intimidating presence. It has been plausibly argued, for example, that some of the weaknesses of Angus Wilson's later novels, with their panoramic coigns of vantage and their vaguely experimental techniques, derive from his exposure to the 'fierce young smartyboots' (Jonathan Raban's phrase) of the UEA campus, where he held a part-time appointment in the 1960s and 1970s. Raban, in particular, had a hunch 'that his time at the UEA . . . may have led him into an agonising misreading of the value of his own work'. Yet the university lecturer at large in the columns of a Sunday newspaper could very often contribute to a raising of the intellectual tone. Take, for example, the seventieth birthday tribute to Wilson by his colleague Lorna Sage commissioned by the *Observer* in 1983, an appreciative but by no means uncritical piece, which hails him as 'an authority against authority', notes that his early novels seem to be slipping mysteriously out of reach, connects this up with the political climate of the day ('The reasons are doubtless to do with the pervasive revulsion against the political doings of that Other Wilson, which discredit, it sometimes seems, any liberal values that happened to be canvassed at the time'), and brackets him with Empson as another pursuer of 'complexity, ambivalence, diversity, and matters of conscience'.

Projections of the male media don, usually seen as glib, sexually adventurous and morally ambiguous, start turning up in British fiction from the mid-1960s onwards and reach an early high point in the persons of Dr Howard Kirk, the opportunistic and nest-feathering sociology lecturer of Malcolm Bradbury's *The History Man*, and Professor Morris Zapp, the jet-setting American theorist of David Lodge's *Changing Places* (both 1975). Bradbury and Lodge themselves represent the *ne plus ultra* of the breed – non-Oxbridge (Bradbury took his first degree at the University of Nottingham, Lodge at University College London), long-term friends and collaborators, so inextricably linked in the popular imagination come their early 1980s heyday that Lodge once received a telephone call from a fan asking that he settle a bet by admitting that he and Bradbury were the same person. In fact, though several of their novels explore vaguely similar territory, in that they are set in universities and use these institutions as a prism through which non-academic concerns can be intermittently glimpsed, there are substantial differences between them: Lodge always seeming to be more interested in academic nitty-gritty; Bradbury more of an ambassador on literature's behalf, and, during the 1980s publishing boom, an ardent proselytiser of English fiction, whose merits he believed to be consistently underrated.

To the casual observer of the 1970s and 1980s literary scene Bradbury, in particular, is a thoroughly protean figure, here glimpsed reviewing for *Punch*, there found chairing the judging panel of the Booker Prize, now turning aside from a scholarly introduction to a reprint of Holbrook Jackson's *The Eighteen Nineties* to appraise a reissue of the bound volumes of the *Left Review*. His contribution to the *New Review* symposium on the state of fiction is entirely characteristic: enthusiastic where everyone else is downbeat; filing 1,500 words where everyone else settles for 500; beginning with an announcement that this is a topic on which he holds such passionate views 'that a brief statement will hardly do for them', singling out a dozen younger writers who have shown 'remarkable vigour and innovation'. Surely, the reader thinks, as one clutch of names (Christine Brooke-Rose, Alan Burns) succeeds another (A. S. Byatt, Ian McEwan), they can't *all* be that good? But if Bradbury's criticism sometimes reduces itself to a talent for picking winners, and his own role to that of the wily impresario, this is not to diminish the enormous impact that he had in the 1980s as patron and propagandist – a role so zealously kept up that he was sometimes in danger of obscuring both his own talents as a novelist and his contribution to some of the cultural and political debates of the day.

Written at the rate of one a decade, as spiritually at home in the mundane English 1950s as in the fractured landscapes of post-glasnost Mitteleuropa, Bradbury's half-dozen full-length novels have a unity that belies their sporadic appearance. This has less to do with their near-identikit setting – either on a university campus or on some semi-academic jaunt to foreign climes – than with what might be called their ideological underpinning. For, without exception, they are about the idea – or even the ideal – of liberal behaviour, and the consequences that trying to live like a liberal may have not only for one's sense of self but for the communities of which one is, however imperfectly, a part. An ideal, more to the point, that requires constant bouts of self-examination and the measuring up of one's responses against a series of more or less impossible yardsticks. If, as John Gross once put it, liberalism is really only a false isolate, 'a loose cluster of interests held together by expediency, local circumstances and piecemeal humanitarian goodwill', then each of Bradbury's six male leads is driven by a neurotic itch to define himself on its terms. Professor Treece in *Eating People is Wrong* (1959) thinks himself 'a liberal humanist who believes in original sin'. James Walker, the novelist hero of *Stepping Westward* (1965), sent to teach creative writing in a Midwestern university, embodies what one of his American hosts calls 'a very English brand of liberalism, a faith of unbelief'. Nearly three decades later, Francis Jay in *Doctor Criminale* (1992) is still eagerly marking himself down as 'a late liberal humanist . . . liking my convictions soft, my faiths put to doubt, my gods upset, my statues parodied, my texts deconstructed'.

False isolates notwithstanding, where does Bradbury's liberalism come from? Like most forms of liberal behaviour forged in the 1950s' provincial furnace – Bradbury secured his first job at the University of Hull's adult education department – its authenticating spirit is E. M. Forster: several times referred to in the early novels and hailed by Treece's 'difficult' proletarian student Louis Bates in his essay on the Movement-era literary landscape as 'our old figurehead'. In fact, to read more than a paragraph of Treece's fitful efforts to define himself, or rather to avoid that definition, is to be returned to the essay entitled 'Mr Forster's Good Influence' that G. D. Klingopulos supplied to the final volume of the *Pelican Guide to English Literature* (1961). Klingopulos, a card-carrying Leavisite and *Scrutiny* scene-sweller, has no trouble in establishing Forster's appeal to the average post-war liberal humanist. There is talk of an 'attractive, though not easily imitable, intellectual shrewdness, delicacy and responsibility', an acknowledgement that the questions Forster asks are, essentially, the questions that a free society needs to consider, and to solve, if it wants to remain free. How, to particularise, is one to remain true to a generous impulse in a world which imposes mere conformity and where individualism is increasingly suspect? How can men and women achieve proper relationships with each other while avoiding the dangers of selfishness and self-sufficiency?

These are all questions in which Bradbury's heroes take a genuine, if constitutionally erratic, interest: Treece and Walker, nervously at large in their university common rooms, sometimes seem to think of nothing else. Worryingly, their liberalism has none of Forster's rigour, its circumspection and its unwillingness to settle for easy solutions. Backward-looking, permanently tethered in the lost golden land of the 1930s, when, as Treece once assures himself, 'to be a liberal was something, and people other than liberals knew what liberals were', its signature marks are neutrality, diffidence, a refusal to be drawn, a silent acknowledgement that the world has changed and an awareness that little can be done to reverse the process. In an afterword to a late 1970s reprint of *Eating People is Wrong*, Bradbury noted that 'the liberalism that makes Treece virtuous also makes him inert'. Harassed survivors from the age of good brave causes, clearly defined enemies and moral certainties, his characters are uncomfortably aware that those who live by liberal principles will perish by them too: 'Their own lack of intransigence, their inevitable effeteness betrayed them.' Thus framed, Bradbury's first three novels, culminating in *The History Man*, are not so much studies in liberal behaviour as exposures of its limitations, its fatal inability to bring a moral debate to a proper conclusion, to affirm the standards that would – at least in a world full of fellow liberals who knew what they were about – see it resolved.

Planet Bradbury is crammed to the rafters with people bewailing their own lack of personal magnetism, their self-conscious incapacity for action. Treece, like Leavis before him, pines to send out into the world a little group of disciples formed in his own image, fellow travellers who share 'his own disgusts, his own firm assurance in the necessity for good taste, honest feeling, integrity of motive', feels himself permanently let down. The roots of this dissatisfaction lie in the environment he inhabits ('a cheap commercial project, run by profiteers'), the working man, who is busy swapping his home-grown cultural arrangements for newly available consumer goods ('You thought he wanted a sturdy working-class culture, weaving baskets and singing folk songs' chides a colleague in the sociology department, who has been keeping abreast of Richard Hoggart, 'And all he wants is *The Lone Ranger*'), and, ultimately, humanity itself. The most powerful source of Treece's disillusionment is that he expects 'a thoughtful apprehension of all men by all men' and 'it worried him when he very rarely got it'.

For Treece, it quickly becomes clear, is a man out of his time. The middle 1950s are dissolving under his grasp. The challenges they set up require a tenacity that his brand of anguished liberalism has desperate trouble in maintaining. Faced with a colonial student who belongs to a terrorist society dedicated to ending British rule, Treece decides that he is 'quite prepared to help Mr Eborebelosa be a terrorist, if that really was his fulfilment, and people there seriously felt they had to be terrorists; but surely, in any case, reason would prevail and he'd work in a post office or a government building, creating rather than destroying'. The obvious questions here, which Treece never dares to confront, are: what if reason doesn't prevail? What if Eborebelosa blows up innocent civilians with lumps of thermite? And, if he does so, whose will the responsibility be? Meanwhile, Emma Fielding, the graduate student with whom Treece conducts a curiously emotion-free affair, is bringing exactly the same kind of guilt-ridden *politesse* to Eborebelosa's proposal of marriage: her chief concern is not to tell her suitor what she honestly thinks of him, but to 'avoid lying to a member of a race which had been lied to too much already'. It is left to Treece's colleague Viola Mansfield, a long-term critic of his moral equivocations, to pronounce judgement. Treece, she insists, is an ethical cheat, always espousing the right causes, 'doing the right thing, as it appears under the gaze of the *New Statesman*, or whatever the proper moral agencies are these days', but still leaving every dilemma he blunders into unresolved. 'Life for you is a play with a message.' Treece, who ends up hospitalised with a burst ulcer, abandoned by Emma, and bleakly assuming that 'from this he would never, never escape', would probably reply that it is not his fault, that the 1950s – on this evidence far more disturbed and fragmented than people ever gave them credit for at the time – are simply not a good time to be a liberal, that so many of the areas in which a liberal might have intervened to his, if not to anyone else's advantage, are now closed off by a moral relativism in whose presence rectitude, as one character puts it, 'turns to ashes in our hands'.

Paying tribute to William Cooper's *Scenes from Provincial Life* (1950), a benign influence on his early work, Bradbury later observed that the 1950s 'saw a cult of provincialism'. Like Treece, *Stepping Westward*'s James Walker is out on a limb, coming to terms with the prospect of his own deracination, eyeing the world from the not very enticing promontory of a top-floor flat in a Midlands city. His novels, Bradbury slyly insists, are like their author, dealing as they do with 'sensitive provincial types . . . for whom life was too plain and ordinary to be worth much at all'. A puzzled American reader complains that they 'give me the feeling that you feel a bit exhausted just living'. But what does the 'bland, uncreative' British liberalism that gives Walker his window on the world really consist of? Again, his politics are those of post-war disillusionment. It is not just that all the social forms that have previously kept intellectual and spiritual aspiration alive appear to have lapsed, but that they seem to have done so in the years since he was born. Unlike Treece, whose deficiencies are exposed only to the (more or less) uncomplaining fellow liberals of an English university campus, Walker is about to be judged by a group of people whose liberalism is that much more purposeful and committed. Froelich, the English lecturer who finesses Walker's invitation, sees his guest as both a useful ally in the advancement of his career and a way of stirring up trouble: a role Walker obligingly fulfils by declining to swear the oath of allegiance and making this refusal the subject of a chaotic public lecture, in which he declares that he 'came here to be uncommitted'.

Yet if Walker's liberalism falls disappointingly flat in the public sphere, then its consequences for his emotional life are quite as unsatisfactory. There is a Mrs Walker, and an infant Walker, back in Nottingham, but the novel's finale is given over to a wintry road trip with a rich American girl first met on the boat from England. This, too, sickens and dies after Walker's failure to assert himself when their car breaks down south of the Mexican border. His answer to the parking problem is a car that disappears when it stops, she briskly informs him. In the Mexican garage where, like the car, their relationship grinds to a halt, she says 'there was two of us and you acted like there was only one'.

Stepping Westward features an interesting minor character named Dr Jochum, a refugee from the communist east and the first of several common-room hardliners in Bradbury's fiction to whom words like 'freedom' and 'liberty' have a bitter personal significance. As Walker reaches the climax of his speech, in circumstances very similar to Jim Dixon's lecture-hall meltdown in *Lucky Jim*, he divines that the argument against what he has just said, his refusal to take sides or commit himself to anything beyond his own room for manoeuvre, is Dr Jochum's: 'that the speciality of liberalism is the betrayal of the society in which liberalism is permitted'. Certainly this warning hangs over *The History Man*, whose leading man, the University of Watermouth's sociology lecturer Howard Kirk, is only a fake liberal, an agent provocateur, happy to abandon any of the principles to which he formally ascribes if it suits his own self-interest. Like his forebears, Howard is another upwardly mobile provincial, from a puritan home where education is 'an instrument, a virtuous one' for getting on and doing well. His negative energy, his duplicity and the double standards that allow him to rebuke a student for reading the manuscript of a work in progress entitled *The Defeat of Privacy*, are the result of his reinvention as a souped-up 1960s Marxist. There is a rather ghastly exchange along these lines with his old friend Beamish, whose increasingly conventional attitudes are written off as 'bourgeois'. Beamish claims, as Treece might plausibly have done, that he is trying to 'define an intelligent, liveable, unharming culture'. To Howard, and the hard men of the sociology falange, high on Gramsci and Marcuse and low on objectivity, this is 'evasive quietism'. There follows another immensely pointed scene in which Howard, charged by his head of department with bullying a student with Conservative views, is reminded that there are two sides to every question. 'You'll just sink into your liberal mess if you think that' Howard tells him.

Though always comically aligned, the moral atmosphere of *The History Man* is infinitely harsher than its predecessors: the Age of Aquarius has been and gone; the 1970s are upon us and the stakes are higher; the problems on hand seem to require bold strokes and decisive action rather than well-meaning discussion. 'Politics were fair in the fifties' Beamish suggests to Howard, only to be told that 'that was why nothing got done.' And if the stakes are higher, so the personal fall-out is more injurious. Beamish's first-chapter suicide attempt, in an upstairs room at one of the Kirks' heaving parties, is unsuccessful. But there is no one to hear Howard's wife Barbara as she drives her arm through a window in the novel's closing paragraph. But by this stage Bradbury's target is not so much the Kirks as the institutions which they and their creator – by this time professor of English and American studies at the UEA – might be thought to represent and which allowed them to prosper. Rather than fostering intellectual freedom, self-determination, all those principles of humanist enquiry that the early twentieth century liberal clung to with such enthusiasm, the new world of higher education is helping to kill them off. To Treece a university is 'the one stronghold of values, the one centre from which the world was resisted.' Yet the college lecture halls in which he and Walker lay out their ideological toolkits are full of students who don't read books and regard a degree not as the route to self-fulfilment but as a passport to a white-collar job. 'My friend,' Dr Jochum counsels Walker, 'universities are not better than life. They are just life. It is not you and I who make them what they are. It is the students . . . and the computer . . . and the football team.' Come *The History Man*, on the other hand, the civilising role of academe has been entirely undermined. Conceived as a fail-safe repository for liberal values, for open-mindedness and communal resolve, it has turned into an environment whose centralising forces seem determined to see those values overthrown.

Though published in 1975, and set in the autumn of 1972, *The History Man* looks back to the decade that preceded it. In its skewering of contemporary fads, it is as much an 'anti-1960s' novel as such genre-definers as A. S. Byatt's *The Game* (1967) and Kingsley Amis's *I Want It Now* (1968). Bradbury's later novels, on the other hand – *Rates of Exchange* (1983), *Doctor Criminale* (1992) and *To the Hermitage* (2000) – are thoroughly of their time, more expansive, more hectic, more ambitious and yet somehow more constrained by the enormity of the task that awaits them. Each involves a journey eastward – Petworth's trip to the Iron Curtain capital of 'Slaka', Francis Jay's pursuit of the shape-shifting Criminale, the deliberations of the 'Diderot Project' en route to Moscow – replete with glamorous female seducers and the hint of espionage. Each, too, exhibits Bradbury's great procedural paradox as a novelist, which is the habit, shared with Lodge, of combining high-grade intellectual fireworks with an almost childlike comic sense. Just as the humour in Lodge's early fiction tends to turn on young men's difficulties among the Durex packets, so Bradbury's idea of a joke in *Rates of Exchange* is to have amusing foreigners mangling Petworth's name into 'Pervert' or 'Petwit', giving the second secretary at the embassy a stammer and calling the president 'Wanko'. It is the same in *Doctor Criminale*, where gatecrashers are 'ejaculated' from academic conferences, and *To the Hermitage* where a stopover in Helsinki yields up a chainstore called *Hankki Pankki*. The burlesque tendencies of Bradbury's humour can seem all the more marked when set against the gravity of his themes. Comic-ironic, built on misunderstandings and wounded dignity, these are also novels about the slipperiness of history, in both its pre- and post-glasnost state, and, by extension, the detachment of the English liberal sensibility from the really serious events going on in Eastern Europe. *Rates of Exchange*'s Dr Jochum figure is the novelist Katya Princip, who reads Petworth a terrific lecture on his inherent marginality while insisting on the crucial importance of magical realism in defying the proscriptions of a totalitarian regime. 'Reality is what happens when you listen to other people's stories and not to your own . . . The world is in your own head, and they put it there, with a me and a you in it, so we can make our own stories.'

Petworth, though prone to humiliating gaffes and inexplicably attractive to women, is a passive figure. The feeling, common to nearly all Bradbury's later work, that one is not so much reading a novel as attending to a series of notably well-dramatised intellectual dialogues, is yet more conspicuous in *Doctor Criminale*, if only because the sophistication of its judgements clearly owes less to its twentysomething narrator than to Bradbury himself. Once again there is the Mitteleuropa history lecture, this time courtesy of a mistrustful Austrian academic ('You cannot understand how it was here. Your country has been lucky, your lives have been simple, you have not suffered from our history') and, once again, the exotic charmer, tantalising Ildiko, who joins Francis in the quest while paying special attention to his credit cards. But just as the working man of the 1950s let down Professor Treece by preferring consumer materialism to the genuinely popular culture hymned by Richard Hoggart's *The Uses of Literacy* (1957), so Francis feels betrayed by his Hungarian guide. There is a poignant moment in which Ildiko, let out into the shopping malls of the west for the first time in her life, returns to their hotel with bags full of stars-and-stripes knickers and Union Jack bras. Francis complains that he preferred her Hungarian miniskirt to consumer-kitsch, only to be told 'But that is just from Hungary. These are from the West. They are from shopping.'

There are other let-downs. Criminale, first represented as a late twentieth-century European intellectual of well-nigh Derridean lustre, is revealed as a wily pragmatist, forever covering his tracks and adapting his views to shifts in the ideological temperature. Here in the early 1990s, with the Berlin Wall crumbled to dust and the Eastern Bloc in turmoil, his role is to defend liberal humanism not against Marx but from the ravages of a pluralist age, where commentators talk about 'the end of *homo historicus*, the individual who finds a meaning or an intention in history'. Always, Criminale tells Francis, we need 'a morality, a politics, a history, a sense of self, a sense of otherness, a sense of human significance of some kind. Now we have sceptics who invent the end of humanism. I do not agree.' Neither, you imagine, did Bradbury. But who, or what, are liberalism's enemies? By this late stage in the proceedings, a third of a century into the pursuit, a short list might include institutions – academic institutions especially – Marxists, theorists, late twentieth-century historicist philosophising and, inevitably, people who describe themselves as liberals. By *To the Hermitage*, published on the cusp of the new century but set seven years earlier, the net has widened still further to include technology. This much may be inferred from the presence of two hulking offstage influences: Diderot, in whose honour the collection of travelling academics has assembled – here seen as the father of both the modern novel and the computer – and the as yet embryonic internet. Are we not reaching the day foreseen by Diderot, one of the participants suggests, 'when knowledge will have grown so extremely fast no one individual or system would ever be able to grasp it?' 'It's here already' the arch-deconstructionist Jack Verso insists. 'It's called the World Wide Web.'

The Diderot Project's *raison d'être* – a slogan that now seems almost revolutionary – is to 'put the person at the centre of the universe'. All this, naturally, requires a resonance, a determination – an understanding – that most of Bradbury's creations don't possess. And if liberals themselves, singly and collectively, in their utterances and through their institutions, are responsible for liberalism's chronic vulnerability, then so is the political force that gave them their original impetus. For lurking behind each of Bradbury's novels is the rueful acceptance that most of modern liberalism's enemies – the free market, late capitalism, caucus politics, technological advance – are the creation of its nineteenth-century ancestors. After all, there would be no Ildikos filling their shopping bags with junk without Mr Gladstone. The liberal, Bradbury constantly asserts, is his own worst enemy, his schemes doomed to perish on the rocks of excessive moral scruple, his fine intentions rarely up to the fighting weight of the orthodoxies that seek to rein him in. He is an anachronism, and a dangerous one at that. Trying to do good, he infallibly ends up doing serious harm both to himself and the people around him, while exaggerating the alarming gap between himself and his creator. It is not merely that

Bradbury is an elegist for an ethical code in severe danger of being swamped, a dazzling intellectual high-wire act, or even – to lower the bar a bit – a top-notch slapstick comedian in the Kingsley Amis mould. His real achievement, you suspect, rests on his ability to show just how formidable a force the old-style liberal humanist can be – even here in a winded and ground-down world, somewhere in that endlessly contested space beyond the end of the Cartesian project and the beginning of the World Wide Web.

Bradbury managed to stay the academic course, only retiring from the UEA a few years before his premature death in 2000. Lodge, on the other hand, was a comparatively early escapee, giving up his Birmingham professorship in his early 50s to devote more time to his own writing. These were productive years: a reviewer of *The Practice of Writing* (1996), one of his periodic collections of essays and reviews, calculated that his first decade outside academe had realised three novels, a volume of heavyweight literary criticism (*After Bakhtin*, 1990), several screenplay adaptations of his own and other people's work, including a BBC version of *Martin Chuzzlewit*, a cascade of literary journalism and a weekly 'fiction masterclass' in the *Independent on Sunday* (collected as *The Art of Fiction*, 1992). At one level, it is tempting to see Lodge's bustling post-campus career as a kind of reversion to historical type, remembering that when the bandwagon of English Studies was sent rolling through the university system at the end of the nineteenth century it had a habit of picking its recruits from light literature (Quiller-Couch at Cambridge) or the higher journalism (Churton Collins, Lodge's distant predecessor at Birmingham). While neither of these comparisons stands up to sustained scrutiny, Lodge's interest in what might be called the journeyman side of writing – the fact that many a great novel was produced in deeply unpromising circumstances at so many pence a page – allows his critical work to focus on the hand-to-mouth aspects of creativity in a way that hasn't always commended itself to professors of literature. When writing about Grub Street, after all, it helps to have some understanding of the conditions in which Grub Street operates, and the Lodge who remarks of Martin Stannard's life of Evelyn Waugh that it could have told us more about how much Waugh earned and the nature of his relationships with agent and publisher was drawing attention to a vitally important part of the specimen writer's existence which a more exalted critic would probably have missed.

The commodification of literature argument can be overzealously applied, even to some of the immensely market-conscious literary fictions of the 1980s and 1990s. For all that, Lodge's comments on the economic pressures to which the average – and less than average – novelist is subject, expressed in the essay 'The Novelist Today: Still at the Crossroads?', are no less relevant than when they were first set down. By extension, when, in a discussion of the staging of his play *The Writing Game* at Birmingham Rep, he stops to calculate how many copies of a hardback novel would produce the same sum in royalties, the reader rather welcomes this glimpse of the writer as businessman. Thackeray, you feel, would have been just as interested in the takings from one of his lectures, and the effect is not to diminish the value of what gets produced but to frame it in the context of the modern literary life. If much of Lodge's critical work is built on the supposition that the gap between the university professor and the literary mainstream need not be as wide as the former would like to make it, then his career as a whole is full of bridge-building exercises of this kind. And while the novels display a sophisticated intelligence revelling in slapstick, the essay collections reveal a skilled interpretative sensibility – never more so than in dealing with Lodge's native Catholicism – festooned with all the latest critical gadgetry, but at its shrewdest when writing biographical analyses based in the ancient standbys of 'character', 'environment' and 'temperament'. The Lodge who submits Harold Pinter's *Last to Go* to a 'structuralist analysis' clearly isn't averse to dressing up in the glad rags of literary theory, but on this – and other – evidence he wouldn't want to wear it next to his skin.

The stiff theoretical breeze blowing in from the continent and North America had not gone unnoticed in the 1960s and 1970s. But what might be called the post-value school of criticism, with its emphasis on sign, structure and system, and – eventually – the deconstruction of those systems, quickly ran up against the buffers of Anglo-Saxon pragmatism. The reactions of David Ellis, who spent time studying in France in the mid-1960s, are entirely typical of the time. Of Lacan: 'Try as I might, I could not see how he was relevant to the novels, plays or poems which interested me, or to anything I might want to say about them.' Barthes seemed slightly more interesting, if only through his insistence that many of the practices we regard as 'natural' are highly contrived, but he was not much taken by Foucault and even less by Derrida. Similar caution is expressed by the Oxford admissions tutor – in all likelihood Jonathan Wordsworth – who interviews the precocious Charles Highway in Martin Amis's *The Rachel Papers* (1973): 'for Christ's sake stop reading all this structuralist stuff. Just read the poems and work out whether you like them, and why.' Curiously enough, until at least the late 1970s the general reader would have been just as likely to find the names of Lacan and Derrida in the *New Musical Express*, where they were zealously inserted into analyses of the post-punk music scene by critics such as Paul Morley and Ian Penman, as in the *New Statesman*. It was only in the early 1980s that Derrida's portrait appeared on the cover of the *London Review of Books* and his name in the title of a Top 30 single by the rock band Scritti Politti, and that debates about the nature of the Oxford English syllabus were reported in the national press.

Lodge's stance on these manoeuvrings combined, on the one hand, the somewhat cautious interest of the professional critic and, on the other, the faint bewilderment of the creative writer. A review of a collection of interviews with various leading US theoreticians not only itemises some of the implications of this collective 'obsession' – its widening of the gap between secondary and tertiary education, its questioning of the canon and the humanist values gathered within it – but also notes some of its institutional consequences: 'The very difficulty and esotericism of theory make it all the more effective for purposes of professional identification, apprenticeship and assessment.' The theorist, in other words, is like the Leavisite but with less comprehensible jargon. As for Lodge's own critical response, some of its ambiguities can be detected in his collection *Working with Structuralism* (1981), whose title, he suggested, could more appropriately have been 'Living with Structuralism', a statement in which the enthusiasm of the critic, who applauded a new expository tool, and the novelist who realised the threat it posed to his art, are uneasily combined. In several of the literary essays he produced in the early 1980s – see in particular those assembled in *Write On* (1986) – there is a fretful little battle going on between critic and creator, with the latter constantly hinting that what the former says is undermining his position. Nowhere is this struggle more flagrant than in the spectacle of Lodge reflecting on some of his own fiction. 'In the last instance' he comments, apropos some densely argued deconstructionist principle, 'I can't go along with this radical decentring of the literary text. It simply doesn't answer to my experience of writing a novel.'

If Lodge seems ultimately to have believed that, whatever our ability to dissect texts and dismember the artifice that is fiction, sooner or later a phrase like 'artful mimicry' will be the reader's only honest reaction to a book, then there were plenty of literary dons for whom these debates offered a heaven-sent opportunity. One might note, by way of illustration, the role played in the Theory Wars of the early 1980s by the then Oxford English tutor Terry Eagleton. It was Eagleton who took a leading role at the 1980 conference, officially designated 'The Necessity of Theory', which debated the need for a compulsory first-year paper for undergraduates (this at a time when, as one of his colleagues remarked, they were likely to be ignorant of the primary texts) and who concluded an accompanying *New Statesman* article with the stirring cry: 'Oxbridge would be ill-advised to be complacent. The real root of these recent stirrings is nothing less than a muted, pervasive crisis in the whole meaning and function of "literature" and "criticism" in the West, one not unconnected with wider ideological turmoil.' It was Eagleton, too, who presided over the meeting of the Oxford Literary Society addressed by Colin MacCabe, author of *James Joyce and the Revolution of the Word*, the non-renewal of whose Cambridge fellowship was thought to reflect suspicion of his interest in the latest news from Paris and Yale. Present at this gathering myself, I can recall Eagleton introducing his guest with a clenched-fist salute and the words 'This man's had a hard time. He needs your support.' Dr MacCabe spent the next hour innocuously deconstructing some very obscure passages of Shakespeare; his listeners departed with the feeling that the opportunity to perpetrate a little genuine cultural mischief had been inexplicably passed over.*

Hindsight, abetted by *After Theory* (2003), soon reveals why Eagleton was so avid to attach himself to this kind of presumed dissension. Even a card-carrying Marxist – a category Eagleton unflaggingly occupied during the 1970s – could see that by the early 1980s the leftist

* For an example of the penetration of literary theory at student level, see *White Room*, later the *Radical Review*, issued irregularly from St John's College, 1981–2. As well as publishing fiction and poetry, this featured discussions of such topics as 'Post-Sexualism', 'Reading (Absent) Character' and 'The Post-Structuralist as Bodhisattva'.

project was running into trouble: let down by the regimes who professed attachment to it and a widespread acceptance that the top-down collectivism of its economic philosophy had simply failed to deliver. Such signs of radicalism that broke across the 1980s landscape came almost entirely from academe, and they assumed their most combative focus in the newly created realm of 'critical theory'. A clutch of (mostly) French philosopher-artists who believed not in 'meaning' but a multiplicity of interpretations, who delighted in exposures of hierarchy and gender imbalance, who aimed to reduce a text to a fine powder of politico-sexual assumptions: all this was meat and drink to a man who had long ago reached the stark conclusion that capitalism was finished, and the even starker conclusion that hardly any capitalists, and scarcely anyone living under capitalism, had noticed. If nothing else, Eagleton's critique of postmodernism rests on a great deal of prima facie evidence from a non-academic world in which the specialist rarely treads. He notes, for example, that the postmodernist mistrust of norms, values, hierarchies and standards looks suspiciously like some of the more stringent brands of economic liberalism. Worse, the 'universality' that most contemporary theorists reach out to embrace – the globe envisaged as a sprawling and resolutely non-occidental hypermarket where boundaries dissolve into the ether and custom diminishes – is contradicted by events on the ground: mysteriously, in a world supposedly getting smaller by the moment, the number of seats around the UN table is on the increase.

What does Eagleton find to praise? Above all, the lure of theory's close readings, its preoccupation with issues that 'belles-lettrist gentlemen' with no concept of hermeneutics always decline to countenance. None of this, though, is to disguise its procedural failings, its habit of overestimating the importance of language (Derrida's famous line about there being nothing outside the text) and its moral evasions, specifically a reluctance to address such vital topics as evil, death, oppression and the nature of truth. However plausible this analysis, the historian of native literary criticism might at this point want to charge Eagleton with a few evasions of his own. For all his sniffiness about the gentleman in the library (which goes all the way back to his 1978 attack on John Bayley in the essay 'Liberality and Order: The Criticism of John Bayley'), there were plenty of people, pre-Barthes, who went in for close readings. The first deconstruction of Dickens's prose in the context of his early training as a journalist was performed by R. H. Hutton as long ago as 1865. And from the other side of the cultural stream that Eagleton assumes to divide the pre- and post-theoretical world, he might want to consider just how much the hierarchical, autocratic and in some cases practically religious air of the Derrida cult owes to bygone critical hierophants such as Leavis. What remains in the wake of this painstaking dissection is the spectacle of a jaunty and somewhat old-fashioned Catholic moralist niggling away at post-modern deracination ('The creature who emerges from postmodern thought is centreless, hedonistic, self-inventing') and relativism ('Anyone who seriously believed that nothing was more important than anything else . . . would not be quite what we recognise as a person'). In the end, like Bradbury and Lodge before him, he falls back on 'intuition', a quality whose existence the average theorist would probably want to deny altogether. And if the neo-Marxist commune which Eagleton sometimes seems to be advocating as an antidote to the world's ills looks as if it would be quite as dreary as the international hypermarket model, then Eagleton is still capable of demonstrating just how great a racket the Marxist critic can continue to kick up, three-quarters of a century and more after such spectral forebears as Edgell Rickword and Christopher Cauldwell set to work.

The Unschooled Reader

Every so often in a branch of popular culture where 'literariness' is rarely given houseroom – in a line uttered by a mid-evening sitcom actor, or a fragment of a pop lyric – there comes a moment when what might be called the ghost of a literary sensibility drifts tantalisingly into view. One of these interludes turns up in the Beatles' 'Eleanor Rigby' (1966) in the line in which poor benighted Miss Rigby is described as having a face which she 'keeps in a jar by the door'. It is an extraordinary configuration, what the Beatles scholar Ian MacDonald calls 'the single most memorable image in the Beatles' output', and likened by A. S. Byatt to 'the minimalist perfection of a Beckett story'. But where did it come from? What accumulation of influence, inspiration and instinct caused it to jump, fully formed, into Paul McCartney's head? This enquiry takes on a deeper significance in the context of the Beatles' songwriting as a whole, for it would be fair to say that, in their seven-and-a-half-year stint as recording artists, John Lennon's is, lyrically, the sharper voice, and that the majority of McCartney's words, seen simply as words, are at about the level of a school magazine's sixth-form poetry supplement. Which is not to patronise them, merely to say that they are, quite naturally, designed to work in conjunction with the visceral tug of the music by which they are framed, as in the wholly arresting line in 'I Saw Her Standing There' (1963) where the singer's 'heart went boom' as he 'crossed that room'. The words to 'Eleanor Rigby', on the other hand, are something different – sparse, imagist, much closer to poetry, capable of existing on their own terms.

The pop lyric has always been a good place to search for, and indeed to conceptualise, the buried literary sensibility – that odd feeling for the biting phrase or the eye-opening metaphor regularly displayed by people with little in the way of formal education. McCartney left the Liverpool Institute at 18 with a single A-level. Lennon attended art school but seems largely to have pleased himself in terms of the curricula on offer: the self-conscious intellectualism of some of the late 1970s post-punk bands who sang songs based on their favourite Russian novels is altogether beyond him. Yet the Beatles' records, though derived – at any rate at the start – from the tradition of rough-hewn black rhythm and blues, are full of brisk little nods in the direction of 'literary culture'. There was even, in 1966, a single called 'Paperback Writer' – again written by McCartney – which (correctly) identifies the paperback revolution of the post-war period as part of a wider social trajectory typified in the title of Jonathan Aitken's progress report, *The Young Meteors* (1967). There is nothing structured, or even particularly deliberate, about this engagement. Rather, it consists of *objets trouvés*, flotsam and jetsam picked up along the way: the copy of *Jude the Obscure* that McCartney may, or may not, have come across on a friend's bookshelf while in the early stages of composing 'Hey Jude' (1968); Nancy Mitford's biography of Louis XIV (1966) offering a title for Lennon's 'Sun King' on *Abbey Road* (1969); the anthology belonging to McCartney's stepsister Ruth which drew his attention to the nursery rhyme by the Elizabethan playwright Thomas Dekker reproduced on the same album's 'Golden Slumbers'. Most significant of all, in this comparatively crowded territory, is 'I am the Walrus' from 1967's *Magical Mystery Tour*, a testimony to Lennon's interest in the quirky, surrealist side of English literature, clearly indebted to Lewis Carroll's poem 'The Walrus and the Carpenter', referencing Edgar Allan Poe and plausibly interpreted as a kind of counter-cultural-cum-anti-establishment checklist. Of equal significance is the lack of precision, exemplified by Lennon's misremembering of the poem on which the piece is based. As he later acknowledged, he had forgotten that the Walrus is 'the bad guy'.

But this is the way in which the Beatles – pop-cultural savants in a world which they were helping to create even as they responded to it – operated as a creative unit: the television constantly on in the background, the colour supplement regularly unfurled, myriad stimuli continually adding to the inherited weight of half-remembered nursery rhymes, childhood memory and historical association, often coming together to produce surprisingly 'literary' metaphors such as the banker in 'Penny Lane' (1967), the coin in whose pocket is 'a portrait of the Queen'. Although it is possible to follow this strain into the 1970s and beyond, there are important distinctions to be drawn. While pop music had in the 1960s been largely a vehicle for working-class self-advancement, it was rapidly colonised by a contingent of more middle-class performers whose intellectual interests frequently leached out into their song-writing. There is, for example, nothing 'buried' about the literary sensibility on display in Howard Devoto of Magazine's 'A Song From Under the Floorboards' (1980), which robs its lyrics wholesale from Dostoevsky's *Notes From Underground* and is even dedicated to 'F. D.', in Joy Division's 'Dead Souls' (1979), in the Ballardian backdrops to Siouxsie and the Banshees' early records, or the surprisingly large number of items namechecking such writers as Nabokov (the Police, 'Don't Stand So Close to Me'), Balzac (Blur, 'Country House') or Camus (the Cure, 'Killing an Arab'). Much more interesting, in that the influences are felt rather than advertised, is the work produced by the band of late 1970s singer-songwriters who, though leaving school in their mid-teens, maintained an autodidact's interest in books and, drawing inspiration from a variety of miscellaneous sources, ended up producing intensely 'literary' songs. The Fall's uncompromising songwriter Mark E. Smith was once quoted to the effect that what he had seen of the literary world encouraged him to regard it as 'evil', but the lyrics of 'The Classical' (1982), with its lines about 'destroying Romantics' show how effectively Smith could have intervened in that world had he thought it worth his while.

Nowhere, perhaps, is this self-cultivated feeling for literature more apparent than in the work of Paul Weller, whose very earliest songs, composed in his late teens as a member of the Jam, reveal not only a nodding acquaintance with various twentieth-century texts, but are sometimes oddly poetic in their texture. When in 'Standards' (1977), a song about the limitations imposed on life by the corporate machine, he warns 'You know what happened to Winston', the reference is to *Nineteen Eighty-Four*'s Winston Smith. The Thatcher-baiting 'Town Called Malice' (1982) takes its title from Nevil Shute's *A Town Like Alice*, while 'Billy Hunt' (1978), about a self-deluding fantasist who yearns to develop 'bionic arms', after which 'the whole world's gonna wish it weren't born' is the natural descendant of Keith Waterhouse's Billy Liar. And while much of the lyrical content is standard for the milieu (girls, social observation, not letting the adult world grind you down), every so often comes a romantic evocation ('the tranquillity of solitude', the 'greenbelt fields that made us feel free') or a stark, alliterative phrase straight out of a novel (Billy's desire to 'satisfy any whim that I wanted to'). Like many an English pop-pastoralist – the key influence here is Pink Floyd's debut album *The Piper at the Gates of Dawn* (1967) – Weller had clearly read *The Wind in the Willows*, which informs both the Jam's 'Tales from the Riverbank' (1981) and his subsequent solo album *Wild Wood* (1993). These influences are all the more effective – that is, they work better in the context of pop music – for being self-instilled. A Weller who had been sent to university and encouraged to sign up for a creative writing MA might well have written some decent poetry, but he would probably not have been able to produce a song like 'That's Entertainment' (1980), which has some claims to be regarded as a highlight of late twentieth-century English popular art.

CHAPTER 17

Beyond the Publishing Crisis

> Of course novels will go on being written, just as poetry goes on being written; and, of course, from time to time, a good or even a superb novelist will emerge. But soon the novelist will find, as the poet has found already, that the majority even of 'educated' people have become totally uninterested in whatever freakish thing it is that he is trying to accomplish.
>
> Francis King, *New Review*, 1978

However prodigious the talents on display, however clamorous the shouts of the new men and women knocking at the door, and however great the volume of abstract glory that attaches itself to the act of writing, most literary epochs end up reeking of insecurity, convinced that the creative torch lit a generation or two back is in danger of being snuffed out, that the whole sanctity of literature, both as an art form and, more narrowly, as a profession is being called seriously into question. Plenty of early Victorian readers, after all, looked back with regret to the age of Fielding, Johnson and the *Rambler*, and thought Dickens a vulgar comedian. The same reservations had been expressed forty years before over *Prometheus Unbound*. In the 1970s the suspicion that this was not a good time to be a writer hardened into certainty. A certainty, moreover, that seemed to be abetted by the material conditions in which books got written. It was an age of book-trade surveys, some of them written by publishers (Per Gedin's *Literature in the Marketplace*), others produced by academics (John Sutherland's *Fiction and the Fiction Industry*), all of them making a more or less specific connection between what was thought to be the depressed state of contemporary literature and what was assumed to be the debilitating effect of the commercial realities that underpinned it. Loss of collective nerve affected most areas of British life in the 1970s, a time of political uncertainty, industrial unrest and economic turmoil. For the non-best-selling writer, here in a world of raging inflation and diminishing returns, the awareness that times were bad was sharpened by a conviction that the bloom had gone off literature as a profession. As well as being economic, the crisis was also creative, and, to a degree, existential. All this, necessarily, had a profound effect on the various public statements that writers allowed themselves in the era of the three-day week and the 1976 IMF bailout. Given any kind of collective forum for their disquiet, the general tone adopted could come very close to despair.

One such forum was a 'symposium' on 'The state of fiction' which filled very nearly half of the 128 pages of the final number of the *New Review* in the summer of 1978. The participants – a rather impressive collection of novelists, reviewers and other interested parties – were invited to answer two questions. How would they describe the development of English fiction in the previous ten years? And what developments did they hope for, or anticipate, in the next ten? What follows, barring a few eternal optimists such as Malcolm Bradbury, is pretty much a howl of pain. The overwhelming conclusion is that 'serious' fiction is in sharp decline (no one, predictably, takes much interest in the non-serious kind). 'The straight novel . . . will virtually perish' John Braine predicts. 'I do not know how the serious novel will survive' Angus Wilson maintains. As for the explanation of a collapse that was thought to be both aesthetic and commercial, various culprits were reliably to hand. They included the galloping Americanisation of a once proudly independent industry ('Try not to include many English references which would not be readily understood by a wider audience' the novelist David Benedictus was advised by his publishers), a lack of enthusiasm for promising new work, a rapid worsening of the economic circumstances in which the average novelist was forced to labour, a stagnating industry reluctant to adopt new business practices that might enable it to compete more effectively, and a more general air of cultural indifference extending to outright malaise in which overproduction and falling sales went hand in hand. Too many books, as one correspondent put it, chasing too few readers. With a full-frontal assault apparently in progress on both the writer's livelihood and his, or her, room for creative manoeuvre, the Dunkirk spirit was much in evidence. 'Survival is the name of the game' Stan Barstow declared. 'Survival on the best terms one can manage.' 'One soldiers on' David Benedictus echoed, 'beset by financial anxiety and the need to take on ephemeral work.'

In some ways the problem went deeper even than this. Lurking behind several of the contributions is the suspicion of what might be called a crisis in professional confidence, a feeling that the novel specifically, and books generally, have ceased to occupy the position that they held in civilised society fifty or a hundred years ago, that what had previously – at any rate at its upper levels – been a fairly glamorous calling had been despatched to the cultural margins. J. B. Priestley, for example, had been one of the great public figures of the interwar era, whose wartime broadcasts rivalled Churchill's in their popularity. The Priestley of his late-period reminiscences, on the other hand, advises the younger writers of the day to err on the side of caution. Go in search of orthodoxy, fit neatly into the 'Eng Lit pigeonhole' is Priestley's no doubt ironic message, never oppose the establishment ('which after all may have a prize waiting for you'), eschew the unpopular cause and keep one eye on America. 'You might *make it*' Priestley enjoins, while adding the comment 'if there is still much to make'. Priestley was in his 80s when he wrote this, but the assumption of a deeply diminished prestige occurred to many a younger practitioner. At its heart, more ruminative commentators insisted, was a widening fracture between writers and their audience, a suspicion that in the final quarter of the twentieth century the gargantuan sales still awaiting a very small proportion of the contemporary talent pool were scant recompense for the genuine conduit that had existed between the novelist of a bygone age and his readers; a compact rendered that much more powerful by the limited number of personnel involved.

William Cooper's contribution to the *New Review* gathering looks back elegiacally to the 'symbiotic' relationship between Victorian novelists and their audiences, alleging that its distinguishing mark was that each 'cared' about the other. 'What percentage of the contemporary public equivalent to the public who loved Dickens and George Eliot is concerned above all whether in their inner lives they are being true to themselves, about whether they are being truly authentic?' To Cooper, for whom the blame for practically any iniquity can be laid at the door of modernism, the villain of the piece is the Modern Novel, 'with its dominant preoccupations with the individual's inner experience on the one hand and aesthetics on the other'. A variation on this line was filed by Kingsley Amis in a radio interview in the early part of 1979. The young Amis, his interviewer reminded him, had seemed to feel that British culture was the property of an exclusive club. The modern Amis seemed to regret its newly acquired democratising tendencies. 'You can't share real culture equally' Amis replied. 'There aren't enough brains to go round, really, and when 100,000 people, instead of say 10,000 people, study the Victorian novel, what those 100,000 are getting is a kind of shadow, a simulacrum, of what the 10,000 lucky ones, the ones fit for it, used to get.' But surely, the interviewer presses him, wouldn't it be a better world if more people read Victorian novels? Amis professes himself 'not really sure. Among the people I talk to about novels, my own and others, it's clear that only a minority of them know what a novel is.'

Whatever misgivings the writer may have had about the people who read, or did not read, or – if Amis is to be believed – were incapable of reading his books, there remained the much more pressing question of sheer visibility, the kind of public figure that the writer cut in an increasingly crowded landscape, the simple business of being seen. A certain kind of author – usually, but not always, one habituated to playing the publicity game – had done well out of the new media dispensations of the 1950s and in particular the advent of television. Beverley Nichols, ever the composer manqué, had been invited to play one of his preludes on 'one of my ridiculous morning television programmes', where the pressures of live broadcasting produced an attack of nerves ('I made a complete hash of it. I got as far as the sixteenth bar and couldn't go on, so in sheer panic I modulated back to the beginning and began all over again'). Somerset Maugham was reverently interviewed on commercial television and encouraged to 'Look at Life' for the *TV Times*. At the upper end of the arts-world spectrum – for example the territory colonised by *Monitor*, the BBC's flagship arts programme, which began broadcasting in the late 1950s – standards were exceptionally high. To watch reruns of some of the early series is to be struck by the rarefied nature of the discussions and the curious homogenising process that the BBC seemed able to bring to the range of accents and social backgrounds on display. Alan Sillitoe, the son of a Nottingham labourer, sounds positively middle class, while Simon Raven (Charterhouse and King's College, Cambridge) and Kingsley Amis (City of London School and St John's College, Oxford), found conducting a somewhat stagey *conversazioni* in a Swansea pub about the sociological basis of *Lucky Jim*, have clearly been plucked from the Goodwood enclosure.

With certain prominent exceptions, the writer inducted into the (relatively) classless and technically innovative world of television tended to treat the experience with a high degree of suspicion. The 1960s novel is full of 'serious' writers venturing into the jungle of studio discussions and high-profile documentary-making and finding the natives distinctly unfriendly. Fielding Gray, the hero of Raven's *The Judas Boy* (1968), narrowly escapes with his life from the machinations surrounding a series entitled 'This is History'. But sharp operators, even those who regarded the medium as vulgarly intrusive, quickly became adept at manipulating it for promotional purposes. Evelyn Waugh made two celebrated BBC television appearances at this time, each of which he carefully stage-managed as a means of projecting the defiantly out-of-date persona of his latter days to a wider audience. 'Will the studio be very hot?' he innocently enquired in advance of his debut on John Freeman's *Face to Face* in 1960. 'Will I need to wear my tropical clothes?' There was a memorable exchange in which Freeman wondered why it was that, given his love of privacy, his guest had agreed to subject himself to an interrogation watched by millions of viewers. 'Poverty' Waugh shot back. 'We are being paid to talk in this deliriously happy way.' When a second interview was proposed for *Monitor* in 1964, Waugh consented with the proviso that it should be conducted by 'a pretty gal'. Elizabeth Jane Howard, to whom the task fell, was greatly to his taste. 'When is Miss Howard going to take her clothes off?' he is supposed to have demanded between takes. Encouraged by his interlocutor, he then inveighed against the 'gibberish' of modernism. It was a bravura performance, which undoubtedly helped sales of Waugh's autobiography, *A Little Learning*, published later in the year.

Early 1960s arts television continued to offer a place to the writer, and not always in the formal setting of the interview or profile. One might note, for example, the success of the BBC's literary quiz show *Take It or Leave It*, directed by Julian Jebb, in which the actor Peter Eyre read unattributed passages of prose and verse and a four-person panel speculated on the authors' identities. Half a century later A. S. Byatt could still recall the excitement of travelling to Manchester to record with her fellow panellists:

> Much the most amiable presence was John Betjeman – it was he who said the audience liked it when we got things wrong. Angus

> Wilson was very brilliant, though possibly the best guesser was Antonia Fraser. Julian put a lot of effort into persuading Elizabeth Bowen – she had a bad stammer – but finally she agreed. And there was Brigid Brophy and many more. I think the recordings were mostly destroyed – if they had been archived they would have been of enormous interest (and amusement). Cyril Connolly got cross because they took to choosing passages from things he was a specialist on, or had reviewed, and when he didn't get them he felt humiliated and sulked.

Cheering as this exposure was, the arts world of the 1960s increasingly came to be defined by its attitude to the burgeoning counter-culture. Here, with one or two exceptions, the 'serious' writer scored badly. There were, of course, several connections between 1960s pop culture and the world of 'straight' literature. John Lennon published two collections of surrealist doggerel, *In His Own Write* (1964) and *A Spaniard in the Works* (1965), with Jonathan Cape, while the Rolling Stones made a desultory attempt to film Dave Wallis's *Only Lovers Left Alive* (1964), a sci-fi epic in which the young take control of the world after the older generation has succumbed to mass suicide, with a screenplay by Keith Waterhouse and Willis Hall. From the other side of the fence, Kingsley Amis and Philip Larkin both liked the Beatles, Larkin praising the early recordings *With the Beatles* and *Help!*, but regretting the mid-1960s change of direction, Amis countering that 'they went on being all right longer than you say, up to Sgt Pepper, no?' Iris Murdoch, too, was a fan, telling her friend Brigid Brophy in May 1967 that 'the Beatles jointly ought to be Poet Laureate.' But in general the writer – certainly the writer over 40 – was either a curious and/or horrified observer of the late 1960s explosion of music and alternative behaviour and, as such, despatched to the margins in coverage of what became the decade's obsession. Where a writer cast in the Kingsley Amis mould – Amis senior was a former Labour voter who spent the 1960s steadily drifting rightward – came into his, or her, own was in the adversarial context of the television discussion programme. There was a famous 'London edition' of the conservative US columnist William F. Buckley's *Front Line*, in which Amis, assisted by the yet more right-wing-leaning John Braine, took on a pair of leftist students over the question of capital punishment.

There was one area of 1960s literature, alternatively, in which links to the emerging counter-culture were more than simply vestigial. This was popular poetry. Not only were the 'Liverpool' or 'Mersey' poets as much a part of the mid-1960s cultural scene as Liverpudlian music, but there was a direct relationship between the world of performance poetry and contemporary pop. Liverpool Scene began life as the Mersey poets Roger McGough, Brian Patten and Adrian Henri, accompanied by a guitar player. McGough then switched to the Scaffold, together with his fellow Liverpudlians John Gorman and Paul McCartney's brother Mike McGear, and enjoyed a UK number one hit single with 'Lily the Pink' in 1968. Forty years before, the popular conception of the 'poet' had been of a grave Georgian eminence striding plus-foured through the heather before recruiting himself at a Sussex pub, but come the mid-1960s it had mutated into the figure of the surrogate pop star inveighing against the Vietnam War from the stage of the Royal Albert Hall or publishing brightly coloured pamphlets with titles like *Fab Gear Groove*. All these factors worked their effect.

By the early 1970s, consequently, the writer was less of a public figure than he or she had been for perhaps a century and a half, while the efforts to increase interest in, and sales of, books seemed destined only to consolidate an existing audience rather than to expand public interest in literature. As Rayner Heppenstall noted, the National Book League's 'Bedford Square Book Bang' of 1971 was memorable for the large number of people who turned out for 'M. Drabble's traditional novelists'. His own assembly of avant-garde experimentalists, among them the novelist Alan Burns who 'looked forward with enthusiasm to the day when novels would be written by computers', fared much less well. Naturally there were exceptions to this rule. The Poet Laureate Sir John Betjeman was by this time well on the way to becoming a national treasure, esteemed quite as much for his attacks on modernist architecture as for his televised jaunts around the route of the old Metropolitan railway. But the writers who commanded the widest public audiences were generally those who had moved on into other fields. Only a tiny fraction of the fans of Malcolm Muggeridge's television documentaries would have read or remembered the novels and pieces of reportage with which he had begun his career in the 1930s.

If there was one writer capable of defying this trend it was Kingsley Amis who, almost uniquely among the novelists who had come to prominence in the 1950s, managed to maintain, and even to extend, his public profile in the decades that followed. The mark of Amis's adroitness was his ability to supplement an already considerable income by way of advertising. In 1975, for example, knowing his client to be strapped for cash, his agent suggested a part-time career in product endorsement, 'provided the product was absolutely right'. The initial list concentrated on the drinks trade, and included such brands as Martini, Campari, Dubonnet and Smirnoff, but it was Sanderson Fabrics who eventually photographed him and his then wife Elizabeth Jane Howard in a newly furbished room beneath the caption 'Very Kingsley Amis. Very Sanderson.' Other commissions followed, for drinks companies and W. H. Smith. As one of his biographers drily remarks, 'If Amis saw these money-spinning activities as a threat to his authorial dignity, he never said so.'

The 'crisis in publishing' – at any rate at the serious end of publishing – was a post-war cliché, but of what precisely did it consist? Business analysts who inspected the performance of the more visible trade publishers in the late 1970s invariably diagnosed a stagnation born of over-reliance on outdated and largely unreformed business models. American publishers, after all, had spent the previous decade restructuring and consolidating, merging smaller firms into conglomerates, integrating mass-market paperback houses and hardback imprints into single entities and streamlining their production and distribution arrangements. Their UK equivalents, with certain exceptions, were still strictly demarcated, with a variety of independent, medium-sized operators – Hamish Hamilton, Chatto & Windus, Jonathan Cape, Faber & Faber – pursuing prestige through the publicity generated by hardback sales and income by selling subsidiary rights to paperback firms. Overseas markets were in decline as American competition made its way into the old Commonwealth territories. At home, cuts in library funding had begun to undermine a hitherto failsafe source of subsidy for hardback fiction. Meanwhile, the books themselves were becoming more expensive to produce. The retail price of a hardback novel crept up from 21s in the old pre-decimal days to £4.95 or even £5.95 at the decade's end. Even this was felt by some publishers to be uneconomic. And to price increases and declining sales could be added the hindrance of a distributive chain that, like some of the publishers who supplied it, was beginning to show its age. Until the early 1980s, the prospective purchaser of a newly published book was offered a choice between the notoriously lightly stocked local branch of W. H. Smith or one of the hundreds of small independents, where the ordering up of an obscure item could take anything from a few days to several weeks.

However hidebound and retrogressive when examined from the angle of business efficiency, the UK publishing industry was, in many respects, a very different animal from its 1950s forebear. Book-trade analysts who examined the lists of books published and the range of interests and preoccupations on display generally noted a reduction in the number of titles and the near-extinction of formerly successful genres. A few best-sellers aside (Betjeman, Hughes, Larkin) poetry was commercially negligible by the end of the 1970s. It was calculated that fewer verse collections were published in 1980 than biographies or even mathematical treatises. Secker & Warburg, one of the few substantial firms with a recognised poetry list, and a part-time poetry editor, publishing in runs of 500 with no paperback sales, was thought to spend £25,000 a year on its programme and recoup a bare £15,000. Serious fiction seemed to be going the same way; the volume of titles falling to half the number published in 1939, genre everywhere triumphant and the average sale of a hardback novel by a reputable novelist put at between 2,000 and 2,500 copies. All this led to an understandable anxiety amongst book-trade pundits. What were the consequences of commercial stagnation for individual creativity? Did the book, in fact, have a future? Brigid Brophy wrote a brisk polemic along these lines, arguing that literary novelists were now engaged in a constant round of self-censorship, fearing to antagonise their publishers by producing innovative or experimental work. 'Which would you rather be?' she demanded. 'Good or published?' A respectable chance of a respectable sale was no longer enough. In the future, as in the past, talent might have to subsidise itself. How else had Firbank succeeded other than by 'the improbable chance of literary genius and a private income falling to the lot of the same baby'?

By coincidence this harangue appeared in a magazine – an early number of the relaunched monthly magazine *Granta* – which carried several intimations of the way in which the literary world was about, or had already begun, to change. One of them was Cape's advertisement for 'a remarkable new novel set in India during the time since independence', Salman Rushdie's *Midnight's Children*. Another was a short story by Martin Amis, then at work on *Money* (1984). A third was an ad for the Faber showcase volume *Introduction Seven*, featuring the first published work of Kazuo Ishiguro. All three writers were to play a distinctive part in a literary renaissance – as much commercial as creative – that was already getting under way at the moment Brophy filed her self-censoring jeremiad. The boom in 'serious' publishing that characterised the 1980s and early 1990s has no single cause. Rather, it consisted of a variety of developments both inside the publishing industry and beyond it which, taken together, had the capacity to transform the atmosphere in which (relatively) highbrow novels were written, issued and received. The most obvious was the emergence of a new wave of English and Commonwealth novelists – Amis, Rushdie, Ishiguro, Timothy Mo, Peter Ackroyd, Graham Swift, Julian Barnes – nearly all of them born in the period 1945 to 1955, and nearly all of them men, whose most significant works appeared in the half-decade between 1980 and 1985. *Midnight's Children*, for example, appeared in 1981; Swift's *Waterland* in 1983; Barnes's *Flaubert's Parrot* in 1984. To the advantage of a significant body of new work produced by a significant body of new writers could be added a series of promotional initiatives designed to take the writers involved beyond the narrow confines of the bookshop and into the wider cultural firmament. The Book Marketing Council's 'Best of British Young Novelists' attracted widespread press attention in the summer of 1983, as did the near-simultaneous publication of Anthony Burgess's compendium *99 Novels*.

Equally fundamental changes were starting to affect the publishing and bookselling industries. By the early 1980s the reconfiguration so long anticipated by book-trade pundits had begun to take shape. Medium-sized firms banded together (Chatto & Windus, Jonathan Cape, Bodley Head) or were assimilated by larger concerns (Hamish Hamilton, Hutchinson, Michael Joseph). American money moved eastward, most symbolically in Rupert Murdoch's purchase of William Collins. There was also – provided they were sufficiently capitalised and the business model worked – space for new independents: Bloomsbury Publishing, co-founded by Cape's former editorial director Liz Calder, was a media sensation on its launch in the summer of 1986, one of the first genuinely important newcomers since the feminist house Virago in 1973. Irrigated by inward investment, and with more money to spend on advances and publicity, the new publishing houses of the late 1980s had a self-confidence that their cash-starved predecessors from the previous decade altogether lacked. They were also able to benefit from changes in the somewhat antiquated world of bookselling, marked by the opening of the first Waterstones in 1982; a chain which developed exponentially throughout the 1980s until its eventual purchase by W. H. Smith in 1989.

But if books, and their authors, were fashionable in the 1980s to a degree scarcely seen for a quarter of a century, their steady climb towards newspaper front pages was assisted by intense media interest in the prize culture that began to dominate 1980s book publicity. The Booker Prize, established in 1969 and first won by the former controller of the BBC Third Programme, P. H. Newby, with *Something to Answer For*, had become steadily more newsworthy throughout the 1970s. By 1980, when William Golding's *Rites of Passage* held off the challenge of Burgess's *Earthly Powers*, it had become a public event; a rise consolidated by the hotly contested judging process of 1981 when *Midnight's Children* narrowly defeated D. M. Thomas's *The White Hotel*. However much disparaged by purists, who alleged that it led to the production of essentially factitious novels – what Richard Todd once termed the 'gratuitous exoticism' of a novel like Penelope Lively's *Moon Tiger* (1987) – written to a formula likely to appeal to judges, the Booker undoubtedly had an unprecedented effect on book sales. Twelve years after Rushdie, Roddy Doyle's *Paddy Clarke Ha Ha Ha* was thought to have earned £6 million for its publishers, Secker & Warburg, including hardback sales in excess of 400,000 copies.

If more books were being sold and read, by publishers who now had the resources to promote them effectively, then the critical environment in which they were received was also subject to change. The late 1980s brought a boom in print journalism, built on Rupert Murdoch's defeat of the print unions and the advent of computerised technology. Newspaper arts coverage expanded; there was proportionately more space for reviews. By 1988, for example, the *Sunday Times Books Section* was a discrete, sixteen-page supplement to the main paper with a staff of five. The *Independent*, founded in 1986, was noted for its literary coverage, featured a daily book review at the foot of its leader page and employed a celebrity critic – at first Anthony Burgess, later Auberon Waugh – to occupy the Friday spot. Other newspapers followed suit, and yet by far the most influential publication associated with the 1980s publishing revival was a literary magazine. In its original incarnation, *Granta* had been a Cambridge student paper, and it was from King's College, Cambridge that Bill Buford, an American postgraduate at work on a PhD, issued the first number of the new series in 1979. In fact these academic credentials – early numbers were printed and typeset by the university library – were misleading. While the Cambridge address was retained for over a decade, the magazine's links with the university's English department – notwithstanding the pride of place given to the Cambridge don George Steiner's novella *The Portage to San Cristóbal of A.H.* in the second number – were comparatively slight.

At this point the enterprise was funded by the Arts Council's East Anglian office and a collection of private supporters. A list of 'honorary patrons' appended to the inside front cover included the poet Anthony Thwaite, his biography-writing wife Ann and, somewhat incongruously, Rugby School. Already, though, Buford had given notice of the kind of territory which *Granta* would increasingly explore and the kind of attitudes that would come to colour its editorial stance. Issue three, which contained new work from Angela Carter and Russell Hoban and a prepublication extract from *Midnight's Children*, was prefaced by a polemical introduction in which most of post-war English literature was condemned out of hand. According to Buford, vast swathes of the writing 'of the Fifties, Sixties, and even much of the Seventies . . . lacks excellence, wants drive, provides comfort, not challenge'. The antidote lay in fashionable Americana of the kind written by Raymond Carver (featured in issue four) and Richard Ford. The fourth number unveiled what became the standard *Granta* format: a fat paperback, as much as 300 pages long, attractively laid out and, at £2.25, cheaper than most soft cover novels.

In trying to assess the magazine's steady trajectory of achievement over the next half-decade – regular publication, professional distribution, the move to proper premises in Hobson Street – one is constantly having to balance the element of genuine risk-taking (*Midnight's Children*, for example, was the work of a little-known writer who had published one poorly received novel six years before) with carefully managed opportunism. The celebrated 'Dirty Realism' number of 1984, which made Buford's reputation as an importer of hot American talent, brought together Carver, Ford, Jayne Anne Phillips and Tobias Wolff – all of whom went on to make substantial reputations in the UK. Three decades later, especially given what we now know about Carver's well-nigh collaborative relationship with his editor, the tag looks bogus, a marketing opportunity rather than an attempt to establish a more or less homogeneous *galère* of up-and-coming transatlantic fiction in some kind of relief.

On the other hand, there was no denying *Granta*'s success. This, in the context of literary magazine publishing, was simply unprecedented. Circulation, now overseen by Penguin, rose towards the 100,000 mark in the late 1980s: to find an equivalent it was necessary to go as far back as the headiest days of *Penguin New Writing*. None of this, though, was enough to silence Buford's critics. There were complaints about editorial high-handedness: 'the drawing rooms of literary London have resounded to the laments of senior novelists who, asked for contributions at length and in haste, have found them rejected without explanation and by return of post' the *Sunday Times* once alleged. Much more wounding was the charge of cliquishness and the suggestion that far from encouraging new talent, Buford was merely adept at making existing developments in literature work to his own advantage. Few neutral observers, perhaps, would have gone as far as the rival editor who declared that '*Granta* is a business success because it publishes exclusively established writers and journalists and is serviced by a coterie of London publishers and top-shot agents who put their illustrious clients at the magazine's disposal with minimum fuss and maximum reward.' At the same time, the frequency with which an issue carrying work by Amis, Barnes and Rushdie was succeeded by one offering work by Rushdie, Barnes and Amis was noted even by disinterested critics. Neither was Buford interested in bona fide new writers: a former editorial assistant revealed that the number of contributions taken from the 'unsoliciteds' pile during the sixteen years of his tenure was precisely nil. In some ways this exclusiveness was merely the mark of Buford's success. Whether or not they were genuine discoveries, the writers he championed early in his career stayed loyal. Between 1984 and 1995 each of Amis's novels enjoyed prepublication exposure in *Granta*. It was also a symbol of a much wider determination to promote certain kinds of writing at the expense of others. Taken as a whole, the domestic contributions to the forty-nine numbers of the Buford era – he resigned in 1995 to become the *New Yorker*'s fiction editor – have a tendency to harbour bloke-ish male writers of the Amis/Barnes school. Certainly, very few women ever appeared there to advantage. At its best – for example 1989's 'Death' issue, with memoirs from William Cooper and John Gregory Dunne – it was very good: prescient (in its interest in Eastern Europe), adept at introducing British audiences to emerging international talent (Milan Kundera, Mario Vargas Llosa). At its worst it was faddish and packed with overfamiliar faces. On the other hand, a similar charge sheet could have been drawn up for *Horizon*.

Granta's considerable éclat shouldn't blind us to the part played by less flamboyant operators on the 1980s scene, whose influence was sometimes out of all proportion to their decidedly un-*Granta* like sales. 'If *London Magazine* shuts down' Anthony Powell wrote in his journal, 'nothing else whatever of that sort will ever take its place.' Plenty of younger subscribers would have agreed. Julian Barnes, trying to sum up its attractions, noted the distrust of coteries, international awareness, its attempts to keep pace with developments across the arts, the space offered to debutants as well as established writers. Like *Granta*, the *London Magazine* relied on the efforts of a single editorial eminence, but Alan Ross (1922–2001) was a markedly different proposition from Buford: self-effacing, self-contained, sometimes reduced to near-silence by the fits of depression to which he was periodically subject. In sole charge since 1961, when one of his early contributors was Evelyn Waugh (who confessed to Nancy Mitford that he had reviewed her latest novel for 'a funny little paper run by Evelyn Gardner's niece and a beaver whose name escapes me – Rouse? Rose? He calls me Evelyn'), Ross had by this time settled on what he diffidently termed 'a more or less considered formula' – stories, three or four clumps of poems, a memoir or critical essay trailed by reports from abroad, notices of current exhibitions and thirty or so two-column pages of book reviews. But there was also space for drawings, portfolios of photographs and extended treatments of theatre and cinema, as well as the long-running series 'Living in London', 'Living out of London', 'Leaving School' and 'Developments in Style'.

Run on a shoestring, underwritten by substantial subsidy from the Arts Council, and even in its balmiest days rarely exceeding a circulation of 4,000 copies, the *London Magazine* had all the advantages – and one or two of the drawbacks – of being a one-man band. The twenty-fifth anniversary volume is an extraordinary concoction – poems by Plath, Larkin, Heaney and Walcott, Auden's 'Hammerfest', stories by William Trevor and Peter Carey, Keith Vaughan's 'Last Journals'. On the other hand, a subsequent attempt to move with the times, when the magazine was briefly taken up by a commercial publisher, given a four-colour jacket, an increased print run and proper distribution, was not a success. Ross, when it came to it, would only play the magazine game on his own terms. As such he was uninterested in rehiring the famous names (William Boyd, Graham Swift, Paul Theroux) whose initial reputations he had helped to make, and deeply suspicious of contemporary razzmatazz. One of the few things calculated to 'drive him wild with rage', according to one obituarist, was mention of *Granta*, which he refused to take seriously, claiming that it took no risks but merely promoted modish writers who had already made their reputations elsewhere.

Ross died in 2001, still in harness, the magazine surviving in various forms but bereft of its animating spirit. If by the time of his death he was a complete anachronism, then he also demonstrated what a formidable proposition a one-man editorial band operating in an atmosphere more or less unchanged since the days of Connolly and Lehmann could be. Not the least of his achievements, for example, was the magazine's publishing imprint, London Magazine Editions, which maintained a sporadic existence until at least the early 1990s. While the books it sponsored – small-circulation and warily promoted – tended to be the memoirs of a particular kind of Ross crony, often elderly literary men of a pre-1939 vintage (Julian Symons's *Notes from Another Country*, Roy Fuller's *Souvenirs* and *Vamp Till Ready*) or collections of previously published *London Magazine* series, Ross's taste in fiction was capable of accommodating anything from Graham Swift's short stories to J. L. Carr's *A Season in Sinji*.

From nearly all these manoeuvrings there arose the question of affiliation, milieu, geography even. The *London Magazine*, in its latter days, was edited out of an ancient shed in South Kensington. The early *Granta* was metropolitan in everything but its postal address. Simultaneously there were plenty of provincial literary magazines capable of playing a part in the 1980s–90s boom. In many cases their locations were arbitrary, merely a case of where the editors happened to be living at the time: the distinguishing mark of *Argo*, founded in 1979 by a pair of Oxford postgraduates and published biannually for the next decade, is just how *un*-Oxonian it seems, much more likely to be interested in translations from the French, modern Israeli writing, reviews of fiction that might not even be available in the UK. But there were other magazines that made a positive virtue of this sequestration – the Lincolnshire-based *Sunk Island Review*, for example – leading, at their outermost extreme, to a select cadre who used a distinct regional identity as a stick with which to beat what they imagined to be the inadequacies of a cliquish and self-serving London literary scene.

Chief among these was *Panurge*, edited by the novelist John Murray from a farmhouse seven miles outside Carlisle, which managed twenty-five issues in a combative career that extended between 1984 and 1996. Although it published a fair amount of criticism and reportage, from the very first the magazine specialised in the short story; the more obscure the author the greater the chances of him, or her, being published – 'brilliant work by people you've never heard of' as one of the early editorials put it, with further showcasing of little-known talent provided by occasional anthologies (see *Move over Waxblinder! The Panurge Book of Funny Stories*, 1994) and compilations. If *Panurge* had a weakness, whether edited by Murray or, between 1987 and 1993 by David Almond, it was that very few of these discoveries went on to make distinctive careers. A notable exception was Julia Darling, who published a collection of short stories under the magazine's imprint (*Bloodlines*, 1995) before moving on to Penguin. Murray would probably have argued that these failures proved his point, that London publishers preferred to talent-spot in their own backyards. He signed off with a bumper valedictory number nearly 100,000 words in length, arguing in a final editorial that such 'cottage industries' were no longer economically viable, calculating that he had managed to pay himself £11 a week during his time in the editorial chair and thanking his wife, whose full-time job had kept him afloat. There were regional publishing houses capable of riding the 1990s wave: Birmingham's Tindal Street Press, for example, which launched the early careers of Alan Mahar and Clare Morrall. But here in the new commercial environment of the post-Thatcher years, such enterprises needed a degree of organisation and financial backing that Murray and his dogged band of helpers, irascibly adrift in their Cumbrian backwater, did not possess.

One advantage of the boom in print journalism was that it extended the generational range. The slight air of fustiness that attended books pages in the late 1970s, when, as one observer put it, newspapers were still full of literary editors printing reviews by chaps they had sauntered round Cambridge quadrangles with at the time of the Two Cultures debate, was replaced by an emphasis on youth: it was quite usual for a 30-year-old publishing his first novel to find it reviewed by half a dozen critics even younger than he was. With youth, inevitably, came a certain amount of asperity. The late 1980s, for example, were marked by a distinctive revolt against one or two of the senior figures of the post-war era: ageing eminences such as Kingsley Amis and Iris Murdoch were sometimes startled to find the respect in which they had formerly been held turning into a robust and crisply expressed dissatisfaction, although Amis, for one, still held to the belief that age was a defence against serious insult. 'When you're old enough you can get away with piss' he told his friend Robert Conquest shortly before publication of *Difficulties with Girls* (1988). But these could be trying times for the senior novelist. *Private Eye*, noting the hostility with which certain critics greeted Murdoch's *The Message to the Planet* (1989), suggested that 'the treatment handed out to poor Dame Iris does no more than symbolise a great deal of accumulated resentment. Book-reviewing in this country is beginning to look like a blood sport again.'

There were one or two senior reviewers for whom it always had been. Given the four and a half decades which he spent teaching at Oxford, latterly as Merton Professor, it is tempting to write John Carey (b.1934) down as a classic example of the media don. In fact, a glance at the contents of his solitary miscellany *Original Copy* (1987), which collects many of his contributions to the *Sunday Times*, instantly establishes him as a metropolitan critic on the Hamilton pattern, not least because of his attitude to a profession which in ordinary circumstances he might have been expected to defend. As it is, Carey's celebrated essay 'Down with Dons', provoked by Hugh Lloyd-Jones's *Maurice Bowra*, is a blistering attack on what he calls the 'insulating effect of donnish uppishness'. A career academic, who made his original reputation as a Milton specialist, Carey's reviewing style – a mixture of calculated asperity sometimes descending into outright rudeness – would doubtless have startled anyone who came to his work by way of *The Violent Effigy* (1973), his pioneering study of Dickens's imagery, or his equally prescient book about Thackeray. He once remarked that Lady Diana Cooper had 'a talent for scavenging that would have done credit to a coyote', professed himself appalled by Bowra's bad manners, his perpetual showing off and the thought that all this was excused by the figure he cut, and quotes with approval the reader who wrote to commend his review of Diana Mosley's *Loved Ones* on the grounds that 'she needed a poke in the nose'.

The inseparability of Carey's literary judgements from his social judgements is entirely consistent with one of the recurring themes of his criticism, the idea that, as he once put it, 'English writing in the twentieth century has persistently catered for minorities and elites to the exclusion of a large potential readership of ordinary, intelligent people who have developed, over the years, a thoroughly understandable dislike of "culture" and the "cultured".' Opponents of modernist excess nearly always have him cheering from the touchline, and he wrote a revealing essay on Larkin, praising his attacks on Pound and Picasso for being 'in contradiction of human life as we know it' and declaring that 'the normal reader, coming upon this, feels like cheering at the spectacle of sanity coming back into critical discourse'. What does he admire in Larkin? A short answer would be his intelligibility, his dislike of show-offs and bohemians, his siding with the common man 'who pays good money for a book and expects to be entertained in return', and for his 'punch and subtlety' – two very Carey-like qualities, it has to be said. Naturally he is appalled by structuralism, whose wilder ideas 'pretty clearly call for a spell of sedation and devoted nursing', and David Lodge is awarded top marks for suggesting that the aim of Derridean deconstruction is 'the mystification and intimidation of the reader'.

All this might suggest that Carey is an extremely uncomplicated kind of critic, a personal-response man with his likes and dislikes and a very small patch of neutral ground in between. And certainly Carey on 'Evaluation' is a kind of object lesson in relative values: the only real judge is God, and in the absence of God how can judgements retain their credibility. The real usefulness of value judgements, consequently, will emerge only when we have acknowledged them to be subjective. It is the same with his middle-class materialism, ever critical of 'affluent soft-headedness' and remarking of Jeremy Seabrook, who lamented the educational process that took him to Cambridge and detached him from his parents' world, that 'gifted children of ungifted parents must either outgrow them or remain stunted'. Simultaneously, these displays of bourgeois self-confidence embody a fundamental shrewdness about human motivation – see, for example, his assessment of Beatrice Webb, of whom he notes that 'she liked repression because she was repressed'.

As for the source of this belligerence, the clues lie scattered throughout his recent autobiography. The youngest son of a quintessentially middle-class family from south-west London, whose once prosperous father had been badly hit by the Depression, Carey is a distinctive example of the bright scholarship boy drawn by his ability along thoroughfares where the scholarship boy had hitherto rarely strayed. Some of the most scathing passages of his memoirs are reserved for Christ Church College, Oxford, which appointed him to a temporary fellowship in the late 1950s, where the distinguished economist Sir Roy Harrod declines to speak to him across the dinner table, the college staff enjoy being patronised by their blue-blooded charges and even the architecture is 'an object lesson in how to make people feel small'. Infuriated by the closed scholarship system which, as it seemed to him, promoted mediocre privately educated talent at the expense of genuine live wires from the grammar schools, Carey turned into an academic class-warrior, circularising likely-looking English teachers with the aim of getting them to send him their brightest pupils, while doing his best to modernise the limited range of set books that might greet them on their arrival and disparaging those nineteenth-century classics whose merits he thought were being taken on trust: *Idylls of the King*, for example, was written off as 'high Victorian bunkum'.

Bracing as much of this is, the amusement to be gained from these irruptions of temperament is always sharpened by an awareness of the ironies that lurk beneath. At one point, for instance, he ticks off the Matthew Arnold of *Culture and Anarchy* on the grounds that Arnold as a thinker is 'at best useless and at worst malign. Every thought that comes to him is drenched in the assumptions of his social class' while ignoring the fact that the same could surely be said, *mutatis mutandis*, of a critic who admits being drawn to the material that produced *The Intellectuals and the Masses* (1992) after coming across one or two of Virginia Woolf's less enlightened remarks about the servant problem. If one of Carey's charms as a critic is this ability to have it both ways, without seeming to notice that the trick is being played, then another is his studied self-confidence, the note that V. S. Pritchett admired in Orwell's use of the word 'unquestionably' when making judgements that could seem all too precarious. As for drawbacks to this class-consciousness, they lie in his reluctance to examine one or two of its implications, to concede that not all virtue is bred up in the green-houses of the south-west London sprawl or even to allow that the idea of English social class is rarely as homogeneous, as innately cut and dried, as it can seem from the outside. Carey's exceptionally astute biography of William Golding falls halfway into this trap by contrasting Golding's time at Marlborough Grammar School, which left him with the feeling that he was 'not quite a gentleman', with the advantages of the public school down the road. True, no doubt, but the Old Marlburian John Betjeman was mocked on exactly the same grounds by Oxford friends who had been to Eton and Winchester. But Carey, you feel, has invested too much emotional energy in Golding, chained himself too tightly to his subject's own mythological image, to be able to admit this relativism, and the best weapon for carving up the English social system is invariably a chopper.

Something of the same absorption informs Carey's most celebrated tour de force, *What Good Are the Arts?* (2005), several of whose conclusions have their roots in the essay on evaluation filed a quarter of a century before: all cultural judgements are, of their very nature, provisional, and there is no unarguable method of proving that Proust is superior to last week's best-seller; art neither exalts nor debases, and neuro-scientific attempts to establish universal standards of perception are so much garbage; reading and writing will not make you a better person, and neither – whatever Bloomsbury and Jeanette Winterson may say – is literature a substitute for religious belief. All this is written up with a fine, caustic fury – Ms Winterson effortlessly disposed of for using art as a vehicle for what, to Carey, is her own smug superiority, Iris Murdoch's theory of great art's 'essential selflessness' found to be 'spectacularly wrong' – in which the mark of Carey's ability is that he can follow this frenzy of statue-tumbling with a thoroughly disarming essay on literature's manifest superiority to any other art form and appear to get away with it. In the end, though, a faint air of disingenuousness hangs over the proceedings. No doubt there is no universal standard capable of demonstrating that one book is better than another, or that one artist is a genius and another a fraudulent hack. On the other hand, it would take an exceptionally trusting reader not to recollect that Professor Carey spent nearly fifty years of his life serving an institution at which judgements of this kind were – presumably – taken rather seriously.

Inevitably, one man's wasted life may be another's declaration of intellectual honesty, but again the all-art-is-useless line is immediately called into question by the substantial number of books that can be seen to have engineered some shift in the way that societies organise themselves. Where, after all, would the reform of the early twentieth-century Chicago meat-packing industry have been without Upton Sinclair's *The Jungle*, or the abolitionist movement without *Uncle Tom's*

Cabin? In the last resort, polemics of this kind can only be written from a position of strength. And here there are interesting continuities with Carey's distant predecessor in the Merton chair, Sir Walter Raleigh, another of those anti-academic academics whose rhetorical flourishes are only enhanced by their just happening to be Oxford professors. In much the same way, 'Down with Dons' could only have been written by a paid-up member of the cadre it affects to despise. None of this in any way detracts from the vigour of Carey's attack, his habit of summing up the face a particular writer raises to the world in a sentence, as when he writes of Chesterton that he had 'a body like a slag heap, but a mind like the dawn sky'. And he is always capable of reining in his prejudices when something in him is stirred. Ultimately, Evelyn Waugh's snobbishness, his malice and his airs cease to matter because his novels are funny, and even Lady Diana Cooper turns out to display 'such dauntless trust in the supremacy of herself and her class that it commands, in the end, grudging respect'.

If Carey was a moonlighting don, keen to demonstrate that he could double up as a journalist, stalking his quarry by way of the breezy generalisation and the pithy one-liner, then James Wood (b.1965) sometimes seemed like a journalist avid to bring to newspaper books pages some of the techniques of the lecture room. A rather old-fashioned lecture room, too, as the somewhat quaint academicism of his style ('What a piece of writing! What an amazing opening!') would not look out of place in some of Arthur Quiller-Couch's early lectures, and the fustiness of some of his critical language ('marvellous and alchemical translation', etc.) occasionally makes it seem closer in spirit to a late Victorian belles-lettrist. Although Wood's early career, mostly on the *Guardian*, where he was eventually given the title of 'chief literary critic', involved a certain amount of bread-and-butter reviewing, his real forte – again, unusually for a literary journalist – was Cambridge-style practical criticism: stripping the engine of a book down to its component parts with the aim of establishing just exactly how a piece of prose works at bedrock level to bring off its effects, the way in which, as he once put it, a novel 'teaches us how to read its narrator'. While each of Wood's first collections, *The Broken Estate* (1999) and *The Irresponsible Self* (2004), are full of dazzling exercises along these lines, the work in which he comes closest to adumbrating a theory of narrator-reading is the primer *How Fiction Works* (2008). The mark of Wood's dexterity, as chapters on 'Detail', 'Language',

'Character' and 'Dialogue' rapidly succeed each other, is his ability to draw useful lessons from the spectacle of a major-league talent getting it wrong. The James of *What Maisie Knew* is able to oscillate between its heroine, the wider community in which she operates and the writer himself, by virtue of James's mastery of the point of view (a discussion which, by the way, takes us back to Percy Lubbock's *The Craft of Fiction*). The John Updike of *Terrorist*, on the other hand, is convicted of stuffing in so much character-establishing detail that he ends up playing his creations false.

This close engagement with (and undoubted mastery of) his texts gives Wood's work an authority not often found outside the seminar room. If there is a drawback to these pageants of stately prose, now more often found in American periodicals after Wood's move to America to a job on the *New Republic* and, later, a part-time professorship at Harvard, it is the faint hint of companionability, the feeling that he is taking Flaubert, Nabokov, Joyce and the other heroes of the modernist canon out into the book-lined study of his mind and simply hobnobbing with them. There is, too, a way in which Wood's progress from close reading to mighty conclusion tends to rely on grand-sounding *obiter dicta*, which certain other Cambridge-bred close readers would want to subject to rather more scrutiny than they get: 'Metaphor is analogous to fiction because it floats a rival reality'; 'The novel is the virtuouso of exceptionalism: it always wriggles out of the rules thrown around it.' To say that this proceeds out of a heightened self-consciousness about the nature of criticism and, by implication, the value of the critic, is not to complain about the sometimes vertiginous standards on display, or of the demands being made on the reader. Yet Wood's habit of pronouncing august taxonomic judgement on absolutely everybody who strays beneath his lens can sometimes seem faintly superfluous. Arthur Benson, for example, dragged into one of *How Fiction Works*' ornate footnotes, can't merely be 'the writer A. C. Benson'; he has to be 'the minor English writer, A. C. Benson'. What sometimes undermines this exacting brand of Olympianism is that the critical tools on display become so finely calibrated that they only work at the very highest levels of literature. A review of a run-of-the-mill good-bad novel would, you feel, be rather beyond him – not a paralysing disability by any means, but it could not have been said of, say, V. S. Pritchett.

Wood tended to restrict himself to the canon, or to those angling towards it, but there were other critics at work in the 1990s determined to venture as far beyond it as was consistent with the demands of the mass-circulation newspapers in which their reviews appeared. The subjects of *Pandora's Handbag*, the solitary collection of the work of Elizabeth Young (1950–2001), published shortly after her premature death – Irvine Welsh, Poppy Z. Brite, Robert Mapplethorpe – wear their counter-cultural credentials like so many rosettes, and were selected, you sometimes suspect, for their ability to man the right side of the barricades rather than for any merits that they might have possessed. Zealously pursued as these enthusiasms were, there are several drawbacks to the Young approach to contemporary literature. Most obviously, it demands the construction of a rigid and reductive model of recent British culture, in which the 1950s can never have a good word said about them, and the 1960s are a model of egalitarian probity, only for the seeds of a liberal revolution to be uprooted by the 'aggressive dominatrix politics' of Mrs Thatcher. Then again, Young's approach requires dramatic causes célèbres, over which the battle between free speech and censorship could be endlessly refought – her particular totem pole is A. M. Homes's faked paedophile memoir, *The End of Alice* (1996).

What she excelled at, on the other hand, was the outpouring of imaginative sympathy – see, for example, her brilliant and curiously personal appreciation of Anna Kavan, a career heroin addict effectively criminalised by the drugs legislation of the late 1960s, in which Young's own psycho-medical problems – she died of hepatitis C – hover in the background. Rueful and self-effacing, the voice that arises from her best work is an unusual one for a late twentieth-century literary journalist: modest, confidential, somehow spirited in its occasional sadnesses. One reads her work not (as with Carey) to be swept aside by the vigour of some of the judgements, or (as with Wood) to be admitted into some celestial amphitheatre where an exceptionally well-informed tour guide is conducting a series of *conversazioni* with the ghosts of the past, but to admire the spectacle of a critic who is merely curious, plagued by uncertainty, occasionally seduced by the charms of material that may not stand the test of time, but always redeeming herself by a conviction that the activity on which she is engaged is a central part of life.

Mrs Thatcher and the Writers

> The Lefty is an intellectually disreputable and morally desensitised person whom the Labour Party tolerates within itself.
>
> Kingsley Amis, letter to *Encounter*, November 1968

> There are, of course, many Britains, and many of them – the sceptical, questioning, radical, reformist, libertarian, nonconformist Britains – I have always admired greatly. But these Britains are presently in retreat, even in disarray; while nanny-Britain, strait-laced Victorian values Britain, thin-lipped jingoist Britain, is in charge. Dark goddesses rule; brightness falls from the air.
>
> Salman Rushdie, *New Statesman*, May 1983

The radicalism of the 1950s had very often been wished upon it by journalists, conceptualised and burnished up by newspaper symposia to the point where it became entirely factitious. Certainly there were card-carrying members of the Labour Party among the literary groupings of the era of Anthony Eden and Harold Macmillan; certainly there was opposition to Suez, a general distrust of the Conservative Party and sympathy for the theories of cultural fragmentation and communal drift advanced by Richard Hoggart in *The Uses of Literacy*, but in general a rough and ready pragmatism was the order of the day, and of the qualities valued by Kingsley Amis, John Wain and their contemporaries, 'commitment' comes a long way down the list: the reluctance of several of the decade's big hitters to contribute to Tom Maschler's *Declaration* in 1957 tells its own story. Amis, in fact, is a prime example of some of the equivocations on offer at the time, on the one hand the author of a Fabian Society pamphlet entitled *Socialism and the Intellectuals*, which predicted that its author would continue to vote Labour 'to the end of my days, however depraved the Labour candidate may be and however virtuous his opponent', on the other already beginning to make ominous noises about the likely impact of 'progressive' policies in the field of higher education and suggesting that a proposed expansion of the university would lead to an inevitable collapse in standards.

Over the next twenty years most of these equivocations fell away, to reveal a literary landscape that was at once more politicised and polarised than at any time since the 1930s and in which, almost uniquely, most of the running was made by the right. One of the features of British intellectual history in the period 1964–79 is the regularity with which so many distinguished former anti-Conservatives publicly jumped ship. The historian Hugh Thomas, who had begun his career as the editor of a statue-tumbling symposium (*The Establishment*, 1959) ended up as Mrs Thatcher's *chef de cabinet*. Paul Johnson, a former editor of the *New Statesman* and right-hand man of the Labour prime minister Harold Wilson, was by the early 1970s firmly established as a critic of trades union excess. Amis, meanwhile, spent the 1960s steadily tracking rightward, voting Labour for the last time at the 1964 general election, and producing a celebrated article ('Why Lucky Jim Turned Right') for the *Sunday Telegraph* in which he attributed much of the era's political unrest to 'the frustrations of trying to get on in a competitive society where most people, by definition, cannot get on very far'. To Amis, the left-winger's complaints about the unfairness of 'the system' are merely an excuse for his, or her, laziness and stupidity. A cross letter to *Encounter*, written the following year, establishes these views in a generational context. 'Yes, quite a number of people have progressed from Left to Right as they grew older. Not enough to satisfy me, though.'

There were several reasons for this abandonment of socialism, even socialism of the shrimp-paste tint associated with Harold Wilson and James Callaghan. Some of it had to do with a general dislike of the liberalising attitudes of the 1960s, for which a reforming Labour Home Secretary, Roy Jenkins, was thought to be partly responsible. Rather more stemmed from an instinctive suspicion of what were seen as the robber barons of the Trades Union Congress – the *Enemies of Society* of Johnson's 1977 polemic. The ambivalence of the domestic left's attitude to such litmus tests of right-wing opinion as the situation in South East Asia and the blighted hopes of the short-lived Prague Spring of 1968 were roundly disparaged. The point about Alexander Dubček, the deposed First Secretary of the Czech Communist Party, Amis wrote, was that 'he was the only good sort of communist other than a dead one: the sort that looks forward to the dismantling of communism, whether or not he retains the name.' But quite as close to the heart of this contempt for the Wilson years was the idea that they had helped to lower standards, not least in the world of education. The idea that the left had presided over a wholesale betrayal of the nation's young continues as far as J. L. Carr's novel *Harpole & Foxberrow, General Publishers* (1992). This contains an uncannily prophetic chapter in which an irascible schoolteacher named Shutlanger, sacked by his local education authority, establishes 'The Margaret Thatcher Academy', whose principles are summarised thus:

> Special terms for intelligent hard-working pupils.
> No reduction of fees for families supposing themselves to be deprived.
> Idlers, bullies and backsliders assaulted daily.
> New educational theories unwelcome.

While the literary right had had its doubts about Edward Heath, Conservative Party leader since 1965, on the grounds that he was essentially a trimmer, too keen to negotiate with institutions which needed either to be fundamentally restructured or simply overthrown, Mrs Thatcher's triumph in the Tory leadership election of February 1975 stirred general agreement that she was, as Anthony Powell was later to put it, 'the answer.' Amis's correspondence from the late 1970s with his friend Philip Larkin echoes to the steady drip of approbation. 'Bloody good about Mrs Thatcher' Amis informed Robert Conquest, a celebrated critic of the Soviet experiment, early in 1976 after the new Leader of Her Majesty's Opposition had made a bracing anti-communist speech. Taken to dinner with her a year later, he reported back to Larkin that 'I thought her bright and tough and nice, and by God she doesn't half hate Lefties.' Larkin who, unlike Amis, had never made this incremental transit across the political spectrum, was, if anything, even more enthusiastic. 'Thatcher's team seems as bad as she is good' he pronounced on the recently assembled Shadow Cabinet in July 1978, while two years into her first administration the University of Hull's veteran librarian noted that 'la divine Thatcher is planning to slim the universities. None is to be closed (shame!)'.

And it was not just that the literary right approved of Mrs Thatcher's assault on the trades unions and her plans for higher education; their admiration was enhanced by the fact that, almost to a man, they found her physically attractive. 'What a superb creature she is – right and beautiful' Larkin declared in December 1984, after declining the offer of the Poet Laureateship. 'I find Mrs Thatcher very attractive' the then 76-year-old Powell recorded after a dinner convened for literary sympathisers at the Ladbroke Grove house of Hugh Thomas in October 1982, 'if not at all easy.' Making covert enquiries among his fellow guests, a glittering assemblage of High Tory talent that included Larkin, V. S.Naipaul and the Peruvian novelist Mario Vargas Llosa, he noted that 'physically desirable was the universal answer among all those questioned'. Three years later, at a dinner at Downing Street when he found himself seated next to the prime minister, Powell returned to the chase, deciding that her general appearance seemed to justify a comment recently made by the French president François Mitterrand – by no means an admirer – to the effect that 'she has the eyes of Caligula and the lips of Marilyn Monroe'. Wilting in the heat of her dinner-table conversation, Powell confessed himself 'taken back to age of nineteen, sitting next to a beautiful girl, myself quite unable to think of anything to say'.

Why should Mrs Thatcher have thought it worthwhile to sit down to dinner with a collection of sympathetic novelists, poets and historians (along with Powell, the guests assembled for the prime minister's benefit included Iris Murdoch, Stephen Spender and Hugh Trevor-Roper)? Plenty of British writers, from Thackeray to Evelyn Waugh, have occasionally enjoyed hobnobbing with senior politicians, but the two evenings so assiduously recorded by the author of *A Dance to the Music of Time* are almost unprecedented. The explanation lies in the peculiar circumstances of the 1980s, a deeply divided and monumentally contested age, in which for the first time in nearly half a century writers found their political opinions a subject of more than usual interest to the world at large. It was the era of Salman Rushdie's 'Mrs Torture', as featured in *The Satanic Verses* (1988), of the public rebuke of Ian McEwan by the *Sunday Times*, of mass signature letters to the *Guardian*, and earnest conversations amid the elegant furniture of Lady Antonia Fraser's and Harold Pinter's house in Campden Hill Square, where the anti-Conservative 'June 20 Group', as it was christened by newspapers, held its meetings. But it was also an era in which, for all its parliamentary majorities, the right was supposed not only to have lost the intellectual high ground but to positively glory in the reputation for philistinism which this forfeiture entailed. Margaret Drabble remembered dining at the Savoy in the early 1980s with a party that included a Tory arts supremo and mentioning that Arnold Bennett had enjoyed the hotel's cuisine so much that an omelette had been named after him. 'And is Arnold Bennett here tonight?' this cultural titan blandly enquired of a writer who had died as long ago as 1931. In this context it made perfect sense for Hugh Thomas to wish to expand his employer's horizons, encourage her to meet people who might be useful to her and whose brains she could pick.

Significantly Mrs Thatcher's opponents were quite as absorbed by her physical presence and the shock waves sent out by her personality whenever she walked into a room as any rightward-travelling senior novelist. Hilary Mantel, who first caught sight of her as an 18-year-old student, when the then Secretary of State for Education came to dinner at her college hall of residence, remembered 'a space opening around her as people stood back to look because she was a phenomenon' (the visit is written up in Mantel's novel *An Experiment in Love*). But however fascinated, appalled or disbelieving, the left found itself faced with the considerable difficulty of how best to represent Mrs Thatcher, whether as a social or cultural force, in print. The temptation was to deride her as anti-intellectual, a philistine, entirely uninterested in the life of the mind. The words put into her mouth by Michael Dibdin in his novel *Dirty Tricks* (1991) are entirely typical of the tenor of the time: 'And don't for Christ's sake talk to me about culture. You don't give a toss about culture. All you want to do is sit at home and watch TV. It's no use protesting. I know you. You're selfish, greedy, ignorant and complacent. So vote for me!'

In fact, much of the evidence suggests that Mrs Thatcher was a great deal more culturally astute than her critics on the left gave her credit for. How many modern prime ministers, for example, would be able to greet a distinguished poet by quoting one of his poems back at him (as happened to Larkin) or take the trouble to appoint a bona fide writer – in this case Lord Gowrie – to the post of arts minister. At the Downing Street dinner of 1985 Powell and his host discussed Dostoevsky. Could Tony Blair have done this? Or Gordon Brown? Mrs Thatcher may have read books because people whose opinion she respected counselled her to (she apparently took up *The Possessed* on the advice of Malcolm Muggeridge, who told her it would help her understand Russia), she may have scorned the kind of mid-1980s artistic 'happenings' sponsored by the Greater London Council, but of all her failings, real and supposed, philistinism comes fairly low on the list. Neither was she content to bask in the adoration of her right-wing literary acolytes if she disagreed with them. Amis, presenting his hero with a copy of *Russian Hide and Seek* (1980), a dystopia which imagines a future Britain under Soviet control, was given short shrift. '*Not* a very accurate prophecy' Mrs Thatcher is supposed to have lectured him.

To pin down someone so divisive, so self-evidently larger than life and at the same time so indisputably real in a form so open-ended and provisional as the novel, required a degree of objectivity that much of the late 1980s fiction trained on the Thatcher phenomenon did not possess. Thatcher-man, who muscles his way on to the fictional scene at about the time that his inspiration saw off the National Union of Mineworkers, in such novels as Julian Rathbone's *Nasty, Very* (1984), David Caute's *Veronica, Or The Two Nations* or Terence Blacker's *Fixx* (both 1989) is almost without exception a corrupt, proletariat-exploiting, Darwinian suburbanite gleefully transporting his neuroses and inadequacies into a world where they will be properly appreciated. Picaresque, heartless, upwardly mobile, Thatcher-man's negative vitality often ends up working against the novels in which he features, for his ultimate effect is to confuse the moral landscape in which he is supposed to be operating; what was intended as satire comes close to glorifying the thing it seeks to disparage. As for the woman herself, it is significant that her most effective fictional appearances are nearly always oblique – in Philip Hensher's novel about a disaffected House of Commons clerk, *Kitchen Venom* (1996), some of which she narrates, or Alan Hollinghurst's *The Line of Beauty* (2004), in which she turns up at a Notting Hill dinner party. Even in Mantel's controversial short story 'The Assassination of Margaret Thatcher' (2014), she is – literally – a walk-on ('high heels on the mossy path. Tippy-tap. Toddle on. She's making an effort but getting nowhere fast') straying into the sights of a hitman's rifle, and by this stage in her career an almost mythical figure, forever hanging slightly out of reach, for whom the techniques of realist fiction seem sadly inadequate.

CHAPTER 18

Making a Living III 1970–

Kingsley is frankly very short of cash for the taxman at the moment.

Kingsley Amis's literary agent Michael Sissons, letter to his US publisher, 1972

If that's all you earn, why do it?

Question to the novelist Paul Bailey, school visit, 1976

One novel aspect of the 1978 *New Review* symposium on the state of fiction was the readiness of the contributors to discuss money. If one counts the considerable number of pleas for the speedy introduction of Public Lending Right, then perhaps a fifth of the fifty-six writers questioned chose to use an enquiry framed largely in aesthetic terms to air some concerns that were narrowly economic. Given the number of participants and an understandably wide age range (late 20s to late 60s), no single pattern prevails. And yet, almost immediately, one or two general observations can be made. The first is that, notwithstanding the presence of devout optimists – John Braine noted that 'the pickings from the straight novel aren't very great, but there *are* pickings' – the overall tone is profoundly pessimistic. The second is the distinction between novelists of an older generation, who had begun their careers in the 1940s and 1950s, and those who had started work ten or fifteen years later. Peter Vansittart (1920–2008), comparing the literary scene of the late 1970s with the circumstances in which he had published his first novel in 1942 (688 copies sold), professed himself 'fairly hopeful', suggested that there remained 'lively freedoms for ambitious novelists without a fan club' and declared himself 'surprised by the number of publishers still prepared to back him'. The loudest howls of pain, on the other hand, came from writers in early middle age who had made their initial impact back in the early 1960s. Among these, Auberon Waugh confessed that he had given up writing novels six years previously in 1972, when his fifth exercise in the genre ended up earning a grand total of £600, on the plausible grounds that 'it is not possible to bring up a young family of four on this sort of earning, and it is not possible to hold down any sort of regular journalistic engagement if one is to take three months off every year to write a novel'.

The real interest of Waugh's apologia lies not merely in its candid admission of defeat, but in its underlying assumptions. Chief among these is a belief that novel-writing is a calling that needs to be factored into a host of other professional commitments, and that any novelist worth his salt writes at the rate of a book a year. In a later paragraph, Waugh offers a precise financial context. As a journalist, he tells us, he manages to earn nearly £20,000 a year – a sum which, he allows, may seem enormous to those who earn £5,000, but, after tax and school fees, secures only a moderate middle-class livelihood. 'There can be no question of any system of artistic patronage producing this sort of money and such grants as the Arts Council can make would only be enough to ensure an extremely modest standard of living, somewhere well below the average weekly wage.' Significantly, the two young British novelists of whom Waugh approves – Martin Amis and Piers Paul Read – are those who have solved the problem of fiction's exiguous returns: Read by writing lucrative non-fiction and Amis by doubling up as literary editor of the *New Statesman*. And yet Waugh's complaints can seem relatively restrained when set against the *j'accuse* filed by Jeremy Brooks in his account of the fate of his most recent novel, *Smith, as Hero* (1964). Brooks had been writing fiction since the late 1950s. *Smith, as Hero*, he tells us, had favourable reviews in all the Sunday newspapers and weekly magazines, and even spent a few weeks on the best-seller lists: 'after fifteen years of writing, I had the beginnings of a reputation'. The book earned £800 in hardback (the advance, not recovered by royalties) and something over £400 in paperback – a total of nearly £1,300, Brooks calculated, for a work that had taken three years to write. After this setback, Brooks revealed, he had opted to use up his creative energies in the theatre, films and journalism. Especially irksome was what he perceived to be the difference between his own and other literary cultures:

> If I lived in practically any other country, such success as I had would have been enough to keep me and my family fed while I got those other novels written. But in England 'best-seller' (unless one writes in a popular genre) means that all the public libraries, rather than just some of them, buy copies of the hardback edition; and there, apart from a handful of rich eccentrics, one's sales stop.

Not all the *New Review*'s respondents, it should be pointed out, are quite so gloomy as this. Paul Theroux notes that he is 'glad there *is* money in fiction, because if there were none, no one would bother'. On the other hand, to browse the substantial body of evidence for the material conditions of the average literary life in the 1970s and early 1980s is to be astonished by just how little money it was apparently possible to live on and the complex financial obstacles which had to be negotiated merely to establish the conditions in which books could be written. These impediments are particularly noticeable in those novels of the period which have novelists as their central characters. Francis King's *The Action* (1978) features a writer named Hazel Saunders, whose misfortune it is to be threatened by a libel suit by a woman who imagines that she has been caricatured in one of her books. Hazel, it becomes clear from a conversation between her publishers, is a top-notcher in her profession – '"As good as Muriel [Spark] any day." "Or Maggie [Drabble]." "Or even Iris [Murdoch]."' Yet, in the course of a conference at the chambers of the grand legal eminence to whom the case has been referred, when the question of Hazel's financial resources is discreetly raised, the reader quickly comes to appreciate the fact that Hazel is living in virtual poverty. In fact her income consists of a legacy worth £400 a year and £20 a week from renting her basement; her literary earnings are put at between £400 and £500. Whereupon any thought of defending the case collapses on the grounds that Hazel will not be able to defray her costs.

That Hazel was, materially, in the same position as her creator is confirmed by a passage in King's autobiography where he reflects on the difficulty he had in establishing himself as a writer once he had resigned from the British Council and returned to the UK with the aim of living the freelance literary life. It became increasingly difficult to make ends meet. The roster of part-time employments King added to what he saw as his principal job of novel-writing included a weekly novel round-up for the *Sunday Telegraph*, reading for the publishers Weidenfeld & Nicolson, a television column for the *Listener* and cooking for the lodgers admitted into his Brighton house. In the midst of juggling these various tasks, he would 'often give way to regret, even despair. By resigning from the British Council, all I had done was to exchange one treadmill for another even more gruelling.'

And King, it should be emphasised, was a long way from being a Grub Street hack. In his day he was one of the most highly regarded novelists of his generation, whose book jackets come dripping with praise from Angus Wilson, Paul Bailey and A. S. Byatt. His tragedy was that the economic conditions in which he laboured forced him to squander his talents on book reviewing and theatre criticism. He was very far from being alone in this plight. Even more so than in the immediately post-war era, the 1970s and 1980s, with their raging inflation and pressure on middle-class incomes, were a time when writers' incomes signally failed to keep pace with the cost of living. Advances for 'serious' work were almost uniformly low. Throughout the 1980s the standard Secker & Warburg contract for a first novel allowed for a payment of £750. Certain precariously financed independent firms went much lower than this. Colin Haycraft, the managing director of Duckworth, wrote to Penelope Fitzgerald on the acceptance of her first novel, *The Golden Child* (1977), wondering if an advance of £200 was acceptable; 'No, but I haven't the courage to say no' Fitzgerald scribbled on the letter. The deal went ahead, if only because at this stage in her career Fitzgerald had nowhere else to go. As late as the mid-1980s Duckworth was still offering £200 to their debutants. This was extraordinarily bad, even for the time, but even a hot fictional property could consider himself or herself fortunate to attract anything approaching a four-figure sum. Ian McEwan remembered being offered £1,000 by Jonathan Cape's talent-spotting publisher Tom Maschler to develop his early short story 'Home-made' into a novel, a scheme eventually abandoned in favour of the collection *First Love, Last Rites* (1975). This compares very favourably with the £250 offered to Martin Amis for *The Rachel Papers* (1973) at almost exactly the same time. More serious writers, though they could expect to attract better down-payments than the up-and-coming were always conscious that their earning powers were declining in relative terms. Reflecting on the £2,000 offered for her ninth novel in 1980, and remembering the £50 earned by her debut in 1958, Isabel Colegate decided that 'allowing for inflation, there doesn't seem much in it'.

But if 'serious' fiction still seemed mired in the pay scales of a bygone era, then the outlook for the freelance literary journalist, keen to enhance his or her income by reviewing for newspapers or writing short essays for weekly magazines was correspondingly bleak. In the early 1980s, for example, a 1,200-word comment piece commissioned by the *Daily Telegraph* might attract a fee of £150. A feature article for a weekly such as the *Spectator* would bring in half this; a standard-size book review perhaps £50. Rates of pay offered by smaller-scale literary magazines were lower even than this – £30, say, from the *London Magazine* for a 1,200-word review of four novels, rising to £50 for a full-length critical article, several thousand words in length, or a short story. There were, of course, substantial sums to be made out of journalism, even in the cash-strapped 1970s. Roy Jenkins' biographer reveals that when Jenkins lost office as Chancellor of the Exchequer after the general election of 1970 he was immediately able to fix up a series of lucrative newspaper assignments. These included a run of long (10,000–15,000 word) biographical essays for *The Times* at £1,500 a throw and regular book reviewing for the *Observer* at £120 a commission. Buttressed by these emoluments, Jenkins' annual income had reached £35,000 by the end of the 1972–3 tax year, barely a seventh of which was contributed by his parliamentary salary. On the other hand, Jenkins was a major public figure whose views on the great issues of the day were eagerly sought by editors. No straightforwardly literary man or woman would have been able to command anything like this kind of money. The contracts offered to freelance critics contributing set numbers of book reviews or critical articles to the art sections of national newspapers – when they were offered – rarely amounted to more than a few hundred pounds a year.

Against the catalogue of woe offered up by contributors to the *New Review* symposium should be set the fact that throughout the 1970s and early 1980s there were still enormous sums of money to be made out of 'serious' writing. The total sales tallies racked up by Iris Murdoch's novels make impressive reading: 242,000 copies of *Under the Net* (1954), 148,000 for *The Flight from the Enchanter* (1956), 223,000 for *An Unofficial Rose* (1962). A note from Chatto & Windus's managing director, Norah Smallwood, in 1982 advised her that £200,000 of royalties lay awaiting her instructions. Even here, though, at the very top of the fictional pile, there are serious distinctions to be made. Very few English novelists in the 1970s, for example, could have expected to earn as much as John Fowles, yet a detailed investigation of Fowles's income reveals significant discrepancies and imbalances. In 1968 we find Fowles recording in his diary that Maschler has offered £8,000 for *The French Lieutenant's Woman* (1969), 'which he says is the highest Cape has ever given outside the Len Deighton and Ian Fleming thriller class. The papers these days are full of the plight of the novelist (financially) so it seems a little unreal.' Six years later we join him at dinner with his literary agent, who estimates probable income from his new book, *The Ebony Tower* (1974), 'in the £80,000–90,000 area'. Then in February 1977 there is an extraordinary week in which negotiations over the film rights for *The French Lieutenant's Woman* and various publishing deals for the newly completed *Daniel Martin* (1977) produce total payments of half a million dollars ('I feel like Midas more exactly than most people could ever realise'). Five years later, with *Mantissa* (1982) complete, there is another bumper payout when Little, Brown offers $250,000 for the US rights and Maschler chips in with £40,000 for the UK edition. But, as with the negotiations over *Island in the Sun* that had made Alec Waugh his fortune a quarter of a century before, the significant aspect of this largesse is how much of it comes from beyond the domestic market. Amid the stratospheric sums bandied about by American publishers and film barons, the domestic offer for the publishing rights of *Daniel Martin* was a much more modest £25,000. Fowles himself admits that Maschler 'overpaid' for *Mantissa*.

If there was still money to be made by the serious writer, then, increasingly, it came at second hand, from America, from film deals or TV work – eminently worth having, but far beyond the aspirations of the vast majority of writers bent on the bread-and-butter task of putting words on paper for the benefit of British readers. Simon Raven, for example, enjoyed a highly successful career in the 1970s and 1980s – his income in 1980 and 1981 was put at between £70,000 and £80,000 – but the money came mostly from screenwriting commissions on the TV dramatisation of Trollope's *The Pallisers* (this was supposed to have brought in £100,000), *Edward and Mrs Simpson* and adaptations of Nancy Mitford's *The Pursuit of Love* and *Love in a Cold Climate*. The ensuing three-year jaunt around various upmarket continental watering holes, which eventually realised a novel signed off from 'Deal . . .

Corfu . . . Venice . . . Cannes . . . Athens . . . Rome . . . Monte Carlo . . . Dieppe' had nothing to do with the relatively meagre rewards from his books. Six years later the accountants calculated that he was indebted to his publisher to the tune of £28,000.

Martin Amis once remarked that when success comes to an American writer it changes his life, but that when it comes to a British writer he might just nervously buy a new filing cabinet. Frequently the home-grown novelist of the 1970s who struck it lucky, or at any rate began to move up the ladder of literary achievement in a way that accorded to his notion of just desserts, discovered that the rewards were still relatively meagre. J. G. Farrell's later career is a case in point. Farrell began the decade in his usual precarious financial state, living in a two-room flat in Chelsea, about to publish his novel *Troubles* and the beneficiary of an Arts Council grant of £750 'with which to go on writing'. The novel was well reviewed, but sold fewer than 2,000 copies, although it subsequently won the Geoffrey Faber Memorial Prize, worth a providential £250. By this time the author was in India, researching what was to become *The Siege of Krishnapur* (1973) and still irremediably hard up. A letter to his literary agent Deborah Rogers in December 1972 urged her to arrange a contract with Weidenfeld & Nicolson, to whom he had jumped ship from Cape, 'and get some money soon. I've just realised that I'm running low.' Then, a year later, came Farrell's first substantial stroke of luck when *The Siege of Krishnapur* won the Booker Prize. Avid to bite the hand that fed him, and keen to return some of the slights to which he imagined he had been subject during his apprentice years, Farrell made what the *Bookseller* described as an 'unmanly' speech, criticised privilege and the public schools (one of which he had attended himself), the royal family and the prize's sponsor, and recalled his time living in a rented greenhouse at £1 a week. The £5,000 prize money, he declared, would be used to research his next novel – a full-scale study of colonial exploitation, built around the fall of Singapore in 1942.

There followed a deluge of foreign-rights sales and film options, after which Farrell departed for the Far East. Still, though, the financial awards available to a successful novelist – even one who had won the Booker Prize – failed to match his expectations of them. By 1976 he was complaining to Rogers about a 'minuscule option payment' that had just arrived ('for a film that I don't particularly want made') and exploring the possibility of buying a house. A £10,000 mortgage, he calculated, would cost him £2,000 a year in interest payments. This, he decided, 'reduces my hopes of house-owning to a heap of ashes, as I obviously couldn't persuade Sir George [Weidenfeld] to produce £4,000, the minimum I'd need per year, given the speed at which I produce books'. Whatever tactics Rogers may have employed to bring Weidenfeld up to the mark were clearly ineffectual, as in early 1977 Farrell dispensed with her services ('Our difficulties stem, it seems to me, from the fact that the agent's duties towards his author are not clearly defined') and resolved to handle the work in progress, now titled *The Singapore Grip* (1978), himself. By mid-1978 the financial situation had improved: Weidenfeld agreed to pay £20,000 for the book with £5,000 on delivery. In July, having been 'forced to register for VAT', Farrell moved to the Republic of Ireland in order to take advantage of its favourable tax rates for artists, and bought a house overlooking Bantry Bay by means of a £5,500 deposit and a mortgage to cover the remaining 75 per cent of the purchase price. A year later he reported that he was 'working on a new novel night and day to try to pay for this house', and on 10 August 1979 he informed his editor at Weidenfeld that 'barring some unforeseen disaster' he would deliver the new book by the end of the year. The unforeseen disaster came the very next morning when, fishing for pollock, he was washed off a rock by a freak wave – the outlier of a storm heading for the Irish coast – and swept away to his death.

No reader of Farrell's voluminous diaries can ignore the vein of resentment that runs beneath their surface: the unhappiness of a man who thought that he was worth more than he received and that, by implication, there were other writers at work for whom this process operated in reverse. The pressures to which moderately successful writers who earned their living solely by the pen were subject in the 1970s and early 1980s took several forms. One of them was sheer overproduction, that impulse to keep the pot boiling at whatever cost. Francis King, for example, published ten books between 1970 and 1979; Kingsley Amis managed nine. Each, left to themselves, would probably have preferred the long stretches of time that Fowles was able to devote to *Daniel Martin*, 300,000 words in length and composed over a period of several years. Another was the search for new outlets. The market for short fiction continued to evaporate. Of the nine stories included in Ian McEwan's second collection *In Between the Sheets* (1978), four had been previously published by his regular sponsor the *New Review*, one brought out obscurely in America, one bought by the small-circulation intellectual monthly *Encounter* and another by the even smaller-circulation and Arts Council-funded *Bananas*. Only 'Sunday March 199–' had acquired a reasonably upmarket berth in *Harper's*.

Aspiring short-story writers of the period who preferred cash to prestige were often tempted by the vastly superior rates offered by adult magazines: see, for example, McEwan's as yet uncollected piece 'Vaginismus', which appeared in Paul Raymond's *Club International*, and Martin Amis's 'Debitocracy', a dystopian story about a future world where sexual passion has been vanquished, which graced the November 1974 issue of *Penthouse*. Finally, there was the struggle to obtain part-time employment of a kind that would subsidise the production of more serious works without exhausting the writer to such a degree that the serious work fell by the wayside. For most of the up-and-coming writers of the late 1970s the solution lay in journalism. The three years spent on Amis's breakout novel *Money* (1984) were effectively underwritten by overseas assignments for the *Sunday Telegraph* and the *Observer*. The stack of novels and biographies that made Peter Ackroyd's name in the 1980s were preceded by stints as literary editor, managing editor and later film critic of the *Spectator*. Timothy Mo, uniquely for a contemporary novelist, reported fights for *Boxing News*. For a small, undeviating handful, Farrell-like self-sacrifice and frugality were the order of the day. The *Vogue* journalists who came to interview McEwan after the publication of *First Love, Last Rites* were admitted to a clammy basement flat.

But all this was about to change. One dramatic effect of the early 1980s publishing revolution was a substantial increase in the amount of money available to an elite band of home-grown 'literary' novelists. Between 1983 and 1995, for example, such writers as McEwan, Mo, Kazuo Ishiguro, Graham Swift and Jeanette Winterson were reliably reported to have received advances for individual books of as much as £250,000. While the writers who benefited from this newfound largesse were only a tiny proportion of the talent pool, there was a significant knock-on effect, and a general improvement in the contract terms that publishers felt able to offer fledgling authors. A promising first novel, with a canny agent behind it, was capable of fetching £10,000 or more in the febrile conditions of the early 1990s.

If these developments were of only limited value to the middle-ranking novelist who made only a proportion of his or her income from writing fiction, then the simultaneous changes in the world of arts journalism were an important compensation. The boom in broadsheet journalism, which began with the arrival of the *Independent* in 1986 and continued well into the mid-1990s, had several advantages for the literary freelance. Not only were there more outlets – for a brief period in 1989–90 the UK boasted no fewer than five quality Sunday newspapers – but arts supplements grew in size; there was more space for reviews and correspondingly inflated rates of pay. The *Sunday Times* paid as much as £400 for a 1,000-word review in the 1990s. At the *Mail on Sunday*, whose defiantly upmarket *Night and Day* magazine ran from 1993 to 1999, the rate could rise to £500. 'Name' writers did even better. In the late 1980s, for example, Anthony Burgess was engaged to write a weekly book review for the *Independent* at £600 a piece.

All this was a far cry from the austerity of the previous decade. So, to a degree, were the retainers offered to journalists whose loyalties the newspaper in question thought it important to secure. While the sums available were dependent on the paper's wider resources – the *Sunday Times* paid as much as £8,000 a year – the result was that, for the first time in half a century, the rewards on offer to a sharp operator who wrote for several different papers were worth having. A freelance critic with an annual contract for the *Sunday Times* who, additionally, reviewed for a daily newspaper while keeping his, or her, hand in with the weeklies, could earn between £15,000 and £20,000 a year from literary journalism. There were not a great number of these journalists, and – as in publishing – the boom was swiftly followed by a period of retrenchment, but their very existence demonstrates quite how much the world of Grub Street had changed since the bleakly remunerated vistas of the early 1970s, when J. G. Farrell could complain that the *Spectator* had cut its reviewing rate to £10 a contribution.

Little of this could have happened without the emergence of another factor crucial to the increase in certain writers' incomes in the 1980s and 1990s. This was the influence acquired by a small but immensely powerful group of literary agents who, in an era where more money was suddenly available, and publishers competed for prestige titles, had no hesitation in exploiting the position in which they found themselves. A capable agent, backed by a sympathetic, or at any rate malleable, publisher could transform an author's earning power. Iris Murdoch, for example, whose un-agented novels had traditionally been published by Chatto on a £10,000 advance with fifty-fifty royalty splits, found herself in 1984 in the hands of Ed Victor. The advance for her next novel, *The Book and the Brotherhood* (1987), increased fivefold. But for an example of what a resourceful agent could do for a high-profile writer in a favourable marketplace one need only turn to the transformation wrought upon Kingsley Amis's finances by Jonathan Clowes. Youngish, and with a reputation for being go-ahead, Clowes had replaced the firm of A. D. Peters in the mid-1970s. The final contract negotiated by Peters had been for Amis's novel *The Alteration* (1976) for an advance of £7,500. Clowes's first step was to move his client to a new publisher, arranging a two-book deal with Hutchinson for *Jake's Thing* (1978) and *Russian Hide and Seek* (1980), worth £35,000. In 1980 he brokered a second two-book deal for *Stanley and the Women* (1984) and *The Old Devils* (1986), increasing the advance to £60,000. *The Old Devils'* victory in the 1986 Booker Prize enhanced Clowes's bargaining power and he was able to negotiate a further two-book deal for *Difficulties with Girls* (1988) and *The Folks That Live on the Hill* (1990) worth £200,000. Clowes's declared aim at this time was, by means of books, journalism and television adaptations, to get his client's income up to £200,000 a year. A trawl through Amis's finances in the last five years of his life shows just how close he came to achieving this: £160,000 in 1991; £192,000 in 1992; £218,000 in 1993; £173,000 in 1994; and £80,000 in 1995, the year of his death. In half a decade Clowes had arranged work for his client to the value of £822,000. There was a final coup in 1995 when, disappointed by the £40,000 Hutchinson had offered for *The Biographer's Moustache*, Clowes persuaded HarperCollins to pay £135,000 for a two-book deal – a contract which, as Amis's biographer relates, 'baffled' rival publishers who knew it to be economically unviable.

Given Amis's earning power in the last years of his life, it might be wondered why he left such a relatively modest estate (£616,000). The answer lay in his extravagant lifestyle. Although living with his ex-wife and her third husband in a house in north London, he contrived in the month of February 1993 alone to spend £315 on taxis, £432 at the Garrick Club and £1,038 on drink. Of the £172,854 of gross income amassed in 1994, £133,000 was siphoned off in expenses. Amis, in other words, needed an income of this size, and having earned it, spent it. Asked by an interviewer in the mid-1980s what he laid out his money on, he replied 'Oh, mortgages, horrible things like that.' Divorced from his second wife, Elizabeth Jane Howard, he made the unwelcome discovery that 'all of a sudden the bit of fat you've accumulated over the years is gone and you have to start again'.

Not all those in Amis's position were so fortunate, and the literary landscape of the 1970s and 1980s is littered with the bones of senior literary men and women who, having failed to set aside money when the going was good, found themselves contemplating old age in conditions that occasionally amounted to something very near penury. Cyril Connolly, who died in 1974, bequeathed an overdraft of £27,000; a trust fund had to be got up for his heirs. Beverley Nichols lived out his last decade on an income of £6,000 a year. Simon Raven, beset by libel writs for his scurrilous memoir *Is There Anybody There? Said the Traveller* (1991), and massively in hock to the publisher of his seriously underperforming *First-Born of Egypt* novel sequence (1984–92), was eventually admitted to an alms house for impoverished old gentlemen, where preference was given to, among others, 'decrepit or old Captaynes either at Sea or Land' and 'Souldiers maymed or ympotent'. John Braine, who died in 1986, spent all but the final months of his last years in a tiny bed-sitter and ate his final Christmas dinner in a community centre, surrounded by down-and-outs. But perhaps the most poignant casualty was Angus Wilson. In 1983, disillusioned with Mrs Thatcher's Britain, Sir Angus, Knight of the realm and president of the Royal Society of Literature, had made a dramatic TV appearance in which, found descending the steps of the Garrick Club, he declared that he felt undervalued as a writer and was departing for France. The move was a disaster. Wilson wrote no more, lapsed into dementia and was eventually brought back to England to live in a nursing home. His income for 1988 consisted of a pension from the UEA of £325, another pension of £2,695, £573 from Public Lending Right, £4,437 from various private schemes and literary earnings amounting to £7,300 from a film option and an advance on a short-story collection. The Royal Literary Fund chipped in with a grant of £5,000 but the nursing home cost £1,160 a month. Wilson's long-term partner and principal carer, Tony Garrett, had little in the way of savings and was dependent on Wilson's income. As Wilson's biographer Margaret Drabble put it, the remainder of his life – he died in 1991 – was 'going to be a close-run thing'.

* * *

And there were other, younger casualties. It would be difficult to find a more cautionary tale from the world of late 1980s and early 1990s publishing than that of Richard Burns (1958–92). A winner of a mid-1980s 'New Authors' competition sponsored by *The Times* and Jonathan Cape, he was taken up by Cape's editorial director, Liz Calder, and, having published two well-received novels, *A Dance for the Moon* (1986) and *The Panda Hunt* (1987), followed Calder to the newly established firm of Bloomsbury. Already, though, there were signs of trouble ahead. In May 1989 he fired his agent, Xandra Hardie, in a letter pointing out that in the four years she had represented him he had earned only £6,300. 'This may not be your fault, but it is an unbearable situation, particularly when every other writer I know – some perhaps better than me, but many who are not – earns much more' he declared. 'I cannot assess my market value but if it is really so low then I ought not to be writing at all.' With a new agent in place and a five-figure deal negotiated for *Fond and Foolish Lovers* (1990), his career seemed to have taken a turn for the better, but the book failed to recoup its advance. Bloomsbury offered a meagre £3,000 for its successor, and it took a £7,000 grant from the Arts Council to avoid a financial meltdown when the bank called in an overdraft. In August 1992, a week before the publication of *Sandro and Simonetta*, and the day before his thirty-fourth birthday, he hanged himself in the house he shared with his wife and family on the outskirts of Sheffield.

The obituaries dwelt on the suggestion that Burns, in some sense, imagined himself to be a victim of a literary marketplace that ignored his promise. A former editor noted that 'anything you said merely confirmed his suspicion that there was a London literary mafia that organised everything for its own benefit, that if you lived in Sheffield you might as well live on the moon for all the notice anyone took of you'. Did Burns, when it came to it, kill himself because he had failed to obtain the financial success he thought his writing deserved? It is tempting to make a direct connection between the two, and yet biographical accounts suggest that he had a depressive streak; there had been an earlier incident, in which he attempted to slit his wrists, five years before. Then there is the fact that at the time of his death his financial troubles were prospectively at an end: he had recently been appointed to the University of Lancaster's creative writing department at a salary of £20,000 a year – probably as much as he had earned from his entire literary career. If his death highlighted anything beyond the torment of a remarkably talented man at the end of his tether, it was the skewed economics of fiction publishing. As his agent pointed out, strictly speaking he was no worse off than the hundreds of other writers condemned to labour in the shadow of the famous names of the Waterstones display case: 'If everyone in his financial position committed suicide, there'd be no novelists left.'

But the effect of the mid-1980s explosion in publishers' advances was grotesquely to exaggerate this divide, and to create a professional world whose facade, once penetrated, revealed a landscape in which the super-rich and the relatively hard up worked on side by side. More than one critic remarked that the difficulty of being a novel-reviewer in the 1930s was that the quality of the books that came the reviewer's way was so very varied. The same point could be made in strict economic terms of Kingsley Amis and Richard Burns, each of whom gave their profession as 'writer' in reference books, each of whom expected to see his books reviewed in the same newspapers (and could expect to be employed, albeit at different rates, by their literary editors) but whose annual income differed by a factor of nearly twenty to one. The reader who knows his way around the late Victorian publishing scene may be forgiven for thinking that the world in which a Richard Burns could despair of writing 'serious' work capable of making him an income on which he might be able to live does not differ in any essential regard from the world of *New Grub Street* a century before.

On the other hand, Gissing's all-purpose hack journalist Jasper Milvain transported into the literary marketplace of the early twenty-first century would have his work cut out. The newspaper industry hit its peak at the end of the 1990s; thereafter readers migrated to the internet and circulations declined. With them went the once abundant space for arts journalism and high freelance payments. By 2014 the *Independent* had reduced its rate to £100 for a 700-word review – less than the fee on offer in 1986, the year of the paper's foundation. The literary man or woman looking to supplement his or her meagre earnings from books was much more likely to turn to university teaching. That the economic conditions of the 1980s and 1990s were a statistical blip, after which the general rewards on offer to writers continued their long-term decline, is borne out by the most comprehensive recent enquiries into literary incomes, undertaken by the Authors' Licensing and Collecting Society (ALCS). Analysing the 1,700 responses to its 2005 questionnaire, ALCS concluded that the typical income for a professional author was one-third below the national average wage, that median earnings were less than three-quarters of this sum and that significant inequalities existed: the top 10 per cent of authors earned more than 50 per cent of the total income, while the bottom 50 per cent earned less than 10 per cent of it. Wounding comparisons were made with a 2000 survey conducted by the Society of Authors, showing that while mean earnings had risen slightly from £16,000 to £16,500, median earnings had plummeted from £6,333 to £4,000. Sixty per cent of those who regarded themselves as 'professional' authors needed a second source of income, while the 'typical' income of a professional author at the start of his or her career – those between 25 and 34 – was a mere £5,000.

By the 2013 survey, on the other hand, these meagre rewards were beginning to look highly desirable. The number of 'professional authors' who earned their income solely from writing had fallen to 11.5 per cent, while the typical income from writing had fallen by 29 per cent in real terms since 2005. The median income for 'professionals' was put at £11,000 – nearly £6,000 below the figure identified by the Joseph Rowntree Foundation as 'the income level considered to be a socially acceptable standard of living'. As for who was earning what, of the 121 novelists who responded to the 2005 ALCS survey, the median income was £13,000. There is a rather dreadful moment in *New Grub Street*, in which Reardon, having deposited the manuscript of what he knows is a worthless book, stands looking at his publisher's windows. 'Do they suspect in what wretched circumstances I am?' he wonders. 'Would it surprise them to know all that depends upon that budget of paltry scribbling?' But it could be argued that Reardon, at any rate in his bachelor days, is better off than many of his modern-day equivalents, living in London on a cheap rent and able to subsist on the proceeds of books whose composition does not rob him of his self-esteem. The 'serious' twenty-first-century novelist who wishes to write in whichever way his aesthetic spirit points him usually finds that he can only do this by doubling up as a teacher of creative writing. On the other hand, once literature became a trade, dependent on the whims of the market, this kind of outcome is inevitable. The point about Reardon, as even the most sympathetic of his friends concede, is that his novels – 'clever', rarefied, relying for their impact on scraps of human psychology – are, as Gissing puts it, 'not of a kind to win popularity', dealing as they do 'with no particular class of society (unless one makes an additional class out of people who have brains)' and, lacking these qualities, attract exactly the sales they deserve. The same judgement, however much one may regret it, could be made of Richard Burns.

CHAPTER 19

Enemies of Promise

> Emily's face has become thinner, even more Virginia Woolf-ish, her nose apparently longer and her eyes more distant from the action, so that she looks strangely like an icon. She has the aspect of a writer – serious, a little worried about where it's going, but also – I am reading way too much into this – the comfort of belonging to a superior caste, people who write about funny domestic misunderstandings, people who make up history, people who write about detectives who drink too much while still able to solve crimes, people who see pathos in autism, people who write about how to overcome sex addiction, people who write the autobiographies of sportsmen and sportswomen, people who write their own *Bildungsroman*, retired politicians who rewrite their careers, people who write about tasty ten-minute recipes, people who write about the failings of men, people who write celebrity novels, people who write comic novels, people who write spy novels, people who write epistolary novels. Writing is still highly esteemed, even more so than reading.
>
> Justin Cartwright, *Lion Heart* (2013)

> We must answer a question sometimes put by certain literary diehards, old cats who sit purring over the mouseholes of talent in wait for what comes out. 'Is this age', they pretend to ask, 'really more unfavourable to writers than any other? Have not writers always had the greatest difficulty in surviving?' . . . The answer, if they wanted an answer, is yes.
>
> Cyril Connolly, *Enemies of Promise* (1938)

No literary period is ever quite distinct from the one that follows it: the behemoths of a previous age invariably survive to haunt and sometimes embarrass the inhabitants of the next – the grand Victorian panjandrum Sir Edmund Gosse, for example, persisting into the era of Joyce and Eliot, Hugh Walpole topping the best-seller lists in the epoch of Geoffrey Grigson's *New Verse*. Yet there usually comes a time when the survivors realise that the game is up and that a chasm now separates them from the Elysian Fields of their youth. And so Sir John Squire, sitting down to write to his old secretary Grace Chapman on the eve of his seventieth birthday party in April 1954, was sharply conscious of the fact that while the Garrick Club would undoubtedly be crammed to the rafters with 'good fellows', Shanks, Chesterton, W. J. Turner, Lynd and Hardy could not be among their number; like these ornaments of the 1920s, and like the *London Mercury* and its campaigning editorials, Georgianism was dead. This, in terms of literary chronology, was the world of the Movement – shortly to be unveiled to readers of the *Spectator* by J. D. Scott – the New Men of C. P. Snow's and William Cooper's novels and the upwardly mobile scholarship boy anatomised by Richard Hoggart's *The Uses of Literacy*. At the same time, had he made a study of the new landscapes stretching out on either side of him he would no doubt have been struck by some of the resemblances to what had gone before.

What would Squire have made of the literary world of the early twenty-first century, could he by some miracle have been set down in it and encouraged to sum it up in a Parnassian editorial note or two? He would certainly have remarked its cosmopolitanism, and the march upon its citadels of writers who were neither provincial nor metropolitan but international, equally at home in two or three literary communities and with a foothold in half a dozen more. He might have thought that the old-style literary culture over which he had fitfully presided, small-scale and centralised, had ceased to exist or, if it had, could no longer be described as distinctively English. From his own particular vantage point – that of the diehard controversialist – he would probably be startled by its lack of rancour, the absence of any real aesthetic divide or the conviction, fought over by implacably opposed cultural blocs, that the business of literature ought to be conducted in a certain way and that to wander from this primrose path was heresy. And he would undoubtedly have deduced that the lack of conflict derived from a lack of authority, the absence of any influential arbiters of 'taste' and a wholesale fragmentation of a reading public to whom these arbiters used once to appeal.

Ninety years on there is, in terms of sheer cultural impact, no equivalent to the Sitwells, or Middleton Murry's attacks on *Georgian Poetry*, or the early numbers of the *Criterion*. There are writers bent on publicising themselves, and for whom column inches double up as literary criticism; there are still polemics and hatchet-jobs; there are still upmarket intellectual magazines with sophisticated readerships – the *London Review of Books*, say, or *Areté* – in which can be detected the glimmerings of a cultural stance greater than the sum of their accumulated journalistic parts; at the same time, none of them works in quite the same manner, operates with quite the same degree of attack, or, in a landscape yet more fragmented than its 1920s predecessor, can hope to achieve anything like the same measure of wider resonance. In the same way the 'movements' of the past thirty years have generally been brought into being by vague generational association rather than the pressures of literary politicking. If the loosely affiliated group of novelists headed by Martin Amis (b.1949), Salman Rushdie (b.1947), Ian McEwan (b.1948) and Julian Barnes (b.1946) became such a dominant force in the 1980s – a dominance that persisted into the 2000s and to some extent endures today – it was the result of a particular combination of cultural and economic factors, together with new ways of publicising books and a newfound concentration on the 'literary novel'. Similarly, if anything links the fashionable younger writers who have come to prominence since 2000 – Zadie Smith, David Mitchell, Ali Smith – it is their reliance on the techniques of what the critic Richard Bradford has called 'domesticated postmodernism', here defined as a relish for avant-garde procedural devices that is never allowed to impede the commercial prospects of their books.

Perhaps this is merely a way of saying that many of the complaints that tend to be levelled at the literary world of 2016 could have been filed in 1926, and that several of the devitalising forces assumed to be at work in the age of Amazon's Mr Jeff Bezos, illegal downloads and the three-for-two front-of-store promotion existed in embryonic form in the era of Eliot and Priestley. Certainly for every contemporary critic who laments the tide of celebrity memoirs and ghostwritten novels crowding out the bookshop tables – the *biblia abiblia* of the Victorian purist – there was a disdainful 1930s forebear complaining about the undeserved attention lavished on Asquith's letters to his mistress Hilda Harrisson or *My First Life* (1935), the autobiography of the 'society drug addict' Brenda Dean Paul, serialised with maximum éclat in the *News of the World*. The lists of speakers at the *Sunday Times* 'book exhibitions' of the Baldwin era may extend to such thrusting young intellectuals as Graham Greene, Aldous Huxley and Stephen Spender but they also harbour celebrity chefs and England cricket captains. Did Douglas Jardine write his own autobiography or employ some deferential journalist to knock it into shape for him? We shall never know. The same point could be made of the migration of 'serious' criticism to the universities, then in its infancy but, in the hands of Richards, Leavis and Empson, showing every sign of being about to hurtle towards a ripe maturity. It could also be made of that very common complaint about 'taste' being inculcated by pundits whose qualifications might, if closely inspected, be called seriously into question. Nine decades later, the gap between a Book Society, administered by such mainstream figures as Walpole and Priestley in cahoots with a handful of commercial sponsors, and the Richard and Judy Book Club may not seem quite as wide as it seems.

Or perhaps the gap is wider than some observers of the middlebrow book world might assume, given that Walpole and Priestley, however much posterity might be disposed to mock them, were in touch with the intellectual forces of the day, genuinely convinced that they were embarked on a civilising mission, that literature, in what even then was a world of ever-proliferating media, mattered in a way that cinema and television could never hope to emulate. But whether or not Squire would have approved of TV book clubs and celebrity endorsements, he would certainly have appreciated some of the profound changes that have affected recent literary culture, changes so elemental as to make the long-term observer wonder whether such a thing as old-style literary culture still exists. Some of these developments, naturally, are to do with technology, but an equally large number have their basis in what might be called the transfer of power, a process in which technology originally played only a comparatively small part but has now come thoroughly to dominate. To comprehend the transformation of the English literary landscape over the past thirty years it is necessary to see book publishing in strictly economic terms. From this angle, the book, or rather the manuscript of the book, features as raw material, created by its primary producer, the writer, and brought to the market by its secondary producer, the publisher with the aid of a third party, the distributor. Already there is a complicating factor at work, which is that, historically, the 'value' of certain books has been judged by aesthetic rather than fiscal criteria, meaning that the results are likely to be measured in terms of prestige rather than cash receipts. On the other hand, the most impenetrable highbrow novel ever published is – something that highbrow novelists are sometimes reluctant to admit – ultimately an economic unit, with a balance sheet to match.

For the greater part of book-trade history this production line was simplified by the doubling up of some of its component parts. Until the early part of the nineteenth century, for example, many publishers were booksellers who undertook the distributive function themselves, by selling the items they published in their own shops and employing their own representatives to unload them on other retailers around the country. Except in very unusual cases – Dickens, for example, who was such a successful proposition that he could make his own terms with anyone he chose – power lay with the publisher, and very little in the late Victorian book world could be achieved without him. Yet the steady industrialisation of the book trade to meet the demands of the rapidly expanding mid-Victorian reading public quickly began to jeopardise this control over what the average nineteenth-century reader read and what he or increasingly she could expect to pay for it. The principal distribution channel for the Victorian novel in three volumes, generally priced at a guinea and a half and beyond the means of most potential purchasers, was the circulating library, whose take-up of a particular title not only guaranteed a substantial part of its print run but, at any rate in moral terms, dictated a fair amount of its content (George Moore's *Literature at Nurse* (1885) is a sarcastic account of the threat to a literary career posed by the disapproval of the eagle-eyed Mudie's censor). The stranglehold on 'taste' exerted by Mr Mudie and his henchmen was eventually overthrown by the advent of the single-volume novel priced at six shillings, but this did not mean that publishers recovered the ground that had been lost in the process. Even by the early twentieth century book wholesalers and the larger booksellers were engaged in a constant struggle for better terms – discounting, say, or the common 1920s practice of thirteen copies counting as twelve; if there is a common theme to the memoirs of the interwar publishing scene left by Alec Waugh, Anthony Powell and Douglas Jerrold, it is the sheer precariousness of publishing 'literature' at a profit while allowing the author to make a living out of his, or her, trade.

Much of the history of the twentieth-century book trade, consequently, can be viewed as a war of attrition between the various parts of the publishing process in which the embattled figure of the publisher seemed steadily less able to match the fighting weight of his opponents. In the hothouse conditions of the 1980s, when the reconfiguration of the industry ushered in an era of high advances and cut-throat competition over who would have the honour of publishing Ian McEwan or Martin Amis, the new power broker was neither the primary producer of the item being brought to market nor the secondary producer but their intermediary, the literary agent, formerly a minor cog in the book-world wheels, now transformed into an altogether commanding figure, and, as such, frequently consulted in the near-continuous rounds of company restructurings. Then, in the 1990s, a final and perhaps irrevocable transfer of power was negotiated by publishers themselves, in the unilateral action that brought about the collapse of the Net Book Agreement (NBA), the trade-wide regulation whereby books, with the exception of copies distributed through book clubs and limited amounts of stock marketed at discount to public libraries, were sold at the price printed on their jackets. In retrospect, as many of the publishers involved came later to admit, this was a classic example of an industry sacrificing long-term advantage for short-term gain. Its immediate consequence, here in the pre-internet age, was a glut of heavily discounted best-sellers in bookshops, but its long-term effect was to create an ideal marketing environment for the sale of books online by the internet retailer. Amazon's book division, it is fair to say, could not have existed in its present form without the fall of the NBA.

Twenty years later, in a market that has largely decamped to cyberspace, anyone trying to write, or promote, or sell a book is compelled to operate in an environment where the distributive tail wags the manufacturing dog, and in an industry that is dominated and increasingly controlled by a third party entirely detached from the creative and manufacturing process – a third party, moreover, able, by virtue of its dominant position in the market, to siphon off most of the profits for itself. The senior novelist, noting this transfer of power and resources, frequently congratulates himself on having begun his career in a more hospitable age. As David Lodge puts it in a passage from his recently published autobiography, the abundance of laptops, emails and e-books threatens 'to dissolve the connection between writing as a profession and the book as a mechanically reproducible commodity, which has existed since the invention of the printing press, and to render obsolete the interlinked system of publishers, agents, printers, booksellers and copyright law that for more than a century has provided a relatively firm framework within which writers have pursued their vocation and earned income from it'.

One consequence of this revolution is that books, for perhaps the first time in literary history, are cheap to buy, and at times – as many an author has noticed to his chagrin when touring the download sites – obtainable gratis. On the other hand, the availability of large amounts of best-selling paperbacks at £2.99 a unit at supermarket checkouts or online bargain bins does not mean, as one or two starry-eyed pundits occasionally suggest, that publishing has suddenly turned 'democratic'; it means that more copies will be sold – or, worse, simply dispersed – of fewer titles; that publishers will concentrate their energies on hitting the jackpot rather than encouraging fresh but not necessarily commercial talent; and that 'choice', rather than being stimulated by the existence of a mass audience with more money to spend, will eventually be seriously restricted. At the same time, if it is ever more difficult for a first-time author to be taken on by a commercial publisher, then the route to 'authorship', here in an age when one can self-publish one's work at the click of a couple of buttons, is ever more navigable. Never, it might be said, has it been easier to become a writer, and never has it been harder to make an income out of that desirable state.

As for the other consequences of the technological revolution for old-style literary culture, one of them, naturally, is the effect on literary journalism. The professional book reviewer still flourishes, of course, albeit in a much more limited and poorly paid environment, but in an era of declining print circulations, 'criticism' – when it is not merely masquerading as endorsement – continues to migrate in two contrary directions: to university English departments, where, professionalised and encoded, it is of little interest to the general reader; and to the online forum where, unregulated and un-authenticated, it takes a bewildering variety of forms and offers a bewildering variety of registers and shifts in judgement. But the decline of the critic – either into a harassed print reviewer with insufficient space to tease out the complexities of the artefact before him, or an enthusiastic online amateur who protests his inability to 'relate' to the central character of the novel under discussion and imagines this to be a fault of the book – is perhaps secondary to the implications of a literary culture increasingly governed by a computer screen, where distraction arrives at half-minute intervals and sustained engagement with a text is more or less impossible to accomplish. Then there is the sheer proliferation of the materials from which this new literary culture is constructed. No one over the age of 40 – no one at any rate old enough to have experienced a literary world made up entirely of books, newspapers and reference libraries – can roam the world of the blogosphere and the online symposium without thinking that there is too much of everything – too many books, too much criticism of them, too many reviews, too many opinions, too many reading groups, too many book clubs, so many literary prizes that any vaguely competent novel comes garlanded with two or three endorsements from the judging committees, that we are drowning in a sea of data where an instant reaction is always liable to crowd out mature reflection, where anyone's opinion is as good as anyone else's and the fact that the distinguished man of letters in the *Wall Street Journal* thinks Cormac McCarthy's *The Road* a work of genius is of no interest at all to the Amazon reviewer who awards it a single star for lacking bite.

On the other hand, complaints about the torrent of secondary literature are as old as literature itself, certainly older than the internet. In the late 1960s, John Gross professed faint alarm at the existence of an anthology edited by a leading American scholar entitled *44 Essential Articles on Pope*. 'None of this represents wasted labour' Gross decided, 'but what are we going to do when there are forty-four essential *books*?' Nearly half a century later a decent-sized bibliography of Pope criticism would probably extend to several pages. If nothing else, this exponential hike in the volume of materials from which literary criticism is fashioned inhibits the kind of intelligent generalising which, however inimical to the specialist, is of value to the ordinary reader anxious for a lesson or two in the ability to discriminate. As it is, most non-university critics invited to compile, say, a history of the English novel since 1945 would probably decline the offer, scared off in advance by the near-insoluble dilemmas of where to begin, who to include (and by extension leave out) and the large number of extraneous influences which need some kind of consideration. In these circumstances the critic – the academic critic especially – understandably finds it easier to specialise, to wring the last shred of meaning from a solitary text or a single writer and his work, leading to the uncomfortable spectacle of work that seems to be written not to fill a space but to inflate a CV. No doubt the three full-length studies of the novels of Hanif Kureishi currently available, each offering plot summaries and synopses of reviews, have much to recommend them to the undergraduate embarking on a course in contemporary literature, but wouldn't one be enough?

And if, on the one hand, this evolving literary landscape resists assimilation, then, on the other, it takes an increasingly equivocal view of the idea of authorial, critical or indeed textual autonomy. This, we are constantly informed, will be a collaborative world, where writers and readers interact, where a reader can, if he or she desires, intervene in a book and transform its construction into a communal experience. The novelist Kate Pullinger once produced an entertaining projection of the conditions of novel-writing in the 2050s in which the writer offers instalments to an audience of online subscribers, each of whom supplies comments and plot suggestions that will be taken on board and used to shape the writing of the next episode, and whose names will appear in the acknowledgements once the book is complete. Again, there are interesting continuities with bygone arrangements. Much early Victorian poetry, after all, was essentially collaborative, with drafts circulated to small private audiences and lines tried out on sympathetic friends. Victorian novelists, too, publishing in monthly instalments and sensitive to their subscribers' concerns, could often be found directly responding to reader pressure. On the other hand, the argument against genuinely communal work of the Pullinger kind is usually that of sharply diminished quality. Some years ago, for example, BBC Radio Four featured a week of short stories whose authors had developed their contributions in collaboration with a series of West Midlands reading groups. Whatever their individual merits, over them all hung the faintly depressing, uniform scent of work that had, effectively, been manufactured by committee.

Naturally, in a world where 'taste' has fewer guardians, and those of them who survive are much less influential than before, where there is no single mainstream but a mass of contending rivulets, in which the power which writers, critics and publishers used to exercise has migrated to a solitary distributor, the question of the literary audience becomes that much more problematic. There have always been different kinds of readers who read different kinds of books, but another consequence of the technological revolution in publishing may very well be a marketplace in which different kinds of readers read different versions of the same book. Not long ago, for example, armed with the results of a survey published in the *Bookseller* which showed that 90 per cent of book buyers now read e-books, with genre and commercial fiction comprehensively outselling 'literary fiction', the novelist Fay Weldon suggested that authors should 'abandon their dignity' and write alternative versions of their work suitable for the e-book audience. 'Writers have to write now for a world where readers are busy, on the move, and have little time for contemplation and reflection' she declared. 'The writer has to focus on writing better, cutting to the chase and doing more of the readers' contemplative work for them.' Press reporting of these remarks was, inevitably, accompanied by a second survey showing that the amount of time spent reading long-form texts is in decline and, as a result of digitisation, reading is becoming more intermittent and fragmented. Kindle readers are apparently significantly worse at recalling events in a mystery story than those reading in paperback.

A book-world conservative would probably suggest that it is a mark of our obsession with technological advance that this kind of thing gets nodded through with only the mildest of head-shakes, and that in a properly regulated world governments would insist that Kindles be marketed with the words 'Warning: this device will make you stupid.' Yet, a glance at the last century or so of literary history shows that Weldon has a point, or rather two points – one of them about the way in which the form of literature changes in response to the technological and commercial processes available, and another about the gulf which separates the animal known as 'literary fiction', the kind of novel which is entered for the Man Booker Prize, and the genres hoovered up by the specimen e-reader. It was Evelyn Waugh, writing over half a century ago, who noted the existence of a link between the words on the page and the implement that transmits them, that, to particularise, the boiled-down, staccato prose pioneered by Hemingway in the 1920s is intimately linked to his habit of composing straight on to the typewriter. Commercial pressures, too, have always dictated the length of novels. Late Victorian writers did not abandon the novel in three volumes in a sudden collective aesthetic revolt but because the circulating libraries – the principal purchasers of 'serious fiction' until the early twenty-first century – decided that they were no longer economically viable.

And if Fay Weldon is correct in noticing the way in which literary forms calibrate themselves both to market conditions and technological developments, then she is also right to draw attention to the widening gap between what gets known as the 'serious novel' and the 'fast-moving event-driven stories' of the online bargain bin. A useful exercise guaranteed to drive an iron spike into the soul of the highbrow is to look up any book written by a 'serious novelist' that has been well reviewed in the national press and see what the cyber-critics made of it. In four cases out of five, Andrew O'Hagan or Will Self or Paul Auster will have been convicted by the amateur audience of being impenetrable, overly clever or – a rather peculiar insult, but there you are – 'literate'. And fair play to the Amazon reviewers, you might say, for there are no exact standards in literature and surely anyone who buys a book is entitled to say what they think of it, however much more august authorities might regard this opinion as worthless. The 'literary novel', whose demise has been several times proclaimed in the past few years, would sell far more copies and attract far more attention beyond newspaper books pages if it didn't habitually come served up in a light sauce of snootiness – if, in fact, it didn't refer to itself as a literary novel in the first place.

A certain type of reader might think that he, or she, was being patronised by e-lite versions of 'serious' novels, and that, like the proles in *Nineteen Eighty-Four*, to whom pornography is supplied in sealed packets, they were having their tastes judged in advance. A certain type of writer, on the other hand, might be simply embarrassed by the intellectual sleight of hand required. It may very well be that the modern literary landscape is occupied by two increasingly distinct audiences, but a writer who believes that the act of reading is anything more than a way of passing time will probably want to try to bring them closer together rather than force them farther apart.

If, as is sometimes suggested, the literary world is in the middle of a revolution, then it is worth asking exactly on whose behalf the gates of that old, prelapsarian citadel of hardback novels in tiny print runs, literary journalism and Leavisite sneering at manifestations of popular taste are being stormed. A certain kind of reader does very well in a landscape of cheap books of whose merits, or their absence, no serious questions are asked. So do the self-published and the self-publicising. And so, above all, does the online monopoly for whose ultimate benefit the racket is conducted. But what about the writers? How do they get on? Where do they find the leisure and the funding to produce the books on which any literary culture, whether staffed by Dickens, Thackeray and Charlotte Brontë, or a gang of crowd-funders and cyber-collaborators, will eventually be judged? This may be a good age in which to be reading books, or selling books, or preventing other people from selling them, but is it a good age to be writing them?

All of which takes us back to Cyril Connolly's *Enemies of Promise*, an attempt to identify, albeit from the vantage point of 1938, some of the snares that lie in wait for apprentice writers, and the many impediments strewn across their path – all that random environmental baggage whose cumulative effect is to prevent them from producing the books that they burn to write. Like much of the raw material that went to make up the Connolly myth, *Enemies* is several things altogether – a rueful evocation of his Etonian and Oxonian adolescence, a pitiless exploration of his own neuroses and an open hold for a bumper cargo of lapidary epigrams, simultaneously an apparently objective analysis of the conditions in which literature gets written, in which Connolly sets out with the aim of establishing what qualities, or strokes of fortune, are required to enable a book to last ten years, and a study of one particular author and his attempts to fulfil this task. If there are victims then one of them – or so we infer from the demoralising downward march that turns his exemplar 'Walter Savage Shelleyblake' from a young man of promise into a magazine hack seduced into writing an endless succession of reviews for 'Mr Vampire' of the *Blue Bugloss* – is Connolly himself.

Enemies of Promise is divided into three parts: a scorching hundred or so pages of literary criticism in which Connolly anatomises the contending styles of the 1930s ('The New Mandarins', 'The New Vernacular', etc.); a final third sorrowing over his Georgian boyhood; and, sandwiched between them, a section entitled 'The Charlock's Shade', in which Crabbe's poem 'The Heath', a region where 'the thin harvest waves its withered ears', is pressed into service as a metaphorical lexicon:

> There thistles stretch their prickly arms afar,
> And to the ragged infant threaten war;
> There Poppies, nodding, mock the hope of toil,
> There the blue Bugloss paints the sterile soil;
> Hardy and high, above the slender sheaf,
> The slimy Mallow waves her silky leaf;
> O'er the young shoot the Charlock throws a shade,
> And clasping Tares cling round the sickly blade;
> With mingled tints the rocky coasts abound,
> And a sad splendour vainly shines around.

Here, Connolly goes on to explain, is the literary world of the 1930s in miniature. Crabbe's 'thin harvest' may be taken as the achievement of young authors, the 'withered ears' their books and the 'thistles' politics. The 'Poppies, nodding' are drink, daydreams and diversion, the 'blue Bugloss' the clarion call of journalism and the 'slimy Mallow' that of worldly success. The 'Charlock' doubles up as sex, and the 'clasping Tares' are the obligations of duty and domesticity. The 'mingled tints' are the varieties of talent and accomplishment which duly appear, and the 'sad splendour' is that of their evanescent promise. 'These enemies of literature, these parasites on genius' require detailed examination, Connolly then informs us, for they are 'blights from which no writer is immune'.

Not all of this can go unqualified. Connolly, let us remember, was writing in the year of Munich. When he suggests that 'a writer must grow used to the idea that culture as we know it may disappear and remain lost for ever or till it is excavated, a thousand years hence, from a new Herculaneum' and that at any moment the schools of Athens may be closed and the libraries burnt, he is not talking about the retreat of newspaper arts pages and the squeeze on publishers' lists, but the prospect of Armageddon. And when he insists that the writer must be 'a lie-detector who exposes the fallacies in words and ideals before half the world is killed for them' he is reacting to some highly specific threats to civilised life that no serious person who put pen to paper in the late 1930s could altogether ignore. At the same time he is always worth reading on the more mundane pressures experienced by the man or woman in search of, as he rather grandiosely puts it, 'the truth that is always being clouded over by romantic words and ideas or obscured by actions and motives dictated by interest and fear', if only because the reader senses that he has felt them himself, that the accidie he diagnoses as one of the great stumbling blocks placed in the writer of the Auden era's path can be traced back to the *New Statesman* critic in the Chelsea flat squandering his talent on this week's fiction round-up when he should be writing the great masterpiece that will put Proust in the shade. Or rather not squandering it, because there is a counter-argument lurking behind the satire of Walter Savage Shelleyblake which urges us not to forget the importance of the *New Statesman* critic tapping out his 1,000 words on the Nonesuch Press *Boswell* and the forces he represents.

And so, to revert to the Connolly model, what snares lie in wait for the young writer of today? Creeping domesticity, marital obligation, interest-only mortgages, all the urgent summonses of hearth and home encapsulated by his immortal phrase 'the pram in the hall' are more easily avoided now than they were eighty years ago: significant others don't always require to be taken to the altar; neither do they necessarily want children; there are other options; other relationship choices to be made, although as someone once pointed out, the most promising sexual state for a modern writer to inhabit is that of the gay man or woman – overheads are lower and you have a ready-made subject to write about. As for the 'thistles', politics, too, is not the drain on a writer's energies that it was in the era of Jarrow and Spain. The last decade in which there was any real sense of a political divide that extended into literature was the 1980s, an age in which Mrs Thatcher dined with right-wing acolytes such as Kingsley Amis and V. S. Naipaul while her left-leaning opponents wrote multi-signature letters to the *Guardian* about spending cuts and the miners' strike or caballed in Lady Antonia Fraser's drawing room in Campden Hill Square. Certainly the most recent assemblage of literary opinion on a great political issue of the day – the *Authors Take Sides on Iraq* volume of 2004 – was a rather muted affair, in which dislike of the Blair government alternated with a suspicion that the days when writers could be expected usefully to contribute to debates of this kind were gone.

What about Mr Vampire and the review columns of the *Blue Bugloss*? The snares of literary journalism are more easily avoided for the simple reason that in an era of declining print circulations and negligible fees there is a lot less of it to be had – so little, in fact, that the thirtysomething novelist looking up from the reviews of his under-publicised first novel to contemplate the looming spectacle of the second, while wondering how much longer he will have to endure his part-time job in a public relations agency, would quite like to know where this particular enemy of promise can be found, so that he can have the pleasure of experiencing some of its supposedly injurious effects for himself. What has really changed, perhaps, in the three-quarters of a century since Connolly set to work are some of the fundamental structures through whose agency literature gets produced. These are less to do with the publishing industry's periodic reconfigurations than with the manner in which the modern literary world's talent pool finds itself being cultivated. Broadly speaking, the two most significant developments with the capacity to alter the outward face that 'literature' presents to the world are the rise of creative writing MAs and the employment by university English departments of novelists and poets to teach them. The aspiring writer of the Connolly generation, on coming down from Oxford or Cambridge, where he had generally read an arts subject, marked time as a school-teacher or a private secretary or compiled fiction round-ups for weekly magazines before embarking on his first book. He, or sometimes she, was effectively an amateur, or at any rate self-taught, whose knowledge of the world he was attempting to infiltrate was picked up as he went along. His tutors, such as they were, tended to be literary editors, publishers' readers or older writers met socially, and the advice they gave was strictly informal.

Consider, for example, the early career of Connolly's little-known but by no means unsuccessful friend, Esme Beresford de Courcy Littlejohn (1905–82). Like Connolly, Littlejohn was educated at Eton, where he knew Brian Howard and Harold Acton but failed, alas, to get his prose poem 'Les Mouers Atroces' accepted for the *Eton Candle*. Upon leaving Balliol College, Oxford, where he secured a third-class degree in modern history, drew polished sketches of his contemporaries for the *Isis*, persuaded Aldous Huxley to address the college essay club, and was several times entertained at Garsington, he secured temporary employment in the office of a London publicity firm. Introduced by an old school-friend to the literary editor of the *Spectator*, he made his debut in 1929 with a review of another old school-friend's first novel. More work of this kind soon followed, and with the encouragement of a wealthy uncle, who allowed him a small private income until such time as he was able to establish himself, he set up as a writer of light historical biographies, their subjects including such figures as Madame de Stael, Sydney Smith and Lillie Langtry. His contribution to *Spain: Authors Take Sides*, although ambiguous, was generally thought to express qualified support for Franco. By the late 1930s, by now married to a baronet's daughter and living comfortably in South Kensington, he was making a steady £1,500 a year.

Contrast this with the progress of Esme's great-grandson Hugo (b.1985). From an early stage, and mindful of the tug of ancestry, Hugo was determined to 'be a writer'. To this end, in his late teens he began to post small fragments of poetry and prose on an online website of his own devising. With the help of a supportive English master he was able to acquire a place on the English literature BA course at the University of Loamshire, where he wrote a much-admired final-year dissertation on textual hermeneutics, before moving on, at the age of 22, to a creative writing MA at the same establishment. Here he had the great good luck to be taught by the Man Booker-shortlisted author Terence Frisk, author of *Droop, Dahlias* and *In My Window Box* (Hugo thinks Frisk 'quite a good writer' but 'rather old-fashioned in his approach') and the award-winning poet Sally Marjoribanks, and also to have one of his short stories printed in the department's annual anthology, *Spring Buds*. Happily, this was noticed by an agent who attended the launch party and within a year of leaving the University of Loamshire – he was at this point working part-time in the local branch of Waterstones – Hugo had his first novel, *Come and Lie With Me*, accepted for publication. The advance, sad to relate, was a mere £5,000, with the result that Hugo, now aged 27, shortly afterwards accepted an offer from his alma mater to return to its creative department as an assistant lecturer. Here he spends a great deal of time attending departmental meetings, standing at the photocopier, keeping up with the jargon ('discourse', 'platform', 'textual engagement' and so on) and conciliating the egos of his students. His second novel, the provisionally titled *Sighs and Whispers*, is still incomplete. On the plus side, he has been asked to organise an interdisciplinary conference to be attended by several internationally distinguished writers, which it is hoped will help to advertise the exciting new partnership the university has recently entered into with the local council and East Midlands Arts, with the aim of establishing Loamshire as a 'cultural hub'.

What is the essential difference between Esme and his great-grandson? The one, it might be said, treated the business of writing as an amusing and profitable way to make a living; the other is thoroughly professionalised, as accomplished a technician in his way as an engineer or the celebrated soda-siphon manufacturer Ezekiel Littlejohn (1823–92), Esme's own great-grandfather, a former ploughboy who by his solid industry and perseverance first put the family on the map. At the same time, there are other discrepancies. Esme, for example, spent much of the early 1930s travelling in parts of the world that were, at this time, more or less off the map (*Tipping the Bearer*, his account of an excursion to the interior of Mali is still worth reading even today). He also fought in the Second World War, latterly in Military Intelligence where he was supposed to have had dealings with the secret services. Someone with a feel for the period, and a knowledge of upper-class life in the interwar era, could write an entertaining biography of Esme. But it is very unlikely that, sixty years hence, one will be written about Hugo, who seems set to see out his days in further education, writing occasional novels that will, however much zest he brings to them, inevitably reflect the protocols of the organisations he serves and on whose behalf he labours. Hugo, in other words, has been institutionalised, turned into one of literature's civil servants, a process which, it might be argued, is far more of a threat to the survival of any kind of literary culture than cyberspace or online collaboration.

None of this is Hugo's fault. He wants to be a writer, and these, generally speaking, are the hoops through which the apprentice has to jump in order to succeed in an ever more crowded professional marketplace. The role of 'man of action' which so many bygone practitioners of his craft so desperately coveted, is denied him by the radically altered world into which he was born. Neither is it the fault of university English departments, which are full of distinguished writers producing excellent novels, merely an acknowledgement that in a world now technologically conditioned to a point where most writers can never hope to make a living out of their work they are a necessary evil – a sort of glorified employment bureau which at any rate prevents Novelist X, or indeed Hugo Littlejohn, from having to work in a bank. But whether he, or she, teaches at the University of Loamshire, works for an advertising agency, or juggles various kinds of increasingly ill-paid journalism, the contemporary writer is fated to discover that most of the conditions that attend his or her professional life – from the modes of modern publishing to the vengeful ghosts of the technological machine – are enemies of promise. As for their cumulative effect, this can only be to inhibit the writer's ability to say the things that people do not wish to hear – which might be defined as one of the main functions of literature, in this or any other age.

Illustrations

First picture section

Second picture section

1: Anthony Powell en route to Holland, 1958 (© Powell family); Powell in old age with a young fan, The Chantry, Somerset, 1994 (© Sally Soames)

2: Poet and critic D. J. Enright (© Chatto & Windus Archive); novelist Alan Sillitoe, early 1960s (© Ruth Fainlight); 'The One Subject Man' cartoon from *Punch* (© *Punch* Archive)

3: 'Kingsley Aimless' and 'The Senile Club' cartoons from the *Spectator*, both drawn by the young William Rushton, 1962 (© *Spectator*)

4: Poet, editor and critic Ian Hamilton, 1980s (© Matthew Hamilton); Philip Larkin and Anthony Thwaite in Norfolk, 1970s (© Ann Thwaite)

5: Alan Ross, 1990s (© Jane Rye); J. L. Carr, 1980s (Author's own collection); J. R. Ackerley at home, 1940s (© Estate of J. R. Ackerley)

6: Malcolm Bradbury and David Lodge, University of Birmingham, 1978 (© Paul Morby); Angela Carter and Lorna Sage, 1980s (© University of East Anglia Archive)

7: A. S. Byatt, *c.*1964; Iris Murdoch, early 1960s (© Chatto & Windus Archive); Writers' Tour of North Wales, 1969 (© Dame Margaret Drabble)

8: Author photograph of Richard Burns on the dustjacket for his novel, *Fond and Foolish Lovers*, first published in 1990; John Carey, 1970s (© John Carey, 1980)

Notes and Further Reading

Unless otherwise stated, the place of publication is London.

Introduction

1 For obituary notices of Deborah Rogers, see *The Times*, 4 May 2014, and *Guardian*, 4 May 2014. Richard Bradford discusses the shift in favour of modernism in 'A Brief Essay on Taste', *Is Shakespeare Any Good? And Other Questions on How to Evaluate Literature* (Oxford 2015). Roy Jenkins' conversation with Léopold Senghor is reproduced in Anthony Powell, *Journals 1987–1989* (1996), 168–9. On the critical reception of Elizabeth Taylor's *In a Summer Season*, David Kynaston, *Modernity Britain: Book Two: A Shake of the Dice 1959–1962* (2014), 256.

1. *Landscape with Figures*

1 For general surveys of the early twentieth-century literary scene, see Philip Waller, *Writers, Readers & Reputations: Literary Life in Britain 1870–1918* (Oxford 2006), John Gross, *The Rise and Fall of the Man of Letters: English Literary Life Since 1800* (1969) and Frank Swinnerton, *The Georgian Literary Scene 1910–1935* (1935). Rickword's *New Statesman* review of J. C. Squire's *Selections from Modern Poets* is reproduced in Alan Young, ed. *Edgell Rickword: Essays and Opinions 1921–1931* (Manchester 1974), 39–41.

2 On the immediately pre-1918 book trade, Mary Hammond and Shafquat Towheed, eds. *Publishing in the First World War: Essays in Book History* (Basingstoke 2007). Geoffrey Grigson remembers the influence of Edmund Gosse in *The Crest on the Silver* (1950), 120. For W. L. Courtney, see Alec Waugh, *The Early Years of Alec Waugh* (1962), *passim*. Harold Macmillan's wartime reading is described in D. R. Thorpe, *Supermac: The Life of Harold Macmillan* (2010), 50–1, 57. On Henry Deacon Ritchie, see *Hal* (privately printed, 2010).

3 For Blunden on the sales of *Retreat*, Carol Z. Rothkop, ed. *Selected Letters of Siegfried Sassoon and Edmund Blunden, Volume I 1919–1931* (2012), 197.

E. M. Delafield's account of her childhood is taken from L.A.G. Strong, ed. *Beginnings* (1935), 66–7. On the Poetry Bookshop, see John Lehmann, ed. *Coming to London* (1957), Penelope Fitzgerald, *Charlotte Mew and her Friends* (1984) and 'The Poetry Bookshop' (1988), reprinted in *A House of Air: Selected Writings* (2003), 154–70, and Walter Allen, *As I Walked Down New Grub Street: Memories of a Writing Life* (1981), 23–4. Hermione Lee discusses Fitzgerald's abiding interest in Monro and his legacy in *Penelope Fitzgerald: A Life* (2013), 29–30, 299–306.

4 John Sutherland's essay 'The Victorian Novelists: Who were they?' originally appeared in *Critical Quarterly*, 1988, and is reprinted in *Victorian Fiction: Writers, Publishers, Readers* (Basingstoke 1995), 151–64. For educational backgrounds in the interwar era, see Graham Greene, ed. *The Old School* (1934). Orwell's letter to Cyril Connolly of 14 March 1938 is reproduced in Peter Davison, ed. *The Complete Works of George Orwell, Volume Eleven: Facing Unpleasant Facts: 1937–1939* (1998), 127. On the social background to 1920s literary London, see Alec Waugh, *Early Years*, 158–9. For the writer as a public figure in the interwar period, David Newsome, *On the Edge of Paradise: A. C. Benson Diarist* (1980), Rupert Hart-Davis, *Hugh Walpole* (1952), Bryan Connon, *Beverley Nichols: A Life* (1991), Michael Davie, ed. *The Diaries of Evelyn Waugh* (1976), 311. For Penelope Fitzgerald's memory of Walter de la Mare, *A House of Air*, 184. A. J. Cronin summarises his pre-literary career in Strong, ed. *Beginnings*, 48–61.

2. *The Georgian Twilight*

1 For Georgian poetry generally, see Robert H. Ross, *The Georgian Revolt: Rise and Fall of a Poetic Ideal 1910–1922* (1967). On Murry's attacks on the Georgian movement, Frank Swinnerton, *Figures in the Foreground: Literary Reminiscences 1917–1940* (1963), 63–73. The portrait of J. C. Squire draws on Patrick Howarth, *Squire: Most Generous of Men* (1963), Alec Waugh, 'J. C. Squire', in *My Brother Evelyn and Other Profiles* (1967), 157–61, and Dudley Carew, *The House is Gone: A Personal Retrospect* (1949). Geoffrey Grigson remembers calling on Squire in *The Crest on the Silver*, 77. For Osbert Sitwell's *Chapbook* article, 'Jolly Old Squire and Shanks's Mare's Nest', see John Pearson, *Facades: Edith, Osbert and Sacheverell Sitwell* (1978), 150–1.

2 For Sassoon's and Blunden's view of Georgian poetry, see Rothkop, ed. *Selected Letters of Siegfried Sassoon and Edmund Blunden*, *passim*. A representative selection of Shanks's criticism can be found in *Second Essays*

on Literature (1927). On the young Margaret Roberts's recitations of Drinkwater and de la Mare, Charles Moore, *Margaret Thatcher: The Authorised Biography, Volume One: Not for Turning* (2013), 31. For Dudley Carew's Georgian summing-up, *The House is Gone*, 152.

3. Dancing on the Hecatomb: Modern Movements

1 George Saintsbury's letter to T. S. Eliot of 11 February 1923 is reproduced in Valerie Eliot and Hugh Haughton, eds. *The Letters of T. S. Eliot Volume 2: 1923–1925* (2009), 53. On Patrick Hamilton, see Bruce Hamilton, *The Light Went Out: A Biography of Patrick Hamilton* (1972), 30–1. For Dudley Carew's view of Georgian verse, *The House is Gone*, 101. Grigson discusses his conversion to modernism in *The Crest on the Silver*, 115–22. On C. S. Lewis, Humphrey Carpenter, *The Inklings: C. S. Lewis, J. R. R. Tolkien, Charles Williams and their friends* (1978), *passim*. For Powell on M. R. James, *Under Review: Writings on Writers 1946–1990* (1992), 274. C. K. Scott Moncrieff, quoted in Jean Findlay, *Chasing Lost Time: The Life of C. K. Scott Moncrieff: Soldier, Spy and Translator* (2014), 106–7. Swinnerton, *Figures in the Foreground*, *passim*.

2 Robert Ross reproduces Frank Rutter's 'Nine Propositions' in *The Georgian Revolt*, 197. Edgell Rickword, review of Virginia Woolf's *The Common Reader*, reprinted in Young, ed. *Essays and Opinions*, 201. For Eliot on *Wheels*, see Ross, *The Georgian Revolt*, 193–4. On Middleton Murry, Swinnerton, *Figures in the Foreground*, 63–73.

3 On the Sitwells as an operational unit, see Pearson, *Façades*. For individual portraits, Philip Ziegler, *Osbert Sitwell* (1998), Victoria Glendinning, *Edith Sitwell: A Unicorn Among Lions* (1981) and Sarah Bradford, *Sacheverell Sitwell: Splendours and Miseries* (1993). A more recent study is Richard Greene's *Edith Sitwell: Avant-garde Poet, English Genius* (2011). Brian Howard's letter to Harold Acton about his visit to Edith's flat is reproduced in Marie-Jaqueline Lancaster, ed. *Brian Howard: Portrait of a Failure* (1968), 89–93. For Scott Moncrieff's *The Strange and Striking Adventures of Four Authors in Search of a Character*, see Findlay, *Chasing Lost Time*, 245–6. Orwell's review of Edith's *Alexander Pope*, which originally appeared in *The New Adelphi*, is reprinted in Davison, ed. *The Complete Works, Volume Ten: A Kind of Compulsion: 1903–1936* (1998), 184–6. For 'Marrakech', see *Volume Eleven*, 416–21.

4 For Eliot's interwar prestige, see Anthony Powell, *To Keep the Ball Rolling: The Memoirs of Anthony Powell: Volume Three: Faces in My Time* (1980), 190, Lancaster, ed. *Brian Howard*, 292, Edgell Rickword, *Calendar of*

Modern Letters review of *Poems, 1909–1925*, reprinted in Young, ed. *Essays and Opinions*, 180–4. For Powell's later view of Eliot's personality, see *Faces*, 190–2. On the *Criterion*, see Julian Symons, '*The Cri*' in *Critical Observations* (1981), 119–23, and Valerie Eliot and John Haffenden, eds. *The Letters of T. S. Eliot, Volume 3: 1926–1927* (2012), *Volume 4: 1928–1929* (2013) and *Volume 5: 1930–1931* (2014).

5 On Rickword and the *Calendar of Modern Letters*, see Alan Young's introduction to *Essays and Opinions* and Gross, *Rise and Fall of the Man of Letters*, 254–6. Malcolm Bradbury, quoted in Young, ed. *Essays and Opinions*, 7. For modernist influence on Brian Howard, Lancaster, ed. *Brian Howard*, 275. On Huxley, Powell, *Under Review*, 315. Firbank's effect on the younger writers of the interwar era is discussed in D. J. Taylor, *Bright Young People: The Rise and Fall of a Generation 1918–1940* (2007), 253–5, from which this account largely derives.

Hugh Walpole: The Perils of Success

1 For Walpole, see Hart-Davis, *Walpole* and Alec Waugh, 'The Nail in the Coffin – Hugh Walpole', *My Brother Evelyn and Other Profiles*, 128–40. Swinnerton prints a selection of Walpole's letters in *Figures in the Foreground*. Constant Lambert's joke is taken from Stephen Lloyd, *Constant Lambert: Beyond the Rio Grande* (2014), 194. Berlin's letter to Elizabeth Bowen appears in Henry Hardy, ed. Isaiah Berlin, *Flourishing: Letters 1928–1946* (2004), 193–6.

4. Highbrows, Lowbrows and Those In Between

1 On the background to commercial publishing in the 1920s and 1930s, Douglas Jerrold, *Georgian Adventure* (1937) and Alec Waugh, *Early Years*. For Blunden's complaint about Richard Cobden-Sanderson, Rothkop, ed. *Selected Letters, Volume II*, 34.

2 The details of Hodder & Stoughton's publishing activities in the interwar era are taken from John Attenborough, *A Living Memory: Hodder & Stoughton Publishers 1868–1975* (1975). On the Book of the Month Club, Hart-Davis, *Walpole*, 299–300 and Jerrold, *Georgian Adventure*. For the 'star reviewer', see Swinnerton, *Figures in the Foreground*, 173–81. For testimonies to Bennett's influence, Powell, *Under Review*, 112–14, and Malachi Whitaker in Strong, ed. *Beginnings*, 200.

3 Caroline Pollentier discusses the 'light essay' in '"Everybody's Essayist":

On Middles and Middlebrows', Kate Macdonald, ed. *The Masculine Middlebrow 1880–1950: What Mr Miniver Read* (2011), 119–34. On Lynd, see Sean McMahon's introduction to *Galway of the Races: Selected Essays* (Dublin 1991), and the posthumous selection *Books and Writers* (1952).

4 For the reviewing climate of the 1930s, Orwell, 'In Defence of the Novel', in Davison, ed. *Complete Works, Volume Ten*, 517–22, and Graham Greene, *A Sort of Life* (Harmondsworth 1972), 145. On Priestley, Vincent Brome, *J. B. Priestley* (1988) and Judith Cook, *Priestley* (1997). Grigson writes about his encounter with Priestley at the Café Royal in *The Crest on the Silver*, 163–4.

5. The Pink Decade

1 For literary responses to the events of autumn 1931, see Stanley Olson, ed. *Harold Nicolson, Diaries and Letters 1930–1964* (1980), 31–3, Anne Olivier Bell, ed. *The Diaries of Virginia Woolf, Volume IV: 1931–1935* (1982), 45. Orwell, 'Diary: Hop-picking', in Davison, ed. *Complete Works, Volume Ten*, 230, Alec Waugh, *A Year to Remember: A Reminiscence of 1931* (1975), 149–87.

2 On 1930s literature generally, Valentine Cunningham, *British Writers of the Thirties* (Oxford 1988), Andy Croft, *Red Letter Days: British Fiction in the 1930s* (1990). For the book world's leftward slant, see Orwell, 'Inside the Whale', in Davison, ed. *Complete Works, Volume Twelve: A Patriot After All: 1940–1941* (1998), 86–115, Jerrold, *Georgian Adventure*, Anthony Powell, 1985 *Observer* interview with Miriam Gross, reprinted in *An Almost English Life: Literary and Not-so Literary Recollections* (2012), 196. Sean French discusses Patrick Hamilton's Marxism in *Patrick Hamilton: A Life* (1993), 149–57, 270. Alec Waugh recalls his interest in 1930s politics in *The Best Wine Last: An Autobiography Through the Years 1932–1969* (1978), 63–9. For Orwell's review of *Caliban Shrieks*, Davison, ed. *Complete Works, Volume Ten*, 381–2.

3 On Sassoon's and Blunden's dislike of Stephen Spender, Rothkop, ed. *Selected Letters, Volume II*, *passim*. Edgell Rickword, interview with John Lucas, in John Lucas, ed. *The 1930s: A Challenge to Orthodoxy* (Hassocks 1978), 7.

4 Sid Chaplin's invitation to a party at Orwell's house in Kilburn, Mrs Rene Chaplin to author. Beverley Nichols' abortive trip to Glasgow, Connon, *Beverley Nichols*, 178. On Orwell and the 1930s Labour Party, Robert Colls, *George Orwell: English Rebel* (Oxford 2013), 51–7. For Heppenstall and the 'proletarian stunt', Jonathan Goodman, ed. *The*

Master Eccentric: The Journals of Rayner Heppenstall 1969–1981 (1986), 69. Brian Howard's career in the 1930s is extensively covered in Lancaster, ed. *Brian Howard*.

5 For *Left Review*, see Julian Symons, 'Keeping Left in the Thirties', *Critical Observations*, 124–7, Rickword interview with John Lucas, *A Challenge to Orthodoxy*, 3–12. On Marxist literary critics of the 1930s, Philip Bounds, *British Communism and the Politics of Literature 1928–1939* (2012). For the Left Book Club, see Paul Laity, ed., *Left Book Club Anthology* (2001).

6 On Chesterton and Belloc, Ian Ker, *G. K. Chesterton: A Biography* (2011), A. N. Wilson, *Hilaire Belloc* (1984) and Joseph Pearce, *Old Thunder: A Life of Hilaire Belloc* (2002), Evelyn Waugh, diary entry of 6 November 1936, Davie, ed. *Diaries*, 412.

7 For Grigson, Symons and the poetry scene of the 1930s, see Grigson, *The Crest on the Silver, passim*, Julian Symons, 'Deadly Rustic: The Two Geoffrey Grigsons', *Critical Observations*, 82–9, and the latter's memoir *Notes From Another Country* (1972), 52–69. Larkin's letter to Monica Jones, Anthony Thwaite, ed. *Selected Letters of Philip Larkin 1940–1985* (1992), 309.

6. *Making a Living I 1918–1939*

1 The definitive account of Gissing's early struggles is Pierre Coustillas, *The Heroic Life of George Gissing, Part I: 1857–1888* (2011). For Bennett's earnings in the 1920s, see James Hepburn, ed. *Letters of Arnold Bennett I: Letters to J. B. Pinker* (Oxford 1966), and Margaret Drabble, *Arnold Bennett* (1974). On Benson's income, Newsome, *Edge of Paradise*, 322–4, 369. For Squire, Howarth, *Squire, passim*. For Allingham, Julia Jones, *Fifty Years in the Fiction Factory: The Working Life of Herbert Allingham* (Chelmsford 2012). Hayward, John Smart, *Tarantula's Web: John Hayward, T. S. Eliot and their Circle* (Wilby 2013). Orwell's 'Confessions of a Book Reviewer', Davison, ed. *Complete Works, Volume Eighteen: Smothered Under Journalism: 1946* (1998), 300–2.

2 There is extensive discussion of Walpole's earnings in Hart-Davis, *Walpole*. For Hugh Kingsmill, see Richard Ingrams, *God's Apology: A Chronicle of Three Friends* (1977), in particular 126–7. For details of Straus, Alec Waugh, 'Ralph Straus' in *My Brother Evelyn*, 96–104.

3 On publishers' advances, Greene, *A Sort of Life, passim*, French, *Patrick Hamilton*. Orwell's letters to his literary agent, Leonard Moore, are printed in the various volumes of Davison, ed. *Complete Works*.

4 On the American market in the interwar era, Connon, *Beverley Nichols*,

134–7, Hart-Davis, *Walpole*, 188–93. For Maugham's early adventures in Hollywood, Selina Hastings, *The Secret Lives of Somerset Maugham* (2009), 266–70. Walpole's film work, Hart-Davis, *Walpole*, *passim*. Anthony Powell's stay in California is described in *Faces in My Time*, 46–71.

5 For Walter Allen's early career, *As I Walked Down New Grub Street*. The summary of Alec Waugh's fortunes is taken from *The Early Years of Alec Waugh*, *A Year to Remember* and *The Best Wine Last*.

7. *University English I*

1 On Raleigh and Quiller-Couch, Gross, *Rise and Fall of the Man of Letters*, 179–89. There are interesting details of Q's early life in his posthumously published *Memories and Opinions: An unfinished autobiography* (Cambridge 1945). For the background to the university teaching of English generally, Stephen Potter, *The Muse in Chains: A Study in Education* (1937).

2 For Oxford English in the interwar period, see Humphrey Carpenter, *The Inklings* and *J. R. R. Tolkien: A Biography* (1977), and A. N. Wilson, *C. S. Lewis: A Biography* (1991). On undergraduate opinion of the syllabus, John Carey, *The Unexpected Professor: An Oxford Life in Books* (2014), Kingsley Amis, *Memoirs* (1991), 45, 52–3. For an account of the University of Birmingham's English department, Allen, *As I Walked Down New Grub Street*, 31–4.

3 The early history of Cambridge English is covered in Ian MacKillop, *F. R. Leavis: A Life in Criticism* (1995) and John Haffenden's *William Empson, Volume I: Among the Mandarins* (Oxford 2005). The Isherwood quote is from Haffenden, *William Empson*, 179. For the Leavises and *Scrutiny*, see MacKillop, *F. R. Leavis*, G. Singh, *F. R. Leavis: A Literary Biography* (1996) and Francis Mulhern, *The Moment of Scrutiny* (1979).

8. *Late Bloomsbury*

1 Powell, *Under Review*, 89. Raymond Mortimer's *Dial* essay is reprinted in S. P. Rosenbaum, ed. *The Bloomsbury Group* (Toronto 1975), 241–5. For Frances Partridge's definition of Bloomsbury, Anne Chisholm, *Frances Partridge: The Biography* (2009), 364–5. Leonard Woolf, 'group of friends', quoted in Regina Marler, *Bloomsbury Pie: The Making of the Bloomsbury Boom* (1997), 23. Strachey's account of the Anglo-French poetry society is reproduced in Michael Holroyd, *Lytton Strachey: The New Biography* (1994), 496–7. Noel Annan on Keynes, quoted in

Marler, *Bloomsbury Pie*, 59. The Spender quote is from Rosenbaum, ed. *Bloomsbury Group*, 261.

2 On MacCarthy, see David Cecil, ed. *Desmond MacCarthy, The Man and his Writings* (1984) and Hugh and Mirabel Cecil, *Clever Hearts: Desmond and Molly MacCarthy* (1990), from which the majority of the quoted references are taken. Julia Strachey's description of him is taken from *Julia: A Portrait of Julia Strachey by Herself and Frances Partridge* (1983), 195. For Raymond Mortimer's criticism, see *Try Anything Once: Selected Writings* (1976). There are numberless glimpses of Mortimer in Frances Partridge's several volumes of diaries.

3 On the Bloomsbury revival, see Marler, *Bloomsbury Pie*, *passim*, and Victoria Glendinning, *Leonard Woolf: A Biography* (2006). For Frances Partridge's view of Bloomsbury in the immediately post-war era, *Everything to Lose: Diaries 1945–1960* (1985). Anne Chisholm discusses fictional representations of Ham Spray in *Frances Partridge*, 231–3, 248–9. For David Plante on the Bloomsbury legend, see *Becoming a Londoner: A Diary* (2013), 197, 241, 362.

9. *Editors at War*

1 On the 1940s literary scene, see Robert Hewison, *Under Siege: Literary Life in London 1939–45* (1977) and Andrew Sinclair, *War Like a Wasp: The Lost Decade of the Forties* (1989).

2 Anthony Powell, reporting a conversation with Peter Parker, *Journals: 1990–1992*, 224. Walpole's diary entry is quoted in Hart-Davis, *Walpole*, 426. Evelyn Waugh, *Brideshead Revisited: A Revised Edition with a New Preface* (1960), 9–10. Nicholas Moore's comment occurs in an essay contributed to Jane Williams, ed. *Tambimuttu: Bridge Between Two Worlds* (1989), 61. For Maclaren-Ross's career in the 1940s, Paul Willetts, *Fear and Loathing in Fitzrovia* (revised edition Stockport, 2005). On Wilson, Margaret Drabble, *Angus Wilson: A Biography* (1995).

3 Connolly's 1964 essay, 'Fifty Years of Little Magazines' is reproduced in *The Evening Colonnade* (1973), 375–86. For Orwell's letter to Lehmann, Davison, ed. *Complete Works, Volume Ten*, 483.

4 On Connolly, Clive Fisher, *Cyril Connolly: A Nostalgic Life* (1995), Jeremy Lewis, *Cyril Connolly: A Life* (1997), Michael Shelden, *Friends of Promise: Cyril Connolly and the World of Horizon* (1989) and the portrait in Julian Maclaren-Ross, *Memoirs of the Forties* (1965), 55–80. Among various selections of his journalism, see in particular *The Condemned Playground* (1945) and *The Evening Colonnade*. For Connolly's own view of his personal

life, David Pryce-Jones, ed. *Cyril Connolly: Journal and Memoir* (1983). Auberon Waugh, quoted in J. A. Sutherland, *Fiction and the Fiction Industry* (1978), 99. Julian Symons's criticisms of *Horizon* are taken from *Notes from Another Country*, 130. Kingsley Amis's *New Statesman* review of *Previous Convictions* is quoted in Lewis, *Cyril Connolly*, 518–19.

5 For Tambimuttu, Williams, ed. *Bridge Between Two Worlds*, *passim*, Maclaren-Ross, *Memoirs*, 135–52, Derek Stanford, *Inside the Forties: Literary Memoirs 1937–1957* (1977) and Ian Hamilton, 'Tambidextrous: The Presence of *Poetry London*', in *Walking Possession: Essays and Reviews 1968–1993* (1994).

6 On Lehmann, Adrian Wright, *John Lehmann: Pagan Adventure* (1998). The Lehmann family background is covered in Selina Hastings, *Rosamond Lehmann* (2002).

10. *Waiting for the Barbarians*

1 On the last days of the Left Book Club, see Laity, ed., *Left Book Club Anthology*. Alec Waugh's conversation with A. D. Peters and its consequences, *The Best Wine Last*, 235–6. For an overview of literary life in the immediately post-war period, Smart, *Tarantula's Web*, *passim*.

2 On Norman Collins, see Ed Glinert's introduction to the Penguin Modern Classics edition of *London Belongs to Me* (2008). Orwell's review is reproduced in Davison, ed. *Complete Works, Volume Seventeen: I Belong to the Left: 1945* (1998), 399–401.

3 For Orwell's *New Statesman* and *Nation* fiction round-up of February 1941, Davison, ed. *Complete Works, Volume Twelve*, 435–7. The fragment of 'A Smoking-room Story' is included in Davison, ed. *Complete Works, Volume Twenty: Our Job is to Make Life Worth Living: 1949–1950* (1998), 193–200. Muggeridge on Orwell's funeral, quoted in D. J. Taylor, *Orwell: The Life* (2003), 9.

4 Amis's mature view of *Nineteen Eighty-Four* is contained in a letter of 5 April 1969 to M. G. Sherlock, Zachary Leader, ed. *The Letters of Kingsley Amis* (2000), 710–11. For the Raymond Williams quote, *Orwell* (1971), 57. Carey on Orwell and Thackeray, *The Unexpected Professor*, 313. Amis on Orwell's air of 'passionately believing', quoted in Blake Morrison, *The Movement* (Oxford 1980), 93. John Wain on the audience for poetry, 'The Strategy of Victorian Poetry', *Twentieth Century*, May 1953, 388–9. For Bradbury on the 'ordinariness' of the post-1945 fictional landscape, see his afterword to the 1978 Arrow paperback reissue of *Eating People is Wrong* (1959).

11. *Making a Living II 1939–1970*

1 For Orwell's *Manchester Evening News* column of 5 July 1945, Davison, ed. *Complete Works, Volume Seventeen*, 210–12. On Paul Brickhill's sales in the 1950s, George Greenfield, *Scribblers for Bread: Aspects of the English Novel Since 1945* (1989), 117, 124. Peter Cheyney's sales figures, ibid., 113. Paul Scott's financial dealings with his publishers are extensively covered in Hilary Spurling, *Paul Scott: A Life* (1990). On J. L. Carr, Byron Rogers, *The Last Englishman: The Life of J. L. Carr* (2003). For Roger Angell's letter to Pritchett, Jeremy Treglown, *V. S. Pritchett: A Working Life* (2004), 211.

2 On Waugh's earnings in the last decade of his life, Selina Hastings, *Evelyn Waugh: A Biography* (1994), *passim*. Richard Ollard discusses A. L. Rowse's earnings in an appendix to his *A Man of Contradictions: A Life of A. L. Rowse* (1999), 330–2. For the diary entry of 21 September 1967, see Ollard, ed. *The Diaries of A. L. Rowse* (2003).

3 For Amis's advance for *Lucky Jim*, Leader, *The Life of Kingsley Amis*, 281. On Burgess and *The Worm and the Ring*, Andrew Biswell, *The Real Life of Anthony Burgess* (2005), 234. Raven discusses his contract with Anthony Blond in *Boys Will Be Boys*, 44–5. Isabel Colegate remembers the publishing arrangements of her early books in an introduction to *Three Novels* (1983).

4 The quotation from Beverley Nichols's diaries is taken from Connon, *Beverley Nichols*, 249. Raven describes his television interview with Amis in *Boys Will Be Boys*, 144–5. For Burgess's career generally, see Biswell, *The Real Life of Anthony Burgess*. On Maclaren-Ross's financial straits in March 1960, Willetts, *Fear and Loathing in Fitzrovia*, 278–80. For J. G. Farrell's career in the 1960s, Lavinia Greacen, *J. G. Farrell: The Making of a Writer* (1999). Raven on his prospects for 1963, *Boys Will Be Boys*, 196. For Raban's early adventures in literary journalism, *Of Love and Money* (1989), *passim*.

Alec Waugh: The First Best-seller

1 The sales figures quoted in the opening paragraph are taken from Greenfield, *Scribblers*, 116–17. For an account of *Island in the Sun*'s composition and acceptance, Alec Waugh, 'Island in the Sun', *My Brother Evelyn*, 323–40. For Evelyn Waugh's comment about Alec 'never drawing a sober breath', Auberon Waugh, 'My Uncle Alec', *Spectator*, 12 September 1981, reprinted in William Cook, ed. *Kiss Me, Chudleigh: The World According to Auberon Waugh* (2010), 292–5.

12. *New Men*

1 For Raven on 'Amis man', see 'The Kingsley Amis Story', *Spectator*, 17 January 1958, reprinted in *Boys Will Be Boys* (1963), 12–14. Carey's review of *Children of the Sun* can be found in *Original Copy: Selected Reviews and Journalism 1969–1986* (1987), 39–44.

2 Amis's letter to Edith Sitwell of 24 March 1954 is reproduced in Leader, ed. *Letters of Kingsley Amis*, 380. For the letter to Larkin of 3–8 July 1958, ibid., 395. Amis describes the radio interview with Powell in *Memoirs*, 151–2.

3 On Amis and the 'lower-middle-class gentlemanly conscience', Martin Green, *A Mirror for Anglo-Saxons* (1961), 120–3. For Amis's complaint about Virginia Woolf, letter to Larkin of 12 January 1948, Leader, ed. *Letters of Kingsley Amis*, 156. 'The Experimental Novel was about Man-Alone . . .', see William Cooper's British Council pamphlet *C. P. Snow* (1959). Julian Symons discusses post-war developments in British art and letters in 'The Little Magazines and the *Review*', *Critical Observations*, 111–13.

4 On the Movement, Morrison, *The Movement*, supplemented by Zachary Leader, ed. *The Movement Reconsidered: Essays on Amis, Larkin, Gunn, Davie and their Contemporaries* (Oxford 2009). J. D. Scott recalled his original *Spectator* article in 'A chip of literary history', *Spectator*, 16 April 1977. Evelyn Waugh's letter to the *Spectator* of 8 October 1954 is quoted in Leader, ed. *The Movement Reconsidered*, 6–7, as is the quotation from for Anthony Thwaite's, ibid, 254.

5 For press attitudes to working-class fiction of the 1950s, see Harry Ritchie, *Success Stories: Literature and the Media in England 1950–1959* (1988), *passim*, Stan Barstow, *In My Own Good Time* (Otley 2001) and Richard Bradford, *The Life of a Long-distance Writer: The Biography of Alan Sillitoe* (2008). For further details on Sillitoe, *Every Day of the Week: a Celebration of the Life and Work of Alan Sillitoe*, transcripts of addresses given at a British Library memorial meeting of April 2011 (Lewes 2012). 'The One Subject Man' is included in William Hewison, *Types Behind the Print* (1963).

6 Stuart Holroyd remembers his alliance with Wilson and Hopkins in *Contraries: A Personal Progression* (1975). For Wilson's own view of the 1950s, see *The Angry Years: The Rise and Fall of the Angry Young Men* (2007). The quotation from Elizabeth Young is taken from *Pandora's Handbag: Adventures in the Book World* (2001). For Isherwood's visit to England in 1960, Katharine Bucknell, ed. *Christopher Isherwood: The Sixties: Diaries Volume Two: 1960–1969* (2010), 59–60, 77. John Lucas recalls

his early life in *Next Year Will Be Better: A memoir of England in the 50s* (Nottingham 2010).

13. Common Readers: The Mid-century Audience

1 For Nella Last's reading habits, Richard Beard and Suzie Fleming, eds. *Nella Last's Peace* (2009), *passim*. Alan Sillitoe, *Life without Armour: An Autobiography* (1999), 30. On the 'Dickens atmosphere', Humphry House, *The Dickens World* (Oxford 1941), 16–17. Orwell's 'Charles Dickens' is included in *Inside the Whale and Other Essays* (1940).

2 For Allen Lane and Penguins, see Jeremy Lewis, *Penguin Special: The Life and Times of Allen Lane* (2005). John Gross, *A Double Thread* (2000), 176. Richard Hoggart, *The Uses of Literacy* (1957), 258.

3 Anthony Blond discusses the economics of post-war literary fiction publishing in *The Publishing Game* (1971), 68–80. For evidence of juvenile taste in the 1940s and 1950s, Gross, *Double Thread*, David Lodge, *Quite a Good Time to be Born: A Memoir 1935–1975* (2015), Keith Waterhouse, *City Lights* (1994) and Alan Johnson, *This Boy* (2013).

14. Metropolitan Critics

1 For Kingsley Amis's trip to London of November 1954, described in a letter to Philip Larkin, see Leader, ed. *Letters of Kingsley Amis*, 412. The quotation from Clive James's letter to *Private Eye* is reproduced in Sutherland, *Fiction and the Fiction Industry*, 40. Symons on reviewing standards, *Critical Observations*, 112. Raban, *Of Love and Money*, 41. For Claire Tomalin's memories of working on the early 1970s *New Statesman*, see *Several Strangers* (1999), 33–7.

2 For Miriam Gross, *An Almost English Life*. Keith Waterhouse's early adventures in Fleet Street may be followed in *Streets Ahead* (1995). David Holloway, quoted in Sutherland, *Fiction and the Fiction Industry*, 95.

3 On Ackerley and the *Listener*, see Peter Parker, *Ackerley: A Life* (1989) and Neville Braybrooke, ed. *The Letters of J. R. Ackerley* (1975). Karl Miller describes his career as a literary editor in *Dark Horses: An Experience of Literary Journalism* (1998). Frances Partridge's account of meeting him at a party is recorded in *Hanging On: Diaries, Volume 3: 1960–1963* (1990), 87. For a selection of Martin Amis's *New Statesman* reviews, see *The War Against Cliché: Essays and Reviews* 1971–2000 (2001). Ackroyd, quoted in Sutherland, *Fiction and the Fiction Industry*, 90.

4 For Enright generally, see Jacqueline Simms, ed. *Life by Other Means: Essays on D. J. Enright* (Oxford 1990). A selection of his criticism can be found in *Poets and Conspirators* (1966). For Brigid Brophy's literary journalism, *Don't Never Forget* (1966) and *Reads: A Collection of Essays* (1989). On Ian Hamilton, Alan Jenkins, introduction to *Collected Poems* (2009) and David Collard, 'Ian Hamilton's Brilliance, Busted: Remembering the *New Review* forty years on', *Times Literary Supplement*, 2 April 2014. Rayner Heppenstall's description is taken from Goodman, ed. *Master Eccentric*, 43. For Julian Symons's verdict on the *New Review*, *Critical Observations*, 116–17.

5 There is a good account of the *New Statesman* end of the early 1970s reviewing scene in Richard Bradford, *Martin Amis: The Biography* (2011), 117–30, from which Clive James's remark about the 'alternative to academia' is taken. Jonathan Raban on James's reviewing style, *Of Love and Money*, 40. Peter Ackroyd's review of Erica Jong's *How to Save Your Own Life* appeared in the *Spectator*, 7 May 1977.

Lady Writers

1 Simon Raven, 'Scheherazade: The Menace of the Sixties', *Spectator*, 31 December 1965. Colin Haycraft, quoted in Lee, *Penelope Fitzgerald*, 249. For Fitzgerald's TV interview with Robert Robinson and her categorisation, ibid., 277–9. Larkin's letter to Charles Monteith about Barbara Pym is included in Thwaite, ed. *Selected Letters of Philip Larkin*, 375. For Iris Murdoch's account of her dealings with the press, Peter J. Conradi, *Iris Murdoch: A Life* (2001), 424.

15. Reaching Out

1 The programme for the 1936 *Sunday Times* 'Book Exhibition' is reproduced in Rupert Hart-Davis, *The Power of Chance: A Table of Memory* (1991), 90. On the 1962 Cheltenham Literary Festival, Leader, *The Life of Kingsley Amis*, 485–6.

2 For the Arts Council's funding of literature in the post-war era, Charles Osborne, *Giving it Away: Memoirs of an Uncivil Servant* (1987), *passim*. On the controversy surrounding subsidy of the *New Review*, Sutherland, *Fiction and the Fiction Industry* 138–43. For the New Fiction Society, ibid., 143–7.

3 There is a detailed account of the writers' tour of North Wales in

Drabble, *Angus Wilson*, 382–8. For Iris Murdoch's involvement, Conradi, *Iris Murdoch*, 497. 'The Road to Nowhere', Shiva Naipaul's account of his experiences on Humberside, appeared in the *Spectator* of 18 February 1978 and is reprinted in *Beyond the Dragon's Mouth, Stories and Pieces* (1984), 230–6. For literature funding in the 1980s, Osborne, *Giving it Away, passim.*

16. *University English II*

1 For post-war Oxford and its ornaments, see John Lowe, *John Sparrow: A Portrait* (1999), Adam Sisman, *Hugh Trevor-Roper: The Biography* (2010), Leslie Mitchell, *Maurice Bowra: A Life* (2009), and Hugh Lloyd-Jones, ed. *Maurice Bowra: A Celebration* (1974). Kingsley Amis remembers Lord David Cecil in *Memoirs*, 101–7.

2 On the later Leavis, see MacKillop. *F. R. Leavis*, David Ellis, *Memoirs of a Leavisite* (Liverpool 2013), and David Holbrook, 'Disciples and Enemies: F. R. Leavis', *London Magazine*, June/July 1992. The exchanges between George Lyttelton and Rupert Hart-Davis are taken from Rupert Hart-Davis, ed. *The Lyttelton Hart-Davis Letters: Correspondence of George Lyttelton and Rupert Hart-Davis, Volume Six: 1961–62* (1984), 161–2, 177, 179. Julian Symons's review of *Anna Karenina and Other Essays* is reprinted in *Critical Observations*, 108–10.

3 On the post-war expansion in university English departments, see MacKillop, *F. R. Leavis*, 333–6. Margaret Drabble's description of the University of East Anglia in the late 1960s appears in *Angus Wilson*, 363. Lorna Sage, *Women in the House of Fiction: Post-War Women Novelists* (Basingstoke 1992). For David Lodge on institutionalisation, 'A Kind of Business: The Academic Critic in America', in *After Bakhtin: Essays on Fiction and Criticism* (1990), 175–84. Lodge writes about his early career in *Quite a Good Time to be Born*. Raban quotes taken from Drabble, *Angus Wilson*, 441, 575. Lorna Sage's *Observer* tribute to Wilson, ibid., 577.

4 For Bradbury, see David Lodge's exemplary tribute, 'Malcolm Bradbury: Writer and Friend', in *Lives in Writing: Essays* (2014), 165–97. G. D. Klingopoulos, 'Mr Forster's Good Influence', Boris Ford, ed. *The Pelican Guide to English Literature, Volume 7: The Modern Age* (1961), 263–74. Bradbury, afterword to 1978 Arrow paperback reprint of *Eating People is Wrong*, 296. 'Cult of provincialism', ibid., 292.

5 Lodge's literary journalism can be approached in the collections *Write On* (1986), *The Art of Fiction* (1992), *The Practice of Writing* (1996) and *The Year of Henry James* (2006). David Ellis on Lacan, *Memoirs of a*

Leavisite, 93. For Lodge's remarks about 'the very difficulty and esotericism of theory', *After Bakhtin*, 181. On the Oxford conference of 1980, see Craig Raine's amusing essay 'Gossip', *Haydn and the Valve Trumpet* (1990), 491–4, which reproduces the quotation from Terry Eagleton's *New Statesman* article of 6 June 1980.

The Unschooled Reader

1 On the Beatles' lyrics generally, Ian MacDonald, *Revolution in the Head: The Beatles' Records and the Sixties* (revised ed. 1997). Mark E. Smith's comments on literary life are made in the course of an interview featured in the promotional video *Perverted by Language* (2003). For Weller, see *Surburban 100: Selected Lyrics* (2007).

17. Beyond the Publishing Crisis

1 For Priestley's advice to the young writer of the 1970s, *Instead of the Trees: a Final Chapter of Autobiography* (1977), 27–8. 'Writing and Warning: An Interview with Kingsley Amis', *Listener*, 15 February 1979. Beverley Nichols's TV appearances, Connon, *Beverley Nichols*, 250. On Evelyn Waugh's interviews on *Face to Face* and *Monitor*, Martin Stannard, *Evelyn Waugh: No Abiding City: 1939–1966* (1992), 430, 477. *Take It or Leave It*, A. S. Byatt to author.

2 Kingsley Amis discusses the Beatles in a letter to Philip Larkin of 24 June 1981, Leader, ed. *Letters of Kingsley Amis*, 925. For the *Firing Line* debate, see his *Memoirs*, 159. For Heppenstall and the National Book League's 'Bedford Square Bookbag', Goodman, ed. *Master Eccentric*, 70–1. On Amis's product endorsements, see Leader, *The Life of Kingsley Amis*, 642–3.

3 For the state of the early 1980s publishing industry, *Granta 4: Beyond the Publishing Crisis* (1981). This contains useful essays by, among others, Brigid Brophy, John Sutherland, Blake Morrison and David Caute. On the impact of literary prizes, Richard Todd, *Consuming Fictions* (1996), *passim*. For *Granta* in the Buford era, 'Big Issues', *Sunday Times Books Section*, 26 February 1995.

4 On Alan Ross and the *London Magazine*, see the memoir by Jeremy Lewis, *Grub Street Irregular: Scenes from Literary Life* (2008), 317–29 and Ross's anthology, *25 Years of the London Magazine* (1986). Anthony Powell, *Journals 1990–1992*, 144. For Evelyn Waugh's letter to Nancy Mitford,

Amory, ed. *Letters of Evelyn Waugh*, 559. John Murray's valedictory editorial, 'Our Final Issue', appears in *Panurge: Café Royal* (1996).

5 *Private Eye*'s review of Iris Murdoch's *The Message to the Planet*, 13 September 1989, is reprinted in Francis Wheen, ed. *Lord Gnome's Literary Companion* (1994), 169–71. Much of Carey's literary journalism from the 1960s and 1970s can be found in *Original Copy*. His social background and early career is outlined in *An Unexpected Professor*. For James Wood, see 'The Secular Wood' in James Ley, *The Critic in the Modern World: Public Criticism from Samuel Johnson to James Wood* (2014), 171–205. Elizabeth Young's best essays from the period are collected in *Pandora's Handbag*.

Mrs Thatcher and the Writers

1 On Kingsley Amis's rightward drift, Leader, *Life of Kingsley Amis*, 559–63. The letter to *Encounter* of November 1968 is reproduced in Leader, ed. *Letters of Kingsley Amis*, 704–7. The latter is also the source of Amis's remarks about Alexander Dubček. For Amis's approval of Mrs Thatcher, ibid., 787, 840. Larkin's comments can be found in Thwaite, ed. *Selected Letters of Philip Larkin*, 584, 680, 726. For Powell's accounts of the two dinner parties of October 1982 and March 1985, see his *Journals 1982–1986*, 40–1 and 139–42. Hilary Mantel remembered her first sighting of Mrs Thatcher in 'Mrs Thatcher and the Writers', BBC Radio Four, 18 June 2015.

18. *Making a Living III 1970–*

1 For Francis King's early career as a freelance writer, see *Yesterday Came Suddenly: An Autobiography* (1993), 207–13. Penelope Fitzgerald, quoted in Lee, *Penelope Fitzgerald*, 249. Isabel Colegate, introduction to *Three Novels*. John Campbell discusses Roy Jenkins' literary earnings in the early 1970s in *Roy Jenkins: A Well-Rounded Life* (2014), 364–5.

2 On Iris Murdoch's sales and income, Conradi, *Iris Murdoch*, 560. For Fowles, Charles Drazin, ed. John Fowles, *Journals: Volume 2* (2006), 49, 149, 212–13, 268. Details of Simon Raven's income in the early 1980s can be found in Michael Barber, *The Captain: The Life and Times of Simon Raven* (1998), 216–22. For Farrell in the 1970s, Greacen, *J. G. Farrell*, *passim*.

3 For Murdoch and Ed Victor, Conradi, *Iris Murdoch*, 560–1. On Kingsley Amis's earnings, Leader, *The Life of Kingsley Amis*, 736–7. Connolly's

financial misfortunes are covered in Fisher, *Cyril Connolly*, 407, 412. Raven, Barber, *The Captain*, 241–2. For Beverley Nichols's income in his last years, Connon, *Beverley Nichols*, 293–4. On Wilson, Drabble, *Angus Wilson*, 642–60. For a sympathetic account of Richard Burns's career, see Ian Katz, 'Chronicle of a Death Foretold', *Guardian*, 14 December 1992.

19. *Enemies of Promise*

1 On Squire's seventieth birthday party, Howarth, *Squire*, 280. For 'domesticated postmodernism', see Richard Bradford, *The Novel Now* (2006), *passim*. David Lodge, *Quite a Good Time to be Born*, 2. Gross, *Rise and Fall of the Man of Letters*, 214.

Acknowledgements

Most works of non-fiction have other works of non-fiction lurking silently behind them. In this case a decisive influence was exerted by John Gross's *The Rise and Fall of the Man of Letters* (1969) and Philip Waller's *Writers, Readers, and Reputations: Literary Life in Britain 1870–1918* (2006), both of which offered valuable ideas as to how the history of bygone literary periods might be approached. In fact, I count the discovery of Gross's pioneering study in a second-hand shop in Sussex nearly thirty years ago as one of the great Damascene moments of my professional life.

Throughout the writing I have benefited from the advice of a large number of friends and fellow workers in what George Gissing used to call the valley of the shadow of books. Professor John Carey recalled details of the development of Oxford English in the post-war years. Anthony Thwaite was happy to share his memories of a 1950s literary scene in which he played a prominent part, and I am grateful to Dame Antonia Byatt for allowing me to make use of her recollections of the 1960s literary quiz show *Take It or Leave It*. Of the many other people who responded to requests for information, I should like to thank Dame Margaret Drabble, Jeremy Lewis, Professor Richard Bradford, Andrew Holgate, Paul Willetts, John Lucas, Richard Davenport-Hines, David Lodge, Hugh and Mirabel Cecil, John Powell, Jane Rye, Deirdre Levi, Matthew Hamilton, Alexander Waugh, Ruth Fainlight, Nicola Swords, Rosie Price, Nick Llewellyn, Peter Parker, Jeremy Noel-Tod, Andre Gailani of *Punch* Ltd., Hannah Lowery of the University of Bristol Arts and Social Sciences Library, Patricia McGuire, archivist, King's College, Cambridge, Justine Mann of the University of East Anglia Literary Archive, Professor Christopher Bigsby and Alison Cullingham, Special Collections Librarian at the University of Bradford.

Parts of Chapter Four originally began their life as an introduction to a new edition of J. B. Priestley's *Angel Pavement* published in 2012, while versions of parts of Chapters 10 and 16 originally appeared in the *Times Literary Supplement*. I am grateful to their respective sponsors, Great Northern Books and Sir Peter Stothard, for permission to reprint this material

Many literary editors and journalistic sponsors steered relevant books in my direction. They include Boyd Tonkin, Arifa Akbar, Katy Guest, Paul Laity, Mark Amory, Sam Leith, Ian Hislop, Lucy Lethbridge, David Propson, Jonathan Derbyshire, David Wolf, Alan Jenkins, Anna Vaux, Roz Dineen, Michael Caines, Claudia Fitzherbert, Nancy Sladek and Robert McCrum. Particular thanks to Tom Fleming for his willingness to procure copies of ancient reviews from the *Literary Review*'s archive.

This book is dedicated to John Gross, without whose example it would not have been written. But I should also like to acknowledge the contribution – direct and indirect – of several writers whose help and encouragement over many years became even more apparent to me once they were no longer around to offer it. They include Sir Malcolm Bradbury, Dame Beryl Bainbridge, William Cooper, D. J. Enright, Francis King, Alan Sillitoe and Peter Vansittart.

At Chatto & Windus, Alison Samuel and Jenny Uglow commissioned the book and Clara Farmer and my indefatigable editor Juliet Brooke saw it through. David Milner brought invaluable expertise to the copy-editing process. I should also like to thank my former agent, Gill Coleridge, and my current agent Gordon Wise. Much love, as ever, to Rachel, Felix, Benjy and Leo.

D.J.T.

Index